A SACRED OATH

A
SACRED
OATH

MEMOIRS OF A
SECRETARY OF DEFENSE DURING
EXTRAORDINARY TIMES

MARK T. ESPER

wm

WILLIAM MORROW

An Imprint of HarperCollinsPublishers

Sources for the materials that appear in the appendix: Department of Defense.

Sources for the photographs that appear in the art insert: courtesy of the author (page 1); Official DoD Photo by Staff Sgt. Brandy Nicole Mejia (page 2, top; page 3, top and middle; page 4, middle and bottom; page 6, middle); Official DoD Photo by Sgt. 1st Class Teddy Wade (page 2, middle); Official DoD Photo by Staff Sgt. Carl Greenwell (page 2, bottom left); Official White House Photo (page 2, bottom right; page 7, middle); Official DoD Photo by Lisa Ferdinando (page 3, bottom; page 5, top and bottom; page 6, top; page 8, middle and bottom); Official DoD Photo by Sgt. James E. Harvey (page 4, top); Official DoD Photo (page 5, middle); Official White House Photo by Shealah Craighead (page 6, bottom; page 7, top); Official DoD Photo by Staff Sgt. Jack Sanders (page 7, bottom); and Official DoD Photo by Carlos M. Vazquez II (page 8, top).

HarperCollins books may be purchased for educational, business, or sales promotional use. For information, please email the Special Markets Department at SPsales@harpercollins.com.

FIRST EDITION

Library of Congress Cataloging-in-Publication Data has been applied for.

ISBN 978-0-06-314431-6

22 23 24 25 26 LSC 10 9 8 7 6 5 4 3 2 1

To my wife and best friend, Leah, and our children,
Luke, Jack, and Kate.

And

To the West Point Class of 1986, with whom I swore
my first oath to the Constitution on July 1, 1982,
and for whom "Courage Never Quits."

And

To the men and women of the U.S. Department of Defense,
who honor their sacred oaths each and every day,
and in whom our great nation's safety, security,
and future is entrusted.

I, Mark Esper, do solemnly swear that I will support and defend the Constitution of the United States against all enemies, foreign and domestic; that I will bear true faith and allegiance to the same; that I take this obligation freely, without any mental reservation or purpose of evasion; and that I will well and faithfully discharge the duties of the office on which I am about to enter. So help me God.

Mark T. Esper
Oath of Office as Secretary of Defense
The White House
Washington, D.C.
July 23, 2019

CONTENTS

A SACRED OATH

A MEETING LIKE NO OTHER

"Can't you just shoot them? Just shoot them in the legs or something?" he asked.

I couldn't believe the president of the United States just suggested the U.S. military shoot our fellow Americans in the streets of the nation's capital. The moment was surreal, sitting in front of the Resolute desk, inside the Oval Office, with this idea weighing heavily in the air, and the president red faced and complaining loudly about the protests under way in Washington, D.C.

When I accepted the job as secretary of defense the previous year, I knew I would face tough issues—questions of war and peace, for example. But never anything like this. The good news—this wasn't a difficult decision. The bad news—I had to figure out a way to walk Trump back without creating the mess I was trying to avoid. This wasn't how I ever thought the first week of June 2020, or any week for that matter, would begin.

Monday, June 1, 2020, started like most others. I arrived early at the Pentagon after hitting the gym, did a quick review of the day's intelligence, and then picked through my read-ahead book for the tab on my 8:00 A.M. meeting—the Secretary's Weekly Policy Review, or "swipper" as we called it. This meeting included the civilian and military leadership of the Department of Defense (DoD), from the Office of the Secretary of Defense (OSD) and Joint Staff to the service secretaries and their uniformed chiefs—the four-star heads of the Army, Navy, Marines, Air Force, and Space Force.

Before the pandemic, we gathered in the large Nunn-Lugar conference room opposite my office on the E-ring of the Pentagon and sat around the big wooden table—the deputy secretary of defense to my right and the chairman of the Joint Chiefs of Staff to my left—by rank, with aides and assistants lining the walls. The table could fit nearly two dozen people. In the era of COVID, however, we now met by secure video from our desks.

I initiated the swipper my first week in office. It would be that one meeting where we combined the important work of going through our organizational priorities, as a joint team of civilian and military leaders, with the more immediate matters of pending issues and current events. It would also help me close the civilian-military divide that had opened over time. About halfway through the June 1 swipper meeting, my secure phone rang a few times and then stopped.

One of my assistants in the front office must have picked it up, I thought. Moments later, I saw General Mark Milley drop off the screen, which was unusual for the Joint Chiefs chairman. My phone soon rang again, and I discovered exactly why he had vanished so abruptly. Milley was spun up; he had urgent news.

General Mark Milley is a barrel-chested soldier with dark bushy eyebrows who hails from the Boston area. A standout hockey player in school, he graduated from Princeton in 1980 and was commissioned as an armor officer. After forty years of Army service, he had multiple combat tours and a lifetime of experience under his belt. He carried a stern look on his face that belied a quick sense of humor, and he could fill a room with his booming voice, which often spoke in exclamation points and language not always made to be taken literally. The president, ever drawn to appearances, would often say he was "straight out of central casting."

I turned the meeting over to my deputy and took the chairman's call. Milley was unusually animated now, and rightfully so. Minutes earlier the president had called him, he said, in a fury over what happened in the streets of D.C. the prior evening, when more than a thousand people gathered to protest the killing of George Floyd—as was happening around the country. Protesters marched through the streets and gathered in Lafayette Park, right across from the White House. Fires were lit, windows were smashed, and people were hurt as some in the crowd grew violent. The chaotic scenes played over and over on television and undoubtedly caught Trump's attention. The president thought his administration "looked weak" and wanted something done.

I asked General Milley to come up to my office. The fact that Trump called him was unusual, and Milley's quick summary was very troubling. I was anxious to sit with him and tease the conversation out, to understand *exactly* what the president said. The general arrived quickly. His demeanor was very serious, his face ashen. I wondered how many times in his years in the military he had ever looked this way.

"The president is really angry," Milley said. "He thinks it's a disgrace what happened last night. He wants ten thousand troops deployed to stop the violence. I told him I had to speak with you."

"Ten thousand troops, really, he said that?" I asked.

"Yes, sir," he responded with a serious but slightly wide-eyed look. "Ten thousand."

I shook my head in disbelief. I knew some of the protesters had become violent and damage had occurred—including to the historic

Episcopal church directly across from the White House. Vandalism is never acceptable, but the perpetrators were a small minority in a much larger crowd. Law enforcement, as well as some D.C. National Guardsmen who were on duty to support them, suffered injuries; otherwise, they had things under control. I'd received updates throughout the weekend, but there were no urgent calls for additional troops.

"Where did the number ten thousand come from?" I asked Milley. He didn't know. In any event, Milley and I both understood that deploying active-duty forces into the nation's capital was a terrible idea, and if anything it would likely incite more violence. We also knew it was impossible to send this many in twelve hours. It took the most elite units in the U.S military a "few hours" to deploy, and they were our most ready forces.

Minutes later, a member of my staff came in to inform us the president called a snap meeting for 10:30 A.M. to discuss the protests. Milley and I were already scheduled to be at the White House at 11:00 A.M. for a call with the nation's governors regarding the ongoing civil unrest. We looked at each other and grimaced, silently acknowledging that we were in for another interesting morning.

Milley and I trudged over to 1600 Pennsylvania Avenue that morning for what turned out to be a very heated encounter with the president. It was loud, contentious, and unreal. We did manage to avoid a terrible outcome—the one that Trump wanted—but we were shaken, and it wasn't even noon yet.

As we briskly left the meeting and crossed the threshold into the outer office where the president's schedulers sat, Milley put his thumb and forefinger tightly together, close to his face, leaned in, and whispered to me that he was "this close" to resigning on the spot. So was I.

...

What transpired that day would leave me deeply troubled about the leader of our country and the decisions he was making. I was worried for our democracy. At that point, having served as Donald Trump's secretary of defense for about a year, I had seen many red flags, many warnings, and many inconsistencies. But now we seemed on the verge of crossing a dark red line. We had walked up to these thresholds in the past, but never one this important, and never with such rage.

At times like this, I asked myself why I didn't resign. This was the existential question of the Trump administration: Why did good people stay even after the president suggested or pressed us to do things that were reckless, or foolish, or just plain wrong? Why did we remain even after he made outrageous or false statements, or denigrated our people, our departments, or us?

I wrestled with these questions many times during my tenure, and especially in the months following the events of June 1. It demanded a lot of soul-searching, reaching back into my upbringing, my education at West Point, and my training in the Army, studying historical examples, speaking with my predecessors in both parties, thinking hard about my oath, and talking it through with my wife. On more than one occasion, Leah would say to me, "As your wife, please quit. As an American citizen, please stay."

Quitting in outrage would have made me feel good in the moment—it would have saved me a ton of stress and criticism. News outlets and social media would likely hail me as a "resistance" hero. However, I didn't think it was the right thing to do *for our country*. And as I told a reporter once near the end of my tenure, "my soldiers don't get to quit" when the going gets tough, so I won't either. I agonized nonetheless. Many of us did.

There was another major concern I had to factor in to the equation: Who would replace me? There likely wasn't enough time for the president to nominate and the Senate to confirm a new defense secretary. Nevertheless, Trump could certainly place a true loyalist as acting secretary. And given enough time, real damage could be done. We saw this earlier in the year when he installed Ric Grenell as the acting Director of National Intelligence. There were a number of people in the administration who would willingly do Trump's bidding, and probably even his more extreme dictates, and it deeply concerned me.

As readers of this book will learn, the president or some of his top White House aides proposed to take some type of military action in or against other nations on multiple occasions during the nearly eighteen months I served as secretary of defense. Other recommendations were so careless that they easily could have provoked a conflict. Some of these proposed actions are still unknown to the public. Some could even have led to war. On each of those occasions, sober minds pulled us back from the brink. What would happen, I wondered, if we were all gone?

Some of the decisions made by the Pentagon leadership after I left, other actions attempted but not consummated, and, even further, matters reportedly discussed at the White House in mid-December to use the military to enable a recount would later validate my concerns. And of course, nothing was more troubling than the horrific Trump-inspired assault on the Capitol on January 6, 2021.

I stayed because I didn't want our military politicized, let alone shooting civilians or collecting ballot boxes. I also didn't want to start any unnecessary wars, break any alliances, or compromise our nation's security. I stayed because I thought it was the right thing to do, and because I knew we would do our best to do the right thing as long as I was secretary of defense. I say that reluctantly, knowing it may come across as vainglorious, but it was how I felt and what

I believed. We had a sacred oath to the Constitution, after all, not to the president or a party. It was about the country and our values.

In the end, the answer always came back to staying and fighting the good fight, the necessary one. To get some important things accomplished for the country and the military in the time I had, which we did. But also, to stop bad things from happening, which we also did on a number of occasions. I was never concerned about being fired, only about being fired too soon. This was the high wire I had to walk until Election Day. In order to do so and keep the Defense Department out of politics and the military out of elections, however, I would need a new game plan after June 1, 2020. Donald Trump would not make that easy.

This book aims to tell that story—the story of my decisions and perspectives during one of the most chaotic, difficult, and consequential periods in modern American history. An extraordinary period where we fought a global pandemic the likes of which the world hadn't seen in a century; dealt with the greatest domestic unrest in two generations; battled aggressive actions by hostile powers and terrorist groups around the world; confronted novel challenges from peer/near-peer rivals* in a new era of great power competition; began transforming the U.S. military through implementation of

---

* Army Doctrinal Publication 2.0—Intelligence, published in July 2019, describes a "peer threat" (or "rival" in this context) as "an adversary or enemy with capabilities and capacity to oppose U.S. forces across multiple domains worldwide or in a specific region where they enjoy a position of relative advantage. Peer threats possess roughly equal combat power in geographical proximity to a conflict area with U.S. forces." At the beginning of this century, China and Russia were considered by a majority of national security experts to be "near-peers" who lacked certain capabilities or capacity that could challenge the U.S. military in a material way. Recent modernization efforts by both countries, especially China, has prompted many of these same experts to begin describing one or both of these countries as "peer threats" to the United States.

a new National Defense Strategy; and endeavored to do all of this while dealing with an idiosyncratic, unpredictable, and unprincipled commander in chief.

This was not a position I ever expected to be in when I was a young boy growing up in a small coal-mining town forty-six miles southeast of Pittsburgh. My birthplace, Uniontown, was founded on July 4, 1776, not far from Fort Necessity, a small circular stockade built by George Washington during the French and Indian War. General George C. Marshall, the area's favorite son, was born and raised in Uniontown. His home, which later became the site of the local VFW, was no more than a quarter mile from where I first lived. Marshall and I used to play in the same creek that ran between our homes, I'd muse, though with about ninety years of time between our boyhood exploits.

In the 1960s, Uniontown was about seventeen thousand strong and its diversity was marked by the various places of worship dotting the city, each identified by the ethnic groups that attended them, and the foods, customs, language, and histories their congregants brought to our tight-knit community. People from this blue-collar area were generally conservative, patriotic, and hardworking. We were considered Reagan Democrats in the 1980s. By that time, unfortunately, the collapse of the steel industry, which had begun in the previous decade, had hit the region hard. Many coal mines went under too, taking thousands of jobs with them. This was a historic change, from which most small towns in southwest Pennsylvania would never recover.

My late father, Tom, was a welfare caseworker for the state. His family had emigrated from Lebanon at the turn of the century. He had seven brothers and sisters, all of whom spoke Arabic and continued some of the traditions of their homeland. My mother, Polly, was a homemaker who traced her roots back to County Cork in Ireland. Her maiden name was Reagan, and she claimed to be part of the Reagan clan that came to the States in the latter half of the nineteenth century and gave us our fortieth president. I wasn't so sure about her story, but I wasn't about to say my "ma" was telling tales. Besides, I liked the notion of somehow being related to someone who would turn out to be one of our greatest presidents. She was an identical twin, and with seven older brothers and sisters of her own, it was quite a circus when the family came together.

I was born in 1964 and grew up during this period with my three younger sisters, Patty, Donna, and Beth Ann. The Vietnam War was ending, the local economy was crumbling, but at least the Pittsburgh Steelers were winning. I attended public school and played varsity sports year-round. In western Pennsylvania, that meant football, basketball, and track. I was a B+/A- student, but never made the National Honor Society. My life would change, however, when I came across a school catalogue for West Point in my guidance counselor's office.

I didn't come from a military family. Far from it. And with no major bases nearby, there was little connection to the armed forces. I did, however, read military history, watch classic World War II movies like *Patton* and *The Longest Day,* and play soldier with my friends in the backyard, but that was it. As I read that catalogue, West Point called to me with its pictures of cadets in gray uniforms, promises of military training in the summer, and engineering classes in the fall, not to mention the appeal of serving my country as an "officer and gentleman." The adventure, the challenge, and the academy motto of "Duty, Honor, Country" all resonated deep within me. I knew immediately it was where I had to go, where I needed to be. West Point was the only college to which I would apply.

A little over a year later, in July 1982, with freshly cut hair, an awkwardly worn uniform, and my first hectic day nearly under my new belt, I raised my right hand and swore my first oath to support and defend the Constitution of the United States against all enemies. More than one thousand other young, scared men and women from across the land would join me on that large, grassy field known as the Plain that hot summer day. It was an important moment for all of us. The Long Gray Line would continue.

My four years at West Point provided the foundation that would allow me decades later to stand up against a president who undermined our nation's institutions and traditions, had little respect for the truth or propriety, and put himself above everything else. The academy's purpose of developing "leaders of character" who valued integrity, put country and mission first, and—as the Cadet Prayer asked God to do—"Make us to choose the harder right instead of the easier wrong," all ran counter to Donald J. Trump's way of doing business.

My many years of public service in uniform and out, in the United States and abroad, in wartime and peace, constantly reinforced the importance of the timeless values drilled into us at West Point.* They were fully internalized long before I ever returned to the Pentagon and public service in 2017, and well before I would continually face off against the forty-fifth president of the United States. This moral, ethical, and professional compass would guide me as I took on one of the most demanding jobs, during one of the most difficult epochs, in one of the most tumultuous administrations in American history, and it would make all the difference in the world.

---

* For more detailed information on my life and career, please visit my website, marktesper.com.

CHAPTER 1

FIRST DAYS, EARLY WARNINGS

When President Trump came to office in January 2017, war with North Korea was a real possibility. I didn't fully realize this as I went through the confirmation process to become the twenty-third Army secretary, nor did I fully appreciate that Trump was playing carelessly with the matches that could ignite a conflict, one the world hadn't seen since the last war in Korea. It would be at least that bad.

The Senate confirmed me as secretary of the Army in mid-November by an 89–6 vote. I was grateful for what would become increasingly rare bipartisan support, and was sworn into office on November 21, 2017. I had worked on Capitol Hill for many years, particularly in the Senate, handled a range of policy issues in the private sector as well, traveled extensively abroad in both capacities to meet with foreign leaders and address issues up close, and, of course, served in the military. As such, I brought a great deal of defense, foreign-policy, and business experience to the position—more than two decades at this point, not counting my time on active duty. I knew many of the senators, so I also believed the vote reflected a reputation I had built for being bipartisan, even-keeled, and reasonable. I considered myself a traditional Republican with conventional views—a fiscal conservative, social moderate, and defense hawk who believed in free but fair trade, protecting the environment, legal immigration, and limited government—who worked across the aisle.

Stepping into the secretary of the Army's historic office on the second floor of the Pentagon's E-ring was like coming home. I remember as a young captain working in the War Plans Office on the Army Staff in the mid-1990s that the "secretary's office" then was hallowed ground. The highest I traveled in those days was to brief the three-star head of Army operations. Yet here I was twenty-one years later, sitting behind the large, ornate "Taft desk," with pictures of General George C. Marshall—my hometown hero—staring down on me. I felt privileged to serve my country once again. It was hard to imagine.

The key to success in any organization, and especially at the most senior levels, is getting the right team aligned and working together. Fate gave me Ryan McCarthy as the Army under secretary, General Mark Milley as the Army chief of staff, and General Jim McConville as the vice chief of staff of the Army. This lineup would make all the difference and was key to everything the four of us would accomplish in our nineteen months together. What each person brought to the team spoke volumes about how quickly we could deliberate, discuss, decide, and act.

Ryan McCarthy grew up in the Chicago area and attended the Virginia Military Institute. After college, he commissioned in the infantry and later served with the Army Rangers in Afghanistan. He then spent several years in the private sector and had a brief stint on Capitol Hill before reporting to the Pentagon to work as a special assistant to Secretary of Defense Bob Gates for a few years. In 2011, he left the DoD to take a senior role in the defense industry, before becoming Army under secretary six years later in his midforties.

Of medium height and build with a close-cropped haircut, Ryan leaned into the challenges we faced together. Whenever a problem arose, he would always pull me aside quietly, lean forward, and quietly say, "Mr. Secretary, I need to talk to you about something. . . ." I valued his ability to identify problems early, tease them out, and then propose solutions to get them fixed.

Jim McConville rounded out the Army's leadership team. He hailed from Quincy, Massachusetts, graduated from West Point in 1981, and became an aviator soon thereafter. With blue eyes that squinted as he spoke in his thick Boston accent, McConville commanded at multiple levels, served in both Iraq and Afghanistan, and distinguished himself as the longest serving and one of the most capable combat commanders of the 101st Airborne Division. McConville also brought valuable Pentagon experience to the job, having served previously as the head of Army personnel (G-1) and the chief of legislative liaison. McConville's and Milley's paths in the Army had crossed many times in the past, so they already had a strong working relationship.

The most important relationship, however, is the one between the secretary and the chief of staff. There is a large, heavy, wooden door that separates the secretary's and the chief's offices; it is a physical metaphor for their relationship. There are horror stories of past occupants who openly bickered or never spoke to each other. File cabinets, large potted plants, or anything else that could obstruct this passageway often blocked the door during these times. The Army would suffer as a result, with the civilians and uniformed personnel drawing battle lines on what is otherwise an integrated staff.

Milley and I made a different commitment—to keep the door open. Over time, we would take it to a new level, often transiting back and forth between each other's office multiple times a day to discuss issues, share information, or plot a way forward on some tough matter. It was a close relationship we would carry forward as secretary of defense and chairman, and one that few understood or appreciated. It made our relationship unique in the history of defense secretaries and chairmen, I suppose.

McCarthy, Milley, McConville, and I realized early on the special chemistry among the four of us that could give us the chance to do big things—long overdue and necessary things—with the Army. We just needed to stay focused on the mission and work together. We had some common bonds that facilitated this: we all served in the Army; we were all combat arms officers; all four of us had deployed and been in combat; and we were all willing to do what was necessary to improve the Army's readiness and position the force for the future.

The only thing that divided us was that both Milley and McConville were from Boston and Patriots fans, and I was from the Pittsburgh area and favored the Steelers. Counting Super Bowl wins and who had won or lost each week became important. More seriously, we sometimes spent time together outside of work, often joined by our wives. In many ways, it had the feel of being junior officers again in a battalion—committed to the team, focused on the mission, and having fun doing both.

When I arrived in November, however, our focus wasn't on the Army's future. The immediate challenge was the situation on the Korean peninsula, the readiness of our forces in South Korea, and the very real prospect of war with the Democratic People's Republic of Korea, or DPRK, as the North is more formally known.

In July 2017, four months before I took office, North Korea launched its first missile capable of reaching the United States. If they were able to mount a nuclear weapon atop one of them, then this was a very serious threat. U.S. Forces Korea in Seoul took reciprocal actions intended to send a warning message to Kim Jong Un, the DPRK's young authoritarian leader, but it failed to deter further firings. North Korea would continue missile launches into the fall and added a nuclear test in early September.

As the public rhetoric between Trump and Kim increased and sharpened, planning and preparations ticked up at the Pentagon, and military options were fine-tuned. North Korean officials would call Trump "Mr. Evil President," as Trump dubbed Kim "Little Rocket Man." This name-calling was petty and dangerous, doing nothing to resolve the differences between our countries. Tensions continued into the fall. A week after my arrival in late November, North Korea conducted another missile test.

General Milley had been holding near weekly readiness meetings with the Army Staff to ensure the units programmed to fight in Korea were fully prepared. We were also participating in field exercises, computer simulations, and all manner of training events in South Korea with our allies. The Army was also quietly sending leaders from U.S.-based combat units on temporary duty to "walk" the operational area where they might be deployed.

It was all very real and very serious, and Milley and McCarthy—as acting secretary of the Army pending my confirmation—had done a solid job in the months leading up to my arrival to get ready. We still had a lot of work to do, though, and it wasn't solely about combat units either. We had to procure and ship munitions to the theater, rehearse evacuation plans for civilians, exercise our communications networks, and ensure our logistical systems—which would move everything. from ammunition, food, spare parts, and other items forward to backhauling casualties, damaged equipment, and other items rearward—would function in the heat of battle. I worked on the war plan twenty-two years earlier, so it was a little strange and unsettling to see it being updated and rehearsed with such urgency.

In late January, about two months after becoming the secretary of the Army, I traveled to Redstone Arsenal in Huntsville, Alabama. I wanted to see and discuss a few things there, but my primary purpose was to meet with General Gus Perna, the head of U.S. Army Material Command—and eventual chief operating officer for Operation Warp Speed—to understand better the Army's logistical preparations and readiness for war with North Korea.

I was sitting with Perna in his office when an urgent call from the Pentagon interrupted our meeting. What could this be, I asked myself? The person on the other end informed me that the president was ordering a withdrawal of all U.S. military dependents from South Korea, and he was going to announce it that afternoon. I couldn't believe it. I asked if something had happened in Korea. Did Kim shoot a missile at Hawaii? Were North Korean armored units moving to the DMZ? Did they sink an American ship? Did Pyongyang fire a ballistic missile at the United States? What?

Only a few weeks before, Trump and Kim were taunting each other about the capabilities of their respective nuclear arsenals. It was the American president who would spook the world on January 3, 2018, with a series of tweets, culminating in one that said "Will someone from his [Kim's] depleted and food starved regime please inform him that I too have a Nuclear Button, but it is a much bigger & more powerful one than his, and my Button works!"[1]

And now we had a possible evacuation order. There was nothing to explain it. There was nothing to warrant it. I asked them to "check with the SecDef's office," follow up on these core questions, and to "start leaning into the problem." I would call back in an hour for an update with key leaders. I set down the phone and told Perna the news. He was stunned too.

There were more than 28,000 U.S. military personnel stationed in Korea, plus another 7,000 family members. Evacuating them all, along with 11,000 other DoD noncombatants, would be a challenging task. I had visited our troops there two weeks earlier. The command briefed me on their war preparations, which included plans to evacuate *all* Americans from South Korea, a number that approached close to 190,000 people.[2] It was a daunting task that was complicated and overwhelming, and which would take far longer than anyone preferred. The message I just received gave me no sense of timing for evacuating our families, but this was small potatoes compared to the bigger issue at hand.

Evacuating all American military family members was such an unexpected and dramatic move that many would likely interpret it that war was on the horizon, if not imminent. It would probably trigger a panic that would affect the South Korean economy, its stock market, air transportation, and a range of other things. U.S. citizens in Korea would want to leave as well, and likely request U.S. government assistance. Many other countries would probably follow suit, which would heighten the sense of panic throughout Korea and the region.

Most importantly, what would North Korea think? Kim would probably view a U.S. evacuation as a prelude to conflict. Even if he was unsure, prudence would demand he put his military on alert, get his ships to sea, and disperse his aircraft. Therefore, the critical question asked how exactly Kim would react. Would he stand down? Negotiate? Conduct more missile tests? Call for snap military exercises? Or would he strike first, targeting Seoul in a bloody assault? Maybe even seize the city of 10 million and then sue for peace before the United States could act with sufficient force. Would this be like the beginning of World War I, where we all stumble into a bloody, years-long conflict? Nobody knew, but this was a dangerous game of chicken, and with nuclear roosters no less. If the president was going to announce an evacuation, then, we needed to be ready for war.

As quickly as the warning found its way to me in Alabama, it also went away. I never received a clear explanation, but, apparently, somebody talked the president out of sending the tweet announcing the evacuation of Americans from South Korea. Crisis averted. War avoided. I was dumbfounded at the time as to what was happening, and why there was this back-and-forth decision making over a matter of such import and consequence.

My experiences later as secretary of defense enabled me to imagine someone on the White House staff, or maybe even a talking head on Fox News, goading the president into action, a series of moves that could lead to the outbreak of war. I would have to wrestle with and navigate these dynamics for eighteen months. Too many people played too often to the president's whims, and it seemed that too few were willing to consider the second-, third-, and fourth-order consequences. This wasn't simply Trump pushing over one domino, but possibly a series of black tiles that led in different directions, with other players—such as North Korea or China—able to tumble other sets of dominoes, maybe even more troubling ones. As such, these things needed careful deliberation, with Congress and our allies, but that simply wasn't how this White House tended to operate.

War with North Korea remained the top international concern

for me during my tenure as Army secretary, followed closely by Afghanistan, as it was my job to make sure our ground combat units were manned, trained, equipped, and prepared for what would be a bloody and violent fight. Who knew when another doomsday tweet might come? We had to be ready.

Fortunately, tensions in northeast Asia with North Korea began easing in early 2018, once Trump took a more diplomatic approach toward Kim. Nuclear testing stopped, as did long-range missile tests. This new tone would culminate in the very first meeting between the leaders of North Korea and the United States, in Singapore in June 2018. Many complained that Trump gave Kim what he wanted—a high-profile meeting that raised his stature—and received nothing in return. That is true in many ways, but Trump's engagement did get us off the warpath and kept things under control through the end of his term. That was a good thing. I had watched Presidents Clinton, Bush, and Obama try similar approaches dating back to the early 1990s with no real effect. Why not try a different diplomatic tack, especially when nuclear weapons are on the table?

With the early drama of a forced emergency withdrawal of American family members and government workers from the Korean peninsula behind me, I focused on writing a clear, concise two-page vision statement for where I wanted to take the Army during my tenure, and then developing the plans to implement it. We had to get the Army in much better shape and ready for the difficult future we saw ahead of us, especially if it meant a fight against China or Russia.

CHAPTER 2

AN ARMY RENAISSANCE

For years the war had lasted. Americans were killed and wounded in the thousands. People were tired. With the conflict behind them, the last thing they wanted to think about was preparing for the next fight. Nevertheless, on January 8, 1790, President George Washington delivered his first annual message to Congress. Washington had learned some important lessons about war and peace over his lifetime.

He told Congress, "To be prepared for war is one of the most effectual means of preserving peace." Washington was no warmonger. He had seen more death and destruction than anyone should. However, to ensure the young nation's security, he understood the importance of having a ready and capable force that could defeat its enemies, and thus deter the malign intentions of others in the first place.

Nearly two hundred years later, another great American president, Ronald Reagan, would capture Washington's maxim in the simple and eloquent policy of "Peace Through Strength." It would be our fortieth president's guiding principle as he rebuilt the U.S. military in the 1980s to confront the Soviet Union. As a result, the Cold War would end less than a decade after Reagan's inauguration.

In 2017, nearly thirty years after staring down the Soviets and defeating the world's fourth largest military in the 1991 Gulf War, the U.S. Army wasn't well prepared for war against the countries that could do us the most harm. In fact, while China and Russia modernized their armed forces to defeat ours, our high-end warfighting advantages eroded. After sixteen years of conflict in Afghanistan and Iraq, the continuous back-and-forth deployment of brigade combat teams to places like Europe and the Middle East, and a dramatic reduction in annual defense dollars over several years, the Army was tired, broken, and old. We were still very capable, but we weren't where we needed to be, nor were we on the right path, to preserve the peace, fight and win against the likes of China, and maintain America's role in the world for the next thirty years.

Once General Mark Milley became Army chief of staff in August 2015, he made readiness his top priority. At the time, the Army's nondeployable rate—meaning the percentage of soldiers unable to go to war—was an unacceptably high 15 percent. Five percent or lower is a solid mark to hit. Moreover, out of fifty-eight total brigade combat teams—the standard war-fighting maneuver unit of the Army—the number considered fully ready was in the single digits. These units, which averaged four thousand to five thousand soldiers each, needed to be above 50 percent. Times were tough, and the future didn't look better.

Meanwhile, the Army was still heavily reliant on the foundational combat systems of the Reagan buildup decades earlier: the Abrams tank, Bradley fighting vehicle, Apache attack helicopter, Blackhawk utility helicopter, and Patriot air-defense system. Army leaders improved them all over the years, but upgrades can only go so far. The service tried in the past to introduce new systems but failed miserably with projects such as the Crusader mobile artillery system and the Future Combat System family of vehicles. The department wasted billions of dollars with little or nothing to show for all the money and effort. Acquisition of major end items had a terrible legacy. It was the result of bureaucracy, an insatiable appetite to add an insufferable number of requirements to a program, inefficient processes, and a weak business culture.

The Army had become really good at fighting insurgents and terrorists over the last sixteen years. To meet the demands of the times, the types of combat units critical to winning wars against threats like North Korea, let alone China and Russia—heavy armor, artillery, and air defense, for example—had to learn to fight like the light infantry. For many, the daily tasks of maintenance, gunnery, and maneuver training went by the wayside; fighting as a combined arms team atrophied; being concerned about enemy aircraft, electronic surveillance, and long-range missiles waned. The last decade and a half was about counterterrorism, convoy security, foot patrols, and running checkpoints.

To make matters worse, the Army lowered recruiting standards at times. This would solve the immediate manpower shortage problems resulting from the conflicts in Iraq and Afghanistan but created deeper challenges down the road when it came to maintaining readiness, good order, and discipline.

Ryan McCarthy and I arrived in 2017 and, with McConville and Milley as our uniformed counterparts, began mapping out plans to address all these issues and more, even before we were confirmed.

An emphasis for Secretary of Defense James Mattis was improving the readiness and lethality of the armed forces. President Trump would deliver on his plan to increase funding for the military and, with Congress's help, this would continue for three good years. We knew if we did anything with these much needed dollars, we had to keep improving current readiness while effecting a dramatic shift to modernize the force.

By the end of my first six months as Army secretary, I had written a new vision statement for the Army.[*] General Milley cosigned it with me to demonstrate that the Army's civilian and military leaders were equally committed to the path charted. Both a clear vision and the partnership had been lacking for years.

In two short pages, I covered not only what we wanted to achieve by 2028 but also the ways and means to get there. The vision emphasized the centrality of the American soldier and their leaders, and the importance we placed on remaining committed to, and living by, the Army's values.

We also spoke to the need to grow the force to more than five hundred thousand active-duty soldiers. This would not only give us greater capacity but also allow us to reduce the strains on our soldiers and their families by spreading the burden of frequent deployments. A deployment cycle typically alternated between a nine-month tour abroad, followed by an eighteen-month stay at home, and then another nine-month deployment.[†] To improve further our soldiers' professional experience and quality of life, we planned to implement a new market-based, talent-centric personnel

---

[*]   For the 2018 Army Vision, see Appendix A.

[†]   The military shorthand for this cycle is called the "deploy-to-dwell" ratio. In numerical terms, we wanted to achieve a ratio of 1:3 and no less than 1:2 for active-duty forces, and higher for the National Guard and Army Reserve, in order to sustain readiness.

system that would better optimize the Army's manpower pool. This initiative would go a long way to retaining more of our service members by giving them greater say when it came to where they worked, what they did, and how often they moved.

The vision made clear that we now faced a new range of future threats, beginning with China, and that we had to focus training on high-intensity combat operations under the constant surveillance that would mark conflict with the People's Liberation Army. This type of warfare was on the other end of how we had fought the last sixteen-plus years—low-intensity warfare—so it would be a dramatic and overdue shift.

The challenges we cited in making this shift began with the fact that technological change was accelerating and that we would face continued downward pressure on our budget. We are seeing that today. As such, I wanted to prepare the Army to pursue needed reforms that would free up time, money, and manpower to put back into our top priorities. Moreover, to be successful, the vision affirmed our objective of standing up a new command that would focus Army acquisition to modernize the force, our biggest challenge.

The vision statement would be the road map for the Army's "renaissance"; we would also use it as a yardstick to measure our progress. I'm proud to say that we started the ball rolling on all the major items included in the vision and accomplished many of them in the time we had. However, it wasn't easy, especially with everything else occurring in the world and in Washington, D.C.

In 2018, the U.S. Army failed to meet its recruiting goals. This was the first time it happened in over a dozen years. It was easy to attribute the misfire to a very strong job market, which typically works against the armed services when it comes to recruiting eighteen-year-olds graduating from high school, but there were other issues at play.

The Army probably reached too high the year prior by trying to grow too fast, failing to recognize the challenge presented by an expanding economy that offered America's youth more opportunities. By the time I arrived in November 2017, the Army's active-duty personnel target was 483,000, which translated into an annual recruiting goal of 80,000. Congress lowered that number further, but the Army still came up short.[1]

It was troubling to learn what the data and people outside of Washington told me as I dug into the problem. We were sacrificing quality for quantity. Too many recruits received waivers for histories of drug use, bad conduct, breaking the law, medical problems, or even mental health issues. All this did was create problems down the road. To me, quality took priority over quantity any day of the week, even if that meant a smaller Army. Therefore, if we were to meet all of our recruiting goals, we needed to be more innovative and commit more resources. More importantly, the answer wasn't to lower standards. People want to believe they are part of something special, something elite if not unique. Our answer was to *raise* the standards.

Traditionally, 95 percent or more of Army enlistees are high school graduates, the top category. Two-thirds score in the top half in verbal and mathematical aptitudes. However, the DoD allows up to 4 percent of recruits to come from the lowest tier, Category 4. We immediately cut that in half, allowing no more than 2 percent. Further, a failed drug test now meant automatic disqualification. We also removed prospective recruits with indications of mental health issues—such as "self-mutilation" or suicide attempts—as well young people who committed serious crimes. These actions and others mostly took care of my quality concerns.

We were also conscious of extremism in any form entering our ranks. The Army carefully screens new recruits for any tattoos or body markings that suggest membership in or support for extremist organizations. We also conduct social media and other background checks as warranted. The Army had some bad experiences in the past, and every year would come across a small number of cases. We worked hard to keep those corrosive views and behaviors out of our ranks by swiftly dealing with these cases. We expected America's soldiers to be committed to one organization, the U.S. Army; loyal to their fellow service members, regardless of race, ethnicity, and gender; committed to defending the country; and sworn to an oath of supporting the U.S. Constitution. It was that simple.

When it came to missing our recruiting numbers, we were also late to discover the serious problems in our recruiting operations, beginning at the Pentagon. We uncovered issues of mismanagement, poor leadership, and squandered dollars that caught the attention of lawmakers on Capitol Hill. Some marketing ideas had very low returns on investment. All of this prompted us to investigate—and eventually conduct a complete overhaul of—the operation. This took months and months to sort out, and in the meantime, our recruiting was suffering.

Eventually the team brought forward a series of recommendations to completely transform our recruiting operations, including hiring a different marketing firm, initiating a new ad campaign, and making other changes that would at least get us even with our competition—the other armed services.

We were also facing some alarming demographic changes in the country that were a warning sign for me, and should be for the nation's leaders. Studies were telling us that 71 percent of the 34 million seventeen- to twenty-four-year-olds in the United States could not meet the military's entry requirements, most often due to obesity, drugs, physical and mental health problems, misconduct, or aptitude. Worse yet, only around 1 percent of the population that could qualify—the other 29 percent—had some interest in serving. When you did the math, it meant that the Army, Navy, Air Force, and Marines were all competing for the same three hundred thousand to four hundred thousand young Americans.[2] Therefore, when you throw in the fact that our marketing, branding, and appeal seemed weaker than the other services, the Army was in a bad position.

We were also sensing declining support among parents and other "influencers"—teachers, counselors, coaches, pastors—for their children to join the Army, which we attributed to the long wars in Iraq and Afghanistan, and too many TV shows, stories, and movies portraying service members as "broken heroes" who wrestled with severe combat injuries and PTSD. It wasn't accurate, and it had a negative effect.

We knew that if we were to stay ahead of the trend lines, we had to shift the narrative and change our game. This meant overhauling our marketing campaign to portray more of the noncombat skills—such as medical technicians, mechanics, cooks, truck drivers—that the Army needed, and that were often less dangerous, more interesting, or provided a better transition to the civilian job market for young people. It meant going online, in all forms of social media, and requiring recruiters to use Instagram, moves that would pay off in 2020 once COVID shut down many recruiting offices. It meant reducing TV ads in favor of targeted advertising on Facebook and Twitch. It also meant putting money behind unconventional ideas coming out of Recruiting Command that would make the service look cooler and more appealing, from the creation of a competitive Army CrossFit team to the establishment of an Army eSports cadre that would participate in online competitions.

As I pushed this notion of an Army "renaissance," we all believed that reinstating the World War II–era "pinks and greens" uniform—the iconic Army attire of the greatest generation—would be a big morale booster for the force. It would remind everyone of our tremendous history, help burnish the Army's appeal, and strengthen our connections to society. Dan Dailey, the sergeant major of the Army, was the real leader on this initiative. He made the case that we should issue this classic uniform to our recruiters first. Dailey was right. One of my favorite days as Army secretary was approving the return of this historic uniform.

The composition of our recruiting teams also needed to change to give them local appeal with local knowledge. This meant getting our sergeants and officers in Recruiting Command back to the towns, cities, and states where they grew up. I spoke with a recruiter once in Boston who was originally from New York City. He wanted to be assigned to his old stomping grounds, but a colleague of his, who was from Boston ironically, was already there. You would think we could simply swap them out.

We also needed more women in recruiting and more people of color. I met once with the recruiting team responsible for the broader Denver area. We had only one woman for that entire metro region at the time. Go figure. It wasn't all bad, though. When I visited a recruiting headquarters in Los Angeles, I was pleased to see that the command was quite diverse.

Finally, our efforts needed to expand across the country and across demographics. We viewed ourselves as "America's Army," and if that was the case, then we needed to represent better our fellow citizens we swore an oath to defend. Yet we faced, and still do, some troubling facts. To begin, nearly 80 percent of recruits have a relative who served, which suggests military service has become somewhat of a family business. And second, an inordinate number of recruits—41 percent—come from the South.[3] We needed to broaden our recruiting base.

In the fall of 2018, we developed a "22 City" initiative, which meant going to nearly two dozen of America's largest cities to recruit—going to where the young people are, especially urban areas where many high school graduates were looking for more and different opportunities. By doing this, we would broaden our reach into other regions, and into many states that didn't have as much identification with or exposure to the U.S. military. We realized it would take time, but we needed to start somewhere, sometime, before the recruiting pool became too narrow, too regional, and too hard.

The Army's leaders fanned out to many of these urban areas. I personally visited cities ranging from Boston and Pittsburgh to Cleveland and Atlanta, and to Denver and Los Angeles. The purpose was to hear from our recruiters on the ground, to speak with mayors, governors, and other leaders, and to spend time with local media at each stop. After nearly two years of effort, the Army saw a 15 percent annual increase in recruiting from these cities from where we began in 2017. It was a good start.

Taking a long-term perspective, I said at the time—and still believe today—that one of the greatest challenges facing our country going forward will be ensuring a strong bond between the less than 1 percent of the U.S. population that serves in uniform, and the other 99 percent we are sworn to defend. With fewer and fewer young Americans both able to serve and interested in military duty, with our recruiting pools not well represented across the country, and with service becoming more of a family business, we risk a military increasingly isolated from the broader American public it serves. We need a national effort, led by our elected leaders, sports figures, celebrities, entertainers, and other well-known influencers, to join with the armed forces and help address these trends. This side of the civilian-military relationship coin is too important and too consequential to risk.

In my multiple jobs at the Pentagon over a quarter century, the position of Army secretary was by far the most fun, the most productive, and the most rewarding. Having the opportunity to be back among young soldiers one day, and to turn around and make decisions that will shape the Army for decades the next, was quite the joy and privilege.

Leah felt the same way. We had the chance to leverage our experiences from my twenty-one years in uniform to make a difference for the soldiers and their families. Leah was by my side through thick and thin to help move things forward, whether it was improving job opportunities for spouses, expanding child-care capacity, or simply ensuring new moms received the recuperation time they needed in Army hospitals after giving birth. She was the voice and conscience of Army families for me, and I'll be forever grateful for the time she spent with me in D.C. and on the road meeting with spouses, taking issue briefs, and developing new ways to take better care of the families.

Unit readiness is largely shaped by four factors: having enough time and resources to train for your assigned tasks; ensuring the right number and type of soldiers are in your units; possessing the correct numbers and types of equipment; and maintaining a sufficient level of serviceability of that equipment. The confluence of all these assessments, plus a commander's evaluation, constitutes a unit's readiness level. In early 2017, only a few out of the thirty-one active-duty brigade combat teams were fully ready to deploy. To quickly improve this, we dug into every element of readiness.[4]

Mandatory training—the classes and instruction often directed from above, including from Congress—had grown ridiculously high since I commanded an infantry company in the early 1990s. It now took the typical unit at least forty days to complete all this instruction. I served in both Army National Guard and Army Reserve units as well. If you are a traditional reservist, you only have about thirty-eight days in a normal year to begin with to train. How were the Guard and Reserve going to find time for their unit training if they had to complete nearly six weeks of required individual training first? It was impossible.

Some of these mandates were completely unnecessary; most gave commanders little say in how to adapt the training, if at all, to their unique situation. It also frustrated our soldiers. We asked them to be willing to fight and die for their country in wartime, and then we treated them like children in peace. However, this is what happens when higher headquarters tries to manage centrally from the top down, and often does so in reaction (or overreaction) to an incident or trend.

One of my favorite examples of BS training and unnecessary requirements was a program called the Travel Risk Planning System, or TRiPS. Over the years, well-intended bureaucrats eager to help reduce accidents associated with soldiers doing normal stuff such as taking road trips or driving home over a long weekend, developed this checklist to help soldiers assess their weekend plans. Every person was required to do a TRiPS assessment, even if you lived in a nearby town and wanted to visit your parents. Nearly all were complaining about TRiPS. It had become a monster.

I never had to deal with it during my time in the service. It was the sergeant's job back then to know when his/her soldiers were taking leave or a weekend pass, and then discuss their plans with them as necessary. So, on a long plane flight overseas once, I asked my staff to pull up the TRiPS program online so that I could apply for a weekend pass. I wanted to see if it was as bad as the troops were telling me. I logged in and began the series of questions. Thirteen minutes later—yes, thirteen minutes—the system denied my pass and instructed me to see my chain of command. TRiPS died that day.

We eliminated several dozen mandatory training, inspection, reporting, and other requirements beginning in the spring of 2018. It had a big effect on training time, and in the confidence we were expressing in our junior leaders, but it still took a while to get the bureaucracy to purge these programs and this tendency from the system. Too many people don't like change, and many more are afraid to take a little managed risk.

We then worked hard to improve collective training, which is military jargon for when everyone trains together as a team. The National Training Center (NTC) was the Army's premier training site, with thousands of acres of open land in the California desert for Army brigades to go head-to-head in a mock war fight for two-plus weeks against a heavy armored force that fought like the Russians. Developed in the 1970s to prepare the Army to fight the Soviets, it was the next best thing to actual combat.

I had gone through an NTC rotation as a lieutenant in the 101st Airborne Division decades earlier, so I understood the demands it placed on units. Most would agree that the NTC was critical to the Army's swift defeat of the fourth largest army in the world during Operation Desert Storm in 1991. However, over the last ten years, the NTC adapted its program to meet the needs of units deploying to Iraq and Afghanistan. There weren't nearly as many "high intensity" rotations as in the past, and certainly nowhere near enough as we entered this era of great power competition with China and Russia. The plan was to return to these types of heavy operations, with lessons learned from the Russians' actions in Ukraine (for example, incorporating the use of drones) and elsewhere, and then completely max out the number of rotations to the NTC.

These are a few of the major initiatives we pushed. And when coupled with a significant increase in training dollars and other actions—such as personnel policy changes to keep units together longer—the number of brigade combat teams fully ready to deploy by late 2018 had increased 400 percent.

After graduating from West Point, I had attended the Infantry Officer Basic Course at Fort Benning, Georgia, for about five months. The course prepared me to lead a forty-plus-man platoon. Ranger school awaited me after that; it was there that I learned a great deal about leadership and infantry tactics. It built upon my earlier graduation from Airborne school to become a paratrooper, and later Pathfinder school, Air Assault school, and, much later, Jungle training. I had nearly a year of individual schooling under my belt before I took command of my first platoon in the spring of 1987. I was well prepared to do my job, but the same wasn't true for our newest soldiers, which was obvious when they arrived at their first duty assignment.

Too often, many of these young privates would show up at their initial unit underprepared to meet the demands of an active-duty Army brigade combat team. Many weren't fit enough, didn't possess all the right skills, and usually didn't understand tactics well. This placed a burden on the sergeants now responsible for them; it would take a lot of time and hard work to get them ready. General Milley and I had a different vision, a simple one: ensuring that our newest soldiers were ready to deploy the week they arrived at their first assignment.

To do this, we would have to overhaul basic training and add more money and people. It would end up being the biggest change to basic and advanced infantry training since 1974, and a big part of our renaissance. The results were impressive.

Achieving our goal meant extending basic and advanced training by over 50 percent, to twenty-two weeks, which made it one of the longest (if not *the* longest) in the world. Initial reports in early 2019 showed a 50 percent reduction in attrition and injuries, with significant improvements in physical fitness, land navigation, and marksmanship skills. The additional training time and a significant reduction in the drill-sergeant-to-trainee ratio drove these results.[5]

In November 2018, I went to Fort Benning to observe the new program up close. The trainees were employing all infantry weapons, conducting hand-to-hand combatives training, and performing a variety of other tasks critical to modern warfare. I watched from a catwalk twelve feet above a series of ceiling-less rooms as groups of four young infantrymen stacked against a concrete wall, readied themselves, and then conducted a live-fire clearing of multiple rooms. It was incredible. As the rifles of entering soldiers fired one round after another with precision at the targets, they looked more like experienced professionals than they did new recruits. They could have fought side by side on day one with the paratroopers I once led.

There was a great deal of excitement regarding this change. I would learn months later that the active-duty units assigned this new batch of soldiers were equally impressed. The reports I received said they quickly integrated because they were as fit as the old hands, were proficient on nearly every weapon, understood tactics, and had mastered basic soldier skills. This was a sea change. We decided quickly to expand basic training for other branches, such as armor and cavalry.

While the changes to basic and advanced training would take

time to propagate throughout the force, the physical fitness training we incorporated into the new infantry basic and advanced training proved itself out and promised its own renaissance in combat fitness for the entire Army.

Since 1980, the Army used the three-event Army Physical Fitness Test (APFT), consisting of push-ups, sit-ups, and a two-mile run, to gauge soldiers' fitness. It was a simple test that could be administered anywhere, but it wasn't too hard to prepare for or excel on. Most troubling, though, was that it had little correlation to the fitness needed by soldiers in wartime. This had to change.

Years before my arrival as Army secretary, the service began experimenting with a replacement for the APFT that would be based on our wartime experiences in Iraq and Afghanistan, more than a hundred critical "warrior tasks and drills" required of soldiers, and modern fitness regimens. We also had good data on how, where, and why soldiers suffered physical injuries. For example, we knew that musculoskeletal injuries—broken bones, muscle strains, and cartilage tears—prompted more battlefield evacuations than enemy action. We were seeing similar things during training. Many of these injuries—which reduced deployability and combat power on the ground in war zones—were preventable through proper technique training, practice, and strengthening. As such, an improved fitness regimen could help units maintain higher levels of readiness, effectiveness, and deployability.

Born from these studies and assessments was the Army Combat Fitness Test (ACFT). The six-event ACFT would mimic the skills, movements, and other physical tasks associated with combat, and would measure attributes such as power, agility, endurance, and speed. Whereas the current APFT was only around 30 percent relevant to combat movements and tasks, the ACFT was well over 70 percent.[6]

We also made the test both age- and gender-neutral, with performance standards pegged to the soldier's military occupational specialty. This was consistent with direction given to us by Congress, a fact seemingly disregarded by a couple of liberal senators who have worked to delay the ACFT's implementation and lower its standards.[7] Nonetheless, the new test reflected the realities of the modern battlefield and resonated well with our younger soldiers. We knew that many could meet the test's high standards, and with hard work and proper training, nearly all should be able to do so. I saw several personal examples of that happening to make me confident in this decision. A female sergeant on my staff who probably weighed no more than 110 pounds and who could barely pass the test at first, ended up exceeding the infantry standard on a few parts after several months of training. It would just take time, effort, and commitment.

The ACFT was only one aspect of our plans to transform the Army's fitness culture. We also wanted to put sports trainers, physical therapists, nutritionists, and other specialists down into our brigades and battalions to help units and individuals be the best they can be. We called this part of the plan "holistic health and fitness"; it promised to "optimize soldier readiness, reduce injury rates, improve rehabilitation after injury, and increase the overall effectiveness of the Army."[8]

In short, we looked at the Army as a professional sports team—"tactical athletes," we called them—that needed to understand the importance of nutrition, sleep, strength training, flexibility, and aerobic fitness—to be the most lethal and ready players on the modern battlefield.

I approved the new fitness test in the summer of 2018 after taking and passing it myself. I was convinced it would deliver on its promises, as would our holistic health and fitness plans. During my tenure as Army secretary, I traveled around the Army and conducted morning physical training with the troops quite often. Our younger soldiers were generally on board with the new test; many had grown up doing CrossFit and other high-intensity workouts. Older soldiers were less enthusiastic and concerned, which wasn't a surprise. This would be a major change for them, so we set the implementation date out a couple of years to give everyone sufficient time to train. Nevertheless, at the end of the day, we had to ensure our soldiers were as healthy and fit as modern warfare would demand.

To prepare the Army for high-intensity conflict against China and Russia, we also had to begin reshaping the force. The insurgencies of the past fifteen years put less emphasis on "heavy" units, such as tank brigades, and combat systems, such as short-range air defenses and long-range artillery.

The most lethal Army ground formation is the armored brigade combat team (ABCT), which has over 4,500 soldiers, 85 Abrams tanks, and 150 Bradley fighting vehicles. These units carry quite the punch and would lead the fight in a major ground war. Infantry brigade combat teams (IBCTs) could deploy more quickly but weren't nearly as potent or operationally mobile as an ABCT. Therefore, we began rebalancing our force structure by converting two IBCTs to ABCTs. Meanwhile, we launched new programs to build longer-range artillery systems and mobile air-defense battalions, and looked at other ways to make the ABCTs even more robust, such as adding additional mechanized infantry companies to their formations, along with electronic warfare and cyber capabilities.

We also worked to resurrect a fourth corps headquarters that would focus on Europe to improve our command and control and help organize the war planning and preparations of our NATO allies. Despite the need, the Obama administration deactivated V Corps (commonly known as Fifth Corps) in Germany in 2013, about eighteen months after announcing the withdrawal of two brigades and seven thousand soldiers from Europe. A year later, Russia annexed Crimea and occupied eastern Ukraine. In February 2020, the Army announced the V Corps reactivation and basing at Fort Knox, Kentucky, with a small forward headquarters established months later in Poland. The uncasing of the corps flag came on the heels of the largest deployment of U.S. forces to Europe in decades. Our NATO allies were happy; so were we.

On top of all this, however, we had other changes to make to our force structure and doctrine. We experimented with a new Multi-Domain Task Force in the Indo-Pacific designed to counter China by integrating conventional military capabilities with cyber, information, and electronic warfare functions. We also began studying whether and how to restructure our fighting formations. Do we stick with brigade combat teams, go back to the division structures of the 1980s, or move to something completely new? These were important issues to dig into if we were going to win in the years to come.

By March 2019, we were seeing big increases in readiness. The Army's nondeployable rate shrunk to 6 percent and the readiness of our active-component brigade combat teams reached a high of 74 percent, with half of all brigades (both active and Guard) considered ready. At the same time, our investments in expanded basic training, new fitness tests and health regimens, more armored brigades, and other changes were showing real promise in reshaping the Army for the future.

While the Army knew how to train for combat, it did not have a great track record when it came to modernizing the force. The

Reagan buildup in the early 1980s saw the introduction of the so-called Big 5 weapons systems designed to defeat the Soviets. These systems crushed the Iraqis twice yet were still in use more than three decades since their introduction. The service needed a new mix of speed, lethality, survivability, and mobility that only modern technologies, such as robotics and AI, could provide.

To avoid the abysmal failures of the past, we also needed a new acquisition system that could deliver. This was the backdrop behind the Army's Six Modernization Priorities and the establishment of Army Futures Command (AFC). Both were critical pillars in this renaissance we were working to effect.

General Milley was the natural leader for advancing readiness through training. However, when it came to modernization, Ryan McCarthy shined. He really immersed himself in the issue, bringing the right combination of enthusiasm, knowledge, experience, and determination to the task.

In 2018, we made the biggest change in the Army's structure in over four decades—since 1973—when we established the AFC in Austin, Texas. With McCarthy in the lead, we had spent months going over the organizational purpose and structure, the roles and responsibilities, the systems and processes, and all the way down to how we would choose the cross-functional teams to lead each of our modernization priorities. I also had to select the commander, which ending up being the very capable General Mike Murray. For the first time in the Army's history, one commander was driving concept development, requirements determination, organizational design, science and technology research, and solution development.

This change didn't come easy, however. We had a lot of resistance from within the Army, including from some of our acquisition professionals, who saw this as a threat to their programs and prerogatives. When some didn't get their way, they went to the Hill or leaked to the press all the nefarious reasons that Futures Command would fail, and how it would harm the service. It was a lot of bunk, and it caused unnecessary delays and friction.

One of the reasons so many major Army programs failed in the past was that the acquisition system itself was broken. It wasn't due to a lack of good ideas, able professionals, or extraordinary effort. We had all of that. But overall, the acquisition system was risk averse, prone to say no to new ideas and yes to more process, and constantly demonstrating that classic bureaucratic tendency to protect turf and budget. At the end of the day, however, it was Army capability and soldier effectiveness that paid the price for this behavior.

Another issue we had to sort through was the constant tension between the demands of today and the needs of tomorrow. Modernization had suffered in the past because those organizations charged with thinking about future war and its requirements became burdened with today's problems, such as combat operations in Iraq or the conflict in Afghanistan. In short, the present was constantly elbowing out the future.

To address this dynamic, it was decided when we created AFC that all of those organizations responsible for future warfare, identifying enemy tech trends and investments, studying advanced operational concepts, and so on would be assigned to AFC and would not be allowed to work on current problems. Futures Command could work only on issues and programs beyond the five-year Future Years Defense Program. It wasn't a hard black line, but it was a very good demarcation point to protect the future from the present, and vice versa.

To guide AFC's work, the Army established a clear set of modernization priorities that we publicly committed to not change. During my many years on Capitol Hill and in the defense industry, I saw the services' priorities constantly shifting. This made it hard for the private sector to be a good and helpful partner.

One of the things my many years as a senior defense executive taught me was that companies need predictability, clarity, and commitment from the DoD. This means a clear objective, a long-term plan to achieve it, and dedicated funding over several years. With these things, industry is more willing to spend its own money on research and development, hire the right people, retool factories, and do all those things that are essential to competing, winning, and delivering on a contract. When the DoD, or Congress by extension, fails to provide these things, you get more risk—meaning fewer bidders, and all of whom tend to bake more time and cost into their proposals to offset the uncertainty. For the Pentagon, this often means higher prices and schedule slips. Not surprisingly, these were the hallmarks of some of the Army's epic modernization failures.

The six priorities critical to modernizing the Army were straightforward. First up was *long-range precision fires,* focused on improving the range, accuracy, and lethality of the cannon artillery and missiles needed in an Indo-Pacific fight. Second was *next-generation combat vehicles,* a new optionally manned tracked combat system to replace the Bradley fighting vehicle; these would be critical in the intense urban warfare we envisioned. *Future vertical lift* was our third priority. We needed a new helicopter fleet with greater range, speed, and survivability if they were going to fly against Chinese air defenses in the western Pacific. Fourth up was the *Army network,* a broad term for ensuring we had a resilient and secure tactical communications network that would work against Russian and Chinese jamming and intercepts—something ISIS and the Taliban never had. *Air and missile defense* was our fifth priority. Because the wars in Iraq and Afghanistan required more foot soldiers, and our enemies didn't have air assets, we cannibalized these units to free up troops and money. This was shortsighted, though, and the Army now needed to rebuild these capabilities. Moreover, in an era of cruise missiles and drone swarms, we needed directed energy systems that could provide a "deep and cheap" magazine that missiles couldn't offer. Finally, the last of our top six modernization priorities was *soldier lethality*. The infantry usually suffered the largest numbers of casualties on the battlefield. We were committed to changing this by providing our soldiers advanced rifles, next-generation vision systems, and improved body armor.

To find the monies necessary to fund our six modernization priorities, and the thirty-one programs associated with them, we couldn't rely solely on new funding. The Army vision statement I released in June 2018 made clear we would face budget pressures in the future and twice said that we would need to make tough decisions when it came to spending.

I'm sure many thought these were throwaway lines, but I had been in Washington a long time and understood the budget math when it came to the nation's debt, the annual deficit, and future trends. By early 2021, the national debt was over 100 percent of gross domestic product, at nearly $28 trillion. For years the federal government has been spending more money each year than what it received, thus creating an annual deficit that accumulated over time into the overall debt.

Compounding this problem is the fact that each year, a larger and larger share of federal dollars was going to spending for programs such as Medicare, Medicaid, and Social Security as America ages and health-care costs continue to rise. Moreover, the interest the U.S. government pays to finance this debt is also growing. In 2019, all this so-called mandatory spending—programs based in law that run on autopilot—was over half of government expenditures.

With defense spending around 3.3 percent of GDP and about 15 percent of all federal spending, it was only a matter of time before these numbers were pushed down even further, all at a moment in history when we needed a solid decade of healthy defense budgets to transform the U.S. military. It was hard to see, though, how sufficient levels of defense spending could be sustained going forward, especially the 3 to 5 percent annual real growth in defense dollars—funding that needed to be predictable, adequate, and on time (meaning by the beginning of the new fiscal year)—that I was advocating.

Meanwhile, China was increasing its defense budget at no less than 6 to 8 percent annually.

This was the impetus behind my hard push for the Army to reform and make the tough choices. I used to say that the best time to fix your roof was when the sun was out, and during the early Trump years, the weather was great. Mistakenly, that's when most organizations relax and see the problems, if at all, as something in the distance. We needed a way to pressurize the system and apply the heat to find as much money as possible to sustain the renaissance. There might even be the chance to teach the service some better budget habits, and hope the lessons and the momentum would endure.

When I sat down for my first budget meeting in early 2018, the staff laid out a large sheet of paper filled with a single multicolored box. Inside the box were smaller boxes, with dollar figures coded to the colors of each square or rectangle. It looked like a large game of Tetris with all the colors, sizes, and shapes. As a briefer pointed to the graphic, he told me how much of our annual $182 billion was for people, for operations and maintenance, for military construction, for overseas contingencies, for basic training and modernization, and for health care, for example. Sitting upright in his chair, the officer told me what I could adjust, what I couldn't adjust, and what I shouldn't try to adjust. It was tedious and complex, but necessary to understand. Where you put your time and money, after all, says everything about your priorities.

"Okay," I said when the team finished. "How many of our thirty-one programs in our top six modernization priorities are we funding?" Blank stares froze across the table. The briefer hemmed and hawed a bit, then started down the path of "Well, sir, we've been working this for almost a year, the budgets always start out pretty tight, as we looked at this. . . ." Yada yada yada. My BS meter went off. I stopped him and said, "Just tell me the number." It was astounding to hear that it was such a small percentage of our overall budget.

What happened was that the bureaucracy—Milley called it "the machine"—took over and did the same thing it had done the previous year, the year before that, and the year before that. Add a little here, trim a little there, and call it a day. There was no real prioritization; there was no bold shift; there was no appreciation that the Army's future was at stake, it seemed. In short, while McCarthy, Milley, McConville, and I were out beating the drum about transforming the Army, modernizing the BCTs, and preparing for a future fight with China, the bureaucracy had never jumped on board. Everyone was protecting his or her program and share of the pie.

"You need to start over," I said to the group. "Go back, rank and stack every single one of our five-hundred-plus modernization programs in priority order, and then come back in and tell me why each and every one is more important than our new modernization goals." I added, "Because as of today, the thirty-one modernization programs will be funded first, and we'll simply cut or reduce programs from the bottom of the five-hundred-plus-program list upward until we can afford the remaining programs at the top." The room went silent; people stiffened in their chairs; folks glanced nervously at one another from the corners of their eyes. The tension in the large, dimly lit room went from zero to one hundred.

I also told them not to feel beholden to finding savings only in the accounts that needed more funding. In other words, if we need more dollars to put into acquisition, then we will go to the acquisition account first, but we would also go to the operations and maintenance, personnel, and other budget lines if need be. "Everything is going to be prioritized, everything is going to be looked at, and everything is on the table. We have to be ruthless," I said. Milley, McCarthy, and McConville were all on board, and that made a big difference.

The teams scrambled off and came back in a few weeks. We started to review the first program on the list when someone from my congressional affairs team chirped up and said, "Sir, this program is important to Representative _____," he said. "If you touch this, then we'll have a fight on our hands." "I get it," I said matter-of-factly, without reminding folks that I had worked on the Hill for several years. I expressed confidence that "nearly every one of our programs has some type of congressional interest, sponsorship, or angle." I said, "But if we let politics be a determining factor, we'll never cut or trim a program, we'll never free up money, and we'll never reform."

And thus began what became known as "Night Court."

We began going through hundreds of programs, week after week, hour after hour. We canceled, cut, trimmed, delayed, and asked every question we could to get to ground truth. General after general, colonel after colonel, and occasionally a major, stood up to brief. We grilled many hard. Some we praised. Others we criticized. Everybody had the chance to speak. We kept asking: Why do you need this? How does it compare to a top six modernization priority? Why do you need a new one? How much longer can you drive the old one? Does the war plan say we need that many? Why? Why? Why?

We learned a lot about the Army. The "machine" thoughtlessly, on autopilot, consumed billions of dollars, buying equipment simply because it was on an organizational chart. Thousands and thousands of dump trucks, forklifts, and trailers, and now they were asking for new models, all to replace the current ones that often sat rusting, rarely moving, in motor pools. Our wartime experiences showed we rarely used all this stuff. Forklifts, for example, were often provided by the host nation, or they could be leased. We needed to look at these types of options, not just buy more. I would often say, "The Bradley fighting vehicle is decades old, and we've reached the end of its upgrading. If we have to fight the Russians in ten years, or the Chinese in twenty, would you rather have new forklifts and dump trucks, or a new fighting vehicle?"

We reduced Army watercraft by 50 percent, canceled programs for new rubber boats and cyber-proofed surveying instruments, scrutinized Army museums and institutes, and froze new hires for our civilian workforce. We spared few things outright. We went deep, we went broad, and we went hard. We also went after military construction, figuring out that there was really no prioritization there either. Everybody seemed to be logrolling, calculating who would be next to get a budget increase or project *they* wanted, instead of what the Army needed to prepare its soldiers or win the next fight.

Several weeks, five-hundred-plus programs, and over fifty hours of personal time later in Night Court resulted in us finding at least $25 billion in savings, with the accounting still ongoing. We had eliminated or reduced 186 programs to fund our modernization initiatives as well as such things as expanded basic training, a new recruiting campaign, and a complete overhaul of our physical fitness program.

The hard part now was selling it to Congress. To do so, I gave McCarthy the green light to go to the Hill weeks before the budget rollout to start briefing them. It was unconventional, and actually not permitted by standard practice, but we needed to inform the chairmen and ranking members before the administration delivered the budget to Capitol Hill. That way we could answer their questions up front—privately, quietly—before 186 program cuts dropped in members' laps. Giving them our numbers and rationale would also help them fend off the press, upset colleagues, angry constituents, corporate lobbyists, and others.

By the time the budget arrived at the House and Senate on March 11, 2019, the final amount saved over five years would be $31 billion. Every single one of the top thirty-one programs bundled under our six new modernization priorities received the money it needed. It was all about implementing our own vision for the Army. Most lawmakers respected that. Enough of them would get behind our plans as well.

At the end of the day, Congress supported all of our 186 proposed cuts and reductions except one. The major disappointment was our plan to delay the purchase of Block II CH-47 helicopters for five years, until we could determine whether we needed them, even though the current facts and data told us we really didn't. In our efforts to prepare the Army for high-intensity conflict against the Chinese or Russians, we needed a new type of heavy-lift aircraft. We needed one that could fly farther, faster, and with heavier loads, and which was less vulnerable to modern air-defense systems. That wasn't the CH-47, in my view.

Don't get me wrong. I had nothing against the CH-47 Chinook. It was a very capable aircraft. It was what carried other soldiers and me behind Iraqi lines in the opening days of the Operation Desert Storm ground offensive in 1991. However, like so many other Army systems, we didn't see it holding up well in the future. Moreover, we already had 10 percent more of them in the inventory than we needed. Rather than keep spending billions more on an aircraft we didn't need, we decided to put those dollars into developing new helicopters. A few lawmakers felt differently, regrettably. So much for putting our soldiers and readiness first.

The importance of congressional support for our efforts was more than the dollars-and-cents facts that we were freeing up money for the future. It sent an important message to the Army that our efforts, our hard work, the tough decisions we were making, would be rewarded. It was helpful in terms of purging bad habits from the system and working to adopt better ones.

The Army would continue our Night Court proceedings into the fall, and then into 2019. By the spring of that year, only a few months before I would become secretary of defense, we canceled another forty-one programs, and delayed or reduced thirty-nine more, to find an additional $13.5 billion in savings. The good news was that we never found fraud or waste; these were good programs. We simply needed to put their dollars into higher priorities. With the budget relatively flat at around $178 billion, we knew that we had to keep digging deep or risk the future.[9] Our efforts were paying off.

As we rolled into 2019 with our modernization initiatives moving forward nicely, I wanted to make the upcoming year about replacing the clunky Army personnel system with one based on talent management. We needed to go from an "up or out" philosophy to a "perform or out" approach. This would be a major change for the Army—the personnel pillar of the renaissance—but it was long overdue and much needed. It would go a long way toward advancing our credo of putting people first.

Vice Chief of Staff Jim McConville was passionate about the issue of talent management, which made him a perfect battle buddy when it came to reforming the personnel system. Not only did McConville bring a war fighter's perspective to the task, but he was also a functional expert as the former head of Army personnel—and as the father of adult children who were serving.

Under McConville's and my direction, a Talent Management Task Force was formed to turn what the four of us often called "an industrial age personnel system" into a digital one for the twenty-first century—and one that promised to do a far better job of meeting the needs of the soldier, the family, commanders, and the Army. We went about setting up a market-based, talent-focused model that gave commanders and soldiers (beginning with the officer corps)—the buyers and sellers, respectively—more say in their careers, their timelines, and the assignments they took.

Within the constraints of a military system where the needs of the Army still had to come first, there was no reason that we couldn't give people more say in their careers. Past studies and ongoing pilot projects demonstrated that a market-based system would work more efficiently, and with higher rates of satisfaction, than the current command-directed one.

The system wasn't completely broken, but it could be a whole lot better. In a volunteer force, people vote with their feet, and we were often losing too many top performers. In 2018, soldiers didn't make decisions to stay or go based solely on their career; now their duty location, their spouse's job prospects, and their children's schools were also factors.

We needed to give our service members the opportunity to stay at one duty station longer than three years if they wanted to because, for example, their wife or husband had a great job, they loved the schools, the community was wonderful, or aging parents were nearby. Homesteading may make them less competitive than peers who were willing to move and experience more of the Army, but that's a decision they could make as adults and professionals.

Leah and I moved four times between 1990 and 1995. It's not bad when it's just the two of you, an apartment's worth of household goods, and a young child, but it's really tough when you're asking your older kids to change schools two or three times as teenagers. And of course, Leah couldn't get a full-time job commensurate with her degree and work history. Companies knew she was married to an Army officer; they simply didn't want to invest the time in someone who likely had to leave in a couple of years. We needed to adjust our personnel system to these realities.

By May 2019, the leadership team was speaking publicly about the Army Talent Alignment Process Program, which would allow officers to search and apply for jobs across the Army. They would post their résumés and any other information they felt relevant to the assignments they were seeking. Commanders, conversely, would be able to see applicants and make better choices about who served in their units. They could attract top talent by posting things such as their command philosophy, training regimen, and the expectations they had of their subordinates. We began the inaugural iteration of this program in the first half of 2019, and the initial feedback was very good.

That summer, we also piloted a new multiday approach to selecting battalion commanders based on the NFL's Combine. Under this new system, selected officers underwent "a series of cognitive, non-cognitive, and physical assessments," such as fitness tests, assessments of verbal and written communications skills, and a double-blind interview with a panel of senior officers.[10] We knew the first major gateway to becoming a future commander and senior Army leader began with battalion command. As such, picking this initial pool of leaders was critical to the future of the service. We had to get it right. You must select officers who not only will excel at the battalion level but also have the potential to be a general officer who could perform at the four-star rung. This change turned out to be a dramatic and historic one that is already exceeding expectations.

There were several other initiatives we were pursuing as well, such as giving service members the opportunity to take yearlong unpaid sabbaticals without being penalized, and making it possible for soldiers to make seamless transitions between the regular Army, the National Guard, and the Army Reserve. I had made these switches over my twenty-one-year career, and it was needlessly difficult. Building ease and flexibility into career management could go a long way toward keeping people in the service.

All these things were good ideas, but the top issues for many families were spousal hiring and child care. Military spouses were the most overqualified and underemployed group of people in the country, I felt. It was an unfortunate by-product of an Army system that moved people frequently, and sometimes to states and locales that didn't recognize their credentials, want the professional competition, or need their skills. It was a bad mix of things that worked against spouses and families.

We went about approaching this problem by making professional license reciprocity a condition for installation investment decisions, working with members of Congress on federal mandates or state-level assistance, and other initiatives. I also worked with my fellow service secretaries to write all fifty governors to inform them that "family issues," such as the quality of local schools and license reciprocity for spouses, would be factors when our services evaluated future basing questions.

We made some progress, but not nearly enough. It would take becoming secretary of defense to add more heft to this push, but even then, I didn't accomplish all that I had hoped.

There were some obvious and simple solutions available, such as mandating through federal or state law that states must recognize a military spouse's professional credentials for up to three years when they arrive due to military orders, and creating a business tax incentive for hiring a military spouse. We couldn't seem to get much traction on either of these with lawmakers, though, which was frustrating, especially with so many elected officials talking the talk. Many states did recognize a military spouse's professional license, but not all. It was disappointing.

One great story comes to mind, and it shows the tenacity and spirit of military spouses. In October 2019, while visiting Wright-Patterson Air Force Base in Ohio, Leah met a woman named Bri McKinnon at a spouse luncheon. Bri had earned a teaching degree in special education in Washington State, but said Ohio made it "almost impossible" for her to get a job, even though she was credentialed and positions were open. Unwilling to give in, Bri took up the fight. After two years of meetings, constant travel, and testimony, she persuaded state lawmakers to draft, approve, and deliver a military-spouse reciprocity law to the governor's desk, which he signed in early 2020. Bri's leadership and tenacity made all the difference for countless numbers of military spouses in Ohio.

However, I couldn't expect our spouses to lead the charge, nor could I blame local, state, and federal governments for all our challenges. Even on our own installations, the civilian hiring process was long and complicated. On one of my first overseas visits as secretary of the Army, I did a town-hall meeting with families at Camp Humphreys in South Korea. The session was held in the chapel, an interesting location once the discussion broke down into tough talk from spouses, seated in one set of pews, directed at the installation staff, seated in another.

The spouses were rightly angry about a hiring process that took over 130 days on average to get someone working. Many on the installation staff thought that was quick, but it was terrible. The Army needed to get the process down to no more than 45 days. Who can wait more than four months to take a job?

However, these timelines were the average across the service, so I started a very tedious process month after month going through every step of the hiring system to cut out wasted time. Whether it was background checks, drug tests, or multiple review boards— you name it—we looked at it. We reduced it to under 90 days in the Army, and even that was excessively long.

The extended hiring process made it difficult to tackle the biggest issue for many families: child care. Some people thought we needed more on-base facilities, but that wasn't the main issue. When you looked at locations with long wait periods (months)—such as the Washington, D.C., area or Hawaii—the first problem that jumped out was the fact that some child-care facilities were only 70 percent or so filled. The 30 percent vacancy rate was due to a lack of child-care providers, and that was because the civilian hiring system was so slow. The reforms we put in place, like a centralized background check process and getting direct hiring authority, began fixing this.

Addressing the supply side of the equation could take us only so far in the near term. We also had to look at the demand side.

Reducing bureaucracy and timelines became my focus for my nineteen months as Army secretary. I kept with it as secretary of defense too. The demand on the DoD child-care system was too great to accommodate the needs of our service members under a first-come-first-served basis. Too often, junior enlisted personnel couldn't get on-base child care because the children of DoD civilian workers filled many of the slots. So I directed that military children take priority over the children of DoD civilian employees. Prioritizing military children rankled a good many civilian employees, but our first obligation had to be to our service members, especially our junior enlisted.

We had to put our service members first. Many lived on base, which made driving back and forth off base twice a day to drop off and pick up their kids a hassle, and sometimes a hindrance to the service member's work schedule. It could be a round trip of more than thirty minutes each time. Second, most civilians employed by the DoD either grew up in the area where they worked or rarely moved, so they had established friend and family networks to help them out. Military personnel who were coming and going every three years or less didn't have this advantage. And finally, some of our service members worked unusual hours, including getting up early in the morning for physical training, which made having access to the on-base child-care center to accommodate these things important to their work performance.

Mission accomplished for me would have been having sufficient on-base child care for those service members seeking it, plus the ability to do hourly care, and finally the option to have 24/7 services for those bases and career fields that needed that type of flexibility. The same was true for improving the Exceptional Family Member Program, a system by which a service member with a child in need of specialty care or medical attention would get easier access to both. Moreover, the family's needs would be taken into far greater account when assigning the service member to a new post. Each of these programs worked well at different installations around the

U.S. military, so I knew what was possible. We needed to adopt, adapt, and standardize them across the armed forces. We had settled on a plan for hourly child care in the fall of 2020. I wish we could have implemented this plan and the other things on my watch.

Some changes like this were hard for obvious reasons, but others seemed unnecessarily difficult. During my visit to Hawaii in August 2020, Leah learned that local commissaries and post/base exchanges did not allow patrons to wear fitness clothes, like gym shorts and yoga pants, inside the store. Needless to say, spouses were quite upset. After all, this wasn't the 1950s.

We heard stories of military wives returning from a fitness class who had to drive all the way home to change before going back out to pick up a gallon of milk or pump gas at the exchange. Another spouse recounted a story of how a Marine denied a mom and her seven-year-old boy from entering the commissary because the child was wearing "workout clothes." This was ridiculous. We ask the families to put up with short-notice moves, long deployments, missed holidays, and all of the other rigors of military life. Why make anything else more difficult than necessary?

I came back from the Hawaii visit and asked my Personnel and Readiness Office to draft a memo authorizing the wear of fitness clothes to commissaries and exchanges on all bases, provided they were clean, modest, and serviceable. They then sent the memo around to other OSD and service offices for coordination and comment. To my surprise, none of the armed services supported the change. They argued it was their business. "Okay," I said, "if it's your business, then go ahead and change it so that I don't have to." We waited weeks to see movement. Nothing. My staff told me the uniformed leaders "are concerned about good order and discipline of their service members." I understand, sort of. "But the spouses and children didn't join the military, so why not let them wear fitness clothes?" Silence.

We made one final adjustment to the memo, then, that gave the service secretaries the authority to waive the relaxed attire standards for military personnel. Still, no one approved. I had had enough. In October I decided to send out my own directive with no support whatsoever from the services. Many considered this a trivial matter for a secretary of defense to concern himself with, but it was the right thing to do for our families, and an important signal to send to our leaders. If we were going to talk the talk about taking care of families, so to speak, then we needed to walk the walk. In addition, I was confident that good order and discipline would survive in the U.S. military. The lesson of this story is that even the simplest things at the Pentagon are difficult to change. Sometimes you have to just do it.

I don't know whether any other Army secretary or defense secretary spent as much time on family issues, but having lived it, heard it, and committed to take it on, I couldn't let the issue go. I can only hope we made a difference for some military families, especially the spouses.

Aside from serving in an infantry battalion, nowhere else did I have more professional satisfaction than my time as secretary of the Army. As I said before, it was a great opportunity and experience. Leah and I really enjoyed being back and working with a wonderful group of uniformed and civilian professionals, while also being able to accomplish a good deal in the time we had. I went to work every day as if it was my last, and every day we moved the ball farther down the field.

I was blessed to have Ryan McCarthy, General Mark Milley, General Jim McConville, SMA Dan Dailey, and many others on the team with me. After nineteen months of hard work together, I felt we had launched a true Army renaissance that would resonate and endure long after we left. We were well on our way toward restoring the service back to the war-fighting posture it needed to be in if we were to fully realize George Washington's and Ronald Reagan's view—that the best way to preserve peace is by being ready to fight and win the war.

In time, I would come to realize that my experiences in the Pentagon as secretary of the Army, and the relationships I had built both there and beyond—with General Milley, the OSD and Joint Staffs, combatant commanders, the National Guard, members of Congress, international leaders, and others—would serve me well in the challenging times ahead as the twenty-seventh secretary of defense.

_____

CHAPTER 3

WAR WITH IRAN BEGINS IN IRAQ

_____

The United States and Iran were one misstep away from open con-flict. Planes, drones, and ships from both countries' air forces and navies traversed the contentious waters of the Persian Gulf, on it, beneath it, and above it. Proxy forces funded and directed by Teh-ran spread mischief throughout the region, while Washington and its allies worked their own shadow war to blunt and counter these malign actions. It was hard to believe we might find ourselves in *another* Middle East war.

President Trump appointed me acting secretary of defense on June 24, 2019, smack dab in the middle of this evolving milieu—America's most serious set of confrontations, friction, and heated rhetoric with Iran in decades.

I was not the person expected to take the job of defense secretary. Although I had been serving as the secretary of the Army—one of the three service secretaries at the DoD—Trump had selected

Patrick Shanahan, the deputy secretary of defense, months earlier. Pat was a tall, blond, thirty-year veteran of the Boeing Company, where he had led many of its trademark programs. He was a sharp leader and capable engineer with a good sense of humor. I had known Pat before he arrived at the Pentagon and liked him. His strong business skills were a good complement to what former Marine general Jim Mattis brought to his role as secretary of defense.

Secretary Mattis spent a lot of time on the road during his tenure, which I suspected was his strategy to avoid Trump and whatever requests might be made of him. This left Pat responsible for the occasional cabinet meetings and other engagements with the president. As such, a rapport developed between Shanahan and Trump. So when Mattis resigned in late December 2018, Pat was the natural successor as deputy, and he became the acting secretary of defense on January 1, 2019.

In May, four months later, Trump announced that Shanahan would become the next secretary of defense. There was some skepticism on Capitol Hill about Pat, but most expected his eventual confirmation. Not long after that, however, scrutiny into his personal life involving his ex-wife and children brought to light a dark period that prompted him to step aside. I felt bad for Pat. He had put his heart and soul into the job and was getting things done, but the beast that was Washington, D.C., was chewing him up, much like it did so many other people. It was one thing to dig into a nominee's past, but doing so in a way that harms a person's family was over-the-top. Nobody deserves that.

I was at an Army Senior Leader Conference in D.C. on Tuesday, June 18, when an aide pulled me from a meeting and told me the president wanted to speak with me. Although I was occupying the third highest position at the Pentagon, my responsibility was the training, manning, and equipping of the U.S. Army. I did not

interact with the president often; that was the secretary of defense's
role. However, Trump and I had met and talked a few times in
the past, at a tank plant in Ohio, and at a Dignified Transfer of a
fallen soldier at Dover Air Force Base, which is where service members killed abroad in combat are welcomed home—back to U.S.
soil—by their comrades, senior officials, and grieving families. I
also met the president at the White House on a few occasions, and
during events like the Army-Navy football game. He also saw me
do television interviews a couple of times, and called to congratu-
late and tell me I "did a great job" on one of them. So over time we
had developed an easy rapport.

During our conversations, he would ask for my views on any
number of issues, most outside my purview as secretary of the
Army: "Do you think we should be in Iraq? Tell me about your
thoughts on Afghanistan? How is the southwest border wall coming along? What do you think of Pat Shanahan? General Mark
Milley? What about China? How do you feel about NATO?"

My previous government and private sector jobs gave me a broad
and deep background in foreign policy and national security, so I
felt confident offering up my views and perspectives. Back then,
I found the president easy to speak with, curious, and willing to
listen. My experience at the time was far different from the carica-
tures in the press. Then again, my interactions at that point were
limited.

As I walked to another room to take the call, news outlets reported that Shanahan was stepping down. Uh-oh. I could put two
and two together. We knew Pat's nomination was wobbly, and
there was speculation that I was next in the queue, but that was all
it was . . . speculation.

I was standing in a large, empty classroom when the call came
in from the White House. I paced back and forth with nervous

energy, like a soldier on guard duty, the phone pressed to my ear, anticipating the conversation I would soon have. The phone line briefly cackled, and as always happens before the president gets on the line, a voice formally announced: "Mr. Secretary. . . . the pres-i-dent." It was so serious and formal that you couldn't help but be awed by the moment.

President Trump jumped on the line and immediately said, "Hello, Mark, how are you," drawing out the words a little longer than usual.

"Fine, Mr. President," I responded. "How are you, sir?"

He was on speakerphone; I could hear the faint voices of others in the background. The president was in an upbeat mood and play-ing to the moment. We exchanged a few other niceties, and then he went to the point of the call. Trump said that "Pat Shanahan is withdrawing from the nomination," and added that "it's a shame what he is going through. . . . It's terrible," he said. "So unfair . . . Pat is a good man."

I agreed, as I listened intently and gazed at the floor in front of me.

The volume and pitch of his voice quickly changed again. You could feel the energy in the line as he began, speaking not just to me, but also to everyone gathered in the Oval Office. Without pausing as he spoke loudly into the phone, the president said, "Mark, I want you to become my secretary of defense. I got a whole room full of people here who think you will do a great job! So do I. What do you say?"

I stopped my pacing. I was now standing in this stark white room, with empty worktables all about, the phone pressed into my right ear. It was all very quiet, and lonely, as his words came through the line. Although I had known this question was coming, I was still humbled and taken aback, aware of the history of the moment. Here I was, a young man from southwest Pennsylvania who left home at eighteen to attend West Point and become an Army officer, finding myself thirty-seven years later, with the president of the United States asking me to become the nation's next secretary of defense. I would be stepping into the job my hometown hero, George C. Marshall, assumed in September 1950, and doing so as one of the youngest secretaries in many years.

The only answer I could give was "Yes, Mr. President," followed by: "It would be an honor and privilege to serve my country as secretary of defense."

With that, Trump thanked and congratulated me. My words slightly echoed in the empty classroom. Trump then said, "Let's meet very soon to talk. I'm excited to have you on board. You'll do great."

"Thanks, Mr. President. I look forward to it," I replied.

And with a quick "Okay, great, see you later," Trump ended the call. I started pacing again, thinking about all the things I needed to start doing.

There was no "formal interview" per se, but that was not unusual. All presidents manage these things a little differently, depending on whether they know the person, the recommendations of their closest advisers, the circumstances at the moment, and other factors. Unlike many of my predecessors, I was already in the administration, serving as secretary of the Army. I had a track record in the executive branch and with Congress, knew many who were close to the president, and even had a relationship with first daughter Ivanka and son-in-law Jared Kushner.

Moreover, the president and I had talked several times in the past—both in person and on the phone—so he knew where I stood on a variety of issues, including ones where we disagreed, such as NATO. Yet, because those conversations were often one-sided, I didn't know or fully appreciate his views on several matters that would become friction points between us. I would have, however, a couple of weeks on the job before the president formally nominated me to talk further, share my views on other issues, and to get his agreement regarding my style of work and access to him.

I immediately called my wife, Leah, to share the news. We both couldn't believe how far we had traveled together. From two kids on a blind date in Nashville in 1988, to Washington, D.C., three children, and thirty years of marriage, she was the best person to share that journey with, and Lord knows I would need her by my side in the days ahead.

After my calls, I gathered my immediate team in the classroom and told them we had to get back to the Pentagon. I spoke privately with General Milley, the Army chief of staff and my right hand, for a few minutes too. The president had already selected him to be the next chairman of the Joint Chiefs of Staff. It was reassuring for both of us to know that we would be working alongside someone that we knew and respected. "Battle buddies, again," we'd say. He congratulated me, spoke briefly about how we would both be playing at a much higher level now, with far more scrutiny, and then joked about "buckling up for a crazy ride ahead." How prescient.

I quickly headed back to the Pentagon to meet with Shanahan, taking calls from National Security Adviser John Bolton and others as we sped toward Arlington. Pat graciously congratulated me as I entered the building, saying, "You'll do great" and offering to do everything he could in the short time we had to get me up to speed. With the withdrawal of his name as secretary of defense, Pat also decided to resign as deputy secretary of defense. He seemed relieved. I was happy for him in that regard.

Once Pat stepped down, I would become the acting secretary of defense, given that the secretary of the Army is next up in the line of succession. I would be taking over before formal Senate confirmation.

To ensure the transfer of power was as orderly, legal, and low risk as possible, we picked Sunday, June 23, at midnight, as the handover point. I would be responsible after that. Before then, I would shadow Shanahan in his daily duties—keeping my eyes and ears open, and my thoughts to myself. After all, there is only one secretary of defense at a time, and I didn't want to confuse the chain of command or my future colleagues by commenting on matters while Pat was still in charge. This was especially important given the growing tensions between the United States and Iran, and the crash course I would soon get on the rigors of the job and the unpredictability of the president.

America's relationship with Iran is a long and sordid one. Formal relations between the two countries dates back to the mid-nineteenth century. Interactions were generally positive through the end of World War II. Mohammad Reza Pahlavi, the shah (king) of Iran, who came to power in 1941, was strongly pro-American. As the Cold War emerged, this was important to the United States, given Iran's strategic location in the Persian Gulf and its long border with the Soviet Union.

In 1953, Iranian sentiment toward America turned after the United States and the United Kingdom organized a coup that overthrew the government of Mohammad Mossadeq, the popular prime minister. Growing tensions between him and the United Kingdom were empowering the Communist Party in the country, which risked pushing Iran into the Soviet orbit. This prompted Mossadeq's removal.

Pahlavi became more authoritarian over time and undertook

initiatives to modernize Iran that created tensions with conservative groups. By the late 1970s, large anti-Shah demonstrations were common. In early 1979, Iranian hard-liners overthrew Pahlavi and replaced him with the popular Ayatollah Khomeini, who established the Islamic Republic. In less than a year, an antiwestern theocracy had replaced a pro-American monarchy in a critical part of the world. Iranians angered by the United States' long-standing support for the Shah seized the U.S. embassy and took dozens of Americans hostage in November 1979. The Iranians held fifty-two of them captive for 444 days.

The United States and Iran have had no formal relations since then. Rather, conflict has marked the relationship over the last forty years, most notably the 1983 car bomb attack that killed 241 U.S. service members in their Beirut barracks. The U.S. embassy in Lebanon had been bombed a few months earlier by Hezbollah, a militant Shia group founded by Iran, leaving 17 Americans dead. And in 1988, the USS *Vincennes* accidentally shot down an Iranian airliner, killing 290 passengers and crew.

Limited naval actions by the United States against Iran in the Gulf marked the late 1980s. The 1990s saw the Clinton administration embargo the country, with Congress piling on additional sanctions.

In late 2002 the United States accused Iran of pursuing nuclear weapons work, a charge buttressed by a U.N. assessment months later that said Tehran failed to report "certain nuclear materials and activities" that are associated with a bomb-making program.

Throughout the 2000s, Iran provided Iraqi militias with weapons, training, and equipment to support their insurgency against the United States. Such was the state of play between Tehran and Washington as the Trump administration came to power in January 2017.

...

Even before the election, Trump repeatedly vowed to extricate the United States from the 2015 nuclear agreement with Iran— formally known as the Joint Comprehensive Plan of Action—and the five permanent members of the U.N. Security Council, plus Germany.

He called the 2015 pact a "horrible deal" and "the worst . . . ever negotiated." Many Republicans in Congress agreed, as did Israel and several Gulf Arab states. Critics said the agreement threatened the security of the United States, never really ended the regime's nuclear efforts, and gave Tehran cover to advance a covert nuclear program. They added that the deal was not sufficiently verifiable and didn't provide adequate access to Iranian nuclear sites for international inspectors.

The Iran nuclear deal was not a good one. It gave away too much up front in terms of unfreezing their funds and providing sanctions relief, without getting nearly enough when it came to the scope of the agreement, its duration, and the verification mechanisms. Trump was correct that the Iranian regime couldn't be trusted, which is why these shortcomings made the deal so misbegotten.

In addition to proscribing their nuclear weapon development efforts, Trump also stressed the importance of dealing with their ballistic missiles and sponsorship of terrorism throughout the region, both of which threatened U.S. forces in the Middle East and partners like Israel and Kuwait. While the nuclear concern was a legitimate and existential one for neighboring countries, it was still a future proposition. Iranian ballistic missiles and Tehran's support for terrorist groups were serious issues the United States and our partners faced daily.

The agreement with Iran should have covered all these things. I assume the Obama administration believed the nuclear part of the deal, even with its shortcomings, was the best they could get from

Tehran. But was it? And why wasn't more effort made to get the Israelis, Saudis, Emiratis, and others in the region on board?

Before finally exiting the agreement in 2018, President Trump said, "It is clear to me that we cannot prevent an Iranian nuclear bomb under the decaying and rotten structure of the current agreement," adding that "the Iran deal is defective at its core. If we do nothing we know exactly what will happen."[1] At the same time, the White House imposed a broad range of sanctions on Tehran.

If I had been in the cabinet prior to Trump's exit from the Iran deal in 2018, I would have recommended we first try to handle the pact as a treaty, and send it to the Senate for the chamber's advice and consent. In addition to being the proper way of addressing an agreement of this importance, such a strategy would have better exposed the deal's weaknesses and fundamental lack of support. After all, it was doubtful the nuclear deal could get a majority of votes in the Senate, let alone the two-thirds required for approval.

The Senate's rejection of the 2015 deal would have set the stage to draft an improved version of the agreement, working hand in glove with Democrats and Republicans on Capitol Hill. Once completed, we could have reached out to our Gulf partners and European allies to further refine the plan and forge a new consensus.

Trump, instead, left the agreement and launched a "maximum pressure" campaign that imposed tough economic sanctions aimed at strong-arming Iran back to the negotiating table. The administration wanted to conclude a new deal that would address the weak points in the original pact. GOP allies in Congress and America's partners in the Middle East praised the president's move. Many Democrats in Congress and the United Kingdom, France, and Germany—three of the agreement's cosigners—opposed it. Their continued support for the 2015 deal likely incentivized Iran not to reopen the troubled agreement.

Secretary of State Mike Pompeo and I publicly said on many occasions that Washington was willing to sit down with the Iranians and talk, without precondition. I never heard from Tehran, or our allies, and I don't believe Pompeo did either. Realistically, this game plan would always be an uphill slog as long as the existing agreement still enjoyed some U.S. domestic and international support. As such, I concluded the path we were on could well result in a military confrontation.

Nonetheless, the maximum pressure campaign certainly had an impact on Iran's military programs and support to foreign proxies, because it put a squeeze on that country's economy and cash reserves. Funding for their armed forces took a hit, as did their support for some external groups involved in terrorism. However, unilateral U.S. pressure was unlikely to bring Tehran back to the negotiating table anytime soon. With the Europeans on their side, and the possibility that Trump could be a one-term president, Iran was willing to bear the pain and simply hold on. They hoped a new administration in 2021 would return to the old, bad deal.

It was still only 2019, however, and U.S.-Iranian relations were now at another historic low. In April, the State Department labeled the Islamic Revolutionary Guard Corps (IRGC) a "foreign terrorist organization" for its long-standing support of extremist groups throughout the region. The IRGC is a unique branch of the Iranian armed forces responsible for safeguarding the country's political system while also coordinating and supporting Iran's external operations. The IRGC is also a powerful player in Iran, with activities and influence throughout the country's economic, political, and social structure. Its leaders often have access to the highest levels of the government.

Washington also threatened that month to sanction countries that continued to purchase oil from Iran, putting further pressure on Tehran's stressed economy. Weeks later, the United States deployed B-52 bombers and a carrier strike group to the Middle East amid concern that Iran was planning some type of regional offensive. That same week, Tehran declared it would be reducing its commitments under the nuclear deal.

Tensions were escalating quickly in the Persian Gulf.

Never one to undersell his intentions, President Trump warned on May 19 that conflict would be "the official end of Iran."[2] On that same day, militia groups aligned with and funded by Tehran fired rockets at the U.S. embassy in Baghdad.

Two commercial tankers were attacked in the Gulf of Oman on June 13. Secretary of State Pompeo declared that Iran was responsible, a charge they denied. A few days later, the president of Iran said his country would increase uranium enrichment if other countries failed to protect it from punitive U.S. economic measures. That same day, Trump placed additional sanctions on Iran's economy and the Pentagon confirmed that one thousand more troops would deploy to the region for defensive purposes following the attack on the oil tankers.[3]

And on the evening of June 20, two days after the president asked me to be secretary of defense, Iran shot down a U.S. Air Force Global Hawk, a $200 million unmanned aircraft that was flying a surveillance mission in international airspace over the Strait of Hormuz.

Trump's national security team—Pompeo, National Security Adviser John Bolton, Pat Shanahan, Joint Chiefs Chairman General Joseph Dunford, and I—met over breakfast on the morning of the twenty-first to discuss options and develop a recommendation to present the president.

I wasn't completely new to the group. I had known and worked with John Bolton since our days together in the George W. Bush administration. With graying hair and his telltale bushy white mustache, John was a force of nature in D.C., having established himself over many years as an attorney, diplomat, political commentator, and foreign policy hawk. John was a national security expert who was blunt, principled, and unyielding. He was a good fit for the national security adviser role.

Mike Pompeo and I shared the common background of being in the same West Point class of 1986. We hadn't known each other at the academy, but we had dozens of mutual friends. Mike served in a cavalry unit in Germany upon graduation. He earned a law degree from Harvard and practiced in D.C. after leaving the Army. He then tried his hand in business back home in Wichita. I really befriended Mike and his wife, Susan, when he arrived in Washington as a freshman Republican congressman from Kansas in 2011. With salt-and-pepper hair and a stocky build, Mike was a conservative, a foreign policy hawk, and a man of deep faith, and he had a wry sense of humor to boot.

General Joe Dunford was your classic Marine. Tall and fit with a close haircut, Dunford grew up in Boston, attended Saint Michael's College in Vermont, and commissioned into the Corps the same year he graduated college. From there he commanded at every level and led a regimental combat team during the 2003 invasion of Iraq. He later commanded the International Security Assistance Force and U.S. Forces Afghanistan in 2013, after which he became commandant of the Marine Corps in 2014. Less than a year later, in 2015, President Obama selected him as the next chairman of the Joint Chiefs of Staff, the nation's highest military position.

Dunford and I had become acquainted when I was Army secretary. He was very helpful then, and even more so as I took on the role as secretary of defense. He spoke softly and wielded a deft hand when it came to doing his job and managing all the personalities in his orbit, from the president to the Joint Chiefs to everyone else around him. I always found his advice to be wise, candid, and insightful, and I relied on him a good deal.

Everyone agreed on the importance of responding firmly to the unwarranted attack, and all felt it was essential that the national security team bring the president a unanimous recommendation. Bolton and Pompeo pushed for a very strong response. Shanahan and Dunford weighed in from the other side. The group eventually agreed, as the president himself later announced publicly, to strike three targets and take some additional measures.[4] I remained silent out of deference to Pat, but privately felt the final action agreed to was still disproportionate. We could send the same message to Tehran with fewer casualties on their side. High losses could lead us to tit-for-tat escalatory actions, and who knew where that would take us.

A National Security Council (NSC) meeting—which meant the president would attend with his appropriate cabinet members and top advisers—convened later that morning, at eleven in the White House Situation Room. Bolton opened the session by discussing its purpose and presenting the unified recommendation of the three principals. Shanahan offered a few preliminary comments before turning the substance of the discussion over to Dunford. The general began by restating some of the overarching policy goals that had been agreed to in the past, followed by the purpose of any military response, and then walking the president through the various options, pausing to elaborate on the one recommended by the team. The room full of advisers was silent as he spoke. Shanahan sat closest to the president, to his left, followed by me, and then the chairman. Dunford had a very calm, steady, and low-key demeanor, locking eyes with the president as he spoke. He did his best to present the case and keep the president focused as Trump bounced from question to question.

As he often did, Trump would interject with specific questions about the operation, such as "How many planes will you use?" Or "What is the [economic] cost of the damage that will be done?" He also piped up about our forces in Syria, looking at Dunford and Shanahan, and directing both to "Get them out!" This issue would come up repeatedly over the next several months.

General Dunford gently steered Trump back to the issue at hand and made clear that, while the timing would limit casualties, "we should expect that Iranians will be killed." He added that it was "possible some Russians could be killed or injured" as well. The chairman and Trump went back and forth on how we would know there would be Iranian losses or not. The president didn't seem overly concerned as much as he was curious. None of the lawyers in the room raised any questions either. Dunford put some other options out there that didn't involve killing people, but Trump wanted a very tough response. He kept saying, "We need to hit them hard. We need to make them pay."

Trump then fixated on the cost of the U.S. drone, why it was so expensive, what its capabilities were, and so on. He wanted to strike something of more value, like an accountant keeping the books. Dollars were the metric, it seemed, more than the message we were trying to send or the policy outcome we wanted to achieve. However, when it comes to retaliatory attacks, the aim isn't to run up the score; that could get you into a worse situation. Rather, you want to signal determination and keep upping the ante until the other side folds.

Trump approved the recommended strikes nonetheless, and without hesitation. As we all began shuffling out of the cramped room, the president was upbeat and confident. Groups of two or three folks gathered and remained behind to discuss specific items. You could feel the energy. We all knew that the contest with Iran was entering a new phase.

The attack would begin later that day, after dinner in D.C. I joined Shanahan, Dunford, and others in the secretary of defense's office around then. General Dunford had just begun speaking with Trump on the secure phone when I entered; he was discussing estimated casualty numbers with the president as Shanahan listened in. The DoD legal office had apparently provided a casualty estimate to the NSC that said up to 150 people could be killed in the attacks; this report then made its way to the president. Technically that number was correct—*up to* 150 people *could* be killed.

Dunford did his best to reassure Trump that the casualties would be less than that. He pointed out, for example, that "we will hit the targets at night, Mr. President, after most of the people have gone home for the day." Dunford had been down this road before, though, with the earlier strikes on Syria coming to mind, and knew where this was heading. The irony of the discussion wasn't lost on us either—seven or so hours earlier Trump seemed to be pressing for more aggressive action, now here we were, minutes before the "Go/No Go" call needed to be made, and the president was waffling. "I don't know, general," he said. "A hundred and fifty is a lot of people. They shoot down an unmanned plane, and we kill a hundred and fifty. It doesn't seem right."

Trump's unease and skepticism were evident in his voice. I could envision him sitting there with his arms folded, the left side of his face tightened up in a cynical look, frowning, and shaking his head. To his credit, Dunford was quick to add, in his steady voice, "Mr. President, if you're not comfortable with the plan, then you shouldn't approve it." He was right about that, of course.

While General Dunford and the president spoke, the rest of us in the room were quietly asking one another about this legal assessment, who had seen it, what exactly did it say, and so forth. No one had. Amazing. Pat Shanahan, slightly pale and bleary eyed from fatigue, turned, looked at me with a half smile, and slowly shook his head. I couldn't tell whether he meant the mission was canceled or he was simply sharing (with me, the "new guy") his seeming frustration with what was a routinely haphazard decision-making process. I would learn over time that it was the latter.

The military's practical estimates, based on years of experience and insight, focused on what was *likely* to occur. This was different from the legal assessment, which listed the ranges of what *could* occur, that made its way to the president. Dunford was doing his best to make the case for action; it was an unexpected position to be in for someone who, Trump unfairly alleged to others in the past, wasn't "aggressive enough." Bolton jumped in as well, working to counter the president's repeated concerns about "body bags" of Iranians being beamed all over television. It didn't matter, though. With the "150 casualties" number locking in the president's mind, he was getting cold feet.

Pompeo, who was now on the line, pushed back, pressing for the operation's approval. He came in forcefully behind Dunford's best case. You could hear the growing frustration in Mike's voice as the small group of us at the Pentagon stood around the secure phone on Shanahan's desk to hear the conversation. Pompeo spoke quickly, his pace quickening, pressing that "We need to respond, Mr. President." He put forward his best arguments, one after another, which practically devolved into pleas to do something. It didn't matter at this point. Trump's mind was decided. He rationalized that we could always strike later. The president canceled the attack.

I thought later about these first forty-eight hours and the lessons I could take from them. I lauded Bolton for pulling the team together, getting us all behind one recommendation, and then presenting a unified front to the president. That was good and needed to continue. My sense too was that he and Pompeo were more willing to use military force against Iran than the Pentagon. Most troubling for me, however, was how to read the president. In the morning, he was gung ho to hit Iran, and to do so harder than anyone had recommended, but less than twelve hours later he completely reversed his position. Is this, I wondered, how things often played out?

The president was right to consider proportionality, and maybe the team should have spoken more loudly about it at the 11:00 A.M. meeting. General Dunford, though, did a really good job with this. That said, I was personally concerned that even a couple of dozen Iranians killed was too many when responding to the shoot down of an *unmanned* drone, so in the end I was fine with calling off the specific mission.

However, we still had a message of resolve that we needed to send Tehran, and we needed to restore deterrence. Failing to do both would likely guarantee more Iranian bad behavior as they continued to push and test us. Rather than calling off the strikes and walking away from the incident, we should have hit some other targets that would have achieved our purposes without any killed. But we didn't, and history moved on, arguably setting us up for more trouble ahead.

Over the weekend leading up to the Sunday evening handover with Shanahan, it was clear that we could soon be back in the Situation Room presenting military options again for the commander in chief to consider. The president would likely look to me for a recommendation if that happened. I was determined to make one even if I wasn't asked. Given the weighty issues of war and peace that I could soon face, I wanted to make sure that my thought process was principled, disciplined, and thorough.

Prior to my confirmation hearing before the Senate Armed

Services Committee weeks later, the committee required me to answer hundreds of advance policy questions. One of them dealt with the use of military force, and the factors I would "consider in making recommendations to the president."[5] My reflection that weekend would evolve into the following response I provided the Senate:

> In evaluating whether the use of military force is appropriate, I would consider a variety of factors, but principally the threat to the United States, including its imminence; the nature of the U.S. interest at issue and its importance; whether nonmilitary means have been considered and are being integrated into any proposed response; whether we would have a clear and achievable objective for using force; the likely risks, costs, and consequences of the operation; whether the proposed action is appropriate and proportional; the views of the Congress; the willingness of foreign partners to support the action; and the legal basis in domestic and international law.

I would carry this statement—the "Nine Considerations" for the use of military force—around with me during the nearly eighteen months I served as secretary of defense, and I would refer to it when the situation demanded. I didn't view it as a mechanical checklist but as a guide to aid my thinking and help formulate my recommendations. After all, every situation is unique and requires judgment and discernment. I just wanted to make sure I kept faith with the Department, the Congress, the American people, and myself.

The Sunday midnight transition with Shanahan went off without incident. The next morning, I started early as the acting secretary of defense, beginning with an 8:00 A.M. meeting with my civilian leaders, the service chiefs, and the combatant commanders. The purpose of this session was to introduce myself in this new role, discuss my leadership style and priorities, and to lay out my expectations of the command team.

I had already drafted an Initial Message to the Department, which my front office would send out to everyone in the DoD that morning, but I wanted to elaborate on some of the main points in that note for those gathered.* I made clear that carrying out the National Defense Strategy (NDS)—the Pentagon's plan to implement the president's National Security Strategy and modernize the U.S. armed forces—was my top priority, with our goal being able to fight and win our nation's wars, should deterrence fail. My focus was on China, then Russia, in that order.

I also stated what I would say in my formal message, that "I place great importance on a commitment by all—especially Leaders—to those values and behaviors that represent the best of the military profession and mark the character and integrity of the Armed Forces that the American people admire." I added that we all must "stay focused" on the mission and "remain steadfast in your pursuit of excellence." And I finished by urging everyone to always strive to "do the right thing"—a saying that would become my touch phrase, along with the more practical "follow established process and precedent" in the difficult times ahead that were not yet known to me.

On July 1, 2019, upon my return from a NATO meeting in Brussels, I held a ninety-minute secure call with U.S. Central Command, the four-star geographic command responsible for all operations in the Middle East. I wanted to discuss Operation Sentinel, an initiative to ensure freedom of navigation and commerce—important long-standing principles of U.S. foreign policy—in the Persian Gulf in light of recent actions by Iran to threaten commercial shipping. I

---

* For the Initial Message to the Department, see Appendix B.

would pause with concern later in my tenure when others in the administration pressed, without regard to these well-established tenets of U.S. foreign policy, to interdict Iranian or Venezuelan ships arbitrarily on the high seas.

General Frank McKenzie, the capable CENTCOM commander, briefed the plan. McKenzie was from Alabama, attended college at The Citadel, and commissioned into the Marine Corps in 1979. He was an infantry officer who commanded at multiple levels, with deployments to both Iraq and Afghanistan. McKenzie served a few tours in the Pentagon, with his last being as director of the Joint Staff beginning in July 2017, which is where I first met him. He took the helm of U.S. Central Command in March 2019.

I liked McKenzie. He was an able leader with a steady hand who operated in a very complex and demanding theater. At any one time, he had to deal with Shia militia forces attacking us in Iraq, a potential ISIS resurgence in Syria, Taliban operations in Afghanistan, and the ongoing confrontations with Iran from Yemen all the way to Lebanon. On top of all that, he also had to deal with me constantly pressing him to reshape the theater for the future while looking for ways to free up forces that I could retask to deal with China. He had a tough job but handled it well.

McKenzie's basic concept for Operation Sentinel was to increase maritime and overhead surveillance at both ends of the Strait of Hormuz, and then farther up into the Gulf as well. We would do this with a combination of U.S. naval vessels, manned aircraft, and unmanned surveillance drones. I believed if we could deter Iranian bad behavior in the first place, we could avoid an accident, provocation, or intentional act that could lead to real conflict.

I spoke with Pompeo during our weekly call and updated him on our plans to activate Operation Sentinel. The key now was getting partners to join us. Defense was working this angle, but we really needed State to push it hard, which Mike agreed to do. We would all have a tough job, though, with the French working quietly behind the scenes against us to keep our other European partners from joining, concerned that doing so would anger the Iranians.

I also shared with Pompeo some of my recent discussions in Brussels regarding Afghanistan and the Intermediate-Range Nuclear Forces (INF) Treaty*; we also talked about our continuing challenges with Turkey, especially their purchase of the Russian S-400 air-defense system. Afghanistan and Turkey would be tough, enduring issues for us during my nearly eighteen months in office.

Mike and I developed a good working relationship early on, and that approach resonated throughout both departments. Some would say it was one of the most positive eras of collaboration between State and Defense. It was certainly true compared to my time at the DoD from 2002 through 2004, when Defense Secretary Donald Rumsfeld and Secretary of State Colin Powell clashed on a routine basis, like Caspar Weinberger and George Shultz before them in the Reagan years. Mike and I built our interactions on not only our personal friendship but also the similar approaches we often took when it came to dealing with the issues in our respective portfolios.

Our close collaboration occasionally caused concern among some at times, and it was the subject of a misinformed news story or two, but we would often get a good laugh out of these. Mike would hear from folks on his side complain that he was "yielding too much to Esper and DoD," and I would hear the opposite from

---

* According to the U.S. Department of State, the INF Treaty was a 1987 agreement between the United States and the Soviet Union that eliminated both countries' ground-launched ballistic and cruise missiles with ranges of between 500 and 5,500 kilometers, and their associated launchers, support structures, and equipment within three years after the treaty entered into force in 1988.

people who followed defense matters. To me, that meant we had the relationship about right.

By August, the national security team's principal focus shifted to Afghanistan, and the possibility of concluding a peace deal with the Taliban. Meanwhile, we kept a watchful eye on Iran and their malign behavior throughout the region. Our biggest areas of concern were their provision of ballistic missiles to the Houthis in Yemen, their arms shipments into Syria, their continued threats against Persian Gulf shipping, and the growing belligerence of the Shia militia groups in Iraq that they were supporting and directing.

Though the rhetoric between Washington and Tehran had abated some, tensions were still high. While our main attention moved elsewhere, Iran's did not. At the Pentagon, we expected Trump's failure to respond to the drone shootdown would encourage increasing provocations from Tehran. Indeed, the pieces were falling into place that would eventually aggregate and escalate into a major confrontation—the most serious in decades between the United States and Iran.

This first experience with the president jump-started a fast, chaotic, yet necessary learning process for me. As I would assess over time, Trump's instincts weren't always wrong about the policy or end state he wanted to achieve. However, the odds of success were spoiled or the goal tarnished by the process he often followed (little to none); the strategy he usually pursued (narrow and incomplete); the consensus he normally built behind it (minimal and insufficient); and the manner in which he generally communicated it (coarsely and divisively). In short, the ends he often sought rarely survived the ways and means he typically pursued to accomplish them. This often made all the difference.

CHAPTER 4

CIVILIAN CONTROL AND REFORM OF THE PENTAGON

"The vote just came in and it was 90–8. That's a vote we're not accustomed to," President Trump said as he introduced me before the nation on July 23, 2019, from the Oval Office.[1] It was a resounding bipartisan vote, one that only three other Trump cabinet officials would receive (and they were all in 2017, when the administration was young). The president and I spoke privately later, and he said, "Ninety to eight. Huh, maybe I should be concerned?" Maybe.

The president was very generous in his remarks that afternoon. He described me as "outstanding in every way" and said, "no one is more qualified." Trump flattered me with his comments, but I was most appreciative of the fact that Tim Kaine, my senator from Virginia, and a Democrat, had introduced and vouched for me at my confirmation hearing. He gave me one of the greatest compliments anyone could by describing me as a leader of "sound character and moral courage." His endorsement was a selfless act of bipartisanship that gave me real hope that there were still leaders in Congress, especially ones who could get our nation's lawmakers working together once again.

As I entered the Pentagon the next day, the stir in Washington over the lack of confirmed leadership at the DoD was finally ending. There were still concerns about the relationship between the uniformed military and their civilian leadership, however. These were real, but mostly about the interactions in Washington, D.C., among the Department's civilians, the armed services, and the combatant commands. The DoD has eleven combatant commands, each with a geographic (e.g., European Command) or functional (e.g., Space Command) mission. They are comprised of units and personnel from the armed services and led by a four-star general or admiral who provides command and control of military forces in peace and war.[2] Importantly, the operational chain of command runs from the president to the secretary of defense, and then to the combatant commanders.

There was never any doubt about civilians being in control—this is both a fact and a principle based in law, practice, history, and culture. It was a sacrosanct matter drilled into our military leaders from day one. Yet, I did have concerns that the combatant commands had grown too powerful. Restoring the proper civilian-military balance was an issue that I would work hard to achieve.

In November 2018, the congressionally directed National Defense Strategy Commission published a dire warning that "the security and wellbeing of the United States are at greater risk than at any time in decades" and that "America's military superiority . . . has eroded to a dangerous degree." After summarizing the key threats and challenges facing the United States and its armed forces, the commission stated that "healthy" civilian-military relations were essential to address these matters. It then surprised many by reporting on a "relative imbalance of civilian and military voices on critical issues." In its report, this bipartisan group was troubled that "civilian voices were relatively muted on issues at the center of U.S. defense and national security policy."[3]

During my tenure as Army secretary, I faced this imbalance. It was frustrating and hindered my ability as a senior civilian leader—number three in the Pentagon chain of command, no less—to perform my statutory duties. The combatant commands' influence—usually backed by the uniformed Joint Staff—on my authority to man, train, and equip the force for deployment, to include medical preparations and who I could send abroad, were the most egregious examples. It was incredible how much authority had been whittled away from the services, and their civilian leaders, over the years.

Air Force Secretary Heather Wilson, Navy Secretary Richard Spencer, and I had written letters to OSD leadership and raised these issues during meetings, asking for relief with specific proposals, but none ever came. The Joint Staff, advocating on behalf of the combatant commands, kept pushing the issues off or watering down the text to preserve the position and "prerogatives" of the four-star commanders. It wasn't until I became defense secretary that I could address these problems. It took some time and effort, but in December 2019 I issued my first directive effecting some of these changes to re-empower the civilian secretaries.

Wilson, Spencer, and I—the "three amigos," as we called ourselves—worked together on other tough issues. For example, we took on an OSD medical bureaucracy that tried to leverage congressional mandates to reform the health-care system as a way to subsume our operational medical personnel, units, and resources. We also worked together to improve acquisition programs and share workload, whether it was developing hypersonic missiles for our respective services or swapping ideas on body armor for the troops. No good idea was off the table, and no parochialism had a place on it. We were putting readiness, capability, and common sense above all else, even if it affected our budgets and missions.

Some of my best times as Army secretary were the moments I spent working with my fellow service secretaries. Our biweekly breakfasts and after-hours get-togethers really built a strong rapport among our services and us. Beyond our individual goals, we really hoped to demonstrate the good that came to the Defense Department when the three of us worked together. Competition and rivalry often made for contentious relationships in the past between service secretaries. We aimed to change that.

Another problem that Wilson, Spencer, and I faced was getting complete, accurate, and timely information about force management and operational matters. My primary source for receiving information, such as combatant commanders' requests for forces and their operational employment abroad, was through the Army chief of staff. General Milley attended weekly sessions in the "tank"— the conference room where the Joint Chiefs of Staff met—and briefed me on what was going on. He was conscientious about this, but none of this information ever came through the civilian side. In other words, I usually had to rely upon secondhand updates from my senior military adviser to learn what was happening. These matters often affected important things such as my force, my budget, my training cycles, and my readiness.

The National Defense Strategy Commission report took a similar view. When it came to issues such as operational deployments and global integration, decision making at the Pentagon had to be "nested under higher-order guidance from civilians." In the report's view, failure to give due consideration to the "relevant political-military dynamics of force management shifts" involved could influence readiness and produce terrible strategic results.[4]

As Army secretary, with all my years of experience in the Army, in the Pentagon, in Congress, and in Washington, I—as well as Spencer and Wilson—could provide useful counsel, or at least be a sounding board for some of these matters. At a minimum, basic information could help me "look over the horizon" and prepare Army units for what may be asked of them down the road.

The commission report explicitly stated, "The issue here is not that the existing Title 10 responsibilities of the secretary and his civilian advisers are inadequate, but that they have not been used effectively, and that responsibility on key strategic and policy issues has increasingly migrated to the military."[5] How damn true. Since I wasn't involved in the process as secretary of the Army and I had never been invited to these forums, it was unclear to me how much OSD civilian appointees participated in the process. What I later learned was disheartening.

Once I became defense secretary in July 2019, the first thing I did was bring together the leadership team at the top. They had balkanized over the years into roughly four groups: OSD civilians, Joint Staff, combatant commands, and the services. Existing Pentagon processes both reflected and exacerbated this breakdown.

In my first couple of weeks as secretary of defense, I made immediate changes to begin getting everyone to think and function as a team. First and foremost, I made the National Defense Strategy our focus. The purpose of the NDS is to translate, refine, and develop the military guidance needed to implement the National

Security Strategy that is produced by the White House. Published in January 2018, the NDS was clear-eyed and straightforward that the DoD's mission was "to provide combat-credible military forces needed to deter war and protect the security of our nation" and that, if deterrence failed, the U.S. military had to fight and win on the modern battlefield.

The NDS said the U.S. had now entered a new era of great power competition, with China and Russia as our strategic competitors, but that we found ourselves in a position of "strategic atrophy" after nearly two decades of focus on low-intensity conflict in Iraq and Afghanistan. We had also burned down a good deal of readiness that left the force with major challenges. The strategy also said that the U.S. military operated in an "increasingly complex security environment" that is "defined by rapid technological change."

These facts, coupled with sharp funding decreases and unpredictable defense budgets during the Obama years, saw our military advantage erode as China and Russia used the same period to modernize and expand their capabilities. The fact that the People's Republic of China now has the largest navy in the world is the starkest evidence of this.

At the same time, Beijing was chipping away at the international rules-based order that helped ensure security, stability, and prosperity for many countries; its excessive and illegal claims over the South China Sea being a prime example of that. The NDS asserted, "The costs of not implementing this strategy are clear. Failure to meet our defense objectives will result in decreasing U.S. global influence, eroding cohesion among allies and partners, and reduced access to markets that will contribute to a decline in our prosperity and standard of living."[6]

The NDS prioritized three major lines of effort for the DoD to be successful: "First, rebuilding readiness as we build a more lethal

Joint Force; Second, strengthening alliances as we attract new partners; and Third, reforming the Department's business practices for greater performance and affordability."[7] There were several goals listed under each line, but like many documents of this nature, phrases such as "evolve innovative operational concepts," "deepen interoperability," and "organize for innovation" were catchy and sounded good, but didn't give enough direction for one to achieve the vision set out for the Department.

The challenge of any sound strategy is to operationalize it. And in the case of the NDS, this meant turning these broad lines of effort and lofty goals into actionable objectives that we could define, measure, assign, and track over time. Implementation is the tough task of any strategy, and I made this my top priority.

To effect this, the second major change I made was to have two large team meetings on Mondays. The first one in the morning included the OSD, the Joint Staff, and the service chiefs and secretaries. Rather than having a forty-minute free-for-all, we would lengthen the meeting to ninety minutes and have a more structured agenda that focused on the next two week's events and the Department's priorities.

Since I did this successfully as secretary of the Army, I knew the pace, scope, and detail of the particular objectives I wanted to cover, such as readiness, modernization, reform, allies and partners, and people. Later, once we figured out our plans to implement the NDS, we added topics such as Developing Counter UAS Systems, Digital Modernization, and Reveal/Conceal Strategies. In the end, I wanted no more than twelve topic areas, so that I could revisit each priority every quarter to check on progress, while giving those implementing these initiatives the time and space to work in between updates.

The last half of the meeting would include briefings by my heads of legislative affairs, public affairs, and any undersecretary on matters they wanted to raise. We then went around the room for other issues. Finally, we reviewed the dreaded "task tracker." During my time as Army secretary, the previous version of this meeting had often frustrated Wilson, Spencer, and me. When we did have substantive discussions that resulted in an action, nobody seemed to be recording and tracking these decisions. One of us would ask a month or two later, "What is the status of _____ that we agreed to several weeks ago?" Blank stares would carpet the room, like we were in the Twilight Zone. So no progress was ever made, it seemed. Everybody kept doing what they wanted to do. We changed this too. There was no escaping a tasking now and no running from a progress report, and the metrics we established for each.

The other meeting added to our Mondays was an afternoon session on NDS Implementation. To be successful, I needed all the right players in the room. That meant not only the service leaders and undersecretaries who participated in the morning session but the combatant commanders as well. We set the time for ninety minutes in the middle of the day to be as fair as possible for those commanders calling in from different time zones abroad. It was this weekly forum where we discussed much of the hard work associated with reviewing war plans, developing supporting strategies, and discussing specific NDS operational issues. Unlike my experience as secretary of the Army, the civilian secretaries would be at the table.

Finally, I began meeting with the service secretaries every two to three weeks. I wanted to give them the opportunity to raise issues directly with me, for us to discuss matters that affected more than one of the services—such as housing, diversity, or COVID response—and for me to update them on any emerging operational issues. I didn't get any regular face time with the secretary of defense when I was secretary of the Army, but the one or two times that I did, I found it very helpful when it came to receiving guidance on major issues, feedback on something the Army was doing, or flagging an issue for Mattis or Shanahan to be aware of. The service secretaries appreciated these sessions for all these reasons, but also because it empowered them to go back to their services and speak with more authority. In my mind, this was not solely about making the building run more effectively, but also about reaffirming the principle of civilian control and improving civilian-military relations.

Writing a strategy and implementing a strategy are two very different things. The DoD published the NDS in January 2018, just a few months after I arrived for my fourth tour at the Pentagon. But for our equipment modernization plans, I had no sense from my Army perch that the DoD was advancing the strategy, or that we had a plan to do so. Indeed, when the NDS Commission published its report months later, in November 2018, it stated that the strategy "points the Department . . . and the country in the right direction, but it does not adequately explain how we should get there." They were right.

Deputy Secretary David Norquist, General Joe Dunford, Eric Chewning—my new chief of staff—and I sat down in late July 2019, right after my confirmation, to discuss the way ahead. NDS implementation was the topic. After getting ninety votes from the Senate, I felt I had a strong endorsement from Congress to pursue this end. And with the advantage of having served in the building as Army secretary, I had sufficient perspective and a lot of ideas about how to do it. The NDS wasn't perfect, but it was very good, and I didn't want to waste time reviewing, updating, and tweaking it. There would be time for that later.

The key now was to flesh these ideas and others out as quickly as possible, seek input broadly, and then finalize to implement before too much time passed. If we could make real progress over the next year, then we would have accomplished something significant. Chewning pointed out that we might have only a year or so anyway before the election cycle slowed things down.

David Norquist began his career as a budget analyst for the Department of the Army after graduating from the University of Michigan. He later worked on Capitol Hill, which was where I met him, before going back to a more senior role in the DoD. In 2006 David became the CFO for the Department of Homeland Security in the Bush administration. He later joined a public accounting firm before returning to the Pentagon as the comptroller in May 2017. The Senate confirmed him as deputy secretary of defense a few days after me. I had really come to know David when I was secretary of the Army. He is incredibly smart, analytical, and thorough, with a good sense of humor and a surprising knack for communications messaging. He made a good partner and sounding board for me.

I was fortunate to have Eric Chewning as my first chief of staff. I became acquainted with him while I was Army secretary, and was impressed. It was only later that I would learn he was working on Wall Street when 9/11 happened. He enlisted, went to Army Officer Candidate School, and became a military intelligence officer, serving in the famed 1st Cavalry Division in Iraq. After the Army, Eric worked for McKinsey & Company before returning to the DoD in October 2017 to be deputy assistant secretary of defense for Industrial Policy. When Pat Shanahan became the acting secretary, he elevated Eric to the chief of staff role. I decided to hold on to Eric once the Senate confirmed me, despite some pressing me to bring in "my own guy."

On top of all this great experience, Eric was a serious thinker, a very good manager, and an even-keeled colleague. The first half of my tenure was not nearly as demanding as the second half, though we had our moments of high stress in different ways. I'll never forget when Eric burst into my office once after a particularly rough morning. Something wasn't going well and I figured it was more of the same. "Can today get any worse?" I mused.

To my surprise, it could. Eric's eyes widened and his voice grew anxious. "Sir," he said, "please come with me. We have an unidentified aircraft in the Washington, D.C., airspace." He added, "NORTHCOM and others have been trying to contact it for quite some time." Next up was a "nose bump," where our fighters conduct a movement in front of the aircraft to get its attention, Eric said. Failing that, more drastic measures are part of the protocol. "If it doesn't change course in the next few minutes," my chief of staff said, "you may need to give the order to shoot it down."

Time was ticking away, so we hustled down to another room where a computer screen displayed a graphic of the region's airspace. I could see the unidentified plane, as well as the military aircraft and other capabilities we had available. I also had the NORTHCOM commander on the line. I had rehearsed this scenario in my first weeks on the job, but now this was the real thing. As I heard the chatter on the open line, I prayed that we would get the pilot's attention. With little time left on the countdown clock before I would have to give the shoot down order, the plane veered off and continued away from the White House and the Capitol. Whew! This wouldn't be the last time we'd go through this, though.

We had a Senior Leader Conference coming up in early October. This is an annual meeting where all the four-star combatant commanders, uniformed and civilian service leaders, and OSD undersecretaries meet to discuss a variety of issues. Too often, these gatherings didn't deliver a high return on investment. In my view, if we were going to bring all the commanders to D.C., and ask other leaders to commit to a full day as well, then we should get real value out of it.

With that, I decided that I would work with my Policy office* and my Strategic Initiatives Group to fine-tune the National Defense Strategy implementation ideas I was developing. We would send them out a week or two in advance for the commanders to review. We could then discuss them in detail at the conference, with the aim of locking them down before the day ended. The schedule would be aggressive, but we didn't have the luxury of conducting the long, tedious, drawn-out processes typical of the Pentagon.

By the time the conference arrived, we had developed what would eventually become the Top Ten objectives critical to implementing the NDS. I kicked off the morning session by stating my primary focus: "war fighting." We couldn't afford to get this wrong, I told the group. Collective and coordinated advancement of the Top Ten objectives would get us there. These objectives flowed from the NDS's first two lines of effort: building a more lethal and ready force; and strengthening allies and growing new partners.

After some final opening comments that emphasized "taking care of our people," "living our values," and "remaining apolitical," I turned to the hard work of the day, which was reviewing and

---

* The Office of the Secretary of Defense (OSD), depending on administration, includes at least six core elements, each of which are led by a Senate-confirmed undersecretary: Acquisition and Sustainment, Budget and Financial Management, Intelligence and Security, Personnel and Readiness, Research and Engineering, and Policy. The Policy office's responsibilities include national security policy formulation, coordination, and implementation; strategy, plans, and capabilities development; and homeland defense and global security, among other things.

fine-tuning each of the implementation objectives I had dissemi-
nated in advance.

The final Top Ten list that we agreed upon that day were as
follows, accompanied by an associated timeline and lead agency or
office responsible for their completion:

- Review, update, and approve all China and Russia plans;
- Implement the Immediate Response Force, Contingency Response
  Force, and Dynamic Force Employment enhanced readiness
  concepts;
- Reallocate, reassign, and redeploy forces in accordance with the
  NDS;
- Achieve a higher level of sustainable readiness;
- Develop a coordinated plan to strengthen allies and build partners;
- Reform and manage the Fourth Estate [defined below] and DoD;
- Focus the Department on China;
- Modernize the force—invest in game-changing technologies;
- Establish realistic joint war games, exercises, and training plans;
  and,
- Develop a modern joint warfighting concept and, ultimately,
  doctrine.

Lastly, I spoke to the NDS's third line of effort, the one that I
expected would be the toughest for everyone—reform. My plan
was to "improve our business practices, become more efficient, and
free up funding" by "digging deep into the Fourth Estate, the combatant commands, and the armed services, in that order." This got
a lot of people's attention, especially the combatant commanders.
I suspected some folks thought I wasn't really serious about this
topic, but my former Army colleagues in the room knew better.

My first major push when it came to reform was to take a Night

Court approach to the so-called Fourth Estate—the collective name for DoD agencies and activities that are not part of the military branches, ranging from the OSD and the Joint Staff to the Defense Logistics Agency and Missile Defense Agency. There are more than two dozen of these organizations, and they include more than 380,000 people and spend more than $100 billion—nearly 15 percent of the entire DoD budget—annually.

I would learn that some of these agencies had become an avenue through which a combatant command could get funding for "engagement" activities with countries in its area of responsibility—a connection unknown to several of us. Any increase in defense agency budgets to support these back-door initiatives often came at the expense of service plans and budgets, without an enterprise-wide evaluation of alignment with our established priorities, return on investment, or the opportunity costs associated with these activities. This needed close and immediate attention.

I was going after $7 to $10 billion in reform of the Fourth Estate in the coming year, and we were making good progress, but this amount wasn't nearly enough to pay for our modernization plans and other initiatives. Moreover, I didn't have the time to continue doing reform meetings week after week—the pace I had largely been keeping since I became secretary of defense. What we needed at the OSD level was a completely different management system, and the type of leadership model that can spend every day and week driving efficiency, oversight, and effectiveness.

As a result, we developed a novel management structure that put Chief Management Officer Lisa Hershman in charge of the Fourth Estate. We gave her control over the "budget and personnel" of these agencies, while leaving the operational activities the responsibility of each group's undersecretary. For the first time, the Fourth Estate would now have to participate in the annual budget build and Program Objective Memorandum process just like the services. This would be the accountability and control we desperately needed.

David Norquist and I were able to find $5.7 billion—a few billion short of what I wanted—after four months of work in the fall of 2019. We spent a good amount of time—a few hours each week we were in town—boring into these agencies. I told Hershman that she had to "find *at least* $5 billion more" for the following year. Meanwhile, there would be no growth in the Fourth Estate, and no bills imposed on the services. Hershman was confident she could deliver on the additional savings, and the service secretaries were pleased to learn their budgets wouldn't be raided again.*

The second avenue for reform scrutinized the combatant commands. I'm not sure they had ever been analyzed in detail, if at all, but I was confident we could find savings. Unfortunately, some of the commands viewed cost cutting and reform as things the Pentagon did to fund *their* operations. Not all of the four-stars saw a role for themselves when it came to reform.

Neither view was correct, of course. We all had an obligation to be good stewards of the taxpayers' dollars. We were making solid progress on the first-ever DoD audit—a priority for me—but still had a couple of years to go. I told the combatant commanders that "finding efficiencies and savings will be a big part of your reviews."

Moreover, I saw these reform initiatives not only as a means to free up funds for modernization of the force but also as one of my

---

* Congress eliminated the chief management officer position in 2020 after many years of dissatisfaction with the outcomes it failed to achieve, but we made the case to the defense committees that having a single person in charge of the Fourth Estate, if only for the administrative and budgetary purposes I enacted, showed promise. We were working on this when I left office that November.

first acts to assert greater civilian control by imposing accountability and fiscal discipline on the combatant commands.

What we found as we dug into the issue surprised us. Each command's plans, operations, structure, and budgets were driven by an accumulation of orders, policies, and other instructions over the years, coupled with their assigned missions—which were often self-written—and the specified and implied tasks derived from all of the above. These tasks numbered in the several hundred; some topped one thousand. While scores of them were administrative, many were substantive tasks that were no longer necessary, no longer made sense, were out of date, or were too broad; but they drove resource demands nonetheless. The commands were dutifully implementing them with people, assets, and funding. All of this needed scouring in detail, and each command's mission statement needed to be reviewed, fine-tuned, and approved by the secretary of defense. General Milley and the Joint Chiefs took this on with appropriate involvement by my civilian Policy shop.

Finally, I called upon the armed services to dig deep to find savings. I privately sensed that the large annual increases under Trump were ending, which regrettably proved to be true. So we needed to get ahead of the curve on our budgets. Each of the services was at a different stage in doing this, with the Army out front and the Navy lagging. The Air Force's efforts were in between, and complicated by the pending birth of Space Force in December 2019.

All the armed forces had modernization plans, with some more aggressive and forward-looking than others. To pay for this, each of the services had plans to divest systems that were no longer needed or sufficient for the future fight. They were also looking for money from the OSD. "I'm not prepared to give you more money, or change the budget allocations between services," I often told them, "until we have updated war plans for China and Russia, a new Joint Warfighting Concept, and clear evidence that you've done the hard work of reform in your departments first." I didn't have "free money" to throw around, didn't want to reward bad behaviors, and certainly didn't want to invest in a particular area only to find out later that we were headed in a different direction.

Instead, I focused on investing in the top eleven modernization initiatives that we had identified as the game changers for all the services.* These technologies, such as artificial intelligence, hypersonics, quantum science, biotechnology, directed energy, microelectronics, and 5G networks, would ensure our continued overmatch—a military concept that values having overwhelming advantages (superiority) over an adversary to a more significant margin as critical for national security—in the future. Indeed, we put billions of additional dollars into these areas, making the Fiscal Year 2021 budget submission the largest research and development funding in the Department's history. And the FY 2022 budget that we built the following year, in 2020—the same one the Biden administration delivered to Congress in 2021—was even bigger when it came to research and development.

Additionally, we released modernization road maps for these technologies. For example, we accelerated the development of hypersonics, with plans to start fielding them in 2023 by ramping up flight testing, with over forty flight tests planned in the next five years. And when it came to microelectronics and 5G, we improved our access to advanced commercial and specialty microelectronics—later working to "re-shore" high-end chip production in the United

---

* The NDS directed the department to "modernize key capabilities" in order to "address the scope and pace of our competitors' and adversaries' ambitions and capabilities." The technology areas identified as critical to NDS implementation were microelectronics, autonomy, cyber, 5G communications, fully networked command, control and communications, space, hypersonics, quantum science, biotechnology, artificial intelligence (AI), and directed energy.

States—and leveraging the power of 5G for our mission sets. As part of this effort, we initiated large-scale experiments to test and evaluate 5G communications capabilities at twelve DoD bases, working alongside industry partners.

On AI, which many experts (and I) believe will change the character of warfare for generations to come, we sped up the fielding of AI capabilities at scale to meet war-fighter needs through the Joint Artificial Intelligence Center. After all, my view was that AI would afford decisive and enduring advantages to whoever harnessed and mastered it first. And we had to be first.

To do so, we established the first official chief data officer under the chief information officer, issued the first DoD Data Strategy to guide improvements on the availability and reliability of Department information, and created the first-ever AI Ethics Principles to ensure the United States is the global leader in the responsible development and use of AI. Finally, we took additional steps to support management operations by developing platforms for senior leaders to interact with live data. If there was one technology critical to winning the future against China and Russia, it was AI, and we had a lot of work to do.

In early July 2020—less than a year after the Senior Leader Conference—I would deliver a ten-minute video update on our progress in meeting these objectives, and was pleased to report that we had achieved a good deal on most of them.[8] With many in the Department distracted by the social unrest that occurred just weeks prior and other things that were happening at the time, I felt it important to celebrate their efforts and progress, and to keep everyone focused on the critical work of continuing to implement the

NDS. It was also important to let Congress, the think tank world, and the media know that the Pentagon understood what its mission and top priorities were, and that we continued to press forward.

However, I knew in October 2019 that in order to get as far as we hoped by midsummer 2020, when I would give my NDS progress update, I needed empowered and engaged civilian leadership driving these efforts. I also stressed the importance of the group becoming a closely knit leadership team that worked "far more closely together, far more often" to accomplish our shared goals.

There was some rumbling in the building about the meeting changes and process adjustments I had already made, so I wanted to address the issue head-on. "Civilians are in charge," I said, "and to do their jobs effectively, the secretaries, undersecretaries, and others need to be involved in the relevant processes" that had either stagnated or excluded them. In addition, I told my secretaries that "I need civilian leaders who are engaged and prepared to assert their proper roles." As the old saying goes, "When in charge, take charge." They got the message.

In September 2019, *Defense One,* an independent trade publication that covers the national security landscape, published an article entitled "Two Cheers for Esper's Plan to Reassert Civilian Control of the Pentagon." All three authors had been advisers to other defense secretaries. They astutely made the point that "civilian control is a *process,* not simply a person." They added, "Civilians are losing control over key processes that manage war plans, deployment decisions, and the programs that determine what kind of military the U.S. builds for the future."[9] They weren't entirely correct about the last point, but they hit the mark on the first two items.

Over the succeeding months, beginning in the fall of 2019, the civilian leadership in the OSD and the services would start reasserting control and involving themselves in the processes where appropriate and necessary. For example, our war plans needed updating. If war is an extension of politics, and the political objective must be kept in mind at all times during war—as that timeless maxim by the nineteenth-century Prussian general and military theorist Carl von Clausewitz goes—then the civilian political leadership must ensure the plans and preparations being made by the military to achieve that political outcome are aligned and credible. This is why I felt so strongly about personally reviewing and updating the war plans, as well as about ensuring my civilian appointees were leading this process.

That meant my Policy team, led by John Rood, had to be intimately involved in the process. There was organizational resistance by some on the Joint Staff who viewed war planning as the military's exclusive domain. Rood was having some challenges breaking through. It ultimately took me having to review and approve a flow chart for war planning to make sure Rood and I felt comfortable about Policy's role and insertion points in the process. We eventually succeeded, and everything was in much better shape after that, once the new system took root.

In-progress reviews of the evolving Russia and China war plans would be a necessary and recurring agenda item at the Monday afternoon NDS sessions with the combatant commanders and the leadership team in the Pentagon. The Policy team was now leading these reviews. Moreover, having the four-star combatant commanders in the room was important because we all agreed that conflict with a peer/near-peer rival would be global in nature, and not limited to either Asia or Europe.

Conflict would also not be limited to geographic domains. Having Space Command, Strategic Command, Transportation Command, and Cyber Command also attend was essential. And of course, Northern Command was vital to protecting the homeland, especially U.S. airspace, from enemy aircraft and missiles.

Another major issue that demanded greater participation from civilian leaders was global force management and the deployment of the armed forces. The secretary of defense is the only person in the DoD with the authority to deploy military units. Deployment orders that captured the detailed information necessary to send forces around the globe are the instrument for doing this. Large binders containing these orders arrived at my office about every two weeks for my review and approval.

These proposed deployments are studied by the affected services and combatant commands, and adjustments are often negotiated to get everyone to concur. It was not unusual to receive "non-concurs," if a command or a service believed that some aspect of a deployment would cause them serious hardship or present a very high risk. Some commands played the "significant-risk" card—which inevitably attracted everyone's attention—too often.

What troubled me early on was not the give-and-takes of this process, but that the only persons in the room to explain them to me was the uniformed Joint Staff. They would march into my office, sit down at the large conference table, and start walking me through the various orders. In the early days I would ask, "Where's Policy? What's their view?" or "Why isn't Joe Kernan [the undersecretary of defense for intelligence] here? What does he think?" I would be given a quick answer, and a reminder that "his office signed off on this." But that wasn't what I asked. I wanted to hear straight from the stakeholders, and I wanted the Policy team (and others) in the room as well to verify policy alignment and offer their views.

The same thing occurred with deployments that I knew impacted the services, all of them. I would often ask, "What do the chief of naval operations and Navy secretary say? How about the Army—McConville and McCarthy?" What I found is that most of these orders were being agreed to at levels below them. Sometimes the uniformed chiefs were not in the loop, and usually the service secretaries were not apprised. This all had to change. I wanted to hear from the principals, especially the civilians, when there were disagreements, and I wanted a healthy debate and discussion. It wasn't good enough on matters of such importance to simply have some officer on the Joint Staff represent the services' views.

Just like with our war-planning processes, there was some initial resistance. But it didn't take long to make this change happen and get everyone comfortable with this new normal. We eventually added other OSD civilian leaders as well depending on the issue, but it was another early effort to restore the proper balance in civilian-military relations at the Pentagon.

Along these same lines, I would later approve a new Global Force Management Allocation Plan (GFMAP), which further aligned our force allocation to the National Defense Strategy. This also caused some stir. The GFMAP better balanced the interests of the services and the combatant commands and shifted forces to higher priority missions. We also increased the "deployment to dwell" ratio—the proportion of time a unit is deployed abroad versus the time spent at home—for many units so that service members had more time at home to recover and train, and more time with their families, before going abroad again.

Also importantly, we increased the size, scope, and readiness of our Immediate Response Forces (IRF) to make them more operationally available and flexible. We now had forces from all the services packed and ready to go to war within a few days' notice. The next evolution of this new preparedness posture was to begin "no-notice" callouts where we could verify and evaluate IRF units' readiness to deploy, fight, and win. Such readiness exercises would offer good training too, while also making us more operationally unpredictable to the Chinese and Russians.

Other areas where I saw my civilian undersecretaries take the initiative and play a very important role were the two Top Ten objectives that required development of a coordinated plan to "strengthen allies and build partners" and the department to "establish realistic joint war games, exercises, and training plans." These initiatives were related to one another, as well as to our new operational concepts associated with the IRF. And not surprisingly, they also generated their own share of internal pushback.

In my assessment, the combatant commanders' training and exercise plans weren't always of the quality and caliber I expected. General Milley shared this view as well. Too often, it seemed, the commands sacrificed the quality training that really improved the readiness and integration of the joint force* with our allies and partners at the altars of volume and fanfare. The metric for success had seemed to become counting the number of events year over year, regardless of their value, instead of assessing the units' ability to fight and win together after the training. These events were also costly.

To meet the demands of our strategy, we needed to return to a more centralized and traditional stance regarding the training, exercise, and evaluation of our forces when it came to readiness and

---

* The DoD defines the term "joint force" as a force composed of elements, assigned or attached, of two or more military departments (e.g. Army, Navy) operating under a single joint-force commander. A geographic combatant command such as European Command, for example, is a joint force, as it is assigned or attached forces from more than one department similar to the DoD's other combatant commands.

deployability. By the spring of 2020, Undersecretary Matt Donovan, Milley, and I were meeting monthly to track and push this initiative, which wasn't moving as quickly as I liked. The Joint Staff
was overwhelmed with several major projects, including COVID
and the development of the Joint Warfighting Concept, but Milley
was trying to juggle this task as well.

I also asked the chairman to "establish a Joint Staff training and
exercise validation team" that could "travel the globe, make assessments, and report back to us." This would help "validate" the IRF
and Dynamic Force Employment concepts we had developed and
began implementing, and "give us timely and accurate assessments
on IRF readiness."

Matt Donovan was the Undersecretary for Personnel and Readiness; he brought a great deal of civilian and military experience
to the role. He served thirty-one years in the Air Force, worked on
Capitol Hill, and then served as undersecretary of the Air Force beginning in August 2017. His thoughtfulness and willingness to effect change, even though it seemed many of those working for him
resisted it, always impressed me. Donovan was working these initiatives hard. Despite our efforts, he would later share with me his
nearly daily struggle with the Joint Staff when it came to OSD policy, guidance, and oversight. Their views on the military role at the
Pentagon were deeply rooted, he conveyed with some annoyance.

Some of the geographic combatant commanders also resisted the
changes I sought. In their minds, I suppose, Pentagon-directed major force exercises would reduce their ability to conduct dozens of
their annual "exercises." I continued to emphasize with them that
"I value quality over quantity" and reemphasized the importance
I placed on war fighting. I had done my share of these "engagement exercises" with allies, as I called them, during my service in
Europe. They had little training value, but were great for photo

ops and diplomatic talking points. However, these engagements were also costly and time-consuming. In my view, they needed to be "consolidated and/or reduced" if we were to fund the return to training exercises of the "size, scale, and quality necessary to validate and practice our joint war plans." It took a while, but we were finally making some progress by the time I left.

The one Top Ten task that probably stoked the most pushback from the combatant commanders, however, was the Policy team's efforts to develop a single, coordinated plan to strengthen allies and build partners. James Anderson, who succeeded John Rood as the acting undersecretary of defense for policy in the spring of 2020, worked for months to develop what became the Guidance for the Development of Alliances and Partnerships (GDAP)—a strategy that was the first of its kind.

Anderson arrived at the Pentagon in 2018 with a solid professional background. He began his career as a Marine Corps intelligence officer and later served in OSD Policy, from 2001 to 2009. Along the way he earned a Ph.D. from Tufts University, worked at D.C. think tanks, and taught at the National Defense University and George Washington University. He was vice president for academic affairs at the Marine Corps University prior to his confirmation as assistant secretary of defense for Strategy, Plans, and Capabilities in August 2018. I knew James before his arrival at the DoD and always found him to be smart, thorough, and professional. He was a real team player with a serious approach and demeanor, which made it good to have him running the Policy shop.

While Russia and China are developing asymmetric capabilities, such as hypersonic missiles and space weapons designed to offset our strengths, America's great advantage is its global network of allies and partners. We have dozens of them; Russia and China have only a few, and those are of questionable quality. To optimize this advantage, however, the DoD needs to speak with one voice. Too often, the regional priorities of the combatant commands and the parochial interests of the armed services drove our international engagements. For example, it was not unusual for various DoD leaders to propose to a foreign military that they make different weapons systems an acquisition priority over others: a Navy secretary would ask them to buy a new ship or missile, an Army chief would urge a new ground vehicle, an Air Force leader might propose a new plane, and the geographic commander might push for something totally different, all within a matter of several weeks. Nobody was doing this purposefully to undermine the Department, but it would confuse and frustrate our allies and result in unnecessary delays that sometimes played into a country's own bureaucratic tendencies. With limited resources, and seeking clear direction from the United States, these types of interactions tended to reduce a partner's war-fighting effectiveness and interoperability with us. The GDAP would fix this.

It would enable us to prioritize and align our security cooperation activities to build partner capacity, better articulate the DoD's needs for their priority war-fighting roles, and help them shape their militaries into more capable forces. The four pillars of this program were key leader engagements, international professional military education, the state partnership program run by and through the National Guard, and Foreign Military Sales. All were successful programs, and we had plans to take each to a new level, such as expanding the highly successful International Military Education and Training program—where allied and partner service members typically come to the United States for training or schooling—by growing it 50 percent over the next five years.

Strategies like this that threaten the status quo tend to generate resistance and anxiety. Some people simply don't like change.

Others see their programs under threat, scrutiny, or simply losing out. The entrenched bureaucracies—military and civilian alike—tend to push back. As such, it took us months just to get the geographic commands to prioritize the five to eight countries each would put in its top tier. The State Department could never come around to doing this, telling us instead that "all countries are important." Hmmm. This was frustrating. After all, the DoD is supposed to take its foreign policy lead from the State Department. James Anderson provided that leadership notwithstanding, and after going around and around for weeks trying to resolve the commands' issues with little success, he delivered the GDAP document to me.

I was never one to seek 100 percent consensus, just 100 percent opportunity for everyone to share their views. We heard them out. Now it was time to move forward and do what was best for the greater good. I signed the GDAP in October 2020 and delivered a major speech on it that same month.[10] A couple of senior leaders from President Biden's Pentagon would later compliment me privately on the GDAP, so I was encouraged that it too might endure the transition and the resistance of a few combatant commanders.

A few final thoughts on civilian-military relations. Based on my experiences over many years, both at the Pentagon and on Capitol Hill, I believe Congress has a critical role to play in empowering the civilian leadership at the Pentagon and helping restore the balance of power there. First, the Senate needs to do a much better job in quickly vetting and confirming DoD nominees. It's great that the secretary of defense typically gets confirmed in the first days of an administration, but it then takes months, if not an entire year, to get the whole team of political appointees confirmed and in place.

Moreover, failing to replace civilians quickly over time, once the first wave moves on, is also detrimental to civilian-military relations and civilian control. With civilians not in key positions at the Pentagon, the uniformed professionals on the Joint Staff and in the combatant commands will fill the vacuum, bolstered by their large staffs, the force of their processes, and an unbroken leadership continuity that is rarely confounded with the challenge of open positions.

Second, combatant commanders should testify before Congress or meet with members and Hill staff only with their OSD counterparts alongside them in most cases. This would reaffirm civilian primacy and control of the military and give the necessary perspective of civilian leadership at the Pentagon to their congressional overseers.

Another important way in which Congress can affirm constructive civilian-military relations is to give deference to reform initiatives put forward by civilian leadership and not be swayed by uniformed leaders from the services or combatant commands making end arounds to protect their turf or advance their agendas. The quickest way to undermine civilian leadership is by empowering this type of bad behavior, which not only harms civilian control of the military but also dampens any real enthusiasm to take on serious reform at the DoD. At the end of the day, it is the secretary of defense who sees the entire landscape—region by region, domain by domain, function by function, present and future—and who is the most capable and responsible person for making the trade-offs and adjustments necessary to ensure our nation's security.

Next, the House and Senate Armed Services Committees should support installing civilians at most of the defense agencies. When I was secretary of defense, I began moving in this direction by appointing the first civilian head of the Defense Security Cooperation Agency in years, replacing the job previously held by a three-star officer. Civilians should lead the Defense Logistics Agency, Defense Contract Management Agency, and Defense Health Agency, much as they do at the Defense Contract Audit Agency and Defense Commissary Agency. In short, unless there is some compelling reason otherwise, any organization that begins with the word "Defense" should be led by a civilian, preferably one with longtime, relevant private sector experience in that field or industry. An added benefit of this move is the opportunity to reduce the total number of general officers in the services, another endeavor I pursued.

Finally, Congress should jump-start a multiyear process to assess the cumulative effect of the various congressional requirements and enacted laws over the preceding decades—beginning with the 1986 Goldwater-Nichols Act reforms—and determine which provisions watered down the roles, responsibilities, duties, and authorities of civilian leaders and distorted the balance of power between the services and the combatant commands. In the days following my departure from the Pentagon in November 2020, I privately raised this idea with the chairmen of both the House Armed Services Committee and the Senate Armed Services Committee. I remain committed to work with them to get this important initiative off the ground, and stand ready as a private citizen if Congress wants to take me up on this proposal.

CHAPTER 5

TEHRAN ESCALATES

We sat in absolute silence, watching the screen, as the most significant military strike of the Trump administration unfolded before us thousands of miles away. One that threatened the prospect of violent retaliation, but one we felt we had no choice but to conduct. It was a bold action that would change the landscape of the Middle East, and constituted a major test of Donald Trump as commander in chief.

On September 14, 2019—just under two months after I was confirmed as secretary of defense—Iran launched drone attacks at a major Saudi petroleum refinery at Abqaiq. It was a complex strike that targeted two sites and demonstrated Iran's capabilities. Abqaiq is one of the most important oil production facilities in the world, so a successful attempt to knock it out would affect not only the Saudi economy but global oil prices as well. While the Houthis took credit for the attack, the launch point for the drones wasn't Yemen.

The attack shocked the Saudi leadership. They saw it as unprecedented and feared these strikes marked the beginning of a broader campaign by Iran against them. I quickly met with General McKenzie, the CENTCOM commander, and my leadership to discuss how to strengthen Saudi defenses and reassure them of our support. The biggest asset the Saudis needed were air defenses. We already had multiple Patriot batteries deployed to Saudi Arabia, but McKenzie and the Saudis wanted more. The problem was, there was only so much in the Army inventory, and I couldn't afford to commit most of them to one theater.

The Saudis had a sufficient number of Patriot batteries, but too many were inoperable due to poor maintenance—as with other Saudi systems—a sticking point for me during my tenure. Most of the remainder focused south toward Yemen. Now Saudi Arabia had to worry about the Iranian threat to their east and northeast as well. This was particularly troubling given that Iran possesses the largest and most diverse inventory of ballistic and cruise missiles in the Middle East. These systems are accurate, with most able to reach Iran's immediate neighbors, and some capable of striking southeastern Europe.[1] They would be a top challenge for the United States and its partners if war came.

While I committed some additional U.S. air-defense assets, I immediately asked McKenzie and John Rood, the undersecretary for policy, to reach out to our NATO allies. Many of them had Patriots or other compatible systems that could help us fill the air-defense gaps. However, except for one country, Greece, none stepped up to help the Saudis, even after months of asking.

The Saudis also requested that we initiate our operations plan and significantly increase an array of resources for their nation's defense, broadening our commitments in a way that would result in a significant increase of troops to the theater. They would push on these matters for months and months, even during my meeting in Riyadh with the crown prince, Mohammed bin Salman, and in their later correspondence to the White House.

The situation didn't warrant such a move yet, and I was confident the president wouldn't support it. After all, he had been spending years pressing to get out of the Middle East, not commit *more* forces there. We also had to be careful about sending the wrong signals to Tehran, and the unintended consequences if we erred. Nobody wanted war, but what might look like defensive U.S. support to the Saudis from our perspective could appear to be the first phase of an offensive campaign against Iran from their view. Such a misreading of the situation might force them to take preemptive action. On the other hand, not doing something might well embolden even more Iranian aggression. Finding deterrence, the sweet spot between inaction and provocation, was always a challenge.

Rather than implementing the full plan, we decided to deploy those forces that were needed to "open the theater." These are logistical, transportation, and other noncombat units that take a long time to deploy and set up but are critical to receiving, processing, and supporting combat units flowing into a theater of war. Getting them in place now would help reassure the Saudis and save us a great deal of time should things go bad later. We also could do so without spooking Tehran too much.

On Friday, September 20, 2019, General Dunford and I appeared before the media in the Pentagon Briefing Room to announce that air- and missile-defense units and other assets would soon be flowing to the region to help defend the Saudis, reassure our partners, and deter further Iranian aggression. Behind the scenes, we continued working with U.S. Central Command on refining military options to present the president should the situation escalate. This process would continue through the fall.

Meanwhile, the State Department was working hard to get our European allies on board, prodding Britain, France, and Germany to publicly place blame for the attack on Iran, and urging Tehran to halt the provocations. The timing was particularly tricky given the upcoming meeting of the U.N. General Assembly in New York, and Iranian president Hassan Rouhani's attendance, but the three European leaders put out a helpful statement on September 23.

On October 3, the national security team met with the president in the Situation Room. General Mark Milley was on board by now. He became chairman of the Joint Chiefs of Staff on September 30 after General Dunford's well-earned retirement. The president sat at the front of the small room. Behind Trump's black-leather chair—on the opposite end of the room from the large video screens—hung a presidential seal the size of a large serving plate. I, then Milley, sat to his immediate left. Across the narrow conference table, and the various wires and phones strewn across it, the vice president, secretary of state, national security adviser, and others faced us. More staff sat along the walls behind their principals. As much as we tried to keep these meetings small for the sake of operational security, the more others managed to find a way in.

Everyone arrived before the president, which presented a good opportunity for some final small talk. We managed to clear some space at Trump's end of the table so that we had room to lay down graphics and other material in front of him. The president usually arrived on time, often dressed in his standard blue suit, white shirt, and red tie. He entered in a very businesslike manner, scanned the room, and greeted everyone as he proceeded to sit.

The meeting began with a short discussion about the tense situation on the Turkey-Syria border, and how State and Defense were working to keep both sides apart, propose solutions to tamp down Ankara's fever, and maintain stability in the area. I had spoken privately to my defense counterpart in Turkey about these things a few times over the preceding weeks, but it was clear Turkish president Recep Tayyip Erdogan was determined to carve out a safe zone in northern Syria—a long-standing ambition of our NATO ally. Pompeo and I presented our updates in a very brief, matter-of-fact way. General Milley added some details about the force levels on the ground, and the disposition of American personnel in Syria. Trump responded by repeating his long-standing desire to withdraw U.S. forces from the country once and for all, following the physical defeat of the ISIS caliphate in Syria several months earlier.

Unbeknownst to us at the time, the Turkish military would cross the Syrian border to the east the following week and accomplish its goal. General Milley (like Dunford before him) and I opposed this move, as well as the president's desire to hastily withdraw all U.S. forces from Syria, and counseled Trump regarding both issues prior to a call he had with Erdogan a few days before the Turkish incursion. However, the best we got from the president was agreement that the U.S. military would not provide any support to the Turks. Upon Milley's recommendation, we decided to immediately withdraw from the border area a few dozen soldiers who would have otherwise been trapped in the combat zone between the opposing forces.[2]

After the Turkish assault, I publicly criticized Erdogan's actions and his country's behavior as an ally, also noting that Erdogan seemed resolved to conduct the invasion when he spoke with Trump.[3] Later, with help from key members of Congress, we would be surprisingly successful in persuading the president to reverse himself and permit the retention of sufficient U.S. forces in eastern Syria to continue our support to the Syrian Democratic Forces, ensuring the enduring defeat of ISIS, helping to protect Iraq, and keeping a close eye on the Iranians.

Back in the Situation Room on October 3, we then pivoted to Iran—the purpose of the meeting. I told Trump that "the chairman and I want to walk you through an updated set of options that target multiple Iranian assets, each with a varying degree of impact, estimated casualties, level of difficulty and risk, and anticipated response." He looked at me and nodded.

We used a "heat chart" that was developed by Dunford and modified by Milley to brief Trump. It was challenging to keep the president focused. I had been in enough meetings now to experience it multiple times. A discussion would stop stone cold and pivot as a new thought raced through his head—he saw something on TV, or somebody made a remark that threw him off track. Somehow, we often ended up on the same topics, like his greatest hits of the decade: NATO spending; Merkel, Germany, and Nord Stream 2; corruption in Afghanistan; U.S. troops in Korea; and, closing our embassies in Africa, for example. My first full exposure to this behavior was at a principals' meeting in Bedminster, New Jersey, in August 2019 that was supposed to focus on the Afghan peace agreement.

The conversations were like a pinball machine—you knew where the silver ball would begin and end its journey, but the path in between was chaotic, bumpy, and unpredictable. And to stretch the metaphor a little further, depending on who got bumped during that journey, you would either gain or lose points with the president. That was how meetings with Trump transpired. As such, we thought something very simple and visual would not only help us explain these complex military matters but help us control the narrative, like putting guardrails on the inside of the pinball machine, right down the narrow middle.

I set down the chart in front of the president on the conference table, and he quickly leaned into it. You could see his eyes darting around the large graphic, with its colored boxes and lines. To fill the space and avoid unrelated questions, I quickly explained to Trump that "the easier options are on the left side of the chart, with options of increasing difficulty and consequence as you move to the right, with the far right option being the most difficult, dangerous, and destructive." We literally used a colored bar that ran across the graphic and morphed from yellow to red, getting "hotter," as you looked left to right to visually identify the escalating options.

At the top of the page, in a larger font, we listed key objectives the president said repeatedly. I read them off for all to hear, since we had handed out only a few of the graphics. It began with "No war with Iran" and "No nuclear weapon for Iran." We wanted to remind the president of what *he* said, let him know that we were listening, and ensure others in the room—especially the war hawks like National Security Adviser Robert O'Brien, and to a lesser extent Secretary of State Pompeo and Vice President Pence—were all reminded of the president's views. Sometimes other cabinet members, like Commerce Secretary Wilbur Ross, would be present, and offer their full-throated support for tough action. Go figure. We wanted to baseline everyone attending to these key principles—the ones Trump personally approved—in case the discussion became muddy, as it often did. In my view, if we had these wrong, then this was the time to change them. Nobody ever challenged this formula.

At the bottom of the page, beneath each option, we listed the estimated Battle Damage Assessment for each target set. I made clear that "these include estimated casualties—both civilian and military." I had added this after our experience in June, when the president called off the strike in response to Iran shooting down the U.S. drone. In short, we wanted to be very clear about the key details of these options, from the common strategic aims to the unique tactical considerations, so that there were no misunderstandings.

With that, I turned the floor over to General Milley, who began walking the president through each of the options in detail. He would also answer questions such as "How many missiles will that take?" or "How do you know there will be that many casualties?" At times, CIA Director Gina Haspel or someone from her team would speak up and respond to the president.

As he had in June, Trump leaned toward the high end of strikes, those that caused the most damage. He wanted to "take out" Iran's nuclear infrastructure, as he would say. We would acknowledge this, walk him around a small map, pointing out key sites, and then describe in basic terms how we would go about doing that. Trump hunched over the map, his eyes narrowed, looking closely. He would nod and say, "Good, good." He would invariably follow up with something like "Let's do it. Let's go."

I often had to point back to the top of the chart and say, "Mr. President, you said, 'No war with Iran.' If we do this, there is a good chance that we'll be at war with Iran." I'd continue with the seriousness the matter demanded, "And if that's the likely outcome, then we need to prepare for it *before* we begin."

Milley and I would then pivot and speak to everything from the significant buildup of combat power to the extended timelines and other considerations. We would finish with our assessment of the costs, estimated killed, and the likelihood of war. The president would look attentively, pause, lean back in his chair, fold his arms across his chest, and take it in. He would look around the table to gauge others' reactions as well. These things clearly grabbed his attention, like a major league hitter getting a fastball thrown right in front of his chin. The consequences were significant.

Pompeo often didn't say much. He generally preferred the tougher responses too and at times would challenge assessments about the Iranian reaction. That was a fair discussion to have, and we would often turn to the CIA director or the director of national intelligence to offer their views. "How would Iran respond?"—this question always hung heavily in the air. It was an unknown, for sure. However, I contended we should assume the worst and prepare for that likelihood. Invariably, I would say, "Mr. President, since we don't know for sure, then we should prepare for the worst. I don't recommend this [the hard-hitting option], but if that is your decision, we will need time to set the theater, flow in additional forces, and be prepared for all-out conflict." There was too much at stake to simply assume a country like Iran would either roll over or respond lightly to a major U.S. attack.

However, putting more U.S. troops in the Middle East, especially on the scale we would need, was just the opposite of what Trump wanted to do. He was consistent on that matter. When Milley and I talked him through what such a deployment would look like, he would back off.

Robert O'Brien was new to this, having just become national security adviser (NSA) two weeks earlier, on September 18. He was good at praising the DoD for its "great work in pulling this all together." He gave his assessment and then chirped in his support to "hit them hard," which over time became his tedious signature phrase. It made him sound tough and appealed to Trump, but I thought this was reckless and not necessarily the role of the NSA. Rather, his job was to coordinate policy across the departments and ensure all relevant sides were represented, not become an advocate who ran his own agenda, proposed his own plans, or played up to the president. It didn't serve anybody well, including Trump, and only grew worse over time.

I didn't know O'Brien before he became the national security adviser. His résumé seemed light on the experiences and background typically found in NSAs, but he was a smart person with an upbeat demeanor who I thought would grow into the job. I had hosted a breakfast for him at the Pentagon his first week in office to welcome him aboard.

We had a good conversation, and I shared with him the strengths and weaknesses I saw in the current National Security Council (NSC). John Bolton had done a really good job, but I told him that "more coordination and consultation," which was *the role* of the council, "and less direction and involvement in department affairs"— views shared by my cabinet colleagues—"was always welcome."

"I agree," O'Brien said, committing to doing so, and then adding that he intended "to slash the size of the NSC considerably," which would also help limit any meddling.

I told O'Brien that my practice was "to brief you and Pompeo in advance of any issue we have to take to the president to ensure you are informed, solicit your views, and hopefully get everyone's support." This was important to do not only because of the internal politics of the national security bureaucracy, and the dynamics that could unfold with the president, but also because the secretary of state was responsible for overall U.S. foreign policy and the national security adviser was charged with its coordination across the federal government.

"It is always best if the three of us are aligned on matters being taken to the president," I said. Bolton did this well. "And at a minimum," I added, "we at least have to speak to one another before any such discussion." Unfortunately, that wasn't always the case, and it was another problem that would also grow worse over time.

Our first meeting went well, but things inevitably frayed as the NSC, and O'Brien personally, increasingly stuck their noses (and fingers) into the DoD and other departments. They also tended to take hard-core positions on issues that I believed were divorced from practical consequences.

Maybe they felt they had to amplify Trump's views, even if they didn't know exactly what they were—who knew? These tendencies, often dangerous ones, would become topics of discussion at many of the weekly breakfast meetings Pompeo would host at State for CIA Director Gina Haspel, Treasury Secretary Steve Mnuchin, and me. Mike Pompeo later told me he regretted recommending O'Brien for the NSA job to the president.

Back in the Situation Room, General Milley and I advocated a graduated approach based on our stated policy outcomes, in response to the action taken by the Iranians. I also had to calculate the likely consequences of our actions, assess how they could escalate, and think about some of the most relevant Nine Considerations I outlined during my confirmation process. The point wasn't to pick an option today, but to think through the dynamics of them while we had the time.

We also needed to consider broader issues, ranging from the time it would take to build combat power and withdraw American citizens from the region to consulting with Congress and getting the support of allies and partners.

Regarding U.S. forces, I didn't want to put too many in any one region unnecessarily. It seemed like whenever you did that, it was doubly hard to pull them back out once the situation settled down. The commanders would fight to keep them in theater, our partners would complain about feeling vulnerable, some lawmakers on Capitol Hill would say we were "abandoning allies," and you had to consider what your adversary's conclusion might be as well.

Milley made the point, as Dunford had before him, that it's far easier to get into a war than it is to get out of one. I agreed and doubled down. The good news was that Trump didn't want war. He could be a man of many random thoughts and non sequiturs, but he was always clear and consistent about that. That said, the contradiction in his view was that he sometimes believed the United States could act with impunity, that the chance of starting a war was unlikely.

The president often had others in the room, and foreign leaders like Israeli prime minister Benjamin Netanyahu, telling him ███████ ███ ████████████████████████████████████.* Netanyahu would say this to me when I met with him, so I was confident he was telling Trump the same thing.

In my view, that seemed like a big bet to take, especially when there wasn't a pressing need to take it anytime soon. ██████████ ███ ███ ███ ████████████████████████. Even according to Israeli media, ministry of defense officials in Israel reportedly briefed their superiors sometime much later that, while Tehran's nuclear efforts were progressing, Iran was still two years away from assembling a nuclear weapon.[4]

General Milley and I left the meeting satisfied that we had delivered what the president was expecting and needed, and confident that we made all the right points regarding how to think about these matters. However, there was still a palpable sense that too many around the table wanted to strike Iran.

---

* For updates on redactions—to include newly released or modified text—and other information regarding *A Sacred Oath,* please visit my website, markt esper.com.

My combat service paled in comparison to Milley's, but we couldn't help but note, as we headed to our cars after this NSC meeting, the irony that the only two persons in the room that had ever gone to war were the ones least willing to risk doing so now.

Over the succeeding weeks and months, we would continue to refine our planning at the Pentagon. McKenzie would work to improve his defenses and capabilities in the region, especially in Iraq. And we all watched Iran and the Shia militia groups in Baghdad closely.

I traveled to Iraq, Saudi Arabia, and Afghanistan later in October to meet with my counterparts and talk to our people on the ground. In Saudi Arabia, I met with troops stationed at Prince Sultan Air Base, which was our primary reception point into the country. It was outside the range of most Iranian missiles, yet we had to defend it nonetheless.

I spent time with the soldiers operating the Patriot battery to get a good sense of how they saw their mission and the principal challenges they faced. It was a gritty existence in the flat, hot sands surrounding the base. The units were already building berms to help with security, and the soldiers had settled into their daily routines.

As I spoke with the battery commander, I was impressed with her and the many young officers leading our frontline forces. I usually learned a thing or two from those on the ground who were actually making policy happen. It was hard to believe that was me twenty-five years earlier. I felt much older now, but even more impressed by the commitment of the soldiers who spent so much time away from home and in some degree of danger. America should be proud.

In Baghdad, I met with Iraqi defense minister Najah Hassan Ali al-Shammari on October 23 to discuss several issues, including the redeployment of some U.S. forces from northeast Syria and the planned reduction over time of American personnel in Iraq. Al-Shammari was a quiet man who stood a little over six feet tall, with thin, graying hair and a matching mustache. Like me, he graduated from his nation's military academy, spent many years in the Army, and became defense minister in the summer of 2019.

Al-Shammari was an intelligent and well-educated man who understood all the competing factors we were dealing with, but as a Sunni Arab in a Shi'ite-dominated political system marked by violence, tumult, and factionalism, there were limits to what he could say and do. He was pro-American and approached issues as I would expect a career Army officer would, so I didn't let his cautious reticence overly concern me. Rather, the quiet support his ministry was providing to U.S. forces in Iraq and the personal assurances he was conveying to me were helpful.

We had a little over five thousand personnel in the country, with a plan to go down to three thousand by the following summer, and even lower after that. The Iraqi military had improved considerably, which meant we could reduce our training program. Nevertheless, we still wanted to keep other assets around to conduct counterterrorism strikes against ISIS while keeping a close eye on Iran. A complete U.S. departure from Iraq would create a vacuum for Tehran to fill, even though they had a significant presence and influence there already.

I told al-Shammari, "We are committed to helping Iraq improve its security." I added that, while we had no aspirations for a permanent U.S. presence in the country, "we do expect Iraq to provide for our security." This meant an active defense of our bases, and "the arrest of any groups or individuals planning or conducting attacks against us." I pressed him hard on these points.

My team was sure there was at least one person in the room from his side who was reporting back to Tehran. The fun and challenging part of this reality was trying to figure out who it might be as you sat opposite one another sipping strong coffee from small porcelain cups and exchanging niceties. Regardless, I wanted to make sure I was clear about our intentions and resolve. I added, for all to hear, that "we don't want to see Iraq become a battlefield again, nor are we seeking war with Iran," but "we are going to defend our people and interests from any attack, and will hold Iran responsible." I thought that was unambiguous.

Throughout the rest of the month and into December, Iran and Iraq remained a focus as U.S. forces continued to flow into Saudi Arabia. In October, I ordered the deployment of two more fighter squadrons to the region, bringing the total to three thousand additional troops I either extended or dispatched since the Iranian attack on the Saudi oil refinery. Meanwhile, Shia militia groups in Iraq continued their random rocket attacks against U.S. forces based in that country. We remained on guard as Tehran picked up the scope and pace of its bad behavior.

At the same time, developments in Afghanistan with the stalled peace plan, followed by issues with Venezuela and Turkey—notably the latter's incursion into northern Syria—also demanded my attention. My weekly meetings with Pompeo centered on these matters, while my internal discussions with Deputy Secretary David Norquist, Undersecretary for Policy John Rood, and General Milley also focused on the upcoming budget submission, combatant command reviews, and the day-to-day functioning of the department.

I needed to find a new chief of staff as well. Eric Chewning had been running hard for quite some time. He had a young family that needed more of his attention. I completely understood. Prioritizing the kids is a fundamental dilemma for dual-career parents, and it's especially challenging when you're coming into work before the sun rises and leaving after it sets. I often regretted not spending more time with my children when they were younger, so I had a lot of respect for his decision. I just needed some time to find the right person for what is one of the most important positions in the building. This would have to wait for a few weeks, however.

On Friday, December 27, a rocket attack on an Iraqi military base in Kirkuk, north of Baghdad, resulted in the death of an American contractor and injuries to four U.S. service members. Like the eleven previous attacks, this one also had the telltale signs of a Tehran-aligned Shia militia group, which we eventually determined to be Kata'ib Hezbollah (KH). Iran long supported KH, which had close ties to the Islamic Republican Guard Corps. KH was one of the most hard-core and capable militia groups in Iraq.

It was the Christmas holiday break back in the United States, but as soon as reports began flowing in, Norquist, Rood, Milley, McKenzie, and I started meeting on secure phones from our homes to get the details of the attack, strengthen our defenses in Iraq, and begin reviewing military options. A redline was crossed. With an American killed, we had to respond. If not, the next attack would be bigger, and could kill or injure more, an outcome we had to deter. The president was asking for my recommendation.

I spoke with General Milley by secure phone early on the twenty-eighth. CENTCOM confirmed that KH was responsible for the strike, which involved more than thirty rockets. I gave him guidance regarding the range of options—six total—to develop, beginning with going after those directly responsible for killing Nawres

Waleed Hamid, the Iraqi American linguist who left behind a wife and two young sons in Sacramento, California.[5]

General McKenzie briefed the group later that day and, after making some adjustments in consultation with Milley, I approved the plan. We did a final call early the next morning to review the operation one last time. Everything was still a go. The concept was very straightforward—the U.S. military would conduct air strikes using F-15s and precision munitions against KH weapons depots and command centers in Iraq and eastern Syria. Not only would this send a message of resolve, it would also punish them for killing an American and set back any additional plans they were preparing.

Shortly afterward, I called the president down in Florida, where he was staying over the holiday break, to brief him. An aide answered, and after a short wait, the president picked up the secure phone. Trump was always personally engaging. "Hello Mark, how are you?" he said. I told him that I was calling to walk him through our recommended response to the attack that killed the American.

"Good, good," he said. "What do you think?" I outlined the general concept, telling him that "U.S. aircraft would strike multiple sites under the cover of darkness," and that "we are confident that these are KH targets." I made clear that "we will definitely kill some militia, and maybe even some Iranians," but was quick to add, "We still recommended proceeding with this course of action."

In these situations, when we were talking about actual military options, I usually found Trump to be attentive, listening closely, weighing and assessing, it seemed, which was a good thing. He was also more open-minded and he postured less when we met or spoke one-on-one, as compared to a group setting. In the latter situations, he relished the drama and display of holding court and pitting people and sides against one another. As such, I tried to be more laconic and succinct in Oval Office or Situation Room meetings—keeping my powder dry—and saving my best arguments or ideas for more private meetings. I had a better chance of winning the day in more personal settings, enlisting allies behind the scenes, as compared to the melee of bad ideas pushed or supported by his White House sycophants. I wasn't always able to stick to my game plan, however. Sometimes you have to speak up, to draw a line, to push back hard, even if it means jeopardizing your own position in the long run.

Regarding Iraq, I informed the president that the operation would take place before noon that day, December 29—very early in the evening Baghdad time—once we finalized all preparations. Trump was familiar with the general situation and the key players since we had had these discussions before, so he was quick to approve our recommendation. The call wrapped up with him saying, "Good job, Mark. Thanks. Keep me informed."

I spoke with Mike Pompeo a couple of times about the operation, shoring up our partners, and public messaging. We agreed I would call Iraqi prime minister Adel Abdul-Mahdi beforehand, which I did just prior to the strike, to inform him what we were doing and why. Abdul-Mahdi wasn't happy and asked that we call off the operation. He viewed this as "a violation of Iraqi sovereignty" and an escalatory action that could throw Iraq into deep turmoil. In our view, I said, "Iran and the militia groups are the ones escalating things," and he was doing nothing about it. I was clear about "our right to self-defense and the expectation we had long expressed"—including when I had met with him in October—about "the Iraqi government ensuring our security."

The DoD had long been concerned that U.S. military actions aimed at restoring deterrence could force the Iraqi government to expel us from the country. Such an outcome could harm our ability to ensure the enduring defeat of ISIS, prevent increased Iranian control of the government in Baghdad, and monitor/track Tehran's operations in the region. That said, we couldn't tolerate the killing of an American and the increasing belligerence of the Shia militia groups. This too could eventually make our position in Iraq untenable. After all, the goal of the militia groups and their Iranian sponsors was the removal of the United States from Iraq, and from the broader Middle East.

Prime Minister Abdul-Mahdi was a Shi'ite and former member of the Supreme Islamic Iraqi Council, which was based in Iran and opposed the U.S. involvement in Iraq. He faced a near impossible situation balancing all the competing factions in his country. A quiet majority of Iraqis supported the U.S. presence and the relative stability we provided, while a vocal minority aligned with Iran opposed it. Making matters more dangerous, many of the political groups in Iraq seemed to have their own militias they employed to defend their interests. It was tribal warfare on a national scale, and they didn't hesitate to use violence to get their way.

I also called the chairmen and ranking members of the House and Senate Armed Services Committees prior to the attack. I don't believe any of them were in D.C. at the time, and none had secure phone capabilities. However, without breaching security, I was able to inform them about our plans for an appropriate military response to the Kirkuk attack. I assured them the DoD would brief them afterward as soon as possible. They asked good questions, offered advice, and generally appreciated the call. To their credit, no leaks ever came from these four lawmakers in the eighteen months or so that we worked together.

The air strikes went off without a hitch on Sunday morning, with all five sites being hit and suffering extensive damage. Secondary explosions at some locations confirmed our assessment that they were weapons depots. The strikes killed at least two dozen militiamen, including a few KH commanders, with over twice that number wounded. We weren't expecting tallies that high, but then again, they should have known it was an occupational hazard to target Americans.

That same afternoon, Pompeo, Milley, and I traveled to Mar-a-Lago to brief the president. We gathered in a back room of the ornate estate. Chief of Staff Mick Mulvaney, who was already in Florida, and a couple of other White House staffers joined us. Mulvaney and I had worked together a little over four months by now, and I found him to be helpful and reasonable. He was easy to work with, well aware of the internal politics of the White House, and did his best to make the place function.

Pompeo and I were in dark suits, with Milley in his dress uniform, making us all look out of place at the resort as we wound our way through a maze of dark wood, chandeliers, and marble floors. Trump met us in a waiting room, dressed comfortably in a white shirt with a blazer. He was relaxed and in good spirits.

Robert O'Brien and CIA Director Gina Haspel called in for the meeting. The rest of us sat around the large rectangular table, with me at the end, closest to the president, so that I could walk him through the update. Trump slouched forward to listen, with his hands crossed on the table in front of him, as he often did, looking alternatively at me and others in the room. He always seemed to be assessing who was thinking what as conversations ebbed and flowed.

I kicked off the session with an intelligence update, our current force posture, and a quick summary of the additional troops we had moving into the theater to buttress our operations. General Milley briefed the president in detail on the strikes against the five KH sites, and the battle damage assessments we had so far.

Milley went through it quickly, with photos as well to enhance his report. On a couple of sites we conducted both direct hits and offset strikes, the latter meaning we intentionally didn't target buildings where we assessed Iranian Guard Corps personnel were suspected of working. This tactic was an effort to message Tehran while avoiding Iranian casualties that could unnecessarily escalate the situation.

To my surprise, this really angered Trump. He wasn't yelling, but he was both frustrated and mad. He sat there, hunched over, shaking his head, with a grimace on his face, looking up at Milley and saying, "That was stupid" and "Why would you do that," adding that "it makes us look like we can't hit the target." This, of course, wasn't the case, and we were confident the Iranians knew that. The U.S. military had long proven it could hit targets with ruthless precision. This was about messaging and deterrence, and about our knowledge of facts on the ground. This action was about subtlety, something for which Trump was not known.

Milley seemed to take the criticism a little hard and was certainly frustrated. We both were. Pompeo jumped in to help Trump put things into perspective. I tried to pull the brief out of a nosedive by saying, "Mr. President, when you step back, the bottom line is that the operation was very successful. We destroyed five KH sites and killed many of their fighters, and all U.S. planes returned safely to their base." Trump leaned back into his chair and said, "I guess so" in a resigned manner, still wearing the grimace of disapproval on his face.

This was one of the mysteries of Donald Trump as commander in chief. Sometimes he would express concern about being drawn into a conflict, and he was always talking about getting out of the "endless wars." In the same vein, he would call off strikes we had already agreed to. At other times, like now, he would complain we were not being tough enough and want the most aggressive options possible. His views on the use of force swung back and forth like a pendulum, though even a pendulum has some predictability. The president rarely gave us much at all.

We quickly transitioned into a discussion of the military options available in the event Iran or the Shia militia groups—though in many ways they were one and the same—decided to escalate the situation. This conversation included many of the options we had covered in the past, from targets outside of Iranian territory, to those in the waters of the Gulf, and some in Iran proper. We had also discussed going after key leaders of the Shia militia groups in Iraq, as well as Iranian military personnel—namely, Qasem Soleimani, the commander of Iran's Quds Force.

Qasem Soleimani was an Iranian military officer who first saw service in the Iran-Iraq War, where he earned a reputation as a capable commander. He eventually became commander of the Quds Force—a branch of the Guard Corps responsible for special operations outside of Iran. He built strong relations with Hezbollah in Lebanon, and with other terror groups throughout the Middle East and beyond. Soleimani's persona and accomplishments made him a popular figure in Iran. Many considered him the second most powerful person in the country, right behind the Ayatollah Khamenei, Iran's supreme leader. Needless to say, Soleimani had extraordinary influence over Iran's foreign policy and external activities.

In 2007, the Bush administration designated the Quds Force a foreign terrorist organization. Four years later, the Obama administration placed sanctions on Soleimani and other Quds Force officials for planning to assassinate the Saudi ambassador to the United States in Washington, D.C.

Trump raised the idea of going after Soleimani. It was an option first proposed long before Milley and I took up our respective positions in 2019, but that resurfaced every now and then. We all knew that the Quds commander was a key player—indeed, *the* player—when it came to all the mischief that Iran was causing in the region. He had overseen the arming, resourcing, and training of Shia groups throughout the Middle East for years, and helped support or plan operations that resulted in deaths too many to number. The United Nations and the European Union had personally sanctioned him, and the United States designated him a terrorist in 2005.

Soleimani's activities against the United States in Iraq during its insurgency resulted in more than six hundred American service members killed, and many more wounded. In fact, the United States announced earlier in 2019 that "17 percent of all deaths of U.S. personnel in Iraq from 2003 to 2011 were orchestrated by Soleimani."[6] There was no love lost for him at the DoD. We could all support going after him if the situation warranted, but Milley and I recommended a graduated response that first allowed the dust to settle from the day's strikes. After that, if Iran retaliated, we would go about hitting more targets of increasing importance to Tehran.

Milley and I expressed concern that attacks on Iranian soil or aimed at Soleimani could provoke an all-out war, which was another reason to "climb the escalation ladder" one rung at a time until we found the point where Iran backed down. After all, the goal now was ensuring we deterred Tehran. Mulvaney joined in, pushing back with us against any precipitous actions, particularly against the higher-end targets we had identified, the ones that Trump was focusing on.

The president grew irritated again, still smoldering over the "offset strikes." He was frustrated that the ███████ had not taken care of

Soleimani earlier, as they had been pressing to do for months, well before I arrived on the scene in June. He complained that ████ was talking tough but really wanted the United States to conduct the strike, which was a shrewd assessment. The DoD had long expressed reservations about such an action, concerned about consequences ranging from increased attacks against U.S. personnel in Iraq, to Baghdad evicting us from the country, and all the way up to war with Iran. The risks seemed high.

O'Brien weighed in over the phone, picking up on Trump's inclination and doubling down, arguing that *all* the targets should be hit, and that we should "hit them hard" now. Milley and I looked at each other and rolled our eyes. We quickly jumped back into the discussion and urged restraint. "We need to let the next few days play out," I said. "After all, we just took out five sites, killed at least nineteen militiamen as best we knew, and wounded a few dozen others based on early reports." Fires were still burning, and we were hearing the strikes might have killed some Iranians as well. "This was a pretty heavy price for them to pay," we argued. Milley added, "Mr. President, we own the shot clock here; no need to rush."

The "shot clock" reference was a phrase used often at the Pentagon. The point was, we didn't need to act immediately; there was no timer on us. "If we're going to do something big, Mr. President, then we need time to prep the theater and deploy additional forces." We need to be ready for moves 2, 3, 4, and 5, I would often say. The meeting wrapped up with Trump directing us to keep developing the plans in the event KH retaliated.

As the end of 2019 neared, the U.S. intelligence community (IC) was working overtime to figure out what the Shia militia groups and Iran would do next. Anti-American anger in Iraq had shot through the roof, so we had every reason to believe the militia groups would attack again. We started getting information that Soleimani would soon travel to the region to do operational planning in response to the U.S. strikes. General McKenzie had his forces at the highest protection posture, and we stayed in constant contact with State, CIA, and our allies.

We held an update call for the DoD leadership team and General McKenzie on Monday, December 30. CENTCOM gave us their latest battle damage assessment, which was now calculating twenty-five killed, up to fifty wounded, and eighteen to twenty structures destroyed. We also discussed potential next steps in the event of a response from Iran or the militia groups, and different ways by which we might multilateralize our operations, with Policy taking the lead on this.

One matter we discussed briefly, but which would become a more pressing issue in the days following, was ordering the departure of U.S. military family members and nonessential personnel back to the United States from the Middle East for their own safety. While this made sense in the event that things escalated in Iraq, we also didn't want to provoke an attack by sending Americans home. Tehran could interpret this defensive movement to protect civilians as a first step toward a major U.S. invasion of Iran and decide to take preemptive action. It was a real dilemma, but also an issue we all eventually agreed didn't need to be decided just yet.

Later that day at 3:00 P.M., Milley and I joined an update call with the national security team, with Vice President Pence presiding over the session. Though it happened only rarely, the vice president brought a much different tone to the meetings he chaired. They were usually straightforward, focused, and predictable. Pence listened well and asked good questions, and he was always quick with a "thanks" or "great job." He was part cheerleader and part sounding board, though I could never tell how much influence he really had with Trump. He often didn't say much in meetings that the president attended, and he rarely disagreed with Trump in front of us.

That said, I'll never forget when, as our special operators crossed into Syrian airspace on the mission to capture or kill the ISIS leader Abu Bakr al-Baghdadi in October 2019, the vice president asked everyone in the Situation Room to pause for a minute to pray. Pence was an evangelical Christian who would call for such moments on the eve of an important meeting or event.

The president had not yet arrived, but as the large, silent screens flashed various black-and-white images from the Predator Unmanned Aerial Vehicle feeds, the vice president asked everyone to "please take a minute and join me in a short prayer for our troops." We all bowed our heads, clasped our hands in front of us, and listened as he asked God "to watch over our special operators and protect them." It was a memorable moment and said a great deal about Pence as a man of deep conviction and the care he had for our military personnel. I appreciated his thoughtfulness and respected his faith.

We briefed everyone on the latest intelligence and our military options. Meanwhile, the lawyers were working through the legal basis for these plans. Pompeo shared the details of his conversations with regional leaders—all of whom were supportive of the U.S. action the day before—and State's efforts to get a positive statement out of Britain, France, and Germany. I also raised the issue regarding an "ordered departure" of civilians if tensions escalated.

On Tuesday, December 31, following a funeral held for the KH militants killed by the U.S. air strikes, several hundred protesters swarmed our embassy in Baghdad. Chanting "Death to America" and other threatening slogans, they breached the compound, damaged guard posts, vandalized rooms, and lit fires. It was unclear whether they were trying to seize the embassy, but armed U.S. Marines stood guard, keeping a careful eye on the protesters from their fortified rooftop perches.[7]

The first reports of the embassy protest I saw came in shortly after 5:00 A.M. D.C. time on Tuesday, which was early afternoon in Baghdad. Pompeo called me not long after that to discuss security at the compound. Baghdad was our largest diplomatic mission in the world, with thousands of staff assigned. It was also well protected. We were doubly fortunate that many embassy personnel were not at work due to the holiday break. However, we still wanted to make sure the embassy was safe.

Not surprisingly, many of the protesters were members of the Shia militia groups from Iraq's Popular Mobilization Front (PMF). Under Iraqi law, the PMF was an independent military force numbering in the tens of thousands that answered directly to the prime minister. In reality, the militia groups were receiving their instructions and support from Tehran.

The videos of mostly military-age men on the scene gave credence to our internal reports. One of the attackers wrote on the compound wall, "Soleimani is my commander."[8] This not only spoke volumes about the allegiance of the militias but caused heightened concern that they could be armed and prepared to stage a large assault. The fact that the leaders of three of the groups, including KH head and deputy chairman of the Popular Mobilization Committee Abu Mahdi al-Muhandis, joined the crowds added to our consternation.

I remained in constant contact with Pompeo. We weren't going to evacuate the embassy; we needed to show resolve and determination. We also weren't going to allow its seizure. We had to protect our people and our property. My memories of Libya in 2012 and Iran in 1979 reminded me of how important it was to defend them.

Trump was very worried about Embassy Baghdad becoming a repeat of Benghazi—which had become a Republican touchstone against President Obama and Secretary of State Hillary Clinton after militants seized and burned a U.S. compound there in Libya and killed our ambassador. We were all concerned about this. Pompeo and I agreed to put more troops in the Baghdad embassy and to conduct a show of force. The militias needed to understand we weren't backing down.

I spoke to Milley soon afterward and directed CENTCOM to start moving. We quickly deployed approximately one hundred Marines from Kuwait to reinforce our presence at the compound in Baghdad. This would give us a lot of defensive capability. The MV-22 Ospreys the Special Purpose Marine Air-Ground Task Force used to get into Baghdad were tilt-rotor aircraft that could fly like an airplane—with the additional speed and range that a fixed-wing aircraft provides—but take off and land like a helicopter. This gave us the ability to reinforce the embassy quickly and directly. It was an impressive feat of military speed and capability.

We consciously did all of this in a public way so that the Iranians and Iraqi militia groups were aware. Our social media feeds showed video footage of the Marine deployment and landings at the embassy, with heavily armed troops offloading the aircraft and moving into nearby buildings.

To further bolster our defenses and effect the show of force, we put Apache attack helicopters in the skies above the embassy nearly nonstop, with armed drones flying much higher above them. Twitter posts showed footage of the armed Apaches cruising through the dark sky and dropping sun-bright flares over the U.S. diplomatic sector. The aerial display was intimidating, further warning our enemies to keep a distance.

Meanwhile, I remained in contact with the president throughout the day, updating him on the force protection measures we were taking, and the other actions I was considering. He was very concerned about the safety of the embassy, and he was having similar conversations with Pompeo. He feared the militias would seize the embassy. He wanted to "make sure the helicopters are obvious to the Iraqis" on the ground. He kept repeating this. I did my best to reassure him that the embassy was secure. This wasn't Benghazi.

In Washington, D.C., we continued to press our Iraqi counterparts privately and publicly to ensure the security of U.S. personnel in Iraq, and those at the embassy in particular. Trump and Pompeo both called Iraqi prime minister Abdul-Mahdi, who put out a statement urging the protesters to leave.[9]

Trump issued a warning to Tehran via Twitter on Tuesday that "Iran will be held fully responsible for lives lost, or damage incurred, at any of our facilities," adding, "They will pay a very BIG PRICE! This is not a Warning, it is a Threat." He was very agitated by the demonstrations and remained concerned about the embassy. He spoke to reporters later that evening and said the United States didn't want war with Iran. Tehran pushed back, of course, denying any role in the attacks or the protests that followed, calling the U.S. actions crimes, and alleging that America was responsible for all the turmoil in the region.[10]

Not knowing how the situation would unfold in the coming days, I wanted more forces on the ground to support the embassy, help defend bases where U.S. personnel were located, evacuate American citizens if it came to that, and provide us some additional offensive capability if things continued to escalate. I discussed this with General Milley around 9:30 A.M. The nearest large contingent of ground forces was an Amphibious Ready Group-Marine

Expeditionary Unit (ARG-MEU), which totals more than 3,500 service members and is made up of a reinforced Marine infantry battalion and a naval task force that delivers and supports them.

However, the flotilla was in the western Mediterranean; it would take up to ten days to steam close enough to assist. I asked Milley to look at other options, to include deploying the "ready brigade" from the 82nd Airborne Division. They had an eighteen-hour "wheels up" mission for the first elements of their more than 3,000 paratroopers to deploy from Fort Bragg, North Carolina.

The 82nd didn't bring the full punch that an ARG-MEU could, with the latter's combat vehicles and attack aircraft, but the ready brigade could get more troops on the ground quickly. Therefore, in addition to ordering the Marines in the Mediterranean to quickly head east, I directed the 82nd to launch as well. I wasn't waiting for directions from the White House.

On January 1, 2020, the first 750 paratroopers began deploying to Kuwait. In the meantime, we also launched a squadron of special operators to Iraq in the event we needed their extraordinary capabilities. With the forces we had on the ground in Baghdad, not to mention those flowing in, there was little concern among commanders about the militias seizing the embassy.

We also discussed the whereabouts of Soleimani. According to the IC, he was still in Iran but planning to fly to Iraq, Lebanon, and Syria to coordinate and direct a larger series of attacks against U.S. personnel and facilities. Milley and I discussed the security at our embassies in Beirut, Bahrain, and Kuwait City, the latter two because of the number of U.S. troops they were hosting and the problems they had in the past with their own Tehran-sponsored Shia militants. I was concerned about them, so I called Pompeo to discuss this matter with him.

State would later ask for reinforcements for our embassy in

Lebanon given the threat streams they were seeing. Pompeo and I talked about this a couple of times before I deployed a platoon of paratroopers from my old unit in Vicenza, Italy, into Beirut, and held additional soldiers nearby.

A spokesperson for KH reportedly said the Baghdad protests were only a "first step" and called upon the United States to close its embassy and withdraw all its forces from Iraq. If only they knew how much President Trump had wanted to do both. Ironically, their actions were making such a move less likely. For now, the rhetoric coming out of Iran and Iraq, coupled with the intelligence on Soleimani we were receiving, suggested some difficult days ahead. As such, I wanted McKenzie to get all our ships in Bahrain, where the 5th Fleet is headquartered, out to sea. Iranian missiles would find U.S. vessels congregated in port to be easier targets. We had discussed this previously and had a good understanding of where our ships would go—far enough to be safe, but close enough to go on the offense.

I did another quick update call with Pence, Pompeo, O'Brien, and Milley a little after 10:00 A.M. Pompeo informed us that Trump ordered the chargé d'affaires in Baghdad to repel all attacks, and that under no circumstances was the embassy to surrender, reflecting his deep angst over what was happening on the ground. The president's concern about the embassy—and the militants overrunning it as had happened in Benghazi—was consuming him, which in turn made him angrier and angrier about the protests.

I reassured everyone that we had sufficient force to beat back any assault, with the total number of U.S. military personnel at the embassy by the end of the day numbering in the hundreds, and a variety of strike platforms available in the airspace above the compound to provide support.

At 2:00 P.M., we held another update call. For the DoD, the

bottom line was that we were steadily building combat power in Baghdad specifically and Iraq generally. The new reporting about Soleimani planning retaliatory attacks prompted me to send the entire Division Ready Brigade from Fort Bragg. You can never have too much infantry in these situations.

Pompeo reported that things had stabilized in Baghdad. It was nighttime in Iraq by this point, and the local Iraqi forces were finally back in place providing perimeter security around our embassy. None of us had much confidence, however, that these troops would hold the line if the militias returned. Meanwhile, Pompeo was looking to relocate some of his people to our consulate in Erbil, in the northern part of Iraq controlled by the Kurds, where they would be safer. I offered to assist in their movement.

With regard to Soleimani, the most recent reporting had put him in Damascus with plans to travel to Beirut next, and then Baghdad. The intelligence said he was orchestrating multiple attacks against Americans in several locations with "heavy consequences" for the United States. His aim was to get the United States to leave Iraq, much like we had departed Lebanon decades earlier, after the Beirut barracks bombing. However, from our perspective, the consequences his plans might actually provoke would likely result in the United States attacking Iran, not leaving Iraq. Given the president's inclinations, this could mean a large follow-on response, and a good chance that war between the United States and Iran would commence.

We held another internal DoD update on Wednesday, January 1. The situation remained stable at Embassy Baghdad overnight, and by now we had well reinforced the compound. Units from the states continued to flow into theater, naval forces moved into more protected positions in the Persian Gulf, Gulf of Oman, and the Arabian Sea, and we now had heavy Army forces—tanks and fighting vehicles—loading up in Kuwait to move north toward the Iraqi capital.

On the other hand, the Iraqis were not supporting in-country movement by coalition forces. They were ████████████████████ ██ ██. Overall, McKenzie said he was in good shape for the next twenty-four to thirty-six hours, and our partners in the region were lashed up well with his command at the military level.

I began Thursday, January 2, with an early update call to the president. Milley joined me as we ran through the latest intelligence, the security we had at the embassy, our broader force protection measures, and the additional forces we had moving into Iraq to bolster our defenses and capabilities. Trump was in a good place, but still anxious about the embassy, and the threats we were all hearing coming out of the region. He wanted an update on our retaliatory options, with a focus on Soleimani.

Later in the morning, General Milley and I met with the media to update them. One of the issues raised was whether I expected KH to take more actions that were provocative. Of course, by this time we knew that Soleimani was orchestrating an attack against Americans, and we were preparing our own actions to go after him. As such, I responded by recounting the increasing number of attacks against the United States and our coalition partners in the previous months, and said, "So do I think they may do something? Yes. And they will likely regret it." I added later in the media gaggle "if we get word of attacks or some type of indication, we will take preemptive action, as well to—to protect American forces, to protect American lives. So the—the game has changed and we're prepared to do what is necessary to defend our personnel, and our interests and our partners in the region" to include those sponsoring and directing them in Iran.[11] This was my last warning to Soleimani and Tehran.

At 1:00 P.M., we held a conference call with the president, Pence, Pompeo, Haspel, O'Brien, Milley, and maybe Mulvaney. Some White House staff were on the call as well. Milley and I updated everyone on our force posture, which was in very good shape and growing. The conversation quickly pivoted to Soleimani and his plans.

According to the latest intelligence, Soleimani was indeed in Damascus (having gone to Beirut first, contrary to earlier reports) and expected to depart for Baghdad in a few hours. He was reportedly pushing hard for attacks against the U.S. embassy and other sites in and outside of Iraq where Americans were located. Soleimani would likely need to get the final okay from the Ayatollah Khamenei before launching the campaign, the intelligence official briefed. They had every reason to believe Khamenei would approve the plan since Soleimani was recommending it. Moreover, the plan was likely only days away from initiation, based on the IC's best estimates. Regardless, the IC—in fact, all of us—had little confidence that Tehran could restrain the militia groups for much longer than that anyway.

A lot of questions, answers, and comments went back and forth on the line. Most folks were generally in the same places they were the week prior. O'Brien was pushing hard for a full panoply of strikes. Pence and Pompeo were in the same camp, also advocating for a very tough response, but neither was strident about the matter and both were open to less dramatic action. Milley and I were supportive but somewhat reluctant, concerned about how this would play out two or three steps beyond the next one. If we killed

Soleimani, the United States could well end up in a major Middle East war.

The Iranians were a proud people with a track record of responding proportionately in some way, shape, or form to any assault on their country or their citizens. The maximum pressure campaign that was devastating their nation, coupled with the importance of maintaining their credibility with their proxies throughout the Middle East, would likely put additional pressure on the regime to retaliate. The question was: What would their response be if we killed a senior Iranian officer?

In our view, Soleimani was a military officer on an active battlefield he created, coordinating the next round of attacks designed to kill more of his enemy . . . Americans. It was an occupational risk he was taking if he exposed himself, which he had done with increasing boldness in recent years. He was very capable, and indeed unique in many ways, but he was also the head of a foreign terrorist organization. He arrived at this moment in time with the blood of thousands of U.S. service members on his hands. At what point was the U.S. government going to say enough when it came to killing and maiming Americans? What were the moral and ethical considerations of doing nothing, versus doing something? These were just a few of the key questions we had to answer.

Few things are certain in life, and when it comes to matters of war such as we were discussing that Thursday afternoon, the grays became grayer, the risks seem riskier, and the uncertainties become more uncertain. It was good that we were kicking these issues around, and doing so as a team. However, we also needed to find an anchor upon which to make a final decision. In my mind, it often came down to core values, basic principles, established policy, and the goal you want to achieve.

In this case, at this point, the foundation began with the assessment of the IC—those who knew Iran and the Iranians best—followed by our best collective judgment. For me, this had to be consistent with the factors I mentioned, and my Nine Considerations, when it came to making a final recommendation to the president regarding the use of military force. Of the Nine Considerations that I carried around with me, the ones that jumped out immediately centered on the threat to the United States and its imminence; the appropriateness and proportionality of our proposed action; and the likely risks, costs, and consequences of conducting the operation (and not doing so).

The president asked CIA director Gina Haspel her bottom line. Gina was a solid professional with extraordinary judgment and experience. She was also tough but never in a rush to go into a fight unnecessarily. It was one reason the ties between her, Milley, and me were so tight. Her answer couldn't have been clearer or more concise, and she said it with studied confidence and authority: "The risk of doing nothing is greater than the risk of doing something."

That was it for me. General Frank McKenzie had come to the same conclusion earlier. We didn't want to go to war; a majority in that room did not. Nevertheless, Haspel's assessment affirmed my sense that a preemptive strike to prevent an imminent attack on Americans was the right thing to do. If presented with the same situation, but with some no-name Iranian general planning attacks instead, there would have been far less hesitation. Soleimani's stature clearly made a difference, but not so much that we could allow American diplomats and service members to be consciously left in harm's way. This was a core principle that we had to follow—the duty to protect our fellow citizens.

Given the scale and scope of attacks the IC assessed Soleimani was planning, the number of Americans that could be killed and injured would be significant. Allowing that to happen would be immoral. If some of our people were murdered, and we could have prevented it, how could I go to Dover Air Force Base weeks later to greet the flag-draped coffins that arrived home solemnly in the backs of the large Air Force jets, and then sit with the grieving spouses, children, and parents knowing that I could have saved their loved ones?

President Trump quietly soaked it all in, and then listened to anyone who wanted to make a comment. He was unusually focused. The air on the line was tense. It was as if we were collectively holding our breath while waiting for the president's decision. With the uniform support of his national security team, the commander in chief directed the strike on Soleimani for that evening in Baghdad, simply stating, "Okay, it's approved. Let's do it."

Before wrapping up the call, we discussed a few other things. Vice President Pence asked about notifying the Department of Justice and the FBI. Hezbollah apparently had personnel in the United States, and we wanted to make sure law enforcement kept an eye on them in case Tehran ordered their activation. I noted that State and Defense would be considering an ordered departure from countries such as Bahrain, which hosted large numbers of Americans. Pompeo and I would also be making calls to our allies and partners after the strike to inform them and seek their support. Finally, I asked O'Brien for a written White House legal opinion confirming we had the authority to strike Soleimani in Iraq and raised the issue of informing Hill leaders.

CHAPTER 6

AMERICA STRIKES

The Airbus jet flew quietly through the night sky of the Middle East, far above the troubled land below it. Many on board were probably napping, some were likely working, but only a few knew of the special person traveling with them that evening, and the plans he carried with him. His arrival and all that soon followed would mark another chapter in a difficult history.

Soleimani was less than a couple of hours from arriving at Baghdad International Airport. We had hoped to target him in either Damascus or Beirut, but it was difficult to get a good fix on him in either place. Baghdad was different. He seemed to be very comfortable moving around the city, with a sense of unconcerned habit and predictability that we heard troubled his own people. The Israelis had been watching him for a long time, all around the region, and few things had become more routine than his arrival at the Baghdad airport. The landing of the commercial jet, the plane-side pickup by his local militia hosts, the long drive around the airport access road to the exit, plus the fact that few civilians were often in the area, presented an exceptional opportunity.

Still, I was a little uncomfortable with conducting a military operation at the airport. I was concerned that doing so would result in our immediate eviction from Iraq by the government, an action that would affect our longer-term ability to prevent Tehran from fully dominating the country. It would also disrupt our ability to impede Iran's bad behavior in the region, especially the steady flow of arms and missiles west, across northern Iraq, into Syria, Lebanon, and beyond.

Soleimani's plane landed around 12:30 A.M. Baghdad time, on January 3, and taxied into position as it normally did. Soon enough, the Airbus jet came to halt in a lit, open area short of the terminal. As the mobile stairs rolled up to the plane's door near the cockpit, a string of dark-colored cars pulled up in a line perpendicular to the staircase, not far from its base. A few minutes later, the door of the jetliner opened, and a worker seemed to scramble around to ensure it was properly in place. A flight attendant appeared to move around on the inside, just within the door, barely visible from the outside. After what seemed to be a few minutes, Soleimani emerged, offered a friendly gesture to someone, and slowly walked down the metal steps. A few people at the bottom of the stairs greeted him. They shook hands. Their deference to Soleimani was obvious, nonetheless, even at night on the mostly empty black tarmac. This helped us identify both him and the sedan into which he would soon get.

We had real-time overhead surveillance of everything that was happening from deep in the bowels of the Pentagon. It was a small, dimly lit room filled with computer terminals along the walls and video screens in the front. We had to go through a couple of different access points to get to it. There couldn't have been more than a dozen folks there, with mostly military personnel at their workstations. I had invited Mike Pompeo to join us at the Pentagon. Together, Pompeo, Milley, and I watched the operation unfold on a big screen, through the lenses of drones flying high above the airport. Others were at the White House. President Trump was still in Florida.

It took only a few minutes for everyone on the ground in Baghdad to get into their cars and begin the long trek around the airport to the city not far beyond. It was a clear evening, and since it was now ten or so minutes shy of 1:00 A.M. in Iraq, these were the only automobiles on the long stretch of road. We watched quietly as they followed the same route they had many times before. We knew the car that Soleimani was in but were unsure who was with him. A couple of folks guessed quietly at who joined him in the backseat of the sedan, throwing around names of various militia group leaders.

We were confident that it was a senior person from one of the Shia groups, but we didn't know which one, or if some Iraqi government official was with them. The two were becoming indistinguishable, as Iran seemed to slowly consume Iraq over time.

As the cars moved into a long stretch of road designated as the strike area, I was surprised at the speed at which they were now traveling. The streetlights that illuminated the road seemed to flash across the screen with increasing speed. Would this complicate our targeting? Would the missiles hit with the needed precision? Would the cars exit the airport before we had time to strike?

When the small convoy proceeded past the halfway mark in the target area, I started to wonder if there was a complication on the operational end. Did we lose the track? Was there a malfunction? We knew soon enough. A few seconds later, a laconic voice came on the line to announce the release of the missiles. Now, the wait. I could imagine the missiles dropping from the hard points on the drone wings, and streaking downward toward the unwitting target far below, moving through the night sky with incredible speed and force. Meanwhile, the drone's cameras remained fixed and unblinking on the sedan that sped quickly down the empty road.

The time from launch to hit seemed interminably long, and given the speed of the cars, one might have thought they would be well beyond the airport by the time the strike occurred. Soon enough, though, without any last-second visual cue of the missiles closing in on their target, a large explosion mushroomed in the middle of the screen, rapidly expanding in various shades of black, gray, and white, and moving down the highway all the while. It was surreal.

There was dead silence in the room as we all stared at the screen, unsure of what to expect. Seconds went by. The video screen remained obscured by the explosions' effects. More time passed as we watched the black-and-white picture slowly clear, with the long, lonely, curved highway running through the middle of it, and a large inkblot in the center emanating smoke and flames. We soon heard a dry, emotionless voice on the other end announce, "Targets destroyed."

We all exhaled at once, it seemed, as the tension broke. The one thing that passed through my mind at that moment was the word "justice." Otherwise, I kept scanning the cloudy screen; scrutinizing it to make sure a vehicle hadn't somehow escaped the violence, or a person hadn't crawled away from the impact area. I watched for some time. Nothing.

So ended the exceptional life and career of Qasem Soleimani—a general on the battlefield orchestrating his last campaign, the one that thankfully never came to fruition. His passing was far quicker

and less painful than that suffered by the many U.S. soldiers and
Marines he was responsible for killing over the years. From this
moment going forward, no more Americans would die because of
him, and certainly not in the next few days.

I'm not sure who first informed President Trump of the mission's
success, or whether he watched the strike on a live feed that was
available to him. Pompeo, Milley, and I knew there was much more
ahead of us now. There was no time for celebration. We quietly
congratulated one another and those around us. I personally called
and spoke with the mission commanders, thanking them and their
forces for their professionalism and expertise. And then the secretary of state, the chairman, and I discussed some of the next steps
we had to take as we prepared for Iran's next move.

Pompeo quickly headed back to the State Department. I returned
straight to my office.

The pictures from the site that would emerge later showed a
charred, mangled hunk of metal that was once a car, with burned
pieces of it and another destroyed vehicle strewn a hundred yards
up and down the road in a variety of shapes and sizes. DNA samples
taken from the scene, along with a dismembered left hand bearing
a large red stone set in a silver ring that Soleimani always wore,
confirmed his death. Nobody—nothing—could have survived the
precision and violence of the strike.

We would also learn that the attack killed other members of
the PMF, including Abu Mahdi al-Muhandis, a commander in the
PMF who was also deputy chairman of the Popular Mobilization
Committee that oversees it. In 2003, Muhandis had helped form
KH, the Shia group responsible for the rocket attack that killed the
American contractor days earlier. He had been involved in terrorist
activities for decades. In fact, a court in Kuwait sentenced him to

death thirteen years earlier for his role in a series of bombings there in 1983. The United States had also designated Muhandis as a terrorist. Justice finally caught up with him too.

In the days following the strike, thousands of people filled the streets of Baghdad to protest the attack and the American presence in Iraq, demanding the eviction of the U.S. military from the country. While the crowd represented a broader swath of Iraqis living in the city than before, a large number were still pro-Iranian fighters and most were Shias.

On Friday, January 3, the American embassy in Iraq urged all U.S. citizens to leave the country. That same day, President Trump publicly said that he directed the strike because Soleimani was organizing "imminent and sinister attacks" on Americans, and that "we took action last night to stop a war. We did not take action to start a war." One of the takeaways from the intelligence briefings and conversations we had had was that if Soleimani's plans were successful, the size and scope of them likely would have plunged us into war with Iran.

In Tehran, the government declared three days of mourning, with thousands flooding the streets in cities across Iran to grieve Soleimani's death. The supreme leader, Ayatollah Khamenei, paid a personal visit to Soleimani's family and promised a "forceful revenge."[1] Meanwhile from Florida, Trump responded by vowing to strike "fifty-two Iranian sites" if an American citizen or U.S. interests were attacked. The number 52 referred to the number of Americans held by Iran in the 1979 hostage seizure. It was an idea put in his head by Robert O'Brien, and one that clearly had no operational logic behind it. Might we really be asked to find fifty-two separate sites to attack?

These types of statements and ideas troubled me, and others. To think that we would find more than four dozen targets simply because it was a clever rhetorical link to history plugged into a presidential statement was irresponsible. Moreover, announcing it without any consultation with military and civilian leaders responsible for effecting such a mission was disconcerting. If things went badly in the days and weeks ahead, the president was now out on a limb promising to strike fifty-two Iranian targets. If that occurred, there was little doubt that we would be at war with Iran. No country is going to absorb strikes against more than four dozen targets and simply take it. Worse yet, to make this happen—to deliver on the number 52—we would have to put military personnel in harm's way unnecessarily. We needed much more thoughtful deliberation and coordination on these things, and less shooting from the hip.

On Saturday night, January 4, after the IC had picked up indications that the Iranian military, especially its ballistic missile units, were going to a higher alert status—which we expected—Trump warned Iran of more U.S. strikes. He said via Twitter that some of the targets the U.S. military could attack were "at a very high level & important to Iran & the Iranian culture, and those targets, and Iran itself, WILL BE HIT VERY FAST AND VERY HARD."

That same day, I did a check-in call with Eric Chewning, my chief of staff, Chairman Milley, and General McKenzie. The CENTCOM commander reported that all his forces were at an increased level of readiness. He was concerned principally about three potential Iranian responses: a ballistic missile attack, massive rocket attacks by the militia groups, and the targeting of one of our senior leaders in theater. He said the Iraqi military was still working with us, which was a good thing, and that he wasn't expecting Tehran to do anything until after the Iraqi parliament met and voted on whether to demand the U.S. military leave the country.

Most of McKenzie's additional forces from the United States had arrived by then, and he had reinforced some of the embassies in the region. We reviewed our response options once again. Finally, McKenzie reported that he had spoken with nearly a dozen other countries who were with us in the Gulf, and all fully supported our position. Most, though, wouldn't say much publicly. Nobody wanted to get on Iran's wrong side.

Given the escalatory talk on both sides, the White House decided to send Pompeo, the nation's top diplomat, out on the Sunday news shows to articulate our policy toward Iran, de-escalate tensions, and open room for negotiations. This was not what he conveyed, however. That same Sunday, January 5, on board Air Force One, Trump doubled down on his threats toward Iran by telling reporters "They're allowed to kill our people, they're allowed to torture and maim our people, they're allowed to use roadside bombs and blow up our people, and we're not allowed to touch their cultural sites? It doesn't work that way." The president's vow to strike Iranian cultural sites provoked its own little firestorm, prompting me to disagree with him publicly.

I don't know how or why the president latched on to this idea of striking Iranian cultural and historical sites. He usually crafted his Twitter messages and media statements with just one or two other people, or whoever else was in the room with him at the time. They were never coordinated outside of the Oval Office, it seemed, let alone with the departments. While I suspect Trump intended the Friday and Saturday messages to intimidate the Iranians, I thought they were antagonizing and unnecessary. Privately messaging the Iranians would have been more effective.

When asked about this by CNN the next day, I said that the U.S. military "will follow the laws of armed conflict," which prohibit attacking cultural, historic, and religious sites that have no military value. These were the most basic of things that I learned going all the way back to my law and ethics classes at West Point. The president's comments were frustrating because they were wrong and provocative, and they created unnecessary friction between him and his cabinet. They also moved the conversation off topic, as he so often did to his own detriment.

I wasn't trying to rebuke the president, but I did need to make a clear and unequivocal statement to the U.S. military. They needed to hear from me that we would follow the law, our ethical obligations, and our duty as professionals. It was important for our allies and partners to hear as well. After all, we bore the responsibility of leadership in the free world.

The president quickly reversed course on this issue the next day, but he was not happy about my remarks. I had pushed back on him many times in private—going all the way back to my first weeks on the job when I urged the release of security assistance funding to Ukraine, defended the value of NATO, and opposed arbirtrarily withdrawing troops from Korea, for example. I had also made public statements in the past that he didn't like, but this direct rebuke really raised his hackles, friends close to the White House told me. Only a long time later, in retrospect, would I see January as the next phase in our declining relationship, as he realized I wasn't going to echo or support his every claim and statement.

It wasn't long before domestic politics rushed onto the scene. The House would soon be submitting articles of impeachment to the Senate regarding the president's call with his Ukrainian counterpart. Reactions to the strike on Capitol Hill largely divided along party lines. We briefed the House and Senate separately in classified sessions. The biggest issues became the question of "imminence," or how soon or quickly Soleimani's orchestrated attacks might have begun; the executive branch's lack of pre-consultation with

Congress before conducting a military operation; and the legal authorities under which the president acted to employ military force.

The last issue regarding legality went back to the authorities provided President George W. Bush in 2001 and 2003 as he prosecuted the wars in Afghanistan and Iraq, respectively. Many in Congress came to believe that the legislative branch had given the executive too much authority—a blank check—to conduct military operations around the world. The Trump administration defended these authorities as necessary, as had the Obama and Bush administrations before us. However, pressure had grown in Congress to repeal them, and the strike on Soleimani simply renewed the fight between the two branches of government on this matter.

Often not raised by the Congress, though, is the president's Article II constitutional authority as commander in chief, which was also available to him in this matter. Article II allows the president to act without prior approval from the legislative branch, as Ronald Reagan did in his 1986 air strikes on Libya, George H. W. Bush did in his 1989 invasion of Panama, and Bill Clinton did in his 1998 missile strikes in retaliation against al Qaeda's attack on our embassies, to name a few.

The issue of pre-consultation with Congress by the executive was another matter that went back far, far longer than the 2001 and 2003 authorities to use military force. One of its most notable moments in modern U.S. political history was the passage of the War Powers Act in 1973 over President Nixon's objections. Beginning in the mid-2000s, I taught a graduate course on the relationship between Congress and the executive branch when it came to national security, so I knew there would be no immediate resolution to this issue either.

Pre-consultation with congressional leaders was a fine rule to follow, but it wasn't always practical and you had to be conscious about operational security. I was not concerned with any specific lawmaker, but in the most sensitive matters, we typically restricted information to only those who really had to know. In such cases, I felt notification as soon as possible *after* the fact was important, and did so in the Soleimani strike.

In the first hours after the attack, I called the leaders of Congress to inform them about what had happened. I was able to reach all of them except House Minority Leader Kevin McCarthy, who was with the president and receiving a personal update from Trump. My conversations with Senate GOP Leader Mitch McConnell and Democratic Leader Chuck Schumer were straightforward and businesslike. They appreciated the call and my commitment to brief them in more detail. It was difficult to reach Speaker of the House Nancy Pelosi. She was at some type of event on the West Coast, and kept pushing the call back. I eventually got her on the line later that evening.

I generally had positive conversations with the Speaker in the past, but this turned into a ten- to fifteen-minute political rant. I listened patiently to her, interrupting at times to address a statement she made or to steer the call back on topic. Her focus was on Trump and his lack of character. She saw him as "partisan and corrosive," and viewed the strike on Soleimani as "illegal" and "dangerous." She was very concerned that his recklessness was going to "get us into a war with Iran." I told her that we had a strong case for this action and wanted to brief her as soon as possible.

It seemed as if she was talking to others on the line or in the room as some type of political theater, which caused me to be somewhat reticent. She wrapped up, turning slightly apologetic, saying, "I know you're not like the president, Mr. Secretary. I know you know what's right. We're counting on the Defense Department." I listened. She added, "I know you can't respond, but you need to know how my side and I feel." I thanked her for her candor and asked if there was anything else relevant to the operation that I might answer. In a tired and spent voice she said, "No, thank you." "Thank you for your time, Madame Speaker," I responded. And with that, we ended the call.

A few months before, in October 2019, when the United States launched the raid that killed Abu Bakr al-Baghdadi, the leader of ISIS, the president did not inform congressional leaders beforehand either. Some Democrats complained about the lack of pre-consultation then as well. When asked about this, Senate Majority Leader Mitch McConnell, a Republican, simply said, "I wasn't [briefed], but I was in the similar position when President Obama ordered the attack on Osama bin Laden. I was not called in advance then, nor do I expect to be called in advance now . . . but they attempted to let me know before he went public. So the two situations were handled exactly the same from my point of view."[2]

Regarding imminence, this issue was the one that engendered a number of intense views and heated discussions. There was no clean time mark in law or practice that said this minute, those hours, these days, etc., was the demarcation point between something being imminent or not. It was based on several factors, and at the end of the day, it relied on the judgment of the person who had to decide. The attack Soleimani was orchestrating, I was briefed, could occur in a few short days (two or three?), although one couldn't rule out it taking longer. For me, I kept going back to CIA director Haspel's bottom line: the risk of doing nothing far outweighed the risk of doing something. I was convinced the threat was imminent, and so I felt we had a duty to act.

Our allies affirmed the rightness of the president's decision. Pompeo and I began calling our partners in the region, as well as our NATO allies most involved in the Middle East, following the strike. Each one was supportive of the strike and understood the rationale. Their practical concerns focused on whether we were seeking war with Iran—"No," I told them, "just the opposite." And second, whether we were withdrawing from Iraq—also "No. We plan to continue supporting the Iraqis and ensure the continued defeat of ISIS," I said.

Milley and I spoke with the press on January 6, 2020. The chairman got easily frustrated with the second-guessing and political sniping by members of Congress and outside "experts"—we all were—and so when asked about this matter, he made a very forceful and passionate statement:

"I've seen words like, oh, the intel was razor thin. Very, very few people saw that intelligence. He [Secretary Esper] and I saw that intelligence. And I will be happy, when the appropriate time comes in front of the proper committees and anybody else, through history and every—I'll stand by the intelligence I saw, that—that was compelling, it was imminent, and it was very, very clear in scale, scope. Did it exactly say who, what, when, where? No. But he was planning, coordinating, and synchronizing significant combat operations against U.S. military forces in the region and it was imminent. . . . And I—and I know there's a lot of debate out there about all those words and I understand it but I'm not going to go further than that because of the sources and methods. . . . And I know people saying well you're hiding behind and you lie and all that. That's not true. I know what I saw. And—and I think I said publicly previously, and I will reiterate it that we, those of us who were involved in the decision making of that, we would have been culpably negligent to the American people had we not made the decision we made."[3]

Given Milley's role as the seniormost uniformed leader, his comments may have resonated the most. The question of imminence didn't really fade, though, until the Capitol Hill "Gang of

Eight"—the chairmen and ranking members of the two intelligence committees, plus the House and Senate leaders with whom the executive branch shares the most sensitive information—received access to the special intelligence that had been shared with us days before the strike.* There wasn't unanimity in their view of the information as we saw it after being briefed, based on the reports I received, but a majority of members came to understand our rationale. The issue seemed to fade after that.

Much of what drove the questions about imminence was a lack of trust by Democrats and others that the president was being honest. I was sympathetic to this to an extent. The simple fact was that Trump usually exaggerated and often made statements that could not be confirmed; others were outright fabrications. I became ensnared in one of these rhetorical webs on a Sunday morning talk show.

On Friday, January 10, Trump told Fox News that Soleimani planned to attack several diplomatic posts in the Middle East, remarking, "I can reveal that I believe it probably would've been four embassies."[4] Not long before that, Pompeo had told the media the United States didn't know when or where the attacks might occur, but acknowledged that embassies were threatened. This was consistent with my understanding of the intelligence, the reports I was receiving, and precautionary actions we were taking. Embassy Baghdad was obviously under threat, and State had enough concerns about Embassy Beirut that we reinforced that site as well.

---

* The Gang of Eight at the time were Senate Majority Leader Mitch McConnell, Senate Minority Leader Chuck Schumer, Chairman of the Senate Select Committee on Intelligence Richard Burr, Vice Chairman of the Senate Select Committee on Intelligence Mark Warner, Speaker of the House Nancy Pelosi, House Minority Leader Kevin McCarthy, House Permanent Select Committee on Intelligence Chair Adam Schiff, and House Permanent Select Committee on Intelligence Ranking Member Devin Nunes.

In addition, as I mentioned earlier, the safety of our embassies in Kuwait and Bahrain concerned me.

That said, I didn't recall any specific mention of four sites in my briefings and reports from the CIA. Therefore, when I appeared on CNN on Sunday, January 12, I made two things clear: first, that I hadn't seen any specific evidence with regard to the targeting of *four* embassies; and second, that I still believed there were threats against multiple embassies, noting that we had reinforced other diplomatic posts. Regardless, my unwillingness to affirm Trump's specific claim that the intelligence said Soleimani targeted four embassies plunged me into hot water with the president. A trusted colleague told me that some of Trump's friends called to report on me, complaining that I was "undermining" him and "not loyal," and even suggested he "fire Esper" . . . for being honest.

This wasn't the first time I found myself on the spot like this. Maybe I just wasn't savvy enough to answer my way around the question, but I also didn't want to come across as disingenuous. One other example stands out. On October 16, 2019, the president invited congressional leaders to the White House to discuss Turkey's invasion of Syria and Trump's decision to withdraw U.S. troops from the northern part of the country.

The group met around 3:30 P.M. in the large, ornate Cabinet Room, a 1902 addition to the West Wing for the president to meet with his cabinet, members of Congress, and heads of state. The room overlooks the Rose Garden and is less than thirty feet from the Oval Office. Portraits of several presidents, my favorites being Washington and Lincoln, hung prominently on the walls. At the far end were white marble busts of famous statesmen, such as Benjamin Franklin. These were great reminders of the exceptional men who led our country through truly difficult times.

Unlike most of these events, where pre-meeting chitchat sets the tone, followed by a formal opening and exchange of pleasantries, this one went bad immediately. Over thirty people filled the chairs around the long, oval, mahogany table that was a gift from President Nixon in 1970. Members of Congress sat on one side in the heavy leather seats, with staff behind them. The president and his team sat on the side closer to the windows, along with a few GOP leaders. Given the topic of the meeting, I was seated to the president's immediate left, with General Milley to his right.

Trump kicked off the session with a recalcitrant opening, brusquely suggesting the Democrats go first since they "asked for the meeting." Just prior to the session, the House overwhelmingly approved a resolution condemning the president's decision to pull U.S. troops out of northeastern Syria, so the stage was already set for a contentious meeting. Almost immediately, Trump and the Democratic leaders began barking back and forth at one another regarding Syria. The Democrats charged that Trump was jeopardizing our nation's security and "abandoning our Syrian allies." They suggested the president withdrew from Syria as "a favor" for Russian president Vladimir Putin, who was working to consolidate his position in the Middle East.

Trump pushed back forcefully, quickly returning fire and criticizing the Democrats' "Russia witch hunt." The rest of us sat there like spectators watching boxers in a ring exchange blows. Milley kept his head down; this was a bad situation for a uniformed officer to be in. He seemed to be doing his best to become invisible. I looked up a couple of times at the large, gold-framed painting at the north end of the room, above a white fireplace. It was a picture of our Founding Fathers at a meeting of the Continental Congress. I briefly wondered if they ever had a meeting like this one. Things only got worse.

With impeachment proceedings in the House lurking as the eight-hundred-pound gorilla in the room, the exchange between the president and the Speaker of the House—who was sitting right across from him—became particularly nasty. Insults flew between them, with Trump calling Nancy Pelosi "just a politician," Pelosi responding with "I wish *you* were" one. Ever wanting the last word, the president doubled down with a schoolyard-style taunt, calling the speaker a "third-rate politician." Minority Leader Schumer cut in once, trying to calm things down, but another exchange erupted over who "hate[d] ISIS more." At another point, Schumer dragged former defense secretary Jim Mattis, my predecessor, into the exchange by citing the retired general's concern over a resurgent ISIS. Trump responded by dismissing Mattis's view and calling him, as he so often did, "the world's most overrated general." As words were flying back and forth between Trump, Pelosi, and Schumer, everyone else continued to look on uncomfortably.

House Majority Leader Steny Hoyer was seated to Pelosi's immediate left. He leaned over and, in a level, but disgusted tone, urged her to leave, slightly nudging his chair askew as he did. Pelosi quickly stood, pushed back her chair, and leaned forward slightly in her sharp blue dress. Waving her hands like a symphony conductor, and then pointing directly at Trump, she chastised the president in one final flourish—"With you, Mr. President," she pronounced, "all roads lead to Putin!"

Trump was now red in the face, shouting back, and talking over Pelosi as he leaned onto the table. She pivoted about quickly, and as she stormed out of the Cabinet Room with Hoyer right behind her, Trump tauntingly said, "Goodbye, we'll see you at the polls." This was the most unprofessional and uncomfortable exchange I had ever witnessed. It demonstrated a poisonous and dysfunctional relationship that wasn't good for anybody, especially the nation.

Chuck Schumer, the Senate Minority Leader, picked up the questioning as the Cabinet Room door closed. With Pelosi's chair to his left now empty, Schumer leaned over the table, arms folded in front of him, peering over his glasses, and asked the president question after question about Turkey's actions in Syria and our response. Trump responded as quickly as Schumer served. Two New Yorkers going head-to-head. Despite the tension remaining high, both men managed to keep the volume down.

Schumer then asked about "the status of thousands of ISIS prisoners held by the SDF [Syrian Democratic Forces], and how many had escaped." Trump claimed that "few had been freed," and "most of those had been recaptured," which wasn't accurate based on what I had read the previous day. Schumer pushed back, asking how he knew that. As a member of the Gang of Eight, he had access to this level of information, so he probably knew the president wasn't correct. Trump paused for a moment, maybe realizing the same thing, and said something like "I had special intelligence; that's how I know."

For some reason, Schumer turned immediately to me—I was sitting next to the president—looked me in the eyes from across the table, and asked, "Secretary Esper, did you see that intelligence?" The minority leader and I had known each other for some time, so maybe he knew I wasn't going to go along with Trump's story. Regardless, he caught me like a deer in the headlights.

I too paused, thinking about the question, trying to recall my latest intelligence update, and said as matter-of-factly, honestly, and succinctly as possible, trying to navigate this minefield, "I haven't seen that intelligence, but I don't always keep up with it the way I should," or something like that. I was sure my response made the president mad. It had to. I didn't support his story. Yet he never turned toward me or said anything. He just sat there, stone cold, focused on Schumer. I simply had never seen nor heard the intelligence to which Trump was referring.

...

Long after midnight in Baghdad on January 8, 2020, Iran launched sixteen ballistic missiles at two Iraqi bases in retaliation for Soleimani's killing. Eleven hit the Al Asad air base, one struck a base in Erbil but didn't detonate, and four never reached their targets. The first missiles, which were fired from three launch sites in Iran, landed at 1:34 A.M. Iraqi time at Al Asad—5:34 P.M. Washington time. From first launch until the last explosion, at least one more volley would follow over an eighty-minute period.[5] I was meeting with my senior leaders—both military and civilian—in my inner conference room when the missile-defense-warning call activated over the secure phone in my office. One of my assistants rushed down the hallway and interrupted the meeting to get me.

Colorado is the home base for America's missile warning system. In the days following the strike on Soleimani, the threat warning crews at Buckley Air Force Base and Cheyenne Mountain were on high alert. The Space Force's 2nd Space Warning Squadron at Buckley—which operated the six-satellite space-based infrared system that night—would provide the critical early warning for our service members in Iraq to seek cover. The squadron had developed a collection plan to ensure optimal coverage, and once the infrared flares of the Iranian missiles appeared on their screens, they could determine the threat class of the missile. This was critical information when trying to assess the missile's range and payload capability. The automated missile warning system to which they provided the critical information had been in place for years. The squadron constantly rehearsed the system. Now it was sending real warning information through my secure phone.[6]

The squadron quickly counted the number of missiles launched, determined the weapon type, and then estimated their likely impact points. Ballistic missiles are predictable as they follow their programmed trajectory, and these warnings gave our folks on the ground critical time to move into shelters, button up, and take other measures to protect themselves. McKenzie had prudently taken several actions over the preceding days. And in the final hours before the launch, according to a *60 Minutes* news story produced more than a year following the attack, after the Iranians took their last download of commercial overhead imagery of Al Asad for targeting purposes, CENTCOM finished moving dozens of aircraft and hundreds of people off the base to protect them.[7] It was a brilliant move.

With no threat history of Iranian missile launches targeting Iraqi facilities or Americans in-country, Central Command heretofore had not seen the need for anti-ballistic missile systems in Iraq. Indeed, the last time a country attacked American forces with ballistic missiles like this was the 1991 Gulf War.

There were still operations and people at Al Asad that we needed to protect, however, concerned that a ground assault by Iranian-backed militias might immediately follow the missile strikes. With the first launches announced, I shook my head, frowned, and said to myself, "Okay, here we go. . . ." I was very concerned about what might happen in the next ten to fifteen minutes, especially about the fate of our people on the ground, but powerless to do anything to alter the immediate course of events. It would all come down to our brave soldiers and airmen in the impact zone at the air base.

At that moment, I remembered my time during the Gulf War. In the third week of January 1991, the 101st Airborne was repositioning itself farther north and west in Saudi Arabia. We moved under the cover of the ongoing air campaign into what's called an attack position. From there, our role in Operation Desert Storm was to helicopter deep into southern Iraq and cut off the main highway that the Iraqis would likely be using to either reinforce their troops in Kuwait or get them out as U.S. forces approached from the south. Either way, our mission was to block the highway and prevent any movement. This "Hail Mary" play, as some called it, would become one of the deepest air assaults in military history at the time, and the farthest behind enemy lines, and its aim was to close the Iraqis' back door.

While waiting one evening on the airfield to load the C-130 transporters that would fly us to our positions, the air raid sirens went off. We knew this meant a missile launch from Iraq. Since we were most concerned about chemical weapons, we quickly put on our protective masks, checked to ensure they were airtight, and then watched as one, then two, bright lights moved quickly across the night sky to our south. We had nowhere to run or seek cover, so we hunkered down next to our rucksacks and weapons. Soon enough, Patriot missile systems launched in response, and we stared at them anxiously as the interceptors raced toward their targets, arcing upward to destroy Saddam's incoming Scuds. The Patriots destroyed the first missile, then the second one, in bright flashes and delayed booms. This lethal fireworks show would be our big excitement for the night, and a memory I'll never forget.

However, at this moment twenty-nine years later, I could only imagine the fear of our soldiers and airmen at their posts on the lonely Iraqi air base, bracing for what we first believed was a twenty-seven-missile salvo, each with a one-thousand-pound warhead, screaming in on top of them. I quietly asked God to watch over them.

It wasn't until 6:40 P.M. or so D.C. time when the last Iranian missiles hit. Of course, we didn't know then if the campaign was over, only that for now, the last salvo launched from Iran had finally impacted. We were already on the phones with CENTCOM trying to get a casualty and damage assessment but understood it would take time. I knew the outcome of this report would determine whether we were at war with Iran or not.

General Milley and I went to the White House around 7:30 P.M. It was now dark as we rode over to join Vice President Pence, Secretary of State Pompeo, National Security Adviser O'Brien, and a handful of senior staff. We pulled into the driveway, right next to the awning that extends over and protects the West Wing entrance, got out of the car, and quickly entered the building. It was much quieter and less busy than I expected, with few staff bustling around inside or hustling back and forth as they usually do between the White House and the Old Executive Office Building, which was no more than a couple of hundred feet across the narrow drive where the cars parked.

Milley and I entered the room and sat in our usual places to the immediate left of the president's high-backed leather chair at the front of the Situation Room. Pence and Pompeo sat in chairs opposite us, with O'Brien down near the middle. We all stood briefly as Trump entered, and then sat back down as he did. The president was in a good mood, though he was more reticent than usual. Everyone carried a serious look on their face; many had the slight, darkened eye bags that marked the fatigue of a long week. There wasn't much small talk this evening. We were at a significant decision point and a major moment in history.

The president leaned forward in his chair, with his arms folded in front of him, resting comfortably on the table, and said "Good evening, everyone. It's been a long day. So what do we know?" I can't recall whether the CIA provided an intelligence update first, but I summarized that "we know Iran launched sixteen ballistic missiles at two Iraqi bases. Eleven hit the Al Asad air base, where our people are located. The remaining five were aimed elsewhere

and were duds." General Milley chirped in after me, offering details on the types of missiles we believe they fired, the size of the
warheads, and his sense of the amount of damage they can cause.
Milley had a good sense of humor and was known for his occasional wisecracks and sarcasm, even with the president, but tonight
he was dead serious as he explained the damage a one-thousand-
pound warhead could deliver. Everyone listened closely, quietly.

I added, "We don't yet know if the Iranians are done. They
could fire more missiles, so everyone remains hunkered down at
their bases." Chairman Milley and I told the room, "We have nothing confirmed either way" when it came to the number of American
casualties and that "it will take the better part of the evening to
get a solid assessment." Trump listened carefully, taking it all in,
constantly scanning the room as he so often did. There was little
bravado.

O'Brien suggested we implement one of our response options
against Iran now. Milley and I pushed back, arguing as we so often
did that "we own the shot clock." Let's act smartly, not quickly.
"We need to first understand what happened, and second, what
they intended," I said. Pompeo agreed. Moreover, Mike anticipated
that Tehran might reach out to us through Switzerland's embassy
in Tehran, a trustworthy conduit used by the United States to com-
municate with Iran since the 1979 revolution. Tehran didn't want
to go to war with us, but they also had to respond—what would
that be, and what would be their real message, if any?

Understanding both the intent of the Iranian attack and the
damage inflicted "would help us determine the best course of action in response," I said. We needed to assess, first, did they aim to
kill or aim to warn? The Iranians had done the latter in the past
by intentionally shooting missiles far off target, claiming victory in
their media, and then standing down.

Milley and I kept pressing everyone for patience until we got a solid report on our killed or wounded. It was still dark in Iraq; the troops remained dispersed around the base and hunkered down. It would also take the benefit of daylight to get a good assessment. Everyone seemed okay with that, though we were all still anxious to learn what happened. We agreed to reconvene back in the Situation Room at 7:30 the next morning.

After our meeting that evening, Trump tweeted, "All is well!" and said that damage assessments were ongoing, adding that he would make a statement on the attack the following morning.[8] I thought it was important for the president to make a statement that evening, but giving the American people such a positive first report was not appropriate. We didn't know nearly enough about what was happening on the ground in Iraq, and the president knew that too. Given the size and nature of the attack, as General Milley explained, we could have had dozens of Americans killed or wounded. Trump walked himself out on a limb, but he would never be the one to take the fall.

Milley worked the phones all night with McKenzie. Meanwhile, I stayed in touch with him and the White House. Before midnight on January 7 in Washington, the initial report was "no casualties." That seemed hard to believe, and the old military adage that "first reports are always wrong" bounced around in Milley's and my heads. We both agreed that CENTCOM needed to check again.

The second response came sometime after midnight—again, no killed or wounded. Milley and I spoke one more time, and ordered one final check; this time I was really specific. I wanted everything counted. We had reported "no casualties" on the al-Baghdadi raid and then learned that one or two of our special operators incurred minor injuries—not from enemy action, though. This had been enough to create a stir with some in the media. This report had to be

100 percent accurate. Milley completely agreed and was all over it. The sun was up in Iraq, so that would be our best and final count. I went back to sleep for a couple of hours.

When I woke up in the morning, we were still at "zero casualties reported." Incredible. Milley felt that this was a solid number. McKenzie had worked it all night. This would be the number I reported to the president at the 7:30 A.M. meeting.

At the White House meeting, everybody was pleased to hear the news when I told Trump "no casualties." You could see faces relax and smiles emerge. A couple of thumbs-ups cropped up too around the room. It was a good moment, though an unexpected one. The president congratulated me and General Milley, saying, "Great job, great job." Milley was quick to point out that it was really the CENTCOM team all the way down to the soldiers and airmen on the ground being very prudent and aggressive in their active defense, force protection measures, and taking care of one another. Trump asked to pass along his thanks to "General McKenzie and his team."

Milley reported that the Iranian missiles "caused damage at the base to tentage, a building, a helicopter" and so on. In his view, "these were not warning shots. They wanted to kill Americans." I agreed with that assessment. While I was not surprised on one hand, I was on the other. Did Iran really want to risk all-out war with the United States over the killing of Soleimani, a man who had his fair share of enemies and detractors in Tehran?

The government in Tehran falsely reported that the Islamic Republican Guard Corps (IRGC) launched tens of missiles. Iranian news reports said the missile strikes killed eighty Americans. They were obviously playing to their domestic audience. Indeed, Ayatollah Khamenei would later boast that "Iran has the power to give such a slap to a world power shows the hand of God."[9]

In the Situation Room that morning, though, the question was: Do we respond to the ballistic missile attacks or stand down? At this point, our reporting said the Iranian missile strike caused no American casualties; our air strike on December 29, conversely, had killed twenty-five militiamen and wounded over twice that number, and Soleimani was off the battlefield for good.

On the diplomatic front, the State Department was exchanging messages with the Iranian government through our Swiss intermediaries. We had urged Tehran not to escalate after our strike at the Baghdad airport. Iran responded nonetheless. They were now conveying that the evening's ballistic missile salvos were their last action, even without determining the impact of their strike. There would be no further attacks from them; they wanted things to end.

At this point, with the "score" in our favor and our resolve demonstrated, we didn't see a compelling need to strike back. Nobody wanted another war in the Middle East, especially Trump. Therefore, the president decided that we were done too; everyone supported this. Gina Haspel's assessment turned out to be accurate— Iran didn't want a war either. Importantly, no Americans would be killed in the orchestrated attack that Soleimani was prevented from launching. Moreover, we would soon observe Tehran exercising far greater effort to reign in the Shia militia groups in Iraq.

Later that morning, the president appeared before the media, flanked by Pence, Pompeo, the Joint Chiefs of Staff, O'Brien, and me, to update the American people. In his remarks, he noted that Iran was standing down; however, he took a hard line on their nuclear aspirations, recounting the events of the past couple of weeks, criticizing the Iran nuclear deal, and addressing a number of related issues. At the end, he spoke directly to the leadership in Tehran and the Iranian people, extending an olive branch as he suggested

both countries embrace peace and a new way forward. His remarks
sought to close this latest chapter in U.S.-Iranian relations.

About a week later, we started getting reports out of CENTCOM
that U.S. service members at Al Asad the night of the attack had
been medically evacuated to a military hospital in Germany. This
surprised us. The base was supposedly screening everyone for trau-
matic brain injury (TBI), but symptoms could take days to appear,
and the review process itself took a while. The military rightly took
a conservative approach to these issues.

We had learned a great deal about TBI, given the many terrible
years of experience gained in Iraq treating service members injured
by roadside bombs and other explosions. Apparently, the troops
sent to Germany from Iraq were experiencing daily headaches and
other symptoms associated with a concussion, and our military
facilities in Europe were better equipped to accurately diagnose and
treat them.

By late February, the official count of injured troops numbered
110, though "mild" TBI was the diagnosis for a majority of these
cases, and the service members returned to duty. Nonetheless, the
command eventually awarded the Purple Heart to nearly 30 military personnel given the extent of their injuries. The troubling part
of this episode was the accusations coming from administration
critics, and suggestions from the media, that Trump was lying
about the number wounded when he announced "no casualties" to
the press on January 8. That was not true. The president was accurately conveying the report I personally delivered to him, the same
one the chain of command relayed to me a few times the evening
before.

We also weren't aware of the first TBI cases evacuating to Germany before they actually happened. No one at the Pentagon was trying to downplay the injuries or underreport them. We simply didn't know what was unfolding on the ground until a week or so later. I wanted to understand as much as everyone else did why the injuries weren't reported to the Pentagon sooner. This was a matter we would dig into and fix over the succeeding months.

I was disappointed and troubled by the president's careless comment later in January, though, when he downplayed the casualty reports as "headaches" that were "not very serious."[10] A majority did eventually fall into this category, but not all. It wasn't clear if this was part of his braggadocio—that he hit Iran hard and they didn't lay a glove on us in return. If so, the truth interrupted that narrative. I needed to go to the White House, explain to the president the nature of these injuries, and ask him to change his tone. So after a meeting in the Oval Office, I cornered him near the passageway that led to his private room in the back.

I told the president that his "comments aren't playing well with the force" and that "it sounds like you don't care." He pushed back with "That's not true." I told him I understood—after all, I had witnessed him in private moments with injured soldiers and their families, and watched him spend time with them, talk with them, and take pictures—"but that's not what's coming across."

Trump got defensive, pivoting, speaking about the injured troops he met with in the past. The service members he spent time with at Walter Reed were some of the most seriously combat wounded—with limbs missing, badly mangled bodies, and horrible burns; they constituted his mental framework when it came to war injuries. I had met many of these brave warriors too and understood where he was coming from.

But the president didn't get it. He said, "What about the soldiers in World War II? They didn't have these brain injuries; they didn't complain about headaches." Without saying it explicitly, he was claiming these were fictional injuries. He couldn't reconcile the past with what we knew today.

I told him TBI "is not new to the battlefield." It's been around as long as large blasts, blunt force trauma, and other head injuries have occurred, I explained. Medical science, battlefield medicine, and a shortened timeline from injury to hospital arrival had given us the ability to save more people from the horrible and relentless improvised explosive device (IED) attacks against our forces in Iraq. "Most of these service members would have died in the past" from the violent blasts, and the trauma and massive losses of blood that ensued, I told him.

Moreover, unlike burns, lacerations, broken bones, and other visible wounds, it could take time for TBI symptoms to manifest themselves fully, and for the doctors to determine the extent of the injuries. New technologies also gave us the means to look inside the brain and learn a lot more about the heretofore hidden damage IEDs caused. "The blasts from the Iranian missiles striking the base at Al Asad were no different," I said. "TBI was an 'invisible' injury that many of us were still learning about, including me," I added. He stood opposite me listening, but not hearing. He shook his head, either disagreeing or unwilling to accept my explanation. Regardless, the president—as commander in chief—should have demonstrated more empathy for our wounded warriors. Empathy wasn't his strong suit, however.

Weeks later, I went to visit the wounded at Walter Reed hospital, as I tried to do every three months or so. I met a young officer there who was being treated for TBI resulting from injuries he received at Al Asad the evening of the ballistic missile attacks. He was one of the more serious cases, but was thankfully doing much better.

We sat down to talk at one of the tables in a large, cafeteria-style dining area. My wife, Leah, joined us. He described in detail how, as he ran toward a bunker after checking on his soldiers, the blast from an exploding missile knocked him "off [his] feet and threw [him] some distance." It took him a while in the dark of the night, amid all the chaos, to regain his senses, he said, but once he did and stood back up, he "made [his] way into the concrete bunker where others were seeking shelter." Another missile exploded outside a short time later, he added, and the shock wave rippled through the shelter, bouncing off the walls, and jostling everyone about. As he recounted, he "had now been hit twice." Medical test results would later reveal the harm done.

I asked why it took so long to report these cases. God bless him, he said, "Sir, I had soldiers to take care of the next day, and every day after that. Sure, I had headaches and didn't feel right, but if I got evacuated, who would take care of my troops." His sense of duty choked me up. He said it took a few days until one of his fellow officers or NCOs, coupled with his worsening symptoms, persuaded him to report to the medical staff. One thing quickly led to another, and sure enough he was soon on a flight to Germany, and eventually back to Walter Reed.

I would like to say this officer's story was unique, but in many ways it wasn't. It showed the leadership, commitment, and sense of duty our service members were exhibiting during a very challeng- ing and dangerous time. You can't fault a leader for putting his or her people and mission first—that's what we teach them to do. He had his priorities right. However, at some point the leader needs to take care of himself or herself, or everyone else and the mission suffer. This was why he finally sought help, and what helps explain the delays in reporting.

...

By the end of January 2020, as things settled down with Iran, we had the opportunity to consider changes to our force posture in the region. This was something we had begun before the recent events as part of our combatant command reviews.

The DoD's footprint in Iraq was above five thousand service members, and we had been planning to go lower, down to at least three thousand by the summer. Doing so gave us the opportunity to consolidate all our forces onto a few larger bases that we could then harden to enhance force protection. Moreover, now that Iran had demonstrated a willingness to shoot ballistic missiles into Iraq, we needed Patriot and other air-defense systems at these bases, especially against unmanned drones.

General McKenzie's dispersal plans had been extremely effective. Without them, he estimated we would have lost between 100 to 150 personnel and 20 to 30 aircraft.[11] He did a great job, but we now had to do more to protect our people as we looked ahead. The Iraqis kept denying us permission to bring the Patriots in, however. Eventually we decided that force protection trumped diplomatic niceties and bureaucratic gamesmanship, so I directed him to unilaterally deploy and emplace them.

We also took some major long-term lessons away from our experience in early January that built upon work that had already begun. One of them was the realization that too many of our bases and too many of our people in all the Gulf Cooperation Council countries—Bahrain, Kuwait, Oman, Qatar, Saudi Arabia, and the United Arab Emirates—as well as in Iraq, were within range of too many Iranian missiles. For several months, I had laid out on my conference table a large map of the Arabian peninsula with the location of each and every U.S. base and facility in the region. From that perspective, the vulnerability of our troops and families was obvious. Therefore, by the summer of 2020 we initiated several plans and discussions on how to reshape better our footprint for the long haul.

The first initiative involved ending the practice of sending most family members with their service members to countries along the Gulf. The risk was too great, and we realized it was difficult to get them out of harm's way in times of crisis. We didn't want to put the families at risk, nor create a liability that limited our freedom of action. This decision was toughest for the Navy, which had the most family members in the region.

This issue was acute at the 5th Fleet headquarters in Bahrain. Despite the clear missile threat, coupled with an enduring terrorism concern on the ground, too many senior leaders at the base were convinced that "the Iranians would never attack us." The Bahrainis were great hosts and very good partners, but we still couldn't afford to ignore the facts. It would take two to three years to draw down our family members' presence there, but it was the responsible thing to do.

Ending accompanied assignments scratched the surface of what we needed to do strategically for the 5th Fleet. When you stepped back, looked at the map, and considered the short distance to Iran, the time it took for a ship to get from Bahrain into the open waters of the Arabian Sea to the south—especially through the constricted and often contested Strait of Hormuz—and the growing Chinese activity in the Indian Ocean, the headquarters and our forces were out of place for the threats, challenges, and missions we faced in the future.

We now seemed trapped in an operational cul-de-sac at the metaphorical end of the street with a bad neighbor next door. The Iranians had developed a vast array of missile capabilities that could overwhelm most defensive systems, leaving U.S. bases vulnerable. We were also subject to the continuous threat of Iranian proxies on the ground in some countries. Locating the headquarters and our forces *inside* the Persian Gulf, or at least near Iran, makes much less sense today, especially given the growing importance of the Indian Ocean.

It was important that we maintain a presence in the Gulf to contain Iran and support our friends in the region. We wanted to remain the security partner of choice (as compared to the Russians or Chinese) for the Gulf Cooperation Council states and Iraq. However, to do this most effectively going forward, we needed the protection, confidence, and flexibility that distance provides to our bases, people, and forces.

Therefore, the second major initiative we started working on was a plan to consolidate and move many of our bases and facilities in the frontline states farther west and south, away from Iran. The airfield at Prince Sultan Air Base in Saudi Arabia was a first step, but even that base was still too close. This would be a multiyear effort developed by CENTCOM, in coordination with our regional partners, and involved changing our basing and operational protocols so fewer forces were exposed on a daily basis. We would also look to harden established sites and develop deception measures to increase force protection. This was a major reason many of us felt the Iran nuclear deal should address Tehran's missile programs.

Third, we also needed to return forces back home, especially headquarters and operational centers that could function equally well from the United States. CENTCOM operated out of Tampa, Florida, and proved the value and effectiveness of this model over the years.

I also didn't see the need to maintain more than sixty thousand American service members in the Middle East; we needed many of them elsewhere. By the fall, we had finalized plans to start reducing our footprint in the region, a long-sought goal of mine that was critical to implementing the National Defense Strategy. Patriot batteries were set to return to the United States from Saudi Arabia in 2021, followed by other Army assets, a Marine task force, Air Force aircraft, and more. We would further reduce our footprint in Iraq below three thousand, to include downgrading the three-star headquarters in-country.

I also determined that a permanent stationing of an aircraft carrier in the Middle East was not necessary given all the other ground-based aircraft we had in the region. The same was true for other naval assets in constant demand by CENTCOM. We would use Dynamic Force Employment operations from our IRF and other Navy assets to surge when necessary. Our plans cut the U.S. force presence in theater nearly in half, from its peak in January 2020, to the low forty thousands by the summer of 2021. The savings would allow us to invest in several of our modernization priorities, while reducing the churn on the services and their people.

Regarding 5th Fleet, I asked CENTCOM to look at locations around the rim of the Indian Ocean, out of the range of (most) Iranian missiles, in order to relocate the headquarters, support infrastructure, and the ships.

General Milley and I also made a run at extricating the United States from the Multinational Force and Observers mission in the Sinai, Egypt, but we ran out of time. We had a few hundred soldiers there helping other countries "supervise the implementation of the security provisions of the Egyptian-Israeli Treaty of Peace" signed in 1979.[12] This mission had outlived its usefulness after four decades, at least for the United States, given the much improved state of relations between Egypt and Israel. My combatant command reviews were revealing missions like this and others, such as the Kosovo Force international peacekeepers in the Balkans, which were important when begun in 1999 but could now be performed without the United States. It seems the only thing harder than getting out of a war is getting your forces out of a peacekeeping mission whose raison d'être has passed. We needed to focus on China and Russia, and at least give our troops a break.

Finally, a major war with Iran would ultimately require the collaboration of all U.S. allies and partners in the region who saw Tehran as a threat. The successful prosecution of a campaign to defend against Iranian attacks, and then go on the offensive with equal success, would require a high degree of command, control, and coordination. As such, we would need much better unity of command and unity of effort—two long-standing principles of war, and something the region certainly didn't have enough of—to ensure a positive outcome should war come. This is why I launched the process of changing the Unified Command Plan (UCP) to move Israel from the European Command (EUCOM) into Central Command, where it belonged.

The UCP, which the DoD updates every two years, sets forth basic guidance to all combatant commanders. The plan "establishes combatant command missions, responsibilities, and force structure; delineates geographic areas of responsibility for geographic combatant commanders; and specifies functional responsibilities for functional combatant commanders."[13] Past objections to moving Israel into CENTCOM centered on the politics of asking Arab military leaders to work with their Israeli counterparts in CENTCOM forums, but the growing and common threat of Iran, coupled with the easing of tensions between some Arab capitals and Tel Aviv over time, and then the rapid advancement of the Abraham Accords, which jump-started the process of normalizing relations between Israel and countries such as the United Arab Emirates, made this operationally prudent move possible.

There was a fleeting, final concern from some in the Pentagon that making the move now was "out of cycle" for UCP modifications, but bureaucratic timelines shouldn't postpone good ideas, especially those involving the conduct of war. And so a UCP change that we first raised in early 2020, coordinated with the State Department over many months, discussed with Israel in the fall, and that I quickly approved soon thereafter, finally became a reality by the end of the administration.[14] It was one of the quicker actions we were able to get done.

Things calmed regarding Iran after January 2020, at least for a while. The country never left our radar screens, however. Occasional rocket attacks from militia groups against our bases or embassy in Iraq, tough talk from the government in Baghdad about reducing the American presence in the country, and infrequent comments by senior Iranian leaders about the United States kept us on our toes. It created an opportunity just the same, to keep reshaping the theater consistent with the NDS and my overarching focus on China, then Russia, as well as my reform agenda that would enable it.

The situation did not calm down in Washington, though. Things only got worse—more unpredictable, more uncoordinated, more outlandish—as processes began breaking down, hard-core loyalists arrived in the West Wing, and the darker, uglier side of some in the White House became more and more obvious.

CHAPTER 7

THE POLITICS OF BUILDING
A BETTER NAVY

The aircraft carrier nearly filled the entire periscope lens. The waterline, wave tops and all, were apparent about halfway up the photo, visible both near and far in the circular view. The object of its fixation was completely unaware it was being stalked.

It was a snapshot straight out of a Hollywood World War II movie, with the submarine's periscope focused on a far-off ship, watching carefully, quietly, from beneath the sea. The difference was that this picture was only a few months old. And the vessel at the other end of the American periscope wasn't a Nazi battleship, it was a Chinese aircraft carrier.

Without a doubt, the U.S. Navy is the most capable maritime force in the world. It has served our nation extremely well for almost 250 years. The purpose of the sea service is to guarantee America's security and safeguard our interests in the maritime domain, which includes ensuring freedom of navigation and commerce. These principles underlie America's security, economy, and the international rules-based order that has proven so successful.

China wants to rewrite these rules to their advantage. Beijing seeks to control critical waterways and expand its claims over fishing areas and undersea oil fields. It wants to exert veto power over the economic and security decisions of other nations in ways that challenge their sovereignty.

To do this, China is modernizing and growing its armed forces. When Beijing talks about fielding a world-class military by 2049, the purpose is to displace the United States as the global superpower and push us out of the Pacific. Beijing has studied how we fight (as has Moscow) and is developing a full range of capabilities designed to counter our strengths and maximize their own. For example, China is investing in long-range missiles, hypersonic weapons, and unmanned submarines as cost-effective counters to American naval power, intending to use these systems to destroy our aircraft carriers at great distances.

China's nefarious behavior would only grow worse should Beijing achieve its modernization goals and build a military better than ours. We cannot let that happen. Hence, while the U.S. military fights as a joint force, retaining overmatch in the Indo-Pacific begins with the Navy.

In the context of our National Defense Strategy, the Pentagon's overarching plan to transform the DoD to deal with the threats of the twenty-first century, the challenges we face in the future are clear enough. We know the capabilities the Chinese are building. Moreover, we have a good sense of their strategy, operational plans, and timeline. Given all the facts, data, and trends, the United States is behind when it comes to building a joint force that can fight and win by the mid-2030s.

Transforming the military to deal with Beijing, however, faces its own unique headwinds—and politics—within the Navy and the DoD, on Capitol Hill, at the White House, and in D.C. and beyond.

The shipbuilding plans of the Navy have been an interest of Congress since the earliest days of the republic. Ostensibly, to understand the Navy's direction better, Congress requires the submission of a thirty-year shipbuilding plan each year with the proposed defense budget. The law assigns the defense secretary this task, but often the Navy submits it on behalf of the DoD, and in some years the Pentagon delivers it late (if ever). Not all defense secretaries reviewed the Navy's plans. I took a different approach.

If the Pentagon is submitting a plan of this importance to Congress—one that charts the structure of the future Navy—then I wanted to be knowledgeable about and confident in its content. After all, I owned it at that point. Moreover, the reports I was getting about the Navy's plans didn't assure me. As such, I decided that my OSD team, the Joint Staff, and I needed to get involved. So, I put a hold on the Navy's submission.

Despite a few lawmakers' specious claims that my delay would affect their ability to craft the next year's defense bill, Congress had a solid understanding of what the Navy was building over the next half decade; the Department updates and submits this information annually. The theatrics coming from some congressional representatives over my decision to delay the plan's submission was simply the politics they played to their base and the money this industry brought. To some, this was about jobs and reelection, not strategy or building the best Navy possible. I planned to submit the thirty-year shipbuilding plan, but given the NDS and our focus on China, I felt it was more important to get the plan right than get something to Congress on time.

...

In December 2017, the Navy released a future force structure goal that called for building and maintaining a fleet of 355 ships. The service completed this assessment in 2016, well before the NDS was developed. Critics of the plan said that the 355-ship goal supported the admiralty's desire for a 12-carrier fleet, with a battle force built to protect and support them. Therefore, they took the number of other vessels required to enable 1 carrier, multiplied it by 12, added a few other ships that didn't fit neatly into the number, and . . . voilà—out came 355. That explanation is probably too simple and too cynical—though I had watched the Army do something similar with its 10-division force in the mid-1990s.

Nonetheless, members of Congress representing shipbuilding interests decided to make that force goal the law in December 2017, and they reinforced it in 2018 with another statute mandating no fewer than 11 aircraft carriers in the fleet. The system was taking care of the key stakeholders and itself.

I began raising questions about force structure and readiness with the Navy early in my tenure, as we tried to maintain enough carriers in the right place, at the right time, for the right duration. The precipitating event was the delayed departure of the USS *Harry Truman* from Norfolk, Virginia, in August 2019. An electrical malfunction prevented the aircraft carrier from getting to sea for three months, which caused me to extend the USS *Abraham Lincoln*'s stay in the Middle East, which prompted another set of compounding readiness and maintenance concerns.

The Navy was in a bad place when it came to readiness. On any given day, about one-third of the roughly three-hundred-ship fleet was at sea, which was impressive given their challenges, but the trend lines weren't good. The Government Accountability Office (GAO) reported in 2017 that ship conditions continued to decline and readiness had worsened. The Navy was burning down future readiness to meet the current demands of the combatant commanders.

The operational geographic commanders of CENTCOM and EUCOM, for example, wanted these ships on patrol in their areas of responsibility to support operations. More importantly, they wanted to send a message to our adversaries about the reach and capabilities of the U.S. military. I respected what the Navy was doing, but maintaining such a pace was not sustainable, and the future fleet would end up paying the bill.

However, the combatant commanders didn't bear all the blame for the Navy's readiness problems. The service had made several bad decisions too, such as reducing crew sizes, which resulted in fewer sailors available to do maintenance at sea (thus necessitating longer in-port repairs), not ordering enough spare parts, and failing to build training into some ships' schedules. A follow-up report by the GAO in 2019 suggested the problems were worsening.[1] Fixing all the issues would take billions of dollars and many years.

Aircraft carriers—the crown jewels of the fleet—were in a category all by themselves. During most of my tenure, the Navy could only deploy two carriers out of eleven simultaneously. At some points there were none at sea—which was risky and irresponsible—and on a few rare occasions, there were three or more. I would readily give up having three at sea if it meant never hitting zero again.

Given the total number of carriers in the inventory, we should have three on station most months out of the year, but the best the Navy could really sustain was two. After going through another few weeks with no carriers deployed, I told Admiral Mike Gilday, the chief of naval operations (CNO), in the summer of 2020 to plan on two carriers deployed all the time. This would be the new policy, and they needed to figure out a way to make it happen without hurting current or future readiness. I would do my part by continuing to challenge the combatant commanders' requests. The Navy Secretary, CNO, and I discussed this often. I knew a continuous two-carrier presence wouldn't be achievable anytime soon given the maintenance schedules, but I didn't want my successors to go through what I did.

Extended periods of scheduled maintenance and months-long work-up blocks for the carrier crews and aviation drove much of the challenge with these ships. U.S. Navy aircraft carriers are incredibly impressive, can project American power abroad, and are probably the most lethal weapon system afloat, but I wasn't convinced that for the amount of money the nation poured into them we were getting a high enough return on investment. I certainly wasn't convinced they would survive in a war fight against China the way the admirals envisioned their employment.

The other challenge was the opportunity cost of investing in a carrier versus other platforms, particularly when the Department is facing budgetary headwinds. The USS *Gerald R. Ford,* the first in a new class of aircraft carriers, will cost nearly $14 billion based on current estimates (and up to $20 billion with everything it needed to go to war, such as its embarked air wing) and take at least fourteen years to build, by the time it's complete and fully ready to deploy. With that same amount of time and funding, the Navy could build up to four Virginia class attack submarines. Importantly, the sub will spend more time at sea over its lifetime, is less vulnerable to the enemy, and can deliver lethal effects with near impunity.

After a hearing before the House Armed Services Committee on February 27, 2020, and some drama in Congress over my decision regarding the shipbuilding plan, Acting Navy Secretary Thomas Modly came to brief me on the final Integrated Naval

Force Structure Assessment (INFSA), which was the Navy's plan for its future fleet. Tom, a 1983 graduate of the Naval Academy, became undersecretary of the Navy in December 2017. He spent seven years on active duty as a helicopter pilot, a couple of decades in the private sector, and took over as acting secretary in November 2019. Tom was good with the numbers and called things the way he saw them.

Despite all the work, I saw nothing bold in the Navy's plan and not enough of what my OSD experts and external think tanks thought was important to deal with a future China. The INFSA was still built around the myopic 12-carrier paradigm, despite both Modly and former Navy secretary Richard Spencer privately expressing their concerns about the carriers' cost and utility in a China fight. Modly thought we should have fewer carriers, which would free up billions of dollars for other needed ships.[2]

Spencer had taken a similar approach. He pushed hard for so-called light carriers, where existing Marine amphibious ships were loaded solely with F-35 stealth fighters, and able to deliver an aerial punch from the sea. Both secretaries were on the right path but faced resistance from the uniformed side and select members of the Armed Services Committees. It seemed to all of us that the admiralty and certain members of Congress were as attached to the aircraft carrier in 2020 as their predecessors had been to the battleship prior to World War II.

This phenomenon was not unique to the Navy; each of the services had their cultural fixations that prevented them from preparing to fight the next war. However, the amount of money and effort the Navy poured into a carrier-centric fleet at the opportunity cost of so many other things, coupled with their growing vulnerability, was the quiet complaint whispered to me by many other members of Congress, think tank experts, and former Pentagon officials.

Regardless, Modly endorsed the plan, proudly stating that the CNO and the Marine Corps Commandant developed it, and did so without involvement by the secretary of the Navy. That was strange, I thought. I knew where Tom stood on the carriers and other key parts of the report, so why endorse this plan? Moreover, what was the purpose of civilian leadership if they weren't going to get involved with something as important as the future of their service?

Tom was candid about something everybody knew: the Navy's plan to build a 355-ship fleet by 2030 was not budget-informed, and equally important, industry and the shipyards could not logistically support it. He would press for an additional $5 to $7 billion annually, and I would push back, asking from where I should take that money. All the services needed more funding to modernize, and we had to build out space, cyberspace, and other things first on top of that. At least the Army and Air Force were scrubbing their budgets to free up funding. I saw little of that from the sea service. So I wasn't about to reward bad behavior simply because the Navy didn't want to make hard choices. That was the onus I put on Modly, and to his credit, he jumped on it.

Not surprisingly, the Navy's proponents inside and outside the building took up the charge that the Navy needed more of the budget pie; they felt they were receiving the smallest share; plus, they argued, the China fight was a maritime one. Both points were incorrect. According to the Pentagon comptroller, the Navy was receiving *more* funding than any other service, and even then was only spending 11 percent of their $205 billion annual budget on shipbuilding. Having gone through the Night Court process with the Army, I knew that if the Navy leadership could all get on the same page, they could find the additional money. The new incoming secretary, Ken Braithwaite—a former Navy aviator and retired rear admiral turned business executive whom the Senate confirmed in May 2020—would do just that.

Regarding the China fight, the service's argument was unfair to the rest of the force. Of course the Navy would play a much larger role in the Pacific. But to win against China, or any adversary for that matter, a joint approach incorporating the Army, Air Force, Marines, Space Force, Cyber Command, and others was necessary. These were the things that I, as secretary of defense, had to balance.

I wasn't opposed to allocating more of the budget to the Navy, but before making any adjustments I wanted to do three things. First, I wanted to approve an updated war plan for the Indo-Pacific, so that I knew how the commander planned to fight and win. That would give me a better sense of what the services needed to procure. Second, I wanted a new Joint Warfighting Concept, so that I better understood how we planned to conduct warfare in the coming decades, and how that would affect the force mix. And finally, I wanted to see internal reforms by the services. We had an obligation to spend the American taxpayers' dollars well. It is too easy to forget about that and ignore the hard work of reform when Congress is showering dollars down on you. I needed to see that commitment first, and it was important that others inside and outside the Pentagon saw it too.

After my February 2020 House Armed Services Committee hearing, Representative Joe Courtney (D-CT) complained about the lack of a shipbuilding plan and the Trump administration not delivering a strategy to build a 355-ship Navy. Although he was being both partisan and parochial, he was right about this. I couldn't account for my predecessors, however. It was true that the Navy was prioritizing readiness over growth for all the right reasons.

Admiral Gilday was concerned about having a "hollow Navy," and so was I. I committed to deliver a credible plan to build a bigger, better Navy, but I wasn't going to be cowed into submitting a plan I didn't support.

Many people in Washington who were involved in Navy issues often cited Trump's support for a 355-ship fleet as talking point number one to increase the Navy budget. It was true, but in my nearly eighteen months as secretary of defense, the president never raised this issue with me. Rather, he complained constantly about the USS *Ford* and how overpriced and broken the carrier was: "the catapults don't work," which wasn't true; the "elevators are broken," which was partially true; and the "island" on the flight deck from where air operations and other ship functions are controlled "looks really bad—it's stupid" because it was positioned too far aft of ship instead of near the middle. I had answers to these gripes—I had visited the *Ford* in Norfolk early in my tenure—and tried to explain the issues to the president multiple times. He listened but never heard.

The most important thing always seemed to be about the image and "the look," as he called it. With the USS *Ford,* it was such an issue that he proposed we "move the island" closer to the middle of the ship. Imagine the time and cost to do that. As he spoke about it, Trump would gesture with his hands, parallel to each other, farther apart, then closer, like a football referee measuring the distance in inches or feet to get a first down.

He then pressed several times to cancel the entire multiship purchase, often throwing his hands up in the air as he said it, and then tucking his head and waving his hand in a "forget it" gesture to show his frustration. "It looks horrible," he said, and "it will never work." He said he once spoke to a chief petty officer on the *Ford* who agreed that the new catapults were bad. "Steam, he told me. He prefers steam catapults," Trump would say, emphasizing the word "steam" with an exaggerated pronunciation as he said it.

With regard to the elevators, the president recounted his experience with this type of system from his real estate days. "One glass of sea water. Just one. That's all it will take. Once it splashes on those elevators they'll never work," he would say in a disgusted manner, arms out to his side like a polar bear, once again shaking his head in disapproval. The Navy disagreed. Nonetheless, I shared his frustration with all the dollars the service was sinking into the *Ford*, and the continual delays.

On multiple occasions, the president complained that the U.S. Navy ships "look ugly," while the Russian and Italian ships, for example, "look nicer, sleeker, like a real ship." Maybe so, but as I told the president in defense of the Navy, "Our ships are built to fight and win, not win beauty contests; we prize function over form." That didn't satisfy him. In retrospect, it probably angered him.

He wanted to see ships that looked more like yachts. At his request, I once brought along a picture book of ships from various navies, laying it out on the Resolute desk in front of him. He would flip through the pages like a billionaire shopping for a new yacht . . . naturally . . . studying each and every one. He would point out features he liked—"See that line," he'd say, "it's nice and clean" as he passed his index finger slowly across the ship's picture from the bow to the stern.

On more than one occasion, the Navy had to bring over their ship experts to the White House to explain the design of our surface vessels. It never made a difference. These were the Navy issues that kept Trump's attention, not building a 355-ship fleet. It was such a waste of time.

Robert O'Brien was a self-stylized "navalist" who also believed in growing the Navy. He didn't have any practical background but was passionate about the topic. At one point, very early in the administration, it was reported by many he was actively lobbying to become secretary of the Navy. That said, he was helpful in managing the president's desires to kill the Ford class carriers, but presented his own hobbyhorses that I had to beat back, such as spending up to $500 million per ship to resurrect a half dozen mothballed Perry class frigates from the 1970s. He wanted to put them in the water simply to raise the ship count for a few brief years, it seemed. This wasn't the way to grow capability either; we would have wasted over $3 billion simply to say we had more ships than the Obama administration.

Too often, people get fixated on the number of ships. Quantity is important, but so are quality, capability, affordability, and sustainability. These were things O'Brien, who in his role as national security adviser with no budget, program, or operational responsibility (let alone actual experience), didn't seem to appreciate. Over time, once he had a peek at the future naval force we were designing at the Pentagon, and how we built these factors into the plan, he became so enamored with it that he began to claim it as his own, I was told, overstating his personal involvement behind the scenes to others and a gullible press.

These were the dynamics of Navy shipbuilding with which I had to deal, as I'm sure some of my predecessors did as well. The challenges we faced building a future fleet were sharper than most other issues, it seemed, but epitomized the constant headwinds we confronted across the DoD when it came to modernizing the force: the internal politics of the Navy, its various tribes, and friction between its civilian and military leadership over future structure, especially with regard to aircraft carriers; a focus from some in Congress that was all about jobs and maintaining the status quo, rather than helping the DoD make tough decisions and build a truly capable Navy; the internal politics of the White House, and the interests and ambitions of the various players, including an Office of Management and Budget that wanted to trim defense spending; and the hidden role that industry, unions, associations, retired officers, and others played as liaisons among these groups, and as advocates on behalf of "their" programs.

All these factors—individually and in combination—hurt the Department, hindered our war-fighting capabilities, and weakened our national security. I wondered if my counterpart in Beijing faced similar challenges.

We needed to build a Navy *larger* than 355 ships, beginning with more attack submarines. We also needed aircraft carriers, no doubt, but I wasn't convinced that we had the size, type, or number right. Richard Spencer's idea of building light carriers had a lot of appeal, and it could help address the incessant requests of combatant commanders. A mix of both made sense; it gave you more options and capacity, and it would be more affordable, especially if you deployed nuclear-powered carriers against your higher-end and most complex adversaries and deployed light carriers toward the other end of the spectrum.

Given all these factors, I could not accept the Navy's plans. They seemed to be a product of internal Navy logrolling among the various tribes—surface, subsurface, aviation, etc.—to keep their share of the Navy budget largely unchanged. Insiders were confirming this to me. The plan also seemed trapped in the war-fighting constructs of the past, not adequately reflecting where we needed to be in a future fight against China.

I turned to Deputy Secretary of Defense David Norquist to lead a study to assess a range of future fleet options designed to maintain our overmatch. The team included participants from the Navy, Marine Corps, Joint Staff, and the OSD, as well as outside advisers and experts. They began their work in the spring of 2020.

As the team looked at different solutions, I wanted their future fleet proposal to optimize the following attributes: distributed lethality and awareness; survivability in a high-intensity conflict; adaptability for a complex world; ability to project power, control the seas, and demonstrate presence; and finally, the capability to deliver precision effects at very long ranges.

At the same time, I told them the fleet design must be affordable in an era of tight budgets, sustainable over the long term, and operationally ready and available at higher rates. These were all issues we currently faced and would continue to deal with.

What they developed was a more balanced Navy of over 500 manned and unmanned ships that we called Battle Force 2045. The work was a testament to Norquist's inclusive style and analytical approach. So much so that he (and later Navy Secretary Braithwaite) was able to get the CNO and the Navy's senior leaders on board. The plan would reach more than 350 traditional line ships prior to 2035—the year China aimed to fully modernize its military. And the entire battle force would be completed by 2045, four years prior to Beijing's goal of building a world-class military. Importantly, we had a credible path for reaching these numbers in an era of fiscal constraint.

Under the proposal, Battle Force 2045 would comprise a much larger and more capable submarine force. There was a broad consensus on this, and I publicly said, "If we do nothing else, we should invest in attack submarines." The Navy must begin building three attack submarines a year as soon as possible. Subs were the clear advantage we had to sustain, and yet current plans didn't put sufficient value on them.

The tough issue was the aircraft carriers. We made clear that nuclear-powered carriers would remain our most visible deterrent, but we didn't need to build an entire Navy around them, and we needed to take a serious look at light conventional carriers. The study pointed to as few as eight big carriers, complemented by up to six light ones, which seemed like a good mix, especially if you readjusted the existing basing plans for carriers to better meet the more demanding operational needs in the Pacific.

The future force would comprise between 140 and 240 unmanned and optionally manned surface and sub-surface vessels that could perform a wide range of missions, from resupply and surveillance to mine laying and missile strikes. These ships would add significant offensive and defensive capabilities to the fleet at an affordable cost in terms of both sailors and dollars. We just needed a reluctant Congress to give the Navy the authority to develop these systems more aggressively.

Next, we determined that the future fleet needed more and smaller surface combatants. Adding 60 to 70 lighter combatants would not only increase capacity to conduct distributed maritime operations but also free other critical assets for more efficient mission distribution.

We also made strategic lift and logistics vessels a priority. They are key to getting ground forces to the fight and sustaining distributed operations, so I felt strongly that they should be included in the study. I also didn't want the Navy or Congress to forget about them. Success in conflict can come down to simple logistics, but it's not sexy, and so it's often overlooked . . . until it matters.

We knew that Battle Force 2045 would be a more lethal, survivable, adaptable, sustainable, and larger force than we have seen in decades. It was the naval force needed to deal with China. Achieving it over the long run would not be easy, however. Parochial interests, budget uncertainties, infighting, industrial capacity, and other competing factors would challenge us.

Money was always an issue, but once Secretary Braithwaite came aboard in May 2020, he was committed to making reforms that would free up billions of dollars. With that good faith effort, I decided to match his initiative with funding harvested from ongoing DoD-wide reform efforts.

If the Department pursued all these initiatives, and Congress made some adjustments as well—such as returning unspent appropriations dollars to the Navy rather than letting them expire—we could match the average percentage of dollars spent annually for new ships during the Reagan buildup. We wouldn't be able to begin building more ships for a few years, but starting was achievable in the next five. It would take that long for the shipbuilders to improve shipyard capacity and grow their workforce to meet demand, they told me when I met with them.

I introduced Battle Force 2045 in a major speech on October 6, 2020. Norquist and his team, along with Braithwaite and the Navy, had done extraordinary work over the previous half year to get to this point. In the final weeks, though, O'Brien and the NSC were nipping at both men's heels for more information, suggesting that the White House unveil the initiative.

Chief of Staff Mark Meadows even got involved. Indeed, he and I got into a yelling match not long after I briefed Battle Force 2045 to the public. He had the nerve to ask in a phone call, "Who are you to make a major announcement about the Navy?" "I'm the goddamn secretary of defense!" I shouted back, as I stood above the secure phone at my desk. There was a brief pause—I imagined him turning red and eyes watering, as so often happened when he was confronted—and then he said, "Who gave you the authority?" "The Senate confirmed me, and Congress gave me full authority, direction, and control over the Department of Defense under Title 10 of the law, that's who," I charged back.

He really wanted to know who at the White House gave me the approval to move forward. I didn't need anyone's approval, as I said. Moreover, my future naval force structure plans were wholly consistent with Trump's views on building up the military. In a normal administration I would have briefed the relevant players and coordinated our roll-out plan in advance. But I couldn't risk doing that with this White House team, however.

Mark Meadows became Trump's fourth chief of staff in March 2020. Meadows hailed from North Carolina and was elected to Congress in 2012. He is a Tea Party Republican who quickly established himself as a founder of the ultraconservative House Freedom Caucus. In his early sixties with gray hair, a slight heavy set, and a ruddy look at times, he is a 100 percent Trump loyalist. He seemed committed to two things: getting the president reelected and doing what the president said. It was never clear to me which of those two came first, but there were indications at times that his own personal political ambitions and policy aims factored into both as well.

With my last response to Meadows, he went silent. I hung up.

I couldn't believe these were the things I had to argue about with the White House. I looked up at the portrait of George C. Marshall that hung above my desk and shook my head in amazement after this call with the White House chief of staff. Did Marshall have to deal with such BS as well? I wondered. This was why I didn't want anyone in the White House involved at this point. Battle Force 2045 was a serious piece of work done by a committed group of defense professionals. My concern was that allowing the

NSC to get involved, especially a few weeks before the election, would politicize it. We already saw that happening. Building upon the reported fund-raisers O'Brien attended alongside Trump for many months, he was now making solo political trips throughout the fall, and nearly right up to November 3.

On October 21, the national security adviser traveled to Portsmouth Naval Shipyard in Maine. During his remarks he said the U.S. Navy plans to put hypersonic missiles "on all . . . Arleigh Burke-class destroyers" and new attack submarines. Oh really—who in the Navy said that? I called up Navy Secretary Braithwaite after I read about it in the paper. He was unaware of this. It looked like O'Brien was freelancing again. Even the media was smart enough to know that doing this "would be a significant expense and would likely tie up shipyards for years to come" as one article read.[3] An expert from a prominent think tank called it a "terrible idea." One theory was that, after denied the chance to roll out Battle Force 2045 personally, he was looking for other ways to burnish his credentials and position himself to be the next secretary of defense.

Less than a week later, on October 26, O'Brien was on the road again, this time visiting Fincantieri Marinette Marine Shipyard in Wisconsin, an important electoral state. He toured the facility and gave a speech highlighting the Navy's award of a $795 million contract to the company to begin building the new Constellation class frigates. These trips by the national security adviser weren't the DoD's idea, but I was concerned that his visiting key states just weeks before the election, and talking about the military, risked tainting the apolitical reputation of the armed forces I was working hard to maintain. We were concerned about guilt by association, especially when the speaker not only talks about contract awards but also suggests the Trump administration will spend millions building more ships in their state if they vote for him.[4] These visits raised serious questions from government ethics experts and watchdog groups about potential violations of the Hatch Act and other improprieties, though I don't believe any charges were ever brought against him or others.[5] It all just seemed improper and unnecessary.

Meanwhile, O'Brien was reportedly leaking to the press that he was the driving force behind the plan to modernize and expand the Navy. Indeed, on December 9—after I left office—he coauthored an opinion piece with the director of the Office of Management and Budget touting our future fleet plans.[6] Such a piece should have been written by a senior Pentagon official. For nearly a year, though, O'Brien seemingly wanted to play "Navy Secretary" from the White House, causing a good deal of personal friction with Navy secretaries Spencer and Braithwaite. Now here he was trying to claim ownership of Battle Force 2045, despite never having been involved with the study. It was complete BS, yet *Politico* and others bought the story hook, line, and sinker.

I simply wasn't concerned about the administration getting credit for this future fleet initiative by the fall of 2020. I just wanted Congress to embrace the plan we put forward. A White House role would taint it. Battle Force 2045 needed to endure because it was the right naval force structure for the future, and some key stakeholders were now behind it. Moreover, with Beijing rapidly increasing its maritime capabilities, we couldn't afford to lose any more time.

Politics aside, which is where we wanted them, Battle Force 2045 was the right way forward for the U.S. Navy and the entire joint force. It was wholly consistent with the NDS, which was driven by the White House's overarching strategy, and it addressed China's plans and ambitions. It was a daunting task, for sure, but we were confident that our plans met the operational and non-war-fighting attributes necessary to ensure the Navy's continued success for decades to come. The key now was keeping the Navy in the boat and rowing hard in unison with the OSD, while building industry and congressional support on Capitol Hill to see Battle Force 2045 implemented.

I was disappointed to read in June 2021 that the Biden administration's Fiscal Year 2022 budget request would result in less real spending for the Navy—a 3 percent reduction for shipbuilding—than the previous year. Worse yet, it included funding for only eight Navy ships, four of which are support vessels. This stands in stark contrast to the original FY22 budget we built for Battle Force 2045, which called for twelve ships to be procured, most of which were warships, followed by increasingly more ships annually in years 2023 through 2026.[7]

The only way to build a bigger, better Navy—the one we need to retain overmatch, if not dominance, for the next thirty years—is to procure more ships year over year over year. And the only way to pay for it is through increased appropriations for shipbuilding, internal Navy reforms to secure additional funding for the budget lines necessary to sustain a larger fleet, and legislative changes that would allow the sea service to keep its unspent dollars and retire older vessels.

Failing to do so will mean that we will yield the waters of the Indo-Pacific to China over time, a development that will harm our security, our economy, our diplomacy, our commerce, and the international rules-based order that helps underpin them all.

CHAPTER 8

THE AFGHANISTAN DILEMMA

The uniformed pallbearers carried the flag-draped metal container slowly down and off the lowered back ramp of the large, gray C-17 transport plane. They marched in quiet unison to a whispered cadence across the concrete tarmac of Dover Air Force Base in Delaware.

The Old Guard soldiers—with the silver, rectangular "carrying case" firmly in hand—first passed a lineup of senior civilian and uniformed officials, two or three rows deep, all of whom either saluted or placed their hand over their heart as the dignified transfer from the airplane to the awaiting transfer vehicle took place. With white-gloved hands, they then carried the fallen hero past the family members seated beneath a small canopy, not more than forty yards from the rear of the plane, and watched as the case was carefully loaded into the van in front of them. Many sat there stunned; most wiped away tears throughout; others at times cried out to the deceased.

One final salute was rendered by all as the large, dark gray vehicle slowly pulled away. Everyone held one another tighter. It was always very solemn and very emotional. And the military's act of welcoming home America's fallen sons and daughters one last time from combat abroad always made the nation's far-off conflicts very real for those who had to live with the consequences, especially the families.

Getting out of Afghanistan and ending the "forever wars" was a core Trump promise. One had to give the president credit for wanting to fulfill the commitments he made during the 2016 campaign. We were long overdue for getting out of that conflict. We had spent too much time and too much money, and lost too many lives there.

During my tenure as Army secretary, dignified transfer ceremonies at Dover AFB were unfortunately still somewhat common. There was nothing more difficult than to meet the wife or husband of the soldier lost, and try to console them while their young children ran about seemingly oblivious to what had happened. The spouses nearly always put on a tough face, though I often imagined they were more in shock than anything else.

I usually asked to hear their personal stories, tales that the sterile career summaries we were provided could never capture. You could see a young widow's face light up ever so briefly when she recounted those private moments: where they first met, their wedding day, the birth of their first child, and so forth. Better yet were the humorous moments they shared, when everyone would get a quick chuckle out of a funny story well told, forgetting for a brief moment the nightmare they were now living.

Leah would sometimes join me at Dover. She experienced it all through the lens of an Army spouse and mother, remembering the time she saw me off to war and then didn't know whether she might get that slow knock at the door. She was really good with the family members, especially the parents who often attended as well. We ached for them too, and their sorrow made real that adage that no parent should ever have to bury their child. It was terrible, and no words or gestures could ever truly comfort them. We did the best we could. It was time to end this war.

I found writing condolence letters to the families of those killed in action—as well as to the loved ones of those many other soldiers who would die each week from things like car accidents, suicide, or illness—difficult and depressing. As a result, I also started writing "happy letters" to soldiers recognized for their accomplishments, performing volunteer work in their community, or putting their own lives at risk to help others, among other things. Stories of soldiers rescuing people from a burning house or organizing a major charitable event in their spare time helped offset the losses for me. I would bring this practice with me to the secretary of defense's office. I still wrote to families whose sons or daughters were killed in combat, but thankfully, no further wartime deaths in Afghanistan happened during my tenure after we signed an agreement with the Taliban in February 2020.

Many uniformed personnel in the Pentagon had strong feelings the other way about Afghanistan. To many, it was unfinished business. It was a place where they had invested significant parts of their lives and careers; many of them lost friends and colleagues in the mountains and valleys of that tribal country. You had to respect this, and admire it as well. Afghanistan was a noble effort, and nobody assigned there had fought in vain, but it was also costly and distracting us from the bigger, growing challenges of China and Russia.

That said, we really needed to make sure that Afghanistan never again became a safe haven for terrorists to plan, prepare, and conduct attacks against the United States. That was the original reason we went there in 2001—and no attacks from that mountainous, landlocked country had occurred in nearly twenty years—so we had an obligation to continue that record.

Most Americans probably couldn't find Afghanistan on a blank map before the tragic events of September 11, 2001. That horrific day shook our nation and our sense of security unlike any other except Pearl Harbor. In contrast to the surprise attack on December 7, 1941, 9/11 was a ruthless assault by terrorist hijackers against civilians. It was mass murder on a scale we had never seen before. We were all vulnerable now, it seemed.

Since that terrible day, and the Bush administration's subsequent decision to eliminate al Qaeda and the Taliban government that was protecting them, the United States invested a great deal of its time, resources, and people to help the Afghans organize a new government, establish a democracy, and build a country. The United States was joined in this endeavor by many other nations, primarily from Europe, who wanted to see Afghanistan become a normal state that could sustain and protect itself.

Beginning with the Taliban's ouster in late 2001, the U.S. troop presence grew from 2,500 that December 2001 to 100,000 by August 2010. In short, as the Taliban grew and combat operations increased, so did the U.S. troop presence . . . as did U.S. casualties. The numbers would begin to decline year after year after that as the United States changed its strategy and Afghan security forces played more of a role. By the time President Obama left office in 2017, U.S. forces in Afghanistan totaled around 8,400.

In August 2017, Trump announced plans to deploy additional

forces to Afghanistan, increasing the number to about 14,000. This move ran completely counter to remarks he had made on the campaign trail. The media quickly jumped on this reversal, citing a range of his past comments such as "Let's get out of Afghanistan. Our troops are being killed by the Afghanis we train and we waste billions there. Nonsense!"[1] In announcing his turnaround, Trump declared, "Conditions on the ground, not arbitrary timetables, will guide our strategy from now on."[2] Nevertheless, as with so many things in the Trump administration, that would change again.

By the time I became secretary of defense in July 2019, Trump wanted out immediately. He would continually claim Jim Mattis talked him into deploying more troops, promising that the war would be over on his watch. He would mock the former secretary of defense's comments about the Afghans' commitment to their country, mimicking Mattis by dipping his chin to his chest and lowering his voice to say " 'Sir, they are fighting for their country,' " and " 'They are great fighters.' " Trump would then respond to himself, saying back to everyone gathered around him, "They only fight because we're paying them" and claimed, "They are the highest paid fighters in the world."

Trump would go on to complain about the "trillions of dollars" we wasted "in that hellhole" and how "corrupt" the Afghans were, especially President Ashraf Ghani Ahmadzai, often citing without proof the "extravagant mansion he owns" in Dubai. Trump was certainly right about the corruption in Afghanistan. It was rampant, and reached from the highest persons in the country to the lowest.

In Trump's view, Mattis was a "terrible" secretary of defense who duped him by promising victory on one hand and, on the other hand, warning that if we didn't fight the terrorists in Afghanistan, we would be fighting them in America. Mattis had boxed him in, the president complained, and "never delivered on anything." This was another example of how Trump's views of a person could swing from one extreme to another, and usually—eventually—for the worst.

I first learned of the near final deal between the Taliban and the United States in late June 2019, not long after the president named me acting secretary of defense. Few in the DoD were aware of the arrangement that Zalmay "Zal" Khalilzad, a seasoned Afghan-born diplomat appointed by Secretary of State Pompeo to be the U.S. special envoy to Afghanistan, was negotiating to find a peaceful resolution to the war.

I was fully in favor of crafting a political end to the conflict. Nobody, but for the Afghans themselves, paid a heavier price than our military personnel. The contours of the plan briefed to me by Pompeo still lacked some key details and had little support across the interagency, meaning the other relevant departments and agencies of the executive branch. I pressed Mike about circulating the draft for review. I was new to the club at that time, so it wasn't clear to me yet that there was a lot of tension between him and then National Security Adviser John Bolton.

Pompeo was fully on board with sharing the draft with the DoD. He invited General Dunford and me to a detailed brief on July 15, 2019, at the State Department. We sat in a small conference room, where others on his team joined us, including from abroad via secure video. They walked us through the deal as it stood, the expected next steps, and the likelihood of success on the key sticking points. Mike would often say, matter-of-factly in his baritone voice, twiddling a pen as he did, "None of us trust the Taliban" and "It's not a perfect agreement—never will be" but that "we need to get them talking." I agreed. Peace was certainly worth the chance.

There was not going to be a military solution to Afghanistan that would ever meet our aims.

Mike had a good sense of humor, often accompanied by a short, half-smiled chuckle, but meddling from the National Security Council really angered him. He ranted to me about it on a couple occasions. The NSC had a historical reputation for getting too much into DoD (and other departments') business, so I empathized. In his view, though, the NSC "didn't want to study the plan as much as kill it." Putting it into the NSC process would "give Bolton and his team" a chance to "dissect it," and "leak its shortcomings" to the media and the Afghanistan hawks on Capitol Hill, who would then oppose it, Pompeo said.

I was still new to the team—the Senate had not even confirmed me at this point—so I soaked in Mike's assessment and thought about the DoD's role in this unfolding drama. In addition, if NSC staff was quick to leak sensitive information involving State, then I should expect similar treatment for Defense. Time would prove out this conclusion. Mike was right about GOP opposition on the Hill, but the other fact was that most lawmakers from both parties wanted to see the United States leave Afghanistan. We understood this too.

Leaks were a chronic problem in the administration. Much of the information being disclosed to the media at the time seemed to be coming from the White House and was focused on internal policy disputes—Afghanistan, Syria, Turkey, and Venezuela, for example. This was Pompeo's concern; soon it would be mine as well. The individual motivations for the leaks ranged from advancing a preferred policy outcome to enhancing the leaker's own role or credentials to currying favor with the president. It was a noxious behavior learned from the top. The president was the biggest leaker of all. It turned colleague against colleague, department against department, and it was generally bad for the administration and the country.

By early 2020, leaks coming from the West Wing had become far more personal in nature—attacks on others within the executive branch to settle scores, position themselves for future jobs, or to burnish their own record by denigrating colleagues. Alex Azar had NSC staff constantly alleging to the press that he was mismanaging the Department of Health and Human Services and its response to COVID; they also stirred the pot between Azar and the administrator for the Centers for Medicare and Medicaid Services. Others attacked CIA director Gina Haspel for allegedly maintaining ties with senior officials from the prior administration. Some went after me for not being "loyal" to the president or "not fully supporting his narrative" on a variety of issues.

Meanwhile, leaks about plans and policy matters were on the rise at the Pentagon. Whether planning to deploy additional troops to the Middle East or reducing our footprint in countries such as Iraq, some government employees who felt differently leaked information—often classified—to the media. In many cases, these were just options under development at a much lower level for the DoD's leadership to consider. The problem of illegal leaks became so bad, and had jeopardized our national security so much, that I felt compelled to launch a DoD-wide investigation in the summer of 2020. This was accompanied by a sustained effort to remind our uniformed and civilian employees of their obligations to protect classified information, and to educate them on why and how best to do so. None of this was about muzzling whistleblowers or clamping down on the activities of a free media, as a few alleged. It was all about curtailing the unauthorized release of classified information that harmed our nation's security or put our troops at risk, while also weakening the trust and confidence our foreign partners had in us.

In other cases, people leaked one-sided information to Capitol

Hill or to the press in order to undermine options under internal consideration to reform the Pentagon, trim the budget, or cancel programs that had outlived their usefulness. This aspect was less about strategy and policy, and more about their own agency budgets, missions, or jobs. Either way, it was detrimental to internal deliberations aimed at doing what's best for the DoD and the country.

These leaks also damaged trust within the building, making people far more reluctant to speak up and share their views. Nobody wanted to see their name in the morning news, especially when the words were so often twisted, misinterpreted, or taken out of context. In the Trump administration, this could get you blacklisted or fired.

Very early in my tenure, I took a scheduled call from John Bolton. As I was about to pick up the phone, a half dozen people—military assistants, policy experts, and strategy managers, for example—piled into my office to listen in and take notes. I was baffled. I felt perfectly capable of taking my own notes, and I didn't want either Bolton or me to feel constrained because there was an audience on the line as well. We needed to have candid conversations. For example, the privacy of these calls enabled me to get agreement from Bolton and Pompeo to stop reaching out directly to my commands or my leaders, which had become a problem by the time I took the helm of the DoD. These calls were also good opportunities to discuss politics, share rumors, or maybe even commiserate. Staff didn't need to be in on all of this. Moreover, I didn't want my team accused of leaks. I asked everyone in my office to leave, which become the new standard for my phone calls with cabinet members.

Ironically, someone later "leaked" this change to the media, and anonymously—of course—suggested it was an example of me not wanting my staff to hear when Bolton, Pompeo, or others told me how to run the DoD. How ridiculous. Worse yet is the fact that someone in the media would even print such a fabricated story. This was how low things were becoming.

The bottom line is that I didn't want to get in the middle of the feud between NSC and State. I was friends with Mike and John, having worked with them both in the past, and would need their support to be successful. More importantly, we needed to make our organizations and engagements work for the good of the country. At the time, I simply wanted to ensure the DoD had the opportunity to scrub the Afghan peace plan in detail and talk with Zal before it was finalized. Pompeo was completely on board with this.

My team received a draft not long after Dunford and I met with the secretary of state. Its high points included a commitment by the Taliban to take a series of steps "to prevent any group or individual, including al-Qa'ida, from using the soil of Afghanistan to threaten the security of the United States and its allies." The required actions included preventing terrorist groups from recruiting, training, and fund-raising in Afghanistan; not issuing them visa, passports, or travel permits; and directing Taliban members not to cooperate with any such groups or persons.[3]

John Rood, the undersecretary for policy, had serious concerns about the plan. In his view, the agreement was heavy on commitment by the United States to withdraw its forces down to zero, but light on how the Taliban would deliver on their obligations to break from al Qaeda and work in good faith on a peace agreement with the government in Kabul. John made very good points, but not everyone shared his views. Regardless, I asked him to go back to Zal and look for ways to tighten up the areas that concerned him.

The biggest issue at the principals' level was the obligation to withdraw all U.S. military personnel from Afghanistan by May 2021. I didn't support an arbitrary timeline. We all agreed that the Taliban couldn't be trusted to hold up their end of the deal.

Meanwhile, the two biggest levers we had over them were the U.S. military presence and our ability to inflict violence upon them. These were also the most important things to the Afghan government, in addition to U.S. economic assistance, logistical and maintenance support, and the $5 to $6 billion we paid them annually to man, train, and equip their forces.

Rood came back to me with additional concerns about going to zero U.S. troops. If we did that, he argued—setting aside an arbitrary date—then how would we be able to maintain a counterterrorism presence in the country? In my view, if the Taliban lived up to their end of the deal—broke with al Qaeda, denied them safe haven, and committed to keeping terrorist groups out of Afghanistan—then we shouldn't need a counterterrorism force there. I thought that was unlikely to happen, though, which is where a "conditions-based" catchall would once again kick in and allow us to suspend our departure (and even return troops).

The key for me was to get agreement that our departure would be conditions based, and to make that known publicly and privately, especially with the Taliban. We also needed Trump on board with this. Once we had that catchall covering the entire deal, then I could get on board. The fact was that General Scott Miller, our commander in Afghanistan, was in the process of reducing the U.S. footprint in-country anyway, from around 13,500 to something much lower. He wasn't giving away capability, he simply found organizations and people that weren't critical to the mission, and started sending them home as an efficiency and force protection measure. He wanted to go deeper—down to nine thousand or so—but this would involve consolidating some of our bases.

In my view, if we could get the Taliban to agree *not* to attack our forces while we implemented a reduction we had planned to do anyway, that would be a good thing. This was another reason to support the deal in my mind. What was interesting, however, was the position I found myself in between the president and my own civilian political appointees. Trump wanted out of Afghanistan immediately but didn't want to sign a "bad deal." Nobody ever wants to sign a bad deal, but this really didn't make sense, given what was on the table. If the president wanted completely out, and the Taliban were promising not to attack us while we did so, then why not sign up for that? For Donald Trump, however, the words "bad deal" were a trigger to stop acting, stop thinking, and go in a completely differently direction. I didn't support signing on to bad deals either. I just found it hard to reconcile his position.

On the other hand, my Policy shop argued this plan "wasn't a good deal" because of the commitments we were making up front and the lack of detail underlying the actions the Taliban had to take. Pompeo and Khalilzad were clear-eyed about the agreement's shortcomings and were not necessarily optimistic about its prospects, which were views I shared, but at least it started us down a different path than we had been on the past nineteen years. It was worth a try after nearly two decades of fighting and over 2,300 Americans killed.

The bottom line for me was simple: the only way the conflict in Afghanistan would ever end acceptably was going to be through a political agreement between the two warring parties. There was no obvious military solution; we had tried that. This wasn't a great deal; it wasn't even a good deal. For me, though, it was a "good enough" deal. Good enough, that is, to get the process moving forward, get both sides in a room, get them all talking, and see where it goes from there. I used to say to the media that it would be a long, winding, bumpy path, with plenty of ups and downs and starts and stops along the way, but the important thing was that everyone kept moving forward.

Maybe more importantly, I didn't see Afghanistan as a strategic priority beyond ensuring it never again became a safe haven
for terrorists to attack America. We needed to focus on China and
Russia. To do that, I needed to shift time, attention, and resources
to the Indo-Pacific, as well as to reposition forces in eastern Europe. So as imperfect as it was, I supported the State Department's
efforts to negotiate a peace agreement.

On Friday, August 16, 2019—just three weeks after the Senate
confirmed me—the national security team met with Trump at
his Bedminster, New Jersey, golf club. Acting Chief of Staff Mick
Mulvaney was already on-site, along with Gina Haspel and White
House Legal Counsel Pat Cipollone, when General Dunford and
I arrived. It was a little strange driving onto the club grounds in
black Suburbans and exiting the cars in dark suits and uniforms
while Bedminster members of all ages frolicked in the nearby pool
and foursomes golfed on the other side of the clubhouse.

John Bolton arrived a little after us. He had come aboard Air
Force Two with Vice President Pence. John and I quickly said hello,
and he pulled me aside to ask quietly, "When did you find out about
this meeting?" "Yesterday," I said. He paused, told me that he had
"just found out this morning about it," and said that State was trying to "cut the NSC out of the process." He then quickly asked my
views of the Afghan deal. While we were talking, a White House
aide called out that "POTUS is en route." We moved toward our
chairs.

The meeting began a little after 3:00 P.M. in a security "tent"
erected inside a large, empty wing of a club building to protect us
from electronic eavesdropping. The tent was no longer than two
picnic tables in length, with just enough room on the sides for

people to walk by and grab their seats. The president arrived in good spirits, dressed in a white shirt, blue sport coat, and slacks, and took his seat at the end of the narrow table, nearest the entrance. I sat next to him, with Dunford to my right. Pence, Pompeo, and Bolton sat opposite me, in that order.

After Trump greeted everyone, Pompeo kicked off the discussion by outlining Zal's efforts over the previous months and then hitting the key points of the agreement. The secretary of state was realistic about the proposal and presented a sober assessment of its prospects, adding that it was "not a perfect deal" and he "did not trust the Taliban." Trump asked a few questions, zeroing in on the unequal numbers of prisoners listed for exchange between both sides. The president didn't think that a 5-to-1 exchange made sense—"not a fair deal," he said. I looked across the table at Bolton furiously taking notes on a large legal pad.

When the conversation turned to me, I told the president that the DoD supported the plan, contingent on a conditions-based approach. I also added in my two cents about not trusting the Taliban, but thought the deal was "good enough" to give peace a chance. "We can always hit pause if the conditions aren't being met," I added. General Dunford agreed. I had consulted with him and the military chain of command a few times leading up to this moment, and they were on board with my approach. Besides, I said to the group, we were "in the process of reducing our numbers anyway."

It was clear that Bolton opposed the agreement. John cited specific concerns about the May 2021 departure date for U.S. forces, especially the fact that no residual "counterterrorism capability" would remain in-country if implemented as written. All agreed that this would be a major issue on Capitol Hill for such Republican hawks as Lindsey Graham, Tom Cotton, and Liz Cheney. But what would the Democrats say and do?

We didn't stay on topic long at any point during the meeting. Trump started bouncing from issue to issue, getting more and more fired up as he ranted about corruption in Afghanistan, Ghani's alleged mansion in Dubai, and inevitably, his complaints about Jim Mattis. He then leaped around the world like a bullfrog jumping from lily pad to lily pad. The president disapprovingly asked why we were putting more troops in Poland, asking, "Do we really want a Fort Trump there?" He already agreed to both, Bolton reminded him. The president complained there were too many U.S. troops in Europe and that "NATO is ripping us off." I told the commander in chief that our troops going to Poland were "rotational forces"— not permanent ones—that help "deter the Russians and reassure our allies," and that I was initiating a global review of our military footprint around the world.

My NATO comment triggered the Germany soundtrack, which was mostly about Chancellor Angela Merkel and how Berlin was "not paying its fair share" when it came to defense. He told the story about his first meeting with Merkel, and how she asked, "What are you going to do about Ukraine?" regarding U.S. military and financial support. To which he quickly responded, as he told it, "What are *you* going to do about Ukraine?" In his view, Germany was "closer to Ukraine than we are," and it's a "big buffer" for the Germans against Russia. "They should be paying Ukraine more than anyone," he proclaimed. I would hear this monologue several more times during my tenure.

The president was wound up now, sitting in his chair, arms alternating between outstretched at his side as he spoke, and folded across his chest as he finished a point. He also kept looking up and down the table to read people's reactions. His volume pitched between high and higher. He pivoted from Germany to issues such as leaks in the government; how to handle the media; the U.S.

presence in Africa; and military exercises in South Korea. I tried to respond to issues as they applied to the DoD, but the president wasn't listening. I probably should have just sat there quietly, like everyone else. He moved quickly from topic to topic as if on auto-play, eventually coming back to the proposed peace deal and the domestic politics surrounding it.

I had only been on the job for a few weeks now, and had departed for a weeklong visit to Asia on August 2, so this was my first encounter with Trump in this mode; it wouldn't be my last. Some of the things he was proposing were outlandish—such as a "complete withdrawal of U.S. forces from South Korea" or the pullback of *all* military and diplomatic personnel from Africa. "Shut down the embassies in Africa," he often said, "and bring our people [U.S. diplomats] home." None of this was in our nation's interests, and as I calmly responded with facts, data, and arguments, I saw some irritation in him—I was the "new guy" pushing back.

I knew right then and there that this job would be far more challenging than I had anticipated, to say the least. Less than a week after the Bedminster meeting, on August 22, I would have another early dustup. In my first televised interview, the reporter asked if I considered the press the "enemy" of the American people. The reporter was clearly trying to gauge my independence by juxtaposing me with Trump, who had already labeled the media an enemy. I replied, "The press is not the enemy in my book."

When questioned about Trump politicizing the military with campaign gear at rallies, I added that we don't allow buttons, hats, etc., on military uniforms. Period. My first interview as secretary of defense ended up catching the attention of the White House, as would many more that followed, but my message to the media was that I was my own man and that I wanted to work with them.

The meeting that Friday afternoon in Bedminster ended a little before 5:00 P.M. without a hard decision. Trump seemed to be
leaning toward supporting the agreement, but only if he could pitch
it as a "wonderful deal." This, of course, was in contrast with his
earlier comments. Now, he was somehow going to will the "bad
deal" into a "wonderful deal." Just as I was figuring out that the
quality of the deal was the most important thing to Trump, he was
now demonstrating how he could personally, magically, change the
character of that deal in his mind.

Moreover, I learned one other important thing that day. Near
the end of our meeting, Trump said he wanted any public statement
we might release about the peace deal to say that the U.S. would
be at "zero [troops] in October" 2020, just before the election. November 3, 2020, was the lens through which he viewed the agreement. It was an important takeaway for me.

The team that had met at Bedminster had a follow-up session in the
Situation Room on Friday, August 30, with Vice President Pence,
John Bolton, and Zal Khalilzad all calling in from abroad this
time. The discussion largely picked up where we left off in New
Jersey. The principals still held their same positions. Pompeo outlined to the president the final plan as it was at that point, which
was mostly unchanged from the version briefed weeks earlier, and
he recommended we "move forward" on it, as imperfect as it was.
Trump listened closely.

The president looked at the large screen and asked Bolton, who
was in Warsaw, "Would you sign it, John?" Trump knew Bolton
drew the hardest line on the proposed agreement. "I would not,"
John responded. He ticked off the reasons, but gave some ground

by telling Trump he "can support going down to 8,600 troops and then wait" for the Afghan elections. We "can decide what to do next after that," he added.

Bolton made clear we couldn't trust the Taliban and cited his concerns about the lack of an enforcement mechanism. He made several good points, many the same as my Policy team. I too was fine with going down to 8,600 and pausing. General Scott Miller was reducing the number of troops in-country anyway. I acknowledged Bolton's position but restated my view that we pursue the deal "provided that further reductions in U.S. forces were conditions based," and that we stick to that approach. Without it, we would squander the leverage that a continued U.S. military presence and the threat of force gave us.

Trump was now more curious than before about the optics of the deal, the reaction of the Democrats, the backlash from Republicans, and the views of his base. As I mentioned earlier, large majorities in both parties on Capitol Hill supported leaving Afghanistan and were looking for a way to do so without losing our hard-fought gains. I spoke up and proposed we "invite congressional leaders in to discuss the plan to build some bipartisan support, or at least dampen opposition." There were a couple of positive nods around the table, but otherwise the group sidestepped the suggestion as the conversation moved on. Too many people took their cues from the president, and he wasn't biting. He never really saw the value in this type of outreach, even if it was just for show. This wasn't the last time I would make such a recommendation, nor the last time the president would ignore it.

Congressional outreach was such a simple thing to do, and an important one when you are considering a peace deal to end America's longest war. Starting and ending wars are significant decisions for which you want broad bipartisan support, especially if you want to bring the American people along with you.

Trump then caught everyone by surprise by declaring, "I want to meet with the Taliban" here in Washington. We all sat there stunned for a moment, carefully looking around at one another, and then at him to see if the president was serious. He was. Trump asked Pence what he thought, to which the vice president rightly cautioned that we give the idea more thought.

Trump then said he wanted to meet with Ghani too, proposing separate meetings in D.C. with him and the Taliban leadership. So, we can meet with the Taliban but not congressional leadership? I thought disgustedly. Ever the showman, Trump believed this would bring great focus to the matter at hand and, though this was never said, cast him as an extraordinary diplomat and businessman who could close any deal. None of us liked this idea.

As the president went around the room, we each tried to dissuade him in different ways. I recommended against it, reminding him that "the Taliban have the blood of American service members on their hands, not to mention their role in the death of nearly three thousand civilians killed on our own soil on 9/11." It was not appropriate for the president of the United States to meet with them, I added, and said, "It will not go over well with the troops and their families." It didn't sit well with me at all. I didn't see how General Dunford or I could possibly participate in this.

Bolton broke the serious tone of the room when the president asked what he thought. I knew John long enough to anticipate his view—no way—but he surprised us with a wisecrack about making sure any Taliban that visit the White House first walk through "the world's most powerful magnetometer." Everybody got a chuckle out of that, but those of us who understood the ruthlessness of the Taliban knew what they were capable of doing.

The president then transitioned to a quick discussion about how to craft the message about his proposed meeting with Ghani and the Taliban. Trump would often look up into the air, chin raised, as he searched for the right words, then drop his head, and say, "How about . . . 'The president has agreed to a meeting'" and then, "Wait, wait, . . . let's say 'he's looking forward to the meeting.'" Pence and he went back and forth a couple of times, the vice president in his even tone trying to steer Trump in a better direction with suggestions phrased as questions, such as "Would you meet with President Ghani first?"

The meeting soon ended with the president's approval of the peace deal and a quick discussion about security assistance for Ukraine. Regarding the visit by Ghani and the Taliban, it was still on, though Trump later put out that he wanted it moved to Camp David, and that all of us were to join him. I couldn't believe this was happening. We were actually going to sit down with the Taliban at the president's historic Maryland retreat, like old friends?

There was no way Dunford and I could join him. The Taliban had killed and wounded more than twenty thousand U.S. service members in Afghanistan since 2001, and that's just counting the physical wounds of war. Not only couldn't I personally do it, it would be terrible for any secretary of defense or chairman of the Joint Chiefs of Staff to be sipping tea with these terrorists, especially while we still had troops in a combat zone. It would be breaking faith with them, their families, and our veterans.

It was not lost on many of us, either, that the eighteenth anniversary of the 9/11 attacks was coming up in a week or so. This idea was terrible in so many ways.

On Thursday, September 5, a car bomb killed a dozen people in Kabul, including an American service member. Trump was furious the Taliban would do this as he planned a meeting with them at Camp David in a few days to finalize the peace deal. In a series of tweets, he both announced the meetings had been planned for the upcoming Sunday and then canceled them, stating that if the Taliban "cannot agree to a ceasefire during these very important peace talks, and would even kill 12 innocent people, then they probably don't have the power to negotiate a meaningful agreement anyway."[4] With that, not only was Camp David off but so too were the talks. It also relieved me of a difficult, early decision about what I'd do if faced with the order to join him and the Taliban at Camp David.

Peace talks would pick back up in December 2019, however, not long after Trump made a surprise visit to Afghanistan over Thanksgiving.[5] As the talks between the United States and the Taliban ramped up again in Qatar, Zal and team went to work. The two biggest issues they would face were the process of entering into intra-Afghan negotiations and achieving a visible reduction of violence, the issue that prompted Trump to halt the talks in September.

On February 5, 2020, I had an update call with my team back at the Pentagon, with General Miller calling in from Afghanistan, and General McKenzie from CENTCOM in Tampa. General Miller confirmed that the negotiating teams had reached agreement on a final text, which was what we were hearing in D.C. It was nearly identical to the version State shared with us the previous summer.[6] The Taliban also committed to start intra-Afghan discussions on March 10, 2020. These talks wouldn't begin until September 2020, though, mostly due to disagreements over prisoner swaps.[7]

Before the United States signed the agreement, however, we wanted more proof that the Taliban was serious. As such, we required a weeklong reduction in violence before inking the accord. If all went well, both sides would sign it on the eighth day. I asked everyone once again for their views and recommendations. General Miller was satisfied with the deal from an operational perspective given that there were off-ramps, a dispute resolution mechanism, and sufficient military capability remained on the ground. Coming from him, that meant a lot to me. Generals Milley and McKenzie also supported the agreement.

I asked General Miller about the Afghan National Defense and Security Forces (ANDSF). He believed that "they will support the deal with sufficient handholding." They were the DoD's key partners, and our biggest concern. We needed them on board to make the plan a success. They would be instrumental in providing security throughout the country, and for us more specifically. While U.S. and coalition forces provided their own internal protection, the Afghan forces were responsible for external security, and their outer ring of protection at our various locations was very important.

Of greater concern were insider threats, the so-called green on blue attacks that had occurred in the past when Afghan soldiers turned on their American counterparts and gunned them down in cold blood. This often "happened when the Afghans were under stress," General Miller said, and the Taliban was able to get one of their fighters into the local forces or "turn" a current member. Either way, it was deeply troubling, broke the trust between our militaries, and caused a great deal of turmoil and tension in the ranks. It was one thing to fight and die alongside your Afghan partners; being targeted and attacked by them was horrendous and unconscionable.

Finally, I was concerned about the Afghan Army's staying power and willingness to fight. What would happen as our numbers went lower and lower? The ANDSF experienced an inordinate number of desertions every month as it was, but they were still able to field a sufficient number of troops to sustain the fight. And their commandos were very good. Would it all fall apart with the U.S. departure? And what about Afghanistan's political leadership? Would they cut and run too? Corruption was rampant in Afghanistan and, as the saying goes, a fish rots from the head down.

President Ghani always seemed more concerned about himself than his country, as were many other senior government officials, it appeared. It was hard to believe the Afghan military—at least the average soldier—would put their lives on the line if the country's political leaders were unwilling to do so. As in most things, it always comes down to leadership, and the Afghan people deserved far, far better than what they had over the years.

By mid-February, both sides finalized the agreement. On the twenty-first of that month, Pompeo announced that we "have come to an understanding with the Taliban on a significant and nationwide reduction in violence across Afghanistan." Moreover, he added, "Upon a successful implementation of this understanding, signing of the U.S.-Taliban agreement is expected to move forward" with "the signing to take place on February 29."

It was important to the president, indeed to all of us, that the Taliban demonstrate seriousness regarding this deal, and the reduction in violence was the metric. Moreover, the reduction in violence would also signal whether the Taliban leadership could really exercise control over their fighters. This was something important for us to know. We would quickly find out that they could.[8]

By the end of the month, Pompeo was on a plane to observe the signing of the agreement in Doha by Khalilzad and his Taliban counterpart. Meanwhile, I flew to Kabul to speak and stand alongside our Afghan partners and NATO Secretary General Jens Stoltenberg, a symbolic reaffirmation of our support for the Afghan government and our transatlantic allies who bravely served alongside us for so many years. Many Afghans were anxious about the deal. Some were angry that the United States signed it without their participation; others opposed it outright. The bottom line was that we needed Afghanistan's political elites to get behind this plan. I addressed this in my public remarks.

We knew Ghani privately rejected the deal and was reportedly working through proxies to undermine it, despite saying all the right things publicly and privately to us. At the time of our ceremony, he and Afghan Chief Executive Abdullah were locked in a bitter dispute over who had won the 2019 presidential election. Now, from Ghani's perspective, the United States was pushing him into negotiations with the Taliban that could result in a new government where he had no role. As such, we had strong reason to conclude these contradictory behaviors from him would continue long after the ink was dry in Qatar.

The U.S. obligations under the agreement included a phased withdrawal of all American and foreign forces within fourteen months, which worked out to be May 2021. The first steps called for a reduction to 8,600 U.S. troops, and a proportionate cut in number by the allies, over the next 135 days, coupled with the closure of five military bases. These actions had already begun, and we were all quite comfortable with this lower number, so the United States had no trouble agreeing to this.

The United States and the Taliban also agreed to halt offensive military operations against each other (and our allies), although we reserved the right to take defensive actions in support of our Afghan partners if the Taliban attacked them. With that understanding, we would now be able to continue our reductions without the threat of the Taliban attacking us.

At the press conference in Kabul, I made clear that "we are fully committed to supporting the [Afghan forces] throughout this process" and that "we reserve all the rights of self defense." For the record, I added that "this will be a conditions-based process" and that the standard for me was that "Afghanistan again never becomes . . . a safe haven for terrorists to threaten America."

We didn't stay much longer after the press conference. The team was anxious to get me to the airport. There was chatter in intelligence channels before departing D.C. about efforts to target me during my visit—which was very unusual—so we took additional security precautions going into and departing Afghanistan, and made several other operational adjustments. General Miller personally involved himself in my security.

It was one thing to be concerned about my own safety, but I also dragged around many other folks on these trips, so I was particularly concerned about them. We trimmed some of our team before leaving Washington. Jennifer Stewart, my new chief of staff, then spoke privately with the others and, to their credit, they still wanted to make the trip. We all felt it was important to be on the ground in Afghanistan during this historic moment, and to show our support for the Afghan people and the peace process.

I was similarly concerned about our traveling press. Jonathan Hoffman, my head of public affairs, briefed them at the airport prior to departing D.C., giving them the choice to go or not. I spoke with them briefly as well. Jonathan told me later that all went, which I respected. Fortunately, the trip happened without a hitch.

Jen Stewart took over from Eric Chewning as my chief of staff in January 2020. Jen came from the House Armed Services Committee, where she was the staff director under Representative Mac Thornberry. A graduate of Miami University in Ohio, her home state, she was a strategic thinker and policy expert with a great deal of common sense, keen political insight, and an even keel. She had a big heart and a great smile that the day-to-day grind of the job couldn't suppress. Not only did Jen have many years on Capitol Hill, but she had also worked in the Pentagon previously, as a top adviser to General Dunford when he was the chairman of the Joint Chiefs. I had also known her for years and felt fortunate to get someone with her stature and skills on the team. She would prove invaluable in the long months ahead.

Back at the Pentagon on March 2, I informed the press that the United States was beginning to draw down its forces in Afghanistan consistent with the peace deal. Meanwhile, the Taliban announced, "As per the [US-Taliban] agreement, our mujahedeen will not attack foreign forces but our operations will continue against the Kabul administration forces."

I commented, as I so often would, that "we will take this one day at a time" because the peace process will be a "long, windy, bumpy road" with all kinds of starts and stops along the way.[9] Such a journey is not uncommon in the history of peace processes that ended wars. However, while you are always skeptical of your adversary's commitment to the deal, in this case we also had to worry about Ghani's reported efforts to scuttle the agreement. Worse yet, we had a second president who was increasingly undermining the agreement.

I never believed President Trump bought into the peace plan. He just wanted out of Afghanistan, saying so in nearly every meeting I attended with him on this topic. It was a main reason I would say publicly and repeatedly, as I did not long after the deal was signed, that not only was the deal a "conditions-based agreement," but if we assessed that the Taliban was not honoring it and "if progress stalls, then our drawdown likely will be suspended, as well." After all, complementing the deal's carrots of sanctions relief, international assistance, diplomatic recognition, etc., that would come to the Taliban—assuming they were part of a new, unified Afghan government—if they fully lived up to the deal, were the sticks of a continued U.S. and allied presence in Afghanistan and a resumption of offensive military actions.

Regardless, the only variation on Trump's "get out" narrative was whether he wanted U.S. troops withdrawn by May 2021 (per the agreement), by the end of 2020, or prior to the election (as he mentioned in August 2019). Not surprisingly, as 2019 rolled into 2020, and November 3 neared, getting all (or at least most) of our forces out of Afghanistan sooner rather than later became Trump's singular focus, *not* implementing the peace agreement. This was obvious to everyone, including the Taliban, I bet. As such, his words and decisions would squander our leverage with them and undermine the prospects for achieving an enduring peace in Afghanistan that would benefit the Afghan people and better safeguard America's long-term security.

CHAPTER 9

COVID—A TRAGIC, EPIC FIGHT

As I spoke with the reporters huddled in my small office on the Air Force jet, a news story flashed across the muted screen. Mystery virus hits America! It was early morning on January 22, 2020, and we were flying to Pensacola, Florida, to visit the Navy. News coverage reported on the first confirmed case of coronavirus in the United States. A man in his thirties from Washington state had developed symptoms after returning from a trip to China, which had recorded its first death from the virus less than two weeks earlier on January 11.

A reporter gestured to the story on the screen and, amid the sound of rushing air that noisily occupied the cabin, asked me if I was tracking this person's case. I was not. It had just appeared in the media yesterday, and I had not dug into the details of this unfortunate man's story. This anecdote, however, became fodder for the hard-left partisans who often dominate parts of Wikipedia to characterize it as an example of me "downplaying" the seriousness of COVID as part of the Trump administration narrative. If only we knew what this new virus really was in January 2020, let alone had a coordinated message regarding it. Nevertheless, we were tracking the virus. The DoD had been monitoring it at least since mid-January, when there were only a few hundred cases worldwide, and none in the United States.[1]

In addition to the DoD, the IC was watching the virus. According to Bob Woodward in *Rage,* Trump was briefed on January 23 that the intelligence experts "had a pretty benign take on the coronavirus,"[2] that it was "'just like the flu'" and unlikely to become a global pandemic.[3]

Within days, the Defense Department activated its pandemic response plans. By summer, more than forty-seven thousand National Guardsmen and thousands more military medical personnel were committed across all fifty U.S. states and its territories. Tragically, by the end of February 2021, a year after the first death in the United States due to COVID, more than five hundred thousand Americans had succumbed to the virus. It would be the first global pandemic of its kind in a century.

Some of the DoD's first actions in response to the pandemic began on January 29, 2020—six weeks before President Trump would declare a national emergency—when the military received the initial planeload of Americans evacuated from China at March Air Reserve Base in California. We quarantined and cared for them for several weeks. This event marked not only the DoD's first public role in the virus but also the beginning of a close relationship between the DoD and the Department of Health and Human Services (HHS), one that would eventually transition into our joint work together on Operation Warp Speed. Most Americans weren't paying attention to the virus at this point in late January, and many of those who did probably didn't take it seriously enough.

The Pentagon did, however. On February 1, before the first person in the United States would die from COVID, we implemented our global pandemic response plans, as already mentioned. We could see where this virus *might* go, and we wanted to stay ahead of it. Many of us at the DoD understood from a careful reading of history the devastation that disease can inflict on populations and on military units in particular. The close quarters of military life often allows easy transmission. For most of military history, disease was the biggest killer during wartime, not combat.

During Operation Desert Shield in the fall of 1990, a bug of some type ripped through the infantry battalion that I had deployed with as part of the 101st Airborne Division. We were in defensive positions in the north of Saudi Arabia, out in the middle of the gritty desert, expecting a cross-border assault by the Iraqis. However, it wasn't Saddam's Republican Guard that knocked us back. Rather, it was a virus that crippled the battalion for days, with many of us confined to a medical tent, with IVs in our arms, as we each sweated it out for twenty-four to forty-eight hours, passing the bug along from soldier to soldier. We were technically "combat ineffective," and there was nothing we could do except let it play out in the harsh environment of the desert. "Combat ineffective" was exactly what we couldn't afford to let happen to the U.S. armed forces in 2020.

I quickly outlined my three priorities for the Department regarding COVID: first, protect our service members, our department civilians, and their families; second, ensure we maintain our national security mission capabilities and readiness; and third, provide full support to the whole-of-nation, whole-of-government response to the virus.

On January 30, a week after that initial U.S. infection, we issued our first Force Health Protection Guidance memo for dealing with COVID-19; there would eventually be thirteen total over a period of several months to keep the force up-to-date and healthy.[4] These went to service secretaries, service chiefs, and combatant commanders—each of whom had extensive medical staffs and resources—on how to protect oneself and others from COVID.[5] The early and continued issuance of guidance memos to the Department would prove vital to the military meeting my three priorities.

The White House soon established its Coronavirus Task Force. One of its first tasks was determining how best to keep travelers from China out of the United States and how to bring American citizens home from abroad. As HHS Secretary Alex Azar warned the president about the possibility of a global pandemic, his department sought masks and ventilators from the DoD, both of which we had in our strategic stockpile. On January 31, Trump restricted travel from China, a prudent move that prompted some to unfairly call this action "xenophobic."

February would be a big month for the DoD as we ramped up our efforts in multiple areas, including how best to support domestic authorities dealing with this new virus. Meanwhile, my commanders around the world had to make their own independent assessments of countries in their area of responsibility as well, especially those where there were high concentrations of U.S. service members *and* the infection rates were growing quickly, such as Italy and South Korea.

At the same time, the number of Americans returning from abroad increased significantly, with the DoD helping the State Department arrange flights, and then working with HHS to isolate and care for over three thousand people at thirteen military installations in multiple states. More than one thousand of our fellow citizens were flown home from Wuhan, China, alone. Hundreds more would come in from infected cruise ships. The virus seemed inescapable.[6]

Despite all this, some would later try to say the Pentagon was playing down the virus in the early days of the pandemic, which was never the case. We were leaning into it hard, neither downplaying nor exaggerating the threat. In the large meetings where we would discuss issues, there were a few folks, though, who were very concerned and felt we should do more. Some believed we should basically shut down the military by pausing all recruiting, in-processing, basic training, field maneuvers, and other activities critical to maintaining readiness. That was not realistic, nor was it warranted, and our outcomes over time would demonstrate this to be the case.

Others didn't see any reason for concern, reflecting a nonchalant approach taken by elected leaders from both political parties. Speaker of the House Nancy Pelosi said in late February that "there are no indications of widespread infections in the United States" and encouraged people to go out in public to San Francisco's Chinatown, while the president said, "The Coronavirus is very much under control in the USA."[7]

Even the person who would become our nation's most trusted expert on COVID, Dr. Anthony Fauci, the director of the U.S. National Institute of Allergy and Infectious Diseases and the chief medical adviser to the president, was saying in mid-February that the virus was low risk. Fauci reportedly chuckled at healthy people who wore masks, saying that only "sick people" should be wearing them.[8] Two weeks later, on national TV, Fauci would say, "Right now, at this moment, there's no need to change anything that you're doing on a day-by-day basis. Right now the risk is still low, but this could change."[9] Such was the state of play in late February 2020. In early March, Fauci's assessment would completely pivot.

Not surprisingly, the growing political grandstanding over the virus eventually found its way into the Pentagon. A *New York Times* story on March 2 falsely reported, based on one anonymous source who wasn't even in the meeting, that I "urged . . . commanders overseas not to make any decisions related to the coronavirus that might surprise the White House or run afoul of President Trump's messaging" on COVID.[10] That was complete BS. The commanders had the authority to do what they needed to protect their troops, per my earlier guidance.

Two days later, General Milley and I testified under oath before the Senate Armed Services Committee that the *Times* story was "completely wrong. It's bad reporting, at its worst." I told the committee that one thing I did request of my commanders was that "if you're going to make a very big decision, a high-profile decision, give me a heads-up, because I want to make sure that we're integrated across the interagency, that HHS knows, that State knows— indeed, the White House knows, and that Congress knows, because that's what I've got to do. I've got to make sure we're integrated."[11] There was no way we were putting politics or messaging before protecting the troops and my other priorities. General Milley completely confirmed my story, as did Army Secretary Ryan McCarthy and my head of public affairs, all of whom were in the room— unlike the single anonymous source the *New York Times* relied on.

The precipitating event was that General Robert Abrams, the commander of U.S. Forces Korea, was considering declaring a public health emergency for all American service members in South Korea as his caseload crept into double digits. Making such a declaration gave him more authority to enforce restrictions aimed at preventing the spread of coronavirus, which was the smart thing to do. I just wanted him to inform me before he acted, so that we could make sure the State Department—who also had personnel in South Korea, for example—and others were aware. He needed no approval from me to act.

Beyond just being sloppy reporting that aimed to cast the shadow of politicization on our efforts, the *Times* story was a harbinger of how political COVID would become. Issues of face mask wearing and social distancing would eventually divide along party lines, and between red states and blue ones. We worked hard to stay out of this, and to keep a low profile. I was disappointed that even after our testimony and other information was presented to the *New York Times*, they still allowed this false narrative to keep appearing in their paper for months to follow, and decided to not even mention our sworn testimony to Congress. To this day, the *Times* has never corrected the story.

On March 11, just days after several states announced their first cases—and a week before the president would introduce new national guidelines to control the spread of the virus—we restricted all travel for DoD military and civilian personnel and their families effective March 13. This ban applied to all persons going to, from, or through areas that the Centers for Disease Control and Prevention (CDC) labeled as a Level 3 danger. This included all forms of official travel, including permanent changes of station, temporary duty, and government-funded leave.

For military personnel, this restriction also included personal leave and other nonofficial travel. Days prior, Alexis Ross, my deputy chief of staff, whom I had assigned to be acting undersecretary for personnel and readiness while Matt Donovan awaited Senate confirmation, also issued our fourth instruction to safeguard the health and well-being of the force, as well as comprehensive guidance to establish new protocols for the seven hundred thousand civilians in the DoD workforce who would suddenly be working remotely.

The travel ban had a dramatic impact on the force, shutting down an entire ecosystem that spanned dozens of countries, tens of thousands of families, and hundreds of bases worldwide. Moreover, we had to extend it at least twice into the summer, but with modifications. We couldn't afford to enable the spread of the virus, however. For example, Italy was a hot zone in March, so we were very concerned about allowing families living there to move back to the United States on a normal rotation, and possibly bring the virus to an uninfected base on American soil. We had to stick with the priorities I laid out, in the order I presented them.

We also began social distancing at the Pentagon, wiping down furniture, conducting meetings by video conference, and so forth. We directed many DoD employees to stay home, so we had less to worry about there. And we all took hard looks at our schedules and planned trips. Most of the latter were canceled, as were meetings with outside visitors. My chief of staff, Jen Stewart, established new protocols on who could visit our front office and who could enter mine. We were taking this all very seriously and adopted rigorous practices, as compared to the White House.

Also on March 11, the president announced that the United States was suspending all travel from Europe. That same day, the World Health Organization declared COVID-19 to be a pandemic. I was at the White House one of the times the issue was discussed, having stayed behind following a meeting on a different set of topics with Trump.

Vice President Pence led the large group into the Oval Office after apparently meeting with them separately in the Roosevelt Room, just across a narrow hallway in the West Wing. Top leaders from HHS and the CDC, along with NSC staffers, the communications team, and other White House staff quickly packed the Oval. I stood along the wall nearest the Rose Garden, having stopped not far from the outer office after my meeting with the president ended.

A half dozen wooden chairs sat immediately opposite the Resolute desk in a semicircle around Trump, the couches and seats farther back were also filled, and people stood along the walls. Though Trump had many bad days, he also had some good ones where he was reasonable and in positive control. For this issue, the president sat squarely behind his historic wooden desk, taking it all in, asking good questions, letting others debate.

The room was divided, with a clear majority led by Alex Azar, Dr. Anthony Fauci, CDC Director Dr. Robert Redfield, and Dr. Deborah Birx, the White House Coronavirus Response Coordinator, making the case to "shut down all air travel . . . from Europe." That recommendation took Trump aback—he knew what this meant—and nearly everyone in the room seemed to agree with the doctors.

Treasury Secretary Steve Mnuchin was the lone voice with a different view, sitting just across from Trump, waiting his turn to speak. His opposition to this suggestion was obvious from the slight scowl he wore on his face, and his head shaking gently in disagreement at times as the doctors spoke. When Trump turned to him, Steve made very clear that closing the country would kill the economy. It would result in a "depression," he said in no uncertain terms, and it would take a long time for the nation to recover. He argued that the medical facts didn't justify such an extreme measure, but he was clearly in the minority.

Mnuchin looked for ways to thread the needle—something less than the "all or nothing" approach that was under debate. Steve was incredibly smart, thoughtful, and reasonable. I always found him to be a good colleague, but the odds were against him that day.

Birx led the argument for a shutdown after Redfield recommended it. In her view, "tens of thousands of people had already entered the U.S. and were spreading the virus." Unfortunately, it would take "a couple weeks" for the cases to appear, she said, before hospitalization rates soared. Mnuchin tried to counter again, but Robert O'Brien chirped in from the back of the room that "thousands of people" could die.

Trump wrestled with the matter. You could see him thinking through it, weighing both sides, asking questions from opposing perspectives, deciding which way to go. This was an unprecedented situation, and I felt for him. At the time, the CDC had reported 31 Americans dead from COVID and more than 1,000 infected. Was it more like the annual influenza, which killed anywhere between 12,000 to 61,000 Americans each year, or the devastating Spanish flu of 1918, which took the lives of over 650,000 U.S. citizens (out of a much smaller population of 103 million)?[12]

As emotions started to soar in the Oval Office and the discussion stalled, someone suggested the team reconvene elsewhere and develop some clear options for the president to consider. I didn't join them. I headed back to the Pentagon.

The numbers being reported by the CDC were nothing like what would develop just a couple of months later, but it was early March and most people still had a hard time seeing that far ahead. If Mnuchin was right, and the doctors were wrong, the president would likely cripple one of the best economies the nation had experienced in years. Millions would lose their livelihoods. I'm sure Trump wondered how badly that would hurt his reelection chances, with Election Day less than eight months away.

That said, I'm not sure the president ever fully grasped that how he would lead the nation through the pandemic would also influence voters' views toward him, for good or bad, regardless of how many jobs COVID wiped out. By the end of the day, however, Trump made the right call and shut down travel.

Two days later, on March 13, President Trump declared a national state of emergency as the virus took off. As of February 29, only 1 American had reportedly died from COVID.[13] By the third week of March, more than 300 individuals had succumbed to the virus, with nearly 20,000 confirmed cases. Contrary to what the president was saying, things were definitely not under control.

Over the course of the preceding weeks, we kept getting requests from HHS and the Coronavirus Task Force about releasing respirator masks, other personal protective equipment (PPE), and ventilators from our strategic reserves. Since we had more than enough to support DoD clinics and hospitals around the world, we offered 5 million masks and two thousand ventilators to HHS. We were willing to share despite some initial resistance from our logisticians and medical professionals, but we couldn't seem to get anyone in the interagency to accept them. It was a harbinger of deeper problems that took a fair amount of time—too much time—to address. We never got a good explanation why this was so hard, though I came to suspect it was a combination of bureaucratic incompetence and an overwhelming tidal wave of issues and problems.

There was something else going on within the government, however, which we couldn't explain at the time. The White House replaced HHS Secretary Alex Azar as the Task Force's leader in late February. Alex told me later that the organization was helplessly broken and pointed the finger directly at Pence's office. I had appointed David Norquist and General John Hyten as the DoD representatives to this body; they never reported much progress either. Other DoD folks I had involved in the interagency process also conveyed that there was a fair amount of dysfunction.

By mid-March, the DoD was busy transporting hundreds of

thousands of sampling swabs from Italy in coordination with HHS, working with State to bring Americans home from abroad, and opening sixteen of our coronavirus testing labs to test non-DoD personnel. Meanwhile, our doctors and scientists at our top-tier research facilities, such as Fort Detrick and the Walter Reed Army Institute of Research in Maryland, were busy working on COVID vaccines and therapeutics, including ones that could work against multiple variants. I spent a day visiting with our researchers and was pleased with the progress they were making.[14]

On March 18, the president announced the deployment of the Navy's two hospital ships—the *Comfort* and the *Mercy*—to the hot zones of New York City and Los Angeles, respectively. We had been discussing this within the Pentagon for a few weeks. Both ships were in various states of maintenance, and it would take some time to assemble the doctors, nurses, and other medical professionals who would staff them, but we thought they could help take the pressure off civilian hospitals, especially in New York, which had become the epicenter of the virus in America.[15]

I first needed to make sure I understood how the vessels fit into our contingency plans. I didn't want to end up in a war in the Middle East—after all, this was only two months after Iran fired ballistic missiles at our troops in Iraq—where the hospital ships would be needed, and then find ourselves in a fix to treat our combat wounded. This was what the ships were configured and purposed for to begin with, not to handle infectious diseases. This was also how we came around to the recommendation that we initially use the ships to handle trauma cases in New York City and Los Angeles, as compared to treating COVID patients.

Each ship has nearly one thousand beds, but half of those are organized to stack patients on top of one another a foot or so apart, like in a submarine. There's insufficient separation to treat patients infected with a communicable disease. Most of the other rooms on the ships weren't suitable for an infectious disease either. What the civilian hospitals were getting short on were individual rooms with oxygen inlets, and the associated doctors and nurses. Our proposal was to free up those rooms and medical professionals by having the hospitals send their trauma patients—car accidents, shooting victims, home injuries, etc.—to the Navy ships. An added benefit was that if we needed the ships for another mission, we would save time by not having to go through the laborious process of disinfecting the vessel before sending it on to its next mission. Everyone agreed with this plan.

I was very proud of the Department, and our medical professionals in particular, for how quickly and professionally they were acting. We struggled some at the DoD level, though, to get accurate data across the services on medical matters, such as supplies, equipment, doctors and nurses, and hospital capacity. It was something we would need to improve. And while we were working hard to stay ahead of the pandemic, we also had to keep our eyes and ears open outside the United States, safeguarding the nation's security. That was still job one.

On March 24, I held the first of what would become several virtual town halls for service members, family members, and Department employees to address COVID-19. The chairman of the Joint Chiefs of Staff and the senior enlisted adviser to the chairman joined me. COVID had hit the country hard that month, so I felt it was important we further open the lines of communication to all of the DoD. By this point, we had forty-five thousand service members assisting their fellow citizens across the country who were dealing with COVID. The virus affected every state; it also hit hard many other countries where we had people serving. On the call, I first wanted to thank our DoD employees for helping with testing, supply distribution, and other functions in support of America's governors, but then I wanted to speak to how we were adapting to the pandemic.

The call gave me the opportunity to reiterate my three priorities as commanders and civilian leaders across our 2.8-million-person force worked tirelessly to do their jobs. It also gave me the chance to explain our pandemic policies and answer questions. On a more personal level, I wanted our service members to understand how we continued to evaluate and adjust policies to address a variety of issues, from large personnel movements to individual travel, in order to lessen the burden on them and their families. It was a successful innovation we decided to keep doing.

On Saturday, March 28, I joined the president in Norfolk, Virginia, to see off the USNS *Comfort* and her crew. It would take the hospital ship two days to arrive in New York, where the governor was reporting more than fifty-two thousand confirmed cases and over seven hundred people dead. It was a tragedy on a massive scale.[16]

The president was in an upbeat mood as we flew down to the large East Coast Navy base on Air Force One. He always enjoyed the pomp and ceremony of the military, and being around all the uniforms. It fueled his ego as commander in chief. As we walked along the pier toward the stage, admiring the destroyers and other warships docked there, the president pointed proudly at each, saying, "Look how great they look" and "How beautiful." His coat flapped in the wind as he pumped his fist a couple of times as he spoke. Then he quickly pivoted to the USS *Ford* aircraft carrier, like an old eight-track player jumping songs, and began complaining about the ship. I had tried multiple times in the past to address these matters, but by now had given up.

Just as I thought the conversation would continue south, he

turned toward the *Comfort*. She wasn't a warship, but she was an enormous vessel that conveyed strength and mass. Trump valued these symbols. The image of this great white ship, with large red crosses painted atop and along it, became his focus. He forgot about the *Ford*. Instead, he asked me a few questions as we approached the *Comfort*—"How many doctors and nurses are on board? How many patients can it hold? How long will it take them to get to New York City?" The president was in a good mood again.

Trump's remarks before the small crowd gathered along the pier were uplifting and complimentary of the military, as they usually were. The American flags flapping in the breeze behind him, and the enormous white hospital ship not more than a few hundred feet beyond that, presented an impressive backdrop for the event. More than that, the *Comfort*'s deployment was a palpable demonstration of him and his administration helping the thousands of Americans suffering from COVID. Trump's formal remarks—"This great ship behind me is a seventy-thousand-ton message of hope and solidarity to the incredible people of New York"—summed up his bottom line: the cavalry was on the way. His promise was that the U.S. military, and specifically the *Comfort*'s medical crew, would "join the ranks of tens of thousands of amazing doctors, nurses, and medical professionals who are battling to save American lives."[17]

The president turned around and faced the ship after finishing his remarks. I stood next to him, to his right. I congratulated him and said, "Nice job, Mr. President." He said, "Thanks, Mark. It's a great day." We chatted a little while waiting for the *Comfort* to begin moving. Soon she slowly, gently, pulled away from the pier; the ship's horns blasted loudly, breaking the silence of the moment, as sailors waved from the decks. The president raised his right arm and saluted.

I had introduced the president to the small crowd of military personnel and DoD civilians gathered along the pier that sunny day less than thirty minutes earlier. Near the end of my remarks, I thanked the president for his "bold leadership and support to the men and women of the United States Armed Forces."[18]

Seven months later, on November 4, 2020, and five days before I departed the Pentagon, I did an "embargoed, off-the-record" discussion with *Military Times*. When the president fired me on November 9, the publication printed the interview in what Jonathan Hoffman and I believed was a clear violation of the embargo—and without the opportunity to review the transcript for accuracy and completeness—breaking what many, including other reporters I sat with for interviews at the same time who honored the embargo, viewed as a breach of professional journalistic standards. In my conversation with the reporter, though, I challenged her to identify another member of the cabinet who pushed back on Trump as much as I did. I also said that I wasn't one to praise Trump publicly from the podium; others did so constantly—which was my frame of reference—though I probably should have explicitly added the phrase "all the time" or "unless it was deserved" to my remarks. Some in the media decided to cherry-pick a moment here and there, like in Norfolk, where I lauded the president.

Frankly, given the decision I saw him make in the Oval Office to shut off travel from Europe, with all that was at stake, I thought then, as I do now, that he did demonstrate bold leadership on COVID at times.[19] Even Dr. Anthony Fauci would reportedly say Trump's early decisions had been his finest hours—from restricting travel from China on January 31 to doing the same for Europe on March 11, and from the so-called 15 Days to Slow the Spread on March 16 to its extension for an additional month on March 29.[20] His strong support for Operation Warp Speed was also laudable.

But such was the toxic political atmosphere of November 2020. This type of sniping had been picking up since early 2020.

I had spoken on a few occasions with both New York governor Andrew Cuomo and New York City mayor Bill de Blasio, before and after the *Comfort*'s arrival. Both men were always professional with me and were thankful for the military's efforts. I never touched the politics between them and the White House, let alone the underlying personal frictions among all three politicians. I always wanted to keep the military out of politics, including at the state and local levels. Rather, I told both men we were ready to help in whatever way we could—masks, ventilators, hospitals, doctors, nurses, and so on. This of course would be the case in the weeks that followed.

One of the issues I was discussing with both Cuomo and de Blasio was deploying the Army Corps of Engineers to New York City to help build medical capacity in the city, given the exponential growth in COVID cases they were seeing. The head of the Corps, Lieutenant General Todd Semonite, briefed me on a plan to develop what he called alternative care facilities (ACFs). Basically, the Corps could take a dormitory, gym, or other type of facility and build out bed space by creating separate rooms, complete with their own electrical lines for medical equipment, and oxygen hoses to keep patients breathing. I quickly dispatched Semonite and his team to New York to brief Governor Cuomo and lay out their proposal.

The general's ideas were a hit. I wasn't surprised. Semonite was a solid officer. He had held multiple command and staff jobs over the years, serving in the U.S. and abroad, and had now risen to the top of his field—the chief of engineers and the head of the Army Corps of Engineers. Lieutenant General Semonite's plans for New York would become the model across the country. All a governor or mayor had to do was provide the building, and the Corps would handle the leasing, contracting, and engineering to set up ACFs. It was a tremendous effort, and a highlight in the history of the Corps of Engineers.

The first ACF established in the U.S. would be the Javits Center in New York City. With 2,500 beds, it quickly became the largest "hospital" in America—and the U.S. military was running it.[21] Eventually, the Defense Department would assess and design more than 1,155 sites and assist states in building 28 ACFs with over 15,000 beds. The DoD also would deploy dozens of teams of medical professionals to more than thirty major metropolitan areas across the country. The Army Corps of Engineers led the ACF effort, with over 15,000 soldiers and civilians working to coordinate and build these facilities. States wanted to stay ahead of the pandemic in the event that caseloads exceeded local hospital capacity, and we were there to make it happen.[22]

At the end of March, the Javits Center hospital opened for business. The U.S. Army also sent doctors, nurses, and other medical staff from two field hospitals to staff this ACF. Nearly one thousand medical personnel would soon be on site to take care of the ill. Meanwhile, we deployed two other Army field hospitals to Seattle.

The one challenge we had with activating many of the DoD's medical personnel had nothing to do with their willingness to serve, or our eagerness to provide help. The fact was that many of our doctors and nurses were reservists—part-time soldiers, sailors, and airmen, so to speak. Therefore, as we called them up for active duty in New York City, Seattle, and the dozen or so other U.S. cities that needed the DoD's help, or for the hospital ships, we had to make sure we weren't pulling them away from their civilian jobs at hometown hospitals where they were treating COVID patients in a private capacity. We couldn't afford to rob Peter to pay Paul, creating a problem in another locale. The armed services, especially the Army, did a good job managing this, but this type of due diligence took some time to sort through.

The entire military medical community kicked in to help, though. The medical professionals eager to assist ranged from the retired— some of whom came back to full-time work—to newly minted doctors. For example, on March 26, 2020, the Uniformed Services University of the Health Sciences announced that more than two hundred medical and graduate nursing students would forgo graduation ceremonies to join the ranks of their military counterparts faster to help combat the virus.

On March 29, Doctors Fauci and Birx persuaded Trump to extend his 15 Days to Slow the Spread campaign, which had been launched on March 16. The guidelines promulgated by the initiative included steps such as avoiding gatherings of ten or more people; staying away from bars and restaurants; not visiting nursing homes; and the basics of washing hands, disinfecting touched surfaces, and remaining home if you feel sick. The purpose was to "flatten the curve" of the virus's spread to avoid overwhelming hospitals and the broader health-care system.[23]

Trump reportedly was reluctant but willing to try it, aiming for Easter as the date to reopen the country. This was another important decision made by the president, for which he deserved credit, though his words rarely matched his actions after that. Some would argue he was attempting to remain optimistic, to encourage Americans. While there is something to be said for that, it did not justify or excuse his rhetoric. This is where the president fell far short, downplaying the pandemic, declaring it would be over soon, that everything was under control, and delivering false hope. He was saying one thing, but the country—the American people—was experiencing something else. By early April, over 5,000 Americans had died from the virus, and more than 215,000 were infected.

As Trump's language continued to diverge from reality, and the handling of COVID became a partisan political issue, the landscape became trickier for the DoD as well. I still can't explain why, but as we made decision after decision to deal with the virus consistent with my three priorities and established medical guidance, we somehow never ended up in the crosshairs of the White House, even though our actions often ran counter to the president's rhetoric.

For example, on April 3 the CDC issued a national recommendation that Americans wear nonmedical face coverings while in public. Within forty-eight hours, we had turned this guidance into a policy and issued it to the force, becoming the first department to do so. All 2.8 million service members and DoD civilians would wear cloth face coverings on duty when they couldn't maintain six feet of social distance in public areas or work centers.[24]

This policy clashed with the White House, where very few people would wear any type of face covering. Trump was actively resisting masks and mocking those who wore them. He was telling people the virus would simply "go away." He viewed mask wearing as a rebuke of that notion. In fact, when Milley and I would show up in the Oval Office with our masks on, Trump chastised us a couple of times, saying, "The leadership of the great U.S. military shouldn't wear masks. It makes you look weak." The fact was, the leadership of the great U.S. military was trying to set the proper example for my troops, and that meant following our own DoD policies and guidelines.

While we generally were taking the right steps to combat COVID within the DoD, the biggest setback for the U.S. military was the outbreak that occurred aboard the USS *Theodore Roosevelt,* a Nimitz class nuclear-powered aircraft carrier that epitomized American military power.

The first cases of COVID appeared aboard the ship on March 24 as she steamed from a port call in Vietnam to Guam. With the virus spreading like wildfire across the United States, people were very anxious. We still had much to learn about COVID. As big as the *TR* was, the five thousand sailors on board the behemoth still lived and worked in cramped quarters. If COVID was going to break out anywhere in the U.S. military, it was going to be on a Navy ship.

By the end of March, after docking in Guam, the virus had infected more than one hundred sailors. The spread of COVID was likely inevitable, but it was enabled by some poor decisions made by the ship's captain, Brett Crozier, and others—all under significant strain—as documented in the final investigative report by the U.S. Navy. At the time, however, Crozier sent an unclassified email to several admirals and captains that found its way to the media. It painted a grim picture of what was happening on board the *TR,* and said the ship and its crew were not getting assistance, which was not accurate.

As the news of the letter broke on March 30, some stories in the press characterized the captain's action as a "desperate plea for help" to a Navy leadership that didn't care, with some going as far as portraying the ship's status as a gross example of the Trump administration trying to "downplay COVID." Crozier soon became a hero of the left. This narrative took hold quickly, despite there being little basis in fact.

I was in my office prepping for an upcoming meeting when a story about the *TR* appeared on the TV affixed to the wall across the room from me. I called out to my staff, asking them to print off a copy of the captain's letter from one of the various news outlets covering the story, and to get Tom Modly, the acting secretary of the Navy, on the phone. I was nearly done reading the letter when he called.*

Tom was fired up about the captain's actions, incensed with how Crozier had "mishandled" the situation. He was rattling off facts left and right, about how the Navy was "working hard to get rooms in Guam," that "large open spaces are available ashore, but Crozier hadn't fully utilized it," and other important details that would eventually come out in the final report. Modly walked me through all these details, including what the Navy had done over the previous days to assist the TR after first receiving word about the spreading infection.

Tom told me about the "personal calls" he and his staff had with Crozier and others, similar to ones that occurred between the captain and his chain of command out in the Pacific, and everything else that was happening behind the scenes. It seemed like they were doing all the right things. Tom said Crozier "never raised such alarm" and said he "was getting good assistance." As such, Modly and the uniformed leadership were blindsided by the letter, and thought it was both inaccurate and inciteful, which was what really angered him.

I also raised my concerns about the crew's health, and asked what Navy leadership was doing to take care of those infected and to protect the others. Modly and his team seemed to be on top of this, pursuing multiple options at the same time.

Tom wanted to relieve Crozier immediately. My gut was also

---

* Whether or not I had read the letter seemed to become the story for a couple of journalists after I acknowledged in an interview that I did not read the entire note "in detail." (https://www.cbsnews.com/news/coronavirus-military-response-defense-secretary-mark-esper-5-things-to-know/). I had read all but the last page of Crozier's four-page letter when Tom Modly called. The first three pages were more than sufficient, I felt, to understand the captain's situation. I thought these types of story angles landed somewhere between silly and cheap.

telling me the captain had made a serious error in judgment, and had demonstrated an unfitness for command. This was not the skipper of a tugboat based in Honolulu, by the way, but the captain of the largest, most powerful, most visible warship in the U.S. Navy, one patrolling the waters of the western Pacific. If this was how he was going to behave during a viral outbreak that hospitalized a small percentage of his crew, how would he perform in combat if the enemy attacked the *TR*? How would he behave if the ship was burning, with secondary explosions, hundreds of casualties, and possibly sinking? I told Modly that my instincts were aligned with his, but that I wanted to sit down with him and Admiral Gilday, the chief of naval operations (CNO), to discuss the matter and explore all options before he acted.

When Trump heard the news of the letter, he was incensed. I was already at the White House for a separate meeting when the matter came up. We met in his private office, about thirty feet down a narrow hallway from the Oval Office. It was back there that the president ate, worked through papers, and mostly watched the news. It contained a large table that could seat four to six people, but newspapers and memorabilia that people gave him occupied most of it. Across the room from where he sat to eat lunch, a large TV hung on the wall about fifteen feet away. It was constantly on, playing Fox News, which meant that conversations were often interrupted when Trump saw news stories that interested him. In midsentence the president would stop talking, raise his left hand in a gesture to suspend the conversation, reach down to the table for the remote control with his right hand, and immediately raise the volume—listening for a few seconds, and then commenting on what he just heard. It was very predictable.

But now, the president was standing up, posturing, and red in the face as he spoke. He barked that the letter was "terrible" and "inappropriate" and that it "makes the Navy look weak," especially as we were increasingly squaring off against China in the Pacific. I agreed with him. I didn't understand why, cognizant of the efforts by the Navy leadership to assist, the captain felt he needed to write the letter the way he did, and to whom he did, and how it found its way to the media.

Trump started asking if Crozier was going to be fired. Sensing where this might go, I cut him off and said, "Mr. President, I understand how you feel. But let's let the Navy handle it. Let's first find out what happened, and then go from there." Despite Trump's frustration with the captain, he surprised me—he backed off and gave me the authority to handle it as I saw fit. He kept griping about the matter, complaining loudly, but agreed with me to let the service deal with it. The president had heard this speech a few times before from me during the Gallagher episode months earlier—which I will address later in this book—so something must have resonated. I was glad that he was recalling it now and heeding my advice.

I spoke to Tom Modly the evening of Wednesday, April 1. He called me at home after dinner, and we discussed the matter for some time. He had calmed down some by now. Tom still wanted to fire Crozier, though, but told me "the CNO isn't one hundred percent on board with relieving him." Tom wanted to hear my thoughts and said, "Sir, I just want to know if you will support me on this." I told him, "Tom, it's critical that you and Gilday get aligned." Modly needed the brass to support him, or the institution wouldn't hold in the rough waters I saw ahead. We already had lawmakers and pundits speaking out about the matter with few or no facts, which only served to complicate a very difficult and sensitive matter. Tom said the CNO was "getting there."

We also discussed the *TR*'s crew again. The number of infected was more than one hundred and still growing, so I wanted to learn what more he and the Navy were doing to take care of them, and how I might be able to help. Modly said, "We are in pretty good shape. The *TR* is rapidly offloading sailors to facilities ashore in Guam" with the territorial governor's assistance, and "the Navy is dispatching medical teams to assist the crew." He seemed to have his arms around the problem.

Modly and I met the next morning, April 2, and were joined by General Milley and Admiral Gilday. As we sat around the rectangular wooden desk in my office, Modly was fired up again and adamant about relieving Crozier. When Tom became animated, he would get an open, expressive look on his face, and his voice would pitch. Over the previous days, he had once pointed to a pin he was wearing on his jacket lapel that quoted a famous Navy captain during the War of 1812: "Don't give up the ship," it said. In his view, Crozier gave up the *TR*. I appreciated his passion and perspective. The captain's actions seemed to strike deep into how strong Tom felt about the sea service, its history, and its traditions.

As we discussed the matter in my office that morning, Gilday sat quietly, listening to his acting secretary, but not showing any emotion. I liked Mike Gilday and thought he was a serious thinker and reasonable person. I turned to him and asked, "What do you think, CNO? Where are you?" He looked at me and said he "preferred doing an inquiry first," but "will support Secretary Modly" if he wanted to fire Crozier. He was very professional and objective about the matter.

Modly's instincts about Crozier were spot-on in my book. I too had lost confidence in Crozier. However, I also thought we should do an investigation first to get the facts, and to see where else they took us. I told Tom the same during our call the night before. So

I questioned Gilday further about how a Navy inquiry would proceed, the timing and so forth. Experience told me these things were often more complicated than what they appeared to be at first.

General Milley and I were in agreement regarding the matter. We had discussed it a few times before the meeting that morning. Investigations were how the Army handled things, so that was his and my baseline. The Navy, however, had different practices and traditions, and I wanted to be respectful of that. It was not unusual for the sea service to remove ship captains from command on the spot.

There was another twist that I was wrestling with, however, and that touched on the issue of civilian control of the military. I was concerned about overriding my acting civilian secretary in favor of the chief of naval operations. Doing so would not be supporting him and could be interpreted as a lack of confidence, especially since Modly had come out so strongly and publicly on the matter. I knew that as acting secretary, Tom had been struggling to work with the senior navy officers, and I didn't want to set him back in this regard either.

I asked one or two times more about "suspending" Crozier's command and doing a quick inquiry, but Tom came back to the fact that he—and other uniformed members in Crozier's chain of command, he claimed—had "lost trust and confidence in Crozier to command" a nuclear-powered and fully armed aircraft carrier. The meeting ended with my support of Modly's decision, and everyone else in the room also agreeing to stand behind him.

A big part of being defense secretary was making or supporting decisions I knew were going to be unpopular. The decision to remove Captain Crozier was one such instance, but we did so with eyes wide open to the consequences, and braced for the fallout. While this action didn't play well politically, it was more important to remove a commander in whom the chain of command had little or no trust. This is especially true when that person commands an aircraft carrier patrolling the seas near the homeland of our greatest adversary.

Modly appeared in the Pentagon Briefing Room that afternoon and announced that Crozier had been relieved of command. He presented a detailed explanation for his decision and made clear that "Captain Crozier had allowed the complexity of his challenge with the COVID breakout on the ship to overwhelm his ability to act professionally, when acting professionally was what was needed most at the time." Tom added that he had "lost confidence . . . in his [Crozier's] ability to continue to lead that warship, as it fights through this virus, to get the crew healthy and so that it [can] continue to meet its important national security requirements."

Many pundits in the media and lawmakers on the Hill criticized the decision to remove Crozier. A video of the crew giving Crozier a rousing nighttime send-off that later surfaced exacerbated the external noise. This was tough for Tom, and he didn't handle it well. Like Crozier, he lost his composure. This resulted in behavior by him that warranted his resignation after he flew out to the *TR* in Guam—a thirty-six-hour round trip—to speak to the ship's crew. He said things he shouldn't have about the incident and Crozier— such as calling the captain "stupid." I knew it was hard for him, as he loved the Navy very much, but his resignation on April 7 was the best thing for the institution.

The Navy came back to me a few weeks later on April 24, following their preliminary investigation, and recommended reinstating Crozier. I told them I wanted to review the report and related documents before I gave them an answer. I spent the entire weekend poring through the materials, including (surprisingly) pivotal redacted items that had to be corrected and delivered to me at home. My assessment was that a full investigation was needed. The facts didn't justify any final conclusion at this point, and certainly not the one the CNO was making. If anything, it was the opposite. I felt the Navy just wanted to get the issue behind them as quickly as possible. More work was clearly needed, however. Deputy Secretary Norquist, General Milley, and Paul Ney, my general counsel, agreed with my decision.

On the morning of April 28, I spoke with James McPherson, the new acting secretary of the Navy, someone I knew and trusted from his service with me as the Army general counsel, and gave him my assessment. Jim was a very capable leader who knew the Navy, the Pentagon, and the law. I appointed him to the post following Modly's resignation, while we waited for Ken Braithwaite to be confirmed as the next secretary of the Navy.

I shared with him my views on the preliminary investigation and directed McPherson to "conduct a full investigation" and to "take it wherever it goes"—meaning beyond Crozier's actions in Guam, and "anywhere in the chain of command you need to go to get the truth." As McPherson got up to leave the meeting room, I looked him in the eye and added, "Jim, follow your standard procedures and practices, and do the right thing." He knew me well; he knew I meant it. "Yes, Mr. Secretary," he said.

The ultimate outcome of the full Navy investigation I ordered confirmed that Crozier had made errors in judgment that justified his relief.[25] At the Pentagon press briefing on June 19, 2020, when the final decision was announced, Admiral Gilday said, "I previously believed that Captain Crozier should be reinstated following his relief in April, after conducting an initial investigation." He continued, "The much broader, deeper investigation that we conducted in the weeks following that had a much deeper scope. It is my belief that both Admiral Baker [Crozier's immediate superior, the commander of Strike Group 9] and Captain Crozier fell well short of what we expect of those in command."

The CNO added, "If Captain Crozier were still in command today, I would be relieving him. Captain Crozier's primary responsibility was the safety and the well-being of the crew, so that the ship could remain as operationally ready as possible," but both Baker and Crozier "did not do enough, soon enough, to fulfill their primary obligation." In short, Gilday said, Crozier "exercised questionable judgment when he released sailors from quarantine on the ship, which put his crew at higher risk and may have increased the spread of the virus aboard the *Theodore Roosevelt*."[26]

Our collective instincts were correct. That said, if I had to do it all over again, I would have followed my gut and figured out a way to "suspend"—not fire—Crozier, while quickly conducting the investigation I later ordered to confirm or deny our instincts regarding his performance. That was my lesson learned. I was just glad I followed my inner voice and directed the broader investigation that ended up drawing out *all* of the facts.

The *TR* wouldn't return to sea until late May. COVID sidelined the ship for nearly two months. It was not a good chapter in Navy history, and at the time it hurt America's image with our allies and partners in the Indo-Pacific. It also gave China cause to cite their self-proclaimed "efficiency" in handling the virus as compared to the U.S. military. Beijing was already working hard to exploit the global pandemic, and the *TR* incident in particular, to their favor. I eventually had to call Admiral Gilday in May and direct him to get the ship to sea, even if some of the crew needed to stay on Guam until their quarantine was over. It was important that the *TR* get back to duty.

That said, the *TR* episode taught us things about the virus. At its peak in May, over 4,000 sailors had been moved off the ship, and more than 1,100 had tested positive for the virus. However, over half of the sailors who tested positive did not have symptoms, which ended up being an important fact for us to understand and absorb about asymptomatic transmission. We also ended up having few sailors hospitalized, which also told us something about the resiliency of our force, though one chief petty officer tragically succumbed to the virus.

Throughout the first ten months of my tenure as secretary of defense, I generally received good support from Democrats and Republicans alike on the Hill. And as I noted earlier, I had been easily confirmed in the third year of the Trump administration with 90 votes. Nevertheless, my support from the Hill wouldn't completely hold as we marched closer and closer to the election in November.

Despite all that the DoD had done in the previous few months—from providing extensive support to cities and states and bringing back Americans and medical supplies from abroad to accelerating contracts and payments to keep the production lines open at critical defense manufacturers, conducting vaccine and therapeutics research in our labs, and keeping the force healthy—ten Democratic senators decided it was time to attack. In a letter to me on April 27, in the wake of the *Theodore Roosevelt* outbreak, they argued that the DoD's civilian leadership was lacking and had "failed to act sufficiently, quickly, and has often prioritized [combat] readiness at the expense of the health of service members and their families."[27] Really?

Of course, their logic was backwards, which was why it fell short: the health of our service members was integral to mission readiness, which was why I made it priority one. Moreover, the argument simply failed to acknowledge the simple fact that, despite the Defense Department being on the front lines of the COVID-19 fight for more than three months, engaged directly with infected persons, only *one*—as tragic as any loss is—active-duty service member had succumbed to COVID-19.[28] The force and their families were in good shape, considering all that was happening.

I wasn't surprised to learn that Senator Elizabeth Warren (D-MA)—no friend of the military to begin with—led the cabal of ten, which included most of the Democrats who didn't vote to confirm me in the first place. Even less shocking was the fact that some of the signatories were actively posturing to be Joe Biden's running mate in the 2020 presidential election. This all seemed a political act to undermine the Trump administration and burnish their own credentials as campaign attack dogs.[29]

Ironically, I had spoken to governors of the states represented by the senators who signed the letter, and every single one of these governors had thanked me and praised the Pentagon's performance.[30] I often found the governors more reasonable to work with than some of their state's representatives in Congress.

Worse, I was troubled that they not only attacked me but also seemed to drag the institution and our people into the political fray. Their letter disrespected the more than sixty thousand soldiers, sailors, airmen, Marines, Space Force professionals, and National Guardsmen deployed across the nation to fight COVID, typically operating away from their families and usually at risk of their own lives, and I told the senators so in a letter back to Congress.

In that same letter, I pushed back on their "false or misleading assertions regarding the department's response to the . . . pandemic." We had been providing weekly updates to Congress, but neither the members nor staff from many of the offices writing me ever bothered to attend them. The Department has been "ahead of need at every step" and "met or exceeded every request for assistance we have received," I asserted.

We were also running planning drills based on worst-case scenarios of high hospitalization rates across the country, as was happening in New York City, and how we could free up more of our medical professionals, supplies, equipment, and treatment facilities to assist cities and towns hit hard. Doctors, nurses, and field hospitals of all types from the services were on alert to deploy.

What the lawmakers ignored was that the DoD had been fighting the coronavirus since late January, only days after doctors identified the first infected person in the United States. By February 1, 2020, we had issued detailed guidance to senior civilian and military leaders—each of whom have extensive medical staffs and resources—on how to address COVID. All this happened weeks before the first American succumbed to the virus.

We would go on to issue updated guidance several more times through the spring and summer, completely belying the senators' false charge about my "inability or unwillingness to issue clear, Department-wide guidance." These Force Health Protection Guidance memos were also "provided to congressional offices."[31] Moreover, the criticisms that morale was bad in the force and readiness was low were a bunch of bunk. The service secretaries, their chiefs, and the combatant commanders were telling me the opposite, and that's what the data was showing as well.

The DoD's long-standing practice of centralized planning and decentralized execution, coupled with a philosophy of putting trust in your subordinates and delegating to them the authority to make the best decisions for their situation, was the key to our success. With hundreds of thousands of service members spread out in over 150 countries around the globe—from the bitter cold of the Arctic to the hottest of deserts of the Middle East; from the jungles of Latin America to the mountains of Asia; from first-world countries in Europe with advanced medical systems to the poorest on earth in Africa with hardly a doctor in sight—we knew we had to give our commanders sufficient guidance, adequate resources, and the necessary authority to make the decisions best for their operating environment, their mission, and their people.

I came to believe that the criticism the DoD faced at times reflected differing leadership styles and governing philosophies, along with the fact that the military had trained leaders. It was manifesting itself in what was happening nationally. Democrats seemed to prefer a centralized, top-down approach to dealing with COVID-19, where Washington provided and directed relevant policies, authorities, resources, and equipment. They were also more willing to take dramatic measures to lock down the economy—or, in our case, shut down training and operations, even though these moves would affect us for years later. In some situations that was probably necessary. Republicans preferred the opposite approach, one that gave states the freedom to lead with assistance as necessary (or requested) from Washington and allowed more differentiated approaches and room for mistakes. The views and actions of blue state and red state governors often reflected these competing approaches.

We had some of that too in the Pentagon. A story in *Politico* criticized our decision to give local commanders flexibility in dealing with COVID. "Anonymous military officials," again, complained there was a lack of top-down planning and direction, despite the issuance of multiple guidance memos going back to January, implementation of our pandemic response plans, and twice-a-week discussions with senior leaders. That said, I believed in outcomes, not inputs.

A thought piece by the Brookings Institute—which many consider left leaning—buttressed the DoD's approach, asserting that clear direction from the Pentagon ensured the Department was staying ahead of the virus, giving credit to commanders for exercising the flexibility we gave them.[32] Even Dr. Anthony Fauci had advised that, in order to beat the virus, governors should be given clear guidance and then room to implement it.[33] That's exactly how the U.S. military operated, and that's exactly what we did.

All our armed services and combatant commands had extensive, highly capable headquarters, staffs, and medical personnel who ensured the health and readiness of the joint force. In addition, our leaders were well trained and top-notch. I had to trust them, and in the fact that we would be far better off in the long run by giving them the room to do what they do best—think, adapt, and lead based on their unique situations.

The numbers proved us right. By November 2020, the Department was still fortunate to lose only one active-duty service member—out of 1.2 million—to COVID-19. In the broader U.S. population, the ratio was one out of every 3,280 people, a 365-fold difference worse than the DoD. Seven members of the Reserve and National Guard had also tragically died, but it was always difficult to account for their actions when most were serving in uniform only a couple of days a month. Did they contract the virus at home, at their civilian job, or when they were under military authority during a monthly weekend drill? By early October, seven military dependents and fifty-nine DoD civilian employees had also died. Overall, our testing, infection, and hospitalization rates across all categories were usually much better than those of our civilian counterparts across the states.[34]

As spring began yielding to summer, Trump's rhetoric on the virus continued out of step with what was happening across the country.

Having missed the Easter reopening that he so dearly wanted, Trump grudgingly extended the COVID restrictions until the end of April to again try to get control of the virus. Frustrated, the president seemed to pick up the pace and volume when it came to downplaying the pandemic.

When I was with him in the White House and the topic came up, he would shake his head in frustration and complain that "the China flu" or "the plague" had killed "the greatest economy ever." He was right about what the virus did to the economy, but he never spoke about the thousands of lives lost or the people hurt by the virus. He would talk about small business owners—stores, restaurants, gyms—but not about the social fabric of the country being ripped apart. He really kept believing that COVID would simply go away, and that maybe if he kept talking about that happening, it would come to be.

On a few occasions, especially after the USS *Theodore Roosevelt* infection, the president would suggest giving the troops the antimalaria drug hydroxychloroquine to prevent and treat COVID. He was quite serious about it, once saying to me in a slightly hushed tone in the Oval Office, "I'm taking it. I feel great. It's a miracle." He waved his arms around as he spoke. I turned to him said, "Mr. President, I'll look into it. We certainly need to protect our folks." He added, "You'd be surprised at how many people are taking it. Many are taking it. I've heard a lot of good stories about it." "I'll speak to our doctors about it," I replied, "and have them check it out." "You do that," he said with a very serious look on his face, "they'll tell you it's great."

I was not studied on the drug, other than what I was reading in the papers. I was open to anything, pulling the thread on many ideas with my staff during this period to help boost the troops' immune systems, such as possibly encouraging service members to take vitamin D and zinc supplements. True to my commitment to the president, I did raise the issue at one of the Department's next COVID meetings, but the staff doctors were not enthusiastic about it. The president called me once at home over a weekend to follow up on his idea, but thankfully he never really pressed me to administer it to the force.

At the Pentagon, we were hoping for the best, planning for the worst, and dealing with the present. Our three priorities remained intact as we worked our way through each challenge presented by the virus. I never tried to sugarcoat the situation or provide false hope to our folks, which always risked conflict with the White House message, but surprisingly never seemed to catch their attention.

For example, during a May 7 visit to Northern Command in Colorado I told the media, "We are preparing for a second wave and maybe more," and "We don't know what the trajectory of this virus will be."[35] This ran completely contrary to Trump's assertions that the virus was under control and that it will soon "go away." It wasn't the first time I had said something along these lines. In late March, when the president was saying he wanted the economy "opened up and just raring to go by Easter," I was warning all of the DoD in a virtual town hall to "plan for this to be a few months long at least." I was sure saying so would get me in trouble with the White House, but it seemed that during the tough months of the pandemic the media thankfully wasn't trying to stir conflict between the Pentagon and the White House like some would later. Or maybe they weren't paying close enough attention. Either way, this was a welcome surprise.

The fact was, no one knew what course this pandemic would run. We invited Doctors Fauci and Birx to brief us during one of our staff meetings, and we kicked around a series of questions and scenarios to aid in our plans and preparations.

Meanwhile, I had to keep reminding people, especially outside of the DoD, that while the entire country focused on COVID inside the United States, the Defense Department still had to worry about protecting the nation from external threats and safeguarding our interests abroad. The world didn't stop because COVID was rampant in America. In fact, many of our adversaries were looking to capitalize off the virus, from terrorist groups in the Middle East to rogue states like Iran, and to peer/near-peer adversaries such as Russia and China. For us, that meant keeping our service members as healthy and ready as possible—priority number one of three.

At the same time, some outside and inside the Pentagon still thought we should completely shut down recruiting and basic training for all of the DoD. That would have been a major mistake, one that would have taken years to remedy. Creating an empty bubble like that in the personnel pipeline would have significant impacts down the road on manning and readiness. We had seen this before. Fortunately, most of the armed services agreed on this and were willing to make only short-term reductions in the numbers they inducted; this allowed for more social distancing and sufficient medical capacity for testing and treatment. Our results proved this decision to be a prudent one.

Moreover, being secretary of defense isn't all about war plans, foreign policy, and future weapons systems. I was also responsible for a 2.8-million-person force of service members and DoD civilians, which includes the family members of anybody on active duty. That meant we were also responsible for the health, welfare, and education of approximately 1.6 million military dependents. When you add in retirees and others, the military medical system was responsible for nearly 10 million beneficiaries.[36]

In June, we began planning for the fall semester of K–12 classes to restart at DoD schools across the nation and overseas. Part of our strategizing included initiatives to issue over 8,000 laptop computers and establish more than 250 Wi-Fi hotspots for students who couldn't attend class in person. Nevertheless, if we wanted to maximize the readiness and effectiveness of Department employees within the constraints that COVID was currently presenting, we needed to get our child-care centers and schools open.

Most people are probably not aware that the Department of Defense Education Activity operates "160 schools in 8 Districts located in 11 countries, 7 states, and 2 territories." Moreover, there are "nearly 900,000 military connected children of all ages worldwide, of which more than 66,000 are enrolled in DoDEA schools."[37]

Across the military, the Defense Department also "oversees over 800 Child Development Centers" on military installations around the world.[38] Over the course of COVID, our centers had been in various stages of opening. Like the schools, much of this depended upon the health and willingness of adult providers to come to work, and the willingness of parents to send their kids to child care.

By the summer, Trump was pushing hard for schools all around the country to open. We wanted to do the same at the DoD, but the reality was something else. With schools and child-care centers all around the world, we had to take a conditions-based approach—like with so many other things—which would allow local commanders to make the decision based on what was happening in their communities.

With most kids scheduled to return to school in early September, we simply weren't ready or able to open the schools in many locales due to COVID rates and government policies in certain areas. This never made national news, thank goodness. I was concerned that someone in the White House would read about this, report it to the president, and then we'd get an order to change our policy and open 100 percent of our schools and child-care centers, regardless of what was happening with COVID. This would have put the DoD in a tough spot, though I'm confident the health of our kids would always come first.

On top of all this, we were diligently staying in close contact with the states. With the president occasionally sparring with some governors, we knew it was critical to stay out of those issues and keep the lines of communication open. The head of the National Guard, General Joe Lengyel, and later General Dan Hokanson, would speak weekly with the adjutant generals, the top military officers in each state. Meanwhile, I was frequently talking with governors—and had spoken with nearly all of them by the summer, and sometimes mayors as well—to make sure they were getting all the support they needed to deal with COVID.

Across the board, the governors were professional, appreciative, and thankful for our support; politics and their disagreements with the White House never crept into our conversations. I was thankful we were able to stay off the White House's radar screen as we continued this outreach.

By the end of summer, we had been hard at work combating COVID for over eight months. We had provided medical support, PPE, and other supplies to federal agencies working in hotspots around the country in support of the American people. We had offered much of the same to some of our allies and partners around the world. Moreover, through the Defense Production Act, we announced over $500 million worth of contracts to sustain essential domestic industrial base capabilities.

Meanwhile, 125 DoD labs had performed more than 500,000 COVID clinical diagnostic tests—significant numbers at the time—as part of our work to enable the safe deployment of forces across the globe. We were testing an average of 40,000 or more service members weekly, peaking at times to over 50,000, to gauge the health of the force. Yet just when we started to see some light at the end of the tunnel, COVID would rise up somewhere. So off we would send our medical professionals once again.[39] It wasn't hard to figure out that the way to beat this virus—and to end the suffering, fear, and turmoil—was to develop a safe and effective vaccine, and to do so quickly.

CHAPTER 10

OPERATION WARP SPEED

On May 15, 2020, President Trump announced Operation Warp Speed, the administration's national program to accelerate the development, manufacturing, and distribution of COVID-19 vaccines, therapeutics, and diagnostics. It would turn out to be one of the most successful public-private partnerships in history, especially when it came to addressing a national crisis of the magnitude we faced—one that affected nearly every American. It would also turn out to be one of the best partnerships ever between two executive branch departments.

The Warp Speed goal was clear and simple: "produce and deliver 300 million doses of safe and effective vaccines with the initial doses available by January 2021."[1]

The strategy was equally straightforward. The Defense Department and Health and Human Services would work *together* on Operation Warp Speed (OWS), with HHS responsible for vaccine and therapeutic research and development, and the DoD charged with the eventual manufacturing and distribution of the vaccines. Both departments would also work hand in glove with the private sector to accomplish these tasks.

The idea for OWS began with HHS Secretary Alex Azar, a slight, middle-aged former pharmaceutical industry executive with a reputation as a scrappy bureaucratic infighter who often spoke with passion and a bias for action. Alex brought to the Trump administration a solid combination of government and corporate experience. He leveraged both to create a second Manhattan Project endeavor—one that would deploy the full powers and resources of the federal government to bring vaccines into production faster than any of the experts thought possible.

Alex was having a difficult time inside the administration from late January 2020 onward, however. The president was not happy with HHS's and the CDC's performance, Azar's relationship with Vice President Pence and his office was strained, and others within the White House were quietly bad-mouthing him to Trump and the media. The president was asking others, "How is Azar doing?" and "What do you think of Alex Azar?" These were presidential tells that he was seeking confirmation from others that he should fire Alex. It had gotten so bad that by the third week in April, odds were that Alex would be out by May 1.

Azar told me later that his strategy was to seek Mark Meadows's help in shutting down the press leaks, while also "lying low" with the president, meaning he would try to stay "out of sight and out of mind" as best he could until things cooled down. "Let Trump come to you," he once said, "that's when you know the worst is behind you."

On Saturday, April 25, Alex called me at home as he took a walk through his neighborhood. He wanted to enlist my support for his project. His pitch was threefold: first, that we needed to save lives; second, that the country was being devastated economically; and third, that if China or Russia produced a vaccine before the United States, "it could dramatically change the landscape of global influence." We agreed on all three points. We needed to get off our heels and on the offensive as a country.

The third item regarding the international landscape was a clever pitch by Azar to enlist my support, given the rocky relations HHS and the DoD had years earlier when it came to other projects. Interdepartmental history aside, it was true that Beijing was already declaring that the United States and other western democracies were in decline. They were using PPE supplies and the promise of an early vaccine as soft power to court a number of key countries around the globe. I told Alex, "I am having similar discussions about this with my counterparts in Asia and Europe. We need to develop a vaccine first, and then share it as broadly as possible." I would raise the "sharing" issue with him and Mike Pompeo a couple times in the months that followed.

Alex's view was that we were "in an un-resource-constrained environment," and that "we should put everything we have against this." I took in his words as I heard cars passing by and a dog barking in the background of his late afternoon stroll. With Congress already having spent $3 trillion on COVID, and the pandemic raging across the country, I concurred, adding there was "no amount of money that we could credibly spend on vaccine development that wouldn't have a high return on investment."

He then said this effort "should be a whole of government approach," with which I agreed, and that we should organize a "board of directors that involves all of us," with which I disagreed. The board he proposed meant HHS, the DoD, and other departments he was reaching out to, such as Energy, Veterans Affairs, Agriculture, and Homeland Security.

I told Alex I liked the vaccine idea, "and while I'm a team player," I said, "only DoD and HHS should lead this initiative." I added, "A big board will slow things down." Plus, I was also concerned about some of the White House staff who could end up either on the board or inviting themselves to the meetings. I didn't want their bad behaviors and toxic personal politics corrupting what could be the best chance we had to beat COVID and save lives.

"Let's meet early next week, lay out how to operate this, and you and I will chair this and get the job done." Alex agreed. We ran two of the largest departments in the executive branch, and the most relevant ones to the task, and personally got along well. I was confident we could pull this off.

The HHS secretary and I had begun working together in late January, when the DoD opened an air base in California to receive, quarantine, and care for Americans returning from China. Alex and I both had spent a lot of time in D.C. around government and understood how things should work, so simple things like bringing home and taking care of our fellow Americans wasn't as difficult as it might otherwise have been.

We had also both worked in the private sector, which gave us helpful perspectives in the months ahead. Some members of Congress, ironically, objected to political appointees with relevant corporate backgrounds, believing that it somehow corrupted their oath and sense of duty to the American people. Go figure. We found such experience to be an invaluable asset.

Finally, we both had witnessed how badly things can become if departments (and really, the cabinet secretaries) don't work well together. The tone, after all, is set at the top. We were determined to make sure that past mistakes didn't happen again, particularly with the country facing a health crisis of the likes we hadn't seen since 1918.

Azar and I had stayed in touch over the weeks and months as the Pentagon opened additional military bases for returning Americans; provided HHS respirators, ventilators, and other medical items; and orchestrated the delivery of medical supplies from producers abroad. The institutional relationship was working out well, and we had a personal friendship that made things doubly easy.

Our mission now would take both departments' relationship to a new level. We had to deploy the full weight of HHS's scientific and medical expertise, coupled with the DoD's planning, operations, contracting, and logistics skills, and partner closely with the private sector, to develop vaccines faster than any expert thought possible. It usually takes five to ten years to develop, test, and approve a vaccine. We wanted to get it done in under eight months. With that, we launched the largest and most successful biomedical public-private partnership in history.

The first meeting to discuss OWS was by secure video the morning of April 29, a few days after my weekend conversation with Azar. With senior leaders from both departments present, our purpose was to map out how best to organize a massive effort to develop a vaccine for COVID.

We agreed up front again that money was not the issue. Everyone needed to understand that. The White House and Congress, we assumed, would support what we put forward if it made sense and showed promise. Our challenges, rather, were time, science, and bureaucracy, as well as access to supplies and raw materials manufactured overseas.

When it came to the timeline, we knew that we would have to move fast, before more people died. We set an initial deadline of

November 1 for a delivery of first doses of a vaccine with no less than 50 percent efficacy. A combination of factors would eventually push this deadline back to the end of December.

Regarding the science, which was in HHS's wheelhouse, Azar spoke about the need to pursue a wide range of technologies, from traditional vaccines and virus vector vaccines to novel messenger RNA approaches. Having already visited our military medical research facilities in Maryland, I understood some of this based on what they were pursuing. Dr. Fauci was on the call as well and chirped in with his support for a broad, multipronged approach.

Finally, the regulatory hurdles and timelines were a major challenge. With regard to the first, some rules were unnecessarily high and arbitrary. When it came to traditional vaccine approval timelines, we didn't have years to work through the standard process. The senior folks from the Food and Drug Administration (FDA) who were on the call were going to look hard at how to break down unneeded barriers and accelerate the timeline. We all agreed that no steps would be skipped when it came to safety—it would remain sacrosanct—but regarding efficacy, most of us agreed that some immunity was better than none. HHS would take the lead on these things.

Acceleration of production and eventual distribution was another topic. We agreed to pursue multiple vaccines simultaneously, and to begin production contemporaneous with the clinical trials. We were hedging, putting our bets down on multiple paths. In our view, time was far more important than money. If we could save months by starting production of a vaccine as soon as it began the trials—which typically spanned three distinct phases over a years-long period—then we would be that much further ahead, and closer to our deadline, than if we did things sequentially, the traditional way. We would eventually reduce a multiyear process down to several months.

The risk was that we could lose hundreds of millions of dollars if we began production of a vaccine that proved to be ineffective. We would have to throw out the doses like tossing expired food out of the refrigerator. However, in our view, the lives saved if we could get vaccines out one, three, or six months sooner than normal was well worth the financial risk.

Moreover, while you can't put a price on life, assessing the economic impact was something else. Calculations done later estimated that COVID cost the United States billions of dollars in GDP every day the country was shut down. OWS would save lives *and* pay for itself.

The meeting broke up after about an hour. It was very successful, with broad agreement on the general goal, timeline, and strategy. Now, we needed to figure out how to organize OWS and who would lead it. It was obvious to me that HHS should have overall leadership; after all, this was a national health crisis. I committed to provide whatever support the DoD could to ensure mission success; Azar did the same with HHS.

The HHS secretary was impressed with the logistical muscle, project management, contracting, and planning that the DoD brought to every task. He saw that in action when we deployed our medical ships and field hospitals into cities across the United States and when we set up the alternative care facilities like the Javits Center in New York City. Azar was right. This was our sweet spot.

Between our two departments now, we needed to figure out how to organize it. I gave David Norquist and General John Hyten, the vice chairman of the Joint Chiefs of Staff—both of whom were in the meeting—the task to start developing options.

We met again early in the morning on Friday, May 1, a couple days later, in the massive Nunn-Lugar conference room on the E-ring of the Pentagon. Azar and his team came over from HHS. Many of my same folks from the previous meeting were in the room again. This time Jared Kushner joined us too, along with Adam Boehler, a close friend of his who ran the U.S. International Development Finance Corporation. The focus was on leadership, structure, and authorities, followed by how OWS would fit into all the other intra-governmental activities and functions out there.

By this session, I had zeroed in on General Gus Perna as the lead for the DoD. He had worked for me as the head of Army Material Command when I was secretary of the Army. He was an outstanding leader and terrific team player, and he was the Army's top logistician. He also had impeccable integrity and no ego. Too often, important projects fail—especially ones that must share power or work across organizational lines—because leaders fall short in one or more of these attributes. I knew that wouldn't be the case for Perna. He would set the proper tone for everyone on his team who had to interact with HHS, FDA, and other federal agencies.

Azar had not yet decided on his lead for vaccine development, but he would eventually select Moncef Mohamed Slaoui, an accomplished Moroccan-born, Belgian American researcher who was the former head of GlaxoSmithKline's vaccines department. He possessed many of the same attributes that Perna did. Moreover, for two individuals who came from vastly different personal and professional backgrounds, their partnership would make all the difference when it came to OWS's ultimate success. I shared a draft document with Azar about how to organize Warp Speed, allocating duties and responsibilities for each, but Perna and Slaoui largely figured it all out on their own and made it happen.

The last part of our meeting that day was the most interesting. Azar was still having many difficulties with the White House, he told me. Not everyone took COVID seriously. There were "too many cooks in the kitchen," he said, "and the decision making is slow and unreliable." Worse yet, the Coronavirus Task Force was assessing everything "through a political lens," he complained. The infighting that was occurring spilled over into personal friction between several individuals. All of this was hurting the effort. Jared Kushner saw many of the same challenges and obstacles that Azar did. We all feared that a traditional interagency structure would bog down OWS—which was my original concern over a big board—and deny us the opportunity to quickly develop a vaccine that saved lives.

I liked Jared and the approach he took to problems. He was always very pleasant, professional, and businesslike in his manner with me, and worked off facts, data, and sound arguments. This was a very DoD-like and corporate approach. In addition, while he understood politics and was heavily engaged on that front, I never really saw it steer him from the right solution. Tall, thin, and unflappable, Jared was someone I also found able to get things done as no one else could and never saw him play the internal politics of personal destruction like others did. For all these reasons, we worked together well.

Kushner committed to provide top cover for OWS. He was going to run interference for HHS and the DoD—especially with the Task Force—and report directly to the president on our progress. He would also use that lever if others in the White House, or the interagency, started getting in the way. Alex and I would cochair the initiative with a small executive board of our own folks. This would allow us to "make decisions quickly and efficiently with limited relitigation," as we often said. It was a very important moment, outlining the key roles we would play, and traps we would avoid, to ensure we accomplished our mission on time. A simple handshake between us consummated the deal.

Not surprisingly, in the days that followed, some senior officials at the White House were unhappy that the DoD and HHS engineered OWS behind the scenes, unbeknownst to them, and were working without their involvement. One person later told the media, "We were blindsided by it" and "They wouldn't brief the task force on it."[2] Oh well.

Following the president's announcement of Operation Warp Speed in the Rose Garden on May 15, Perna and Slaoui took off running with the OWS ball. Perna would send me written updates every Friday, followed by a face-to-face discussion with Norquist, Milley, Hyten, Stewart, and me each week as well. He would brief us on vaccine and therapeutic development, as well as his efforts to get manufacturing moving and his distribution plans set. At the end of the meeting, I would ask Perna each time if he had everything he needed—people, money, authority, etc.—to get the job done.

We had some initial challenges at the Pentagon getting everyone behind him and OWS, but I quickly put that resistance to bed. I spoke often about my support for Perna and OWS, so the DoD bureaucracy figured out that this was a priority. We continued to have the internal critics who would leak stories and memos to create political mischief, and some in the media would dutifully report it— such as the draft Pentagon memo written weeks before OWS was established that reportedly said there was a "real possibility" that a vaccine would not be available until "at least the summer of 2021."[3] I guess that story was wrong.

I also had David Norquist participating in every senior-level update meeting hosted by HHS. I would occasionally join as well, but David was top-notch and knew how to make things happen if there was ever a need. Moreover, it was essential that we had a second empowered, knowledgeable DoD official at the table to see this initiative through, which became increasingly important as the odds of Trump firing me increased after June 3.

Norquist also played a critical role in identifying the need to protect OWS and the companies involved from cyber spying and theft, working closely with Cyber Command to put appropriate safeguards in place to protect vaccine development from being stolen or compromised by the Russians or Chinese. General Perna told us soon thereafter "security was on track" when it came to "government agencies helping companies" with cyber protection and other needs.

At one of his weekly briefings in early July, Perna reported that vaccine development was "making good progress," with higher-than-expected efficacy (at the time, in the low 80s percentiles), and with a contract for 100 million doses scheduled to be signed with Pfizer later in the month. A Moderna contract would soon follow. This was on top of the 300 million doses of AstraZeneca/Oxford we had contracted for in May. Meanwhile, clinical trials were beginning. Even then, Perna reported "strong confidence that we will get a vaccine . . . on time." As such, he was already speaking with major distributors, whether it was FedEx and UPS, or CVS and Walmart.

A month later, in August, six companies were under contract. Pfizer and Moderna trials were ongoing, and Perna was on track with his planning for manufacturing and distribution. Contrary to what the president was saying publicly, though, the DoD was not going to be part of the distribution system. General Perna was telling me that, barring some type of emergency, he was "100% confident that DoD will not be part of the distribution."

It wasn't that the DoD couldn't do this or opposed doing so. We just wanted to use the established logistical network of the commercial sector that reached all across and in every nook and cranny of

America. In addition, it was a good way to prime the economy and get people back to work. I tried to clarify that with the president on a few occasions, but it never seemed to stick. Later in the summer, I would become concerned that the media would focus in on this contradiction and ask me to somehow explain the president's mis-statements.

We also had issues come up at times that were challenging enough that I had to give guidance or direct a specific action. Some-times it involved use of the Defense Production Act; other times it involved keeping Perna and OWS out of the media spotlight; and at one point in the fall we were asked about distribution policy. The last thing the DoD should be doing is making recommendations on which Americans should be vaccinated first, second, third, or last. This should come from the CDC and the medical community, and it should be discussed with the White House and Congress. I instructed Perna to stay out of this and decline to comment. I didn't want any suggestion that the military was deciding who would be vaccinated or when.

That said, the HHS plans first briefed to me in September put the elderly, medical professionals, and people with comorbidities at the top of the list. Vaccines would be allocated on a pro rata basis to the states and other jurisdictions based on their numbers in each of these categories, because in the early days the number of doses would be limited. The prioritization would remain unchanged up until my departure.

By September, the OWS distribution plan was fairly well devel-oped. In addition to manufacturing vaccines, Perna had also con-tracted for all the associated PPE, syringes, alcohol wipes, and other items needed to put shots into arms. Perna was meeting with the distribution companies, as well as state health advisers, to fine-tune the plans, which numbered 65 when you tacked the state, territory, and big-city plans on top of the national one. He also went about synchronizing and rehearsing these plans. I was scheduled to participate in the November distribution rehearsals, after the operational plan was briefed to me. Everything was coming together according to the strategy.

The distribution plan was complicated in execution, but simple in design. In short, the DoD would coordinate vaccine delivery with each jurisdiction, sending vaccines wherever they wanted—for example, to hospitals, nursing homes, and pharmacies. The private sector supply chain would deliver the vaccines, using well-known companies such as McKesson, UPS, and FedEx. The so-called last mile, which received such negative press early in the distribution process, included pharmacies such as CVS and Walgreens; they would eventually receive their supplies through the Federal Pharmacy Partnership formally activated in February 2021. They planned to administer the shots at their stores and, in some cases, to send medical professionals to long-term-care facilities around the states. Nursing homes, for example, would be a priority care facility.

In his update to me on October 6, Perna felt good about the distribution plans. "It's all about the trials, now," he said, and the ability to get through them and the approval process in a timely manner. Issues had cropped up along the way that cost us some time, but it was important that we have public confidence in the vaccines. "The science should drive the decisions," I said to him. This was something we couldn't rush, of course. The good news was, the OWS team was working well together and according to Perna, they were receiving "no pressure" from the White House. As I asked at the end of every single meeting, Perna told me he had everything he needed from the department and me.

In his last briefing to me on November 4, General Perna told me that "everything is on track" and that the government purchased "over 800 million doses" of various vaccines. He reported that "$12 billion has been spent to date, but the final number will be closer to $26 billion." We all agreed it was well worth the lives saved. The OWS team made steady, solid progress. It was good to hear, and not a bad way for me to leave after moving this forward for more than seven months.

Operation Warp Speed ended up being an overwhelming success. The FDA approved the Pfizer and Moderna vaccines for emergency use in mid-December, two weeks ahead of our deadline.[4] We reduced a process that normally takes five to ten years down to around eight months. And we not only met our time goal, we also doubled our success with *two* different vaccines.

Efficacy for both vaccines was 95 percent or higher, nearly *doubling* the 50 percent standard set by the FDA, another major achievement. With several hundred million doses already purchased, tens of millions were available by the end of 2020. The government had more than 39 million doses on hand by January 1, and it distributed over 17 million doses by January 6, according to the CDC. Moreover, the strategy of purchasing hundreds of millions of doses from multiple companies gave us resiliency in addition to supply.

Notwithstanding the success of OWS's vaccine development and manufacturing, there were challenges in vaccine administration and reporting, but politicians and the media exaggerated the problems in the midst of a heated, partisan, postelection transition period. Much of this was unfair to Perna, Slaoui, and all the other federal employees and military personnel at HHS and the DoD, as well as the commercial companies who worked so hard for over eight months to make OWS successful and get the American people vaccinated.

One of the biggest issues the media covered was the reported delay between doses delivered and shots made. General Perna and his team had rehearsed the distribution plans with the states and other key stakeholders in the fall. But once the vaccines were approved in December, several factors came into play that would aggravate the normal kinks that need to be worked out in the early days of any logistical endeavor: delays in reporting, insufficiently trained staff, health-care workers declining to be vaccinated, lost time in notifying people to get shots, too much time spent on paperwork or answering patients' questions, keeping vaccinated persons on-site to monitor them, and so on.

But another major contributor, to be fair, was also a communications shortcoming by the administration. We simply didn't do a good job with strategic comms—managing the public's expectations, letting them know that ramping up the rate at which we put shots in arms would take time. It would take a couple of weeks alone in some cases, for example, to hire the medical personnel that could deliver the "last feet" of the "last mile" shot in the arm.

These delays led to a bad narrative in the early days and weeks, which in turn fed into the new administration's talking points that they would be the ones to fix Trump's broken program. I was disappointed that the incoming Biden team would later start saying that there was really no distribution plan at all, and that they had to start from scratch. It all seemed to be a concerted effort to tarnish and reject anything associated with the Trump administration. They tried to reset the bar very low by denigrating a lot of hard work by many good people, with the aim of coming back months later to claim victory over COVID. I guess they thought that was good politics.

However, it was pure politics, and it wasn't consistent with Joe Biden's promise to bring people together and unify the nation. All it did was further divide Americans and diminish public confidence in and support for the vaccines. Jeff Zients, coordinator of Biden's

COVID-19 task force, for example, said, "There really was no plan to ramp up the supply of those vaccines."[5] President Biden stated on February 25, "We're moving in the right direction, though, despite the mess we inherited from the previous administration, which left us with no real plan to vaccinate all Americans."[6] Whoever gave the president those BS talking points did not serve him well.

The fact is, more than 16 million doses of vaccine had already been administered by inauguration day. Shots were being given at a rate of several million per week by January 20, 2021, which would become the average pace for the Biden administration through the summer of that year.

In late March 2021, Slaoui would finally weigh in by asserting that 90 percent of the Biden administration's vaccine roll-out plan was the same as the Trump plan. He acknowledged early missteps in the Trump administration's distribution plan, such as the need to better educate the public on the roll-out pace but also commended the Biden team's idea to use sports arenas to help increase vaccination capacity, even if just marginally.[7] Dr. Anthony Fauci agreed with most of this.

It would take a while, but to their credit, the media started reporting the truth that many of the new administration's "accomplishments" and "initiatives" on the vaccine front were attributed to Operation Warp Speed. Some would note that "Biden's playbook for vaccine distribution has relied heavily on a system created by the Trump administration," and that "when Biden called for '100 million shots in 100 days'—a pace of 1 million shots per day—former health officials noted that the U.S. had already exceeded that rate by the week of Biden's inauguration in mid-January."[8]

Anthony Fauci said, "Operation Warp Speed will go down historically as a highly successful endeavor, which allowed us to do things with regard to the timing of it and the effectiveness of it in a way that a few years ago people never would have imagined." He added, "It was a combination, of the fundamental basic science that was done right here at the NIH [National Institutes of Health], as well as places that were funded by the NIH and by the Department of Defense and other government agencies." He was generous in giving credit to both HHS and the DoD.[9]

Despite all the politics of the moment, I am confident that historians will look back upon OWS as the incredible partnership and accomplishment that it was. Not only did it deliver hope to the American people when they needed it most, it delivered on its promise to create a vaccine by the end of the year. With well over five hundred thousand dead to COVID-19, our economy in a poor state, and the social fabric of the country in tatters, a safe and effective vaccine was always going to be our best bet for a return to normal, whatever that will look like in a postpandemic world.

Stepping back and assessing 2020 more broadly, I couldn't have been prouder of the DoD's performance during the pandemic. We held true to our three priorities of protecting our people, ensuring the nation's security, and providing support to the whole-of-nation response to COVID in a multitude of ways. By the time I left office in November, we were fortunate that still only one active-duty service member had succumbed to the virus, with fewer than ten combined for our Guard and Reserve forces as well. Every loss is a tragedy, and we mourned them all. I was thankful that there were so few.

At the same time, we continued to defend our interests, our allies, and our partners against threats ranging from North Korea and Syria to Iraq and Afghanistan. We stood up to increased Chinese military activity in the western Pacific, and continued Russian intrusions into American and allied airspace. Moreover, we proceeded with the full-speed implementation of the National Defense Strategy, and its clarion call to modernize the military, strengthen our alliances, and reform the DoD. We did all of this while also sharing medical professionals, supplies, knowledge, and assistance with many of our foreign partners.

Finally, we stepped forward when the nation called, from the earliest days of the pandemic in January to the present day, to assist the American people in fighting the scourge of COVID in all fifty states and territories. We built health-care facilities across the country, deployed hospital ships, and augmented civilian doctors and nurses across the land with our own uniformed professionals. We brought medical supplies and U.S. citizens back to the States, caring for many of them on our bases while they quarantined. And we worked with HHS to develop, test, manufacture, and distribute vaccines as part of Operation Warp Speed.

Over the course of the year, the DoD committed more than sixty thousand service members to the front lines of the pandemic. Many of them left their homes, their families, and their communities on short notice, unsure of what the future would bring, and they often risked their own lives to help their fellow Americans. We should all be proud of their integrity, their professionalism, and their dedication to duty. I certainly am.

CHAPTER 11

DESPERATE MEASURES

"We have many options for Venezuela, and by the way, I'm not going to rule out a military option," President Trump declared in 2017.[1]

Though Venezuela was on President Trump's mind since my confirmation as secretary of defense in July 2019, it remained on the back burner as tensions continued with Iran through the rest of the year. The operations in Iraq from late December 2019 through early January 2020 seemed to sate Trump's appetite for military action for a while longer. However, talk about acting against Caracas resurfaced not long thereafter as interactions between the oil-rich South American country and Iran deepened. Both countries were evading U.S. sanctions as we looked for ways to shut those activities down.

In 1998, the breakdown in Venezuela's political system brought Hugo Chavez, a charismatic military officer, to power. Chavez promised to end corruption and eradicate poverty, two themes that appealed to the millions of poor and working-class people he considered his base. His socialist policies to improve health care, housing, and economic equality saw temporary success early on, but inevitably resulted in massive poverty, high inflation, and other economic woes. Chavez dismantled the country's democracy during this period, while also suppressing critics, clamping down on the press, and manipulating electoral laws, among other things.

Upon Chavez's death in 2013, Nicolás Maduro, a former bus driver, trade union leader, and member of the National Assembly who had become part of Chavez's inner circle, succeeded him as president. Under Maduro, Venezuela fell into even greater social, economic, and political disrepair. Mass protests resulted the year following his inauguration, prompting Maduro to press down even harder on dissent by using lethal force against protesters, arbitrary imprisonment, and extrajudicial killings, all of which would force millions of Venezuelans to flee the country.[2]

On January 23, 2019, less than two weeks after Maduro began his second term as president, Juan Guaidó—the head of the opposition-controlled National Assembly—declared himself interim president in accordance with the nation's constitution. Maduro quickly denounced this move as a coup sponsored by the United States. Meanwhile, over fifty governments worldwide, including the Trump administration, formally recognized Guaidó as the legitimate head of Venezuela. Russia, China, Iran, Syria, Cuba, and other countries, however, continued to regard Maduro as the nation's leader.

Trump had been fixated on Venezuela since the early days of his administration, with an eye toward using military force to oust Maduro. It was August 11, 2017, when he spoke about the "many options for Venezuela," including military ones, that I cited up front.[3] In his book *The Room Where It Happened*, John Bolton recalls Trump telling him at the White House a year later to "get it done." To Bolton, this meant "get rid of the Maduro regime." Bolton goes on to recount Trump saying, "'This is the fifth time I've asked for it.'"[4]

On April 30, 2019, a little more than six weeks before Trump named me acting secretary of defense, Guaidó led a group of Venezuelan military officials and civilian personnel in an uprising to remove Maduro. It failed due to insufficient support from senior military officers, with dozens of people injured and several killed in the clashes that followed.[5] Maduro blamed Trump for the uprising. Bolton and Pompeo took to the airwaves to praise Guaidó's efforts, condemn Maduro, and criticize Russia for its support, with Pompeo saying, "If that's [military action] what's required, that's what the United States will do."[6]

The failure of Guaidó and his fellow plotters marked the end of a critical phase in the Trump administration's attempts to rid the Venezuelan people of Maduro. This setback seemed to take the wind out of the sails of those who had worked to restore democracy in Venezuela and end the humanitarian disaster. Pompeo and Bolton would occasionally talk about "how close we came" to freeing the Venezuelan people. For Trump, it hardened his view that Maduro was "strong" and Guaidó was "weak." He couldn't see Guaidó as president of the country, let alone able to overthrow Maduro, which dampened his enthusiasm to support him.

That said, getting rid of Maduro still seemed to be a bucket list item for Trump. I never heard him articulate why it was so important, though he did speak at times of the suffering of the Venezuelan people. He would dip his head, shake it slowly, and say in a plaintive tone, "How terrible it must be for those poor people" to live there. It seemed sincere, but knowing Trump as I came to do, I hardly felt this was his main motivation. In his book, Bolton mentions the president's interest in gaining access to Venezuela's oil reserves.[7] I heard Trump talk about this a couple of times myself. He once said "we should get the oil" when military action was discussed, and on other occasions wanted to make sure the United States had "full access"—unfettered as well by any previous agreements with Russia or China—to the country's resources if Maduro was dislodged by us. It was consistent with the view he took about the United States gaining control of the oil fields in eastern Syria when we were dealing with the issue of American support to the Syrian Democratic Forces in the fall of 2019.

Trump simply seemed to view these things as opportunities to make money, which didn't surprise me, given his business background and view of wealth as a metric of success. Such actions were, however, at odds with long-standing U.S. policies and practices and, in most cases, international law.

Bolton once shared with me his view that "it's all about the votes for him [Trump]; there's no principle behind it." John was correct. I recalled from my time as the national policy director on Fred Thompson's presidential campaign in 2007 that Cuban Americans and other pro-democracy groups—in this case, Venezuelan Americans—could really deliver come election time. Trump wouldn't be the first presidential candidate to cater to political groups such as these, especially in vote-rich Florida. There were, however, very good humanitarian and strategic reasons for supporting Guaidó and the opposition in Venezuela.

Maduro was a dictator, and what he and Chavez did to the Venezuelan people was horrific. Furthermore, allowing countries like Russia, China, and Iran to gain, or strengthen, a foothold in the Western Hemisphere was of great concern. However, none of these reasons justified risking the lives of American service members, a view I believe Pompeo and Bolton shared. There were other ways to address these issues. Yet again and again, Trump would ask for military options.

On December 12, 2019, I hosted the weekly breakfast for Mike Pompeo and Robert O'Brien at my office in the Pentagon. O'Brien had replaced Bolton in mid-September, so he was relatively new and eager to learn. These meetings were a good opportunity to discuss a wide range of issues privately, and to make sure we were coordinated. Over time, unfortunately, they would end.

Venezuela hadn't come up in months, but near the end of the meeting O'Brien said his team was working on several items that would be coming our way at some point, one of which was "next steps on Venezuela." I jotted it down as we all stood to depart.

I flew to Europe on December 15 to celebrate the seventy-fifth anniversary of the Battle of the Bulge, sharing the experience with my old unit—the 101st Airborne Division "Screaming Eagles"—in Bastogne, Belgium. On the way home a few days later, my staff informed me that the National Security Council had held a meeting to discuss military options for Venezuela. While the NSC wasn't seeking the kinetic measures that concerned me most, one idea— the interdiction of ships carrying Venezuelan oil—had the potential to escalate into conflict. The second option, a plan to organize a naval show of force in the Caribbean, presented a host of other questions. Pompeo and I had our weekly call on Tuesday morning, the day after my return, so I raised this issue with him. He wasn't tracking these developments, which wasn't unusual—news usually travels fastest in the department most affected—but was going to follow up with his staff.

We shouldn't have been too surprised that the NSC was working on something, however. At the time of the Venezuelan opposition's uprising against Maduro, Trump threatened a "full and complete embargo, together with highest-level sanctions" if Cuba didn't immediately end its support for Maduro.[8] Trump had also pressed in the past for military options to stop the flow of oil between Venezuela and Cuba.[9] Oil was the currency by which Caracas compensated Havana for its support. We would eventually learn that Mauricio Claver-Carone, the NSC senior director for the Western Hemisphere, was pushing a hard line in the White House, and he found a sympathetic ear for military options in O'Brien.

Claver-Carone was a sharp staffer who knew Latin American issues well, especially Cuba and Venezuela. I respected his knowledge and passion for his work, but I was concerned that it seemed too personal for him, given how he spoke about the issues and the references he made to growing up in Miami's Cuban American community.

Nearly two months later, on February 5, 2020, Trump met with Guaidó in the Oval Office. At Trump's invitation, Guaidó had attended the State of the Union address the previous evening. During his remarks on Capitol Hill, Trump praised the interim Venezuelan president and offered the United States' support for him and his people, stating "Mr. President . . . please take this message back that all Americans are united with the Venezuelan people in their righteous struggle for freedom"; this was viewed by many as a personal endorsement as well.[10] This notion was mistaken.

I spoke with Trump for a few minutes right before his Oval Office session with Guaidó on the fifth. He still had serious doubts about the young leader, saying he looked "weak," especially compared to how "tough" and "strong" Maduro seemed. Trump doubted Guaidó's ability to overthrow Maduro. He then pivoted quickly and spoke admiringly of Guaidó's wife, Fabiana Rosales, whom Trump had met at the White House in March 2019. He described her as "very young" and mentioned that she didn't wear a wedding ring.

This seemed to puzzle the president, the curiosity visible on his face, but overall Trump seemed more impressed by Rosales than her husband. I had met neither of them, so I had no insights to offer. I was mainly trying to learn if the NSC had put any outlandish ideas in Trump's head.

Soon enough, Guaidó and his entourage entered the Oval Office, shook hands with Trump and the rest of us, and sat down in the large yellow chairs positioned just a few feet in front of the fireplace. Above the white mantelpiece, hanging on the wall, was a large, gold-framed portrait of George Washington. An interpreter sat between both men, and a foot or so behind them, ready to take notes with a pen and pad.

Three members of Guaidó's delegation sat on the large, pale gold embroidered sofa to the right of the Venezuelan leader. I sat on the couch opposite them, across the dark brown rectangular table that divided us, to Trump's immediate left. Seated next to me on the couch were Commerce Secretary Wilbur Ross, and then Robert O'Brien on the far end. A few White House staffers sat in chairs situated at the ends of both sofas. It was a tight circle, but it was an intimate way to take in and contribute to the conversation.

Guaidó was young and intelligent, with a happy-go-lucky way about him. I didn't see the weakness that Trump did, but Maduro certainly had the stout, blue-collar look that came "straight from central casting," as Trump would often say.

President Trump leaned forward to talk, his long red tie dangling between his legs as he did. He would occasionally look at Guaidó, but mostly scanned the small group around him. The Venezuelan leader sat back in his chair, legs crossed, comfortably taking in what the U.S. president had to say. The interpreter would murmur into Guaidó's left ear, but he didn't need her assistance.

Trump and Guaidó said all the right things about each other and their mutual aims, with the Venezuelan expressing his "thanks to you, Mr. President, and the United States" for supporting "the people of Venezuela and me." Trump nodded his acknowledgment and began asking the young leader a series of questions about the stability of the regime, the state of the economy, and the status of his opposition movement. Guaidó was a good interlocutor who was able to answer Trump's questions, with occasional input from his staff seated on the couch.

At one point, Trump raised the possibility of using military force to oust Maduro, saying something along the lines of "What if the U.S. military went down there and got rid of Maduro?" This made me wince, though my sense was that he was testing Guaidó. The interim president shifted uncomfortably in his chair, caught off guard by the question but doing his best to disguise it. I took a deep breath, focused on Guaidó's face, and awaited his response. How he answered could change the course of history.

Thankfully, his answer wasn't as clear or forward leaning as I feared. "Of course we would always welcome U.S. assistance," Guaidó said, but he went on to emphasize that the Venezuelan people—especially those now living next door in Colombia—"want to take back their country themselves." That sounded good to me. I jumped in and pressed him further on this point, asking, "Mr. President, would your people really be willing to organize, train, and fight?" After all, the U.S. military had experience training foreign forces, and this was a far better solution than using American troops against Maduro. Guaidó gave a roundabout answer that concluded with him saying that "yes, they would." It didn't sound reassuring.

The meeting started running long, so Trump thanked Guaidó and then invited us all to "please go into the Cabinet Room and continue the discussion." I had another appointment at the Pentagon I was running late for, but I knew I had to spend some time in this follow-on session. The president remained interested in military options, and the NSC team was even more enthusiastic about them, so I wanted to steer any conversation on this topic in a different direction. They were all in an echo chamber hearing one another's reinforcing messages. And now Guaidó wasn't really pushing back on the idea. As I said to the president sarcastically before the meeting, I was confident the Venezuelan opposition "would fight to the last American" if we offered them.

We all filed into the Cabinet Room, with Guaidó and his delegation on one side, and our team on the other, with our backs to the Rose Garden. Since I couldn't stay too long, I decided to press Guaidó and his colleagues a little bit harder about their ability to organize an expatriate force in Colombia. Around 4.5 million Venezuelans had reportedly fled the country, and many of them crossed the Colombian border to the west and south to find sanctuary there.

"If some of them could be trained and equipped by the U.S.," I asked, "would they really be willing to fight?" I never heard a solid answer. Rather, they told me such a plan would take a lot of time, would be complicated, and so on. I wasn't looking to take on this mission, but I thought it was more viable and palatable than some of the options proposed by O'Brien and the NSC. In my mind, of course, I was thinking that their real answer was "It would be so much easier and quicker if the U.S. would do this for us." "Okay," I said, "I get it. But setting that aside, Mr. President, would your people fight?" Again, they offered no answer that gave me a high degree of confidence. The failed uprising the previous April kept coming to my mind.

The conversation pivoted from a discussion about some type of large-scale operation to something more akin to a smaller, special operation targeted directly at Maduro. Then, out of the blue, one of Guaidó's colleagues looked at me from across the table and said something like "We have some plans you [the U.S. government] know we are working on, they're just not ready yet." There was some quick reference to Florida too. As he finished the sentence, he smiled, looked away from me, and made eye contact with Claver-Carone, the NSC senior director who was pressing the hardest for military action. Claver-Carone smiled and nodded back. I looked directly at him about fifteen feet away from me, down the table to my left. He turned to me, and as our eyes met, his face immediately went blank. Something was up.

Now wasn't the time or place to dig into this issue and besides, I was definitely late for my next meeting at the Pentagon. So, I thanked Guaidó and his team, stood up, and made my way to the door. The folks remaining in the room stayed for quite some time, I learned later. I probably should have too.

At some point in the days (or couple of weeks) following that meeting, I called Gina Haspel at the CIA and recounted this story. I told her my folks were not aware of any plans under development by the Venezuelan opposition, and asked if she knew of any. She wasn't tracking anything either, but would dig a little further. If she and I weren't knowledgeable of any special operation by the opposition, then who was?

In early May 2020, approximately three months after Guaidó's visit to the White House, two former U.S. Special Forces soldiers led a group of nearly sixty Venezuelan dissidents in a failed attempt to infiltrate the country by small boats, move to the capital of Caracas, seize Maduro, and overthrow the government. Guaidó reportedly approved the operation.

Both the retired American soldier and former Venezuelan military officer tagged as the leaders of the group lived in Florida.[11] Despite the participation of former U.S. service members, and accusations by the Maduro regime that the Trump administration was behind the failed assault, the U.S. government was not involved in this operation, to the best of my knowledge. However, I often wondered if this was the plan referred to by Guaidó's team at the White House back in February and, if so, to what degree was the NSC aware and involved.

Beginning in March 2020, the NSC put Venezuela back on the interagency table for discussion. Over a few meetings during the spring and early summer, O'Brien and his team were pushing hard for some type of military action against Cuba and Venezuela to cut off Caracas's access to goods and cash.

In one of the early meetings, which typically included Pompeo, Attorney General Bill Barr, Gina Haspel, Robert O'Brien, General Milley, NSC legal adviser John Eisenberg, and me, NSC staff pushed the idea of a blockade. I couldn't believe they proposed this. I thought the notion of blockading Cuba died in the Kennedy administration nearly sixty years earlier. I quickly pointed out that "blockades are considered an act of war under international law." I understood that the purpose was to shut off Venezuela's oil revenue, but "we need to find a legal and credible way to do it," I added. Debate went back and forth for a few minutes, but the legal, political, and strategic considerations raised overwhelmed this proposal and it died under the weight of its own absurdity.

Next up was the idea of "interdicting ships that are carrying Venezuelan oil," according to O'Brien. ████████ proposed that the U.S. Navy and Coast Guard identify these ships, stop them, and seize them. This would be the best way to shut off these shipments once and for all, they argued. It was frustrating that every one of these NSC meetings, it seemed, always began with the consideration of military options, rather than on the other end of the spectrum—diplomacy. In all fairness to the State Department, they had done a lot of good work to ensure dozens of other countries recognized Guaidó as the legitimate president of Venezuela, to get the Organization of American States on the right side of the issue, and to apply a wide range of sanctions. Nevertheless, I needed them to explore, or reexplore, other diplomatic initiatives that might further move the needle, and be more of a brake on bad ideas too.

It was fairly common that, prior to these meetings, the DoD would be tasked to "deliver military options to be reviewed" first at the deputies level. This was a complete nonstarter, and something we never agreed to do. In fact, I gave my team orders to *never* deliver military options, and to not even discuss them. This really upset the NSC, but these were important decisions—ones that often involved the lives of American service members—and thus demanded the tightest of operational security. Security was also important to preserving the president's decision-making space at the political, policy, and strategic levels. Too much leaking went on in the U.S. government, especially at the Trump White House, and it was harmful on many levels.

It irked the NSC staff and others, but withholding our slate of options was a long-standing practice of the Pentagon that I was committed to restoring. I did feel it important to prebrief the secretary of state, national security adviser, and CIA director before we went to the president, as well as the vice president and the White House chief of staff if they expressed interest. They were all principals who had important roles to play, and I welcomed their outside perspectives. Moreover, it was helpful if we were all aligned when the chairman and I presented recommendations on the use of military force to the commander in chief.

In the case of interdicting ships on the high seas, this required no "options brief." The U.S. Navy had been doing this for more than two hundred years. The tactics weren't hard, but that didn't mean these operations weren't complex or dangerous. "The bigger issues are ones of legality, risk, and logistics," I would say. The NSC had a blind spot on these considerations time and time again. They often didn't think beyond the first step. So, I would immediately raise the inconvenient questions and issues that few in the room wanted to hear.

I didn't like being the skunk at these parties. I also wanted to see Maduro ousted. However, we had to do it the right way, the smart way. Just the same, I knew this was how White House staff would start branding others—especially us at the DoD—as "foot draggers" who "don't support the president." This was why, I suppose, some people seemed to sit silently on the sidelines of these discussions, reluctant to raise their voices.

I had worked on interdiction operations before as a deputy assistant secretary of defense during the George W. Bush administration, and I knew the issues and challenges. The problem then was the maritime interdiction of weapons of mass destruction. In close collaboration with our allies, we had begun working to detect, track, and stop the proliferation of these systems and components by every mode they moved.[12]

An early opportunity presented itself in 2002, when a Spanish frigate off the coast of Yemen, at our request, stopped and boarded a freighter suspected of carrying Scud missiles from North Korea. The Spanish warship discovered the illicit shipment but had to let the vessel proceed because there was no legal basis under international law for preventing the delivery of the missiles.[13] This episode was an embarrassing setback to our efforts to stop proliferation, but we learned a good deal from the incident, and concluded that diplomatic and law enforcement approaches were usually more effective.

Back in the Situation Room, I decided to open up the discussion in the hope of getting us on a better path. "Okay," I said, "we know how to do interdictions. We can come back at a future meeting and show a framework of how the Navy would do this, but there are some things we need answered up front to aid our planning. First, what will be the legal basis for stopping the ship?"

After a long pause, someone said, "we can figure that out."

"Okay. Next question," I said, "what if they deny us boarding rights?" Again, no firm answer. I kept going. "If we don't get permission to board, are we recommending this be a forced boarding?" I asked. "And if so," I added, "what are the rules of engagement if they oppose us?" I went down this path for a while, asking whether we want to risk U.S. service members being shot? killed? captured? I didn't believe these contingencies were likely, but we would plan for them regardless. These were important issues that everyone, especially the president, needed to understand and weigh.

I then delved into the logistics of the NSC proposal: "Once we have control of this ship, what do we do with it? Where do we take it and who's responsible?" No answer. "Who will captain the ship?" "What are the plans for the oil we seize?" More silence. Also, what will it mean for the United States' long-standing support for "freedom of commerce and navigation on the high seas," and our present policy of condemning Iranian interdictions in the Persian Gulf, if we turn around and do something similar? I'm sure the NSC staff wasn't happy with me, but this is the type of rigorous examination and discussion that these matters demanded. By the end of the meeting, all agreed these issues would go back to their respective departments for work.

In a follow-on meeting that spring of 2020, the president joined his national security team for an update brief on Venezuela. Trump entered briskly. He had a busy day ahead, so O'Brien quickly stated the purpose of the meeting. He then turned it over quickly to his staff, which was unusual. Mauricio Claver-Carone stood up from his seat against the wall in the cramped Situation Room and started laying out the ideas discussed in a previous meeting. He spoke in machine-gun fashion as he focused on the president. At some point, though, he went from a recitation of facts to outright advocacy for aggressive action as he gestured with his hands and paced back and forth behind O'Brien's seat.

I thought he went too far, however, when he said, "Failure to take down the Maduro administration would hurt the nation's security," and then added, speaking directly to Trump, "I don't think you want to see a story in the *Wall Street Journal*, Mr. President, that this happened on your watch."

I thought his comment was inappropriate, bordering on a soft threat. O'Brien doubled down on his staff's pitch and foot-stomped the "urgency" of the United States taking action. It was over-the-top, and all advocacy for what the NSC wanted. Any pretense of the NSC being a coordinating body that represented the departments' views and the best collective judgment of the cabinet completely went out the door that day. None of this was ever agreed to.

Worse yet, the NSC's arguments were resonating with the president before he had a chance to hear from everyone else. You could see it in his head nods. This was dangerous.

Barr, Pompeo, Milley, and I—the president's cabinet members and principal military adviser—sat there waiting for our opportunity to speak. This was not how the NSC should run a national security team meeting; it didn't serve the president or the country well. From my seat in the middle of the table, I lost my patience and blurted, "That's ridiculous" when O'Brien and Claver-Carone uttered their dire warnings. Trump gave me a quick glance. Someone to my left closer to the president (Bill Barr, I thought) voiced an objection as well. Meanwhile, Milley rolled his eyes and shook his head.

The president's head nods and comments put me on edge that we might be stuck with a really bad idea—one that could lead to conflict in South America. The president felt the Pentagon wasn't doing enough on this issue—he had been saying it for over three years, others told me—and I had every reason to believe that the NSC and others kept pushing this notion in his head. So, when the president turned to me and asked, "Mark, what do you think?" I started by listing all that Defense was doing in the region to advance the administration's policy and back up our diplomatic efforts.

"Mr. President," I said, "I know not everyone in the room is aware of what DoD is doing in the region, so let me begin with a quick summary." With that, I started down my list: "The Navy is running freedom of navigation operations off the coast of Venezuela. Air Force B-52 bomber training flights are being flown out of Louisiana and partnering with allied air forces in the region as a show of force." I ticked off a few other items on my list. Meanwhile, I added, "SOUTHCOM and my Policy team have developed plans with others in the interagency—consistent with the strategy developed by the State Department—to address the 'day after' events once Maduro is gone," such as "providing humanitarian relief to the people of Venezuela," I said.[14]

I spoke quickly, anxious to lay down a solid baseline before anyone—especially the president—interrupted me. I finished by stating that the DoD was doing a good deal, but noting that "we have many more nonmilitary cards to play" before we—the national security team seated around the table—started considering more aggressive actions.

Bill Barr, who was looking at me as I spoke, swiveled his chair back 90 degrees toward the president, and leaned back. In an easy manner, he took the conversation in a more positive direction by stating, "We should focus on stopping the flow of drugs into the United States" from South America, and not get distracted by military operations.

Drug enforcement was a topic that Barr seemed passionate about as he cited some important statistics regarding the amount of drugs coming into the country, from where they were coming, and how many Americans were dying as a result of this nefarious trade. All of this resonated with Trump, who leaned in toward Barr and nodded his head in agreement as the attorney general spoke. He listened intently as Bill continued.

There was a "direct connection to Maduro and his regime," Barr argued, with the Department of Justice separately preparing to indict Maduro and members of his inner circle on drug trafficking, money laundering, and narcoterrorism charges. According to Justice, Maduro had turned Venezuela into a transshipment point for moving cocaine out of Colombia and north to the United States. This was the regime's way of collecting hard cash, thus presenting an avenue for the United States to apply pressure.

In Barr's view, Maduro had "weaponized" cocaine to undermine the United States. Illicit drugs were "killing millions of Americans" and harming communities across the country. It was hard to find a family who didn't have a friend or relative somehow affected by this scourge. "Stopping the flow of drugs, and specifically out of Venezuela, is what we should focus on," Barr argued. This really had an impact on the president, and indeed most of us. I recalled friends from high school who became addicted to drugs, and the damage it did to them and their families. Most parents do everything they can to keep their kids away from drugs and the wrong crowd that can lead them astray. This was probably the biggest concern Leah and I had as we raised our sons and daughter.

The attorney general's pitch was a success. The president really liked it. Still looking at Barr, he thanked him, and then scanned the room as he said, "Great points. Good. Good. I like it." O'Brien and the NSC staff sat quietly. Thank goodness we were now talking about enhanced drug interdiction efforts in the Caribbean and eastern Pacific, off the coast of California, instead of something far more dubious. This made a whole lot more sense to me. It was something tangible that could really make a difference, and not solely in terms of putting pressure on Maduro and his cronies, and denying them revenue, but also in terms of keeping drugs out of the country. It also didn't bring all of the legal, political, military, and logistical baggage that the ill-conceived NSC ideas carried. It would take away some from my focus on China and the National Defense Strategy, but the commitment was minimal and saving American lives from illicit drugs was worth it.

I thanked Bill for his idea as well, told him and the president I supported it, and then said, "DoD will quickly work up some plans to get more Navy ships and Coast Guard cutters to the area, and look at some other ways to support this initiative." I would then come back to the White House and brief the president and my fellow cabinet members, I added. We should aim to "announce something in late March or early April," I suggested. Everyone else in the room also seemed to be supportive of Barr's idea, and the fact that we coalesced around something. The NSC still wanted more—and the idea of military interdictions would raise its head again months later—but for now they seemed satisfied that we were all looking to do something bigger "after years of inaction," as I'm sure they would say.

The flow of illegal drugs coming into the country really did trouble the president. It wasn't an issue that came up as often as Germany's unwillingness to spend more on defense, or the presence of U.S. forces in Africa, but he'd often make the case that "drugs are killing more Americans than the terrorists." Trump became very animated when he spoke about this matter, showing a good deal of passion and authenticity. It was a hard issue to ignore when so many communities and families across the country were personally affected.

The White House discussions in February and March resulted in a plan announced in early April to beef up our presence in the Gulf of Mexico and the eastern Pacific. Our goal was to increase interdiction efforts through a 65 percent increase in Navy ships, Coast Guard vessels, and airborne reconnaissance, with more than one thousand additional military personnel to bolster the counternarcotics mission.

Southern Command, under Admiral Craig Faller, did a superb job developing and implementing the plan, enlisting many of our partners in the region to join us. The president visited SOUTHCOM headquarters in Miami on July 10, 2020—a little over thirteen weeks after we launched the initiative—to get an update, celebrate our progress, and thank the troops. In his public remarks, Trump noted the increased results, notably the seizure of more than 250,000 pounds of illegal drugs and the arrest of 1,000 drug traffickers in three months. The president said, "We're determined to keep dangerous drugs out of the country and away from our children," adding that "this is a new operation [that has] not been done before. And this operation has been incredibly successful."[15] Trump was genuinely pleased.

However, despite these accomplishments, the president's frustration with drug trafficking festered. It could take him to extremes. Mexico was his particular focus. The U.S. government estimated that most of the drugs entering the United States were coming across the southern border, with everything from methamphetamines and cocaine to heroin and fentanyl, shipped through our ports of entry. On several occasions, the president would point the finger at Mexico for not doing enough and would threaten them with one type of action or another for failing to deal with the trafficking.[16]

In November 2019, Trump announced plans to label drug cartels in Mexico as "foreign terrorist organizations" after the horrific killing of nine adults and children with dual U.S.-Mexican nationality. When asked about Trump's comments, Mexican president Andrés Manuel López Obrador said, "Cooperation, yes, intervention, no." Mexican foreign minister Marcelo Ebrard, whom López Obrador tasked to lead the talks, expressed concern that applying the terrorist label to drug cartels could enable the United States to take direct action against them, and that he intended to defend Mexico's sovereignty.[17] Ebrard's comments were prescient.

On at least two occasions in the summer of 2020—once in the Oval Office and a second time in his private room just off the Oval—the president approached me about a sensitive issue. Slightly hunched over, with his hands motioning in front of him like a quarterback gesturing for a long snap, he asked me if the military could "shoot missiles into Mexico to destroy the drug labs" and take out the cartels. Standing close to me as he spoke, the president complained that the Mexican government "isn't doing enough," getting irritated as he spoke and adding, "They don't have control of their own country." "If we could just knock them [the drug labs] out," he said, this would do the trick. "What do you think?" he asked.

These conversations were quite troubling, to say the least. On one hand, I shared his concern about illicit drugs being trafficked into our country and respected his passion for wanting to stop this dangerous trade, but asking the U.S. military to shoot missiles into a sovereign country and worse yet, our friend and neighbor, definitely wasn't the way to go about it.

Working hard to conceal my shock at this idea, I said, "Mr. President, we *could* do that, and as much as I want to stop these drugs too, shooting missiles into Mexico would be illegal. It would also be an act of war." I recommended that "we look for more ways to help the Mexican government deal with the problem, such as increasing the training, intelligence, and equipment we are providing them." We should also take another look at ideas that were tabled in the past. But to simply launch air or missile strikes into Mexico "would not only violate international law, it would also destroy our relationship with Mexico and damage our global standing," I said.

Trump took these objections in, pursing his lips as he listened. He then suggested, "We could just shoot some Patriot missiles* and take out the labs, quietly," adding preposterously that "no one would know it was us." He would simply deny we had launched them. I had seen Trump spin his own reality before, so I had no doubt he was confident in his ability to persuade people we had not launched the attacks. However, we didn't live in a world where the United States could strike another country and no one would believe the missiles weren't ours. I also couldn't imagine the president would resist taking credit for the attack anyway. It was nonsense, plain and simple.

If I hadn't seen the look on the president's face, I would have thought it was all a joke. He wanted to get this planned and done by Labor Day—"around then," he said—just a few months away. I was speechless. Trump thought this was the only way we would really stop this terrible trade.

I took a long pause, and then said, again, "This would be an act of war, Mr. President, and there would be no way to keep it quiet."

---

* The president often mistook Patriot missiles for Tomahawk missiles. Patriot missiles are air-defense weapons designed to destroy aircraft and ballistic missiles. Tomahawk missiles are used for land attack, such as he was suggesting in this scenario.

I quickly added, "We can't keep our discussions in this room from finding their way into the press." He nodded in silent agreement, not looking at me but into the air as he thought. I further parried by offering to raise this issue with Haspel and Pompeo, who I knew would agree with me, adding,—"I'll speak with Mike and Gina, and see if they have any good ideas." That seemed to satisfy him and, as would happen so predictably, he bounced to another topic, and I immediately made my way to the door.

Fortunately, nothing further ever came of these conversations. Still, I was troubled. This was not rational thinking. Moreover, it only underscored in my mind later how important it was for me to stay in my post. What if another secretary of defense, my replacement, went along with this? Lord knows there were plenty of people in the mix who thought the president's outlandish ideas made sense.

Indeed, taking issues to the extreme wasn't a behavior unique to the president in the Trump White House by any means. He had surrounded himself with staff who would amplify his ideas or come up with their own preposterous ones, and both their aggressiveness and presence around him would increase through the spring and summer. This all seemed to exacerbate the craziness increasingly emanating from the White House as the November elections inched closer.

The flow of illegal narcotics wasn't the only southern-border issue the president and others focused on; the other was illegal immigration. The Department of Homeland Security (DHS) was making steady progress erecting barriers along the southwest border, yet despite this effort and others, there was a hard-core element in the administration for whom illegal immigration seemed to be the only issue the United States faced. In their minds, no holds were barred, and several of them had direct access to Trump.

I was attending an Oval Office meeting during this same time frame when Stephen Miller, Trump's point man on immigration, approached me about security on the border. I barely knew Miller. He was a slight, unremarkable person with a deadpan gaze that suggested a real lack of humor or warmth. When it came to immigration issues, he was very serious, and, as ridiculous as some of his ideas were, he could often back up his game with selective facts, figures, and arguments to supplement his hyperbole.

He was also a capable speechwriter and well liked by the president, so he had both Trump's ear and his voice. As a result, most gave him far more deference than his actual position and qualifications warranted, and many suspected he would involve himself in personnel issues if someone crossed him. Despite any formal authority, Miller threw his weight around when it came to immigration matters. He also had close ties with equally hard-line professionals throughout DHS and the White House who would enable him.

Standing just a few feet away from the Resolute desk as we waited for the president, and without any pretense of a personal greeting or chitchat, Miller said to me from behind, "We need to get a quarter million troops to the border soon. There is another caravan coming up from the south, and we need to stop it." I turned slightly, looked at him, and chuckled. I thought he was joking. He wasn't. His face never moved.

I paused and then, playing along, said, "I haven't seen any reports about another caravan, and I'm confident DHS can handle it as they've done in the past."

As I started to turn back around, he parried with "This is a big one. CBP [Customs and Border Protection] can't do it. We need to deploy the military. I'm already talking to folks at DHS." In any other White House, someone like Stephen Miller plotting administration actions with a separate federal department would have been fanciful and out of bounds. In the Trump White House, it was just another day at the office.

This was now serious. I turned away from the Resolute desk and toward Miller—who as far as I knew had almost no working knowledge of the military or any experience in uniform—and told him some basic facts. "The U.S. armed forces," I said as I stared into his vacant eyes, "don't have two hundred and fifty thousand troops to send to the border for such nonsense." With that, I turned and walked away.

It was one thing to support DHS at the border by deploying a few thousand folks to provide logistical and other support. The DoD had done this in the past, in Republican and Democrat administrations alike. Even President Biden would extend this mission once he came into office. However, the thought of deploying a quarter million troops—combat units, that is—to conduct an active defense on the U.S. border against civilian migrants was simply outrageous, unless you're Stephen Miller.

General Milley would later remind me of the time we gathered in the Situation Room in October 2019, with other members of the national security team, to watch the live video feed of the successful special operations raid that killed Abu Bakr al-Baghdadi in Syria. Stephen Miller suggested later in the evening that U.S. forces try to locate the ISIS leader's head so that we could dip it in pig's blood—which Muslims consider to be unholy—and parade it around (or some barbarous idea along those lines) to deter other terrorists. Milley and I quickly snapped back at him, stating that doing such a thing was a "war crime," and that "the U.S. military will never do that." Miller didn't respond. Everyone else seated around the large rectangular desk, which was crowded with phones and lap-tops, sat silently, continuing to watch events unfold on the large screen before us. Were they unalarmed by this macabre comment, supportive, or just quietly pleased we swatted it down so quickly?

I returned to the Pentagon after my short conversation with Ste-phen Miller, and at some point in the following days, passed along the story about him wanting to send a quarter million troops to the border to Jen Stewart and General Milley. The idea was so outra-geous, they couldn't believe someone conceived it. I also recounted Miller's comment that he was actually working on this idea with DHS. With that, I paused, turned to Milley, and said, "Chair-man, I know this sounds crazy, but please check the Joint Staff and NORTHCOM to see if they've heard anything about this. I want to be safe about it."

Northern Command is the combatant command responsible for North America, from Mexico to Canada, and is specifically charged with the defense of the country's borders. It provides DoD support to civilian authorities in the United States for hurricanes, floods, wildfires, and other natural disasters. NORTHCOM is also responsible for providing military support for civilian authorities, whether the nation was facing a pandemic, civil unrest, or problems at the border.

Milley returned a day or so later. He entered my office, shaking a batch of papers at me as he said, "Secretary, you aren't going to believe this." Oh no, I thought. The chairman went on to describe how a planning team at NORTHCOM had actually begun work on "a concept to deploy a couple hundred thousand plus troops to the border." They had been meeting with DHS about it, had the basics down on the papers he held, and were moving forward with their plans.

I was shocked. I asked questions no one had good answers for: Who approved this? When did this begin? Why weren't we informed? How far along were they? The best we knew at that moment was that NORTHCOM staff was told by DHS staffers—likely, Customs and Border Protection—that the White House (probably Miller) had directed this, and that DHS understood formal orders from the president were forthcoming.

While I was not surprised Miller was working this, I was frustrated that no one senior at NORTHCOM thought to let us, or anyone at the Pentagon for that matter, know. Why didn't the command appreciate the dynamics of this misbegotten project and immediately press the pause button until they received guidance from *their* DoD leadership? The political ramifications were off the charts, and the impact on the military would be enormous. Imagining the reaction from Congress and the public was unfathomable.

I told Milley to get hold of NORTHCOM immediately, tell them to "shut down the planning, and let them know there was to be no further engagement with DHS on this matter." I added, "If anyone at Homeland Security has an issue with my order, then they are welcome to call me direct."

My phone never rang, and the issue never raised its ugly head again. Thank goodness. We had not yet reached the dark days of June 2020, but issues and ideas like these factored heavily into my personal calculations after opposing the president's use of the Insurrection Act, and the many months that followed.

Meanwhile, we weren't done with Venezuela, not by a long shot. The issue of interdicting ships raised its head again in May 2020, when the United States learned that Iranian tankers were carrying oil to Venezuela, ironic as that was, in exchange for gold. Venezuela was historically one of the largest oil-producing nations in the world, but it was now months away from ending its oil exploration for the first time in one hundred years because of Maduro's social-ist policies, mismanagement, and international sanctions.[18]

It was estimated that approximately nine tons of gold valued at around half a billion dollars was payment for Iran's help in repairing Venezuela's refineries and providing gas additives. The global pandemic had a devastating impact on the oil market, and when coupled with the sanctions placed on both countries, Tehran was looking for new sources of revenue. Meanwhile, Caracas wanted to ensure its supply of gasoline didn't run out. Long lines at gas stations and the other effects of scarcity on its broken economy were provoking daily protests and risked leading to more violent outcomes.[19]

The pair of countries had a relationship dating back at least two decades. In 2007, Venezuelan president Chavez and Iranian president Mahmoud Ahmadinejad declared an "axis of unity" against U.S. "imperialism."[20] The relationship between these pariah states would deepen under increasing pressure from the Trump administration. By 2020, with neither regime on the verge of collapse, the thought that both countries now seemed to be working together more closely than ever before was troubling. There was good cause for concern about this deepening collaboration between them, and with Russia and China as well, especially when it involved a country in our hemisphere. For Trump personally, this was like waving red flags in front of an enraged bull.

We needed to keep the pressure on, and find new ways to advance our policy aims. But we also had to be smart about it. By mid-May, however, with Iranian ships plying the waters of the Atlantic en route to Venezuela with fuel and supplies, the NSC was once again pushing interdiction by the U.S. Navy as the best way forward. This potential use of the U.S. military, with little sense of the consequences, was frustrating.

...

The NSC scheduled a principals meeting by secure video for June 9 to discuss Venezuela again. Many of the same people from the earlier meetings—Pompeo, Barr, O'Brien, Milley, and me—were in the room or on the line, and most of the same questions I raised earlier remained unanswered. However, there was now a fresh twist to this cooperation between Tehran and Caracas. John Ratcliffe, the new Director of National Intelligence (DNI), kicked off the discussion with an overview of the recent developments.

Ratcliffe had just become the DNI on May 26, only a couple of weeks prior. He was a lawyer who had worked in both the private sector and in government. He was elected to Congress in 2014, was reelected in 2016 and 2018, and was regarded as one of the most conservative House members. He was also a Trump acolyte.

Trump announced his intent to nominate Ratcliffe for DNI in July 2019 to succeed Dan Coats, but it was withdrawn, due to objections from lawmakers of both parties who were concerned Ratcliffe might politicize the intelligence community. Trump pressed again in February 2020, this time using the leverage of having installed Ric Grenell—his über-loyal ambassador to Germany—as the acting DNI a couple of weeks earlier to help get Ratcliffe confirmed.

The president often bragged about installing Grenell as the acting DNI. In an Oval Office meeting once, as a few of us sat across from him, Trump leaned back in his chair, clasped his hands behind his head, and with a huge smile on his face said that "installing Ric as DNI was one of the best personnel moves I ever made." As his chair tilted forward again toward the Resolute desk, the president added that members of Congress "are so concerned about what he [Grenell] will do, they're now jumping at the chance to quickly get him out of the DNI office." It's crazy, he said. "They used to have concerns about John Ratcliffe," he said. "Now they don't," as he leaned back in his chair again, entertaining the small group with his legerdemain.

What really grabbed my attention, though, was when Trump said aloud to himself, "I should do this again in the future when I face pushback from a department." I never forgot this comment, and the seriousness with which he said it.

Much of the overview delivered by Ratcliffe, and followed up by the CIA, remained unchanged. Regime elites and senior military officers were still loyal to Maduro, while Guaidó was weaker and losing popularity with the people. Regarding the fuel that Tehran was delivering, the CIA explained that many countries were providing oil to Venezuela. This was the Agency's way of not only presenting all the facts and showing the full contours of the problem but also trying to get folks to think more broadly. Milley and I would often push for the Agency to do this summary up front to baseline everyone, before people around the table started laying down their own "facts" to justify their solution.

The new information was that Venezuela was actively seeking to buy arms from Iran. Tehran had not approved anything specific yet, but the list of items apparently ranged from light arms and small boats to long-range missiles that could reach the United States. The last item was the red flag for most of us on the call. However, the fact that Iran had not approved the sale, let alone prepared the shipment, meant we had time to work this problem. Nevertheless, the NSC proposed again that we pursue a military operation ███████ ██.

Like the previous time, though, key questions about authorities, what to do with the cargo, rules of engagement, and others, remained unanswered. Plus, there was always the possibility that Iranian military personnel could be on board the ships, helping

to provide security, which added an entirely different dynamic to
the NSC's preferred option. State mentioned the possibility of engaging the countries whose ships were transporting the goods, or
under whose flags the vessels were sailing. These were great ideas,
and one of the same strategies we used in the past, so I weighed in
behind this initiative.

As the arms sales issue cycled back around, General Milley
jumped in to note that *if* Tehran decided to sell weapons to Caracas, they wouldn't be the only ones. "Russia and China," he pointed
out, "are the top sellers of arms to Venezuela. Are we prepared to
interdict their shipments as well?" And if we weren't, someone else
piped in, "what prevents the Venezuelans from asking the Russians
to transport oil and other goods for them?"

I followed up, adding that we should better understand the intent behind Caracas's purchase of these arms, and the capabilities of
what they were aiming to procure. "We shouldn't overreact to small
arms and other equipment that can't threaten the U.S., but ballistic
missiles are totally different. That's where our focus should be," I
said. We need to develop a policy approach that is more discrim-
inating, can pass the common-sense test, and will hold up under
scrutiny from Congress, our regional partners, and others, I stated.

In my view, we had to maintain our primacy in the Western
Hemisphere and protect our partners throughout the region. This
meant preventing any arm sales that would threaten such a policy
and create a bad precedent. That said, it didn't mean we should
immediately pursue the military option either.

I suppose my question was too strategic for the moment; the
NSC was still at the tactical level. O'Brien went straight for the
jugular, proposing a military strike on ███████████, a seaport in
northeastern Venezuela, where a large complex for loading and
unloading petroleum products on and off ships is located. "If the

ships are too difficult to interdict, then we should look at disrupting the port where they offload their cargo," he argued. This would further disrupt their energy supplies and provoke more unrest, the NSA said.

The means could be either an air strike or the use of Navy SEALs, he added. From my perspective, we were now clearly in the "no war" category of the redlines I had established in early June, just a few days earlier. I pushed back on this, joined by Milley, and tried to elevate the discussion again—"What are we trying to do here? Stop the shipments? Force regime collapse? Start a war?" The group was losing focus once again. Mike Pompeo often didn't say much in these types of meetings, but he piped up now. "We know what our goal is. It's been our policy for some time now," he said, as he proceeded to outline its main elements.

He was right, we all understood the end state we wanted—the departure of Maduro and the installation of Guaidó as the legitimate president—but somehow we started with interdicting Iranian oil on the high seas and were now discussing a military assault on Venezuela, which had little chance of achieving that goal.

Milley coyly asked the CIA, "What do you think Venezuela would do if we attacked a port?" He was trying to elicit an answer from the CIA for which we knew the answer—which most certainly was a strong reaction that could escalate into a conflict and likely rally the Venezuelan people behind Maduro. The response by the Agency helped pull the discussion away from talk of kinetic action. We pivoted to less direct options, such as cyber operations, or ███████ activities supported by the United States but conducted by the opposition.

General Milley also thought we should look at irregular warfare options, such as the U.S. training and arming of Venezuelan expatriates ████████████████████████████████████

██

██████████████████████████████. The United States had a long
history with these types of operations. It was an idea worth developing. Milley and I had discussed this several times before, which
was why I raised it during the White House meeting with Guaidó
in February 2020. But again this day, as it had four months before,
the idea didn't get much traction.

After every principals committee meeting, the NSC would distribute a Summary of Conclusions memo in the days following the
session. What we discussed, what we agreed upon, and the path
forward were all captured in this document, which also served as
the basis for the next principals meeting. The summaries coming
out of the NSC, however, were often inaccurate. They sometimes
reflected what the NSC wanted to do, as compared to what we all
agreed upon. The DoD and the CIA started calling them out on
this. This time was no different, but dangerously so.

My Policy team received the summary late Friday, June 19, and
according to it, the group agreed to develop kinetic and nonkinetic
options, both overt and ████████, that could disrupt Venezuela's oil
and arms shipments. Options would need to include actions that
would have a material impact on key industrial and other high-
value targets. Furthermore, the NSC directed us to prepare these
options by June 23—four days away—and be ready to brief them
to the president in early July. What? Where the hell did this come
from?

My notes read that we, and all the departments and agencies
present, were supposed to develop ideas to interdict the shipments,
and that these would *not* be kinetic. Moreover, the deadline was
ninety days away, around September 9.

I couldn't believe the NSC was pushing such an agenda. We had

to keep this train on the tracks, but it was getting increasingly difficult to do so. And we still had several months to go until the election.

I picked up the secure line and called Mark Meadows. I knew
where he stood on this issue, but I wanted to confirm it before I
called O'Brien. The chief of staff's mission was getting the president reelected, so he understood that the political downsides of
military action in the weeks before an election outweighed the up-
side in most cases. That was particularly true when the president
had been promising for four years to get the United States out of
"endless wars"—not start new ones. Much of the base wouldn't like
this. I needed to leverage this to walk back the NSC memo and momentum. Meadows was consistent on this topic and responded as I
expected, agreeing with me. He was going to talk to O'Brien about
getting the summary right. I told him I'd reach out to O'Brien as
well. I spoke with the NSA around 6:40 P.M. and put things back
on track.

On August 14, a little over two months after this Venezuela-Iran
principals meeting, news broke that the United States intercepted
four tankers and seized 1.1 million barrels of fuel they were ferry-
ing from Iran to Venezuela. The United States did not employ military force. Rather, diplomatic action under a warrant issued by the
U.S. District Court in early July was used to seize the shipments.

This was a great initiative by Justice and State. It achieved everything that we were originally trying to do—stop the shipments—
without any of the downsides that military action would have
brought. The U.S. government exercised its leverage to persuade
the ships' owners, insurers, and captains to hand over their cargo.[21]
Barr and Pompeo did a great job. I hoped this success would beget
others to explore nonmilitary options first in the future.

While this action was a big win when it came to maintaining

pressure on the Iranian and Venezuelan regimes, the U.S. campaign suffered a major setback at the United Nations. Later that day, the U.N. Security Council voted down a U.S. resolution to extend an arms embargo against Iran that was set to expire in October. The embargo prohibiting Tehran from buying and selling conventional weapons had been in place for thirteen years, but was permitted to sunset in 2020 as part of the 2015 nuclear deal with Iran. Many considered this another fundamental flaw of the nuclear deal, and a main reason Trump opposed it.[22] The U.S. position was to maintain the embargo as long as Iran continued to support terrorist organizations such as Hezbollah. This always seemed eminently reasonable and prudent to me. Now, the sunsetting of the embargo would limit our nonmilitary options when it came to Venezuela.

The issue of preparing military options to strike Venezuela didn't raise its head again that summer. State and Justice's successful seizure played a positive role in suppressing this urge coming out of the White House. Other matters—namely, civil unrest—were consuming the president's attention.

Meanwhile, I continued my weekly NDS implementation meetings throughout June—we had to keep pressing forward. Moreover, with all of the craziness going on in Washington, D.C., I needed to keep the Pentagon focused on more productive things and not get distracted. As such, I held a series of meetings on issues ranging from the reassignment of joint forces around the world, an update to our directed force readiness tables, COVID, and Operation Warp Speed to another iteration of the China war plan and a discussion on the structure of the Space Force.

This newest armed service—Space Force—was responsible for the organizing, manning, training, and equipping of U.S. military capabilities focused on this new domain of warfare. It was a bold initiative that would fundamentally change, in a positive way, the

DoD's approach to protecting space, and our ability to operate there. This was so vitally important to our security, economy, and way of life, given that the Chinese and Russians were weaponizing space as an asymmetric counter to our conventional dominance. I was proud to establish the Space Force in December 2019 and play an active role in its development. It was a historic accomplishment for the Air Force, the DoD, and the country. All of these matters were the issues I really enjoyed working on, and the ones that would make an enduring difference for the nation's security.

One issue did arise in July that caught the attention of the Venezuela hawks, and it would eventually create more friction with the Pentagon. In early June, the government of Cape Verde arrested a Colombian businessman by the name of Alex Saab at the request of the United States on money laundering charges, which he denied. They did so during a layover he had in the archipelago, which is located in the Atlantic Ocean hundreds of miles off the coast of West Africa.

At Maduro's direction, Saab was reportedly on a special mission to negotiate a deal with Iran for Venezuela to receive more fuel, food, and medical supplies. Saab was Maduro's long-standing point man when it came to crafting the economic deals and other transactions that were keeping the regime afloat. The U.S. government was seeking his extradition. As such, this small island country detained Saab as judicial proceedings began.[23]

Saab was a very important player, and access to him could really help explain how Maduro and his regime worked. It was important to get custody of him. This could provide a real road map for the U.S. government to unravel the Venezuelan government's illicit schemes and bring them to justice. Maduro knew this as well, so a full court press was under way by Caracas to get Saab released.

Jorge Arreaza, Venezuela's foreign minister, said at the time that Cape Verde's detention of Saab was "violating international norms and law" and promised to do everything possible to protect him. Comments like this really spooked the officials at State, Justice, and the NSC who were working this case. By mid-July, a variety of rumors were circulating in the interagency: Maduro persuaded President Putin to send Russian special forces to spring Saab from jail; Russian mercenaries in Libya were going to travel hundreds of miles in small boats to either rescue or kill Saab; Venezuelan intelligence was chartering a special plane to fly to Cape Verde to repatriate Saab; and, Iranian Revolutionary Guard troops were preparing similar rescue missions. It seemed that somebody was watching too many *Mission: Impossible* movies on the weekend. I never saw intelligence that backed any of it up.

But as night follows day, these rumors prompted a request for action from the DoD, which I was told came from the State Department. I couldn't believe State was requesting an Amphibious Readiness Group-Marine Expeditionary Unit (ARG-MEU) be dispatched immediately from the Mediterranean to Cape Verde to protect Saab and deter intervention from the Russians, Iranians, and anyone else interested in disrupting the judicial proceedings.

I also felt it was important to extradite Saab back to the United States. However, if there was ever an example of the old saying "swatting a fly with a sledgehammer," this was it. Except that . . . there was no proof that the fly even existed, and the hammer was as large as a carnival mallet.

Most troubling was that nobody could answer the most basic questions. How would the expeditionary unit protect Saab? How would it deter action? Did we have permission to put Marines ashore to safeguard him? Did we have permission to intercept any Russian, Iranian, or Venezuelan aircraft or ships that looked suspicious? How would Cape Verde react to such a large military presence? The questions went on and on and on.

As I was preparing for the June 2020 NATO Defense Ministerial, I asked my senior military assistant, Lieutenant General Bryan Fenton, to track this action down and update me. In my mind, this was not simply another case of using the DoD "easy button"; it was misuse of the armed forces, another one of my new redlines. I picked up the phone and called O'Brien. He was obviously aware of Saab's detention and some of the rumors floating around, but not about the ARG-MEU request. "Robert," I said, "what's being proposed by State is ridiculous. Pulling thirty-five-hundred-plus Marines and sailors, and several ships out of the Mediterranean to sail around an island in circles is a major waste of scarce capabilities."

"You're right, Mark," he replied, and then asked, "What can we do to help here?" Before I could respond, he added, "By the way, DOJ is asking about deploying U.S. military special operators to Cape Verde to protect Saab." How equally fatuous. I went through many of the same questions I had with my team: "Will Cape Verde support the deployment of U.S. forces? Will they allow our people to carry weapons? What is their authority once they arrive?" These and more were all critical questions, yet we had not even asked Cape Verde any of them yet, let alone had answers to them. To his credit, O'Brien got it.

I then said, "Why we are even talking about military options? This is a law enforcement and diplomatic action. We should be engaging on those tracks, and at the highest levels. Why not inform Cape Verde of what we're hearing, and ask them to beef up their own security?" If they can't do it, I suggested, "then maybe we can provide federal marshals, DEA agents, State Department diplomatic security, or whatever law enforcement or civilian security teams are more appropriate to the task." O'Brien listened patiently.

I kept up my line of reasoning, trying to maneuver us into a better approach: "If for some reason we truly assessed the need for a naval presence, I said, why not get the U.S. Coast Guard to support? They have a law enforcement role, after all." These were all reasonable and straightforward questions, I thought. However, with fundamentally different views regarding the nature and scope of the problem, the various departments had developed wildly different solutions.

When I was done, O'Brien said State and Justice were "really concerned, and some in Cape Verde are as well." He heard that the government in the capital of Praia "doesn't want this hot potato" and was doing everything they could to keep a low profile. This meant "limiting the U.S. presence" in Cape Verde, which buttressed my position. According to him, "they would appreciate any assistance we can provide to help them improve their own capabilities," beginning with "assistance to repair a couple of their own coastal patrol ships."

This started making more sense, but the U.S. Coast Guard said they couldn't do it—"no cutters are available right now" was what we were told—so I committed to get my folks at U.S. Africa Command on the mission. I also tasked AFRICOM to look at ways "to help the country improve its domain awareness," which was another concern of Cape Verde. In August 2020, a Coast Guard ship eventually performed a joint patrol with the Cape Verdean Coast Guard to ostensibly monitor and enforce fishing rights.

Within a couple of days, this issue died down, but it wouldn't be the end of it. By mid-October, it was back, with reporting coming out of Cape Verde that the government might soon release Saab or move him to house arrest. State was pushing again for a U.S. Navy ship to patrol around Cape Verde and deter any outside intervention. The Coast Guard once again couldn't provide any cutters in a timely manner. I raised this with Pompeo during a call on October 19, but he said he wasn't aware of this latest issue. Mike was always reasonable on these things, so I didn't believe he supported this idea, but he probably wouldn't oppose it if the DoD agreed to move forward. I made it clear that I opposed deploying a Navy warship.

When James Anderson, my Policy head, came to brief me on this issue before the NSC deputies committee meeting he was attending that week, I told him, "I don't support the proposed action. They first have to show me some evidence that Russia, Iran, or Venezuela is planning to grab Saab, and if so, how the presence of a U.S. Navy ship in the waters around Cape Verde will deter or stop that from happening." There weren't enough warships to go around as it was, and I needed these vessels on patrol in the Mediterranean. General Hyten, the vice chairman of the Joint Chiefs, said that he and Milley completely agreed. Anderson conveyed this message back to the NSC, to which they responded: "Is the secretary of defense saying he will ignore a presidential directive?" I disregarded this taunt, and with that, the issue went away again.

The president fired me a few weeks later. With me out of the way, the Venezuela hawks pressed my successor for a warship, which he quickly approved. Not long after that, the USS *San Jacinto* deployed from Norfolk, Virginia, en route to Cape Verde to keep an eye— somehow—on Saab while supposedly deterring outside intervention. These tasks were still undefined, I was told.

The *New York Times* reported in December that the daily operating cost to keep the *San Jacinto* on station was $52,000. A week before Christmas, the crew of 393 sailors received orders to return home for the holidays. A smart call by the uniformed military, I learned, looking to take care of its service members and their families. Nevertheless, it was also a decision that put into stark contrast the unseriousness of this mission in the first place.

In other words, if Saab was so important (and he was) and the threat of taking him from Cape Verde so real (it wasn't) and the impact of the warship's presence so effective (it also wasn't), the *San Jacinto* should have been kept on station regardless of the holiday. Back in 1990, I had spent Thanksgiving and Christmas in the deserts of Saudi Arabia with my fellow soldiers during Operation Desert Shield. Military personnel from all the armed services have missed holidays at home since the American Revolution. They recognize that if duty calls, and it's that important, then they will answer the nation's call. This mission, however, clearly didn't merit it.

The *Times* described this deployment as another example of "the administration's capricious use of the armed forces," and they were right. They also reported that my worst fear—"an inadvertent Navy clash with Iranian or Venezuelan operatives in a matter best suited for diplomats and international lawyers to resolve"—never happened.[24] But that wasn't my concern at all, because I never thought the threat was real in the first place. I was tired of the DoD being the easy button for somebody's tough problem. All this did was militarize our foreign policy, pull the armed forces away from their core mission, and result in suboptimal solutions.

Finally, to close out this story, it is important to note that Alex Saab was extradited to the United States from Cape Verde in October 2021—nearly eighteen months after this entire drama began.[25] It appears no Russian, Iranian, or Venezuelan commandos ever invaded the central Atlantic archipelago to rescue him.

CHAPTER 12

THE REPUBLIC WOBBLES

On Sunday, May 31, 2020, numerous civil disturbances, some violent, were occurring in multiple cities across the United States. It was unlike anything seen in generations. In the District of Columbia, protesters clashed with law enforcement in Lafayette Park, north of the White House, and pushed down multiple security barricades. According to the Secret Service, between the evening of May 29 and into the early hours of May 31, more than sixty Secret Service officers and special agents sustained minor to severe injuries from the violence (eleven were taken to the hospital), and six of their vehicles were vandalized.

Protesters reportedly broke through a barrier near a line of police and National Guard personnel at Lafayette Square. Multiple fires were set within blocks of the White House. St. John's Episcopal Church, across the street from the White House and Lafayette Park, was set ablaze. A U.S. National Park Service building in the park was also set on fire, prompting the U.S. Park Police (USPP) to request continued D.C. National Guard support—with an increase to 250 personnel—through June 7.

Meanwhile, the District of Columbia requested 100 D.C. National Guard personnel and associated transport vehicles through June 6 to assist with traffic control and to block intersections identified by the Metro Police. Their mission was to ensure the lawful protesters could safely exercise their First Amendment rights and allow law enforcement—not the military—to deal with those who became violent or unruly. The secretary of the Army, who is responsible for the D.C. National Guard, verbally approved this request that same day, after briefing me.

It had been a long, rough weekend, to say the least. It was a period of time that would lead to one of the most memorable encounters I ever had with Donald Trump. Indeed, it was probably one of the most significant meetings a secretary of defense ever had with a commander in chief.

General Milley and I arrived at the Oval Office the morning of June 1, shortly after being summoned by the president, and were surprised to see everyone else already there and seated. This was unusual, since these meetings never typically started with such precision. I sat down in one of the hard wooden chairs in front of the Resolute desk, alongside Vice President Pence, Attorney General Barr, and Chief of Staff Mark Meadows. Behind Milley and me, on the two large sofas facing one another were a variety of White House staffers. Apparently, many of those attending the 10:30 A.M. meeting were holdovers from a previous discussion. Even before we sat down, the president started ranting about the protests.

I had rarely seen him so agitated. He was red-faced, with his arms flailing about in the air when they weren't folded tightly across his chest. Just as he had informed Milley earlier over the phone, Trump said he wanted "ten thousand troops in Washington to get control of the streets" and put down the violence. He kept repeating how "disgraceful" it was that the protests were happening and wanted something done. He thought the violence made him look "weak." "How do you think this makes us look to other countries?" Trump yelled. The president kept going back and forth between these two themes. I searched for opportunities to jump in, answer, or clarify, but in a way that wouldn't further inflame him.

The ten-thousand-troops number came up again; it must have sounded like a nice round number to him, I suppose, so he kept mentioning it, as he did the Insurrection Act.

As many Americans would come to learn, the Insurrection Act, originally enacted in 1807, is actually a set of statutes that govern the president's authority to deploy troops within the United States to put down lawlessness, insurrection, and rebellion. Though rarely used, President George H. W. Bush last employed it in this manner in 1992, at the request of the governor of California, to help quell the Los Angeles riots. President Trump had the authority to send the National Guard to the nation's capital, but would need to invoke the act if he wanted to deploy active-duty forces in D.C. or any other American city—or if he wanted to dispatch the Guard, over a governor's objections, to address civil unrest.

The conversation in the Oval Office was contentious and very fluid. Trump was working himself up, getting angrier and angrier. Barr's and my intermittent comments weren't helping. There would later be speculation that stories printed over the weekend about the Secret Service locking down the White House the Friday before, and hurrying the president and his family to an underground bunker for safety, had made Trump furious. He reportedly felt humiliated at the reports, which undercut his strongman image. Now, maybe, he was going to show them real strength.

Barr, Milley, and I pushed back several times on the idea of invoking the Insurrection Act and bringing in ten thousand active-duty troops. Bill would later claim that he never heard that specific number from the president, but there is no doubt in my mind that was what Trump said in the Oval Office. Regardless, I told Trump "I don't see the need to deploy *any* active-duty forces to the capital"—and highlighted some of the downsides if ordered to do this. General Milley agreed. I added, "There simply aren't that many people committing violence to warrant such a move."

I explained to the president, "We have over a thousand members of the D.C. National Guard available now, and they are sufficient to support local and federal law enforcement." Plus, I said, "Guard military police are also trained and have the authority to participate in law enforcement. It is a core function and an authority that active-duty units don't possess." I had served in the D.C. Guard for several years, so I had a good understanding of their capabilities.

That said, I pivoted again, making the case for law enforcement to play the lead role. "Mr. President, the National Guard is best suited to do this," I remarked, "but this is a job for law enforcement. Law enforcement has the lead. The military should be in the back of the line—behind local, state, and federal law enforcement—and active duty should be dead last."

Trump started erupting again, frustrated that we weren't telling him what he wanted to hear. I glanced at the attorney general, hopefully cueing him to jump in at my last mention of law enforcement.

Barr spoke up again, giving a thorough accounting of the law enforcement assets in the city and his plans to call up more officers from a variety of federal agencies, such as the FBI and the Bureau of Alcohol, Tobacco, Firearms and Explosives (ATF). He thought he could assemble "a few thousand personnel"—enough "to get things under control," he said. The president wasn't satisfied. He kept pushing for more aggressive actions. He wanted active-duty forces.

When demonstrations had started in cities across the country in late May, I asked my team at the DoD to develop a plan to put a few active-duty Military Police (MP) units on alert in the event governors requested assistance. These units could backstop the Guard, just in case the violence became unmanageable or the Guard couldn't mobilize and deploy in time or in sufficient numbers. It was, I felt, a reasonable, measured approach to try to stay ahead of things in the event circumstances spiraled dramatically out of control in some city and a governor needed help, as had happened in Los Angeles in 1992. The team did a good job making this happen with the personnel we had. Later in the summer, we would replicate a similar type of heightened readiness status but using National Guard units instead.

There in the Oval Office, however, Trump kept pressing to use active-duty forces, asking if we had troops ready to go. I tried to explain the MP units we had ready to deploy. I then mentioned the forces available at Fort Bragg, but "none of these are necessary, Mr. President," I said. "Plus, these forces are not right for the mission, and take much longer to deploy than you would think.

"I can get the Guard here fast," I added. It was a stretch commitment I would have to deliver on. Milley jumped in to explain how long it would take to alert, assemble, and deploy active-duty units.

We also had elements of the 3rd U.S. Infantry—more commonly called the Old Guard—on standby at Fort Myer in Virginia. Most Americans are familiar with the Old Guard for the solemn and meticulous sentries it provides for the Tomb of the Unknown Soldier, but they also have a role in protecting the capital as well. The 3rd Infantry were familiar with the civil support mission and located immediately across the Potomac River. However, even they would take hours to assemble, ready, and deploy. Milley and I explained that there was no way active-duty troops could deploy in large numbers to D.C. by nightfall. Still, the president kept pushing.

At one point, Trump turned to General Milley, who wasn't saying much; he was deferring the conversation to the civilians, I suspected, given the topic. Trump loved the strength and power of the armed forces, especially senior officers festooned in their uniforms, which Milley wore well. The president barked, "I want you to be in charge of this, General," meaning the chairman would take command of the operation to restore order in D.C. This caught Milley a little off guard.

The chairman quickly leaned back in his chair, raised his hands in a "don't shoot" fashion, and said wide-eyed, "I'm an adviser, Mr. President. I don't command troops. I'm not in an operational role here." His response stumped Trump, who was obviously hoping for a much different answer. The president didn't understand Milley's role as a statutory adviser to the president and secretary of defense, nor did he understand the different roles and authorities of active duty and Guard forces. But the chairman was right—he had no command authority.

Trump became angrier and was now on his feet, yelling that no one was helping him, that "we look weak," and "the country looks weak."

"You are losers!" the president railed. "You are all fucking losers!" This wasn't the first time I had heard him use this language, but not with this much anger, and never directed at people in a room with him, let alone toward Barr, Milley, and me. He repeated the foul insults again, this time directing his venom at the vice president as well, who sat quietly, stone faced, in the chair at the far end of the semicircle closest to the Rose Garden. I never saw him yell at the vice president before, so this really caught my attention.

Trump shouted, "None of you have any backbone to stand up to the violence," and suggested we were fine with people "burning down our cities."

The president sat back down, still fuming, and turned to General Milley and asked why our soldiers couldn't shoot the protesters. "Can't you just shoot them. Just shoot them in the legs or something," he asked. His question was almost technical, curious as to how that would actually be done, not whether members of the military shooting American civilians in a mostly peaceful demonstration was the right thing to do. He never really made a distinction between the peaceful protesters and the violent ones, not that it would matter in this context. In his mind, wounding the protesters would end things very quickly.

I didn't have to look at General Milley to know his reaction. I was sure it was the same as mine: utter disgust at the suggestion, and a feeling that we were only minutes away from a disastrous outcome. And not for the first time.

The president did not directly order us to deploy ten thousand troops. He did not directly order us to shoot civilians. Trump, for all of his reputation as a decisive executive who didn't hesitate to fire people, rarely worked that way. He mused. He suggested. He complained. He fumed. It was almost as if he didn't really want to own a decision as extreme as the one he was suggesting. He was waiting, it seemed, for one of us to yield and simply agree. That wasn't going to happen.

Still, there was always a chance the president would order us to act, and as things became more and more heated again, I felt we were losing the argument despite our united front. It seemed as if this meeting was escalating toward a showdown, one where Trump—out of character for once—would finally order us to do something, such as send in active-duty troops to crush the protests.

As was so often the case in dealing with the president, my sense was that we needed to get out of the room before that happened. He wasn't hopping from topic to topic as he normally did, which was another red flag for me. As such, I felt the need to put something on the table, give Trump something, enough, to calm things down and buy some time.

To let some pressure out of the room, and preempt a direct order that I couldn't follow, I committed to get some active-duty troops from Fort Bragg *moving toward* D.C. and to *alert* the Old Guard, but to keep them in their barracks. Any movement into the District would require invocation of the Insurrection Act, as the attorney general rightly noted. Milley concurred, adding that they were always close by if the situation got really bad.

I also committed that in the meantime, as our better action, "I will get the Guard moving. We will deploy additional Guard units—five thousand personnel if necessary—into D.C. soonest to help law enforcement get things under control." Barr thought he could gin up several thousand law enforcement officers, so in Trump's mind, I thought, he now had his ten thousand number . . . with *no* active-duty forces. I told Trump that General Milley and I would head back to the Pentagon to start things moving. Getting Guard units from neighboring Virginia, Maryland, and Pennsylvania, was our best hope, but they needed as much alert time as possible.

None of this was actually giving Trump what he really wanted, but it sounded like we were bending his way. Barr chirped in that he would have many more law enforcement officers in town for the coming evening, which helped the cause.

After a long pause that weighed heavily in the air, the president

y four years at West Point ingrained in e the moral, ethical, and professional mpass that would guide me decades er, especially when dealing with an unedictable commander in chief. I strove live by the academy motto of "Duty, onor, Country" as I worked to fulfill y sacred oath to the Constitution.

My service in the first Gulf War with the 3rd Battalion, 187th Infantry Regiment of the 101st Airborne Division, and later as an airborne rifle company commander in Europe, were formative experiences that helped inform and shape my decisions decades later as the nation's twenty-seventh secretary of defense, especially as we worked with allies to deal with North Korea, Iran, Russia, China, and others.

My wonderful family just after my July 2019 hearing to become secretary of defense. It was the apex of a career that began with Leah seeing me off to war, long training deployments, and multiple moves in service to country. The Senate confirmed me 90–8 in a solid bipartisan vote. I told lawmakers that I was prepared to resign if asked by the president to do anything immoral, illegal, or unethical.

This great team assisted me i jump-starting the "Army Renai sance" in 2018, with multiple in tiatives that would modernize a improve the Army for years to com *From left to right:* Me, Chief of Sta General Mark Milley, Under Secr tary Ryan McCarthy, Vice Chief Staff Jim McConville, and Sergea Major of the Army Dan Dailey.

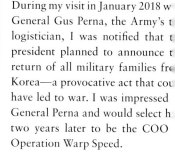

During my visit in January 2018 w General Gus Perna, the Army's t logistician, I was notified that t president planned to announce t return of all military families fr Korea—a provocative act that cou have led to war. I was impressed General Perna and would select h two years later to be the COO Operation Warp Speed.

I enjoyed spending time with our young soldiers, sailors, airmen, Marines, and later, Space Force guardians. They reflected the best of America with their personal stories, insights, and questions. Sessions like these helped shape my ideas to improve the Army's readiness and recruiting, and later, how to address discrimination and bias in the Department of Defense (DoD).

Supreme Court Justice Samuel Alito swore m in as the twenty-seventh secretary of defense July 23, 2019, as Leah held a Bible and our fan ilies looked on. The oath is to the Constitutio not to the commander in chief. President Trum was flattering in his remarks about me but w. surprised to learn that the Senate confirme me by an overwhelming margin. He later sai "Maybe I should be concerned?"

top priority was implementing the National Defense Strategy (NDS). To accomplish that, ... eeded to strengthen civilian control of the military and get the entire leadership team on the ... ne page. Bringing everyone together weekly to discuss NDS objectives, review tasks, and re- ... ve issues was essential. We made a good deal of progress on our Top Ten objectives during my ... hteen months as secretary of defense.

At my first Pentagon press conference as secretary of defense, I repeated my priority of implementing the NDS, with a focus on China. General Joe Dunford, chairman of the Joint Chiefs of Staff during my first few months in office, was a consummate professional and teammate. Together, we would address the president's continued push to withdraw U.S. forces from Europe, Asia, and Africa, while preparing military options to strike Iran.

In Norfolk, Virginia, I visited the USS *Boise*, an attack submarine that had not deployed in four years due to a maintenance backlog. I also spent time on the troubled USS *Ford* aircraft carrier. The Navy faced serious readiness issues. Moreover, I did not believe the sea service was building a future fleet that would fare well against China, so I directed the development of Battle Force 2045.

General Mark Milley became chairman of the Joint Chiefs of Staff during a rain-soaked ceremony on September 30, 2019. The president remarked that the rain was a sign of good luck. We would need it. After twenty months together as Army secretary and chief of staff, our close relationship was crucial in weathering some of the toughest days that the DoD and the nation would ever face.

In my meeting with Iraqi prime minister Adel Abdul-Mahdi in October 2019, I told him that the United States was committed to helping Iraq, but we expected them to protect Americans in the country. A rocket attack on an Iraqi military base two months later left one American dead and four service members injured, eventually leading to the biggest confrontation in decades between the United States and Iran.

Official trips were a great opportunity to engage the media in a less formal setting. I always believed a well-functioning press was critical to the exercise of democracy. As such, we significantly increased the number of press briefings and engagements while I was secretary of defense.

...dia is the most important partnership we need to develop to deal with a rising China. In October 2020, I traveled to New Delhi where Secretary of State Mike Pompeo and I accomplished a ...od deal, including agreements on information sharing, joint training, and new cyber and space ...alogues. These and others were important steps toward building the partnership needed to ...aintain a free and open Indo-Pacific.

Neither Beijing nor Moscow can match the asymmetric advantage of America's allies and partners working together. As China continues bucking international rules and norms, Japan and Korea will become more important to deterring this bad behavior. Pictured with me are the South Korean and Japanese defense ministers, Jeong Kyeong-doo (*left*) and Taro Kono (*right*).

Doing physical training with the troops was a fun and easy way to assess unit readiness and morale, while also quickly building a rapport with service members. After each workout, I would present a challenge coin to those who scored highest on their fitness test and invited tough questions from these great Americans. I also asked them questions in return and learned a lot in doing so.

I frequently visited our wounded warriors at Walter Reed National Military Medical Center to check on them and their families. Leah usually joined me. The optimism, tenacity, and patriotism of our service members always inspired me. I often gained a firsthand perspective as well on what was happening abroad in America's conflicts.

The Afghanistan peace deal was signed in Qatar on February 29, 2020. That same day, I stood alongside Afghan president Ashraf Ghani and NATO secretary general Jens Stoltenberg to express our continued commitment to Afghanistan. I made clear that a "conditions-based" approach was vital to implementing the agreement. President Trump never really supported the deal, and when he wanted to pursue a precipitous withdrawal in October 2020, I opposed it in a classified memo.

President Trump met with the interim president of Venezuela, Juan Guaidó, in the Oval Office on February 5, 2020. I listened closely, asked questions, and was on guard for any talk of U.S. military action against Caracas. The National Security Council seemed eager to employ military force against Venezuela, and I was concerned that such a predisposition could turn into a pre-election "October surprise."

On May 15, 2020, the president announced Operation Warp Speed (OWS), the administration's initiative led by the Department of Health and Human Services and the Department of Defense to accelerate the development, manufacturing, and distribution of a COVID-19 vaccine. One of the most successful public-private partnerships in history, OWS exceeded its goals by producing two vaccines on time, saving thousands of lives, and helping to get the country back on its feet.

A typical Oval Office meeting with President Trump. General Milley and I were similarly seated during our heated sessions with the president on June 1, 2020, when Trump pressed to call in active-duty forces to quell the demonstrations and suggested that the protesters be shot. On June 3, he berated me for publicly opposing the invocation of the Insurrection Act. I believe my action helped calm the country.

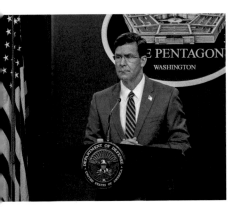

On June 3, 2020, I told the American people that "I do not support invoking the Insurrection Act." The tensions between the president and me had been growing since the previous summer. With protests in over two hundred cities across the country, coupled with Trump's disturbing inclination to call in active-duty forces and "just shoot" the protestors, I felt a clear public statement to the country was needed to stabilize a "wobbly" republic. It worked.

In the wake of June 1, 2020, and the con
clusions we drew from that difficult weel
General Milley and I developed the "For
Nos"—no unnecessary wars, no strategic re
treats, no politicization of the DoD, and n
misuse of the military—as redlines we woul
not cross. Our goal was to follow this gam
plan through the 2020 elections. It would ne
be easy. My sacred oath to the Constitutic
was my North Star.

Working sessions at NATO headquarters in Brussels were critical to keeping the alliance strong and focused. Jens Stoltenberg (*opposite me*) was a great secretary general whom I came to know and trust. Ambassador Kay Bailey Hutchison (*seated to my right*) was very effective in a tough job. The relationship between the three of us, and General Tod Wolters, was important to tackling tough alliance issues, including the president's arbitrary order to reduce U.S. forces in Germany.

I was standing at this desk ju
after lunch on November 9, 202
when Chief of Staff Mark Mea
ows called to say I was fired: "Th
president's not happy with yo
He feels you haven't supporte
him enough. You aren't suffi
ciently loyal." I replied, "That
the president's prerogative," b
"my oath is to the Constitutio
not to him." With that, we bot
hung up.

grudgingly nodded his okay. I thanked God he relented. Trump pointed to Barr and said, "You're going to run this." Barr laconically accepted his assignment, which was more music to my ears. Civilian law enforcement needed to be in charge, not the military.

I was surprised the president finally backed down but knew it was time to get out of the room before someone appealed the decision, as happened so many times on so many other issues in the past. Fortunately, as if on cue, one of the president's aides popped in to notify the group that "the governors are on the line in the Situation Room." Time to go!

The call with the governors was supposed to be fairly straightforward. The president would make some introductory comments about the civil unrest unfolding across the country, and then open up the line for the governors to comment, ask questions, or raise issues. It didn't start well, however. Trump was still fuming from the meeting in the Oval Office.

The president began the call by announcing that "General Milley is here, who's head of Joint Chief of Staff, a fighter, a warrior, had a lot of victories and no losses. And he hates to see the way it's being handled in the various states. And I just put him in charge."[1] While this explained his much earlier call to the chairman, the one that interrupted my Monday morning swipper brief, it was baffling the president said this after we addressed this matter in the Oval not more than twenty minutes before. The only explanation was that he was trying to intimidate the governors and to press them to take tough action. His next set of remarks would prove this was the case.

Milley really hated these comments, however, and I sensed him stirring at the other end of the crowded table. As I heard him say in the White House on more than one occasion, in an attempt to educate others, he was "merely an adviser" who didn't command or control anything.* Reports that Milley engaged in a shouting match with the president on this topic, ever, simply aren't accurate. The chairman was always professional with the commander in chief; he never raised his voice.

But Trump's words at this moment reflected his view and his inclination—to bypass law enforcement (Barr and DOJ, who were legally in charge) and even DoD civilian leadership (me), in order to clamp down on the protesters with overwhelming military force. His words in the Oval Office were exhibit A of this tendency.

Trump then quickly became aggressive with the governors, urging them to "dominate" their cities, arguing they would "look like a bunch of jerks" if they didn't dominate the streets, arrest people, and have them "go to jail for long periods of time." He called out cities from Philadelphia and New York to Dallas and Los Angeles, and argued that "the harder you are, the tougher you are, the less likely it is that you're going to be hit."[2] Trump constantly seemed to conflate peaceful protesters with the anarchists, radicals, and criminals. He obsessed about Antifa.

As his diatribe played on, he talked about the unrest in Washington, D.C.: "If you don't dominate your city and your state, they're gonna walk away with you. And we're doing it in Washington, in D.C., we're

---

* By law, the military chain of command is the president, the secretary of defense, and the eleven combatant commanders. The latter are the four-star military officers responsible for geographic commands, such as U.S. European Command, or functional commands, such as U.S. Strategic Command. These commanders take their direction and orders from the secretary of defense. The chairman of the Joint Chiefs of Staff, by law, is the principal military adviser to the President, the secretary of defense, the National Security Council, and the Homeland Security Council. Though the chairman is the highest-ranking officer in the military, he is prohibited from having operational command authority over the armed forces. The chairman can and does assist the secretary of defense in exercising his command functions.

going to do something that people haven't seen before. But you got to have total domination."[3] My ears perked up. *Is he already walking back the decision he made less than twenty minutes ago to *not* deploy active-duty troops?* I asked myself. *Is he going to announce this now, with the governors? What will he say exactly?* I needed to be ready to respond, to speak, to say something that would buy me, us, the military, some time, some maneuver room, some space.

At the same moment, I knew the clock was ticking on mobilizing Guard units to help support law enforcement in D.C. Without them, the chances of an active-duty call-up were real. Milley and I had walked straight from the Oval to the Situation Room, with no time for a quick phone call to the Pentagon, so no one in the DoD knew what was unfolding, let alone the actions we needed to initiate.

Bill Barr was next on the line. Bill grew up in New York City and graduated with a B.A. from Columbia University, and eventually a J.D. at George Washington University Law School. He had an extensive career, beginning with the CIA, clerking for a judge, working at a private law firm, a stint at the Reagan White House, and a few positions in the Justice Department before becoming attorney general in 1991 under President George H. W. Bush. After a stint in corporate America, he returned to government service in 2019 to serve as AG once again under Trump.

I didn't know Bill before serving with him, but mutual friends spoke very highly of him. I came to learn that Bill matched a keen intellect with a quick wit. He could adroitly pivot from giving you a sober legal assessment to delivering a wisecrack that broke the tension in a room. I had no insight into all the issues between him and the president, but Bill never hesitated to speak his mind and was a good partner when it came to the president's eagerness to use the Insurrection Act.

Barr immediately picked up the president's theme that governors need to "dominate the streets," though he was rightly focused on the "troublemakers" and the need to have enough police to go into the crowds and arrest them.[4] If law enforcement didn't have enough capacity, he argued, then call up your National Guard to show presence, protect buildings, and free up the cops. His message was consistent with what Milley and I had been saying, and what we had discussed with the governor of Minnesota over the weekend, when he eventually called up thousands of Guardsmen to support law enforcement in Minneapolis. This was a good use of the National Guard, and their employment was critical in getting things under control.

Nevertheless, the president kept coming back to "total domination" and the "terrorists" that we needed to go after, and I was still processing his comments about shooting protesters.[5]

When my turn came to speak, I saw an opportunity to get the message out about calling up the Guard under state authority. The numbers deployed across the country were woefully low. I cited the positive example of Governor Tim Walz of Minnesota—a Democrat—for the actions he took days earlier to calm things down in his state—ground zero for the unrest until this point. I thought, if only the governors would make more use of the Guard under their own authorities, then we can avoid further talk of calling up active-duty forces. And then I uttered the words I came to regret.

"Battle space" is an operational term we use all the time in the military. Its colloquial usage is not about the enemy or even the use of force, but about the three-dimensional area in which you have people or assets employed. I made a practice of walking around the Pentagon nearly every week I wasn't traveling, to visit offices, find out what folks were working on, and thank them for their service. It was a nice way to get out of my gilded cage on the E-ring and visit the great Americans in the inner rings of the building who were doing the real work of making the Department run. On these visits, it wasn't uncommon for some young officer to introduce them-self, explain to me their job, and then point to their cubicle and proudly say, "And sir, this is my battle space." The term was that common.

Once, when Milley and I were still at the Army and dealing with sexual harassment and assault at West Point, he pressed the super-intendent to "get control of your barracks. This is your battle space. You must own it and control it if you want to get this problem under control." The phrase was nearly as common as the term "bat-tle buddy," but the governors' call clearly wasn't the place to use it. As I implored the governors to use their Guard to facilitate peaceful protests, I picked up on Trump's and Barr's use of the word "domi-nate" and urged them to quickly "mass"—another military term— the Guard forces and "dominate the battle space" in order to get control of the streets. Milley would use the same phrase a few min-utes later, but the damage was done. Somebody leaked comments from the call to the media, and this was one of them.

In the hours and days following the call, I would be accused by some of urging the military to attack U.S. cities and kill Ameri-cans. That clearly was not true. It was also unfair. Worse, for me it was hurtful because of the great pride I took in the civil-military relations between the American people and the U.S. armed forces. We were the most highly respected institution in the country. Ser-vice members came from all walks of life, from all corners of the nation, and reflected the great diversity of the United States more than any other public institution.

It was inappropriate for me to use those words in that setting for sure. Moreover, part of my job as defense secretary is helping connect the American people to their military, and using the jar-gon of the Pentagon made it sound like the U.S. armed forces were being used for political purposes. It was a mistake and I owned it.

However, those words reflected neither my heart nor my head, and I tried to correct this with the press two days later:

> I was quoted [earlier this week] as saying, "The best way to get street violence under control was by dominating the battle space." And probably all of you who cover the Pentagon hear us use this phrase often. It's something we use day in and day out. There are other phrases that we use day in day out that you'll understand that most people don't understand. It is part of our military lexicon that I grew up with, and it's what we routinely use to describe a bounded area of operations. It's not a phrase focused on people, and certainly not on our fellow Americans as some have suggested. It is a phrase I used over the weekend when speaking with Minnesota Governor Walz. . . . It was his successful use of the Guard in sufficient numbers that really wrested control of the streets from the looters and others breaking the law, so I was giving him credit for that. And he was doing so, so the peaceful demonstrations could be held so that peaceful demonstrators could share their frustration and their anger. That's what I was encouraging other governors to consider. In retrospect, I would use different wording so as to not distract from the more important matters at hand, or allow some to suggest that we are militarizing the issue.[6]

Of course, what I couldn't say at the time, and really wanted to, was that I lost my situational awareness because I thought there was a fair chance that Trump was going to order the 82nd Airborne Division into the streets, and maybe even direct them to shoot the protesters. At that moment, at that time, on that call, I could think of nothing else but this, and the need for governors to call up the Guard, short-circuit the president, and help get this under control.

This was the best way to avoid an active-duty call-up, and a likely disaster.

Once the call wrapped up, Milley and I headed quickly to our cars. We were both a little rattled by the morning's events but had to get things moving in order to prevent some very bad outcomes. We didn't have time to do too much processing. We had to make our way through the brush and the trees right now; seeing the broader forest would have to wait.

The chairman planned on hustling back to his office to begin preparations for the evening with the Army and the D.C. Guard. Before we stepped into our respective vehicles, I verbally approved the movement of troops to bases outside of Washington, D.C., per our discussion with the president, as well as the mobilization of the 3rd Infantry at Fort Myer. However, "no one, no units," I said, "are to step foot into D.C. without my personal approval." Milley understood and concurred. Our eyes met—we knew dramatic things were under way—we also knew he and I had to stay in close touch. We shook hands, and the general jumped into his black Suburban and went to work.

I placed a call to the chief of the National Guard Bureau, General Joe Lengyel, as my SUV sped off from the West Wing. I wanted to get state Guard units moving toward D.C. immediately. Quickly deploying them was the critical part of the plan. Indeed, as soon as I arrived at my Pentagon office, I began calling governors and asking for their help. This would be my principal focus for the next few hours.

CHAPTER 13

A WALK IN THE PARK

Around 5:00 P.M. the afternoon of June 1, I had a conference call with the Army and D.C. National Guard leadership—most of whom were already at the FBI command center downtown near F Street, a short walk from the National Building Museum. All parts of the law enforcement effort were sending representatives there for the evening to enable the command and control necessary to deal with the unrest that was expected. I wanted to do a quick call with the team to make sure everything was set for the night: rules of engagement; necessary authorities; adequate resources; connectivity with law enforcement, and so on.

My plan was to join them at the FBI command center after wrapping things up at the Pentagon around 6:00 P.M. Milley said he would meet me downtown but wanted to first change out of his dress uniform into more comfortable clothing—his camouflage field uniform—as we both expected a long night and had plans to visit the troops scattered across the city. This was a decision he would later regret.

I left the Pentagon on time, and as I neared the temporary FBI command post around 6:20 P.M. or so, I received a call that the president wanted an update on the evening's preparations. The White House expected General Milley and me there immediately. My driver quickly hit the police lights, whipped the armored Suburban around, and sped off toward 1600 Pennsylvania Avenue.

When I arrived, more than a dozen people gathered in the waiting room outside the Oval Office. It was a mixed group of folks, ranging from National Security Adviser Robert O'Brien to first daughter Ivanka Trump and Press Secretary Kayleigh McEnany, along with members of the White House communications team. I asked the president's scheduler what time we were meeting. Someone else piped up and said, "There is no meeting." "Well, then," I said, "I'm heading back to the operations center to check out the security situation for the evening." "No, no," someone else said, "the president is giving a speech in the Rose Garden." He wants members of the cabinet to join him afterward in a walk to the church, she added, "to check out the damage from last night." I didn't think much about it, which was my mistake. I was focused on getting the Guard into the city and getting to the FBI command post before the sun fell.

O'Brien came over and started speaking to me about some international issue we were working. It was noisy in the anteroom of the Oval, with people talking and the TV on, so we stepped into the Cabinet Room and closed the door to chat. I thought that, if I can't get to the command post right now, at least I could get some work done on other issues.

Meanwhile, at some point, no more than several hundred yards away, the USPP began clearing Lafayette Park by force. The police launched the operation prior to the 7:00 P.M. curfew that had been set, and the tactics employed seemed excessive and unnecessary, notwithstanding the violence of previous nights. Many would say that the attorney general issued the order to clear the park, though he denied it. It was never clear to me who approved the operation until a year later, after the Department of the Interior's inspector general issued a report on the actions at Lafayette Park.

I kept moving in and out of the Cabinet Room to talk privately with people. This went on for quite some time until someone said, "The president is wrapping things up. Please line up." We proceeded do so, inside the Oval Office, stretching from the french doors facing east toward the Rose Garden, all the way back into the anteroom—also called the Outer Oval—where the schedulers sat.

Ivanka was looking at a few Bibles sitting on a table—something I had never seen before in the Oval Office—and eventually grabbed one. I wondered what that was about. I had caught glimpses of Lafayette Park earlier on TV as I moved in and out of discussions but had no real sense of what was happening, who did what, how the park clearing was initiated, or what the extent of the action was. I found out when I arrived that we were going to visit the church to check out the damage. But what else? I looked at Milley, who arrived sometime after me, and asked, "What's the game plan?" He had no idea. I'm not sure who really knew.

We stepped out of the Oval Office and walked along the colonnade around the Rose Garden and into the White House proper, before ending up at the State Floor where the Entrance Hall and North Portico—the ground-level entrance facing Lafayette Park—was located. The president met us inside the Entrance Hall. He was in good spirits, much better than earlier. He greeted us, said, "Come on," and asked, "Are you all ready to go?" He then briskly stepped outside onto the North Portico, as I asked him, "What are we doing?" Trump didn't respond as he strode onto the grounds. Though it remained unclear what the plan or purpose of the walk was, you could sense that something dramatic was about to happen.

I turned and looked at Milley. Our glances conveyed our uncertainty. "Let's go and find the troops," I said to him. "Sounds good to me," he responded.

We walked down the driveway, and out the main gate, trailing Trump, with security on all sides. Someone from the communications team asked us to give him some space, so as we wound our way into Lafayette Park, we kept a proper distance behind the president. A large gaggle of press awaited the president just beyond the north entranceway. Aha. Now this was feeling really awkward. "I think we've been duped," I said to Milley. We were being used.

As Trump strode into the park, the media walked backwards before him, taking pictures, and shouting questions. I looked for an opportunity to peel off to visit with the D.C. Guard assigned to protect buildings but was unable to spot them. I couldn't break from the scrum now anyway. It would be too obvious.

Barr, Milley, and I didn't say much as we walked. Soon enough we arrived at the northeast corner of the park, where damage to a small National Park Service building was evident. There was a whiff of pepper spray or tear gas in the air, which burned my nostrils slightly and caught my attention. I never saw or heard any protesters, however.

The crowd of White House staff, cabinet officials, reporters, and security stopped moving and gathered as we crossed onto H Street, which separated the park from St. John's Episcopal Church, our supposed destination. It was also damaged, with graffiti and black smoke stains from fires obvious. We were opposite the parish house when the president stepped onto the sidewalk and turned to face the press.

What would happen next? What would he say? What would he

do? I didn't know. I'm not sure anyone did other than Trump. Part of me envisioned—hoped—that the church's pastor would join the president, that they would greet each other warmly, that they would walk around and inspect the damage, that maybe they would say a prayer together, and then they would jointly speak to the media about repairing the church and healing a troubled country. When I shared that fanciful tale with someone on the White House staff weeks later, they remarked, "W. or Obama would have done that," referring to our previous two presidents, "but not this guy."

I didn't see most of what happened next. I was talking to a member of my staff, still trying to spot the D.C. Guard, as Trump spoke to the media. The next thing I knew, Mark Meadows, Kayleigh McEnany, and Bill Barr had joined him. I sensed there was something really inappropriate evolving, so I tried to move back, away from what was unfolding, yet keeping an eye on what was happening. The press took several photos, and O'Brien joined the president. Trump kept scanning the crowd, though, searching for others. I somehow caught eyes with him through the interspersed people between us. As he stood in front of the church, he made a hand movement from below the waist that beckoned me forward. It was like a third-base coach in baseball giving a batter hitting signals. I ignored the first one, but after another, I felt caught. Dammit. I reluctantly moved into the lineup, at the far end, out of the center frame as much as possible, for a final shot or two.

We then headed back to the White House. My senior military assistant and I broke from the pack and tried one last time to find the National Guard. I wanted to talk with them. We explored the west end of the park with my security detail, but, concerned that we might become trapped outside the White House grounds, we hustled back to regroup with the Trump entourage as they approached the gated north entrance. Once back inside, I quickly made my way to the West Wing, and then to my car, and departed immediately for the FBI command post.

I didn't spend much time thinking about what had just happened in the park. My gut was telling me the whole episode was inappropriate, and that I had made the mistake of being drawn into this highly political moment. While the walk and pictures resonated with many in his base, the context, the pretext, the images, and the message—whatever it really was—was awful. There were clearly lessons for me, but I decided to set the matter aside for later, when I had more time to process and assess it all. Right now, it was getting dark and we had much to do. What happened over the next several hours would make a world of difference for every other day that followed.

While I regretted participating in the entire Lafayette Park debacle, I was both proud and relieved to learn that the Guard played no role in the events leading up to it. As we all learned later, contrary to what the press was reporting at the time, the Guard never directly engaged the protesters, never employed tear gas or pepper balls, and never shot rubber bullets.

By evening, several hundred D.C. Guardsmen protected federal buildings, secured monuments, and blocked key intersections leading to the White House throughout the city. I took a couple of briefings at the FBI command center after arriving sometime around 8:00 P.M. I wanted an update from my team on the additional Guard units flowing into the city, as well as the status of the active-duty forces we alerted. I also needed to understand what law enforcement was hearing on the street regarding any protests, marches, or violence under way or being planned. Shortly after 9:00 P.M., I jumped into a Suburban with Bill Barr to visit a few of our joint checkpoints.

Bill and I didn't talk much on the way about the day's events. Like me, he focused on the night ahead. I shared with him the update I just received regarding additional Guard forces moving toward the city, and he briefed me on what law enforcement was doing. It was good, I thought, that his folks and mine saw us driving around and working closely together.

At the first stop north of the White House, I went to talk to the troops, while Bill went to speak with some of his officers. After a few minutes, several people hanging out on the street, a safe distance from the checkpoint, recognized who we were and started heading toward us. It wasn't clear to me that they were protesters, but a few began yelling while nearby reporters approached us with questions. Barr's security team was concerned, so he ended up getting back into his vehicle and leaving early. I stayed, but walked a block down the street, away from those gathering, to visit another military checkpoint.

After speaking with the soldiers at the second intersection, I traveled with Army Secretary Ryan McCarthy to visit more of our service members. McCarthy was undersecretary of the Army for me when I held the top job in the service, so we knew each other well. He was doing a great job working with Metro Police and the D.C. National Guard in the tough days prior to June 1. Ryan was also the de facto "governor" of Washington, D.C., when it came to the employment of the National Guard within the District. It was his delegated responsibility, and he took it on with great diligence.

Our vehicle moved briskly south through the city, and we eventually ended up at the World War II Memorial, stopping on 17th Street between the memorial and the Washington Monument. It was a dark, quiet night; the area was largely removed from the protests. As we pulled up, I jumped out of the black Suburban and headed toward the troops standing watch alongside the street.

While the service members I met at the memorial were all D.C. Guard, they weren't MPs. In fact, they weren't even Army soldiers. I was surprised to learn they were Air Guard, men and women alike, whom the command pulled from their day jobs as airplane mechanics, admin specialists, and other similar career fields. They were not accustomed to this type of duty, but they did it with great professionalism. I spent a fair amount of time speaking with them, discussing their call-up, the nature of their mission, the tragedy of George Floyd, and other issues. They were inspiring, and it was one of my better conversations of the day.

General Milley showed up not long after me. He had been making the rounds as well. I shook a few more hands, took a picture or two, and then the chairman and I decided to walk to the Lincoln Memorial. We followed the paved path west from the World War II Memorial to visit the soldiers and airmen standing guard at the picturesque monument to our sixteenth president. It would be a good chance to catch up with Milley as we walked. It had been a long day.

Despite all that was happening in the city, the pathway along the south side of the Reflecting Pool toward the Lincoln Memorial was eerily dark and quiet. We had our aides and security personnel around us as we walked, but they were out of earshot. It was a good moment, finally, to reflect on what was happening. We discussed everything from the Oval Office meeting that morning to the clearing of Lafayette Square a few hours before and the next twenty-four hours ahead. The full impact of the day wasn't apparent to us—or at least to me—just yet, but we knew the game had changed. The country also seemed to be losing its footing, and I was very concerned about the president and where he was headed.

Trump seemed unable to think straight and calmly. The protests and violence had him so enraged that he was willing to send in active-duty forces to put down the protesters. Worse yet, he suggested we shoot them. I wondered about his sense of history, of propriety, and of his oath to the Constitution. And then there was his constant concern about appearing weak. How far might that exaggerated sense of insecurity, of that singular need to push back hard and win, take us? Depending on how the protests went that night, we would likely find out the next day.

General Milley was clearly thinking about many of these things too, and the way ahead as well. We held nearly identical views on these issues. The calm of the evening along the quiet path gave us our first real chance to talk. The realization that the White House played us in Lafayette Park for political gain was soaking in, and with it came regret. We were disappointed in ourselves, but we learned an important lesson the hard way. We weren't going to let that happen again.

Our different positions gave us different roles and responsibilities, however. Mark Milley was a uniformed officer and I was a political appointee. I had more freedom to step into the political gray zone and was expected to do so at times. Milley's uniform gave him no such freedom, but it offered him a firm foundation to say no if asked. From our respective perches and different histories, we would inevitably arrive at the same conclusion and develop a new strategy over the coming days that would guide us until the end. It would be a game plan known only to us and a few of our closest advisers. And it would demand discipline, sacrifice, perseverance, teamwork, and integrity if we were to live up to our oaths.

Looking back, it felt doubly strange that a discussion of such importance occurred as we walked toward the memorial of one of our greatest presidents, Abraham Lincoln—the one leader who faced real insurrection over the issue of race in America yet could see and understand the big picture and knew best how to navigate it. Not knowing the future, I had little grasp of the significance of this moment, our strategy, and what would transpire in the coming days and months.

The FBI command post had become a beehive of activity by the time I returned later that night, after my tour of the checkpoints and talk with Milley along the Reflecting Pool. The street in front of the building was packed with law enforcement vehicles, black Suburbans, and police in all types of uniform and gear. Security was very tight. Every threshold—the sidewalk, the front entrance, the inner doors, the elevator—had someone guarding it.

As we walked into the command post on one of the upper floors, the place was abuzz. Law enforcement personnel from across the government filled the room shoulder to shoulder. Many were sitting in front of computer terminals working issues, some were talking in hushed voices in small groups, and still others were crisscrossing the room delivering memos, updates, or simply trying to grab a colleague's attention. A few large screens at one end of the room presented operational data, live news, and video for all to monitor.

The whole gathering made an immediate impression: the low steady rumble of people talking and keyboards clacking; the visual of bodies with guns and badges of all types packed in tight, yet moving about like bees in a hive; the hot and humid air produced by so many people working hurriedly in a space the size of a large living room; and the scent of a warm afternoon mixed with a day's worth of sweat. I said to one of my aides, "If we don't get COVID tonight, we never will."

The DoD had a smaller space on the other side of a large wall that was less packed. I worked my way over there to get an update from the Joint Staff. Of most interest to me remained the flow of personnel into the city, particularly the National Guard. The D.C.

Guard's numbers were above 1,000, but as I learned from my visits around the city, many of these folks were not well trained for the mission if the situation became violent. Their presence imparted an important show of force that helped deter bad behavior by trouble-makers, but if a protest turned truly ugly, I didn't feel that we had enough MPs.

General Lengyel, the four-star head of the National Guard, had done a great job getting other states to commit forces quickly, and many of them were mobilizing. However, several states had their own civil unrest concerns that they were dealing with, making them hard-pressed to assist. The D.C. Guard could generate 1,200 person-nel, so we needed another 3,800 from the states to reach the 5,000 number that I had promised the president. To their credit, we would soon see troops from Utah, Maryland, and New Jersey arrive early, followed by additional forces from another seven states by Thursday.

The Maryland Guard was the first to show up. I had called Gov-ernor Larry Hogan earlier in the afternoon to request his assistance. Hogan had a very even, steady demeanor about him, which I liked, and he was willing to contradict Trump, which I respected. I quickly explained to him what was evolving in D.C. and said, "Governor, I would appreciate whatever Guard forces you can send us to help keep things calm down here." He paused for a moment and, in that same calm tone, spoke about flashpoints in Maryland he was con-cerned about, namely Baltimore.

He then said, "I am always willing to help, but what are they going to be used for?" I told him, "The Guard would be standing watch at federal buildings and monuments, freeing up D.C. Metro PD and federal law enforcement to deal with any violence in the streets."

I could sense his reluctance, and for all the right reasons. I assumed he was on the president's call with the governors that morning, so he understood Trump's mind-set and predisposition to employ the military very aggressively. Hogan did not want his Guardsmen taking on protesters, as he said to me on the phone. I told him, "I get it. I was in the Guard. I understand how best and when best to use them. I don't want that to happen either." However, I added, "If I can't get enough National Guard into D.C. to free up law enforcement, and to help calm the situation, the president will want to send in other troops, and that's the last thing I want to do." Hogan was a real pro about it, grasping the urgency and importance of the situation. He paused again, then said that he wanted to speak with his adjutant general, who oversaw the Maryland Guard, but otherwise gave me a tentative yes.

The governor called me back a few hours later, sometime after the Lafayette Park debacle. As my convoy sped to the FBI command post downtown, Hogan committed to sending me around one hundred Guardsmen that evening. He also wanted my assurance that they would be protecting buildings and monuments, and nothing further. I gave him my word and thanked him for his help.

My earlier calls to Virginia and Pennsylvania that afternoon, however, left me empty-handed. Governor Tom Wolf of Pennsylvania declined to send troops, saying that he faced "civil unrest in Philadelphia" and "can't afford to send any Guard to D.C." I recognized this was a legitimate concern, but I also noted that Pennsylvania had one of the largest Guard forces in the country, with more than eighteen thousand troops. Wolf clearly didn't want to send anyone—you could tell this in his careful tone and measured words—but was cordial enough to dodge my request by suggesting he would reconsider it over the following days. I had no confidence anyone from my birth state would show.

Governor Ralph Northam of Virginia quickly took my call but was also reluctant to send troops "unless [D.C.] mayor [Muriel]

Bowser requested them." He asked me if she had, and I truthfully told him, "No, Governor, she has not, but her police really need our assistance." In fact, the mayor didn't want anything to do with the military, a far different approach than she would take in January 2021. Ryan McCarthy told me that Bowser even refused to take his calls or meet with him—quite unprofessional behavior—so he engaged directly with the head of the Metro Police Department, which ended up working very well. Northam was pleasant and respectful but also turned me down.

I also started dialing Governor Cuomo in New York when my staff told me that I didn't need to speak with him. The New York adjutant general already agreed to send troops, and they were en-route and would be in D.C. by nightfall. I would learn an hour later that the governor directed that they return immediately home. This was disappointing, but not surprising. Democratic governors wanted no part of Trump's plans.

At least twenty-three states, in addition to D.C., would activate their Guard on June 1 to deal with the growing civil unrest in cities across the country. Washington would end up with over 5,100 troops from eleven states joining the D.C. Guard. Their mission included protecting federal property and helping manage crowds in support of law enforcement. Guard leadership considered these missions some of their toughest, but probably never had to perform them in a political environment as toxic as this one.

While the military continued to move forces into the area, federal law enforcement had assembled more quickly. Bill Barr did a good job with this, and I was relieved to see officers from the FBI, the ATF, and other agencies in the streets. Neither Barr nor I wanted to see the Insurrection Act invoked. And I preferred the smallest Guard footprint needed to support law enforcement. If we could get through the night, then DOJ would have enough officers in the city for the subsequent evenings, and the DoD would have enough Guard units to support them. With about seven hours to go until daybreak, things were trending well, but one could never predict how persons bent on violence and mayhem may act once night fell. Or how Trump would react once it happened.

After the staff updated me, I went to a small back office at the FBI command center to talk with my team. Milley, McCarthy, Jonathan Hoffman (my head of public affairs), and a couple of other folks joined me. We shared stories and impressions from the day. While I was aware of the public reaction to the president's photo op at Lafayette Park, Hoffman told me my "battle space" comment was getting a lot of buzz, as was Milley's walk across the park in his camouflage uniform. I had not been back in the Pentagon and hadn't seen the news in hours, so it was hard to get a feel for what was happening more broadly. However, after hearing from the team that evening, two things seemed to stand out: unrest across the country was spiraling, and there was nervousness within the DoD.

The last part surprised me some. It was clear to me what our role was and the part we needed to play, but my public affairs chief's point was that the joint force needed reassurance from its leadership. He was right. The last few hours had sucked me into the tactical state of play—what was happening on the ground in the nation's capital—though I felt it was important to get out and get a feel for things in the city for myself. (For example, the realization that we didn't have enough MPs on duty was an important finding from my evening tour.)

I also wanted to thank and reassure the D.C. Guardsmen. Their leadership yanked them out of their jobs and put them on the streets of the nation's capital amid a lot of fear and uncertainty. The fact was, right now, they were doing more than their job keeping peace on the streets and protecting the monuments. They were all we had to prevent the president from sending in active-duty troops, so I needed them to be strong and confident.

Regardless, I had to get a message out soon to set the right tone and direction for the Department. My message would also provide top cover for the chairman, the services, and the reinforcing messages they wanted to send out, in case the president reacted negatively. The day's events revealed to me how infuriated he was about the civil unrest. I couldn't afford to lose a civilian secretary or flag officer because of this.

I gave Hoffman some guidance on the main points I wanted to hit, that I wanted to review it in the morning, and then get it out by midday, less than twenty-four hours after the police cleared Lafayette Park, and before most service members in the United States ended their workday on Tuesday.

Jonathan Hoffman was from South Carolina and graduated from the University of Richmond and then law school at the University of Virginia. He had spent a decade in the Air Force Reserve Judge Advocate General Corps and was still serving. He came to the Public Affairs job at the Pentagon in May 2019 with a good deal of experience, having served in a variety of senior roles in the George W. Bush administration, working in the private sector doing public affairs and government relations work, and then joining the Trump administration in early 2017 to manage communications for General John Kelly. He had started at the DoD roughly a month before I became the acting secretary, and I first met him the day the president tweeted that I was taking over.

Jonathan was smart, politically savvy, good with the press, and candid with me in his assessment and recommendations, which I appreciated. He was also a quick study with a good feel for what was happening, so he headed out to start putting words to paper for the message we discussed.

It was now after 11:00 P.M., and I had been up since 4:30 that morning, so I decided to make one last spin around the command post and head home. It was a long day, probably the longest in all my years of government service. I had made mistakes for sure, some of my own doing, and others that I should have seen coming. I regretted these, and still do. But as a close friend would later tell me, "Mark, nobody expects you to be perfect. You made mistakes and you'll probably make more. We just expect you to fix them if you can, and do better the next time."

What came to mind on the long drive home that night was the striking contrast in Trump's views toward the armed forces. On one hand, he held the military in high regard. The DoD seemed to be his go-to department for tough problems, for when he wanted things done quickly and well, and certainly to show bold action and determination. The military's role in COVID response, Operation Warp Speed, and building the wall on the southwest border were prime examples.

Trump held the general officers in even higher regard. He loved the uniforms, the badges, the ribbons, the accoutrements. It was all about image and look. He put the flag officers on a pedestal and referred to them as "my generals." For these senior officers, it was a terrible position to be in—upholding the historic tradition of apolitical service with a commander in chief who expected 100 percent political loyalty first and always.

On the other hand, he could be extremely harsh and unfair to them in private. Here we were on June 1, with the president going to the military once again to solve a problem—civil unrest—and expressing confidence in our ability to do so. Only a few weeks earlier, however, the commander in chief had been excoriating the Pentagon's leadership in the Cabinet Room.

...

The Joint Chiefs of Staff and I arrived at the White House shortly before the planned start time of 5:00 P.M. on Saturday, May 9, to give the president an update brief on China. The half dozen or so of us piled into the Cabinet Room and stood behind our seats around the large conference table. Mike Pompeo and Robert O'Brien joined us. The president's chair stood empty in the middle, and behind it were the flags of the armed services, including the newly established Space Force.

We waited quite a while for the president, and then, after a quick heads-up from his assistant in the outer office, who said, "He's coming," we all went silent, while the generals and admirals—in their dress uniforms—stood in a relaxed position of attention behind their chairs. Trump strode into the room with a scowl on his face—not a good sign. He looked down at the floor, his mind focused on something else, as he gave a cursory "Hello, everyone" and took his seat.

With the Joint Chiefs of Staff, the president was usually relaxed. He would smile, look around the room, say hello to those officers he recognized, and then make some laudatory remarks. Not today. I moved quickly to fill the awkward space by greeting the commander in chief in an upbeat manner, trying to shift the dark cloud that entered the room and describing the purpose of the meeting.

I started with a brief overview of the agenda: "Mr. President, thanks for taking time this afternoon to meet with me, the chairman, and the Joint Chiefs of Staff. What I thought we would do today is update you on our plans, programs, and preparations to deal with China, which is the Pentagon's primary strategic focus." I continued, explaining that I would outline the NDS and our implementation plans, that General Milley would "provide a review of our force posture around the globe," and then the service chiefs "will walk you through their top programs, operational preparations, and other hot issues that you should be aware of."

Then, all of a sudden, Trump launched into a twenty-minute tirade. He wasn't screaming, but he was clearly upset. He looked around the room as he spoke, red in the face at times, telling the group that "the great U.S. military isn't as capable as you think," that "we put too much confidence in our allies despite them ripping us off," and that "we can't even win in Afghanistan, a third-rate country."

This last part cued himself to mock Jim Mattis again, imitating the former secretary of defense saying how "the Afghans are brave and they will fight." Trump folded his arms across his chest and again dismissed Mattis as "the most overrated general ever." The president then went on to assert that "the Chinese military is better than us," citing their missiles and the size of their navy. I interjected, saying, "There's no doubt in my mind, Mr. President, that we can beat them," and then adding a quick anecdote regarding the Army's recent test of a hypersonic weapon that hit within inches of its target.

Nevertheless, barely skipping a beat, he continued down his list of complaints, including his old favorite that "the U.S. Navy ships are ugly and broken," followed by a quick recitation of the USS *Ford*'s flaws, and so on, and so on, and so on. I could barely get in a word in defense. General Milley tried as well, but with little success.

The Joint Chiefs sat around the table stone-faced. I was concerned and growing more frustrated. My various ploys to arrest his behavior or change the topic were not having any impact.

The president complained, "For all the money being spent on the military—$2.5 trillion that I gave you to rebuild the military—you can't fight. You can't win." I don't think he believed the last points at all; that outburst was more emotion than anything. But he was convinced about the first part—that he had spent "trillions of dollars" on the military—and furthermore, as he said a few times before in different settings, that "the armed forces have been totally rebuilt" and were better than ever.

The notion that we had a completely rebuilt military was a gross overstatement, of course. We were certainly on the front end of that process and in much better shape since the end of Obama's presidency. Indeed, Trump's push for increased military spending in his first couple of years provided a tremendous boost to our military readiness and allowed for good initial investments into our modernization accounts. Nevertheless, we would need years and years of this type of spending to transform the military into the force required to deal with China in the future.

The president's misconception of the state of the military, marked by his exaggerations, was harmful because he and others in the White House took their foot off the gas and were trimming defense spending just as we were gaining real momentum. Indeed, his Fiscal Year 2021 budget request was several billion dollars less than what the administration asked for and Congress approved for FY 2020 when it came to overall DoD budget authority.[1] My efforts, and those of others in the Pentagon and on Capitol Hill, to explain this to him seemed to always fall on deaf ears.

In Trump's mind, when it came to defense spending, he was done. Mission complete. Russ Vought, the head of the Office of Management and Budget and a fiscal hawk who never seemed keen on increasing the DoD's budget, enabled this view. It was one shared as well by Mark Meadows, who earned the same reputation during his time in Congress. This is where I give Robert O'Brien credit for pushing back inside the White House and advocating for continued investments in the defense enterprise. The fact was, despite the internal advocacy by myself and others, I had little confidence that

Trump would agree to more increases in defense spending—money needed to continue his promised rebuilding of the U.S. military. We had already tried on a few occasions and lost.

Back in the room that late Saturday afternoon in May, however, General Milley and I kept looking for opportunities to push back. We had been through these episodes many times before, so Trump didn't shock us with this one. We did our best with facts, data, and anecdotes, but the president wasn't listening. He was in transmit mode. I also tried a couple of times to get the conversation back on topic or get him engaged with the four-stars. But Trump cut the conversation off and started down another tangent.

This meeting wasn't my idea in the first place. It was an outcome just like this that specifically concerned me. Nevertheless, I had arrived at the West Wing that afternoon hoping it would be a positive experience for everyone. The president rarely met with the Joint Chiefs, so I viewed it as an opportunity for everyone to get to know one another and build some rapport. It was now in a steep nosedive, and getting worse by the minute. The really frustrating thing was that I couldn't stop or deflect it.

My concern grew exponentially about the impact the president's tirade was having on our most senior uniformed leaders, and what they would take away from this meeting. How stupid of the president, I thought, to do something like this. To make false claims and baseless complaints about the capabilities and readiness of the U.S. military to these officers—professionals who had spent their adult lives in uniform defending the country, risking them in many cases, and usually spending long periods away from their families in the process—was reprehensible. I couldn't imagine a worse performance or poorer example by any commander in chief.

Finally, a White House staffer standing alongside the wall behind us said that it was time for the press to come in for some photos and questions. Thank goodness—saved again by the schedule. Trump spoke for less than a minute, but didn't take any questions. He thought this would "drive the press crazy" and create an aura of suspicion. Photos of him, the Joint Chiefs, and me in a special Saturday White House meeting would "get them stirred up," he said. Go figure.

Afterward, I was supposed to join the president, other cabinet officials, and our spouses for dinner. General Milley and the rest of the four-stars were excused. I grabbed Milley privately as the meeting broke and asked him to get the Joint Chiefs all together outside, hear them out, and then talk them down. I suspected they were rattled and angered by Trump's behavior, but needed to know that Milley and I were managing it. The chairman had already figured this out too and intended to pull them aside before everyone went their separate ways. When he did so not long after we spoke, he indeed found the Joint Chiefs in a bad state.

Months later, one of the officers present told me in a phone call that he went home that evening deeply concerned about what he had seen in his commander in chief. The next morning, he said in a very sober tone, he started reading up on the Twenty-Fifth Amendment and the role of the cabinet as a check on the president. He wanted to understand "what the Cabinet needed to consider" and what the process was.

Despite the friction in my relationship with Trump, which had grown over time, I felt I was still able to manage the president and his worst instincts. Moreover, although many things he said and suggested ranged from inappropriate to outlandish, none ever rose to a level that warranted consideration of the Twenty-Fifth Amendment. June 1 was still a few weeks away, however, and

January 6, 2021, was unimaginable. As terrible as this meeting was, I always felt it at least gave the nation's most senior military officers some important insight into what I had to manage and deal with over that long summer and fall, and in the many, many months leading up to both.*

---

* After June 3, 2020, President Trump would turn on the DoD's senior military leaders publicly. On September 7, Trump said that "the top people in the Pentagon" wanted to "fight wars so all of those wonderful companies that make the bombs and make the planes and make everything else stay happy," suggesting that we favored waging war in order to somehow line the pockets of industry. It was wrong and disgraceful. If anything, General Milley and I were often the least likely to support military action. It took angry phone calls from Milley and me to Mark Meadows to try to walk Trump's statement back and prevent future outbursts.

_____

CHAPTER 14

HARD DAYS AND LONG NIGHTS

_____

As the black armored Suburban ferried me into work early on June 2, news stories indicated that no major violence broke out in D.C. after we left the FBI command post late Monday night. That was great news. Hopefully, it meant that Trump wouldn't be pressing us to deploy active-duty troops into the city, and with Guard forces heading toward D.C., we should be in good shape for Tuesday night. Time would tell.

I met with Jonathan Hoffman to review the message to the force that I had asked him to draft. I adjusted it in a few places before taking an update on COVID, followed by a call with the head of U.S. Forces Korea, General Robert Abrams. The country's security after all, let alone the pandemic, didn't rest simply because we had protesters in the nation's streets.

My message, which went out that afternoon, emphasized our oath to support and defend the Constitution of the United States.* This included protecting the rights of all Americans to freedom of speech and to peaceful assembly. I shared my view that people who are frustrated, angry, and seeking to express themselves must be afforded that opportunity. That said, we also had an obligation, when the situation warranted, to uphold the rule of law and protect life and liberty in support of civil authorities. We couldn't allow the violent actions of a few to undermine the rights and freedoms of law-abiding citizens. I went on to remind everyone, as I had done on prior occasions, of our commitment to stay apolitical in these turbulent days.

Before leaving the Pentagon at the end of the day, I took a quick update from several members of my staff. The president's rhetoric was still high and talk of invoking the Insurrection Act remained as protests continued in scores of American cities. The Guard was flowing into D.C. in healthy numbers, at least. Earlier in the afternoon, one of my senior leaders stopped by to update me, saying, "Sir, we're building combat power in the city at a good pace." I appreciated the encouraging news about the National Guard's arrival in the nation's capital, but his words were like fingernails on a chalkboard after my misuse of "battle space" with the governors the day before. I thanked him and then added, "We all need to avoid using our military language in this context." I knew he meant nothing by it—"building combat power" was another common phrase—but we all needed to help one another get our language right.

That evening, as I sat down to knock out the stack of work papers I brought home, I turned on the TV to take in the events from the day. I flipped the channel every thirty minutes or so to get the different perspectives that each outlet was serving up. None of it was good.

---

* For this June 2, 2020, Message to the Department, see Appendix C.

Since I was an early riser, I usually went to bed by 10:00 P.M., but that night I stayed up. As I watched the broadcasts and read the reports my team provided, I grew very concerned. Unrest had broken out in dozens of cities across America, and it was getting worse. Ensuring law and order was important, indeed imperative. But it was important to distinguish between peaceful protesters and violent opportunists. Rather than also working to address the underlying problems and heal the division, however, Trump was fanning the flames of discord, and putting the U.S. military right into the middle of it. Enforcement of the law needed balancing with empathy and understanding.

Civil unrest in United States wasn't a twenty-first-century phenomenon. It had been part of our history since the nation's founding. The rights to petition the government for redress of grievances, to freedom of speech, and to the freedom of assembly are enshrined in the First Amendment. Americans have exercised these rights often over the generations. Indeed, many people today can recall the civil rights, antiwar, and other large-scale protests that occurred during the 1960s and early 1970s.

An integral part of the civil rights movement in America has been to protest the perceived lack of police accountability when it came to misconduct by law enforcement officers, especially the excessive use of force against minorities. In August 1965, police brutality in Los Angeles sparked the Watts riots. What began with a California highway patrolman pulling over a Black man for alleged reckless driving quickly escalated into a series of altercations that spiraled out of control, eventually resulting in six days of violent unrest. Thirty-four people died in the riots. The state had to call up nearly fourteen thousand members of the California Army National Guard to support more than sixteen thousand law enforcement officers to stabilize the situation.

Twenty-seven years later, the largest protest since Watts occurred in Los Angeles when riots broke out after the police officers accused of using excessive force against Rodney King, a Black man, were acquitted by a trial jury. Like Watts, riots occurred over a six-day period, but this time they broke out across several parts of the city. Thousands of people took to the streets from late April through early May 1992, with widespread violence, arson, and looting occurring. Governor Pete Wilson was unable to get the streets under control, so he requested federal help from President George H. W. Bush, who subsequently invoked the Insurrection Act. This federalized the California Army National Guard and authorized federal troops to help restore law and order.

The year 2020 was turning out to be another inflection point in American history when it came to domestic unrest, social justice, and civil rights. On March 13, police killed an unarmed Breonna Taylor in Louisville, Kentucky, after they executed a "no knock" warrant that kicked off an exchange of gunfire. The videotaped murder of George Floyd in Minneapolis on May 25 by a police officer followed this high-profile incident. The officer, who kneeled on Floyd's neck for over nine long minutes, impaired his breathing and killed him. Floyd's murder sparked several nights of protests and rioting in the Minneapolis–Saint Paul area, which then spread quickly to other cities across the country.

By early June, civil unrest had erupted in more than two hundred cities across the United States. Many of the protests included looting, rioting, and arson, resulting in the imposition of curfews in many locales. Meanwhile, several more states had activated their National Guard to support law enforcement, bringing the total number of service members on duty to help deal with the protests to nearly forty-three thousand at its peak.

As I sat at home that Tuesday evening, I started assessing what was happening across the country juxtaposed with the talk inside the White House on Monday. I recalled pivotal moments in American history such as these and reflected upon my oath of office. I also thought carefully about the proper role of the U.S. military in society. With all this circulating in my head, and coming together in a clear way forward, I decided to craft a speech that I would deliver the next morning, less than twelve hours away.

I wanted my remarks to address George Floyd's murder, to reflect upon racism in America, to speak about our sacred oath to the Constitution, and, most importantly, to express my views on the Insurrection Act and the use of the military when it comes to civil unrest. I feared the country was beginning to spiral out of control, that the republic was "getting wobbly," and that somebody needed to put their hand on the wheel, a foot on the brake, and get things under control.

I knew this sounded presumptuous, but Trump couldn't do it, and wouldn't do it even if he could. He was in a fever about law and order and fixated on not appearing weak. He reflexively looked to the military to solve this problem, which likely meant invoking the Insurrection Act and sending in federal troops. This was the wrong answer, and one that could make things dramatically, if not indelibly, worse. I felt it was time to stand up, to break the fever. I began writing around midnight and finished close to 2:00 A.M. I went to bed exhausted but satisfied.

I skipped the gym the next morning and went straight into the office. I had emailed a copy of my remarks to Jen Stewart, my chief of staff, asking her to pull the team in to discuss my draft and the press conference I wanted to hold. The Department—indeed, the country—was in the middle of a crisis, and things didn't seem to be getting better. It was time to stand up and speak out, but I had to do it appropriately, with the right words, the right tone, and the right manner.

This would be a historic moment. I wanted to project calm, steady, civilian leadership at the helm of the Pentagon. I wanted to talk about our oath and our values, conscious of the fact that I was speaking to multiple audiences, ranging from my uniformed personnel and family members at far-flung bases all around the world, all the way to Capitol Hill and the Oval Office, and every small town, city, suburb, and farm in between.

The American people needed reassurance about the DoD's duty and allegiance, and that we were committed to remaining apolitical despite what some might be saying. They had to know and believe we would defend the Constitution, and their rights to peaceably assemble and express themselves. I had to thread several needles in crafting this message, to include not picking a major fight with the White House or appearing to take a political side.

The leadership team gathered in my inner conference room at 8:30 A.M. that morning. David Norquist, General John Hyten, Jen Stewart, Jonathan Hoffman, and a couple of others were present. General Mark Milley wasn't in the Pentagon that morning, so he dialed in for the call, yet uncharacteristically didn't say much during the meeting. Copies of my draft were passed around. It was important to get the unvarnished feedback of this group. I respected them all; we had been through a lot together. They had proven themselves during some challenging times the last many months. I knew the honesty, thoughtfulness, and diversity of their views would help me get the message right.

We want back and forth for some time questioning whether to put this in or take this out of the script. The good news was that everybody was on board with the statement, which was important. Near the end of the meeting, though, somebody raised the issue of the sentence expressing my opposition to invoking the Insurrection Act. They were convinced there would be major fallout if I said it, so, out of caution and concern for me, wanted me to consider it one last time.

We discussed this for a few minutes, with me sharing how strongly I felt about the issue. General Hyten sat across the table from me in the small conference room and provided the thoughtful perspective I had really come to value, saying, "Sir, if that's how you feel, and *it is* a very important statement, then you should say it." And, as he ended the sentence, he nodded affirmatively without breaking his stare. I paused for a moment, took it in, and said, "Good, that's it then," and the meeting concluded. The remarks I had drafted eight hours earlier largely remained unchanged, with a few edits here and there that improved them.

Someone that morning asked whether General Milley should join me at the podium, but that was not going to happen. This had to be a civilian-led moment; there couldn't be any confusion about who was in charge, who was making command decisions, and who was responsible. I was going forward to talk about what I, the secretary of defense, thought when it came to deploying military forces against civilians to deal with civil unrest. These were the views, after all, that I shared with the president. That was my call alone, and I would explain it.

Moreover, much of the recent criticism was about the military being *too involved* in sensitive issues that were under the purview of civilian leaders—highlighted by the deployment of forces to the capital region. I was trying to reassure the American people that the military, through invocation of the Insurrection Act, was *not* the answer to this crisis. As such, it would not make sense to have a military officer at the podium alongside me visually suggesting continued uniformed involvement. General Milley needed to stay away from the briefing, demonstrating the proper role of the military on issues such as these. My entire preparation over the previous several hours, after all, was focused on these matters, and my singular statement as the civilian head of the Department of Defense.

As I stepped up to the podium at 10:00 A.M., I embraced the significance of the moment. The room was sparsely filled due to COVID; most reporters called into an open line. While it is natural to speak to the journalists seated in the room, I wanted to speak to the American people. I opened the book containing my remarks, and with a calm, measured voice, looked straight into the small black camera fifteen yards in front of me—doing my best to ignore everyone else in the room—and began the seven minutes that would ripple across the air waves on Wednesday, June 3, and alter the fates of myself and others.*

I began my remarks by recounting the tragic killing of George Floyd by a Minneapolis police officer. This spark ignited the long festering issues of race and discrimination in America. I stated my view that the officers involved should be held accountable, and I extended condolences to the family and friends of George Floyd from me and the department.

It was important as well to acknowledge that "racism is real in America, and we must all do our very best to recognize it, to confront it, and to eradicate it." I shared my pride in being a member of an institution—the United States military—that embraces diversity and inclusion and abhors discrimination. In addition, while we have often led on this issue, we still had much to do.

I also made clear that everyone in the Defense Department swore an oath to support and defend the Constitution of the United States of America, and that includes freedom of speech and assembly. "The U.S. military is sworn to defend these rights," I said, and "we encourage Americans at all times to exercise them peacefully." I

---

* For the June 3, 2020, Pentagon Briefing Room transcript, see Appendix D.

added, "It is these rights and freedoms that American service members are willing to fight and die for."

The key sentences that drew the sharpest attention—the one where I stated my public disagreement with the president—began as follows:

> I've always believed and continue to believe that the National Guard is best suited for performing domestic support to civil authorities in these situations, in support of local law enforcement. I say this not only as secretary of defense but also as a former soldier and a former member of the National Guard. The option to use active-duty forces in a law enforcement role should only be used as a matter of last resort, and only in the most urgent and dire of situations. We are not in one of those situations now. I do not support invoking the Insurrection Act.

The last sentence would be the focus of Trump's wrath.

I went on to recount the events of Monday afternoon at Lafayette Park. During the Q&A period that followed, I acknowledged that, despite my constant efforts to remain apolitical and stay out of political situations, which I am usually successful at doing, I was not on this occasion.

I took several more questions, but cognizant that I had a meeting at the White House, and one final thing to say to the force, I ended the Q&A.

I turned and looked back into the camera at the far end of the room, and said that I wanted to speak directly, again, to the men and women of the Department of Defense.

I thanked them for their "professionalism and dedication to defending the Constitution for all Americans." I also thanked them for all their efforts and accomplishments over the preceding months. Finally, and importantly, I asked that they "remember at all times our commitment as a department and as public servants, to stay apolitical in these turbulent days. For well over two centuries, the United States military has earned the respect of the American people by being there to protect and serve all Americans."

With that, I walked off the stage and back upstairs to my office, prepared for whatever came next. General Milley, who was now back in the building, was outside my office when I returned around 10:30 A.M. I invited him in to talk for a few minutes. As I sat in the leather chair behind my desk, I felt good—glad that I spoke directly to the nation and confident in what I said. Milley said, "Great job, Secretary," adding that "the press conference went well."

He went on to state the obvious—the upcoming meeting on Afghanistan with the president was "going to be really ugly." Trump was going to "rip your face off"—a favorite Milley phrase. I agreed, telling him that I was not looking forward to it and knew beforehand this would be the likely fallout from my press conference. I grinned and said, "Why don't you and Frank [General McKenzie] just go and brief without me—tell the president I had a dentist appointment," or something like that. He chuckled.

Milley tried to lighten the moment further by joking that the next hour would be like being a plebe again at West Point, enduring the yelling of an upperclassmen for a half hour or so. I smiled at the thought. Back then, I was allowed only four scripted responses. I would have much more to say today.

That was nearly thirty-eight years ago, and it was all somewhat of a big leadership game to test a plebe's mettle and train them how to respond under fire. But it was not a game now. Indeed, the ingrained ideals of "Duty, Honor, Country" were being tested as I never could have imagined back then. I started thinking through how things might unfold in the Oval Office and how I needed to play it—stay calm, stick to the facts, push back where I must, and don't give any ground. I wasn't looking forward to going, but after a couple minutes of strategizing, I stood up from my chair and said, "Okay. Let's go. Let's do it."

The tensions between the president and me had been building since the previous summer, and the gap between us kept growing. His ideas and statements had become even more alarming since beating impeachment. Politicization of the military was a major redline for me. So, as I walked to the other part of the room to grab my suit jacket, I said to Milley with a combination of resolve and peace of mind, "If there's going to be a final showdown, let's get it over with." I expected the president to fire me on the spot, but this issue was well worth it. That said, I felt bad for a moment, saddened by the thought that all the progress we were making to modernize the U.S. military, rebalance our forces around the world, reform the DoD, and focus on China would probably grind to a halt. And what about our military personnel and their families?

I opened my office door and asked my team for a hard copy of my press conference remarks. I wanted to have these in hand, since I knew that someone would try to twist my words. I highlighted a few parts the president might raise, as well as a couple of sentences I might want to restate, and headed to my car for the long drive to the White House.

Milley and I arrived and went first to the Situation Room, where an aide told us that the president wanted to see me in the Oval Office. I walked upstairs and into the anteroom, where his scheduler waved me straight in, with Milley in trail. Trump was behind the Resolute desk when I arrived, sitting straight up in his chair, and stern faced with his arms folded. Mark Meadows sat to his left.

The room was quiet. I walked in and sat down in front of the president. Milley took the empty chair next to me. If I had any question as to whether Trump had seen my remarks, or at least been briefed on them, they vanished when I saw the look on his face.

Trump launched into a tirade almost immediately, questioning why I did what I did, why I said what I said, and accusing me of undermining him. "You betrayed me," he yelled. "I'm the president, not you!" He glared and threw accusation after accusation at me as I sat stone-faced looking straight back at him. He said invocation of the Insurrection Act is "my call, not yours." He shouted, "I'm the president. It's my prerogative." I stared him in the eye and agreed. He roared, "You took away my authority." I held my gaze and disagreed. I responded in a flat tone and direct manner, "Mr. President, I didn't take away your authority." I told him that "I was simply stating my views and recommendation," as I had before. He barked back, "That's not your position to do." Again, I replied, sitting up in my chair, "Mr. President, I didn't say it was my position to do. I said it was my recommendation." Trump grew even more flustered.

The president tried to make the case that the Insurrection Act was needed, once again proclaiming that "the protests are making us"—meaning him—"look weak." I disagreed, responding with the same arguments I had given both on Monday and during the press conference. I said, "I do not believe anything that has happened requires invocation of the Insurrection Act. It would make matters worse and would be terrible for the country."

Trump paused for a moment, and then said, "I can't believe you held a press conference during the hearing." I wasn't expecting this one. A slight tilt of my head and squint of my eyes likely betrayed my surprise. The president was accusing me of purposefully holding the press conference to take national attention off the Senate Judiciary Committee's hearing on the FBI's Russia investigation that began at 10:00 A.M., I would later learn. A former deputy attorney general was supposedly testifying before Senator Lindsey Graham. I wasn't even aware the committee was meeting. But apparently, Trump thought something was going to happen that would validate his claims about the "Russia witch hunt" and I was interfering in his moment of vindication. I let this one go.

The president made another assertion—that I said the military should never be used, that I didn't support employing the National Guard to aid in addressing civil unrest. I told him that was incorrect, that "I did not say that, Mr. President," and paraphrased my media comments back to him. Trump doubled down on this line, yelling back "Yes, you did." So, I pulled my written remarks from the leather portfolio I had resting in my lap, turned to a section I highlighted earlier, waved it briefly in the air, and then dropped it on the Resolute desk. I slapped it down once for effect, and then slid it across the desk toward him, "That's what I said, Mr. President." He glanced quickly down at it, still sitting straight in his chair with his arms folded tensely across his chest, but didn't bother to read. Rather, he sat there speechless. Checkmate. He abandoned this argument.

We went back and forth like this a few more times, like two tennis players in a singles match. Meadows and Milley were in the stands watching, silently. Trump's volleys were loud and angry, while my returns were short, steady, and direct. Finally, he said, "Because of what you did I can't use the Insurrection Act." I didn't say anything. He wasn't completely correct, of course, but I was glad he felt that way, and wasn't about to disabuse him of his conclusion. The meeting ended quickly after that. I stood up, turned, and left the Oval Office. Milley followed me out.

As luck would have it, Milley and I had an already scheduled 12:15 update with the president and other members of the national security team. As we headed toward the Situation Room, I started debating whether I should resign. Milley and I discussed our futures as we walked.

The purpose of the next meeting was to inform the president of our plans to reduce U.S. forces in Afghanistan over the course of 2020, consistent with the agreement we had signed with the Taliban. It was to be a fairly straightforward update. General McKenzie, the commander of CENTCOM, was present to brief everyone. As I entered the Situation Room, Mike Pompeo was sitting in the chair closest the door. He looked up at me as I walked by and said with a half smile, "Courage never quits," which is the motto of our West Point class. I appreciated his empathy and encouragement, and with my own quick smirk mustered a curt "Yeah, thanks" as I headed to my seat on the other side of the table.

The session with Trump began as well as could be expected despite the high tension. Notwithstanding what had just transpired in the Oval Office, I had a job to do—a duty to update the president and field his questions with the assistance of my military leaders. I decided to carry on as if nothing had happened, so I opened the meeting with a review of the overarching policy and the deal the United States had signed with the Taliban. I then delved into our troop strength and basing footprint in Afghanistan at the beginning of the year, where we were that day in the country, and "where we expect to be in the coming months, consistent with the February agreement and our own plans."

I then turned the brief over to the generals to walk through the operational details and issues related to the deliberate withdrawal. As General McKenzie began his pitch, it was clear from the president's comments and questions that he still wanted to get out of

Afghanistan as quickly as possible, despite Pompeo and me repeating the agreed-upon timeline and the importance of a conditions-based approach. Not only did Trump insist on "getting out of that place," but making sure we "don't leave any equipment or bases behind" like we did in Syria, he alleged.

As the meeting was ending, Iran somehow came up. McKenzie acknowledged that he, as the CENTCOM commander, was responsible for that problem set as well. He noted that he continued to "refine options" for the president's consideration if and when needed, and was "updating the war plans" based on guidance from me. This intrigued Trump, prompting him to ask, "What options do you have?" and "What do the plans look like?"

McKenzie had worked to develop and improve a variety of plans for well over a year. He knew them inside and out. In his eagerness to share all aspects of them with the president, coupled with the confidence he expressed in our ultimate success, Trump started misreading the various actions as being relatively quick, easy to do, and costing little. Milley and I had seen this movie a few times in the past, and understood where the president was heading.

Both Trump and McKenzie sat at the end of the Situation Room conference table, with the president at the head of the room and the CENTCOM commander to his immediate right as the briefer. You could see Trump thinking as he eagerly leaned toward McKenzie, like they were the only two people in the room, and begin asking leading questions, such as "How long will it actually take?" and "How hard do you think it really will be?"

Milley and I sat on opposite sides of the long table, a little farther down, but as the questioning picked up, we quickly realized it was time to interject. Nearly simultaneously we spoke up—"Wait, hold on" and "Whoa" were coming across in stereo—to stop McKenzie and get control of the discussion. Otherwise, we risked getting an order to launch military strikes against Iran.

There was never any doubt that our plans would be successful or that we would prevail in a conflict with Iran. The issue, rather, was always at what cost and risk compared to what gain and to what end. You had to look at both sides of the coin. I said as much to the president, as I had in the past, adding words to the effect that "General McKenzie also needs to walk you through the forces required, the elongated timelines, the extensive theater prep, and all of the other details, down to and including estimated losses on all sides."

Milley jumped in quickly behind me, asking McKenzie to tell the president "the rest of the story," walking Frank, Trump, and the rest of the room through a series of questions—ones we had gone through several times before at the Pentagon—such as the numbers of U.S., friendly, and enemy casualties; ships sunk, planes shot down, and installations destroyed; resources required and munitions expended; and so on. They were all estimates, but Trump and everyone else needed to hear them. As McKenzie dutifully answered one question after another, Milley and I would raise other factors, such as war duration, postconflict troop requirements, and the impact on other missions around the world.

The conversation revealed that the president was still itching to act against Iran. This was troubling. But our unrehearsed performance and McKenzie's dry, sober, just-the-facts-type responses were invaluable in teasing out all of the operational issues, concerns, consequences, and unknowns. It was all more than enough to put the president's appetite back on ice. Trump was true to

himself. He didn't want a war in the Middle East, despite some
of the cheerleaders around him in the White House. And without
a very compelling reason right now to risk conflict with Iran, he
rightly realized that the costs outweighed the benefits.

After the meeting, as we walked to our cars, General Milley and
I discussed the near miss we had just had with the commander in
chief regarding Iran. Milley was also angry about O'Brien's comments goading the president into action—pressing the commander
in chief to "hit them hard," as the national security adviser had repeatedly suggested in the past. The chairman then changed tracks
again, leaned close, and whispered to me with some contempt,
"Did you notice how the president barely made eye contact with
you throughout that last meeting? What bullshit." Of course I noticed, especially when I spoke to him. He was still seething and
wanting to fire me.

I remained fine with that outcome if that was what Trump
wanted. I felt good. I had stuck to my principles and stood my
ground. And over the next few hours, I would see that my press
conference had an impact. Things started settling down. The republic was beginning to feel less wobbly.

By Wednesday, the media, their talking heads, and a bevy of retired flag officers were busy commenting about the previous forty-
eight hours, and critiquing the military's role in what transpired
at Lafayette Park. Initial reports are often wrong, but in this case
so were many of the follow-on stories that were published. It was
frustrating to see so many people—including former senior DoD
officials—repeating the false narrative that Trump used *the military* to clear innocent protesters from the park, employing tear gas
and rubber bullets to do so. This was all wrong, and yet it occurred
despite evidence to the contrary. General Milley and I would have

welcomed the courtesy of a private conversation before some repeated or amplified these false claims and accusations, or continued to criticize our missteps in Lafayette Park or on the governors' phone call. It was all too juicy to take a moment to pursue the truth or hear us out first, I suppose.

Milley and I testified before Congress a month later, on July 9, and repeated what DoD officials—beginning with the head of the D.C. National Guard, Major General William Walker—had been saying for weeks by that point: that the National Guard did not engage protesters in Lafayette Park on June 1, did not fire rubber bullets at the crowd, and did not employ chemical agents of any type. The men and women of the National Guard did their duty and never infringed on any Americans' rights to peaceably assembly and express themselves.

Indeed, the inspector general of the Interior Department would report a year later, on June 9, 2021—during the Biden administration—that it was the USPP who cleared the park, and that the Park Police and the Secret Service made the decision to do so. The Guard's mission was to maintain the preestablished and extended security perimeter, which they did.[1]

I left for home around 6:00 P.M. on Wednesday, June 3, tired from three long days, and unsure of my future. Leah was in Tennessee visiting with her parents but cut her plans short and planned to drive the eleven hours back to Virginia on Thursday. As such, I had the night to myself to think about the day's events, and what I needed to do next. I knew in my heart and my head that publicly announcing my opposition to use of the Insurrection Act was the right thing to do. It appeared to have achieved its purpose as a circuit breaker on Trump and the growing unrest, and now I needed to de-escalate the situation further in the time I had.

After a restless night, I made it into the office around 7:40 A.M. on Thursday. As I reached for the top secret classified material that arrived overnight, I looked down at a piece of paper stuffed under the glass on my desktop. It was a copy of Colin Powell's Thirteen Rules of Leadership. I was a sucker for these types of things and would look at it every now and then as a compass check, as we would say in the military, to make sure my personal azimuth was right and proper. Plus, the retired four-star general and former secretary of state would become one of several close confidants of mine in whom I would rely for advice in the tough weeks and months ahead. Powell's rule 1 jumped out at me and captured my thoughts succinctly: "It ain't as bad as you think! It will look better in the morning." So true. Thursday was looking far better than Wednesday. Violence around the country was subsiding, and talk about employing active-duty troops had died down considerably. My public remarks the morning before seemed to break the fever about invocation of the Insurrection Act, exactly as I had hoped.

Now wasn't the time to celebrate or rest on whatever laurels we had earned, however. We needed to keep pressing forward. Mark Milley, Ryan McCarthy, Jen Stewart, and I met that morning. It was time to de-escalate, beginning with the approximately 1,300 active-duty forces in the region. I had already quietly disarmed the National Guard on Tuesday, doing so without consulting or informing the White House.

Now I wanted to get the soldiers from the 82nd Airborne Division back to Fort Bragg as quickly as possible. Approximately 700 paratroopers were at Fort Belvoir, Virginia, about fourteen miles south of Washington, D.C. Other active-duty personnel—mostly MPs from other posts—were located at Joint Base Andrews in Maryland. At this point, even if we were wrong and violence spiked in the city, I didn't want active-duty forces quickly available to the president. We had managed to keep them out of the District so far. Guard forces were now flowing into D.C. in healthy numbers, so I decided to send all active-duty units home. I didn't inform the White House about these actions either. I couldn't trust they wouldn't reverse my decision.

I also felt that this action was consistent with my conversation with the president on Monday. More importantly, I felt a higher duty to the American people, and the relationship between the military and the broader society we serve, to remove active-duty forces from the equation and further signal our understanding of and belief in the proper role of the armed forces under the Constitution.

That evening, White House Chief of Staff Mark Meadows called me at home and proposed that I "send a letter to the president" that would basically say I didn't mean what I said at the press conference; in other words, that "you don't oppose invoking the Insurrection Act." Meadows and I went back and forth about what exactly the letter would say, with me curious as to how ridiculous he wanted this letter to be. Not surprisingly, the president was still angry and itching to fire me, Meadows implied. He thought that sending such a note "would go a long way to calming the president down." Of course, I knew it probably wouldn't, and that the White House would immediately share it with the press and use it against me. Most importantly, it wasn't the right thing to do. I told him tersely, "No, I can't do that, Mark. I stand by what I said." With that, we hung up. Leah had made it back from Tennessee by the time he phoned and overheard our conversation. She couldn't believe it either.

Meadows called me back a little later. This time he took a far different tack with a much more aggressive tone. The Tony Soprano approach. He started by saying, "If you don't send the letter, . . . I will trash you with the press" and that he would go after my integrity. I could picture him on the other end of the phone, getting red-faced as he often did when others challenged him or stumped him with a question or comment. I just couldn't believe he threatened me; at least he was being honest. It really got my Irish up, however. Now I was a double no. I hung up.

I took a third call from Meadows that night, one that pivoted 180 degrees again. In a much calmer tone and pace, he said, "Look, Mark, forget what I said earlier; we're all a little spun up about things. You're an important member of the team. We appreciate the challenges you have over at DoD and what you do. Let's just get through this week and then we can talk later." I didn't buy any of it. I thanked him for his call, and that was that. Bizarre.

I went to bed that evening knowing I had a full schedule of meetings and calls on my calendar, but these days that didn't seem to mean much. Despite Meadows's last call, I still had no idea if I would remain as secretary of defense tomorrow, the next day, or the day after that. I knew how Trump behaved; I had seen it many times before up close. So I was reasonably confident in how the conversation was playing out in the Oval Office about "what to do with Esper." He was likely bad-mouthing me left and right, much like he had with others who crossed him.

David Urban, a West Point classmate and longtime friend, was close to Trump and his campaign staff. He and other friends on that side of the Potomac were telling me the "campaign staff are panicked at the prospect of Trump losing another SecDef," believing that this would "kill his reelection." They weighed in for me from this angle. Pompeo and others reportedly argued on my behalf as well. It was clear to me from my last call with Meadows that I had some unexpected leverage.

Washington, D.C., was still a powder keg, so I was looking for ways to take powder out of it. Friday's focus was on sending troops home, both active-duty and Guard. As important, we were looking for opportunities to show the public, and the protesters, that we were de-escalating. Standing down active-duty troops, disarming the Guard, and redeploying them all were central to that. We made a conscious effort to brief the press, providing them pictures and sharing video of troops leaving the metropolitan region. We felt all of this was essential to calming down the situation, both in D.C. and nationally, which the White House didn't seem capable of doing—a behavior that would repeat itself with the mob assault of the Capitol in January 2021—so we acted again without consulting them.

Early on Sunday, June 7, Trump tweeted, "I have just given an order for our National Guard to start the process of withdrawing from Washington, D.C., now that everything is under perfect control. They will be going home, but can quickly return, if needed. Far fewer protesters showed up last night than anticipated!" I had no idea where this came from. I never received any instructions from him or anyone in the White House.

Furthermore, everything wasn't under "perfect control" at that point. We still had protesters in the city, and we were concerned about any events that could reignite the violence. Therefore, we were working hard behind the scenes with a few states to keep some of their National Guard troops in the District for a few more days, and certainly through George Floyd's memorial service in Texas on

June 9. By Friday, June 12, though, all out-of-state National Guard personnel who deployed to D.C. had returned home.

Trump got "spun up" again on June 11 after watching the protests in Seattle from the night before. He called the Pentagon that morning, pressing General Milley to "act fast" and "hard" because Seattle is going to be "taken over by Antifa" and "[Governor Jay] Inslee is weak."

I had a call with the defense minister of Israel at 9:00 A.M., so Milley reached out to Attorney General Barr and told him what was happening. He asked that Barr get law enforcement involved and that he respond directly back to Trump, which Bill willingly did. The attorney general and I were largely in agreement about law enforcement leading and keeping the military out. I saw Barr a short time after that at a State Department event we were participating in with Pompeo. Milley briefed me before I left for State, so Barr and I discussed the issue to nail down any loose ends. I was glad to hear he already managed to get things back in the box.

A week later, on Friday, June 19, the president called me at home late in the evening. He was in a rage over TV news reports of protesters pulling down a statue in D.C. The secure phone rang in the small office I had set up near my bedroom, about thirty feet away. Its familiar chirp always got my attention.

His call around 11:30 P.M. woke me from a dead sleep. I hustled to my small office as the phone rang, picked it up, and said, "Secretary Esper," in a raspy voice. With no greeting, the president spoke excitedly into the phone: "Statues are being torn down in D.C. They're going after Jefferson and Washington next. You need to get the Guard in there immediately." He was angry as he said these things. I wasn't tracking any of this. I responded with "Yes, Mr. President. I'll get on it immediately and get back to you," and hung up.

I phoned General Milley at home to get him on the case. "Chairman, good evening. I hate to wake you," I said, "but the president just called me. He said people are pulling down statues in D.C. and wants the Guard brought in." Milley wasn't aware of what was unfolding either. Milley said, "I'm not aware of this. Let me turn on my TV and get online." "Okay," I replied, "I'm doing the same." Nothing really jumped out, so I told him I was going to call Mark Meadows and alert him. With that, Milley and I hung up. I then called Meadows and spoke briefly to him, informing him of my call from the president and the actions we were taking at the Pentagon, saying "Milley is looking into it now. He'll be calling me back shortly. I'll let you know as soon as I learn something." "Thanks, Secretary," the White House chief of staff replied.

After my call with Meadows, I got back online and learned that several people toppled a statue of Confederate general Albert Pike, which had been standing in Judiciary Square since 1901. I never heard of Pike and never even knew there was a statue to a Confederate general in D.C.—go figure—but apparently the District had been pressing Congress since 1992 to remove it.[2]

Milley called me back to report that the crowd was fewer than one hundred people and confirmed that only a dozen or so were causing trouble. He said that the Metro Police were on the scene, and that they made no request for military support. In fact, the crowd dispersed after they toppled the statue. The police were tracking them, and there was no intent, it appeared, to pull down other statues.

I doubled back to Meadows, who was pragmatic about this matter. We all agreed the evening's "fire drill" was over, with no need for the Guard to get involved. Meadows was going to call Trump back and update him. The next morning, I saw that the president had tweeted that evening, "The D.C. Police are not doing their job as they watch a statue be ripped down & burn. These people should be immediately arrested. A disgrace to our Country!"[3]

We learned a lot from that long week of June 1 through 7, 2020. As an institution, the DoD and the military proved to be resilient and adaptable, particularly in the face of civil unrest we hadn't seen in decades, and in working with an unpredictable and chaotic White House. We made mistakes, for sure, whether it was my "battle space" comment during the governors' conference call with the president on June 1, or the walk across Lafayette Park later that day. We learned the hard way, owned our gaffes, and made changes.

We erred at the tactical level as well, whether it was the use of helicopters hovering at low altitudes above protesters in D.C., or the employment by a few states of National Guard RC-26 surveillance aircraft in support of law enforcement to track the movements of large crowds. While I wasn't aware of either incident until a day after for the helicopters, and several days later for the other aircraft, I directed immediate investigations into both.

In each case, we determined that policies, procedures, and regulations needed updating, and that we had to exercise much greater care and scrutiny before the DoD deployed forces again in such situations.

Coordination with law enforcement also needed improvement. I directed Army Secretary McCarthy on June 11 to conduct an After-Action Review, which the service describes as "an interactive discussion in which unit members decide what happened, why it happened, and how to improve or sustain collective performance in future exercises," something we did routinely in the Army.[4] Once completed, I wanted the DoD to meet with DOJ to share our findings and recommendations, as well as to make adjustments. This was something I had already discussed with the attorney general, and to which he agreed.

One of the specific things I asked of Barr and Acting Homeland Security Secretary Chad Wolf was that law enforcement not wear green or camouflage uniforms, since that can lead the public to think they are military personnel. This, along with our Military Police lending law enforcement their equipment—namely, riot shields with the words "Military Police" emblazoned across them in large type—partly led to the mistaken conclusion by some early on that the military had directly engaged the protesters in Lafayette Park. I later instructed the Guard to "stop sharing equipment unless you can remove or cover all military markings first."

Milley and I testified before the House Armed Services Committee on July 9, as mentioned earlier; the topic was "DoD Authorities and Roles Related to Civilian Law Enforcement." In the charged political atmosphere of D.C. at the time, even appearing before Congress became a contentious and misinformed affair. The committee invited us to testify on Tuesday, June 2, while we were in the thick of assisting law enforcement with civil unrest in D.C. and other parts of the country. My legislative team began negotiating the details of the hearing—time, date, duration, scope, etc.—with committee staff almost immediately, as they always do.

But some Democrats decided to make this a partisan political issue, and just three days later, as I was getting orders out to redeploy active-duty forces back to their home stations, a Democrat aide told the press that Milley and I "refused" to testify. *Politico* reported this falsehood. Statements followed from Democrats on the committee that Milley and I didn't "respect our constitutional system" or think we needed to "explain [our] actions to Congress."

This was a bunch of BS. I was constantly talking to the leadership of the defense committees. So, I called Adam Smith (D-WA), the committee chairman, whom I had known and respected for many years as thoughtful and reasonable. I complained about these statements and said they reflected politics at its worst—right in the middle of a national crisis when steady, sober, bipartisan leadership was what the nation needed most. Milley and I always made ourselves available to members of Congress, and statements like these simply eroded trust.

Smith was a real pro and regretted some of the comments lawmakers were slinging around in the media and on Twitter; he acknowledged the challenges Milley and I were facing internally. I told him we had to get permission from the White House to appear before the committee, to begin with, and that my team was discussing this with Meadows's office. Smith suspected this.

Despite all the drama leading up to our hearing on July 9, the proceeding turned out to be a relatively serious event. I pulled Chairman Smith aside after the hearing and told him so, and thanked him for doing such a good job managing the session. There was some minor partisanship on both sides of the aisle—some folks can't help themselves—but we were fortunate that the real partisans didn't engage. Milley and I were able to walk the committee through the details and timeline of that first week in June, answering most of their questions.

June was a tough month for the DoD, especially the National Guard. I was never prouder of the Guard than during that period and told them so on multiple occasions later. The soldiers and airmen of the National Guard showed tremendous flexibility, commitment, and professionalism. They bounced from mission to mission—from COVID support and a deployment abroad to civil unrest and natural disaster relief—with enthusiasm, dedication, and skill.

They were building makeshift hospitals in New York, fighting wildfires in California, providing supplies to towns on the storm-battered Gulf Coast, and helping keep the peace in Minnesota. They would leave their civilian employers and families often on very short notice, sometimes not knowing exactly what they were doing, where they were going, or when they would be home.

Tens of thousands deployed across the United States for many months, with thousands more stationed in hotspots around the world for extended tours. It brought a tear to the eye to see these great Americans in action, and it was disheartening to see them drawn into the political fray at times. We all understood our oath to the Constitution, the allegiance we have to it, and our duty to country—as compared to a president or a party—so it was troubling to see these things questioned, and the vital relationship between the American people and its military threatened.

Nonetheless, the challenges and hardships of 2020 made it an epic year for the National Guard—a time when they fully showed their value to America in so many ways, as well as their steady commitment to their oaths and the society we serve. A year in which they stood tall when so many of their fellow citizens had to take a knee or needed a hand. History should remember 2020 as their year.

The week of June 1, 2020, was the worst one of my tenure, and the most challenging period of my professional lifetime. The good news was that my June 3 press conference broke the president's fever, and by Friday, June 5, we had de-escalated the situation in D.C. and across America. The unilateral orders I issued to disarm troops, redeploy active-duty forces, and return the Guard home sent a powerful signal to the country and the White House. These actions also put the onus of responsibility for dealing with civil unrest squarely on the shoulders of law enforcement, where it should be.

The White House didn't like any of these decisions; in fact, they incensed them. Moreover, the president's actions, reactions, and proclivities made clear that I needed to recalibrate how I dealt with Trump and those closest to him. His behavior throughout the week stress-tested the Pentagon's leaders and the DoD as an institution unlike any other time in modern history, but it did not break us. In the end, we successfully reasserted the importance of remaining apolitical and staying true to our oaths.

Beginning with that walk General Milley and I took alongside the Reflecting Pool the evening of June 1, I soon came to fully realize that the president put his reelection above everything else and was willing to do whatever it took to stay in power. People were expendable, principles were pliable, and policies were changed to meet the needs of the moment.

My personal views remained unchanged, however, fixed from my time at West Point and the many years of service that followed: remain true to your oath; put country first; do the right thing; and take care of your people. They were diametrically opposed to how the president operated, thus making continued clashes between us inevitable.

With this vast gulf now so evident, my new strategy became much clearer in the days that followed. By the end of that fateful week, my game plan was largely set. I would play offense inside the Pentagon, making the most of every day I had left to protect the nation, advance the National Defense Strategy (NDS), and get the U.S. military ready for the future. Outside the Pentagon, I would play defense as necessary, making sure to blunt or redirect any efforts that could politicize the military, misuse the force, or undermine the nation's security.

To be successful I would need to stay out of the news. That was the thin ice I had to avoid, and it was made thinner by some in the media who were increasingly looking to report on anything I said or did that differed from the president's position. It would be an unforced error for me to say something that those close to the president could use against me to justify my removal from office.

This dynamic was already playing out in the White House among Trump loyalists who wanted to see me gone. They would leak bad—sometimes false—information about the DoD or me to the media, I would learn later, and then turn around and show it to the president once it was published. "Mr. President, look at what Esper said and did now," I could imagine them saying to Trump, with a gleam in their eye, standing in front of the Resolute desk with a news article in hand. There were many good folks at the White House who labored to do the right thing and to keep the republic on the rails, but for a few key people working there, "integrity" was a word they didn't seem to understand.

As I had said many times, though, I can only control what I can control, and the White House wasn't one of those things. Pentagon briefings were, however. The risk of doing them in the politically charged environment of D.C., with an election just over the horizon, far outweighed any benefit, especially when it was essential to stay off Trump's radar screen.

Simply put, it wasn't worth jeopardizing my strategy to have someone twist my words or write a story in a way that could result in my premature firing. For example, during the first week in August, a few days after I had hosted a Pentagon press conference,

I participated in a virtual interview at the Aspen Security Forum. Near the end of the extended discussion, I was asked about the massive explosion in the port of Beirut that killed more than two hundred people and injured several thousand the day before, on August 4.

Hours after the tragic event in Lebanon, the president suggested the explosion was caused by an attack, which was one of the early theories circulating in the Pentagon and elsewhere. But with the advantage of a day's worth of reporting, I told the Aspen audience that we are "still getting information on what happened," and added, "Most believe it was an accident." This last sentence lit up the media, with USA Today running the headline "Defense Secretary Esper Says Beirut Blast Probably an Accident, Breaking with Trump."[5] Other outlets took a similar angle, playing up the different assessments by Trump and me, with some painting it as the DoD breaking again with the White House. This wasn't true. I was giving an honest assessment based on the latest information available to me, which was more than what Trump had the day prior.

More back-and-forth on this issue would transpire in the days that followed. It was just this sort of media nonsense that unnecessarily put me farther on the wrong side of the White House. Worse, it threatened my strategy by giving the president cause to fire me prior to the election. If that happened, I was confident Trump would put a real loyalist in the job. That would be disastrous for the institution and the country. I could find other ways to get our story out, and I did.

That said, I regretted not doing Pentagon press briefings in the two months before the election. I had restored these sessions when I came into office in July 2019, increasing their frequency over time to the point where we were doing at least two per month on average, when I wasn't traveling abroad. While some critics may pan this number, in a Trump-focused media environment it was the best we could do without risking our standing or our initiatives.

Nevertheless, the partisan atmosphere in D.C. had become toxic to a degree I had never seen during my twenty-five years in the city. Many lawmakers on Capitol Hill, as well as several personalities in the media and think tank world, tried constantly to drag the DoD into the electoral fray or take potshots at the Department. Even commenting on some of the ridiculous things these people were saying would hurt our standing and jeopardize our position. The two-month suspension of press room briefings wasn't, however, the end of my public engagements, interviews, speaking opportunities, or Q&A sessions. I did more public events than ever before in the many weeks leading up to November 3.

With my strategy set, General Milley and I came up with some ideas the week of June 1 that we further shaped into what became the "Four Nos": no unnecessary wars; no strategic retreats; no politicization of the DoD; and no misuse of the military. We could have probably produced a few more, but these four worked for now, and they would hold up well in the following months. As defense secretary, I was the decision maker on all these actions and more, so I would need to be particularly attuned to each and every situation.

Milley and I based our development of the Four Nos on our shared experiences with Trump and his loyalists over the preceding ten months, and the unique situations we found ourselves in on many previous occasions. We had drawn these redlines in one way, shape, or form multiple times in the past year and had managed to both blunt the most egregious ideas coming out of the White House and reshape less onerous ones. But with the president now focused 100 percent on reelection, polling numbers showing Trump consistently trailing Biden by four or more points, the pandemic crushing the economy he prided himself in, and tensions running high, there was no telling what the White House might propose to improve Trump's standing with the electorate and guarantee a win in November.

I now had a strategy (inside offense and outside defense) and metrics (the Four Nos), but had to formulate a timeline. Previous cabinet officers often didn't survive long once they found themselves on Trump's wrong side. I thought long and hard about this, but the answer was quite simple: I would be successful if I could continue advancing this inside/outside strategy through November 3 without crossing any of the Four Nos. It would be tough to make it five more months, especially in this environment. But it was possible. I would later refine this to be "Election Day plus a week" as concern grew about how Trump might use the military in the immediate aftermath of a contested election. As such, I prayed that whatever happened on Election Day, the results be "clear and clean," meaning so decisive in the electoral vote count that a challenge would be insurmountable, and free of any fraud or corruption that could overturn the results or undermine the process. I never envisioned what would eventually happen, but the DoD stayed out of it, nonetheless.

With my new game plan, I looked ahead to the next several weeks. They were brutal. The rest of June and July were fraught with land mines: a new presidential order to withdraw ten thousand troops from Germany, elaborate plans for the military participation in the upcoming Fourth of July festivities, the promotion of Lieutenant Colonel Alexander Vindman, a continued NSC push to take action against Venezuela, and Confederate flags on military bases, to name a few that I will discuss in upcoming chapters.

There were also things I wanted to accomplish, such as addressing diversity and inclusion in the military, continuing to counter China throughout the world, and responding to COVID in a manner that still kept the DoD mission ready but safe. I also needed to keep pushing forward on the NDS, which the president had endorsed—after all, it was the Pentagon's plan to fulfill the military pillar of the administration's National Security Strategy—while doing the day-to-day work of keeping the nation safe and protecting our interests abroad.

The challenge was how to walk through this minefield and do what was right, without setting off an explosion that would upend my strategy and timeline. At the Infantry school at Fort Benning, Georgia, the instructors had taught us to avoid minefields by going around them, not through them. This wasn't an option now, however.

The stress levels in the White House were already high, and a bunker mentality was settling in. Many over there viewed me as "disloyal" and "not on the team," and my traditional cabinet allies couldn't help on issues solely affecting the Defense Department, so I had to play my cards carefully . . . putting the right ones down at the right time in the right way to be successful *and* survive.

It was going to be a long, hot summer. I had to take it one day at a time.

CHAPTER 15

MAKING LEMONADE

"Reduce U.S. forces in Germany to no more than twenty-five thousand service members by the end of September." This was the essence of a presidential directive I received a few days after my June 3 press conference on the Insurrection Act. The memo was dated June 2, 2020.

This instruction, written by the NSC, was the first test of my resolve to stick with my plan and stay on at the Pentagon. It was another cavalier, largely uninformed effort to make breathtaking changes to our national security posture in a fit of presidential pique. In this case, Trump wanted me to develop a plan to withdraw nearly ten thousand troops from Germany, which hosted around thirty-five thousand at the time, to bring them all home, and to get it done in under four months. All of it was folly. Dangerous folly that played into the hands of our adversaries.

Trump had been unhappy with German chancellor Angela Merkel

for a long time. It was no secret, and in many ways it seemed personal. His disgust with Berlin's unwillingness to meet its defense spending commitments made to NATO, its Nord Stream 2 pipeline deal with Russia, and the stationing of tens of thousands of American troops and families on German soil constituted a trifecta that gnawed at him. On top of all this, or maybe because of it, he simply didn't like Merkel. He called her a "weak" leader and someone who had also "played the U.S. for suckers." Many speculated that Merkel's long, successful leadership of Germany, coupled with the fact that she was an accomplished woman, intimidated Trump. Regardless, I was able to observe them up close at the NATO Summit in London in December 2019, and the bad chemistry between them was obvious.

Merkel became chancellor of Germany in 2005. She was not only the first woman to lead the country, but her political views, policy stances, and many years in office earned her the unofficial titles of most powerful woman in the world and leader of the European Union. When it came to foreign policy, the chancellor was focused on two things: strengthening European cooperation and improving transatlantic economic relations with the United States. Merkel's tenure had spanned the terms of three U.S. presidents, beginning with George W. Bush, so far.

Not long after taking office in January 2017, Trump attended the G-7 Summit in Italy and, in May of that year, the NATO Summit in Brussels. His meetings there became very contentious over a series of issues, not least of which was American support for the transatlantic alliance. It was after those engagements that Merkel reportedly no longer saw Washington as a reliable partner. The Trump-Merkel relationship continued downhill from there.

In Trump's view, Germany was taking advantage of other countries, especially the United States, by expecting us to defend them against Russia, while they made business deals with Moscow. And while Washington plowed 3.2 percent of its GDP into defense, Berlin committed only 1.36 percent in 2020. Germany wasn't the only country not meeting its transatlantic defense spending obligations. Of twenty-nine alliance members at the time, only nine were meeting the 2 percent threshold agreed to at the 2014 summit in Wales. Not surprisingly, many of these were frontline states that bordered Russia.

Within days of being appointed acting secretary of defense in June 2019, I had a NATO defense ministerial to attend in Brussels. These happened every few months, so given that Iran had days before shot down an American drone in the Arabian Gulf, and the situation was still simmering, some on my staff recommended I not attend. I couldn't disagree with the logic, but I was concerned about how our allies might interpret my absence. What would it say about my views toward the alliance? About my understanding of transatlantic issues? These questions stood out in the stark background of Trump's dismissive comments about NATO, including his remarks as a presidential candidate that the alliance was "obsolete."

In the end, it was a no-brainer for me. The White House could always reach me if tensions flared in the Persian Gulf. My attendance in Brussels, only days into my appointment as acting secretary of defense, would send a powerful message of support to my fellow defense ministers and NATO.

After two days of meetings in Belgium, I stepped onstage at NATO headquarters for my very first press conference. The large group meetings with my fellow ministers went very well. The same was true of my private bilateral sessions with key allies and with NATO secretary general Jens Stoltenberg. But this would be my first introduction to the public. What would I say? many probably thought. Would I parrot Trump's lines about NATO being "very unfair" to the United States? Would I also threaten an American withdrawal from the alliance? I was sure everyone gathered was curious.

The president's criticism of allied defense spending was not only fair, it was also spot-on. Yet while many of his specific complaints were not technically correct—for example, the U.S. did not pay "70 to 90 percent" of the NATO budget "to protect Europe" and Germany does not "owe NATO billions of dollars" or "owe us a tremendous amount of money for many years back"—the general thrust was one echoed by many of his predecessors, as well as mine.

Indeed, it was President Obama's efforts in September 2014 in Wales that led to a formal pledge from the allies to spend 2 percent of their GDP on defense by 2024. Only three countries at the time were hitting the 2 percent mark. In 2016, Obama would rightly complain about the "free riders" of American security in Europe.

Trump was also right to push the allies hard. And given the poor readiness of many allied militaries and lack of political will in most capitals, coupled with increasing Russian aggression, he was justified in doing so publicly as well. To his credit, the president's effort helped push NATO allies to increase defense spending by $130 billion since 2016 and triple the number of countries meeting their Wales commitment.

Where the president went too far, however, was to threaten an American withdrawal from NATO. This undermined the alliance, greatly worried frontline states such as Romania, Poland, and Estonia, and played right into Moscow's hands. The Russians were always looking for ways to divide the allies, but a unilateral U.S. pullout would be a coup. At worst it would cause NATO to collapse, and at best it would sap credibility from the alliance. It certainly gave reason and room for the French to push for an independent European military capability, a longtime aspiration of Paris that also threatened to weaken NATO.

For me, speaking in Brussels was an opportunity to support Trump's push for greater burden sharing, while striking an independent chord by emphasizing my knowledge of and support for NATO. I began by discussing my time spent working on alliance issues in both Congress and the Pentagon years earlier, and the fact that I lived and served in Europe as an Army captain in the 1990s. I came to Brussels "to emphasize the United States' commitment to NATO," I said. My goal was to strengthen our alliance and improve our readiness. The NATO Readiness Initiative would become a priority of mine.

I shared these same messages with my counterparts in our private meetings. I told them that ensuring NATO's readiness and unity "begins with increased and more equitable burden sharing that meets everyone's investment pledges." I always believed that my experiences with the alliance in a variety of military and civilian roles over the previous twenty-five years or so gave me some credibility with them. It takes time to build a rapport, and with staff constantly around, it is difficult to talk candidly, but I tried to convey my sincere commitment to NATO. I let them know I carried this same message in the White House.

I also committed to be as transparent as possible, and to give them—through the secretary general—as much of a heads-up as possible on any policy changes coming out of Washington. My sense was that they understood this, and it was reassuring to them, but no one really knew if anybody could control Trump's animus toward NATO.

We made progress on NATO readiness, but it was slow. More allies were joining "the 2 percent club," as some of us would call it. Others had decent plans to meet that mark by 2024. As a result, NATO readiness was improving. But Berlin didn't seem to budge. Indeed, in November 2019 the German defense minister announced that her country would reach its 2 percent spending goal by 2031.[1] 2031? That was seven years later than the 2024 completion date they had committed to in 2014. It was a goal they were now pushing off to a future chancellor. It was outrageous and harmful to NATO. It was a target date that might prompt other allies to wrongly follow. It really made a lot of folks in Washington angry and disappointed, including me.

During my Senate confirmation hearing, I made clear that implementing the National Defense Strategy would be my top priority. Of the three main pillars of the NDS—building a more lethal force, strengthening alliances and attracting new partners, and reforming the department to improve efficiency—the third was how I would free up time, money, and manpower to put back into our first two priorities. I was very clear that I would press all of the DoD, including the combatant commands, to do this. Diving deep into the commands was not only a means to free up funds for modernization but also one of my first acts to assert greater civilian control by imposing accountability and fiscal discipline on the four-star commanders.

The head of U.S. European Command was General Tod Wolters, a tall, calm-spoken Air Force officer and accomplished pilot. He had taken over the European Command (EUCOM) in May 2019 during a ceremony in Germany that I hosted, so I knew him already. I found Wolters to be very professional and competent with a serious strategic outlook on his command. He was also a team player who was liked by the allies and easy to work with, essential skills for a senior leader in Europe.

During the fall we talked a few times about the EUCOM review, which my staff slotted for later in the review queue than most other commands. We also discussed changes he was assessing for Europe, given what the Russians were doing, the actions of the allies, and other guidance I had given him. He already had several ideas brewing to improve operational effectiveness, to include keeping Air Force units in England that had been programmed years earlier to move to Germany.

While the NATO Summit in London in December 2019 went as well as most could expect, the bilateral meeting between Trump and Merkel was particularly bad. The president had come into the meeting with Merkel spun up after hearing news of disparaging remarks Canadian prime minister Justin Trudeau made about him at Buckingham Palace the night before. A video caught Trudeau mocking Trump, and a White House staffer showed it to the president that morning. At the press conference with Merkel that preceded their meeting, Trump said Trudeau was "two-faced," adding, "The truth is I called him out on the fact he's not paying 2 percent [of GDP on defense] and I guess he's not happy about it." Other world leaders, such as Boris Johnson and Emmanuel Macron were also in on Trudeau's disparaging remarks about Trump, but the president had a special contempt for the young Canadian, whom he felt was "weak."[2]

I would quickly learn that "weak" was the president's favorite word when describing adversaries or opponents, whether in the United States or abroad. It contrasted sharply with "strong," which was how he regarded himself, and how he wanted others to see him. Trudeau, Merkel, and former U.K. prime minister Theresa May were in the "weak" category. Russian president Vladimir Putin, Chinese president Xi Jinping, and Turkish president Recep Tayyip Erdogan were all in the other column.

Trump sat in a U-shaped semicircle of gray chairs, with Merkel to his right. Both sat at the head of the group. Two pairs of American and German flags dressed up the blue NATO wall behind them. Pompeo sat to Trump's immediate left, followed by me, Mick Mulvaney, Robert O'Brien, and Ric Grenell, the U.S. ambassador to Germany. A flank of German officials sat several feet away, opposite us.

Trump was in an agitated mood, and even more so after having to wait in the conference room for a few minutes for Merkel to arrive. Dressed in his signature dark suit and long red tie, he seemed primed for a fight. While his engagement with the press before his bilateral meeting was generally positive, it belied his mood; he quickly entered the ring once the media left.

As Merkel arrived, and then sat stoically, hands clasped on her lap in front of her, she stared at Trump, who came out swinging. He pressed the chancellor multiple times on defense spending and the Nord Stream 2 deal with Russia. Trump said, "You need to cancel Nord Stream. It's not fair. It's not right that you're dealing with the Russians and we have to pay for your defense." She pushed back, defending the controversial undersea Baltic pipeline, stating, "The project is supported by the EU, and it's almost done." She added, "We must separate politics from business." Trump alternatively raised his eyebrows or frowned, depending on what the chancellor said. The ill feelings between the two were clearly mutual.

Getting nowhere, the president began taunting Merkel, "If you don't cancel it [the pipeline], and won't go to 2 percent [of GDP for defense spending], then we may have to put tariffs on Germany. I don't want to, but I may have to," he teased. This didn't go over well with Merkel. She turned and faced him, arguing that "Germany *is* making progress on its defense spending." Trump knew that wasn't correct and cut her off, interjecting a threat to "put tariffs on all of those wonderful Mercedes flowing into the United States." He smiled slightly at our side of the room as he said it. Merkel stiffened in her chair, and her face drew tight with irritation.

The meeting finished not long after it started, and each side shook hands and said all the right things as everyone left the room.

Pouring fuel on the fire over the two-day event was Ambassador Ric Grenell, who earned quite the reputation as a bomb thrower in diplomatic circles. As such, he and Trump seemed drawn to each other. Ever quick to bash the Germans publicly, Grenell was even more effective behind closed doors with a receptive audience of one. He was the boxing coach at the summit pumping up his prizefighter before the latter stepped into the ring.

I had never met Grenell before, but he approached me briefly in London and introduced himself. With a square jaw and short-cropped hair, he talked briskly when he spoke and had a quick sense of humor. He was also very pro-Trump and had somehow engineered a direct line into the Oval Office. Mike Pompeo found his ambassador to Germany unpredictable and difficult to control, the secretary of state told me, but knew it was something he had to live with. Mike didn't have to endure what many considered Grenell's bad behavior in Germany too much longer, though. Trump would call his ambassador back to Washington in a couple of months to serve as the acting director of National Intelligence.

My conversation with Grenell was friendly, with him rapidly pivoting to the U.S. troop presence in Europe. In his view, he argued, "we should just withdraw some of our forces from Germany, say around ten thousand." He added, "That will get their attention." "Of course it will," I replied, "and many other countries too, including Russia, but for all of the wrong reasons."

I explained to him that I had "a comprehensive review under way to look at our troop presence around the world, and that European Command was on that list." I agreed, "It is important to get

Berlin to the 2 percent funding level, but the challenge is doing so in a way that doesn't harm the alliance, affect our own readiness, or encourage the Russians." I added, "These are all the things we [are] going to look at in the conduct of the review." Our conversation ended when someone poked their head in the room and said, "The president is ready." I left concerned that Grenell was privately pitching this withdraw-ten-thousand-troops idea to Trump. My hunch turned out to be right.

In fact, not long after the London summit, the president raised the issue with me. In the Oval Office several weeks later, he asked after another long rant about German defense spending, "Mark, what do you think about pulling our troops out of Germany? I like the number ten thousand. It's a good number. What do you think?" As I had with Grenell, I said, "Mr. President, I have a review under way to look at our footprint around the globe, to include Europe, which will include Germany." I told him, "I recently discussed this matter with our commander, General Tod Wolters," and that "we will be looking to maximize both efficiency and operational effectiveness, but that we need to be cognizant of the strategic concerns and implications."

The president pressed again, restarting his monologue about the Germans being "delinquent" and "not paying their fair share toward NATO." I told him, "We can accelerate our review." But I added again that we needed to "be aware of how the allies, and especially Moscow, might react to a unilateral drawdown from Germany." Trump went quiet. He seemed satisfied, or maybe he was thinking how the Russian angle might play domestically against him. Either way, I felt I had bought myself some more time. Now I had to get out of the Oval as quickly as possible.

In the weeks that followed, I spoke with Wolters and Milley and asked them to develop some options for my review in the next couple of months, which they did by early March.

While Trump's anger with Merkel often came up, the issue of a U.S. troop withdrawal from Germany largely faded, however. Since we were consumed in early 2020 with Iran and Iraq, and later with COVID, I didn't press the matter either. That is, until the June 2 directive from Trump.

In a note I drafted back to O'Brien in response to the president's order, I made clear again that conducting a responsible withdrawal of this magnitude in the timeline prescribed was neither possible nor prudent. Attempting to move 9,500 service members and their estimated 25,000 to 35,000 family members out of Germany, responsibly, in a little over three months was impossible, and attempting to do so would be grossly unfair to the service members, the DoD civilians, and the families being sent home.

On top of that, I said, it would be extremely difficult on such short notice to identify bases within the United States that have adequate housing, barracks space, school and child-care capacity, medical support, and other things necessary to take care of our people. This would cause a great deal of turmoil for our service members and their families, I wrote, and risked creating instability in the European security environment, breaking trust with our NATO allies and partners, and sending the wrong signals about our willingness to deter Russia.

I proposed we combine the intent behind this recent directive with my ongoing review of the European Command, and allow both to proceed on schedule. I could then return with options and recommendations on posture adjustments. I thought this would serve the president and our national security best.

I never heard back from O'Brien. I'm not sure why the directive was written and sent when it was in the first place, but I assumed that Grenell's constant presence in the White House since returning from Germany and being appointed acting DNI in February

2020—where he could advocate on one issue or another on a daily basis with O'Brien's support—was the key factor. Moreover, I was confident the narrative that "DoD is slow-walking your agenda" or "the Pentagon is dragging its feet"—criticisms by Chief of Staff Mark Meadows and others—was growing. These were views Meadows had brought with him from Congress. And without someone on the National Security Council willing to present the potential strategic and political downsides of such a unilateral move, let alone convene an interagency meeting to discuss it, we were headed for a showdown.

But as the story broke on June 5 about Trump's decision, leaked by the White House for sure, the reporting centered on Merkel's recent decision not to attend the G-7 meeting in Washington that summer despite the NSC's efforts to say it was about Germany's lack of commitment to spending more on defense. The president, by now focused intently on downplaying the spread of COVID in the United States and portraying the country as safe and open for business, apparently saw the German chancellor's decision as undercutting this narrative and personally insulting to him.

Not surprisingly, the announcement of a U.S. force reduction in Germany faced immediate criticism from all corners, including from Republicans on Capitol Hill who believed the move—if taken at face value—would embolden Russia and harm NATO. They were right.

It would be accurate to state, as Trump occasionally did, that restationing ten thousand U.S. military and their family members would be a boost to any local economy in the United States. But one also had to take into consideration the value of the host nation support provided by the Germans, which we estimated to be in the low billions of dollars. Despite me raising this point with him, the president still clung to this notion that stationing U.S. forces in

Germany (and Japan and South Korea) was a financial loser for the United States.

My understanding had been that Berlin was underwriting at least one-third of the cost of stationing American troops in Germany. Some on my staff reported higher percentages. I never saw a thorough accounting of this host nation support. My view was that wealthy countries should contribute *at least* 2 percent of their GDP to defense, and that host nation support should be treated separately, and increased if necessary, so that it was no less than 50/50.

General Milley passed along my guidance to Wolters to prepare an action plan based on the new White House directive, to keep the group very small to prevent leaks, and to be ready to return to Washington later in June to brief me on it. It was a daunting task that was impossible to complete in sufficient detail within the time allotted, but we had a lawful order from the commander in chief. After nearly ten months, I had run out of time and space with the White House. Fortunately, Wolters had already been developing some plans on the matter based on our previous discussions.

On a personal level, I saw this directive as a red flag that I might not be able to implement. In other words, if Trump insisted on a haphazard withdrawal from Germany, I might have to tell him no and see what happened. There was nothing about his order that was illegal, immoral, or unethical—clear lines that I had drawn throughout my career and affirmed again during my Senate confirmation hearing. Previous administrations, including Obama's, had also made significant reductions in Europe.

That said, it was important that we not overreact, that we assess the order carefully and diligently, and that we discuss it as a leadership team in the DoD. I wanted to make sure that my recommendation could stand up to scrutiny—from the White House, the Congress, the allies, and elsewhere. And before I made any personal decision that could upset my game plan of staying in office through the election, I wanted to make sure the recommended strategy made sense to me and was good for the country.

To help frame Wolters's planning, I developed five principles that he had to advance, or at least make no worse: strengthen NATO; reassure Allies; enhance the deterrence of Russia; improve U.S. strategic flexibility and U.S. European Command's operational flexibility; and, finally, take care of our service members and their families. Wolters and his staff went to work and had the broad outlines of a plan—a concept, really—in about two weeks. After a few iterations and a series of adjustments, the final version was nearly ready for presentation to the president.

Robert O'Brien would publish an opinion piece in the *Wall Street Journal* on June 21 defending the president's decision. There is nothing inherently wrong in doing this, except for the fact that nobody in the DoD's senior leadership was aware of it, and some things he wrote were incorrect. But the piece served its purpose, I suppose. A few media outlets reported that O'Brien was now angling to be the next secretary of defense.[3]

According to a June 3 story, O'Brien had "spoken to the president about Esper's television remarks" in the past, citing my "tendency to avoid offering a full-throated defense of the president or his policies," and "presented the president with print-outs that compare[d] his own public remarks on a topic to those of Esper to highlight the contrast." Self-promotion 101.

What the EUCOM plan proposed was to move 11,900 U.S. military personnel, principally Army and Air Force, out of Germany. Of this number, a little over 5,500 service members would be repositioned within other NATO countries, with the balance returning to the United States. Similar units, though, would begin conducting rotational deployments back to Europe from the United States to keep sufficient combat power in theater. We would achieve these numbers by implementing a variety of actions.

To begin, several headquarters would be consolidated in other parts of Europe, to include collocating them with their NATO counterparts in Belgium and Italy. The biggest action would be moving Wolters's EUCOM headquarters and other commands from Germany to Belgium. This would collocate these organizations with Supreme Headquarters Allied Powers Europe, a move that could speed decision making and address a long-held aspiration of some previous commanders.

To improve operational efficiency and readiness, we planned to move engineer, air defense, and other battalion-sized elements out of Germany and reunite some of them with their parent brigades in locations ranging from Belgium to Italy.

The nearly 4,500 members of the 2nd Cavalry Regiment would return to the United States as other Stryker units began continuous rotations farther east into Bulgaria and Romania.* The firepower, sustainability, and enhanced mobility of these units' eight-wheeled infantry carriers would give the United States a more flexible and enduring presence to enhance deterrence and reassure allies along

---

* The 2nd Cavalry Regiment is a U.S. Army Stryker brigade combat team (BCT) headquartered in Vilseck, Germany. A Stryker BCT is a combined arms infantry force structured around the lightly armored, eight-wheeled, infantry-carrying Stryker vehicle. Each Stryker BCT is composed of more than three hundred Stryker vehicles and 4,500 soldiers organized into three infantry battalions, one reconnaissance (cavalry) squadron, one artillery battalion, one brigade support battalion, and one brigade engineer battalion. Stryker BCTs are designed to bridge capability gaps between light (infantry BCTs) and heavy (armored BCTs) forces when it comes to tactical mobility, firepower, protection, and expeditionary speed.

NATO's southeastern flank. I let Wolters know that I was also willing to rotate a second armored brigade combat team, which is a heavier force made up of main battle tanks and infantry fighting vehicles, to Europe, in lieu of the Strykers, if he determined this was necessary, but he was less interested in doing so than I expected.

Additionally, an F-16 squadron and elements of a fighter wing would move to Italy, positioning them closer to the Black Sea region to bolster our allies in an area increasingly contested by the Russians, especially its airspace.

The airmen based in Mildenhall, United Kingdom—personnel responsible for aerial refueling and special operations—would not move to Germany, as Wolters had requested months earlier. Stopping this move would ensure the uninterrupted readiness and responsiveness of these units. My U.K. counterpart, Ben Wallace, was pleased later to hear this and offered his full support.

U.S. Africa Command would also move out of Germany, but work was needed to determine its final destination. I gave guidance to its commander, General Steve Townsend, to assess locations in Africa, Europe, and the United States, following the U.S. Central Command model in the latter case. I personally wanted to get AFRICOM—or at least a forward element of the headquarters—onto the African continent itself. They seemed resistant to any change, however.

The plan would also rotate the lead element of the Army's newly established V Corps headquarters to Poland once Warsaw signed a defense cooperation agreement and burden sharing deal as previously pledged. I pressed Wolters a few times to move additional forces into the Baltics as well, but he was concerned that doing so would give some non-Baltic allies with troops in Estonia, Latvia, or Lithuania a reason to withdraw them, thus forcing the United

States to carry even more of the load. I agreed this would not be a good outcome, so I let this issue rest.

As I studied the plan and discussed it with my leadership team, the most significant thing for me was that it met or advanced the principles I set out for Tod Wolters weeks earlier. Wolters had done a great job. If he hadn't, I would need to steel myself for a contentious meeting with the president. I was obligated to inform him of the downsides of his order and to argue for changes that improved our security posture in Europe, not harmed it. Knowing how frustrated he was with the Germans, I expected this could well be the end of the line for me.

On June 24, I joined the president at the Oval Office for his meeting with the Polish president. Andrzej Duda made this visit a few days ahead of an election back home, hoping that a White House visit—and maybe even the commitment of more U.S. troops to Poland—would give him and his party an electoral boost. Duda was a conservative politician who sported a tight-lipped smile and eager demeanor. He was quick to flatter Trump and yield the floor to him. After all, some said, he flew all the way from Warsaw to get an electoral endorsement from the U.S. president. Needless to say, Trump and Duda got along well, so this was going to be an easy, friendly session.

Before the meeting, I had the chance to update Trump, informing him that I would be briefing him on June 30 regarding our plan to withdraw troops from Germany. Anticipating a request from Duda, the president asked, "Will Poland be getting more forces?" I told him "very few" as part of his recent directive; instead, "some troops would be repositioned in Europe, and some would be returned home to the U.S." He was good with that, and used similar words in his joint press conference afterward.

During the Oval Office meeting, Trump pressed Duda to "sign the [defense] cooperation agreement" that had been pending for months. This agreement was essential to giving our troops legal protections in-country, formalizing the financial support Poland would be providing, and locking in Warsaw's logistical and infrastructure support, among other things. The Poles had been taking their time on this, but I was able to mention it to Trump before the meeting, and he followed through.

I also raised it directly with Duda during the session, after Trump mentioned it, saying, "We need the agreement signed before we can move forward on a few issues, such as establishing an Army Corps headquarters in Poland." This got Duda's attention, so he turned to an aide to his right and asked him about it. As his question was answered, the Polish president nodded affirmatively. He turned back to me and said, "It will be signed in the next thirty days." After months and months of working this issue with his government at various levels, I chalked this up as a win.

I planned a hasty trip to Brussels to meet with Secretary General Jens Stoltenberg at NATO on June 26. The enormous headquarters building was largely vacant due to COVID. Pandemic restrictions meant that I couldn't stay overnight, so we spent the previous day and evening in the United Kingdom, which was fine because it gave me the chance to visit with the various U.S. Air Force units based in Mildenhall, to include discussing race and diversity issues with a group of service members. These were the same personnel that Wolters was proposing we not move to Germany as long planned, so I found the stop very helpful in understanding his recommendation.

Stoltenberg and I met in his office for about an hour. Kay Bailey Hutchison, the U.S. permanent representative to NATO, joined us.

Hutchison was a capable and trusted ambassador who had been in Brussels since 2017 after a distinguished political career in the United States. As if managing relationships among twenty-nine other allies wasn't hard enough, she also had the unenviable task of sorting out what was happening in Washington. State and Defense were usually aligned on issues, but the White House was the wild card that sometimes threw us all off balance.

My meeting with Stoltenberg and Hutchison went well. The three of us sat in the secretary general's private office around a small conference table and had a very candid discussion about my planning. Jens sat upright at the end of the table, with Kay sitting midtable opposite me. I started with the purpose of our meeting, "I want to be as transparent as I can, as I long promised I would, about a presidential directive I recently received," I said. "This order will have a major impact on the alliance. I am doing all I can to make the best of it, but I can't tell you how it will turn out."

There was an unspoken understanding among the three of us that I was riding a tiger back in Washington and doing my best to stay in the saddle while I tried to guide the president in the best direction. Stoltenberg and Hutchison were intimately familiar with Trump's complaints about NATO and had likely seen his mercurial nature up close. When I asked them to "keep this discussion just between the three of us," they understood why.

I told Stoltenberg and Hutchison that "I'm not able to walk you through the details of the plan. We're still not finished, and I've yet to brief the president," which would happen fairly soon. I also said that "I have an obligation, as well, to brief Congress before I walk you and the allies through the details, Jens." Kay, being a former U.S. senator, nodded quietly in agreement. What I could do, however, was "talk about the principles I gave EUCOM to guide their proposals," share some fundamentals of General Wolters's plan, and offer "a few examples" of what we thought would be in the final version. Stoltenberg, in his crisp Norwegian accent, said he understood and committed to "not share this discussion outside this room."

I then proceeded to walk both through the emerging plan. This took several minutes to explain. After I was done and answered a few questions, they agreed that the EUCOM plan would probably meet the principles I had established up front, and that "this could be a real positive for NATO." Jens believed most allies would be supportive; that some, such as Poland and Romania, would be ecstatic; but that Germany, obviously, would not be happy. That said, he thought "Berlin will put the alliance first" and not criticize Trump's decision publicly. In due course, our internal reporting indicated that Stoltenberg's predictions were largely on the mark, though some of the public narrative from Europe was less positive.

Stoltenberg emphasized one area in particular—communications with the allies—once the president made his decision. He said, "Mark, it is very important that you meet as quickly as possible with other countries, especially those affected by the moves, to consult and explain what you are doing" and work to get them on board. I couldn't agree more and told him so. It was the reason I jumped on a plane on such short notice to meet with him, the NATO secretary general, in Brussels. Assuming the president approved the plans, I told him again, "my first stop had to be Congress to brief our oversight committees.

"After that," I said, "I will task my key people," such as General Wolters and James Anderson, my Policy lead, "to brief first the countries affected most," except for Germany. "I owe Annegret [Kramp-Karrenbauer, my German counterpart] a personal call." She had been a good colleague over the many months we worked together. I found her to be pro-defense and pro-NATO, and someone who also believed Germany should contribute more to its own defense. She was easy to speak with, and so we were able to have very candid conversations about alliance issues. When she and I finally spoke, she was as professional as I expected her to be, if not more so.

Concerned that our plans might leak out of D.C., I asked Jens to "please call her confidentially on my behalf and let her know" that I will be reaching out as soon as I can.

Beyond speaking with the German minister of defense, I eventually made myself available for any one-on-one calls my team recommend I personally make, while we planned meetings in the Pentagon for the defense ministers of countries like Romania and Bulgaria.

The three of us talked a little longer in Stoltenberg's office before I told them I had to leave. I needed to get back on my plane for the long flight back to the United States. Both thanked me for making the trip. I told them, "I don't know how things will turn out, but I will do my best to keep you informed." With that we stood up, walked to Jens's outer office door, and shook hands before Hutchison and I headed back out to my waiting car.

On Monday, June 29, I traveled to the White House to brief the president on our plan. General Milley joined me. Also in the room were Robert O'Brien, Mike Pompeo, and Mark Meadows, along with a few other people. I briefed the bottom line up front—"We have a plan to get U.S. forces under 25,000 in Germany, as you directed, Mr. President." In fact, I said, "The EUCOM plan actually proposes to pull 11,900 personnel out of the country." The president, sitting behind the Resolute desk, leaned forward onto it, nodded in agreement, pursed his lips, and said, "Good, good," glancing around to others at the same time, seeking similar nods of approval.

I then outlined the principles I had given Tod Wolters and explained how he went about implementing the guidance, "such as consolidating headquarters, reuniting units that were geographically separated, and rotating troops forward into frontline countries like Romania." The president was pleased. I then turned it over to Milley to discuss the plan in greater detail and to offer up some rough timelines.

The chairman spoke to some of the key units that would be moving. Trump asked, "Will more troops be going to Poland?" His meeting with Duda was still fresh in his mind. I told him that "a limited number of personnel would be going there as part of this initiative, but that other actions to move larger numbers of forces were already under way." I had in mind the return of V Corps to Europe, and the long stalled movement of a so-called deterrence package to Poland.

Milley and I mentioned it would take "a long time" to effect these moves, as well as quite a bit of funding—"in the billions of dollars range." The president seemed unconcerned about the cost, believing, as we had heard many times before, that the Germans were benefiting at America's expense from our presence. Trump thought the withdrawal would save money and believed members of Congress would be "begging me" to put these returning forces in their district or state. He was probably right to some degree on this last point.

About this time, Pompeo jumped in and offered his support, saying, "Mr. President, this is a good plan." O'Brien chirped in his endorsement as well. As was my practice, I had briefed them both a few days in advance to get their input and support. It was important that the three of us get aligned as best and as soon as possible. The president would often play to divisions within the national security team, and that didn't bode well for policies or actions that needed a decision. Unfortunately, this coordination broke down over time, a process that accelerated from the summer onward.

The president asked a couple of times about "bringing all the troops back home to the United States." I was prepared for this, and quickly made the case that "this wouldn't be prudent, given a wide range of strategic, operational, and geopolitical concerns this would raise." Milley added several good points as well, speaking to operational effectiveness, readiness, and other key considerations. Trump yielded both times he raised the issue, seemingly content with the simple fact that we were pulling troops out of Germany, but a return home for all of them was clearly his preference.

At one point, Meadows pressed me and Milley why, with regard to the 6,400 troops we planned on returning to the United States, we couldn't accomplish that in a matter of weeks, which I took to mean sometime before the GOP convention in late August, and certainly no later than Election Day. This conversation had come up at least once before with the chief of staff, and we'd had to explain that the scope of the problem was several times bigger than 6,000-plus troops, as I had done in my conversations with O'Brien. But Meadows was eager to please Trump, and when coupled with his prevailing view that the DoD dragged its feet, this created a lot of unnecessary friction that would worsen over the coming weeks and months.

It was true that, at times, we slowed the process down—so that we could analyze the problem, capture the latest intelligence, staff the matter broadly, and develop options for the president, especially when it involved matters of high risk, consequence, or impact. But that was our job, our duty, and our responsibility, and it was an approach I took throughout my professional career. To suggest, however, as Meadows sometimes did, that these were constant, intentional tactics by the DoD to undermine an elected president was wrong and unfair.

I had lived in Italy as a young Army officer and commanded a rifle company in what is now the 173rd Airborne Brigade Combat Team in Vicenza. I moved my family to and from Europe, and knew it took months before we completely settled in on either side of the Atlantic. Packing up your household goods, getting your car to a port to load on a ship, finding a place to live on the other end, and a hundred other smaller things all consumed a great deal of time and coordination. Wolters told me the quickest a family could move back to the United States was a little over three weeks, which is about the best you could do in an "emergency" situation, he said.

Of course, you still had to figure out where in the United States you were going to move all these people. You couldn't dump several thousand people into a community on short notice and expect the infrastructure—schools, hospitals, housing, etc.—to be able to absorb it all. It was abundantly clear it would be logistically impossible to move 6,400 service members, plus another 13,000 to 17,000 family members, in a couple of months, let alone in a few weeks from a dead start. It would take time to plan, time to coordinate, and time to implement. Meadows wasn't satisfied, but the president was, so I moved the meeting on.

With Trump's formal approval in hand, we started briefing the plan more broadly, beginning with Congress. I called the German defense minister and had a good conversation with her, committing as well to send a team to Berlin to discuss the plan in greater detail with her staff. Others followed with briefings to our allies. And EUCOM began sharing details with the services, especially the Army, which would have the most people in play.

Despite our efforts, we couldn't overcome the White House leaks, the president's comments, and the inclination of many on Capitol

Hill to simply reject anything associated with Trump. It was true that the president's antipathy toward Chancellor Merkel and frustration with Germany were what prompted his directive, neither of which were good reasons at all to withdraw forces. Yet we had made lemonade out of those lemons. Even on the morning of our Pentagon press conference, though, the president would undercut our presentation—the nearly same one I gave him in the Oval Office weeks earlier—by saying "we're reducing the force because they're not paying their bill. It's very simple. They're delinquent." Regardless of his statement, though, it didn't mean that our plans to square that circle weren't reasonable and responsible. Indeed, working from my five principles, Wolters did a really good job. His proposal would improve our posture on the continent in many ways.

The simple fact was that many U.S. forces in Europe were located where they had been at the end of the Cold War, nearly thirty years earlier, when the border between East and West literally divided Germany. But since the end of the Soviet Union in 1991, the boundary with the post-USSR Russia shifted hundreds of miles east as NATO expanded. Most of the U.S. forces necessary to bolster a deterrence of Russian adventurism, however, never moved. I knew this firsthand since I was stationed in Italy in the 1990s and traveled frequently to Germany and elsewhere in Europe for training. This left countries like Romania, Poland, and, especially, the Baltic states vulnerable and uneasy. The EUCOM proposal that we adopted aimed to help address this fundamental problem by moving (more) forces forward into frontline states, even if just on a rotational basis.

We held a press conference to brief the plan on July 29. Mark Milley was traveling, so Vice Chairman John Hyten joined me while General Wolters appeared by video from Europe. The briefing went reasonably well. We covered all the main points, including the five principles I had set down for Tod Wolters, and how he went about meeting or exceeding them. We also made it a point to note that the size, composition, and disposition of U.S. forces in Europe had changed many times in NATO's seventy-one-year existence, and that now was another "inflection point" in the alliance's storied history. We also pointed out that the plan we were presenting was more of a concept than an execution order. It would take months and months to flesh it out in detail, years and billions of dollars to implement, and it would likely change as we continued to work on it.

Indeed, in the weeks following the public rollout, the Army— which heretofore had not participated in EUCOM's planning— would work with the command on a number of changes to General Wolter's plan that would further optimize my five principles without breaching the twenty-five-thousand-troop ceiling in Germany that Trump ordered.

Regrettably, this would mark my last time in the Pentagon Briefing Room. I was on official or personal travel most of August, so July 29 ended up being my last session until the election. The environment in D.C. had become too partisan, and some in the press too politicized, to have serious discussions in the briefing room. As I mentioned earlier, I couldn't afford to have my plans derailed by a few in the media who were looking for gossip, a difference with Trump, or something that would drag the DoD into politics. With sixty days or so to go until the election after my August travels, I didn't need some yellow journalism compromising my strategy. A large majority of the Pentagon press team was a solid group, but we had a few who sometimes did not live up to the standards of their profession.

I would take my fair share of criticism for not conducting press conferences at the Pentagon in September and October. By contrast, the media didn't say much when President Biden went over two months during his first one hundred days in office without holding a press conference—and he is the president of the United States, not the secretary of defense. It's a double standard that plays to the narrative that the media is biased, which is unfortunate. After all, democracy needs a free press, but that press needs to be fair, objective, accurate, and accountable.

Setting aside those who were upset that I put a pause on Pentagon briefings, I still planned to do interviews, talk with the media on background, and take questions at think tanks. Up until that point, we had a very solid track record. I had made engaging with the press a priority from day one, literally.

On July 24, 2019, the morning after I was sworn in, I went down to the press corridor in the Pentagon to meet with the media. I made clear in my conversation with them that they played a "very important role . . . in our society" and helped in "communicating what we [the DoD] are doing" to the American people. I made clear that I looked forward to working with them.[4]

But when they spoke, I took an earful. Many were upset by a few things that occurred in the past, and which I committed on the spot to remedy. First, there had been no press room briefings at the Pentagon for well over a year, they complained. And second, some thought Secretary Mattis's personal example discouraged DoD officials from engaging the media, especially on camera. I told them I would fix both issues immediately—that we would "send out this week updated guidance," which we did a few days later.[5] It was important that the Pentagon's leaders speak to the American people, I told them.

Jonathan Hoffman did a great job implementing this plan and more. By the end of my tenure, I had held nearly two dozen Pentagon

Briefing Room briefings, eight town halls, thirty-two so-called press gaggles, twenty-nine televised or taped interviews, twenty-two off-the-record sessions, sixteen briefings with Q&As at think tanks, nine messages to the force, and eleven major policy speeches. Additionally, I committed to ensuring the media traveled with me on all my official trips, which created far more informal opportunities for them to engage with me and my senior staff.

Press updates started happening every week or so with Hoffman at the podium, and during the heat of the pandemic we had multiple press briefings with senior leaders most days. We had exceeded our own goals, thanks in large part to the press team and my own front office.

This was quite an accomplishment, particularly having to do so in the midst of COVID for ten months. It debunked an opposite narrative a few in the media were trying to generate that we weren't engaging the press corps enough. Others in the press gave us good marks, with Bloomberg crediting the entire team and me for being very accessible, even during the pandemic.[6]

Following the July 29 briefing on Germany, some members of Congress from both parties reacted negatively without even bothering to get briefed by the DoD first. One GOP senator said that removing troops from Germany was "a grave error" and "a gift to Russia." How could that be if U.S. troops were moving hundreds of miles *closer* to the Russian border, and unit effectiveness was improved through collocation? This would be another case study of times I wished members—especially those we aren't able to prebrief—would talk to the DoD *before* they spoke. It would make for a much more serious and responsible debate. After all, this wasn't the first time that an American president repositioned or returned U.S. forces in NATO's history.

In 2012, for example, the Obama administration announced the withdrawal of two heavy armored brigades—the most lethal ground forces in the Army—from Europe. Nearly seven thousand troops returned to the United States, more than what we were proposing in 2020. The fact was, too many people—elected officials, the media, influencers, etc.—couldn't separate Trump the person from the administration's policies and plans. If they thought Trump was bad, then it seemed his policies were bad; if they thought Trump was good, then all his policies were seemingly good. This mind-set was too simplistic, and patently unfair, especially to all those good people in government who were working hard under very unusual circumstances to do what was best for the country. Judgments should be made, instead, on the lemonade that was made, rather than the lemons that were handed us.

On September 25, Chairman Milley convened a meeting to review proposals from the Army to modify EUCOM's plans. I told the service that I would hear them out, but that their recommendations had to abide by my five principles and General Wolters's operational plans and needs. The Army and EUCOM went to work and then presented their recommendations to me in mid-October.

The most significant modification was a recommendation to keep the 2nd Cavalry Regiment in Europe permanently, which meant that approximately 4,500 soldiers and their Stryker vehicles would *not* return to the U.S., as we briefed earlier. The Army was concerned about the long-term cost and wear of constantly moving Stryker combat teams to and from Europe. It was a legitimate concern, but I and others had become big fans of rotational deployments for the strategic flexibility they offered. Secretary McCarthy and General McConville were persuasive, however. My loss of strategic resilience, though, would give Wolters more operational flexibility. EUCOM would be able to push more forces farther east more easily and reinforce them more readily. I approved the modified plan, which offered sufficient offsets in other areas to remain compliant with Trump's original order, later that month.

I hosted separate meetings at the Pentagon with the defense ministers from Bulgaria and Romania in early October. These meetings went well. Both countries were former Soviet states that knew well the heavy hand of Moscow. Carefully and with concern, they also watched what Russia did and was doing in nearby Ukraine. As with other eastern European states, they were anxious to see more American forces in their countries, so they supported the EUCOM repositioning plans, to include hosting the Stryker units.

I also approved what the Army called Deterrence Package 2, a deployment order that had lingered for years. This collection of Army units numbered about 1,600 personnel and included a number of headquarters and commands responsible for long-range fires, air defense, engineers, and logistics, as well as the V Corps headquarters Forward Command Post. These were the type of units, in addition to the assignment of two more Navy destroyers to EUCOM that would be based in Spain, that Wolters needed on a permanent basis. This was due to the fact that they were required in the early days of conflict and could be difficult to deploy from the United States in a timely manner.

I decided not to announce these changes internally, brief the Hill, or share them with the media. These further adjustments would have resonated well with members of Congress, the think tank world, and others, and would have cast our efforts in a far better light. But I was concerned that this news would work its way to White House aides looking to curry favor with the president. They would then rush to the Oval Office, falsely accuse the DoD of some betrayal—even though our plans still met Trump's guidance—and get him to sign an order reversing my directives. It was disappointing that these people had less concern about policy, strategy, and geopolitics than they did in slandering to ingratiate, and that we couldn't entrust them to fairly inform the president. At this point, the best option was to quietly do the right thing.

Not surprisingly, a question that came up a few times in the July 29 press conference was the issue of Trump's order being based on his frustration with Merkel and Germany not contributing more to defense, and not the strategic rationale I presented. They were right, of course; it was something I didn't try to deny. My job from the early days of my tenure was often about making the best out of a bad situation. My challenge now was how to take a poorly thought out decision, reframe it, and shape it into something palatable. If that wasn't possible, I had an obligation to present other options that achieved a similar outcome. On this matter, I felt we were able to make lemonade once again. If we hadn't, I was prepared to push back, and if necessary, get fired, depending on the impacts this directive would have on NATO and our collective security, despite my game plan.

I didn't get a final count before I left office in November, but a couple of members of my staff estimated that, when all was said and done, *all* of the plans I had approved for NATO that fall would actually result in *more* U.S. forces in Europe to strengthen NATO, *more* U.S. forces farther east to deter Russia, *more* U.S. forces in *more* member countries to reassure allies, and *more* operational flexibility for EUCOM, in addition to all of the efficiencies that Wolters would be gaining—but too difficult to immediately calculate—by collocating headquarters and physically reuniting units.

Moreover, we had already stepped up our activities in Europe in 2020 to send a clear message of resolve to Moscow and reassurance to our allies. We sent U.S. destroyers to the Barents Sea, where Russia's Northern Fleet is located, for the first time since the Cold War, and increased the number of American ships deploying to the Black Sea. Meanwhile, we flew U.S. bombers throughout Europe, including through Ukrainian airspace, and conducted one of the largest deployments of U.S. Army ground forces in decades back to the continent for training with our NATO allies.

Regardless of who controls the White House, the United States will continue to face the same opportunities and challenges with NATO that every administration has faced—a great alliance that could be far better if everyone lived up to their spending commitments; occasional squabbles with one country or another, which often present obstacles to the collective good; a persistent effort, led by the French, to establish a European Union force that would compete with NATO; an insufficient commitment to true operational readiness that can respond quickly and effectively in times of crisis; and, most important, an obligation for the United States to lead if the alliance is to succeed.

Working along these lines of effort to improve NATO is necessary but not sufficient if we are to avoid war with Russia in the near term and prepare ourselves to deal with China over the long run. As such, the flip side of the transatlantic coin is the future of Russia. There is no good reason for Moscow to oppose the West, let alone align with Beijing.

Russia is a European country with a shared history, culture, and religion with others on the continent. Moscow has little to none of this with China. With major trend lines continuing to show China's rise and Russia's decline, Moscow risks becoming a client state of Beijing one day. A better alternative for Russia is to become a full-fledged partner in Europe. That was the path many of us hoped and thought they would be on after the Cold War ended, until the revanchist Vladimir Putin came to power in 1999, less than a decade after the collapse of the Soviet Union.

It does not appear that Putin, a wily twenty-first-century autocrat, will be stepping down or voted out of office any time soon. Until then, it is important that the United States and its NATO allies not only show unity, build strength, and demonstrate resolve to deter Putin but continue to support and engage with opposition leaders, the Russian people, and the credible civil society organizations remaining in that country. We must lead with our values and work for the day when a Russian leader who truly believes in democracy, freedom, individual rights, and the rule of law finally comes to power legitimately.

CHAPTER 16

A SALUTE TO AMERICA?

The black, bat-winged bomber passed lazily, ominously, above the Lincoln Memorial, casting a dark shadow over onlookers below. The jagged edges at the rear of its large, single wing cut a sharp contrast with the sky above. The stealthy Air Force bomber capped the overflight on that rainy July 4 celebration in 2019. It was clearly the crowd favorite.

While the matter of withdrawing troops from Germany was first up in the wake of my June 3, 2020, press conference, the annual Fourth of July celebration was right on its heels.

President Trump brought new meaning to Fourth of July fireworks during his tenure. The 2020 Independence Day celebration on the National Mall promised to be another contentious affair. I was serving as acting secretary in 2019 when General Joe Dunford and I joined the president on the podium to watch the festivities and overflight of military aircraft.

I inherited that plan from Acting Secretary of Defense Pat Shanahan and thought the Pentagon put on a reasonable show, given the president's aspirations. There were military vehicles on display around the Lincoln Memorial, and drill teams and military bands from the services were present, but the highlight was clearly the flyover.

Around two dozen aircraft from each of the armed services and the Coast Guard flew westward down the Mall from the Capitol. Despite an unrelenting downpour, it was a nice event and a very impressive display. The thousands attending seemed to feel the same way. The B-2 bomber that flew last that afternoon caught everyone's attention, marking the crescendo of the show. All in all, the event was a success and the criticism about a Fourth of July tribute to the military dried up as quickly as the rains did.

Prior to the event, there was some fuss raised regarding the armed forces' participation and the expectation it would become a partisan political event, but I didn't see the problem if it was modest, not too expensive, and included our military appropriately. The services performed dozens of flyovers and demonstrations around the country each year. We allowed for such events in our annual budgets, which Congress approved. They helped with recruiting, general community awareness, and simple patriotism. In fact, the July 4, 2019, cost to the Pentagon was less than what we spent on the annual Fleet Week celebration in San Francisco.

As I sat at my Pentagon desk in early June a year later, I looked ahead at my calendar for July. The Fourth was always a busy week for the DoD, and recalling the drama that ensued in 2019, I asked where our plans stood to support this year's Independence Day celebration. My front office wasn't tracking this, so my assistant scheduled a briefing with U.S. Northern Command, which had responsibility for the event. I went into the meeting expecting to see the same plan from last year. The presentation caught me completely off guard.

The White House Military Office (WHMO), which handles all liaison and support between the Pentagon and the White House, had been called in to meet with the president weeks earlier. In this meeting, Trump apparently said he wanted a much bigger military presence, something closer to France's Bastille Day celebrations. This would mean more aircraft, more ground vehicles, and more displays, all on a much grander scale. What happened next was never clear, but with the president's approval, WHMO dutifully started things moving, coordinating directly with NORTHCOM. Nobody seemed to think of informing the Pentagon's leadership about what was going on.

The presentation before me was outlandish and politically tone-deaf given what we had just gone through the week of June 1. At a time when everyone was concerned about Trump's politicization of the military and doubts that we could keep the institution out of politics, this would make the problem worse.

The original plan under development by Northern Command, at the White House's direction, called for 107 aircraft—yes, 107 planes—mostly U.S. military aircraft supplemented by privately owned vintage planes, to fly over the White House on the afternoon of July 4. The low-end number was 76 military aircraft. I couldn't believe it. I tried to calculate the cost, the time it would take to fly so many sorties, and the airspace coordination and clearance. It was absurd.

When asked why the planes "are flying over the White House instead of the Mall," the briefers told us that, because of COVID, the D.C. government canceled all gatherings on that large, narrow tract of land that ran about two miles from the Capitol to the Lincoln Memorial. But while the D.C. mayor controlled those grounds, she didn't have any authority over the White House properties.

But still, why "over" the White House? You could still get a good view, if not better, of the aircraft if they flew east to west, straight from Capitol Hill, over the Washington Monument, to the Lincoln Memorial. After all, if people weren't traveling to D.C. for the observances, most Americans will see it on TV. "Well, sir," the answer came back, "the president plans to invite his supporters to a big event on the South Lawn" for a dinner, a speech, and first-class seats to watch the flyover.

Oh my! This generated a new round of questions. "Who's invited? Is this open to the public? Will donors be attending? Will the president ask people to give money to attend the South Lawn event? It's an election year, so is this a political event? Will it be bipartisan?" Our questions went on and on, and nobody had good answers. Red flags were popping up all over.

And then we discussed the vehicles and other displays planned to be on the South Lawn for guests to view. These included a Stryker combat vehicle, a High Mobility Artillery Rocket System, a vehicle-mounted Marine Corps air defense weapon, and mini-planes.

General Milley and I looked at each other and immediately recognized the gravity of these plans. Rather than keep digging into the briefers, who were simply doing their job in response to the White House request, we thanked the team, told them to hold off on any further work, and cut the session short.

I cleared the briefing room except for Milley and a couple of my other close advisers. The sum of what the White House requested was overwhelming. In the wake of what happened in early June—when the Insurrection Act was almost invoked in order to deploy U.S. troops into American cities, when the White House was barricaded and fenced off due to multiple nights of violent protests in the streets of D.C., when the president continually threatened the use of force to deal with protesters, and when serious people expressed alarm about Trump trying to politicize the military—these Fourth of July plans were going to throw fuel on an already incendiary situation.

The Department had gone through this at least once before, when the president signed the so-called Muslim travel ban at the Pentagon (and in the Hall of Heroes no less) in 2017, when Jim Mattis was secretary of defense. It didn't go over well. The DoD had gotten caught up in domestic politics of a very sensitive nature, the type that was laced with charges of bigotry. Protests and legal challenges ensued.

In a matter of weeks, we could have 107 aircraft—more than four times the number than the year before—flying over the White House, where the president and his supporters would be accused of holding a political event. Fighting vehicles, rocket launchers, air-defense systems, and other military hardware positioned on the South Lawn would be seemingly protecting them all; at a minimum they would be political props to convey the candidate's strength, toughness, and seriousness. It was not a good optic for the nation, and it was not a good look for the military. It made *no* sense to any of us at the Pentagon, but at the White House, we would learn, it made all the sense in the world.

Fate was putting a series of minefields in front of me in June and July, and this was next. Some of these things were happening simultaneously. It would take careful footwork not only to avoid stepping on one mine but to avoid triggering another in the process. I had to take each day carefully and deliberately, mindful of all the competing and interlocking issues, and my overall game plan. At the same time, I pressed forward on implementing our NDS Top Ten objectives and pushing Operation Warp Speed along. I couldn't stop doing my primary job just to manage these potential crises.

After the briefing, I asked Jen Stewart to set up a call for me with Vice President Pence to share my concerns. Pence was not just the vice president, he was someone to whom Trump seemed to listen. That doesn't mean that he acted on Pence's advice, but the president did show a certain deference to the former governor of Indiana and longtime representative from the state. In my call with Pence on June 9, I cited all the reasons that an event of this scale, scope, and composition "doesn't make sense politically." I added, "Mr. Vice President, this is going to thrust DoD back into a very bad light, and it won't be good for the White House either." Pence understood politics well, having served decades in this milieu and rising to its heights, so he got it.

The vice president listened intently. I could picture him on the other end of the line, his lips pursed tightly as he took in my words, staring intently as he processed what I was saying, and thinking through his response. He was both thoughtful and cautious in that way. "Mark," he said, "what do you recommend, then?"

"Mr. Vice President, I think we should cancel the event altogether because of the limitations placed on the public attending due to the pandemic. That's our first option and probably the best one," I said. "But I suspect the president won't go for that," I added, "so maybe we either move the large flyover out to Joint Base Andrews, which has an airfield where the annual air show is typically conducted, or we scale down the event in D.C. so that it resembles 2019's Salute to America." There was silence on the other end of the line again as the vice president thought and processed.

Pence asked a few more questions, usually good ones, as he

worked to fully understand the issue and our concerns. As the son of a Korean War veteran and the father of a Marine pilot, he took great pride and interest in the DoD. He and I would often talk about issues facing the armed forces, and he would sometimes share some of his son's experiences with me. The vice president's and his wife, Karen's, concern for our military personnel was genuine. It was something I really appreciated about them.

The vice president listened intently, as he usually did, said that he understood our concerns, and would "think about what you're proposing." I knew I had barraged him with facts and arguments, so I committed to "send a memo putting these issues in writing to help you in any discussion you might have with the president." I also thought this memo would help focus his attention on this very real concern we had and work its way around the White House.

In my formal letter to the vice president on June 10, I wrote that if the White House conducts the July 4 Salute to America as currently being planned, it "would detract from the celebration of the day and risk politicizing the military at a difficult time for our country." To avoid that, we intended to focus the planning on events and activities that celebrate Independence Day and connect the American public with our military personnel and values, I wrote. Therefore, the Department would scope the composition, mix, and scale of aircraft flying in the capital region to no more than what it had provided the previous year. In addition, we would plan for appropriate military static displays at Joint Base Andrews, rather than on the White House grounds, if those were still desired.

Two days later, on June 12, General Milley and I met with Mark Meadows in his large corner office in the West Wing. I was unsure how this meeting would unfold. Meadows could be unpredictable and everyone was still raw from the week before. He greeted us both casually in a soothing voice, marked by his North Carolina drawl. The air in the room was heavy nonetheless. The chief of staff took a seat in a large chair opposite Milley and me. He looked tired as he slumped slightly.

Meadows started off by saying, "Secretary, Chairman, thanks for coming by. It's been a crazy couple weeks. I thought we should take some time to talk through a few things and clear the air." I looked at him, nodded, and said, "Makes sense to me." Meadows said that Chairman Milley and, especially, I were not on good terms with the president, and that he wanted "to help us repair that relationship." Milley sat stone-faced. I remained expressionless as well, occasionally nodding to acknowledge what Meadows was saying, but otherwise not believing that he was concerned about us personally. The White House chief of staff was loyal to the president to a fault and remained fully committed to the task of getting him reelected, as I mentioned before. That meant keeping the team on board and eliminating distractions for the reelection campaign. It was that simple and probably not unlike the mission undertaken by his predecessors in prior administrations at the end of a first term. But couching his pitch in a faux argument that he was concerned about us made it feel very disingenuous.

Meadows wrapped up by asking for Milley's and my "help on a few things." First, he said, "I can't have any more surprises. I need to know if something is going to happen" that would make a splash in the news. Next, he asked us to "lay low in the media for a few weeks until things cool down," to limit press conferences, interviews, and so forth. "And in a couple weeks," he said, "I'll get you in with the president for a private meeting" to do some patch-up work, he said, on the relationship front.

Finally, the chief of staff said, "If you have any issues or concerns with the White House, bring them to me. I will address them."

Meadows stressed that he needed us to be straight up with him so that he could help us. Milley and I didn't say much as he spoke. I thought it important to give Meadows room to speak, which also gave me space to assess what was really going on and what was really being said.

When Meadows finished, he looked at us both, seeking a response as he sat unchanged, comfortable in the chair a few feet away. I said, "Mark, thanks for what you said. I appreciate it. Your asks sound reasonable to me right now." I added, "I'm on board with them, but I have a request." "What's that?" Meadows asked. "That we get the same treatment," I said. He looked back, briefly surprised at my reply, and said, "You will. You have my word."

There was a long pause after that. I decided to take him up on the spot regarding his offer of assistance. So, I jumped back in and said, "There is one particular thing you can help right now with. It's the leaks coming out of the White House. They are undermining the Pentagon and putting us all in awkward positions with the media." The anonymous chatter to the press ran a gamut of issues, from personnel to policy, and all the way to what the president might or might not think about me, Milley, and the DoD. In most cases it seemed to be White House staff trying "to advance their own ambitions or their own agendas." You can usually tell where the leaks emanate from based on who benefits from the story, and it wasn't the DoD. But it was grist for the media mill to "create needless friction between the White House and the Pentagon."

Next, I said, "I'd appreciate your help in keeping the NSC out of my programs and my chain of command," and focused instead on "their proper role of bringing together and coordinating the interagency." I told him of my conversations—plural—with O'Brien on this issue, but that I didn't seem to be getting through to him.

"Pompeo is having similar problems," I added, "and maybe worse than me"—which was based on what the secretary of state and his folks had told me on a few occasions.

To his credit, Meadows responded favorably on both points, noting that he "recently fired a leaker" for bad behavior, and that he too fully endorsed "the importance of following the chain of command." It was important, he said, adding, "I'm a chain of command guy." I wrote these things down. I wanted to believe that both problems would get serious attention, but they only worsened over time, with Meadows reportedly doing his own share of leaking and reaching into the DoD.

General Milley, still troubled by Trump's attempts to put him in charge of civil unrest response on June 1 and sensitive to the social media backlash against him, spoke up about his role, focusing on the "obligation" he had "to provide best military advice." Meadows said he understood but added something to the effect that Milley had to support or be loyal "to the president." Milley shot back immediately that his "duty was *not* to support the president"—as Meadows requested—but "to follow legal orders and his oath." He was trying to educate Meadows, but it caught the chief of staff off guard. Meadows became defensive, straightened up in his chair some, and then launched into a series of arguments that masqueraded as questions. The room started getting tense again.

Milley explained his role well, stressing that, under the law, he was an "adviser to the president and the secretary of defense on military matters." He had "no formal place in the chain of command," he said, which flowed from the president to the secretary of defense, and from there—from me—to either the combatant commanders or the service secretaries.

Milley was doing a good job explaining his role to Meadows, but I didn't want the chief of staff to think my silence, as the chairman spoke, in any way suggested a lack of support on my part for what Milley was saying. So, I jumped in and doubled down on Milley's main points, emphasizing the difference between a civilian political appointee such as myself and a uniformed officer. I pointed out that "I have served on both sides of this line over the years" and that these were "fundamental principles" to the American military tradition and professional ethic, but I felt Meadows didn't really get it, or didn't want to.

Milley and I didn't make much progress on this topic, so I pivoted to another matter. I told Meadows, "My biggest concern at the moment is politicization of the military." He looked at me a little puzzled, slightly tilting his head, so I listed a number of things in addition to the events of June 1 that had the Pentagon and the force spun up and concerned: Confederate symbols, racism in the ranks, use of the military against civilians, and "the celebration being planned for July Fourth." On the last item, I walked him through all the issues we had with the size, scope, and composition of the military's participation, the placement of combat vehicles on the South Lawn, an event for invited guests only, and so on.

Meadows listened but didn't agree. Before responding, though, he shared his unhappiness that I raised my concerns with Vice President Pence, asking in an accusatory manner, "Why did you send a letter to the vice president on this?" I explained why, privately satisfied that my memo achieved another purpose—Pence raised the issue with others in the White House.

Meadows quickly turned back to the main issue, pushing back on our concerns and arguments. I gave Meadows credit for his candor. He simply felt that "the American people paid $700 to $800 billion a year in taxes to fund the U.S. military, so why can't we spend $10 to $15 million to put our military on display for a day?" His response missed the mark, though; it wasn't about the money.

He ignored the points Milley and I had made about politicization of the armed forces. I told him, "I'm completely fine with celebrating our armed forces. That's not the point. There's just a right way to do it and a wrong way." I added, "And what's being proposed is way over the top. The optics are bad, especially after the last couple weeks. It will politicize the military." Meadows shot back, disagreeing with my last comment, and stating that the president wants this." Milley jumped in, arguing that a display like the one being proposed was not what the United States does—it was what authoritarian states like North Korea do.

We went back and forth on this for a few minutes, with no one really wanting to revisit the events of June 1–5. It was a sore spot for everyone, and an open wound for Milley and me. We still regretted what happened on June 1, angry at the White House for playing us, and disappointed in ourselves for not figuring it out beforehand. The chairman seemed to be taking the public criticism especially hard.

With the meeting now running long—well over an hour—it was time to break. Neither side was making any real progress or giving any ground on the Fourth of July plans. Meadows committed to raise our concerns with the president, but I didn't have much faith in his advocacy on our behalf.

I spoke with Mark Meadows again on June 19 regarding the Fourth of July. He said he had spoken with the president a few times and gotten "approval to cancel the static displays on the South Lawn," but the flyover was still a go. I did get the okay to "trim the number of planes" down to 64, however. As much as Meadows probably wanted to take credit for this with me, one was never sure who really pulled Trump back. Was it Meadows? Pence? Or maybe others from whom we had enlisted help on this matter?

Over the next couple of weeks—in the midst of updating our

strategic reconnaissance efforts, signing out deployment orders, and taking briefings on Afghanistan—I unilaterally cut the flyover numbers down even further without informing the White House. In my view, if someone from the president's team wanted to sit on the South Lawn and count the aircraft flying overhead that afternoon, then so be it. I figured the flyover would so entertain them that no one would care. As such, I replaced fighter aircraft with demonstration teams like the Blue Angels, pulled an airplane or two out here and there, and canceled others. I eventually reduced the final number down into the low 30s—closer enough to the 2019 numbers, and a far cry from the starting point of 107.

My last big concern, now that we had eliminated the static displays and combat vehicles on the South Lawn and dramatically reduced the scale of the air show, was how we could depoliticize this event even further so that a flyover of the White House didn't look like a singular tribute to the president. I spent the weekend of June 21 trying to solve this problem. One of the strategies I learned over the years was to, rather than trying to solve the problem as it is, simply enlarge it. Which was what I did.

With a map of the United States in front of me on my desk at home, and a general understanding of aircraft ranges and flight times, I figured that many of the planes—especially the bombers—could easily fly the East Coast south from New England to D.C. I did a rudimentary calculation of the distances between cities and bases, and figured out that if we started early enough, the planes would end up over the White House later in the afternoon, on time. And rather than a tribute to Donald Trump, we could call the flyovers "A Salute to the Great Cities of the American Revolution."

The route would begin at Boston, move south to New York and Philadelphia, and then go on to Baltimore before heading to the capital. Now, the flyover was no longer focused on a single city, and arguably not a single person, but several cities and thousands of Americans. I called my team and they liked it. Milley thought it was a good idea too.

In the wake of what happened the week of June 1, the 2020 Fourth of July celebration planning started off in a really bad place. Too many folks in the White House seemingly promised the president whatever he asked. My team and I worked hard to get this event to a much better position, despite the minefield we were walking in, fully aware of how strongly Trump felt about such displays. I wasn't opposed to honoring our military, but there are right ways to do so, and the right time as well. This was neither the right time nor the right place for much of anything, however.

We arrived at a much better spot in the end, which was a big relief. I managed to avoid another blowup with the White House and possible damage to the military's reputation as an apolitical institution. Importantly, I was able to do so without Trump firing me far earlier than what my game plan called for.

CHAPTER 17

PRIDE, PROMOTIONS, AND POLITICS

The call quickly became heated. "If you don't want him on the list, then you should remove him, but I don't support it. It would be the wrong thing to do," I shouted. Mark Meadows yelled back, "He'll never get promoted." With that, the conversation abruptly ended. We all knew why the president didn't like Alexander Vindman, but the fact that he continued to punch so far down at an Army lieutenant colonel was undignified and wrong.

The National Security Council is staffed with officers from all the armed services, as well as people from other executive branch departments and agencies. Alexander Vindman was one such staffer, an Army lieutenant colonel who served as the director for European Affairs on the NSC beginning in the summer of 2018. I had never met Vindman, but understood from news reports that he had twenty years of service under his belt, including a tour of duty in Iraq.

Vindman and his twin brother, Yevgeny, were born in Ukraine

and emigrated to the United States as young children. Alexander grew up in Brooklyn and attended the State University of New York at Binghamton, where he took part in Army ROTC. After graduation, he was commissioned in the infantry and began his Army career. He later became a foreign area officer and served at the U.S. embassies in Kiev and Moscow. In short, he was a good fit for the NSC job.

In late October 2019, the House Intelligence Committee subpoenaed Vindman to testify as part of the House of Representatives impeachment inquiry of the president involving Ukraine. Vindman told lawmakers that during the telephone call between Trump and Ukrainian president Volodymyr Zelensky that July, Trump asked Zelensky to investigate former vice president Joe Biden, who was running to be the Democrats' nominee for president. He also asked that Biden's son, Hunter, who had ties to a Ukrainian energy company, be investigated.

I wasn't on the call and wasn't even aware it happened until the entire issue appeared in the news several weeks later. Trump's call with the Ukrainian president was on July 25. The Senate had confirmed me just two days earlier, with my first full day as the twenty-seventh secretary of defense on July 24.

I had pressed Trump on several occasions to approve the $250 million in security assistance that Congress had appropriated for Ukraine, and was joined at times by John Bolton, the national security adviser at the time, and/or Mike Pompeo. None of us could figure out what was driving the president's resistance, though his common refrains were that "Ukraine is corrupt," "the allies—especially Germany—should be paying more" to help Kiev, and that "the U.S. shouldn't be spending money to defend them."

My team at the Pentagon didn't understand the White House's resistance either, though they kept pressing their counterparts across the government for answers. As time passed, and their dealings with agencies like the Office of Management and Budget became more contentious, I told my folks to keep doing the right thing, and keep good notes. We foresaw a showdown with Congress if the White House refused to release this assistance, but never imagined the president would be impeached.

In my attempts to get the aid released, I tried every argument and strategy I could muster. I wanted to address the concerns voiced to me by the president but also ensure we followed the law. Trump was impenetrable, however. When he complained about corruption in Ukraine, I told him, "I agree," but pointed out that "they are making progress," and that "tackling corruption is a priority for Zelensky." I said to the president, "Denying him the aid would only undermine Zelensky's efforts to do what you want—clean the place up." Trump would listen, but my words had no discernible impact.

The president would also say, sarcastically, "Our great allies, especially the Germans, need to help. They should be giving the most. Look at the map. Ukraine is a buffer for them" from the Russians. "The allies do need to help," I agreed. I pointed out that they were contributing some, "but they could and should do more." Therefore, I committed to "press them at an upcoming meeting at NATO that I am attending." Still no effect. Trump would stare back with a slight frown on his face. He wasn't buying it.

When he questioned "Why are we even giving them this stuff [security assistance] in the first place," I ran through a series of arguments that failed time and time again: deterrence of Russian aggression; showing Moscow our commitment to our partners; and aiding a democracy under siege. This wasn't a hypothetical either. In 2014, Russian forces had invaded Ukraine and annexed the Crimea.

I then pivoted to the fact that "Congress appropriated the funding, and we don't really have a choice" to not release it. "It is the law, Mr. President," I said bluntly. With his arms folded in front of him as he leaned forward into his desk, he was silent. He didn't seem to care.

And finally, what I thought would be most appealing to him, was the argument that "most of this money went back to U.S. companies anyway, to provide the [security assistance] goods and services Ukraine needed." This funding "created or sustained thousands of jobs in America," I said, recalling this information from the fact sheet provided by my staff. Even this didn't work. In retrospect, I saw my engagements with him on Ukraine as the early days of the tension that would inexorably grow between us over time, and eventually boil over in June 2020.

In sworn testimony that fall, Vindman told Congress that he was "concerned by the call. I did not think it was proper to demand that a foreign government investigate a U.S. citizen, and I was worried about the implications for the U.S. government's support of Ukraine. . . . This would all undermine U.S. national security." Vindman did the right thing and reported his concerns to the NSC's legal adviser, John Eisenberg.

Vindman's testimony was an important part of the investigation, and on December 18, 2019, the Democrat-controlled House of Representatives approved two articles of impeachment against the president. The first article accused Trump of abusing his power by asking Ukrainian officials to conduct investigations that could benefit his reelection bid. The second article charged the president with obstruction by telling administration officials to ignore congressional subpoenas.

The articles of impeachment were submitted to the Senate in January. The upper chamber decided to not call for witnesses or documents in the trial that soon followed. Not surprisingly, the GOP-controlled Senate acquitted Trump of both charges on February 5, 2020.

Throughout the impeachment process, Trump and some GOP lawmakers denounced Vindman for his testimony. Many of these same people also criticized the lieutenant colonel for appearing on Capitol Hill, despite being subpoenaed to do so. Television commentators from the right also joined in the fray. The fact is, Vindman didn't have a choice.

In the wake of these attacks, Vindman expressed serious concerns about the safety of his family, which the Army leadership worked to address. He was also concerned about retribution from the president, and the impact it might have on his career. The service was keeping close tabs on him. Indeed, Vindman met with General Jim McConville, the Army chief of staff, in early November 2019, regarding his situation. McConville assembled a team of lawyers, public affairs officers, and congressional liaisons to aid Vindman with the upcoming hearings. A two-star general was also assigned to assist and take care of him. The Army was doing all of the right things it could.

On February 7, two days after the Senate acquitted Trump, the NSC fired Alexander Vindman. He was walked off the White House grounds that afternoon under escort. His brother, Yevgeny, who also served on the NSC staff as an Army lawyer, was dismissed as well.

Earlier that day, a reporter asked me about possible retribution against Vindman during a press conference at the Pentagon, to which I replied, "We protect all of our persons—service members— from retribution or anything like that. We've already addressed that in policy and other means." I added that "we welcome back all of our service members wherever they serve, to any assignment they are given." I couldn't stop the president from firing Vindman. Nobody could. But we were going to protect him from any retribution beyond that and find a role for him back at the DoD. According to my sources at the White House, the president didn't like what I said, to say the least.

In a tweet the next day, Saturday, Trump alleged that Vindman was "very insubordinate," received poor performance reviews, and "reported contents of my 'perfect' calls incorrectly." Of course, none of these claims were accurate, but this would mark the moment when the president would start talking to me about ending Vindman's career.

At an appearance before the think tank the Atlantic Council the following week, Robert O'Brien was asked about the decision to oust the Vindman brothers from the NSC. He stated that the decision was made by him, not the president. He added that there was "absolutely no retaliation with respect to the Vindmans." He dismissed any suggestion they were fired, simply stating instead that "it was time for them to go back" to the Army. I didn't view any of these statements as completely truthful.

Over the weeks leading into March and then April, the president asked me a couple of times about Vindman: "When will the Army kick him out?" he would say. It was surprising how animated one Army lieutenant colonel was able to make the leader of the free world. I never understood it. The president would then follow up his questions with a long recounting of how Vindman "lied about my perfect phone call," that he was a "never Trumper," and that he was very arrogant and insubordinate.

Trump would again come full circle and ask, "What are you doing about Vindman?" Initially, I could respond with "Mr. President, we'll look into it. We'll do the right thing" and wait for him to hop to the next issue, which he did in nearly every meeting. My plan was to tolerate these occasional rants, unless someone could present a real case, but otherwise let Vindman get on to his next assignment at the Army War College.

The War College, located in Carlisle, Pennsylvania, provides graduate-level instruction to senior military officers to prepare them for high-level assignments in places like the Pentagon. With fewer than 10 percent of all eligible senior officers chosen to attend the War College each year, service leaders consider selection both an endorsement of one's performance and a privilege. As such, when the Army leadership and I said there would be no retribution from the DoD against Vindman, his prestigious assignment to Carlisle was exhibit A.

At a White House meeting on April 21, 2020, Vindman came up again. This time, however, the president pressed harder than ever before. As he sat in the black leather chair at the head of the long table in the Situation Room, he swiveled to his left, looked at me, and began attacking the former NSC staffer. "He lied about my great call," he said, adding that "he made it all up. He's a never Trumper. We need to get rid of him." We went through the routine once again as he recounted all Vindman's alleged transgressions, working himself up in the process until his face was flush and his voice loud. I responded as I did previously, and he pushed back: "But what are you going to do? What will happen to him? Are you going to fire him?" I then said, "Mr. President, for us to take any action along the lines you are suggesting, I need something in writing from the NSC attesting to his poor performance or misconduct that would violate the UCMJ,* and then we'll investigate it."

Trump didn't like that; he paused and glared, and responded by

---

* The Uniform Code of Military Justice, the federal laws that apply to U.S. military personnel.

alleging that Vindman "filed a false report. He confirmed the accuracy of two separate documents that said different things about the same conversation." I responded, in a matter-of-fact tone, "If that's the case, Mr. President, then I need someone in the NSC to write it up, sign it, and send it over to us. We have an obligation at the DoD to follow up on things like this." I looked at Robert O'Brien as I said this, and then glanced over at John Eisenberg, the NSC lawyer to whom Vindman first reported his concerns about Trump's call with Zelensky. Both were sitting silently in the room, unwilling to engage. My quick glances—stares—at them were intended to reinforce the message that it was on them to deliver the evidence.

Around this same time, Army Secretary Ryan McCarthy approached me to say that Vindman was on the promotion list for colonel. The Promotion Board had met in mid-January, before the NSC fired Vindman, to consider eligible lieutenant colonels for advancement. Vindman's promotion would have been based on the officer evaluation reports submitted by the NSC long before Congress called him to testify in late 2019. His ultimate selection for colonel, along with 404 other officers, meant that his performance merited it.

It was as obvious to me, as it was to McCarthy, that announcing Vindman's promotion to full colonel would be like waving a red flag in front of an angry bull. We were headed for a showdown. I was determined to do the right thing, as was McCarthy, so we had to put this issue to rest once and for all. This was no longer about Vindman; this would be about politicization of the military justice system *and* the promotion process.

We had already gone through a similar drama in November 2019, when the president overruled the Navy and directed that Navy SEAL Eddie Gallagher, who was found guilty of posing with an enemy corpse, be restored in rank and allowed to keep his Trident pin. Despite my private efforts—which nearly succeeded with Gallagher and did with another case—and public defense of the military justice system, we had lost this fight.

Previous presidents as recent as Barack Obama had commuted the sentences of service members convicted of crimes, but Trump's actions with Gallagher reached too far and too inappropriately. Basically, Trump wouldn't allow the Navy processes to play themselves out and render a judgment, let alone respect their determination. General Milley and I urged the president on several occasions to stay out of it. It was unfitting for the commander in chief to do what he did, and it caused a lot of ill feelings in the military. We did not want a repeat of this with Vindman.

The Gallagher case was a professional low point for me too. The actions of Navy Secretary Richard Spencer—a friend whom I respected—forced me to ask for his resignation. Richard's patience with Trump had long worn out, and I had spoken to him privately a couple of times to tone it down. I didn't need to lose a capable service secretary in such tumultuous times, but that's what inevitably happened, regrettably. Eventually, though, the drama going on within the service compelled me to get personally involved in their business. I told the press at the time that if folks "want to criticize anyone at this point about reaching down into the administrative processes [to restore Gallagher's Trident pin], then simply blame me. I'm responsible at this point. It's not where I prefer to be, but I'll own it."[1]

I didn't have a problem taking responsibility, but I was troubled that I had broken my own oft stated view that these processes be allowed to play themselves out objectively and deliberately, in fairness to all parties. I simply thought it was unfair to ask a panel of noncommissioned officers to decide an issue of such great political consequence, as the sea service was proposing to do; it would be a no-win situation for them. Maybe I was rationalizing—others can judge—but I also felt the good of the entire Navy wasn't worth one more day of discussion about whether Eddie Gallagher could keep his damn Trident pin or not.

Over a period of several more weeks in April and May, I asked O'Brien and others if they had found any derogatory material regarding Vindman for the Army to assess. General Milley did too. But they never delivered anything. It seemed to be one excuse after another, as if they were just hoping, waiting, for the issue to go away, or for us to just drum something up.

Mark Meadows took an interest in this matter once he became chief of staff, given the president's fixation. When asked, I would say to him "The NSC isn't producing any information for the Army to act on, and without some official allegation to investigate, Vindman's promotion and assignment to Carlisle will proceed." He was not happy, but told me he would engage them as well, and get them moving. It was clear, though, that the NSC had no real evidence or witnesses to offer, as we suspected all along.

But despite what we knew to be the truth—that Vindman didn't do anything wrong—the Army still had an obligation to look into any allegations of bad behavior. This was the Army way. It was the approach Milley and I followed when I was secretary of the Army and he was the Army chief of staff. "Follow the process"; let it work—words I seemed to be saying more often with each passing week. The process wasn't fast, but it was nearly always comprehensive, objective, and fair to all involved.

As the Army conducted its required administrative review of the Promotion Board's report, the NSC finally persuaded somebody to file a report. The council's Resource Management Directorate submitted a memo alleging substandard work performance and behavior by Vindman. The Army immediately opened an investigation as required and went to work quickly. Time was a factor.

According to the Army, the Promotion Board had met in January and completed its work on January 24, 2020. The service now had 180 days to transmit the board results to the Senate. Anything after that would be a delay. This put the deadline around the third week of July. And since it took the White House several days to process the list and forward it to Capitol Hill, my internal deadline to approve the board packet became July 9, two weeks before the congressional due date.

The Army was anxious about my timeline, concerned about leaks and growing outside interest from some in the media and on the Hill. While delays were not common when it came to promotion boards, they weren't terribly unusual either. What Secretary McCarthy and General McConville didn't know was that I was juggling several other White House balls at the time, each of which could blow up on me if dropped. And in the wake of my public break with Trump, if I didn't tackle them in the right order, then I might not be around to deal with any of them.

The Fourth of July celebration had been first in the queue. I was able to put that one largely to rest around the fourth week of June. The matter of withdrawing forces from Germany was directed earlier by the president but wasn't scheduled to be presented to Trump until early July.

Next up was Vindman's promotion, given the internal July 9 deadline I had set. But at the same time, the Army was unraveling over the issue of Confederate base names and flags since George Floyd's tragic murder in late May. They were getting a lot of pressure from within the ranks, which had a higher percentage of African Americans in uniform—over 20 percent—than there was in the nation at large: an important statement about the service's commitment to diversity and equal opportunity. Compounding the problem for the Army, however, was the fact that the Marines had banned Confederate symbols months earlier.

I was determined to take the Confederate symbols issue on, but if I did so right now and the president fired me, then I wouldn't be around to ensure Vindman's name was on the promotion list. And with his promotion on a tight timeline, we had to stand up for Vindman in order to keep politics out of our assignment and promotion boards. Otherwise, it would harm the military as an institution, affecting the troops' confidence in the system and their leaders. I had to keep reassuring McCarthy and McConville that we were going to do the right thing. But Vindman's promotion had to go first.

It took the Army inspector general a little over two months to complete the first inquiry and to determine the NSC's claims didn't warrant taking Vindman's name off the promotion list. I informed Mark Meadows, the White House chief of staff, that we were moving forward with the promotion, which didn't go over well with him.

Meadows did not want Vindman promoted. Period. But he also didn't want the White House to own the decision. He wanted me to exclude Vindman's name from the promotion list. I told him I wasn't going to do that unless the process somehow determined Vindman did something wrong. At the end of the day, the White House also had the ability to remove a name from the promotion list—the president, after all, was the commander in chief. I argued strenuously against doing so, however. Meanwhile, Meadows kept pressing the NSC to produce a witness, which they eventually did.

The single witness presented to the Army in June was a colleague of Vindman's at the NSC. At some point in 2019 they apparently engaged in a workplace argument. Ryan McCarthy told me secondhand that "when the civilian NSC staffer moved to leave the room they were in, Vindman went to the door and stood in front of it." He was apparently blocking his colleague's exit, saying that they "should stay in the room and work out their issues," according to McCarthy, rather than allow the matter to fester. There was no physical altercation, Vindman never threatened the individual, and the two continued working together for months following the episode, McCarthy said.

A news outlet reported the incident as an "allegation [by the NSC] that Vindman had been verbally abusive to a colleague with whom he shared office space" and that the DoD's inquiry "found that the two had gotten into an argument but that it was a minor spat and that they continued to work together afterward."[2] But this "incident" became the basis for a misconduct allegation against Vindman. To further complicate the inquiry, the NSC denied the Army access to the staffer involved in the alleged incident. With only one allegation, no witnesses, and both sides largely agreeing on the facts, the Army disposed of the matter quickly in Vindman's favor.

Meadows called me around 6:15 P.M. on Monday, July 6, a week or so after our earlier conversation about Vindman. I had a busy day working issues ranging from anti-submarine warfare systems to our footprint in the western Pacific, and I had been prepping for a hearing with the House Armed Services Committee, but I had managed to leave the office at six. I was in my car, with my security team, when he called. Meadows first raised with me a news story about a Confederate flag memo that the Office of the Secretary of Defense was staffing (i.e., sending around for coordination) in the Pentagon. Uh-oh.

But as we pulled into my driveway in northern Virginia, the conversation pivoted to Vindman. Meadows asked, "What is the status of the Army's investigation of Vindman." I told him it was done, Vindman was cleared, and that "I will be sending over [to the White House] the promotion board results with Vindman's name on it in the next twenty-four hours or so." I had approved Vindman's inclusion on the board packet earlier that day after a final conversation with McCarthy.

Meadows erupted. In a high pitch, he shouted, "Why didn't you tell me first? How could the Army get this done so quickly? Did the Army speak with other witnesses?" We were quickly yelling at each other on the phone as my black Suburban now sat parked in my driveway. The place where I used to play basketball with my daughter was hosting a showdown with the White House chief of staff. This was a far different game of one-on-one.

I told Meadows, "Yes, the Army was done. The NSC only presented one witness, circumscribed the inquiry, and could produce nothing else." "Then why didn't you call me, Secretary? I would have had them get you something," he shouted. His comment was nefarious. "This has gone on for months. There's nothing!" I barked back, adding, "I can't just pull Vindman's name off the list." Meadows pushed back hard that indeed, I could—that I had the legal authority. He was right, of course, but he completely missed my point. I did have the legal authority, but I couldn't do it because it wasn't the right thing to do. Meadows and I were talking past each other again, but it gave me great insight into him.

He asked for "another week or so" for him to drum up more witnesses, his tone now more of a plea than a demand. I simply said, "No. We're done." This incensed Meadows. He tried to interrupt me. I shouted over him that we were nearly "out of time to get the packet to the Senate." I was going to send it to the White House this week so that his staff had a few days to process it and get it to Capitol Hill. "If you don't want him on the list, then you should remove him, but I don't support it. It would be the wrong thing to do," I yelled into the phone. Meadows shouted back, "He'll never get promoted!" With that, the phone call ended. I climbed out of the car and walked into my house. Another great day at the office.

Meadows phoned me at home about forty-five minutes later. I figured this was the call to inform me that the president was finally firing me. As I told my wife, Leah, at the time, I was fine if that was the case. She agreed. This was a respectable issue to get canned over.

But that didn't happen. Meadows said he had Eisenberg and one other lawyer in his office with him. He accused the Army of conducting an inadequate investigation, and then asked if they could all meet the next day to have the Army brief them on their inquiry. I told him I would check with my general counsel, and if that was allowed, then I didn't have a problem with it. But I reminded him of my decision and my timeline.

My team agreed that a meeting with NSC legal and Meadows was permissible, so we decided to send McCarthy, along with Lieutenant General Chuck Pede, a military lawyer who was the judge advocate general of the Army. Pede was the Army JAG when I was secretary of the Army, so I knew and trusted him as an honest and capable officer who wouldn't yield to pressure. Also joining them was Major General Ed Jackson, the lead investigator. McCarthy was a little frustrated when I first told him that night what I needed him to do but understood better after I gave him an account of my call with Meadows. I told him that I had confidence in their efforts and their inquiry, that I had approved the list with Vindman on it, and that all he had to do was stand firm in the meeting. We were on the right side of this issue.

McCarthy and team went in the next day and indeed held firm. They gave a thorough accounting of their efforts over the previous months, what their inquiry had and had not discovered, and what they were bound to do under the law and regulation. The Army team came out of the meeting unscathed. I heard later that one of the White House lawyers told Meadows that if he pressed too hard, the Army could accuse him of tampering with an investigation, which apparently helped back him off.

I was going to send the paperwork over later that day, but the Army still hadn't shared the diversity statistics that I began asking of all colonel-and-above promotion boards only a few weeks before, in the wake of the diversity initiatives I wanted to pursue. We had that information by Wednesday morning, July 8. I reviewed it, and then directed my staff to send the Army colonel Promotion Board packet, with Lieutenant Colonel Alexander Vindman's name included, to the White House.

Around noon that day, I saw the announcement that Vindman was retiring. I was dumbfounded. We didn't see this coming. I had been asking McCarthy about Vindman's personal status for months. He told me that despite all that was happening, Vindman was holding up fine and was looking forward to the War College. McCarthy hadn't met with him, which was the right thing to do when an investigation is under way and you're in the chain of command. But McConville—the Army's most senior uniformed leader—had, and there was another general officer checking in on him regularly. Vindman was getting a lot of top-level attention and seemed to be doing okay. Just a few weeks earlier, in June, he received a formal update regarding his orders to move to Carlisle for the War College.

At some point much later, Vindman reportedly made public statements that had some of us scratching our heads. One comment that didn't jibe with what the Army's senior leaders told me was Vindman's remark that "at no point did any senior leader, civilian or military, attempt to contact me and indicate that I still was in good standing in the military." Hmmm. He also told CNN, "In certain ways they probably have misrepresented, the secretary of defense, former secretary of defense Esper, probably misrepresented the amount of support I was receiving." This too was curious. The fact is, I don't ever recall making any statements about the amount of support he was receiving, only about my commitment that we would protect him from retribution, which in the end I felt we did to the best of our ability with our support for his highly regarded follow-on assignment and promotion.

I was never briefed on why Vindman decided to retire when he did. There was some speculation that he felt pressure to act because of the impact his case was having on others caught in the fray. On July 2, 2020, Senator Tammy Duckworth (D-IL) had announced that she would block Senate confirmation of over 1,100 military promotions until she received written confirmation that Vindman's promotion wouldn't be stymied.

In my view, it was hypocritical for Duckworth to demand Trump not play politics with promotions . . . by playing politics with promotions herself through the taking of innocent hostages. The fact was, the only person at that point who had held up a promotion was her—more than 1,100 of them, no less. It was at this point in the election season when Democrats were auditioning to become Joe Biden's vice president. Duckworth was as eager as Elizabeth Warren and others to show that she had the "attack dog" bona fides that are often sought in vice president candidates.

In keeping with her partisan approach, she said after Vindman's announced his retirement that the failure to protect him "sets a new, dark precedent that any commander in chief can interfere with routine merit-based military promotions to carry out personal vendettas and retaliation against military officers who follow duly-authorized subpoenas while upholding their oath of office." This was a false statement, of course: the DoD protected Vindman's promotion. Not only that, but he was also being sent to the War College. No new precedent was set either. What was puzzling was that she made this statement *after* Vindman announced his retirement and *after* it became public that his name was on the list. The race for vice president was still ongoing, of course.

A week after Vindman announced his retirement, Duckworth lifted her hold on the promotions. She claimed that she received written confirmation that Vindman was on the promotion list sent to the White House. I never sent her a letter. I don't know who, if anyone, did.

It was wrong for the White House to play politics when it came to military personnel matters, but it was also wrong for members of Congress to do so. We saw this too often—the Vindman promotion and the removal of Captain Brett Crozier as commander of the USS *Theodore Roosevelt* were the most notable examples.

In each case, a few members of Congress would make public comments about matters they had little information about—except, it seemed, what they heard from the media—simply to score political points with their constituents or to advance their own cause. I worked in D.C. long enough to understand that is often the nature of politics, but it goes too far when it's done at the expense of serving military personnel or the institution itself. Those few on Capitol Hill or in the media who did this would be proven wrong in these cases when the dust finally settled, but I cannot ever recall there being any accountability for what they said and the harm it caused.

When it comes to military personnel matters—nominations, promotions, assignments, and other personnel matters—Congress should address concerns and issues that come before them behind closed doors, to get to the facts and consider all the issues first, before talking to the press. I was always impressed by how Senator Jim Inhofe (R-OK), chairman of the Senate Armed Services Committee, and Senator Jack Reed (D-RI), the committee's ranking member, managed the nomination of a senior officer accused of sexual misconduct by a former subordinate. Despite an electrified political environment over this issue, the committee took its deliberations behind closed doors, did their due diligence over a period of weeks, dismissed the allegations in bipartisan fashion, and approved the officer's nomination.

I was disappointed that Vindman decided to retire but respected his decision. The Army as an institution was going to treat him fairly, but he had been through the D.C. wringer like few others. Regrettably, this made him and his family innocent casualties of this whole sordid affair.

The entire Vindman saga revealed another area—military promotions—where we had to be on guard for possible meddling by the White House. Once the president named John McEntee director of the Office of Presidential Personnel in February 2020, we had to be doubly careful.

McEntee had served on the Trump campaign and became his "body man," akin to what the military would call an aide-de-camp, after the election. According to media reports, McEntee was fired in March 2018 after being unable to obtain a security clearance. He returned to the White House two years later in his new role as head of Presidential Personnel, reporting directly to the president, which didn't go over well with either of Trump's chiefs of staff. McEntee was clearly unqualified for the job, but his blind loyalty was likely what attracted him to Trump.

McEntee would not be the first hard-core loyalist to rejoin Team Trump. After the Senate acquitted the president on both impeachment articles in February, more true believers—fresh troops—like Ric Grenell and Mark Meadows began entering the White House. They paired up with the likes of Robert O'Brien, Stephen Miller, and Kash Patel, the senior director for counterterrorism at the NSC, to do Trump's bidding. A darker, more aggressive evolution of the Trump White House was now emerging.

McEntee jumped off to a quick start in his new role by simultaneously moving to install like-minded loyalists in the cabinet departments' liaison offices—those teams responsible to the White House for personnel actions—and scrutinizing the statements and actions of current political appointees.

All the departments were affected, but my sense was that Homeland Security and State had it the toughest. Even Housing and Urban Development wasn't immune to McEntee's tactics, with Secretary Ben Carson's White House notes on this matter photographed once by the media. The captured talking point for his meeting with the president said, "I am not happy with the way PPO [the Presidential Personnel Office that McEntee headed] is handling my agency."[3]

Soon enough, loyalty purges morphed into a weapon that White House staffers wielded to get rid of people in the departments who disagreed with anything they said, even if they were aligned with the president's policies. John Rood at the DoD was a case in point. He supported Trump's national security agenda but pushed back at times against some of the more unreasonable ideas coming out of the NSC: this was a main reason he was pushed out, I later learned. Despite my vocal support, others were denied well-earned promotions, such as the highly qualified Elaine McCusker—who challenged the Office of Management and Budget's decision to hold up the funding for Ukraine—to be the DoD comptroller, and the equally capable Katie Wheelbarger—whose supposed sin was once working for Senator John McCain—to become the deputy in the Office of the Secretary of Defense (OSD) Intelligence and Security directorate.

Worse yet, people were removed from positions simply because the White House wanted to replace them with more hard-core

Trump loyalists, regardless of their qualifications. Tony Tata, for example, was identified to replace Rood as the head of the Pentagon's Policy office. This was also what happened after my departure when they fired James Anderson, forced Joe Kernan—a retired vice admiral and former Navy SEAL commander who was serving as the undersecretary of defense for intelligence and security—to resign, and targeted others before reportedly being urged to stop by GOP lawmakers such as Senator Mitch McConnell. My strategy for dealing with Presidential Personnel was like a game of chess: Don't surrender any pieces easily, but do everything you can to save your most important ones. You have to pick your battles.

When it came to political appointees, it was clearly the president's prerogative to decide who would or would not serve in his administration. Where I drew a hard line was the Presidential Personnel Office's attempts to go after career civilians and uniformed officers. This happened on a few occasions after McEntee installed his people at the Pentagon in October 2020. It was these new loyalists who would eventually implement the orders to remove Anderson and others, and then proceed to purge the Defense Policy and Defense Business Boards.

As if going after current people wasn't good enough, Trump's loyalists once tried to recall retired four-star officers back to active duty to court-martial them for criticizing the president. In early May 2020, stories appeared in outlets like Breitbart that alleged retired Army general Stan McChrystal was advising Democrats on ways to use AI to "track down and counter Trump supporters on social media."[4] This spun the president up.

It wasn't the first time McChrystal was on the wrong side of Trump, though. But this latest report struck a nerve, even though McChrystal had not endorsed former vice president Joe Biden and later told another media outlet that his interest in advising a Democrat-aligned

PAC was about ensuring the accuracy of information leading up to the election.[5] The next thing I knew, Mark Milley and I were sitting in front of the president trying to talk him out of recalling McChrystal to active duty. To make matters worse, by the time we had arrived at the White House, someone in the Oval Office had thrown retired Navy admiral William H. McRaven, the commander who organized the raid to kill Osama bin Laden, onto the bonfire. McRaven had also written things critical of Trump in the past.

The president told Milley and me that he "want[ed] to call them [McChrystal and McRaven] back to active duty and court-martial them" for what they said. "So disloyal," he would say. Milley and I jumped to their defense, arguing that "both are distinguished officers," and that taking such an action was extreme and unwarranted. Doing this "will backfire on you, Mr. President," we said. The discussion went back and forth a little while longer in the Oval Office, with Milley finally figuring out a way to get the president to back down by promising that he would personally call the officers and ask them to dial it back.

At another point, the White House Liaison Office (WHLO) in the Pentagon expressed an interest in "interviewing" the DoD's senior officers, which we saw as code for loyalty tests. We shut this down immediately. The process to appoint an officer to a four-star joint position is a long, well-established one. It does not involve any "interviews" by the WHLO. Approximate transition dates are determined years in advance, and the actual selection begins at the service level at least a year out. The custom is that each service can nominate one individual for any joint assignment coming open.

We kept close track of these positions, and as I went about my travels in the United States and abroad, I tried to meet with the officers the services would likely recommend for one of these jobs. It was a good way to get to know them, without it being a formal interview. I would often conduct an interview process, nonetheless, but I wanted to get as many interactions with the person as possible.

As Jen Stewart, General Milley and I looked at the four-star assignments opening in 2021, now less than a year away, we recognized that the process could really get squeezed if Biden was elected president and had to start from scratch. He might not have all the right people in place to conduct a deliberate and timely process, which usually took up to six months. Two of the first billets to open, for example, were for the command of U.S. Forces Korea and Indo-Pacific Command.

I didn't want to leave the Biden team in a bind by trying to figure how best to select a half dozen officers in a few short months. I wanted to put forward my best recommendations, and they could decide from there whether to accept or reject my selectees. Conversely, if Trump was reelected and I was no longer secretary of defense, I didn't want to put my successor in a fix either.

As such, in October my team presented slates of officers for six service and joint positions for me to consider, interview as necessary, and select. Because my fate beyond November 3 was uncertain, I quickly went through each case, and with the benefit of my knowledge of the officers, the recommendations of their services and my head of personnel and readiness, and discussions with Stewart and Milley, I made my picks.

I ended up choosing the replacements for Indo-Pacific Command and U.S. Forces Korea for a May transition, and Joint Special Operations Command for a July handover. U.S. Transportation Command was set for an August transfer, but because the Senate typically recessed that month, we treat it like a July change of command, meaning that we move up the timeline to ensure we give the upper chamber of Congress sufficient time to act on it. U.S. Southern Command was programmed for a November transition, but the current commander, Admiral Craig Faller, had told me he might retire early, in the summer, so we accelerated that selection as well. Finally, we had to install a new vice chairman of the Joint Chiefs of Staff in November 2021.

We were all aware of the ongoing turmoil with the Presidential Personnel Office and its Pentagon liaison staff, having to swat down their multiple attempts to remove people and purge various defense boards. We also knew there were people on the White House staff who were constantly on the alert for anything they felt smacked of political correctness. That was the conclusion of some when I decided to remove the Confederate flag from our bases in July, and earlier when I put forward the three diversity and inclusion initiatives to deal with discrimination and bias in the ranks.

Finally, there were a lot of knives out for me personally, and some of them had already been inserted by so-called colleagues through the media and with the president. As a result, the fate of my decisions and me after the election was another wild card that was trending negative.

I became increasingly concerned that, somehow, what most of us would consider doing the right thing—putting forward very good officers for promotions into the highest positions of the U.S. military—would get caught up in White House politics or paybacks.

Given these dynamics, we knew these cases would have to be handled carefully, individually, and that the proper scouting of their receptivity at the White House was key. If I remained in office, Milley and I would probably have to walk some of them over, one at a time, to make sure we could get them through the process and to the Senate. If we sensed any resistance, then we'd have to figure out ways to get that person on board. But if the president kept me as secretary of defense, this would be less of a problem.

The more challenging scenario was if I was fired after the election.

If Trump won, then Milley et al. could share my recommendations with the acting secretary of defense, and then he/she would determine what to do with them, to include restarting the entire process. If Trump lost, then Milley et al. would have another option. If he felt that the White House might reject one, some, or all the nominees simply because I—Mark Esper—recommended these officers, then he could sit on them until the Biden team came into office.

The same was true if the reaction by some was to reject nominees because they thought we were playing politics. We were concerned about this because two of the selectees were women: Army lieutenant general Laura Richardson to be the next head of Southern Command and Air Force general Jacqueline Van Ovost to be the future leader of Transportation Command. Both were highly qualified officers—and the best picks for the job. This was not about their gender, but I was concerned that some in the White House would allege that these were "woke" nominations, and act against them.

The president removed me from office before the six promotion packets I approved were acted upon. I learned that somehow Ezra Cohen-Watnick, the new acting undersecretary for intelligence, got his hands on the packets and allegedly tried to scrub them all for "anti-Trump" bias. How someone outside the chain of command and not part of the normal process gained control of these promotion packets was troubling. The Joint Staff was able to get them back, however, but Cohen-Watnick apparently had already found a replacement for one of the officers I selected. This would have been terrible. Milley reportedly went to Acting Secretary of Defense Chris Miller and had this undone.

Three of the packets went forward while Trump was still in office, but two were held back. I'm not sure what happened with the sixth and final recommendation at the time, the one for the next vice chairman of the Joint Chiefs of Staff, though my pick was eventually endorsed by President Biden. I am confident, though, that the Cohen-Watnick intervention further spooked folks about possible White House intervention.

I was pleased to see that President Biden supported the nominations of Van Ovost and Richardson. The strategy had worked. Both officers were confirmed by the Senate in the fall of 2021, becoming the highest-ranking women in the U.S. military, and only the second and third women to run a combatant command.

A couple of critics later tried to claim that the withholding of these packets somehow "delayed" the promotion of these officers, which made no sense since the timing of our actions built enough time into the system on purpose. Moreover, there was no date stamp on these promotions, and no identified "pin on" date like a traditional promotion board.

Someone also wrote that holding on to these promotion packets until the Biden team arrived was "politicizing" the promotion process and hurt civilian-military relations. One suggestion was that we—Milley and I—should have marched these packets over to the White House and fought it out on the spot. These arguments fail to recognize that our strategy actually *prevented* politicization by the White House and protected the officers involved. After all, the president could have selected two other officers for these jobs if the White House learned these positions were opening up, effectively ending the careers of the best qualified ones that I had selected.

Trump certainly did and said things that risked politicizing the military. The Gallagher case was the nadir for the DoD in this regard. That said, I would later tell folks that the Gallagher and Vindman examples were best understood as Trump pressing his thumb into a soccer ball. It's hard to do, and he can cause a small indentation for as long as he keeps his finger in place, but the moment he relents it goes back to its original form. This is the strength of America's institutions, and especially the U.S. military. It is both strong and resilient. And the armed forces' values, ethos, rules, protocols, heritage, and most especially its oath to the Constitution guarantee that it will endure and remain apolitical. No single person, not even the commander in chief, can change the military's DNA.

At the end of the day, as I look back over my nearly eighteen-month tenure as secretary of defense, I am confident that we didn't allow the military promotion system to be politicized. We held true to picking the best qualified officers for advancement, whether it happened through a traditional promotion board system, as it did with Vindman, or whether it transpired through the less formal process that occurs for the nation's most senior officers. The civilian and uniformed leadership at the Pentagon followed established processes, selected leaders based on performance and potential, and protected the institution and its processes from outside political influence.

CHAPTER 18

LOST CAUSES AND IMPORTANT ONES

"Let it go . . . put it in a museum." Candidate Trump uttered these words about the Confederate flag when asked by a reporter in June 2015 whether South Carolina should continue to fly it above its state house.[1] Five years later, he would embrace the opposite position, a stance that would create another flashpoint between the White House and the military.

It was now mid-July 2020, and I had surprisingly survived my objection to invoking the Insurrection Act, reshaped the withdrawal of forces from Germany, scaled down the elaborate celebration planned for the Fourth of July, and sent the promotion of Lieutenant Colonel Alexander Vindman to the White House. It was hard to believe. My game plan was holding. Yet we still had more issues to go.

We had learned about Trump's latest view on Confederate issues the hard way, when Army Secretary Ryan McCarthy told CNN on June 8, on background, that he and I were open to holding a

"bipartisan conversation" about renaming bases and installations
that bear the names of Confederate military leaders. It was an accurate report. We both felt strongly about this issue. It was overdue, and the outpouring of personal stories and emotion coming
from the ranks in the wake of George Floyd's killing was both overwhelming and compelling.

I lived or trained at some of these bases during my military career and was familiar with the other Army installations that bore
the names of Confederate officers. For the most part, I didn't know
much about the men after whom these bases were named, which
was probably true for many military personnel who worked on
or passed through them. Regardless, the common thread running
through all of these Confederate leaders was that they violated
their sworn oaths and took up arms against the United States. It
was that simple.

But changing the names of bases named after Confederate officers was also a deeply political issue that touched on matters of
race, culture, history, law, and so on. I felt that it was an issue for
Congress, the peoples' representatives, to decide. Expecting the
Army to make this decision was passing the buck, because whatever decision the military made would be criticized, challenged politically, taken to the courts, or end up in Congress anyway. It also
risked a great deal of drama that could damage the armed forces at
a time when I was trying to keep us out of politics. So, I was pleased
to see language in the Fiscal Year 2021 National Defense Authorization Act that finally took this issue on in bipartisan fashion.

The president reacted angrily about the report of McCarthy's
comments. Meadows called me on the morning of June 9 and was
upset. He demanded, "Who authorized McCarthy to say what he
said?" I imagined him turning red as he barked into the phone.

"Me," I said. "I approved it." All that McCarthy expressed, I said, "was an openness to have a conversation with Hill leaders on the topic" as I explained our rationale. Meadows shot back, "You don't have any authority to get involved in political issues," which wasn't true, but also wasn't worth debating at the moment.

Well aware that it was still less than a week since I stood before the media in the Pentagon Briefing Room and rebuked the president on the Insurrection Act, I knew I was on very thin ice. Moreover, we weren't ready yet to take on Confederate basing and flags. I still had to figure out the policy, and the best way to implement it.

Equally important, however, was that I had a meeting scheduled at noon that same day to jump-start my three DoD-wide diversity and inclusion initiatives. The high-profile and senseless killings of several African Americans over the previous months, punctuated by the murder of George Floyd in Minneapolis, exposed a festering wound in the ranks of the armed forces that many of us didn't appreciate, but should have.

In the months that would follow, I conducted nearly two dozen listening sessions with our service members as I traveled around U.S. military installations. I would hear the same story over and over. From all parts of the joint force, both in America and abroad, I would learn about the racism and discrimination that so many of our uniformed personnel of color, and their families, had experienced growing up. And in many cases, too many cases, that they were still experiencing while in uniform, on base, and certainly off base.

This was very troubling for me to hear, but it wasn't that hard to understand given that our service members came from small towns, cities, and suburbs across America. Many had dealt with racism prior to joining the military; some came from communities so homogeneous that a person from another race or ethnicity is largely invisible; and still others grew up in households, schools, and neighborhoods that advance all sort of negative stereotypes.

Yet despite everything that the armed services did to bring these young Americans together, to teach them a new set of values and behaviors, and to acculturate them into a merit-based system focused on our nation's security, some degree of prejudice was bound to endure in some of them.

In my talks with service members, the consensus was typically that the military was doing better than American society in general, and that unconscious bias in the ranks was a bigger, more common problem than overt racism. Regardless of how one calculated or categorized this prejudice, there was much more that we needed to do. Tackling this issue wasn't solely about doing the right thing for our service members; it was also the right thing to do for the security of our nation. Ensuring diversity and inclusion was a readiness issue. We needed to recruit the best Americans to serve— regardless of race, ethnicity, religion, or gender. Similarly, a soldier, sailor, airman, guardian, or Marine who feels included, respected, and valued will work harder, stay longer, and fight better.

My discussion that day with the Pentagon leadership was an important moment when I put the issue squarely on the table and challenged all of us to take it head-on. It was just over two weeks since George Floyd's killing. We couldn't solve the issues of race and discrimination in American society that were playing out before us on the news, and I didn't expect Trump to try to do so, but we could confront it in the armed forces. In my view, the military had often led on these issues in the past, and it was time to do so again.

I asked those gathered what else we could do to get out in front of this issue and begin solving problems. There was general agreement that we needed to look at all aspects of military service: from recruitment and accessions, to promotions, schools, command boards, and assignments. We talked some about poor representation in the officer corps, Confederate flags on bases, as well as tasking the inspector general to look at discrimination in the ranks.

These were good ideas, and many eventually made it into our work program, but I wanted to stay away from simply more long-term studies and reports that some recommended. My suspicion was that we had a lot of good ideas before us already. In fact, at one point, after asking to see the previous DoD studies on diversity, I was presented a stack of papers and binders that stood between one and two feet tall. I was told these reports were from previous commissions and study groups over the years. I hadn't realized we had been down this road so many times before. Most disappointing was that the Department rarely implemented many of the recommendations in the various reports. This was why I wanted to focus on concrete actions we could accomplish in the coming days, weeks, and months.

We went around the room so that everyone had a chance to speak, and then I wrapped up by repeating my core view. I challenged everyone to come back to me in a week with some "quick actions" we could implement immediately to demonstrate our seriousness and urgency. Then we needed to look at a range of issues, from the symbolic to the structural, and everything in between, over the longer term. With that, the meeting broke up.

On June 10, Trump tweeted out, "It has been suggested that we should rename as many as 10 of our Legendary Military Bases, such as Fort Bragg in North Carolina, Fort Hood in Texas, Fort Benning in Georgia, etc. These Monumental and very Powerful Bases have become part of a Great American Heritage, and a history of Winning, Victory, and Freedom." He added, "The United States of America trained and deployed our HEROES on these Hallowed

Grounds, and won two World Wars. Therefore, my Administration will not even consider the renaming of these Magnificent and Fabled Military Installations."[2]

We had spent days trying to explain to those around the president, and others outside government who were close to him, about the political benefits of renaming the bases, in the hope they would talk to Trump. We probably called over a half dozen folks to help us make our case. Some, like David Urban—an old friend, West Point classmate, and skilled political operator who orchestrated the president's surprise victory in Pennsylvania in 2016—made this argument more than once to the commander in chief. "It will be something that Obama and Biden never did," he pressed, "and allow you, Mr. President, to claim the high ground." After all, base renaming was going to be in the annual National Defense Authorization Act anyway, I believed, which meant an authority (and opportunity) available to him could be taken over by Congress.

But most important, renaming was the right thing to do, and I wanted to help him get on the right side of the issue, where he was years before. The president's tweets on June 10 closed the door to this much needed change, however. I didn't think Trump was well served by the advice he was getting inside the White House. He would ask General Milley and me many times about this issue over a few months, and our response was consistent—the bases should be renamed.

Meadows and I spoke again on the topic of race and discrimination in the military on the morning of June 11. I continued to share with him the pressure the service leaders were feeling from the ranks. My ideas about a "three-pronged approach" were coming into focus, so I told him that one of the things I intended to do to address the challenges the military was facing was to establish an internal board with a tight timeline to study the issue, including all previous DoD reports, and task them to come back to me with implementable recommendations. I sensed he was a little reluctant, but when I said the board wouldn't report back to me until December, after the election, his support shifted in my favor.

On the Friday of that week, I met with the senior enlisted advisers from all the services, along with Senior Enlisted Adviser to the Chairman of the Joint Chiefs of Staff Ramón "CZ" Colón-López. CZ was a class act who took on this issue head-on; he joined me on some of my sensing sessions with the troops. Engaging with senior NCOs is always refreshing because of their candor and rich perspective from decades in the military. They gave me some good ideas as I started sharing my thoughts with them. Some of these would make it into the directive we would eventually publish.

We regrouped as a leadership team the following Monday as planned. We discussed a few ideas, but nothing really big, and no broader strategy. I raised a few issues that I had dealt with in the past, as both an Army officer in the 1990s and later as secretary of the Army. I never liked the inclusion of photos on promotion boards, for example. It triggered unconscious bias, one way or the other. My concern was that people tended to gravitate to those who look like them. "Ducks pick ducks," as we would often say.

It seemed obvious to me to drop the photo from all promotion boards, with Milley adding that they should be removed from command selection panels as well. I was surprised by the reluctance from the Navy and the Marines, however. They thought removing pictures might lead to *less* diversity. Being a former service secretary, I knew how these boards worked. So I told them that using selection statistics on the back end—once the selectees were chosen but before the promotion list was finalized—was a way to cross-check and assess diversity in the ranks. After a quick discussion on this topic, I thanked everyone for their views and then told them I was going to get rid of the photos. Period.

Privately, I felt that if we couldn't get agreement on something this simple, we were going to have a real challenge on our hands doing the tough things that would make a major difference. I was going to have to drive this issue hard.

Over the weekend I spent a fair amount of time thinking through this issue and some possible strategies. I sensed our opportunity to capture the energy of the moment and everyone's singular attention was fleeting, so we had to act now. I also knew the force was watching closely what we would do; if we paused, it would not go over well, so it was important to show some quick actions to advance diversity and inclusion.

At the same time, I also recognized that quick actions were often the easy ones, the low-hanging fruit that maybe didn't deliver the heavy punches we needed. We had some real systemic and structural changes that had to be made, and that would take longer than a few days or weeks.

We needed an enduring focus on the issues of race, discrimination, and inclusion. This issue was too important for today's leadership alone to study and address. Moreover, regardless of what happened in November, many of us would likely move on by the summer of 2021. We might not be around to see these issues pursued, let alone implemented.

The Defense Department had been dealing with issues of race and discrimination throughout its history, and had done a good job, but at some point the institution took its foot off the gas. Critics would say Trump's Pentagon was all white and all male, and while it's true we could do much better, we also weren't as bad as some would allege. As Army secretary, I had personally selected the first African American superintendent of West Point, and later chose the first African American to serve as Air Force chief of staff, and not because I was pursuing some diversity quota, but because they were the best qualified.

The same was true for women, both during my time as secretary of the Army and secretary of defense. We had several superb professionals at the undersecretary level, such as the head of Acquisition and Sustainment, the chief management officer, and the acting comptroller, and of course my chief of staff. And at the end of my tenure, as mentioned earlier, I would select the second and third women ever to become four-star combatant commanders.

As I thought through these issues more over that weekend, I came up with the following plan to address diversity and inclusion in the ranks: charge the chain of command to come back to me in a few weeks with their recommendations for quick actions we could implement in the near term; organize a more representative internal DoD board to come up with findings and recommendations over the midterm, meaning no later than December; and then establish a permanent outside board comprised of independent experts and thought leaders who could help us address structural, systemic, and cultural obstacles to reform. This last pillar would constitute the sustained, expert focus this issue demanded.

I put my plan on the table at the next Monday morning meeting. I described my vision of three lines of effort, differentiated in time, and by the composition of the groups leading them. I told my team I wanted their feedback soonest. My plan was to announce our strategy in the next week or so. I added that I would be putting a deadline of mid-July, just a month away, for the first set of changes that we would unveil to the force.

This was a big task with an aggressive timeline, just over four weeks away, but I felt I needed to lay down a marker, inject a sense of urgency, and be able to tell Congress and the press we were leading. I also wanted to give the Army something to focus on other than Confederate flags. They were very anxious. I knew the service carried the heaviest burden on this matter, but I kept pressing them to be patient and trust that we were going to address the matter soon.

I also met with the service secretaries. We always discussed a bevy of issues as a team, since so many—such as housing, health care, and COVID—were common to everyone. On diversity and inclusion, I repeated that this was a matter that we civilians needed to lead on. Yes, there were very big morale and readiness issues that the uniformed side was comfortable with and competent in addressing. But this is where civilian leaders, who brought far broader experiences and views to the Pentagon, were better suited—and appropriately so—to lead. I was blessed with a solid group of service secretaries. They were already there.

I asked Barbara Barrett, the Air Force secretary, to lead the second line of effort—a new Defense Board on Diversity and Inclusion in the Military. Barbara was an exceptional leader in her own right who had come to the Department with a proven track record and stellar reputation in the business, academic, and public policy worlds. The temporary board she led would conduct a six-month sprint to develop concrete, actionable recommendations to increase racial diversity and ensure equal opportunity across all ranks, especially in the officer corps. I told her the members of this board, which would be composed of service members of several ranks from each of the military departments, would have the carte blanche and resources to chart their own course until their disbandment in December. However, I didn't want to see their recommendations before November because I was concerned they would be leaked, and that some in the media, the Hill, or the White House would try to politicize her work.

Barbara and I also discussed the third line of effort: establishing a permanent commission to study the issues of diversity and inclusion in the force, and be a ready resource for the Pentagon's leadership. I was aware of the Defense Advisory Committee on Women in the Services (DACOWITS) from my time on the Hill, and I had met with them to discuss a few issues I was trying to advance as Army secretary, such as better policies for pregnant service members. They brought exceptional expertise, and did good work over the years providing independent advice and recommendations on matters under their purview. Barbara had also been a member of DACOWITS earlier in her career. All agreed this was a good model to follow, and thus the Defense Advisory Committee on Diversity and Inclusion in the Armed Services was born as a permanent and independent body of non-DoD civilian experts to work on these issues on behalf of our service members.

I was excited about this plan, and the momentum we were starting to gain in making it happen. I wanted to announce these initiatives and get them rolling *before* I took on Confederate flags. Therefore, on June 18, I released a message from me to all of the DoD explaining our three initiatives, why we were pursuing them, and what we aimed to accomplish. The next day we published a diversity and inclusion directive that integrated all three lines of effort into an action plan.[3]

Separately, I gave Matt Donovan, the undersecretary of defense for personnel and readiness, the task of developing options to address extremism and hate group membership in the ranks, an action that would result in a series of recommendations from him that were approved in November.

It was a historic moment for the Department, being one of the most significant and sustained efforts to address discrimination and bias in our ranks in many years. Doing so made me glad I hadn't stepped down in June. If I had, the DoD would not have launched these initiatives.

I enjoyed the brief moment of satisfaction. It was one of the few that my core team and I had these days. A heavy cloud seemed to be hanging over the DoD since June 3, but it never affected my ability to get things done. Most of what I did, well over 90 percent, was of little interest to the White House, and only the president had the authority to overrule me. As such, I did my best to continue my day-to-day work, including my weekly National Defense Strategy implementation sessions, calls with lawmakers, and engagements with my counterparts around the world. Important meetings on casualty reporting (going back to the Iranian missile attacks in January 2020), with the defense industry, on Operation Warp Speed, and about the development of Space Command—another important administration achievement—also occupied my time. This was the rewarding part of the job and had the added benefit of being wholly consistent with my "inside offense" strategy.

That said, I had to assume that every day was my last. I would often ask Jen Stewart, my chief of staff, "What are the 'must do' items for today in case I'm not here tomorrow?" or "What do I need to sign tonight, before I go home for the day, to advance the NDS or take care of the force?" We couldn't rest; we were going to run through the tape. After months of work, for example, we published a new policy in early November regarding pregnant service members.

As Army secretary, I had learned of anecdotes about female soldiers whose careers were mishandled by the service's personnel system, or their respective leaders, because they were pregnant. This was an issue in the other services as well. Too often, outdated policies and procedural norms not based on medical fact meant that military women had to disrupt their assignments, forgo non-combat deployments, or even relinquish leadership positions—any of which could be detrimental to their career—due to pregnancy. In this day and age, with medical advancements, far better knowledge, and full incorporation of women in the workforce, it seemed like the armed forces were behind the times.

I would often raise this topic with my service secretaries, who conveyed unease and resistance from their uniformed staffs. It was clear there was more concern about liability (which was not unjustified, given some past experiences) than about empowering our female service members. However, I couldn't allow overprotective, outdated assumptions about what women could and couldn't do while pregnant limit their careers, and further risk them leaving the service. We needed to be more flexible. The policy I published, among other things, did away with one-size-fits-all approaches and allowed pregnant female service members to do their jobs—even in deployed settings in the United States or abroad—if they requested it, their commander agreed, and their doctor endorsed it.[4] No more micromanaging individual cases from the Pentagon.

We had several personnel issues like these ahead of us, and I still had an Army leadership team anxious about Confederate flags. I hoped that the announcement on our diversity and inclusion initiatives, though, bought us a little more time.

On June 29, 2020, we briefed the president on our plans to pull more than eleven thousand troops out of Germany and reposition them in other NATO countries and the United States. After the meeting in the Oval Office, I met with Mark Meadows to go over a few other issues.

General Milley was in the Germany meeting too, so I asked him to join me. We sat down in Meadows's office in the West Wing, over-looking the southwest section of the grounds. We started with some small talk, and then I raised the issue of Confederate symbols—flags—on military bases, and the increasing turbulence it was causing in the force.

"This issue is most pronounced in the Army," I said, "because the Marines banned the Confederate flag months earlier, and the Army feels it is playing catch-up." Moreover, I told him, "the Army has several major bases named after Confederate generals, which is adding to the problem." In short, trouble was brewing in the ranks, and the uniform and civilian leaders in all the services were feeling it. General Milley helped by adding his perspective as a soldier, a general, and the leader of the Joint Chiefs.

Meadows listened carefully. He put his finger to his mouth and nodded as we spoke. I knew where Meadows stood. He didn't say so, but my sense was that he saw the Confederate flag as a symbol of southern heritage, not racism. Meadows was also acutely sensitive to anything that sounded like a "cancel culture" action, as he said on a couple of occasions. He surprised me, though, when he said, "To be honest with you, the president would probably personally support a Confederate flag ban," but never went on to explain Trump's opposition to such things now. The answer was obvious, though: the election was a few months away and the president didn't want to anger his base. Someone convinced him that this issue mattered to those voters, though some polling indicated otherwise. It was my sense that Meadows was pushing this logic.

The chief of staff went on to say, now arguing against our recommendation, that "if the military bans the Confederate flag, you will look political." I told him, "This is not a political matter for us, but a morale, cohesion, and readiness issue," and not only for our African American service members. "As leaders, we need to deal with this issue," I added. We were already a diverse force, probably the most diverse department in the government, "but this didn't mean there weren't problems; we had more work to do."

The facts were clear. In the active-duty force of approximately 1.3 million personnel, 82 percent of all personnel are enlisted. Of these numbers, 18.9 percent identify themselves as Black or African American, 16.7 percent as Hispanic or Latino, and 4.5 percent as Asian American. In total, racial and ethnic minorities made up more than 43 percent of the U.S. military. Yet, while minorities were well represented in the enlisted ranks, reflecting American society at large, they were underrepresented in the officer ranks, particularly at the general officer level.

If a sizable minority of the force didn't feel we were addressing their concerns and didn't see their leaders acknowledging them and acting, then they were going to vote with their feet. They would leave the service and were unlikely to encourage others to enlist. And whether they were planning to leave the service or not, it wasn't hard to imagine growing disgruntlement, greater disillusionment, and lower morale. This easily translates into less unit cohesion, morale, and effectiveness if allowed to fester. It was an issue we couldn't take lightly, and one we needed to get in front of quickly. General Milley and I walked Meadows through these issues.

Meadows smartly left the playing field where we dominated and jumped into one where he felt more comfortable: politics. He shared how he handled issues like this in Congress, and then asked, "If you ban the Confederate flag, then where does it end? Where do you draw the line? How do you keep politics out of the military?" These were good points. Flags are very visible symbols, and various ones are claimed by groups and movements on the left and the right. Sometimes long-standing flags and symbols are even co-opted. I wanted none of that in our ranks or on our bases. As I considered the matter right then and there, I came up with an idea that would ultimately become our policy. I would turn the Confederate flag ban inside out.

When Meadows finished, I paused for a moment, looked at him, and said, "You're right, Mark. Those are important issues that I'm concerned about as well." I added, "I have an idea. Give me a few days and I'll get back to you." With that, General Milley and I stood up and left.

I returned to the Pentagon and met with my general counsel, Paul Ney, and later with Matt Donovan, to discuss this alternative approach to get rid of the Stars and Bars and other Confederate symbols on our bases. I first spoke with Ney, to get his legal read on my approach. Much like with Donovan, I had become acquainted with Ney when I was secretary of the Army. The Senate confirmed Paul as general counsel for the Department in July 2018. It wasn't his first tour in the Pentagon, though. He had served in other senior legal positions at the DoD in the past, so between those tours and his private experience he brought a good deal to the role. Paul was also a good lawyer with a lot of common sense who knew how to get an answer to a legal yes instead of a bureaucratic no, as was too often the case in the building.

Paul really liked the idea I was putting forward—to keep the DoD out of politics by publishing a directive listing only the flags *authorized* to be flown on U.S. military bases and installations. We wouldn't ban the Confederate flag explicitly, we just wouldn't authorize it (or most any other flags) to be flown or displayed. Ney doubled down and proposed we say up front that the United States flag—the Stars and Stripes—was the "the principal flag we are authorized and encouraged to display," as the memo would eventually read. This really animated him; you could sense his patriotism. I liked it.

If I signed out a directive affirming the American flag as our principal flag, and didn't allow any others to be flown except those I approved in the directive, how could this administration or a future one overturn it? Who would oppose *only* flying the American flag on U.S. military bases? It was a hard issue to debate, let alone overturn, but that didn't mean some in the White House wouldn't use it against us at the Pentagon. Just the same, I asked Ney and Donovan to start drafting the directive very quietly.

What I really liked about the policy approach we were taking on flags was not only that it addressed the immediate problem— removing the Confederate flag—but that it was a prospective policy that excluded any and all flags that could possibly show a hint of politics. The DoD didn't need to be in the business of deciding which flags were and were not offensive enough for the Department to fly or ban. This was an important way to help keep the DoD out of politics today *and* going forward, and it would at least raise the bar if others in the future wanted to go in the opposite direction.

The team worked hard over the next couple of weeks on the first set of quick action diversity items, and by July 14 I had a memo entitled "Immediate Actions to Address Diversity, Inclusion, and Equal Opportunity in the Military Service" prepared and signed.[5] The directive included a number of recommendations from across the services, beginning with removing photographs from promotion boards, and other actions such as reviewing hairstyle and grooming standards to ensure they were not racially biased, assessing the effectiveness of equal opportunity offices, and training leaders to discuss and address issue of prejudice and discrimination in the ranks. The next day, I joined Barbara Barrett in launching the inaugural meeting of the Defense Board on Diversity and Inclusion.

Separately, I asked Paul Ney on July 10 to reach out to Pat Cipollone, the White House counsel, and share our draft flag memo with him, and to make sure Cipollone shared it with the White House chief of staff as well. Three days later, Meadows emailed me to say he had a couple of edits. I asked Ney to follow up with Cipollone, which he did. Ney and I both thought the changes were fine, especially if we could build support from the White House.

On July 15—a day after at least one news outlet reported that something was in the works—Cipollone called Ney back and said that, despite the edits, he and Meadows didn't want the memo to go out yet. Moreover, they couldn't tell us if they would ever approve its release. It wasn't clear if Meadows was stringing us along, but my sense was that the game was up. The White House wasn't going to support us. I had to decide: do what is right for the armed forces and our people, or play along with the politics of the moment.

I called a meeting with the service secretaries and chiefs for that same afternoon, a few hours after the first meeting of the Diversity and Inclusion Board. We met in the Nunn-Lugar conference room. There was a nervous buzz around the table as I laid out my game plan. I thanked them for their support for how much we accomplished in a few short weeks on race and discrimination. I said it was time to address Confederate flags and symbols.

Rather than banning the Confederate flag, we were going to take a different approach. We were "only going to authorize the American flag and a few others for display on DoD bases and installations." I made clear again that "this is a civilian-led policy issue," and I laid out the four key attributes of our approach: first, it would "affirm the centrality of the U.S. flag" to the military; second, it would be "prospective and keep political and divisive flags and symbols off our bases" into the future; third, it would be "enduring," in that we had determined it could sustain any legal challenge; and finally, it was apolitical.

I informed everyone that my plan was to release the flag memo on Friday, without White House approval, and that I was now giving them a two-day heads-up to have their service-level memos ready to go. I didn't want any extended time gaps between my directive going out and everyone else's. I felt it important that we get them all out the same day and that we all have the same message.

Jen Stewart was directed to review the services' instructions before they went out. Speed, alignment, and unity were important here to show the seriousness with which leadership took the issue, as well as the fact that we are standing together on this issue.

We also couldn't afford any leaks between now and then. Once the memo was out, I told them, the OSD would handle the press and media inquiries. We would also provide them top cover so that they could stay out of the fray. With that, we went around the room one last time for any final questions, comments, or ideas before the meeting adjourned.

The next forty-eight hours or so were tense, not knowing if someone would leak to the media or get word back to the White House. It seemed that every time the phone rang, I expected it was "the call" from the president ordering me to not do anything regarding the Confederate flag. His views on changing the names of bases named after Confederate generals was clear; we took it as an order.

But he never said anything similar regarding Confederate flags. One could argue we were actually doing what Trump supported before becoming president. The fact was, I was still surprised that we made it this far, navigating the minefield of July Fourth, Germany withdrawal, and other issues. Meanwhile, we were making good progress on our internal readiness and modernization agenda while dealing with COVID and keeping the nation safe. The inside/outside strategy was holding. How long could I survive? Friday would be telling.

July 17 came without any major leaks or inquiries from the White

House. Around midmorning, I told Jen Stewart to send out the directive as I picked up the phone to give Meadows a heads-up. His assistant answered the phone but said he was "in another meeting and couldn't be interrupted." I told her why I was calling, and that she should interrupt and give him a note. With that I hung up.

The directive sent throughout the DoD began by restating our mission, duty to the nation, and that which unifies us—"our sworn oath to the Constitution and our shared duty to defend the Nation."[6] The memo reaffirmed the American flag as our principal symbol for display; yet it also authorized the flying of nine other categories of flags, such as state flags, the POW/MIA flag, unit flags, and the flags of organizations of which the United States is a member (e.g., NATO). There was no mention of the Confederate flag.

The guidance memo applied to public displays or depictions of flags by service members and civilian employees in all DoD workplaces, common access areas, and public areas, including several specific areas.

I closed the memo with the same words I used often regarding this issue:

What has always united us remains clear—our common mission, our oath to support and defend the Constitution, and our American flag. With this change in policy, we will further improve the morale, cohesion, and readiness of the force in defense of our great Nation.

Trump was furious as news of my policy change became public.[7] It was not lost on me that the president had declined to denounce the Confederate flag when asked about it by the media in recent weeks. He viewed it as a "freedom of speech" issue that government should protect. In sending out my memo, I wasn't trying to pick a fight with the president or violate someone's First Amendment rights, but in the military those constitutional rights sometimes must take a backseat to good order and discipline, as well as the readiness of the force, and that was my focus.

My friends close to the White House said that while Trump was angry, he wasn't going to fire me. His own reelection still took priority over his desire for retribution. A lot of people, they said, didn't understand why Mattis left over the withdrawal of several hundred troops from Syria—a place most Americans couldn't find on a map, and didn't understand why our troops were there in the first place. But firing Esper because he banned Confederate flags or refused to send active-duty troops into American cities would backfire horribly.

Trump eventually calmed down, but our relationship was even more frayed, and everyone knew it.

I wasn't hiding my disaffection either. On July 7, I recorded a message to the force thanking them and highlighting all of the progress we had made over the previous year when it came to implementing the National Defense Strategy and dealing with the challenges the world threw at us, from conflict with Iran and confrontation with China to the greatest civil unrest the country had seen in decades and a global pandemic the world hadn't experienced in one hundred years.[8] As one news story would astutely report after the fact, "There may be no bigger hint of the strains at play than what Esper is not saying. When he recorded a 10-minute video for troops largely touting his accomplishments and thanking the force he didn't mention the commander in chief once."[9]

As expected, dozens of lawmakers would write me in the weeks that followed, pressing me to allow an exception for LGBTQ pride flags. I had no personal issue with the pride flag, but we had to draw a clear line somewhere. A year later, many of these same lawmakers and outside advocacy groups would urge the Biden administration to reverse my policy. But to my satisfaction and the new administration's credit, the Biden team defended the policy and refused to make any changes to my July 2020 policy memo.

On the other hand, they had unfortunately not yet established the third pillar of my diversity and inclusion agenda—the permanent and independent Defense Advisory Committee on Diversity and Inclusion in the Armed Services. No reason had been given.

Our work was far from done, though. The diversity and inclusion initiatives were a major step forward, but I still had the daily grind of advancing our agenda. Meetings on nuclear command and control, reform of the Navy, space operations, and an update from my China Task Force were on the agenda for the second half of July. These were the best parts of the job.

Finally, Mike Pompeo and I also had an annual "2 plus 2" meeting with our Australian counterparts at the end of the month. The main topic would be China, a topic that was occupying more and more of our attention, for very important reasons.

CHAPTER 19

CHINA, CHINA, CHINA

The vote on the Senate floor wasn't close. Senators Fred Thompson (R-TN) and Robert Torricelli (D-NJ) offered a simple, bipartisan amendment to the China trade bill that would have imposed sanctions on Chinese companies that traffic in nuclear, chemical, or biological weapons systems and components, as well as long-range missiles, selling them to countries such as North Korea and Iran. The last remaining hurdle to a trade bill that would ease China's entry into the World Trade Organization (WTO) failed by 65 votes. It was September 14, 2000.[1]

For years, the United States reached out to China, established formal diplomatic relations in 1979, assisted Beijing's development, and worked to integrate the nation of 1.4 billion people out of isolation and poverty and into the global community of nations where it could prosper and grow.[2] The crowning achievement of this period was China's entry into the WTO in 2001.

The U.S. policy wasn't completely altruistic, and not everyone supported this approach. On an economic level, getting China into the WTO and compliant with the established rules of international trade meant that an enormous market would be opened to American businesses. This would mean economic growth for the United States and jobs for Americans. Many in the Chinese Communist Party (CCP), however, viewed the WTO rules as too unfair, the conditions for joining too harsh, the economic liberalization required too fast, and the transparency rules too onerous. Many Chinese simply didn't like the fact that they were joining a system they didn't help construct.

On a political level, many in the United States believed that economic openness would be the engine that drove liberalization in China. The argument was that, as the Chinese people prospered and their standard of living improved, they would press for political reform that would, inevitably, lead to democratization. This theory, promulgated in initiatives like China's admission to the WTO, had overwhelming bipartisan support in Congress; it was pushed by Republican and Democrat administrations alike; it enjoyed the advocacy of big business, organized labor, and farmers; and it was endorsed by a bevy of other groups. But not everyone was convinced.

A bipartisan minority on Capitol Hill took a more skeptical view. I was working for Fred Thompson at the time, handling China and all his defense and foreign policy issues. In the months leading up to the Senate vote, he argued that the prevailing theory was too simple and too Pollyannaish. If we got it wrong, and the CCP remained in power, we could end up selling them the means of our own undoing.

Thompson and others who expressed deep concern about China pointed to Beijing's human rights record, their suppression of the media and religious groups, threats toward Taiwan, and other reasons that lawmakers should be careful about buying completely into the China liberalization theory. The optimistic view was so strong and so prevalent, however, that a majority of senators defeated the common-sense national security amendment sponsored by Thompson and Torricelli. Not surprisingly, the broad range of concerns expressed by Thompson and other senators two decades ago are still with us today, and are more disconcerting than ever. The China liberalization theory was a failure, as have been our broader efforts to change the CCP's policies and behavior.

An important accomplishment of the Trump administration was its consolidation within the U.S. government of a clear-eyed view that the People's Republic of China (PRC) was not a friendly, benign country, but a strategic competitor—and growing adversary—determined to supplant the United States as the global leader and eager to reshape the international rules, laws, and order in its favor. This new consensus regarding China marked a seismic shift in U.S. policy, certainly signaling a dramatic change from the post-9/11 order. This is the lens through which the administration developed its policies, processes, and messaging toward China.

The administration was also able to focus a growing number of our European allies on the rising threat and challenges that the CCP presented. Nowhere was this more obvious than in the meeting halls of NATO, or in the statements issued by the alliance from 2017 through 2020, where an emphasis was placed on China and specific issues such as Huawei and 5G. The same was true for our efforts to bring together the Quadrilateral Security Dialogue, known as the Quad, the grouping of the four like-minded democracies of Australia, Japan, India, and the United States. These things wouldn't have happened without the continued push by Washington.

Some critics would say that the Trump administration had no

coherent strategy when it came to China. That was unfair and untrue. We had one, and the will to implement it. The president, however, was not inclined to follow it. Indeed, on January 15, 2020, at the signing of the Phase 1 trade deal with China just days before the first COVID case in America would be identified, the president said, "We have a great relationship with China . . . the best it's ever been."[3] It wasn't until later, the final ten months of his administration, once it became clear that COVID was undermining his reelection chances and the global view congealed that China shouldered much of the blame for the pandemic's explosion, that Trump took a hard line toward Beijing on matters other than trade.

Otherwise, Trump was one-dimensional when it came to the PRC. For him, the relationship seemed wholly about the trade imbalance and unfair Chinese trade practices, and even then these matters appeared subordinate to his relationship with Xi Jinping, the autocratic Chinese leader who was taking the PRC in a dark direction. Fortunately, the departments and agencies had been generally following the formal game plan since it was published and had the right people in place to make it happen.

In 2017, the NSC under H. R. McMaster, the national security adviser, and Matt Pottinger, the Asia director at the council who led these efforts, produced two documents—the "U.S. Strategic Framework for the Indo-Pacific" and the "U.S. Strategic Framework for Countering China's Economic Aggression"—that laid out a whole-of-government approach to China. That December of 2017, the National Security Strategy was published. The strategy made clear that China (and Russia) under its Communist Party was a revisionist power that aimed to "shape a world antithetical to U.S. values and interests" and "displace the United States in the Indo-Pacific region, expand the reaches of its state-driven economic model, and reorder the region in its favor."[4]

I was not new to the China portfolio, and the broader challenges in the Indo-Pacific theater. My last active-duty assignment in the Army was as the U.S. Pacific Command war planner on the Army Staff at the Pentagon in 1995 and 1996. In this role, I had responsibility for helping develop, coordinate, and integrate U.S. Army forces and resources required for conflict in the region, with a focus on North Korea and Taiwan at the time.

During my time with Senator Thompson, I did a lot of work on China-related issues, from weapons of mass destruction (WMD) proliferation and the Chinese military buildup to technology theft and espionage against the United States. When I moved to take over the national security portfolio on the Senate Foreign Relations Committee, I took this basket of issues with me. And during my time on the Hill, I had the opportunity to travel to Beijing on several occasions, meet with the PRC's leaders, and to visit our allies in the region, including Taiwan.

I would carry this work forward to my time as policy director for the House Armed Services Committee as well. It was during this period, in the early 2000s, that the small group of us who spent a lot of time on China and related issues sensed a shift under way: members' views toward China were improving at the expense of Taiwan, accompanied by what seemed to be a dramatic increase in Chinese embassy personnel and their lobbyists trolling the halls of Congress. It appeared as if Beijing finally figured out how to play the D.C. game.

When I was a deputy assistant secretary of defense for negotiations policy at the Pentagon from 2002 to 2004, my portfolio included all arms control, nonproliferation, and a broad range of international issues for the DoD. I ended up working a variety of WMD and conventional proliferation matters linked to China, since Beijing was a major trafficker in these items.

I returned to the Hill in 2004 to become the national security adviser to Senate Majority Leader Bill Frist (R-TN), which was probably the best job in Congress for someone who thrives on defense and foreign policy issues, and their intersection with politics at the highest level. Despite a significant focus on Afghanistan and Iraq at the time, China was still a topic that garnered a good deal of attention.

In 2007, a year after I left Capitol Hill, Mitch McConnell, who had succeeded Frist as the Republican leader in the Senate, appointed me to serve as a commissioner on the U.S.-China Economic and Security Review Commission. The commission, which was in a rebuilding mode, included a number of sharp people from both sides of the political aisle, as well as from such key sectors as defense, trade, human rights, and technology. It was a good time to delve deeper into the U.S.-China relationship and the issues facing our country from Beijing. I never considered myself a China expert, but by the end of my tour on the commission I was confident enough to coteach a graduate course on U.S.-China relations at Missouri State University in northern Virginia with Randy Schriver, who later became my assistant secretary of defense for Indo-Pacific security affairs.

About the time my tenure on the commission ended, I went to work at the U.S. Chamber of Commerce, where I served concurrently as the executive vice president for the U.S. Chamber of Commerce's Global Intellectual Property Center and as vice president for Europe and Eurasia. As the Intellectual Property Center head, I had a front-row seat at how China was stealing U.S. ideas, innovations, and all forms of intellectual property on a grand scale. It was devastating to the economy, to companies large and small, and to tens of thousands of U.S. workers. It seemed as if no industry was unaffected, with the cost estimated at between $225 billion and

$600 billion annually.[5] Yet, despite all this theft and other coercive rules Beijing was imposing on many American businesses operating in China, most companies during that first decade of the 2000s still seemed willing to tolerate this bad behavior. The lure of 1.4 billion consumers remained hypnotic.

By the time Trump entered office in 2017, a major shift was under way. Nearly all the key sectors and industries that were fully behind China in 2000 had or were changing their position and their outlook. This transition accelerated after Xi Jinping became general secretary of the CCP in 2012 and began taking the PRC in a far more autocratic direction. The false promise of political reform disappeared as Xi (usually referred to as President Xi in western media) implemented an anticorruption campaign that led to the downfall of many Communist Party officials and instituted stern measures to improve internal party discipline and authority.

Xi also oversaw a buildup of China's armed forces and the development of a more aggressive foreign policy that bullied neighbors, made illegal territorial claims in the South and East China Seas, and used foreign debt as a tool to gain access and influence around the globe. In 2020 alone, a Chinese ship rammed into and sank a Vietnamese fishing vessel with eight persons aboard, an incident similar to one perpetrated against Filipino fisherman the year before; armed Chinese Coast Guard ships routinely escorted Chinese fishing fleets into the exclusive economic zones of Indonesia and the Philippines; and Beijing continued deploying its maritime militia around the Spratly Islands.[6] Meanwhile, the PRC's development and militarization of several geographic features in the waters of the South China Sea were not only illegal and provocative but broke a personal promise Xi made to President Obama in 2015.[7]

Through its Belt and Road Initiative, China is expanding its financial ties across Asia, Europe, Africa, and the Americas, with the ulterior motive of gaining strategic influence, access to key resources, and military footholds around the world. China's first overseas base is in Djibouti, on the east coast of Africa, and the Chinese are actively working to establish more bases from there across the Indian Ocean, and then eastward back toward Beijing. Worse, the PRC is expanding its power at the expense of others' sovereignty. And the smaller the nation is, the heavier the hand from Beijing.

Many China watchers consider Xi an authoritarian leader for clamping down on freedoms, ignoring human rights, and removing term limits on his presidency. That was my perspective as well. As Xi's grip on power tightened, and his direction became clearer, fewer and fewer leaders in the United States had much reason to believe the PRC would change its ways. In fact, China's behavior was getting worse. The China liberalization theory was rapidly collapsing.

Most alarming for the DoD was the incredible growth in the capability of the People's Liberation Army (PLA) since 2000, accelerated by Xi's 2017 goal for the PLA to become a "world-class" military by the end of 2049—the hundredth anniversary of the founding of the PRC.

The Pentagon largely interpreted this objective to mean that Beijing wanted to "develop a military by mid-century that is equal to—or in some cases superior to—the U.S. military, or that of any other great power that the PRC views as a threat."[8] To achieve this end, the CCP committed the people, budget, technology, and disciplined strategic focus to build conventional weaponry in the air, sea, and land domains; to develop asymmetric space and cyber space capabilities; and to both modernize and expand its nuclear forces.

The PRC's midterm objective is to complete its military modernization by 2035. Double-digit annual percentage increases over many years in the PLA's budget epitomized this effort. To meet their 2049 goal, China is also working hard to make their military a more professional force, one that employs modern operational concepts, is structured to be more suitable for joint and combined arms operations, and has a larger overseas military footprint.[9]

The Trump administration's approach toward China didn't begin nearly as strongly as it finished, however. The publication of the National Security Strategy (NSS) in December 2017 was an important first step in setting the background, tone, and direction of the administration with regard to China. The more important document for the Pentagon was its National Defense Strategy (NDS), which translated the NSS into the guidance the DoD needed for military planning, force development, modernization, operational adjustments, training and exercises, global presence, alliance building, and other important defense and war-fighting constructs.

As I've mentioned before, I made implementing the NDS my top priority beginning on my first day. The first of two challenges I faced in doing so was re-empowering OSD civilians to take charge of strategy operationalization and implementation, as discussed earlier. John Rood, and later James Anderson, my Policy leads, understood this. And as supporters of the NDS and civilian control, they were more than willing to take the reins.

The second challenge was the four-star combatant commanders, and mostly the geographic commands as opposed to the functional ones. Some often read the strategy to suit their respective ends. The top-tier countries were China and Russia, but I clearly put the PRC as number one. The U.S. Indo-Pacific Command (INDOPACOM), for example, thought they should get more resources—despite already having the preponderance of assets—since China was in their area of responsibility. Africa Command, on the other hand, worked hard to reframe several of its missions as "global power competition" activities, despite the command being designated earlier as an "economy of force" theater from which resources were to be taken. Central Command was stuck in the middle. Russia and China had a growing presence in their region, but they clamored for more resources based on ongoing operations in Afghanistan and Syria, rocket attacks in Iraq, and potential conflict with Iran.

The fact was, great power competition with China (and Russia) was indeed global in nature, which meant that we couldn't put all our eggs in one basket, or take them all out of another. We needed to make some tough decisions on how, when, and why to reallocate resources and forces between those baskets, though, which meant reducing mission scope, eliminating lower priority tasks, and consolidating resources, while being willing to accept more risk and uncertainty in some places.

On top of all this, we had to keep in mind the resources and budget that had to be committed to our functional commands, such as Space and Cyber—both important, exponentially growing areas—as well as defending the homeland, which was Northern Command's responsibility.

The annual Senior Leader Conference I hosted in October 2019 for all of the DoD's civilian and uniformed leaders was the key moment early in my tenure where we began the arduous task of implementing the NDS, pursuing its three lines of effort, and addressing these issues. The agreed-to Top Ten objectives that gave life to the strategy all touched on China in some way, shape, or form.[*]

For many of these objectives, I asked my Policy team to take the lead in identifying and shaping subobjectives. For example, under the Top Ten objective to "Focus the Department on China,"

---

[*] The Top Ten objectives can be found on page 95.

we developed several tasks that aimed to do just that, beginning with the establishment of a new Defense Policy office on China and the creation of a China Strategy Management Group to better integrate our enterprise and our initiatives. We also created a new deputy assistant secretary of defense for China within Policy. A big part of this office's focus was driving initiatives and internal alignment in the DoD.

First and foremost, we needed updated and approved war plans to deal with any contingencies that could happen, especially regarding Taiwan. Reviewing and approving the plans prepared by each combatant command is job number one for a defense secretary, coupled with ensuring the forces are available and ready to successfully implement the nation's war plans. The pace of technological and geopolitical change significantly affected the underlying assumptions in our plans, and as a matter of urgency, we needed to rewrite them for our top adversaries. They also needed to be updated through the new "globally integrated and resourced" lens we were now applying.

The two flashpoints I was most concerned about were a Chinese attempt to seize Taiwan or compel its surrender and a confrontation in the South China Sea over U.S. military or allied activities in international waters that Beijing considered its own. The particular challenge we face in both scenarios is the ability to quickly build sufficient combat power in each locale to deter an escalation, and if that fails, fighting and winning with such long lines of communication. We started with the planning issue, with my Policy team in the lead. This process would continue right up until my final weeks in office, as we want back and forth refining different aspects of the INDOPACOM plan.

Developing a modern joint warfighting concept (JWC)—a first step to developing new doctrine—was another critical step.

War-fighting doctrine is defined by NATO as the "fundamental principles by which the military forces guide their actions in support of objectives. It is authoritative but requires judgment in application." It is an overall conceptual framework that links theory, history, experimentation, and practical exercises to drive initiative and creative thinking in the conduct of military operations. The new American way of war captured in the JWC is known as All Domain Operations, and it features using large amounts of AI-driven analysis across the five domains of land, air, sea, space, and cyberspace in milliseconds. Each of the services was also tasked with developing subconcepts, such as contested logistics, joint all domain command and control, joint long-range fires, and the information advantage.

The doctrine I learned as a West Point cadet and Army officer was called AirLand Battle. The Army developed it to defeat the Soviets on the battlefields of Europe. To this day I can still cite its key tenets. I wanted that same understanding and emphasis in our professional education for today's force.

AirLand Battle stood the test of time and was still a credible and effective doctrine, but we needed something new. The simple fact that AirLand Battle only dealt with two domains—air and land—and today's military was operating in five—air, land, sea, space, and cyberspace—was evidence enough that new doctrine was needed if we were to prevail on the modern battlefield against the Chinese and Russians. General Milley agreed. He grew up in the Army with AirLand Battle as well. Together we pushed the Army in 2018 to move forward with a new concept based on Multi-Domain Operations, which would become the centerpiece of the effort he and the Joint Staff would begin leading to establish a new war-fighting doctrine for all of the DoD. I was pleased to learn later that the DoD approved version 1.0 of the Joint Warfighting Concept in June 2021.

We also set up a so-called Red Team led by a capable China

hand who would attend all my Strategy Implementation meetings and offer his perspective on the Chinese view, reaction, or position on any number of matters coming before us. His team's job was to think the way that Xi, the Politburo, or a senior Chinese general would, and then tell us the unvarnished strengths, weaknesses, pros, and cons of every critical policy, strategy, and plan we discussed. I relied on this team for their honest assessments and called upon them at nearly every meeting. I routinely received highly classified memos from the Red Team on important technical, strategic, operational, or organizational matters. They involved themselves in all manner of China-related discussions and meetings.

Another "China focus" item was the training and education of our service members on the Chinese military in all our courses. Whether it was a class for new sergeants, or a War College seminar for colonels, I wanted the students learning about the PLA as appropriate to their rank and next job. Junior leaders should be familiar with PLA platoon weapons and tactics, for example, while the colonels and Navy captains should be fluent in Chinese strategy. I was pleased to learn in mid-2021 that the Army was making solid progress on a new publication entitled "Chinese Tactics," which presented an unclassified assessment of the PRC's military organization, strategy, tactics, and capabilities. This is an example of the instructional and informational materials we need.

It was important that we understood a potential foe we hoped to never fight, much like my generation did when we studied the Soviets. I felt so strongly about this as a young cadet in the 1980s that I took Russian as my language at West Point. During the 2000s, many officers studied Arabic. More of our future officers today should be learning Chinese, as well as the languages of our friends and allies in the Indo-Pacific. This was another initiative we worked.

As part of our Top Ten objective to focus the department on

China, I directed the National Defense University to reorient its curriculum by dedicating 50 percent of the coursework to China by academic year 2021. I wanted the university to become a center of excellence for our most senior officers, the one place they could go to become as expert as possible on China and its military.

I also tasked the armed services to make the PLA the pacing threat—the military force against which we needed to organize, man, train, and equip U.S. forces to fight and defeat—in our professional schools, programs, and training, including the Army's National Training Center and exercises such as the Air Force's Red Flag. Identifying the PRC as the pacing threat was the right choice given the effort and resources Beijing was putting into modernizing their military and their war-fighting capabilities, and the fact that they saw *us* as *their* pacing threat.

Even small things mattered when it came to focusing and educating the joint force. We decided to collect articles published in the Chinese media or by PRC-funded think tanks regarding issues in the U.S.-China relationship. These stories were contained under the rubric of "Chinese Perspectives" in our Saturday morning news clips as another important way to push the China focus forward.

My vision was that, if the CCP ever decided years down the road that a military confrontation with the United States was the only way to achieve their strategic aims, at least we would have a generation of officers and NCOs across the joint force who understood the PLA and were as prepared as possible to fight, win, and survive on the modern battlefield.

While I wanted to be prepared for the worst, I was also committed to working for the best. China does not have to be a foe of the United States; that is not what we should want. Therefore, we had to be careful not to make this a self-fulfilling prophecy. To begin, we often stated that our issues were with the CCP, not the Chinese people. Next, we welcomed China's rise *within* the international rules-based order established in the wake of World War II. After all, the United States didn't pursue the 1979 opening, the PRC's 2001 entry into the WTO, and everything else in between just so the CCP could tear the system down and rebuild it in their image. But this was now what we seemed to be up against. The bottom line was that the rules-based order that had been in place for seventy-five years had benefited everyone, and China particularly so, and it would be both wrong and foolish to replace it to benefit one country.

I always believed it was important to open lines of communication and build relationships not only with your allies and partners but also (if not more important) with your rivals, adversaries, and foes. There is no harm done in talking, so I reached out early on to my counterparts in Beijing and Moscow and tried to maintain a pace of meeting or speaking with them every three months or so.

The Chinese defense minister was a general named Wei Fenghe. He had joined the PLA in 1970, at the age of sixteen, and rose over the decades to become commander of the PLA Rocket Force—China's version of U.S. Strategic Command. I had first met him at a dinner Defense Secretary Jim Mattis hosted for our Chinese counterparts at Mt. Vernon in November 2018. Wei had become minister of national defense in March of that year.

Though Wei was my nominal counterpart, we recognized that he wasn't truly an equal when it came to authority and power in his own system. Nonetheless, he was my best point of entry, and I was determined to leverage my interactions with him to further our understanding, interests, and competitive posture.

While it is always difficult to really size up a person—let alone build a rapport—through a translator, I found Wei to be serious and professional. He was also reticent, but I couldn't tell whether that was his nature, or whether he was simply very careful in what he said during our discussions. Our first formal meeting was by video conference, and we met in person again in Bangkok at the Association of Southeast Asian Nations defense ministers' conference in November 2019. Wei also seemed committed to building the relationship and even invited me to visit Beijing in 2021, which I told him I would do.

The important thing was that Wei and I knew each other. We also knew how to get hold of one another quickly, and we had enough of a relationship and mutual respect to discuss difficult matters. This was critically important should a crisis ever occur. I wanted the ability to pick up the phone to explain, warn, question, or simply hear him out so that we could clear the air of any misperception or misunderstanding that might lead to an unintended confrontation or mishap.

As we delved deeper and deeper into the China portfolio during my tenure, I became very concerned about China's cyber capabilities and their growing space abilities. As a result, we made a number of changes and investments in both areas during my tenure to address them.

I was also concerned with China's efforts to modernize and expand the size of their nuclear forces. Beijing was later found to be rapidly building scores of underground missile silos in the country's western desert as it developed its own strategic nuclear triad. The ICBMs that would be placed in these hardened silos would dramatically increase the PRC's number of deployed nuclear weapons, possibly marking a clear shift from Mao Zedong's long-standing posture of maintaining a minimum deterrent against the country's strategic adversaries. Now, it appeared, that strategy had changed as the size and sophistication of its nuclear forces quickly advanced.

We needed much more insight into what Beijing was doing and why. An arms control agreement would give us the opportunity to have these discussions, as well as visit and inspect their nuclear forces—ground, sea, and air platforms—as the Russians and Americans had done with each other for years. Bringing China into the New Strategic Arms Reduction Treaty with Russia was a good way to do this. Using the leverage of Moscow's desire to extend the agreement was a solid way forward. The Trump administration pursued this hard, but ran out of time, having started too late. It was right to extend the treaty, but I was disappointed to see the Biden administration do so for five years (until February 5, 2026) without even trying to get Beijing on board. It was a missed opportunity.

When it came to the conventional balance of power between the United States and the PRC in Asia, China had made enormous gains over the previous two decades, though we still had clear over-match in most areas. Two particular areas stood out, however. One was the PLA's development of land-based ballistic and cruise missiles with conventional warheads.

The Chinese had more than 1,200 of these weapons, many with ranges of well over two thousand miles. This gave them the ability to strike U.S. and allied forces and bases throughout the western Pacific. The numbers they had produced, and continued to build, gave them an advantage in capacity as well that could overwhelm our air defenses. And with the United States constrained from developing comparable systems in the intermediate range of 500 to 5,500 kilometers because of our obligations under the Intermediate-Range Nuclear Forces (INF) Treaty with Russia, we were unable to offset their capabilities with our own equivalent forces. In short, the PLA's missile systems were integral to China's anti-access/area-denial strategy for the western Pacific, and constituted a major obstacle for the United States to overcome if we ended up in a conflict with them.[10]

I supported the U.S. withdrawal from the INF Treaty in 2019, but not because I'm reflexively opposed to arms control. I had worked these issues for years. Arms control has a role to play in our national security tool kit. In fact, the Department's 2018 Nuclear Posture Review points out that we will seek agreements based on certain conditions—namely, that they enhance security and are verifiable and enforceable. Rather, I supported withdrawal because the INF Treaty had outlived its usefulness given Russia's continued noncompliance—a major reason our NATO allies also supported withdrawal—and the constraints it placed on our ability to address the growing PLA missile threat in the Indo-Pacific, a theater notable for its great distances and wide expanses of water.

I was heartened to see in 2021 that the Biden administration supported the position we took on the INF Treaty, as well as the Trump administration's later withdrawal from the Open Skies agreement with Russia and other countries, also due to Moscow's continued noncompliance.[11] These decisions validated our approach toward not only these agreements but our broader national security concerns.

My first trip as secretary of defense was to Australia for the annual 2 plus 2 meeting, along with Secretary Pompeo, to meet with our counterparts and discuss a wide range of issues. China was always a principal topic of discussion. Before departing Sydney for my other stops in New Zealand, Japan, Mongolia, and South Korea, we held a press conference to wrap up our sessions.

In the media briefing, which occurred a day after our August 2 withdrawal from the INF Treaty, I made clear that I wanted to deploy an intermediate-range missile capability in the Asia theater as soon as possible to counter the PLA's advantage. Needless to say, this caught Beijing's attention in a negative way, which told us a lot about the importance of fielding these systems and what doing so meant to them. It was a major reason the DoD decided to invest billions of dollars into hypersonic weapons, new ground-based cruise missiles, and other long-range precision fire systems.

My second major area of concern was the PLA Navy. By 2020, China had also built the largest navy in the world, a threshold they actually crossed in 2015. Meanwhile, the United States declined from a high of nearly 600 vessels during the Reagan era, to slightly under 300 battle-force ships in 2020. Numbers alone, however, do not dictate capability.

The United States deploys more tonnage, meaning larger and more heavily armed ships, and outstrips the Chinese Navy nine to one in vertical launch missile cells.[12] These cells are leading-edge systems for storing and firing a greater number and wide range of missiles, from anti-air to anti-surface guided missiles. These are often the ship's primary war-fighting systems when it comes to long-range defensive and offensive weapons.

Moreover, the composition of both navies is different. While the PLA Navy has an overall fleet of around 360 surface ships and submarines, the United States has far more aircraft carriers, nuclear-powered submarines, cruisers, and destroyers. The Chinese advantage is in more, but less capable, diesel submarines, frigates, and corvettes.[13] Other measures are also important, such as the skills of ones' sailors, the ability to perform joint operations, and experience in conducting sustained deployments. Hence, if given the choice to go with one maritime force or the other in times of conflict, I would go with the U.S. Navy every single time.

That said, China's navy is clearly on the rise. They have been running while we were jogging when it comes to maritime capability, which means at some point they will surpass us in overall war-fighting ability if we don't pick up our pace. With significant increases in their defense budget each year—which has seen significant annual growth over the last twenty years—coupled with exceptional shipbuilding capacity and a unified government commitment by Beijing to increase the size and capability of their naval forces, they have advantages that Washington is either unwilling or unable to match.

As the DoD's 2020 annual report on China states, "In spite of forecast difficulties for China's economic growth in the 2020s, the [Chinese Communist] Party has the political will and fiscal strength to sustain a steady increase in defense spending over the next decade" to modernize the force, "explore new technologies," and ensure it maintains its status as the "second largest military spender in the world."[14]

Washington's commitment isn't keeping pace in comparison. For example, the PRC's defense budget for 2021 shows a 6.8 percent increase over the previous year, while the proposed U.S. budget is roughly flat—which actually ends up being a decrease in spending power due to inflation—with some in Congress pressing for a drastic 10 percent budget reduction. Opponents of increased U.S. defense spending will often argue that America's military budget is more than sufficient. After all, they say, the U.S. defense spending is several times larger than China's. Yet they ignore the details underlying the numbers.

What they fail to acknowledge is that while the United States has a far larger overall defense budget, we also have global responsibilities, alliance commitments, and other requirements that drive costs upward and may not be directly applicable in a conflict with China. Furthermore, when you add in costs the PRC's defense budget doesn't account for (such as military R&D), adjust the price of military personnel/labor between both countries, and then norm spending through the lens of the widely accepted "purchasing power parity" metric, China's defense budget looks far more comparable to ours. Indeed, some reports estimate that "Beijing's military budget is about 87% of America's."[15]

Beijing has other factors in its favor. For example, a 2018 U.N. report put China in the top spot with 40 percent of the world's shipbuilding market (based on gross tons), with South Korea coming in a distant second at 25 percent.[16] According to another report, "Between 2014 and 2018, China launched more submarines, warships, amphibious vessels, and auxiliaries than the number of ships currently serving in the individual navies of Germany, India, Spain, and the United Kingdom."[17] As for the United States, we don't have sufficient shipbuilding capacity right now to materially increase the number of warships we build each year even if we had the money.

For the near term, China is building a navy capable of defending the mainland, the waters surrounding it, and its excessive maritime claims in places like the South China Sea. This is the crowded waterway in the western Pacific through which one-third of the world's shipping passes, carrying $5 trillion in trade annually; it also contains major oil and natural gas reserves on its seabed and hosts enormous fisheries that are critical to the food security of millions in the region.

And of course, Beijing is building a modern military capable of seizing Taiwan, isolating it, or compelling its surrender. Key to these plans are the long-range precision missiles, coupled with satellites and other surveillance assets, that can target U.S. Navy aircraft carriers and other major American warships. By doing so, they put our most powerful vessels at risk, and thus could keep us out of the waters they are aiming to control. Over time, we expect China will build a blue-water navy that can take the fight out of the western Pacific and into the eastern Pacific, and then globally—from the

Persian Gulf to the Arctic, to the Indian Ocean and maybe the Atlantic—to assert themselves and advance their interests.

The future naval force structure called Battle Force 2045 that I presented in the fall of 2020—a year after the 2019 Senior Leader Conference—was designed to ensure the U.S. Navy's predominance for decades to come. As I detailed earlier, it possessed the core operational attributes needed to fight and win against the PRC.* And with more than five hundred manned and unmanned ships, it would be a more balanced fleet with a greater number of smaller surface combatants and an ample submarine force more than capable of handling the Chinese Navy and the future challenges it will present.

As the election heated up in the late summer and early fall of 2020, so did U.S.-China relations. Tensions had been escalating for some time, driven mostly by Beijing's handling of COVID going back to the beginning of the year. There were also sharp and enduring disagreements with Beijing, however, over Taiwan, the treatment of U.S. allies and partners in the region, the confinement and abuse of the Uighur population in western China, and Hong Kong, to name a few. Defense and State had been leading on these matters for a couple of years at this point. In February 2020, for example, I gave a major speech on China at the Munich Security Conference that hit them hard on several of these issues.[18]

President Trump was a relative latecomer to this broad, tough approach. Critics accused him of being soft on human rights issues, taking it easy on China's crackdown on Hong Kong, pulling

---

* These operational attributes include: distributed lethality and awareness; survivability in a high-intensity conflict; adaptability for a complex world; ability to project power, control the seas, and demonstrate presence; and the capability to deliver precision effects at very long ranges.

punches on tough actions against PRC tech giant Huawei, and other things. Indeed, in a rare moment, I saw him chastise Mike Pompeo for being too aggressive in public remarks the secretary of state made about the PRC, asking Mike to "please dial it down" as they sat opposite each other across the Resolute desk. Pompeo paused for a moment, acknowledged Trump's request, and nodded in agreement.

But as COVID hit the United States hard, Trump finally got more on board with his own policy, as I already stated. He was angry about Beijing's handling of the virus, and the impact it was having on America. I suppose it was also easier to blame them for allowing the pandemic to spread in the early days, rather than taking responsibility for how he mishandled it over the course of a year. Lastly, he also wasn't going to let Joe Biden outflank him when it came to getting tough on China.

The United States government, including me, blamed Beijing for not being more transparent about COVID, and not sharing all the information they learned about the virus, its origins, and its spread. Trump brought this up constantly and had been calling COVID-19 the "China flu" for many months. He also knew that COVID had devastated a great economy and was threatening to undermine both his presidency and his reelection.

Over the summer, in July, the DoD conducted a dual carrier cruise—meaning two aircraft carriers performing a joint mission in the immediate vicinity of each other—through the South China Sea. These types of operations aren't common, but they also are not unique—just infrequent. This one captured a lot of media attention, nonetheless, and a good deal of interest from Beijing and our friends in the region. Beijing saw it as a show of force. We thought the operation demonstrated our capabilities and capacity in the midst of a global pandemic—particularly after the sidelining of the USS *Theodore Roosevelt* for several weeks in the spring—when some in China believed the virus brought the U.S. military to its knees. But as we entered the most intense period—the final three months—of an election cycle, I wanted to make sure we were following a more predictable and traditional schedule. Indeed, we organized a secure call with Secretary of State Pompeo not long after the dual carrier operation to discuss these things.

During the first week of September, the Pentagon released its annual report on China's military power, which repeated President Xi Jinping's two major goals for the PLA: to complete military modernization by 2035 and become a world-class military by midcentury. The report further added that Beijing's desire for the "PLA to become a practical instrument of its statecraft with an active role in advancing the PRC's foreign policy" was driving the military buildup. Stories speculating what war between the United States and China would look like began appearing in the wake of this report, further stirring things up.

That same month, we started to see more aggressive behavior from the Chinese Communist leadership and the PLA. Beijing was conducting exercises and deploying more ships to the South China Sea to assert its unfounded territorial claims. At the same time, it was flying more military aircraft closer and closer to Taiwan, and with greater frequency. And in the first half of September, China continued its pressure campaign against Taipei by conducting a large-scale air and naval exercise around an outlying Taiwanese island.

A week later, from September 18 through 19, as the highest-level visit by a State Department official to Taipei in decades began, nearly forty PLA Air Force planes crossed the Taiwan Strait median line—the internationally recognized north-south demarcation bisecting the 110-mile-wide channel east and west between the countries—in a major breach of past practice designed to threaten

Taipei.[19] While all of this was going on, we continued to refine our war planning; it was one of our Top Ten objectives.

On Monday, October 12, the media reported that the Trump administration approved the sale of several advanced weapons system to Taiwan. It was something the DoD definitely supported. We were working on new and more ways—many of which became policy, some of which are not public—to cooperate with Taiwan and help improve their defenses. I was also pressing on Taipei to spend much more on defense, and equally important, on the right mix of forces and weapons . . . the best way to defend against the PLA. China reacted negatively to the arms sales, calling on the United States to cut all military ties with Taiwan, and then promised some type of response for Washington's action if we did not.

The next day, Chinese president Xi Jinping visited a PLA Marine Corps base in Chaozhou City, Guangdong province, and told his troops to "put all [their] minds and energy on preparing for war" and to "maintain a state of high alert," according to media reports.[20]

Between the public rhetoric going back and forth, private feedback we were getting from Americans who work on U.S.-China issues, and intelligence reporting, it was becoming increasingly clear that Beijing was unsure what Washington's intentions were in the fall of 2020. Was it election-year rhetoric, or were we thinking about provoking a military confrontation?

Weeks earlier, James Anderson, Mark Milley, a few others, and I had met with Admiral Phil Davidson at Indo-Pacific Command to better understand his operational, training, and exercise plans over the coming months, through the November election. The activities were straightforward, with standard freedom of navigation exercises and aerial surveillance missions planned. The freedom of navigation operations are particularly important. It was the way by which the U.S. Navy asserted the United States' right—and indeed every nation's right—to fly, sail, and operate anywhere international law allows.

The Navy had done this throughout its history, and it performs these operations today in contested waters all around the world, such as the Persian Gulf. If these operations aren't routinely performed, then it's too easy for a country's baseless legal claims to become a de facto state of affairs. And so, as China's illicit claims increased in recent years, so did U.S. operations. In 2020, the United States conducted more freedom of navigation transits through the Taiwan Strait, a recognized international waterway, than ever before. That said, I wanted to make sure we were neither increasing nor decreasing our operational tempo as we approached November 3; either way could send a wrong signal to Beijing.

One event that did concern me in the fall as Beijing became more jittery was INDOPACOM's plans to deploy larger than normal numbers of ships and aircraft, including bombers, into northeast Asia a week or so before November 3, in preparation for a long planned exercise later that month and into December. The early deployment was necessary due to COVID restrictions and quarantine requirements being imposed upon U.S. forces by our foreign hosts. I understood the command's logic in arriving early, but wasn't comfortable with the timing. I thought it would unnecessarily alarm Beijing to see so many additional ships and aircraft heading toward the area just days ahead of a heated U.S. election. As such, I directed the command to delay the forces' departure until after November 3.

My guidance throughout the fall, after all, was to keep our posture and operations "steady as she goes." Do "nothing more or nothing less than we would normally do," I often said—which included continuing the freedom of navigation operations the Chinese detested—unless some type of external action warranted it, and then we would first discuss the matter. Anything otherwise could send the wrong message to allies, friends, and adversaries in very different and potentially dangerous ways.

Despite our efforts, there was still a risk of confrontation due to a misunderstanding or misperception. The last thing we wanted was a situation, for example, where tensions were so high that a U.S. ship and a Chinese one in the South China Sea—or elsewhere, for that matter—ended up in a bumping match that escalated into shots being fired. And then where would it go from there? Or worse, the PRC might become convinced that the United States was preparing to take some military action against them. Might they be thinking a "wag the dog" scenario was being considered by the White House and act preemptively? Pursuing a confrontation with China was never discussed at the Pentagon, and I never heard the president even mention such a thing, but the Chinese didn't know that. Our job was to look at the situation not only through our own eyes but also through Beijing's lens.

I sat down with my Policy lead, James Anderson, in mid-October to discuss the matter. He had similar concerns given the intel reports, military movements, and escalating rhetoric on both sides. I asked him to send a message to the Chinese from me, that "we understand that you have concerns," and may be confused, but that I wanted to personally assure them that "we are not seeking any type of confrontation" with the PRC. That the situation here in the U.S. should not be misread. We "want to keep the lines of communication between our two militaries open to prevent any misperceptions that could lead to unnecessary friction or conflict."

Following my decision to reach out to the Chinese, we held a conference call on October 22 with Anderson and key members of his Policy team, Undersecretary of Defense for Intelligence Joe

Kernan, General Milley, and Admiral Davidson to discuss a number of INDOPACOM issues, to include the OSD's private outreach to Beijing.

By the time of this secure conference call, James Anderson had come back to report my message was conveyed on October 20 by a civilian political appointee in the Policy office responsible for Indo-Pacific Security Affairs. Anderson said the message was "well received" by the Chinese and that they thanked us for the clarity. I was pleased by the news. The last thing we needed was to stumble into an accidental conflict nobody wanted, especially with the Chinese.

Given this outcome, I asked General Milley to arrange a similar call with his counterpart in the PLA to follow up and reinforce my message, as per our standard practice. Milley agreed. The Joint Staff faced some coordination challenges, so my civilian OSD staff eventually assisted them in arranging the call. All of this pushed the chairman's outreach back to October 30.

This type of coordinated messaging was common at the Pentagon. In fact, sometimes we calibrated it with our peers in other departments, or tasked civilian and military leaders at levels below me to speak with their counterparts as well. Often, other members of the interagency participated in those calls. However, in late September, apparently the State Department cut off most of its contacts with their PRC foreign ministry counterparts, according to my OSD Policy team. This added to the tension and mystery.

Days after his call, the chairman reported that his message was also received well by the PLA. They appreciated our reassurance. All in all, I felt my directed message to the Chinese on October 20, followed by Milley's call on the thirtieth, was the right thing to do. This messaging was all about promoting strategic stability and avoiding unnecessary conflict. I learned months later through a credible source, however, that Trump was unhappy about my decision.

The speculation was that this added further fuel to his desire to fire me. I don't think so, but who knows. And who cares. Better a little careful diplomacy than a confrontation that nobody wants. That was the whole reason I was trying to build a relationship with my Chinese counterpart in the first place, and part of the reason I stayed on board as secretary of defense through the election.

After four years, I felt the United States was in a much better place with China than where we began in 2016. A consensus on China had finally formed. Our country—most of its leaders, institutions, businesses, and others—was moving in a better direction, and it was bipartisan. I was proud that the DoD led this push early on. But it is also fair to say that the coordinated actions of Defense, State, Commerce, Justice, NSC, and others, in accordance with our strategy, solidified this sober, clear-eyed assessment of Beijing's intentions. After all, we knew what it would mean for the nation, and other Western democracies, if we didn't get organized and focused.

Fortunately, the president's inattention to the strategy or his decisions that sometimes seemed to undermine it weren't debilitating. It was tough to build a collective effort with allies and partners in the Indo-Pacific, and especially so with our European allies, when the president was constantly beating them up. It was also difficult to deal more forcefully with your counterparts in Beijing when Trump was proudly citing his personal friendship with the head of the Chinese Communist Party.

The president eventually got more on board with his own China policy in the last year of his administration, as I noted previously. We accomplished a good deal by the end. I just wish we had started as robustly as we finished. We would have moved the ball farther down field if we had.

State, Defense, and others did a good job emphasizing the importance of arms sales to Taiwan, supporting democracy advocates in Hong Kong, citing Beijing's aggressiveness in the South China Sea and the Himalayas, criticizing the PRC for its genocide of the Uighurs in western China, and calling them out for their economic espionage and intellectual property theft. But these actions would have been more effective if we had the full-throated support of the White House and from the president.

Maybe more important, we were fortunate that Trump's heated and escalatory rhetoric toward China in the final months of the administration didn't create a fissure in the bipartisan consensus that had formed in the preceding years. It had taken a long time to get there, and it could have quickly unraveled if either candidate decided to take a different approach toward the PRC for short-term electoral gain.

Looking ahead, the time has also come for the United States to review our One China policy and the various communiqués that undergird it—beginning with the 1979 U.S.-PRC Joint Communiqué—and to update the policy. In the forty-two years since the United States switched diplomatic recognition from Taipei to Beijing, much has changed within both countries, between them, and internationally—politically, economically, and diplomatically. America's One China policy is no longer sufficient. It has been overcome by history and reality, making it an inadequate foundation upon which to rest such an important foreign policy and its supporting strategies going forward. For example, the government in Taiwan is now not only a thriving democracy, but it also no longer claims de jure sovereignty over all of China, as it did decades ago.

Moreover, the PRC has not lived up to its end of the deal. It has used coercion and intimidation to influence Taiwan, as well as other countries that wish to maintain relations with the government in

Taipei. This diplomatic, economic, and military bullying campaign has showed no signs of relenting, and the PRC's flexing of its growing military muscle around Taiwan has increased dramatically in the last few years. This was a main reason we strengthened and expanded the DoD's activities with and around Taiwan.

Beijing has also successfully distorted Washington's One China policy in the minds of many around the world, including in the United States, to serve their own ends. The fact is U.S. policy does not *accept* China's sovereignty over Taiwan as Beijing would like everyone to believe. Rather, the One China policy merely "*acknowledges* that Chinese on either side of the Taiwan Strait maintain there is but one China and that Taiwan is a part of China" (italics added). Washington sought to clarify the U.S. position in 1982, and further reassure Taipei, by issuing its so-called Six Assurances. But much of this diplomatic history is unknown, misunderstood, or forgotten.

A review of U.S. policy toward China and Taiwan should look at the full gamut of issues we now face, and then update that policy in a way that is principled, rationale, defensible, and sustainable. A twenty-first-century policy must better reflect our values, such as our commitment to democracy, freedom, and human rights, which inevitably means being fair to the people of Taiwan and their elected government. For example, there is no good reason Taiwan is not a member of the World Health Organization—especially during a global pandemic—or excluded from other important international organizations.

An updated policy should better reflect reality when it comes to Taiwan's status, restate the importance of resolving the core issue of sovereignty peacefully, and quickly garner the support of other democracies around the world. The challenging part will be to do this without provoking armed conflict with the PRC.

All that said, I walked away in November 2020 feeling good

about the DoD's role in this strategic shift, and the plans we left in place to keep the Department and the nation moving forward. The incoming Biden administration seemed to be saying many of the same things about China that we had during my tenure, and if that continued—and they backed it up with action and sufficient annual increases in defense spending (and maybe even adopted the core tenets of the 2018 National Defense Strategy)—I had hope that as an institution and a country we would continue to improve our position for the challenging years ahead.

CHAPTER 20

AMERICA'S STRATEGIC ADVANTAGE

"There is at least one thing worse than fighting with allies—and that is to fight without them," Winston Churchill famously remarked.

The key to adequate deterrence in the future, let alone being able to fight and win against China, is not only about building a better military, it is about strengthening our allies and growing new partners—a core tenet of the Pentagon's National Defense Strategy.

Allies and partners are an asymmetric advantage of ours that Beijing cannot match. That's why China and Russia are trying to neuter this edge while they work to build their own sets of partnerships, including with each other. That is my concern when I see glimpses of South Korea's seeming drift closer to the PRC. Or when Southeast Asian countries with long-standing ties to the United States hear the siren song from Beijing tugging at them with promises of economic and military assistance.

In my view, East Asia was becoming the epicenter for great power competition, if not geopolitical instability, in the world. Nowhere else but in this region—from North Korea to Taiwan—are the stakes higher, the players bigger, the situation more complicated, and the game more intense. This part of the world contains four of the world's nuclear-capable states, three of the world's largest economies, six of the world's largest or most capable militaries, and a half dozen of the world's most technologically advanced countries, all within relatively close proximity—if not missile range—of one another. Conflict in East Asia would have a devastating global impact, even if the war itself is confined to the likely flash points of the region. The U.S.-Japan alliance is the linchpin of the post–World War II security framework in the Pacific, and critical to ensuring stability in East Asia. Approximately fifty thousand U.S. military personnel are stationed in this maritime nation—the highest number of permanently based service members in any one foreign country—and when you include their family members and other Americans employed there by the DoD, the total is nearly one hundred thousand people. Their purpose is to ensure the theater remains free and open by providing a "ready and lethal capability that deters adversary aggression . . . and enhances regional peace and security."[1]

Postwar bilateral relations between Tokyo and Washington have generally been strong and relatively immune to noticeable swings one way or the other as sometimes happens between the United States and other allies. Moreover, according to the Government Accountability Office (GAO), Japan pays about 38 percent of the cost to keep U.S. forces in Japan, while nearby Seoul pays around 30 percent of the bill to keep 28,500 American troops in Korea.[2] However, while South Korea spent a healthy 2.7 percent of its GDP on defense, Tokyo spends no more than 1 percent. I thought it should be at least 2 percent. This was an issue I would often raise with the Japanese given the increasing challenges we faced from China, especially in the East China Sea.

For nearly my entire tenure, Japan's minister of defense was Taro Kono, an established and capable politician from the Liberal Democratic Party who has been a member of the House of Representatives since 1996. Kono comes from a well-known political family in Japan and earned his college degree from Georgetown University in the United States. Kono spoke very good English, which, when coupled with his keen intellect, affability, and good sense of humor, made him a great partner.

Kono had worked in Prime Minister Shinzo Abe's cabinet in several roles, including a stint as foreign minister before becoming defense minister in September 2019. During the year or so that we worked together, we engaged on a range of issues that had long plagued the U.S.-Japan relationship, such as the U.S. Marine Corps presence on Okinawa, including the relocation of U.S. Marine Corps Air Station Futenma from Ginowan to a less densely populated part of the island; and Japan's efforts to complete the purchase of Mageshima Island—an uninhabited outcrop located a little more than twenty miles from the southernmost Japanese mainland of Kyushu—to support aircraft-carrier landing practice. I also thanked him for Japan being such a gracious host to U.S. forces for so many years, and reiterated our commitment to working with and engaging the local communities where we stationed our troops.

But the bigger issues dealt with international challenges, such as the relationship between Seoul and Tokyo, policy toward North Korea, strengthening the Association of Southeast Asian Nations (ASEAN), building the Quad, and tackling the long-term challenge of China. We would meet whenever possible to discuss these issues, whether in Tokyo, Washington, Bangkok, or Guam.

When it came to North Korea, Tokyo had serious cause for

concern. Pyongyang's missiles could easily range Japan and had been shot into Japanese waters and over one of the country's islands in the past. It was very threatening, especially given the historical animosity between the two peoples since Japan's harsh colonial rule over the Korean peninsula from 1910 to 1945. I always thought that if war erupted on the Korean peninsula, one way or another Japan would end up having missiles fired in its direction. And given North Korea's unpredictable nature, we had little idea if these would be conventional weapons or a missile tipped with a weapon of mass destruction.

As the United States entered into discussions with North Korea, it was important to keep the issue of ballistic missiles in mind for these reasons. It wasn't good enough to simply prohibit the North's work on ICBMs; we needed to proscribe missiles of *all* ranges for the sake of both Seoul and Tokyo.

In addition to the missile and nuclear programs of North Korea that all countries were concerned about, there were matters of unique importance to Japan, principally the abduction of Japanese citizens by the North beginning in the late 1970s. North Korea admitted to some of these criminal acts, but not all of them, and Tokyo was fully committed to resolving the cases. This was another issue always atop the list of items we would discuss bilaterally, and that the United States would commit to putting on the agenda of any talks between Washington and Pyongyang.

Japan was also a critical player when it came to enforcing U.N. Security Council resolutions sanctions against North Korea, disrupting Pyongyang's illicit ship-to-ship transfers of prohibited goods, and hosting other countries who were supporting U.N. activities. It was a team effort to keep the pressure on the North and get them back to the negotiating table.

Finally, there was China. There was no disagreement between the

United States and Japan on Beijing's intentions and plans, or the importance of us standing up to them together. Beijing clearly wanted to dominate the western Pacific and control the sea lanes, which in and of itself was a threat to Japan's sovereignty, security, and economy. But to do this, China needed to secure the so-called first island chain, which is a string of islands enclosing the Chinese mainland that "arcs southward from the Japanese home islands through the Ryukyu Islands, Taiwan, and the Philippine archipelago."[3]

This chain represents a geographic barrier for entry or exit into Chinese waters, and its control is critical in times of conflict. Securing their illicit claims to the many islands caught behind this first island chain, and then defending them, is a major reason Beijing is building out its navy. While the PRC's excessive claims in the South China Sea are often the talk of most countries, it is their claim over the Senkaku Islands, which are under the administration of Japan, that concerns Tokyo most. The Senkakus are a group of uninhabited islands in the energy-rich East China Sea located northeast of Taiwan and west of Okinawa.

In recent years, Chinese ships—both fishing vessels and Coast Guard cutters—have increasingly entered the waters surrounding the Senkakus to push their claims and test Tokyo's mettle. Illegal fishing by China and the harassment of Japanese fishermen in the area is not uncommon. PRC Coast Guard ships have also increased their incursions into Japan's territorial waters. Upping the ante, Beijing recently approved a law for its Coast Guard allowing their ships to take "all necessary measures," which could include using force, to prevent foreign ships from operating in Chinese-claimed waters.

Japan's Coast Guard did a good job pushing back on these incursions. But it was important for me to also affirm publicly Washington's commitment to defending the Senkaku Islands pursuant to Article V of the U.S.-Japan Security Treaty. We also expressed our opposition to any unilateral attempts (meaning by Beijing) to change the status quo in the East China Sea.

It was for all these reasons that Kono and the Abe government were thinking more strategically and more assertively about how best to deal with a rising China. This included collaborating on and considering various PRC-Taiwan scenarios, something we should do more of with our regional partners. China was not just another country that also harbored deep resentment toward Japan because of its own occupation at Tokyo's hand in the first half of the twentieth century, it was now a major player inclined to ignore international rules and norms, and to use its economic and military might to bully and intimidate others, and eventually dominate Asia.

My last meeting with the Japanese defense minister would be in Guam in late August 2020, not long before Prime Minister Abe stepped down and Kono got caught up in a cabinet reshuffle. We were able to discuss several specific items that really showed the increased seriousness with which the Japanese were taking China, including joint war planning, gaming, and exercises. We talked about various ways we could improve interoperability between our forces, particularly when it came to air and missile defense, as well as for intelligence, surveillance, and reconnaissance functions.

Finally, we discussed COVID, how to protect our respective armed forces, and then how to make sure we blocked the CCP's efforts to wield the pandemic as a diplomatic weapon against us in the region. Beijing was working hard to paint the United States as a declining power with a dysfunctional political system. In their view, Washington's handling of the pandemic, as compared to Beijing's, was another instance that showed China's single-party communist model was better and more effective than a multiparty democracy. The sidelining of the USS *Theodore Roosevelt* in the Pacific due to COVID was an example they used against us. In the meantime, they were backing up this rhetoric by offering medical supplies and PPE to countries around the world. Kono and I agreed, as did our other regional partners, that we needed to do everything we could to counter this nefarious information campaign.

When it came to security in northeast Asia, the other critical ally was the Republic of Korea (ROK). The U.S. relationship with South Korea, as the country is more commonly known, was strained by the rhetoric coming out of the White House, however. Over my three-year tenure at the Pentagon, this dynamic and the issues we faced on the peninsula would become a particular concern to me.

Both the United States and South Korea faced an ongoing threat from North Korea and a longer-term strategic challenge from China. I was confident our views regarding Pyongyang were aligned, but I worried that Seoul was drifting into Beijing's orbit, drawn in by the gravitational pull of trade, economics, and geography. The critical issue was whether South Korea would select China as its economic partner of choice while trying to maintain the United States as its security partner, and hope that both approaches are compatible. They aren't, of course, yet this seemed to be the path they were headed down.

The immediate issue facing Washington and Seoul was North Korea. In the last two-plus decades, Pyongyang's development of nuclear weapons and long-range missiles that menaced the ROK were now a threat to the U.S. homeland as well. As such, our first task was enforcement of all U.N. Security Council resolutions as we pursued an agreement that would ensure the complete, irreversible, and verifiable denuclearization of North Korea. At the same time, the horrible plight of the North Korean people, and the oppressive prison state in which they lived, was something none of us could ignore.

More broadly, I saw the alliance as critical to the larger Indo-Pacific region and our evolving posture toward China, even if the North Korea problem disappeared overnight. Both countries are important reasons for maintaining a U.S. military presence on the Korean peninsula.

However, we seemed unable to resolve several issues with our ally despite expending a great deal of effort. North Korea's missile tests in the first half of 2017 prompted the United States to deploy its Terminal High Altitude Area Defense (THAAD) anti-missile system to the southern part of the Korean peninsula as a defensive measure to thicken the existing missile defense architecture. The THAAD system was capable of detecting and intercepting missiles that could threaten South Korea, our troops on the peninsula, and even parts of the United States.

China reacted angrily following the announcement of THAAD's deployment in 2016. Beijing believed the system's radar threatened its own security by being able to track military movements within China. The PRC is South Korea's largest trading partner, so Beijing put an extraordinary amount of economic pressure, in addition to diplomatic arm-twisting, on Seoul to cancel the deployment. Beijing went so far as to cut international flights between the two nations and reduce the number of Chinese tourists visiting Korea. The decrease in tourism alone reportedly cost the South Korean economy billions of dollars.[4]

South Korean president Park Geun-hye stood firm, however, as the United States installed the first THAAD systems in April 2017. The PRC and ROK began patching things up after that, but Beijing had made its point. Over time, it seemed as if Seoul was gravitating more and more toward China, seeking its favor. Was this real or perception? Was it a function of new Korean president Moon Jae-in's government, or was a more fundamental shift under way? This was when our concerns emerged that South Korea might try the impossible by siding with China as its economic partner while relying on the United States for its security.

I visited our troops at the THAAD site in 2018 as secretary of the Army, and their living conditions were terrible. I raised this issue with our South Korean counterparts repeatedly, both as secretary of the Army and secretary of defense. We attributed Seoul's inaction to domestic politics and excessive concern about China. Each time I pressed the matter, my Korean interlocutors asked for more patience to find a solution. At our last gathering at the Pentagon in October 2020, I raised my voice in anger over the issue. After more than three years and no visible progress, my patience with their stalling had run out.

In the large Nunn-Lugar conference room that day, I sat across the table from my counterpart, with our aides flanking us on both sides. I spoke for several minutes, loudly and sharply, looking up and down the table at my Korean allies, who sat stone-faced. I recounted how "I visited this site three years ago, and it was in bad shape then. I was told to be patient because you were working on it." I added, "When I raised this matter again the following year, I was told the same thing. This is not how allies treat allies. This is not how the military takes care of its people." To make it more personal, I asked, "Would you be happy if your sons and daughters lived and worked in these conditions?" The air grew thicker with tension.

As the Korean delegation sat there, trying to figure out what was going on, and how to react, I went on and on about the matter. I finished by turning to General Milley, who nodded as I said the following: "Chairman, I'd like the Joint Staff to conduct a study that assesses the impact of withdrawing THAAD, and presents other options for performing the mission off the Korean peninsula. I'd like that in ninety days." This really got the Koreans' attention, as I expected. Milley responded with a quick and eager "Yes, sir, will do." And that was that. I folded my arms across my chest and gestured for the defense minister to respond.

My performance caught our Korean counterparts off guard. They sat stoically but uneasily in their chairs throughout my monologue, and were now dumbfounded about how to respond. I probably shouldn't have done it—it was not diplomatic—but I felt for our people on the ground, and I had been pressing this matter for years. I needed to shake the Koreans up. After all, our soldiers were not only protecting the United States, they were also defending South Korea. The least our hosts could do was treat them properly. I hoped my outburst would spur them into action. The early reports back told us that it did.

Another major issue, which began in 2018 and bubbled over in the summer of 2019, was the deteriorating relationship between South Korea and Japan, and the effect it had on our collective deterrence in the region. It was frustrating to see these two long-standing allies of ours squabbling between themselves as North Korea tested ballistic missiles and developed nuclear weapons. Meanwhile, Beijing went about flexing its muscles in the waters of the East China Sea and beyond. Even Russia benefited from this dispute. Domestic politics prevented Seoul from containing the matter—the result of a long and horrible history—and impacted the ability of the United States, Korea, and Japan to work more closely together to improve our collective security.

In August 2019, Seoul announced it would not renew an agreement with Japan to share military intelligence. The two nations had signed the pact, known as the General Security of Military Information Agreement, in 2016 as tensions with the North were escalating. An important part of the arrangement was the quick, seamless intelligence sharing it facilitated, especially when it came to urgent situations, such as the launch of ballistic missiles out of North Korea.

The dispute emerged after South Korea's Supreme Court issued rulings in 2018 that Japanese companies must compensate victims of forced labor dating back to Japan's occupation of Korea in the first half of the twentieth century. This infuriated Tokyo, which believed the matter had been settled decades earlier. Japan reciprocated by imposing export controls on Korean chemical exports and taking other actions aimed at the ROK economy. Things continued to escalate from there. In the grander scheme, however, both sides were losing, as was Washington. North Korea benefited from all this internecine fighting, as did China. President Trump would see all of this and shake his head in disgust, questioning again the value of "these great allies," as he would say sarcastically.

I was in the Indo-Pacific region again in November 2019, on a long-planned trip anchored to the ASEAN Defense Ministers' Meeting-Plus in Bangkok that month. The purpose on my trip was to get to know our ASEAN partners better, strengthen our defense ties, and to work with them on a meaningful Code of Conduct regarding maritime behavior in the waters of the region. We were pressing for an agreement that would reinforce the international laws, rules, and norms that ASEAN members and the United States considered essential, and which Beijing was actively working to undermine. China was present too, but rarely mentioned—let alone called out publicly—in these discussions. In some ways, it didn't matter. Everyone knew China was breaking the rules, and that they were our focus. The silence of most countries, however, demonstrated the extent to which they were cowed by Beijing's quiet strong-arming.

This was my second trip to Asia in four months. I had been to

Japan and Korea in August 2019 when the intelligence-sharing dispute was brewing and raised the matter then on visits to each capital.
I stopped in Seoul again, before heading on to Bangkok, to discuss
several issues with my counterpart, to include the intelligence-
sharing arrangement. At breakfast before the start of our business
day, Assistant Secretary of Defense for Indo-Pacific Security Affairs
Randy Schriver suggested an alternative approach when I met with
President Moon later that day. He sensed that asking Moon to reverse himself on the arrangement might be politically difficult, if
not impossible, but suggesting they "suspend" their decision might
be the face-saving way out. This made sense to me, and I saw no
downside to proposing it, as we were getting closer and closer to
Moon's deadline. I offered this framework to President Moon at
our meeting and he seemed to absorb it without making any commitment on the spot. But sure enough, hours before the agreement
was set to expire, the South Korean government announced it would
"conditionally suspend the expiry" of the intelligence-sharing
agreement. A good lesson learned about getting to yes in Asia.

In all my meetings in Seoul, I also raised the issue of burden
sharing. South Korea was a wealthy country, one of the top twelve
global economies. It wasn't fair to ask them to pay for everything.
After all, our forward deployment on the peninsula was about
U.S. security and interests too. However, Seoul could afford to
pay more. Estimates from my team at the DoD were that the ROK
was covering no more than one-third of the costs most directly
associated with the stationing of U.S. forces in-country—a figure corroborated by the GAO at around 30 percent, as mentioned
earlier—such as the employment of local workers and payment for
housing that went back into the Korean economy. According to
the U.S. ambassador in Seoul, many in South Korea mistakenly
thought these funds went to the U.S. treasury.

I thought the starting point should be 50 percent—far less than what President Trump was demanding, but a more equitable place to begin given the challenges we jointly faced. It wasn't worth breaking the alliance over, or even publicly threatening to do so, but with Koreans paying roughly $924 million annually out of a $1.6 trillion GDP, Seoul could afford much more.[5]

We never reached a final agreement on this in 2020. The Koreans dug in. On one hand, they felt the United States had negotiated in bad faith, Schriver told me. After a year of talks, Seoul had agreed to an increase proposed by the U.S. side, only to have President Trump undermine his own negotiators and reject it at the eleventh hour.

On the other hand, South Korea also had legislative elections coming up in April 2020 and President Moon couldn't afford to look weak. However, as insulted as they were by Trump demanding a 400 percent increase in burden sharing to $5 billion annually, Korea failed to see how the 13 percent increase—about $120 million more annually—they proposed that spring was equally insulting to the White House. This made it really difficult for alliance proponents such as Mike Pompeo, whose State Department had the lead on the talks, and me to find a reasonable solution.

With a lapsed burden-sharing agreement in 2020, U.S. Forces Korea was out of money by April 1 to pay for the approximately 9,000 Korean nationals working for the DoD there, as well as logistics support contracts necessary to sustain readiness. To continue to provide our troops and families with workers who supported their life, health, and safety functions, as well as essential logistics, I directed the U.S. military to pay for about 4,200 of the employees' salaries and about $70 million in logistics support. This was an unforecasted bill that affected the services, but we could not leave our people hanging in the wind. State supported this action.

Issues like these would rile Trump up. He would complain that the South Koreans were "horrible to deal with" and pressed multiple times for us to withdraw U.S. forces. Much like his views toward Germany, he believed South Korea was "ripping us off." He constantly cited the trade imbalance, saying that "they sell us Samsung TVs and we protect them; it makes no sense." I would have to explain how the U.S. presence in Korea "is important not only to South Korea but to America as well." We had important interests in "keeping a check on North Korea," which had developed the means to threaten the U.S. homeland. Our presence there helped make sure that Pyongyang didn't do anything stupid.

That said, while I was pleased to see the Biden administration agree in early 2021 to a new Special Measures Agreement with Seoul regarding cost sharing, I still believe we should continue to push for a more equitable burden sharing.

The U.S. presence also stabilized the broader region and helped build the sinews between Seoul and Tokyo that would be so critical in case of a conflict on the Korean peninsula. The Moon government seemed far more willing to set aside differences and talk with North Korea, however, than with the Japanese. This was a problem. It flared dramatically in the summer and fall of 2019 over intelligence sharing, as previously discussed. Trump would point to these tensions and say that South Korea wasn't serious about its security. "Why are they fighting with Japan?" he would ask. Great question.

North Korea was an immediate problem for the United States, Japan, and South Korea, but to me how our three nations worked together to deal with China in the coming years was the bigger issue. Our bases in both countries were great locations to position American forces as we looked ahead. For these reasons, I became very uneasy when Trump talked about the need to pull all U.S. forces completely out of Korea. I was able to make my best case against any such moves by reminding him that I had a global posture review under way—which I did—but that only bought me time. Pompeo jumped in once to help, saying, "Mr. President, you should make that [withdrawing U.S. forces from Korea] a second-term priority." This placated him. Trump responded with "Yeah, yeah, second term," as a Cheshire cat smile came across his face. I knew, however, it was something I couldn't implement.

South Korean domestic politics seemed to be spilling over into other parts of the security relationship as well. The liberal Moon government was hell-bent on assuming wartime operational control of Korean troops during the ROK president's term, which ends in 2022. Since July 1950, the United States has been responsible for control of all forces on the peninsula in the event of war, though the Koreans have a much larger role in that today. However, South Korea wants to be in charge of *all* troops in the theater if war breaks out. It is a creditable approach, and one the U.S. supports, but it should happen only once the South Korean military is ready. If this transition occurs any sooner, it could harm our joint war-fighting effectiveness, which is critical to our deterrence of North Korea.

Operational control transfer was a legacy issue for President Moon, but one that made no strategic or operational sense to rush. We had agreed years earlier to pursue a conditions-based approach whose first principle is to strengthen the alliance's combined defense posture. The first condition requires the Koreans to acquire a number of specific critical military capabilities. Other conditions imposed similar mandates and called for a series of military assessments. There are other issues as well, and South Korea is behind on many of them.

As secretary of defense, I met with President Moon on at least two occasions at the Blue House, his official residence and executive office, to discuss this and other issues. The Blue House was large and ornate, with a broad, wooden, winding double staircase covered in bright red carpeting that led to the second floor, where we usually met. Unlike the White House, the Blue House was quiet and serene. Aides were not running about, as happened continually in the West Wing. When our muted conversations paused as we awaited our escort, you heard nothing but silence.

The large room where we met the South Korean president was decorated with a gold-colored tapestry on the wood walls and a beautiful cream-colored carpeting on the floor. Two rows of square, dark wooden chairs were arranged on opposite sides of the room, facing one another about twenty-five feet apart so that each cohort of aides could see the other. We usually stood in front of our chairs for a few minutes, awaiting the president's arrival. This gave both teams a few moments to greet one another or finish any conversations.

The president would arrive quietly, with no fanfare. He greeted everyone in the room, and then took his seat at the front, between both rows of chairs. My seat was located to his right, with a small table between us. Moon has a quiet, cautious demeanor. Smart, well-informed, and engaging on policy, he occasionally revealed an easy sense of humor with a quick smile as the conversation played on.

Moon was elected president in 2017. His foreign policy aligned with his liberal predecessors by adopting a stance toward North Korea that was softer than that of his political opponents. Regarding the United States, he was once quoted as saying, "I'm pro-U.S., but now South Korea should adopt diplomacy in which it can discuss a U.S. request and say no to the Americans."[6] His policies and actions during the Trump administration clearly reflected this more independent, if not distancing, stance from Washington.

I shared with President Moon the U.S. position (and, frankly, the view of his own armed forces) that "we must continue with the approved conditions-based plan for opcon [operational control] transfer." Too much was at stake, I conveyed in diplomatic terms. "Our joint capabilities are what deter North Korean aggression," I added. If we ended up in a conflict with Pyongyang, "we needed to have the most effective command and control system and leadership in place" to defeat them.

For all of the progress the South Korean armed forces had made over the years, they simply weren't ready to assume operational control. Moon always listened intently and nodded politely, but the president was on a timeline he wanted met by the end of his term in mid-2022.

In a private meeting with the new South Korean minister of national defense, Suh Wook, in October 2020, we discussed this issue at the Pentagon. He was a very professional and capable former general who did his duty, proposing that . I shared with him "my personal commitment to our alliance, and to improving our combined defense posture." All of this meant "we must continue following the long agreed upon process."

We raised other issues as well, the responses to which led me to conclude that, for as much as the political leadership above the ministry of defense talked a good game about readiness and jointness, they weren't fully committed to making the hard decisions needed. Fear of domestic political blowback was too great. Whether it was improving living conditions for our troops at the THAAD site, or supporting our live-fire training requirements in-country, we faced a variety of challenges that affected our readiness.

This political atmosphere created a headwind for other things I wanted to do. For example, I was eager to make changes to our posture on the peninsula that would upgrade our readiness and capabilities, such as replacing many of our permanently based fourth-generation fighters with fifth-generation F-35s. Although I was told ███████████████████████████████████████ ███████████████████████████████, General Abrams, the four-star commander of U.S. Forces Korea, supported getting these advanced aircraft into Korea, especially since the Korean air force already had twenty F-35s in-country.

Abrams liked this idea but thought it would be a political and diplomatic bridge too far, not to mention how North Korea might react. However, I believed this was also manageable if done collaboratively and over time. I proposed instead that we not permanently base the F-35s in Korea, but that we rotate them every six months or so back and forth from different units in the United States. A side benefit, I added, would be that we could keep the crews' families in the States, where they had more stability, including better access to jobs for the spouses. Also important, more U.S. Air Force squadrons would get greater exposure to flying in-country with the Korean air force. This is what we were doing with the Army's armored brigade combat teams, and it was working out fine.

This was a major change for General Abrams to digest, and I'm sure it would have been triply difficult for the Moon government. Nevertheless, Abrams went to work looking at options, and variations of options. He was scheduled to brief me in early December 2020, but of course that was a few weeks after I unceremoniously left the Pentagon.

That said, the politics in the United States at the time weren't right either. With Trump pushing to remove U.S. forces stationed abroad, as he did regarding Korea on many occasions, too many people would have immediately pointed to the White House, cried foul that we were abandoning our ROK allies, and then put up every means of resistance to the DoD adjusting our force posture. Yet all I would have been seeking to do was improve the overall readiness of our fighter squadrons, bring an advanced capability in the F-35 to the peninsula, and give our Air Force families more stability. I also wanted to implement some of the new deployment concepts we had developed as part of the National Defense Strategy.

The key to peace and stability on the peninsula, and an acceptable resolution of the situation there, is strengthening the alliance and our combined defense, so that diplomacy can succeed as the only credible path forward. This will be challenged, though, as long as these U.S.-ROK issues linger. Even with these matters hanging over us, U.S. and South Korean defense cooperation remained robust, especially at the uniformed level. I was always confident we were ready to "fight tonight"—as we would often say—to defend our values, our interests, and our nations.

Also important, however, is the continued cooperation among the United States, South Korea, and Japan, based on our common security interests, especially when it comes to policy consultations, exercises, and information sharing regarding Pyongyang, Beijing, and other regional challenges. Along these same lines, it is essential that South Korea join the Quad. Doing so would not only broaden the grouping as we work to strengthen and deepen it but would also send the right signals to many other countries, especially Beijing, about Seoul's geopolitical position. And beyond our collaboration in conventional areas with these countries, we need to do more together, more quickly, in the space and cyber domains of competition and war fighting, as well as against the gray zone operations by China. These were the things I raised with my Japanese and South

Korean counterparts, including the centrality of leaving history to history, and focusing on the future if we are to be successful.

During my nearly eighteen months as secretary of defense, I was able to build other important relationships in the Indo-Pacific through visits, phone calls, and side meetings at regional forums. I would rack up well over 225 meetings with partners from more than sixty countries around the world, but our focus was Asia. In most of these countries I was also able to meet with presidents, prime ministers, emirs, and kings alike to discuss geopolitics, regional threats, and our bilateral security relationship. Our counterparts were always pressing for a greater U.S. presence, more collaboration and joint exercises, and ironclad commitments to assist in their defense. The importance of American leadership and presence around the globe was rarely more palpable than when I met with our allies and partners, especially those who faced real threats.

The defense minister of New Zealand, Ron Mark, was a pro-American former special forces officer who welcomed me on my arrival in Auckland in August 2019 with a traditional Māori *hongi* greeting, my first ever. Ron was a good partner who leaned forward on issues, which I liked. In Singapore, Ng Eng Hen is an accomplished surgeon with a wonderful sense of humor who became minister of defense in 2011. It didn't take me long to also figure out that he was a wise and extraordinary statesman. And Delfin Lorenzana, the secretary of national defense of the Philippines, was a retired general who served in that nation's army from 1973 to 2004. He was also a good partner who had trained at some of the same U.S. Army schools I had years earlier, which facilitated an easy rapport and a good relationship.

I was also able to visit or meet with partners in Vietnam, Indonesia, Mongolia, Thailand, and Palau, not to mention phone calls I had with other defense ministers and heads of state in the Pacific Island countries—a long overlooked but critical set of relationships. It was an important part of our strategy to strengthen these partnerships.

The good news is that countries in the region were largely aligned with us but seeking greater engagement from the United States. Each conversation had a few common themes: concern about China's plans and ambitions; unhappiness with the PRC's military, diplomatic, and economic bullying; a desire to work more closely and often with the U.S. armed forces, and usually in their country; and a genuine hope that Washington would continue to challenge Beijing and lead in the Indo-Pacific.

The disappointing news was that these partners were reluctant to speak publicly about China's bad behavior or stand up to them in multilateral forums, out of fear of the PRC's intimidation tactics. While there are notable exceptions to the rule, these countries tend to speak out only when parochial interests are challenged and rarely about the overall threat to the free and open order from which they benefit. This is why U.S. leadership was and remains so necessary.

Earlier in the summer, in June 2020, the so-called Five Eye partners of Australia, Canada, New Zealand, the United Kingdom, and the United States held a virtual summit to discuss the challenges facing the region, with a focus on the pandemic. Our discussion centered on how best to help other countries in the Indo-Pacific while also countering the CCP's continued bad behavior and negative COVID diplomacy. Virtual Five Eye meetings among defense ministers were an important development that should be continued beyond the demands of the pandemic. Holding such a meeting semiannually, if not quarterly, would be another way in which we could keep ourselves aligned and advance important initiatives to address the PRC.

Linda Reynolds, the Australian defense minister, whom I met during my first trip to Sydney in early August 2019, organized the first virtual meeting. Linda was a wonderful counterpart who was fluent on all the issues. She and her foreign minister seemed to make a great team. During the year, in between our annual summer meetings, we would often call or text each other. As a result, we became friends as well as colleagues, and had the benefit of our spouses befriending one another as well.

Reynolds's idea for a virtual Five Eyes meeting was brilliant. It was a good way of getting us all together without the challenge of busy schedules and long flights one way or the other. We all agreed on some basic steps we would take together when it came to COVID and China. I also mentioned our continued commitment to conducting freedom of navigation operations in the western Pacific, especially since Beijing was planning large-scale naval exercises in the South China Sea in the coming months. We wanted to make clear not only to these partners but to all our allies and partners in the region that the U.S. Navy was ready and on station, and welcomed their participation in these operations as well.

One of the most important relationships we worked to grow was the one with India, the largest democracy in the world. The U.S.-India bilateral relationship was one the United States had been building for years—through Republican and Democrat administrations alike—and at least as far back as my third stint at the Pentagon, from 2002 to 2004, when I was a deputy assistant secretary of defense in the George W. Bush administration.[*]

There were a lot of sound reasons for Washington and New Delhi to be close partners—two important democracies, shared values, a common respect for the rule of law, and a large and successful Indian diaspora in America. Geostrategically, we have common interests in matters ranging from improving energy security and defeating Islamic radicalism to the future of Afghanistan and, most certainly, the rise of China.

But the history of relations between our two countries still acted like a brake on our efforts. At the time of India's independence from the United Kingdom in 1947, many prominent Indian leaders had positive relations with the United States. The Truman administration also favored India, viewing it as a better long-term partner than Pakistan. But India's neutral stance wasn't received well in Washington as the Cold War heated up. So, in 1954, the more pro-U.S. Pakistan became an American ally under the Central Treaty Organization. In response, to offset the growing U.S.-Pakistan ties, India pursued a relationship with the Soviet Union. India later became a founding member of the non-aligned movement in 1961, in an attempt to avoid taking sides between the United States and the USSR during the Cold War, but too many in the United States still viewed New Delhi with suspicion.

President Kennedy saw things differently, much like American

---

[*]   My first job at the Pentagon was as a war planner on the Army staff from 1995 to 1996, as previously discussed. I count as my second stint at the DoD my work as a major in the National Guard performing weekend (and some weekday) duty at/ for the Office of the Secretary of Defense, Special Operations/Low-Intensity Conflict in the 2001 timeframe. For more detailed information on my life and career, please visit my website, marktesper.com.

leaders do today, with India as a strategic partner to offset the rise of China. As such, the United States publicly supported India during its 1962 border conflict with the PRC, flying in arms, ammunition, and equipment for the Indian military. With Kennedy's assassination in 1963, however, relations cooled again for decades.

It wasn't until 1991, with the collapse of the USSR and the end of the Cold War, that U.S.-Indian relations started warming and allowed for a more natural order of things to develop. The relationship accelerated during the presidency of George W. Bush, and maintained a solid pace during the Obama era. The rapport between Washington and New Delhi would reach a new level during the Trump administration.

One of the newer and more substantive developments in U.S.-India bilateral relations was the establishment of the annual 2 plus 2 meetings between the foreign and defense ministers of both countries. We held the first one of these in India in July 2018. I was fortunate to participate in the second and third sessions in December 2019 and October 2020, in Washington and New Delhi, respectively.

My Indian counterpart was Rajnath Singh, an experienced politician with many years in government who had assumed the defense post in May 2019. Singh was a solemn and reticent minister whom I found to be an able colleague. He was interested in strengthening relations between our two countries and was able to keep his ministry moving forward. This was evident as a border crisis in the Himalayas with China in 2020 heated up. The history of 1962 seemed to be repeating itself.

At our first meeting in December 2019, we were able to get a fair number of things accomplished. Singh and I had good discussions at the Pentagon, making substantial progress in our military relationship and expanding cooperation between our armed services. We launched a new annual exercise in November called Tiger

Triumph that enhanced tri-service coordination and allowed us to exchange a good deal of knowledge and expertise. We concluded what was called the Industrial Security Annex, which facilitates collaboration between our defense industries by supporting the secure transfer of key information and technology. And we also completed three agreements under the Defense Technology and Trade Initiative that we developed to enhance our ability to coproduce and codevelop critical technologies.

In his public remarks, Singh mentioned that these accomplishments—as well as the establishment of communications links between the Indian military and Indo-Pacific Command, the assignment of a liaison officer at our naval headquarters in Bahrain, and the conduct of a defense policy group meeting after a four-year hiatus—were positive steps forward. We had also made progress on maritime domain awareness, an issue of particular importance to New Delhi given the presence of Chinese ships, especially submarines, in Indian territorial waters.

Singh also pressed hard that the industrial relationship move beyond New Delhi simply buying arms from the United States. They wanted much deeper cooperation, as many nations do, such as technology sharing and coproduction. Their aim was to build up their own defense industry capabilities. This was neither new nor unreasonable, though there are inherent challenges. I had heard the same message over the previous fifteen or more years, whether it was during my tenure on Capitol Hill, when I took a business delegation from the Aerospace Industries Association to India in the mid-2000s, or during my industry time at Raytheon.

While this was an issue both sides needed to keep working on together, I was never confident that we could get to the point that India wanted and expected. The U.S. government will always work to protect certain high-end technologies, and American companies will want to do the same out of their own business interests, even from our closest of allies.

We made good progress at the broader meeting with our foreign ministry counterparts too. New agreements on space exploration, a novel exchange program for legislators, and an update on a bilateral trade deal were topics discussed. Pompeo celebrated the inaugural meeting of the Quad in September 2019, and I followed up with a push for the Quad's militaries to begin exercising together, something the Indians resisted. Our private deliberations touched on a number of international topics: Afghanistan, Iran, and, of course, China, to name a few.

During Singh's visit, we were able to host a nice dinner for the minister and his delegation at the Library of Congress, which seemed an unlikely place to hold such an event. My team did a great job setting this up, though. The dinner itself was wonderful, but the majesty of the library and its inner sanctums was a special surprise to see and share with our Indian friends. At the end of the evening, we were able to take them to a section of the library that contained several ancient and historical Indian works, written in Hindi. Singh and his team stopped at different sections of this room to read the books. He and his entourage were impressed by the works and the thoughtfulness of my event organizers. So was I.

When I broke with the president in early June 2020 over the Insurrection Act, I felt sure it would be difficult for me to stay in office through the election. And with the India trip right up against it in late October, the 2 plus 2 meeting was an engagement of such importance that I knew I would regret missing if I was fired early, but as it turned out, I was able to attend.

In the spring, a series of skirmishes developed between Indian and Chinese troops along their shared border in the Himalayas, in the historically disputed areas in Ladakh near the Tibet

Autonomous Region. The renewed friction began in late May 2020, when the Chinese objected to the building of a road by India in the Galwan River valley. The hand-to-hand fighting that took place in mid-June resulted in the deaths of twenty Indian soldiers and at least one Chinese officer, and the taking of several prisoners from both sides, in what marked the most serious conflict between the two countries in many years.

This latest incident seemed to be a transparent move by the PRC to advance its territorial claims during a global pandemic. The Himalayas were another area where Beijing was making excessive and/or illegal claims on territory and waters around its periphery, just as it was doing in the South China Sea. In other parts of the world, President Xi was using debt diplomacy, economic incentives, security cooperation, political strong-arming, and corrupt business practices to gain footholds in key strategic locations, ranging from Africa and Southeast Asia to the Pacific Island countries and South America.

The Indians were standing up to the CCP, and we wanted to help. I reached out early to Singh to offer U.S. assistance. There was some reluctance from New Delhi at first, but we were able to begin with simple information sharing about PLA activities in the mountainous region contested by the Chinese. Eventually, over a series of calls and interactions between our departments, we provided their troops with cold-weather gear so they could better operate in the harsh environment of the Himalayas, and began discussing the acceleration of certain arms purchases.

As September rolled into October, and our 2 plus 2 meeting approached, the Indians' border standoff with the Chinese remained tense despite a series of diplomatic initiatives. On the ground, neither side was budging. This made New Delhi anxious for a positive outcome during our visit.

The success of the meetings was preordained, though, thanks to the hard work of our respective teams in the months leading up to our session. The Indians were gracious hosts during our stay, and the dialogue—which marked the fifteenth anniversary of the first U.S.-India Defense Framework Initiative—went extremely well. Mike Pompeo and I also had the chance to participate in ceremonial events in Delhi, and meet with Indian prime minister Narendra Modi to further discuss the issues covered in our counterpart sessions. All in all, it was a great visit.

A major accomplishment of this third 2 plus 2 dialogue was the signing of the Basic Exchange and Cooperation Agreement for Geo-Spatial Information and Services Cooperation (BECA), which expanded the sharing of this intelligence between our armed forces. The BECA was the last of four key agreements between Washington and New Delhi considered to be crucial to the expansion of strategic ties between our countries. It was particularly relevant and timely, given the situation in the Himalayas opposite the Chinese, while also boosting U.S.-Indian military cooperation more broadly.

Our meetings also confirmed or finalized several other initiatives, such as the establishment of new cyber and space dialogues (again given the common threat of China) and the advancement of maritime security with like-minded nations such as Japan and Australia.

In the open-air press conference closing out our two days of talks, I made clear that the U.S.-India partnership remained more important than ever as we worked to ensure security, stability, and prosperity in a world under siege by a global pandemic, and as we stood shoulder to shoulder in light of increased aggression and destabilizing activities by China.

We had accomplished a great deal and moved the ball considerably forward in the time Pompeo and I had to work with our counterparts. Beijing's aggressiveness helped accelerate things too. The key going forward was to broaden, institutionalize, and regularize this cooperation.

The combined exercise in the Indian Ocean between our two navies in July 2020, which featured the USS *Nimitz* carrier strike group, was important. But even more imperative was India's decision—at our urging—to include Australia in the upcoming Malabar naval exercise among Indian, American, and Japanese forces. Including all members of the Quad in this military exercise, something Beijing opposed and New Delhi had long been reluctant to do, was a major step forward to building the partnerships needed to maintain a free and open Indo-Pacific in the years ahead.

In the grand scheme, when one looks at the arc of history since India gained its independence in 1947, it appears that U.S.-India relations are finally on the right path and making steady progress. There is much that naturally binds our two countries, and these days, the rise of China, which had been foreseen by some decades earlier, is occurring in an ominous way for both countries. If China is the greatest strategic challenge the United States will face in the twenty-first century, and I believe it is, then India is the most important strategic partnership we need to develop to deal with it.

In late August, only two months before the 2 plus 2 dialogue in India, I visited Hawaii, Guam, and Palau. In Honolulu, I spoke at the Asia-Pacific Center for Security Studies about the PLA's growing capabilities, Beijing's efforts to bully other countries and undermine the rules-based international order, and what the United

States was doing in response. My visit to Guam included a tour of our military facilities on the island, a meeting with the governor, and an extended session with the Japanese defense minister to discuss China.

And in Palau, I met with the president of the small but strategic island nation to discuss ways to improve our partnership and keep Beijing out. I also made important phone calls to the leaders of Sri Lanka and Bangladesh, the governor of the Northern Marianas, and my counterpart in Papua New Guinea. These stops and calls built on my earlier travels, when I visited New Zealand and Mongolia—the first time a secretary of defense had visited both since 2012 and 2014, respectively—and other locations such as Vietnam and the Philippines.

A major part of this visit was to get an update from Admiral Phil Davidson, the INDOPACOM commander, on the next iteration of his war planning for conflict with China. The plan continued to improve as we went back and forth on it over several months. Additionally, I wanted to better understand his vision of the theater for the future. Specifically, what would the Indo-Pacific need to look like in 2035, and what should the military footprint and capabilities of the U.S. armed forces and our partners be, if we wanted to ensure our success against a modernized PLA by the mid-2030s?

Our footprint in Asia was heavy in the northeast and too light in the southeast. Much of this was legacy positioning from the end of World War II, coupled with the challenges we continued to face with North Korea. The command recognized this too but, rather than working with the resources they had, they wanted more to spread throughout the region. To improve our presence around the mainland of China, we could look at shifting more assets from another geographic command, but there really wasn't much more available without major impacts in other areas. I pressed them to look at other options within their own control, such as rotational deployments out of Japan or off the Korean peninsula to other parts of the Indo-Pacific. I even pushed them to consider permanent intratheater adjustments, but either the initiative, innovation, or will to do so wasn't there.

Change is hard at the DoD, as it is in many organizations. For too many, change is a threat to them, their budget, or their organization. For others, it is a fear of the unknown or of failing. Some are simply content to stay in their comfort zone. At the Pentagon, the weapon of choice for getting more resources is the phrase "mission requirement," but when it comes to opposing change, the magic words are "increased risk."

Nobody wants to be blamed for a decision that risks the mission or the force. Many recall Secretary of Defense Les Aspin being forced to resign after he refused to provide tanks, armored vehicles, and other equipment requested by the U.S. commander in Somalia not long before the Battle of Mogadishu in 1993. This was the "Blackhawk down" fight that saw eighteen U.S. soldiers killed and dozens more wounded. This story still resonates at the Pentagon. But the fact is, in a resource-constrained world where threats and challenges abound, missions must be prioritized, risk must be managed, and hard decisions have to be made.

From 2019 through 2020, for example, I faced the problem of year-round staging of bombers out of Andersen Air Force Base in Guam. Since 2004, what started out as a temporary deployment of B-1 and B-52 bombers to the U.S. territory morphed into what became known as continuous bomber presence (CBP). The argument to keep bombers in Guam was that it was a mission requirement that deterred bad behavior from North Korea by having a ready capability closer to the Korean peninsula. The bombers also ostensibly reassured our allies that we would fight alongside them in conflict and allowed more training with them too. Removing the aircraft from the theater would create increased risk.

The argument for ending CBP was that it was having a harmful impact on the readiness of our bomber fleets as well as on the airmen who fly and support the planes. Additionally, it limited our flexibility to respond to other parts of the globe by stationing the aircraft in the middle of the Pacific Ocean assigned to a single command. All of this combined created its own level of risk.

I was keen to the readiness argument, but equally important, we needed to fully effectuate the National Defense Strategy. One of my Top Ten objectives included operationalizing the Dynamic Force Employment (DFE) concept. DFE meant the Pentagon would prioritize maintaining the capacity for major combat operations by employing these forces in short sprints and quick, no-notice deployments that make us less operationally predictable and more strategically flexible without wearing out the force. It was also a good way not only to reassure more of our allies and partners but to keep our adversaries off balance as well.

I also wanted to use DFE to evaluate the readiness of our Immediate Response Forces (IRF), those Army, Navy, Air Force, and Marine Corps units that had to be ready to deploy in ten days or less. To make this real, I put over $500 million in the budget for these so-called no-notice operations. I'm not sure the Defense Department had ever done anything like this at the enterprise level, but I wanted to emphasize readiness from the top down.

General Milley and I worked a good deal on this initiative. We wanted to take the operating model used in the Army whereby ready units like the 82nd Airborne Division, which were always on alert, were actually called out on a routine basis. Other services were doing this too. This would evaluate their readiness to see if they could get all their troops and equipment assembled, ready, and prepared to deploy on time. It was this readiness standard that gave us confidence in deploying the 82nd to the Middle East in January 2020.

Finally, I wanted to employ the IRF not only for readiness tests but also for preplanned training events and exercises around the world. In other words, if AFRICOM was planning a multilateral exercise in Morocco and wanted a company of Marines to take part, we could deploy them on a no-notice mission from the IRF. This would result in not only a good readiness test for the DoD but also a good training event for the units and the command.

We had debated what to do with CBP for many months, with neither side yielding to the other's arguments. Then I visited Minot Air Force Base, home of the 5th Bomb Wing, which is the B-52H unit assigned to the base. During my tour I had the chance to walk around, climb up in, and sit in the cockpit of this famous workhorse. It was also a good chance to talk with pilots, free from a crowd. A place to get the facts. We talked about CBP, the Guam mission, and their own readiness. And what they shared with me was the impacts the constant rotations were having on full mission training, crew readiness, maintenance, and families.

I went straight from the hangar to a town hall to speak to the officers, airmen, Air Force civilians, and family members assigned to the base. I enjoyed doing these events. It was a great opportunity to share with them the priorities I had for the Department—and in this case the Air Force in particular—and then have the chance to answer their questions and hear what was on their minds.

Sure enough, during the Q&A session, a spouse spoke up and told the story of her husband, whom the Air Force deployed for several months to Guam on the CBP mission. She recounted how the service extended his tour indefinitely, and about the challenges she faced as a single mom while her spouse was gone. Her story was touching and personal. I faintly recall her holding a young child in one arm with another sitting next to her as she shared this experience with the entire audience. My sense was that we were going to lose this airman and his family when reenlistment time came. As she spoke, I could see the heads of other spouses nodding in agreement.

It was an emotional story, and one I understood well from my service, and Leah's times as a single mom in Italy when my infantry battalion deployed for weeks at a time. Military life was hard, and I always thought it was most difficult for the families left behind. We often said in the Army that you "recruit the soldier but retain the family," and this spouse's tale brought that adage to life. It also reflected what I was hearing from senior Air Force officers in the Pentagon. I left Minot determined to resolve the CBP issue once and for all.

I returned to Washington, D.C., days later and decided to end the CBP in Guam. Indo-Pacific Command wasn't happy. There would be "significant risk," they said, but I had to balance a broader range of interests. Despite all the doom and gloom, other than a few foreboding stories in the military press, life went on without the bomber mission, and with our DFE operations picking up the bomber role as planned. Tellingly, I never received a phone call from any of my counterparts in Asia expressing concern about ending the CBP mission, nor did it come up in any of our meetings. That said a lot.

Within a few short months, we had bombers flying many more missions to Europe, the Middle East, and elsewhere, while still sustaining their operations in the Pacific. Picking up more of these missions was a promise made and kept by the Air Force, and I was pleased to see them go so well. In fact, in August 2020 U.S. bombers flew in formation across all thirty NATO countries in a single day as a show of support to our allies. The operation was called Allied Sky, and it featured the new Bomber Task Forces—the Air Force's name for using bombers to implement DFE—in a demonstration of our strategic reach, operational flexibility, support for allies and partners, and overall war-fighting capability.

But what really hit me was the reaction of the bomber crews. Months later, I was visiting an Air Force installation and noticed that a pilot with whom I was speaking had a tab on his left shoulder sleeve. All the tab had written on it was a date—April 17, 2020, I believe—and so I asked him what it represented. He looked me in the eye and said, "Sir, that's when CBP finally ended for us. Thank you."

In making decisions like these, you have to balance not only the competing demands between different combatant commands but also the tension between the needs of today (as represented by those combatant commands) with the needs of the future (as often represented by the services). I constantly wished more of the senior military officers would take an enterprise perspective, putting themselves in my shoes; some did this better than others. But at the end of the day, it was my job to balance these things, and to make the final call.

CHAPTER 21

UNREST IN THE NORTHWEST

"I want to go in. . . . We need to show them force," the president exclaimed. I couldn't believe it was August 2020 and we were still discussing civil unrest, except now it was Portland, Oregon, not Washington, D.C. Here we were again, back in the Oval Office, talking about sending the National Guard—who the president would need to federalize—into a city against the governor's will. It felt like Groundhog Day.

The president's eagerness to deploy military forces into U.S. cities didn't end in June. The protests in several cities, but especially Portland, seemed to drive him crazy over the summer and into the early fall. Time and again we would end up in meetings at the White House to discuss the ongoing unrest; each time we would need to push back on his proposals to send in the Guard. Bill Barr remained a good ally on this front, as did Acting Secretary of Homeland Security Chad Wolf.

We all seemed to be dealing with something that gnawed at the president viscerally. Much like in June, he seemed to take the Portland protests as personal affronts not only to his authority but to his strength and reputation. Trump would often repeat how the protests "make us look weak," and a "laughingstock," which inevitably were followed by statements that "we need to do something about this."

For me, these were serious but time-consuming distractions to the far more important work of dealing with COVID and engaging my foreign counterparts, not to mention keeping a watchful eye on China, Russia, Iran, and North Korea.

My combatant command reviews were also continuing, especially with Central Command, its long-term footprint, and the deployment of American air-defense assets in the region. We were making good, steady progress. We were also working our way through another iteration of Indo-Pacific Command's updated China war plan. All of this—coupled with Operation Warp Speed updates, finalizing our parts of the Abraham Accords, and video teleconferences with the shipbuilding industry to understand their capacity and needs—was the vital work of the Pentagon. Other important initiatives were also underway.

For example, on Monday, August 10, the White House and the DoD announced a bold plan to accelerate the development of 5G across the nation. We had quietly begun working this plan months earlier, with the aim of freeing up 100 MHz of contiguous mid-band spectrum allocated to the military to share with industry.[1] This idea had been out there for years, but the leadership among the Departments of Commerce and Defense, the National Telecommunications and Information Administration, and the White House couldn't agree on a way forward that addressed everyone's concerns, responsibilities, and objectives.

At the Pentagon, a few of us recognized the importance of 5G to the country for many reasons beyond our nation's security, such as our continued economic growth, technological leadership, and ability to stay ahead of China. Vice Chairman of the Joint Chiefs General John Hyten and Dana Deasy, the DoD's chief information officer, were real leaders on this issue. The faster speeds and reduced latency of 5G would be crucial to a range of industries and cutting-edge innovations, such as self-driving cars, that will rely on 5G, AI, and related systems. I was proud that the team, led by Deasy, took a one- to two-year process and compressed it down to four months while protecting the DoD's core equities. It was an extraordinary feat. And while it would come at some cost to the DoD in terms of altering our operational practices, changing training regimes, and making new equipment investments, it was the right thing to do.

Notwithstanding this accomplishment, Mark Meadows would push hard throughout the fall of 2020 for the Pentagon to essentially award a no-bid contract for a bigger, separate chunk of the DoD's midband spectrum. It was to be written in a way that seemed to favor a single tech company, one that had close ties to power brokers within the GOP. The White House chief of staff wanted this completed by the election and made clear on more than one occasion that Trump was fully behind it.

Neither the Pentagon nor other agency stakeholders supported this unprecedented multibillion-dollar spectrum grab. For Defense, we needed time to assess the impact of this idea on our training, exercises, testing, and the operational ways that we protect the homeland on a routine basis, for example. Moreover, the costs associated with relinquishing the spectrum, developing new capabilities and workarounds, and the risks that all this created were enormous.

We also needed time to assess a claim by the company that it had developed a unique solution called "dynamic sharing," which would supposedly allow multiple companies to operate and coexist in the same spectrum space. Extensive testing and evaluation were needed to validate these functional claims.

Importantly, we made clear on more than one occasion that Defense did not have the authority to award the spectrum. Rather, spectrum management was the purview of the Federal Communications Commission or the National Telecommunications and Information Administration, depending on whether it is a nongovernmental or governmental application, respectively. Meadows pressed just the same. Fortunately, the deliberate churn of our internal processes and continued messaging back to the White House with our interagency counterparts blunted this dubious idea.

That same day the official White House spectrum initiative was announced, August 10, the *Washington Post* ran a story with the headline "Unrest in Chicago and Portland Shows America's Summer of Protest Is Far from Over."[2] Over the preceding weekend, protesters had looted stores in downtown Chicago and set the police union headquarters in Portland ablaze. These things infuriated Trump. At this point in the campaign, law and order was his theme, and these actions struck at the heart of this mantra. In the previous days, as the Department of Homeland Security (DHS) withdrew agents from Portland to de-escalate the situation, things had calmed down some. But the weekend was rough, and on that Monday Trump tweeted, "Portland, which is out of control, should finally, after almost 3 months, bring in the National Guard. The Mayor and Governor are putting people's lives at risk. They will be held responsible. The Guard is ready to act immediately."

Trump called for an 8:00 A.M. meeting the next day in the Oval Office to discuss what to do. I had just flown to South Carolina for a few days off at the beach with Leah. We had not taken vacation in over a year and were not off to a good start that Monday. Tuesday was already looking bad. I should have stayed in D.C., I thought, as I prepped for the meeting. I called into the Oval Office session. Bill Barr, Chad Wolf, Mark Milley, and Ken Cucinelli, who was serving as the "Senior Official Performing the Duties of the Deputy Secretary of Homeland Security," were also present.

Trump was still irritated and started off aggressively, as he typically did. He wasn't one to put an issue on the table and then listen for feedback, or at least give others the illusion of hearing them out first, he went straight to the matter: "I want to go in. . . . We need to show them force!" Barr quickly jumped in, as he should have; this was a law enforcement matter, not a military one. The attorney general was the point person, followed by Wolf; they needed to lead the discussion. In my view, if I was talking, that wasn't a good thing. Being on the other end of a phone line helped me here, but Milley was trapped in the room.

Barr led with "If you do this, more cities will go south," meaning that the unrest and violence would spread. Bill and I had discussed this a few times previously and believed it would be the consequence of sending in the military. He added that law enforcement didn't have the resources to handle this if the violence spread. Trump responded, "The Guard got control of Minneapolis in an hour. We need to show force. I want to go into Chicago with force." Barr kept pushing back, now arguing from a political angle that the violence in these cities was actually working against the Democrats.

The back-and-forth continued, with Barr proposing that Justice and DHS put together a strategy to deal with the violence in a more comprehensive way, and that they would come back to the president in two to three weeks to brief him. This was good. Barr was buying time, the DoD wasn't mentioned, and the president hadn't directed any questions at Milley or me yet. But Trump wasn't persuaded.

The president was unrelenting, saying, "We look weak, and stupid, and pathetic. . . . It looks badly on us." He added, "I'm running for reelection and we have cities burning down. . . . We have to go and do something. We need to be on the offensive. . . . You need to shoot that person [that throws a rock at you]." Oh my God, were we back to talking about shooting people again? I couldn't believe it. I set down my pen and put my hands over my face as I shook my head, a convenient luxury that a distant phone connection provides. I thought . . . hoped . . . that such a notion had left him. Yet here we were again.

The debate wasn't moving along enough, so I felt it was time to jump in and support Barr. Bill and I didn't have the chance to speak before the meeting, but he was spot-on. This was indeed a law enforcement action. There was no need whatsoever for the military, including the National Guard. If a state needed the Guard, then the governors had all the authority they required to call them up and put them to work. Plus, the states weren't Washington, D.C. Any mobilization of Guard units to deploy to another state needed the consent of *both* governors, *unless* the Insurrection Act was invoked, which was something we definitely didn't need or want. In short, Barr's plan needed to succeed. After all, DOJ's success would mean the DoD's success.

Taking a little time to look at the problem more comprehensively, and then coming back with a strategy for the president's review, was the way to tackle tough, complex issues. It also allowed time for things to settle down, and for law enforcement to work the issues behind the scenes. It wasn't the way of this White House, though. "Fire, aim, ready" was the typical approach, and too many folks around Trump enabled that style of decision making. So, with the president still undecided, and having learned that more voices opposing him always helped, I decided to weigh in. "Mr. President,

I support Bill's plan. This is a law enforcement action, and I recommend we let him come back in a few weeks to present it."

I told him that these cities are all different, and in Minneapolis "we had a supportive governor who knew the Guard, and who had all the authority he needed to act." But "these cities all have different histories and cultures and leadership; things we can't change," I said. I followed up with words to the effect of, "And if you go in heavy, with force, then it will spread across the country, and we'll be dealing with this for the next few months. You don't want to own that." Milley had been uncharacteristically quiet throughout the meeting, but helpfully jumped in behind me with facts and stats that downplayed the extent of the unrest and the violence.

Trump watched TV all day long, and that gave him a distorted view—a "soda straw" perspective, we'd say—about what was happening. There really weren't that many people causing violence: it just looked that way through the camera lens of Fox News. The bottom line was that the country wasn't burning—a phrase mentioned by Trump and often used by Stephen Miller to incite him—and that we were basically talking about three cities: Chicago, Portland, and Seattle. And in each of these, the violent actors were a small minority of those on the streets.

The facts never seemed to stop Miller from egging on the president's worst instincts, however, using hyperbole like the "the cities are burning down" and "the governor" or "the mayor" has "lost control of the situation." Miller's implication was that a tough federal response was not just recommended, but necessary if we were going to "save our country from Antifa," as he pressed for invocation of the Insurrection Act. Milley and I tended to ignore Miller, but he somehow seemed to press Bill Barr's buttons in ways no one else could. Not surprisingly, Bill erupted on him again, yelling back, "You don't know what the hell you're talking about," and then making a reference to the 1993 siege of a religious sect in Waco, Texas, by law enforcement and the military. Twenty law enforcement agents were either killed or wounded in the incident, as well as over seventy others. Nobody wanted a repeat of anything close to Waco, especially the attorney general.

The conversation went back and forth a little longer, with both Wolf and Cucinelli finally speaking up as well in support of Barr's proposal. DHS had been bearing the brunt of the work in Portland, with agents defending the federal buildings the violent agitators seemed to be going after. I had spoken to Chad Wolf a couple of weeks earlier, and I knew that his folks were worn down. He too was looking for ways to de-escalate.

In the face of this unified front, Trump finally yielded. He wasn't happy about it. I pictured him sitting behind his desk, with his arms folded across his chest, shaking his head slowly, with a frustrated look on his face. He grudgingly, hesitatingly, said, "Okay, come back with a plan then . . . in two to three weeks . . . but it needs to be an offensive plan . . . and should include the National Guard." He seemed to feel the need to throw in that last part about the Guard. Not only did it reflect his predilection, and indeed his intention, but it was a way to yield the discussion without completely conceding.

Nine days later, on August 20, I was in Colorado to host the changes of command for Northern Command and Space Command. These ceremonies are important events used to inform everyone of the seamless transfer of command from one leader to another, to honor the outgoing officer, and to welcome the new one. It's also a chance to speak about the important roles that NORTHCOM and now SPACECOM play in our nation's defense.

I was especially proud of our establishment of Space Command in August 2019, and its critical role as the war-fighting command—as compared to the Space Force with its manning, training, and equipping duties—in protecting U.S. defense and commercial assets in the heavens by being ready to "conduct offensive and defensive space operations." This ultimate high ground is vital not only to our security but also to the global economy, science, and our way of life.[3] With Russia and China militarizing space, and seeing it as a domain where they could cripple U.S. capabilities in the first moves of a future conflict, Space Command would be a game changer in preventing that outcome. The DoD published a Defense Space Strategy in June 2020 that addressed these matters.

As for Northern Command, they had responsibility for leading the DoD's support to civilian authorities, which meant deploying troops to help during hurricanes, wildfires, floods, and any other type of natural disaster that hits the country. They were also responsible for COVID support across the country, such as helping cities and states set up hospitals, move supplies, and administer tests. NORTHCOM had a very busy, but also very successful, year, and deserved some extra special recognition and attention.

As I reviewed my remarks a few minutes before going on stage at 10:00 A.M., my aide interrupted to say that Chief of Staff Meadows wanted to speak with me about Portland. Portland? I had not heard of anything happening the evening before. Apparently, he was calling to see if the National Guard was "ready." What did that mean? Ready for what *exactly*? I didn't recall Meadows being on the phone call with Trump the week prior, so maybe he was playing catch-up. More likely, however, was that he was reacting to something the president said.

My team told Meadows I was about to go onstage, so he instead tried to call General Dan Hokanson, the new chief of the National Guard Bureau, I was informed later. What was so urgent? I asked at that point. DHS told us nothing was happening anywhere in the country, including Portland, that they couldn't handle. Moreover, if something did, then they would go to Justice first. Chad Wolf and his team were being good partners, and I appreciated that.

They understood our view on the "tiering of forces," as we called it, with Defense being last in the queue. But why was Meadows pushing, and why was he reaching into the DoD? He had told me he was a "chain of command" guy who would work through me, but this was another example where he proved not to be what he said he was. I kept this in mind as we approached November 3.

I was fortunate to now have General Dan Hokanson at the helm of the National Guard. Dan and I had known each other since we were classmates at West Point. Tall and lean with a distance runner's frame—which he did as a top athlete for the academy—he became an aviator after we graduated. Like me, he left active duty after several years, but eventually joined the Army National Guard in Oregon. His experiences after that would serve him especially well in his new role. He served as the adjutant general of the Oregon Guard, made deployments to Iraq and Afghanistan, and was the deputy commander of NORTHCOM. Dan was exceptionally well qualified to be chief of the National Guard Bureau. He was also smart and a team player who was easy to work with, and, importantly, I knew that I could count on him to do the right thing.

By the time the ceremony was over and I was available to talk, the issue had faded. Meadows no longer needed to speak with me. What happened? Maybe he spoke to Barr, who told him of our meeting on the eleventh and the agreement that he would be bringing the president a new strategy in another week or so. Or maybe it was Wolf. Chad had the right approach as well.

I never found out. I ended up having to shut down a more urgent matter regarding Iran that the NSC was pushing at the same time. I'll address this matter later. Nevertheless, the combination of the two issues simultaneously led me to conclude that the president was acting out, and in ways that could produce dire consequences if unchecked. The DoD was once again in the center of the storm and having to apply the brakes.

On Tuesday, August 25, I flew to Hawaii to participate in a number of long-scheduled events: commemorating the seventy-fifth anniversary of the end of World War II; an Indo-Pacific chiefs of defense virtual gathering; and my various meetings in Palau and Guam, as already discussed.

That morning in Hawaii, I spoke with Bill Barr again by phone. He told me the president was pushing him on the Insurrection Act because "he want[ed] to send the Guard into Portland"—so much for Trump waiting for a strategy based on a law enforcement lead—but that he had refused. Neither Barr nor his lawyers "believe[d] that the situation warrant[ed] invoking the Insurrection Act," nor did we. However, he was "concerned about events getting out of control" in cities like Kenosha, Wisconsin, where violence had flared the previous couple of nights after an African American man, Jacob Blake, was shot in the back by police as he opened the door to his car with his three young sons inside.

Barr didn't want law enforcement caught short if things spiraled out of control, so he asked if I could "put one to two thousand Guardsmen on alert around the country for the next sixty days or so." I understood his reasoning, and it made some sense, but doing so presented some challenges. First of all, I told him, "I don't like the optics of National Guard units on standby around the country, prepared to intervene in another state." I added, "It looks like we're enabling the president's worst instincts." In addition, it risked making the DoD "look political" in the wake of June 1.

Given all that transpired, I liked the fact that it would probably take twenty-four hours to get a Guard unit mobilized, organized, trained, equipped, and deployed. That bought time for elected leaders to calm things down, and for me to argue for more law enforcement first. I didn't say this to Bill, however. Barr saw it differently, I supposed—as a way to fend off another call to bring in the active-duty forces. I couldn't argue with that rationale either, but I was still reluctant.

We talked through the issue a little further. The anxiety in Bill's voice was increasing, which led me to believe that Trump was pressing him harder than he was letting on—which in turn maybe meant we were closer to invocation of the Insurrection Act than Barr was revealing. Bill was always on my side on this matter, so I relented and told him, "I'll have General Milley get with the Guard and start working up some options. I'll get back to you after that, Bill."

Milley and Hokanson called me back later in the day. A couple of thousand Guardsmen was more than they felt necessary and more than they could sustain, which confirmed my instinct when Barr first raised it. They were, however, proposing to put one Alabama National Guard Military Police company (which normally numbered around 150 soldiers) on duty for two weeks, and one Guard MP company from Arizona to do the same. The adjutant generals from both states supported this; they just needed to get their governors' okay once I approved it. This wasn't the two-month period Barr was looking for, but it would get us through the GOP convention happening that week, a march planned for D.C. on August 28, and Labor Day weekend. During that time, Milley and Hokanson would work on more sustainable options. I approved the plan and then called Barr to update him. He was good with it as well.

On September 4, a group of us met with Meadows at the White House to brief him on the long-term plan to have Guard MPs available around the country. Generals Hokanson and Milley joined me, with Barr and Wolf on the phone, and Stephen Miller there in person. Hokanson talked everyone through the details, which basically called for four MP companies—two in Arizona and two in Alabama—to be on alert over the next sixty to ninety days. This would get us through the election plus a little longer. Units within these companies would be at a tiered readiness level, with a platoon ready to deploy within two hours of being alerted, for example. This allowed us to manage the force in a way that wouldn't burn them out and shouldn't affect their civilian employers too much.

Meadows liked the plan, as did Barr and the others. General Milley and I were careful to point out a few times that, "even with this approach, when transportation timelines and all were factored in, it would still take ten or more hours after being alerted to get the Guard 'ready platoon' on the streets somewhere." And that wasn't even factoring in getting permission from each state's governor, coordination on the ground with local Guard units, and so on, we added. "That's why," I said, "it's important to have law enforcement—local, county, state, and federal—more ready and available, if not already on the scene." I stated, "We wanted to avoid militarizing the issue." With that, the group broke up with plans to brief the president at 2:30 P.M.

As the meeting with Trump began in the Oval Office that afternoon, everyone was in the room except Barr and Wolf, who for some reason I don't believe joined us by phone either. I kicked things off, saying, "Mr. President, I want to run you through a plan we developed to have a force of National Guard MPs ready to deploy on short notice around the country, if governors need them." I told Trump that we basically had "four MP companies, with two each in Alabama and Arizona, at tiered readiness levels, on alert through at least November 15." The president leaned forward on the Resolute desk, arms folded across it, nodded in seeming agreement as I spoke. I turned to General Milley to explain how the tiered readiness would work, the timelines for alert, deployment, and arrival, and other key factors, just as we set forth in the earlier meeting in Meadows's office. General Hokanson largely sat silently, adding in details at times when Milley turned to him.

The conversation meandered a bit, as it normally did, but the president conveyed his eagerness to send the Guard into Portland. "We're going to need to send them in," he said. "It's out of control up there" in Portland. He repeated his monologue that the unrest makes him "look weak" and the country "look bad." We need to "get tough," he said a few times.

We listened and then responded. I was sitting directly in front of the president with Milley to my left, much like we normally did. We were used to being in the Oval Office and hearing the president talk, but Hokanson was a newcomer to the stage. He was farther off to my left, sitting uncomfortably in his chair, keeping a stone-faced demeanor. When Trump talked about the situation in Portland and using the Guard there, I was tempted to push back and cite the fact that Hokanson served as the adjutant general in charge of all Guard troops in Oregon from 2013 to 2015, but I didn't want to drag him unnecessarily into the fray simply to reinforce points I kept trying to land.

Milley kept trying to make the case that "there really aren't that many protesters, Mr. President," and that "the media is making the situation look worse than it [is]." I picked up the ball and said, "Mr. President, if the military goes in, it will get dramatically worse there and across the country." I added, "Let the mayors of these cities, and their governors, deal with this. They understand the issue best and they have the resources to handle it." Trump acknowledged these things but came back to the necessity to "show force" and not "look weak."

Stephen Miller spoke up from the back of the room, a voice of doom describing a "carnage" that was spreading across America, with cities on fire and Antifa in control. He made it all sound like an apocalypse. In the earlier meeting with Meadows, he had said the United States "risked turning into a dystopia," which provoked a verbal backlash from Barr. In Miller's mind, the barbarians were at the gate, and we should unleash the military.

If there were "only a few" violent protesters, he said in response to a statistic from Milley, then the military "should be able to quickly put them down." Milley fumed at this retort, but I don't recall the chairman shouting back at him as others reported, though I do remember Milley lamenting to me privately after the meeting that he "should have told him [Miller] to shut the fuck up!" The general always took the high road, however, and ignored such stupidity with a simple look of disgust.

Regardless, the fact is that Miller didn't seem to get it. He didn't seem to understand that, for every person you unnecessarily used a heavy hand against, two, three, or four more would rise up in their place. In my view, everything was black-and-white to him, and he couldn't see beyond the next move. Like Trump, the answer to most problems for him seemed to be overwhelming force and its blunt employment. All this did was rile the president back up.

I agreed that we shouldn't tolerate violence. All it did was hurt people, damage property, and impede the peaceful protesters. But you had to separate the large majority of peaceful protesters exercising their First Amendment rights from the small minority of people breaking the law. Trump, Miller, and others couldn't seem to make that distinction. Rather than using an overwhelming law enforcement presence to protect the former and arrest the latter, Miller seemed to want to use the military to go after them all.

Trump picked up the phone and asked an assistant to "connect me immediately with the governor of Oregon," Kate Brown. Once on the line, the president was respectful but doing his best to make the case for her to "get tough." He was practically pleading with her—"Kate, Kate, you need to get tough with them. . . . You need to arrest them if we're going to end the violence." He added, "I'm ready with the National Guard." She too was respectful, and thanked him for his offer to send in the Guard, but said she wasn't in the same spot as him and "didn't see the situation the same way." The call was surprisingly professional: she fended off his arguments and pleas deftly, and ended it after a few minutes.

Both sensing and wanting the meeting to end, I leaned forward in my chair, preparing to stand and leave. Assuming his approval, I said "Thanks for your time, Mr. President. We'll start moving forward on this plan." And with that, the meeting ended. I had no confidence that this was the end of the discussion, however, but I wanted to get out of the room before Stephen Miller suggested another kooky idea or started spinning the president back up. I had been on the end of this yo-yo too many times, doing my best to keep the military off America's streets. It seemed only a matter of time, especially with White House staff like Miller egging him on.

And then, fate intervened. The hundred days or so of protests in Portland that began in late May petered out a few days after the September 4 White House meeting as wind gusts ripping through Oregon and Washington state brought a heavy blanket of smoke from the wildfires burning farther south. The dense smoke that descended on Portland made it hard to breathe and see, so the protesters stayed inside. This lasted only a couple of weeks, but it was enough to break the fever and give law enforcement the opportunity to rest and refit.

While all of this was going on, my pace within the Pentagon didn't slacken. I had to keep moving forward on the "inside offense" part of my game plan. Defense strategy implementation meetings, with a focus on Europe and Africa, occurred, along with budget discussions focused on increasing investment in hypersonics and AI, and improving training and exercises across the joint force. We also had a series of discussions to finalize our proposal for a future naval force, which was enriched by a midmonth visit with the Navy in San Diego to spend a day on an aircraft carrier, and then see a few of the unmanned vehicles the sea service was developing. It was all great stuff.

As September rolled into October, we started becoming less concerned about Trump deploying the military to deal with protesters, and more anxious that he might be tempted to do something on November 3, or the days that followed, if things went badly with the election. There was nothing concrete we could point to, but I had been at this now for months, and I knew Trump's instincts, and the nature of some of the loyalists in his immediate orbit.

None of us at Defense saw a role for the military in the election, other than what we did on the cyber defense front, or what the Guard historically did to logistically support election officials in some states. Trump's rhetoric, though, was setting the stage for him to claim voter fraud if he lost the election. But would he ask the military to get involved somehow? The media was reporting that many people were worried about such a thing, with theories circulating that the president might order the military to collect ballot boxes or oversee state recounts. I thought calling out the military to deal with civil unrest if violence broke out over the election results was far more plausible. Again, I had no indication that anything like the former was being considered, but I knew the president and those closest to him well enough by now to expect anything. We needed to be ready just in case.

On the afternoon of October 22, I had a conference call that invited all fifty state adjutant generals (TAGs)—the individuals in charge of the National Guard in their respective states—as well as the four TAGs from D.C. and the territories, to discuss the upcoming election. I thanked them for all the great work their soldiers and airmen had done so far this year. It was probably the most challenging period for the Guard in over four decades, but an epic one that highlighted the professionalism, commitment, and breadth of skills that the Guard brought to the states and nation.

I acknowledged up front with the TAGs that some Guard personnel routinely supported elections, and some did not. And for those that did, their role was often unique to the state and their electoral practices. I also recognized that they were operating under the authorities of the governors, and not under my legal authority. If I didn't like something they were doing, or that a governor asked them to do, I more likely than not couldn't order them to stop. Rather, I'd have to call the governor and raise the issue with him or her directly.

That said, my request of the TAGs was to keep us in the Pentagon informed about their activities and let us know immediately if they were, or expected to be, directed to do something out of the normal. I expressed my concerns about the optics of service members in uniform on Election Day, and how our fellow citizens, the media, or elected leaders could misinterpret our role. At the end of the day, most people don't understand—and probably don't care—about the distinctions between active, Guard, and Reserve units. In their minds, the uniform makes them all the same, even though they are quite different.

I also asked everyone to keep elected officials, community leaders, and the media well informed too, so as to prevent any misunderstandings about the role and mission of Guard personnel in the days leading up to and following November 3. I implored them to start doing this now and was pleasantly surprised to learn that many had already begun that process in their states.

With that, a couple of TAGs briefed me on the role Guard cyber units were playing in their states to safeguard the integrity of the election. A few others updated me on the logistical support roles they were performing. Sixteen states were asking their Guard units to provide some sort of assistance on Election Day, with another four states involved in cyber security. I took several questions before we wrapped up and then thanked them once again for their efforts.

By the end of October, the anxiety level about Election Day was sky-high, and conspiracy theories involving the military seemed to be everywhere. Some stories out there spoke of possible moves by the White House to seize ballot boxes in contested states and employ the military to hold a new election if Trump was losing, to suspend the Constitution, and declare a limited martial law. More credible was the possibility that hard-core activists on the losing side, right or left, would fill the streets and become violent.

These were crazy days, so I didn't want to take anything for granted. I had watched as the president became more aggressive, egged on by some in the White House, as the election neared and the polls remain unchanged with Biden at a high single-digit lead. I also knew that he often turned to the military when times got tough. So I needed to think through all contingencies, and make sure I had circuit breakers in place in the event things started spinning out of control, as they had in early June.

At my direction, Mark Milley had put word out long ago to the combatant commanders to give us a heads-up at once if they ever received a phone call from anyone in the White House, especially if any unusual requests came with it. This system had worked well in the past for more routine matters, so I knew the commanders would be diligent. With the election looming, however, I was more focused now on the National Guard.

I asked Generals Hokanson and Milley to meet with me privately on the afternoon of October 30, the last Friday before the election. The ostensible purpose of the meeting for scheduling—since many people in the Pentagon had access to my calendar—was to get an update on the Guard MP companies we still had on alert in Alabama and Arizona, as well as any final modifications to the adjutant generals' support to their states over the coming days.

The three of us sat in the large conference room across the hall from my office. Hokanson was seated to my left, and Milley to my right, at the end of the long table. My chief of staff and one other person from my team joined us, sitting in chairs along the broad, back wall. The relative emptiness of the room made it seem quiet and lonely. This was a serious moment.

With the updates on the Guard MP companies completed, I turned to Hokanson and took a deep breath as I thought through the right words to say next. I looked him straight in the eye and said, "General Hokanson . . ." with the formality that our respective positions called for, followed by "Dan," which our thirty-eight years of friendship made more appropriate, and started talking in a very matter-of-fact manner, underlining the seriousness with which I took this next matter. I told him that "if at any point in the coming days—before, during, or after the election—you get a call from *anyone* at the White House, take it, acknowledge the message, and call me immediately." I said, "The same rule applies if you hear of any TAGs or governors getting a similar call." I then asked him to figure out a discreet way to get this last part out, which he said he would.

Without being too explicit, my message was clear: The U.S. military was not going to get involved in the election, no matter who directed it. I would intercede. Hokanson understood. We had known each other since our plebe year at West Point. "Duty, Honor, Country" and obeying our oath to the Constitution were drilled into him, just like me. I could count on him.

The fact was, I needed mechanisms in place—circuit breakers—should the White House try to circumvent me to do something inappropriate. There seemed to be too much of this happening as of late, and I wanted to be ready for anything. I was the sole civilian in the chain of command between the president and the uniformed military, after all, and had a critical role to perform.

Moreover, the whole point of my game plan—the reason that I had taken so much crap over the last several months—was to be in this position, at this moment, to act. The essence of American democracy was free and fair elections, followed by the peaceful transition of power. If we didn't have that, then what type of democracy did we have? It was my goal to protect this precious gift our Founders gave us. That's what our oath to the Constitution was all about.

I had several cards to play if we arrived at that point, but first and foremost, I knew this was a decision for civilian leadership—me, the Senate-confirmed secretary of defense—to make and act upon. Not the general officers. General Milley privately told me that he and the Joint Chiefs discussed such a scenario, and all had agreed to resign if pressed to break their oath. I told him that I couldn't allow that situation to happen. I couldn't allow them to be put in such a compromising position, especially if the presidential order was legal but grossly wrong or inappropriate. This would be a real dilemma, and it would be bad for the republic, the institution, and civilian control of the military if they had to decide one way or the other.

If such an order came from the White House, my immediate

recourse would be to demand a meeting with the president. I would want to hear and understand the directive straight from him, to offer alternative solutions if such were possible, and to voice my opposition face-to-face if he was unyielding. If I was unsuccessful, I would be forced to resign on the spot in protest. But that wouldn't be the end of the line for me.

My next moves would have been a combination of actions, such as phone calls to senior Republicans on Capitol Hill requesting their intercession with the president, followed by a press conference where I informed the country about all that had transpired and continued to unfold. I would present my best case and make an appeal to the American people, their elected leaders in Congress, and the institutions of government to intervene. The point would be to buy time and put pressure on the president to stand down.

November 3 came and went without any incident involving the armed forces. Thank God. I'd like to believe that any temptation to misuse the military in some fashion was tempered by the president's, and his staff's, certain knowledge that I wouldn't do his bidding.

In the weeks and months leading up to the election, close friends and colleagues would ask me my thoughts on the contest. I would simply say that I wanted the election to be "clean and clear," meaning no corruption that could overturn the results, and an electoral vote margin large enough to prevent any serious challenge to the outcome. If we had a repeat of what happened in Florida in 2000, with only a few hundred votes deciding the winner of the contest, that could be an invitation for mischief.

I was relieved, then, to wake up on the morning of November 4 to learn that the election was *not* in fact balanced on a razor-thin margin. Joe Biden was ahead with large enough vote counts in enough states, coupled with strong indications that other open races were trending his way, that it would be difficult for Trump to seriously challenge the results. The American people had spoken and the outcome was obvious, and becoming more certain with each passing day.

That said, I was not surprised by the allegations of fraud and malfeasance that some GOP officials would begin levying. Trump and his campaign did the same and began exploring ways to challenge some of the vote counts. That was part of the process, and it is important to the integrity of any election that credible allegations be investigated. It would delay the outcome, I thought, but not too long, and would most likely not change it.

I never imagined, however, that these challenges would go on and on, and play out through November, December, and January. It was a national embarrassment that undermined our democracy, our credibility, and our leadership on the world stage.

CHAPTER 22

OCTOBER SURPRISES

As October arrived, our political antennae at the Pentagon had to be recalibrated again. We were a little over four weeks away from the election and Trump still trailed Biden in the polls, though things appeared to be tightening some. Around this time of year, the media and political pundits began the quadrennial speculation about October surprises that could dramatically take the election in one direction or another. This was on our minds as well, ever cognizant that use of the military can be a way for a president to wrap himself in the flag and take an action abroad that would have a decent chance of rallying the country around him for a short period. While the White House can take actions such as these to boost a president's ratings, his opponents can launch their own surprises that can tarnish him.

Some thought the report by the *New York Times* on September 27, 2020, claiming Trump paid only $750 in federal income taxes in 2016 and 2017, and that in ten of the previous fifteen years, he allegedly paid no income taxes at all, was the first effort at damaging the president.[1] I was more concerned that someone in the White House would look to do the opposite—boost Trump's ratings—by tasking the U.S. military to do something extraordinary. Something that would cross one or more of my Four Nos. I wanted no part in political maneuverings like this.

These concerns weren't without merit. I had been down this path a few times before. The most recent had occurred a month or so before, as I briefly referenced in an earlier chapter, and it involved Iran.

Iran continued to be a top priority for the administration but took a backseat as the Afghanistan peace deal became the focus of attention in February 2020, followed by COVID from March onward. At the Pentagon, and certainly in CENTCOM, that was definitely not the case. Tensions remained high with Tehran, the Iraqi government was still in turmoil, the fate of the U.S. presence in the country was uncertain, and the militia groups were more unpredictable than ever.

Tehran was trying to keep them under control, though—a good sign that we had restored deterrence—but every now and then one of the groups felt the need to shoot a few rockets at Americans. This was the state of play by the summer of 2020.

On July 7, National Security Adviser Robert O'Brien organized a meeting, chaired by Vice President Pence, to discuss options the various departments should consider taking against Iran to address their uranium enrichment efforts. It was a full meeting, with Mark Meadows, State, CIA, the Office of the Director of National Intelligence, Defense, Treasury, and Commerce attending. O'Brien kicked off the discussion with a visible sense of urgency, his voice pitched and speech rapid. His description of the situation was quite alarmist; his personal assessment seemed far different from what the intelligence community (IC) was reporting. The specific concern was about an Iranian "breakout," which means the time required for Tehran to produce enough weapons-grade uranium for one nuclear weapon. Then, of course, separate from this process is the additional time it takes to design and assemble an actual nuclear device. The IC was confident in their ability to determine these things. O'Brien wasn't. He seemed to think the Iranians were much closer to doing both.

Each of the departments walked through their ongoing and planned actions, with a good discussion on the topic of sanctions. The Treasury, the CIA, and the DoD also reported in. O'Brien was pushing for ███████ and military action, with Pence subtly leaning in behind him, also seeming to support some type of action. I pushed back, asking, "What's the rush? Why act in the next ninety days, if the CIA has confidence in their timelines?" O'Brien squirmed in his chair a little, leaned in slightly, and quickly responded with "The president has an appetite to do something." Aha. Mark Meadows quickly jumped in to contradict this statement, which was both smart and curious. What is going on at the White House? I asked myself. Why do these two have such different views about what Trump wants? Why are we even having this meeting in the first place? We went around and around a few more times discussing other things, with various takeaways from the meeting, and some follow-ups here and there, but there was no directive for kinetic action by the DoD.

About six weeks later, on August 20, I was in Colorado Springs hosting the changes of command for Northern Command and Space Command. This was the same event when Mark Meadows called me about civil unrest in Portland. General Milley showed up about thirty minutes prior to the event, having recently arrived from D.C., and asked to speak with me privately.

We went to a small room that was cluttered with a couple of desks and other workplace items. As he stood there in his dress uniform, speaking in hushed tones, General Milley updated me on a few things. The most alarming matter was a call he received from Robert O'Brien the evening before. O'Brien told him that the president wanted to strike a senior Iranian military officer who was operating outside of Iran. Milley and I were aware of this person and the trouble he had been stirring in the region for a long time. But why now? What was new? Was there an imminent threat? What about gathering the national security team to discuss this? Milley said he was "stunned" by the call, and he sensed that "O'Brien put the president up to this," trying to create news that would help Trump's reelection. The chairman had maneuvered to quickly end the call by telling the national security adviser, "We'll need to look at the intelligence and discuss the matter with CENTCOM. And then I'll talk with Secretary Esper."

I couldn't believe it. I had seen this movie before, where White House aides meet with the president, stir him up, and then serve up one of their "great ideas." But this was a really bad idea with very big consequences. How come folks in the White House didn't see this?

I told the chairman that, for the record, we were *not* going to do anything with this message until I received a written order from the president. If O'Brien called back, he was to tell him that. I would do the same if O'Brien raised it with me. There was no way I was going to unilaterally take such an action—particularly one fraught with a range of legal, diplomatic, political, and military implications, not to mention that it could plunge us into war with Iran—without the opportunity to tease these issues out, discuss them with my fellow cabinet members, and so on. I needed to learn the facts, hear the intelligence assessment, understand the issue we were trying to resolve, and then measure it all against my Nine Considerations. And then, I would want to meet with the president to offer my views and recommendations, and to give him options. That was my duty.

While as surprising as this might be for most, it was not for me. Months earlier, on February 19, I had visited Minot Air Force Base in North Dakota to meet airmen and officers responsible for manning two legs of our nuclear triad. The next day, I traveled to Omaha, Nebraska, to meet with the leadership team of U.S. Strategic Command. On the flight home that evening, I received word that O'Brien wanted the DoD to strike a couple of targets in western Syria.

Apparently the NSC received some type of information that a terrorist(s) was in or near a refugee camp. O'Brien was requesting that we get the location from his staff and quickly organize a strike to "take out the bad guys." Nobody could verify the information, though. Even if we could, there were several issues we had to take into consideration, such as legality, diplomatic impact, collateral damage, and the effect on other missions, not to mention disrupting the uneasy standoff between Russian, Syrian, and Turkish forces in the area. For some on the NSC staff, it seemed that these questions were details that really didn't need to be considered and that the interagency didn't need to be aware of, let alone discuss—as if the Defense Department should just send up aircraft and start shooting missiles at people. This was ludicrous, and it was one of the main reasons I was so concerned—going back much earlier—that, if I resigned my position, who would the president install behind me, and then what would they do? Would they act on these crazy ideas?

I spoke with Milley about this, and later called Gina Haspel and Mike Pompeo. Pompeo wasn't aware of the action, but Haspel was. She was as taken aback as I was and was drafting a formal letter of objection for the record to send O'Brien. I should have probably done the same, but a verbal conveyance seemed sufficient at the time. I would later start putting more of my objections and concerns in written form, however. To close out this matter at the time, I told my folks to ignore the directive. If someone in the NSC wanted this to happen, I would need an order from the president and the opportunity to discuss it with him.

O'Brien's call in late August regarding a strike on the Iranian officer was the last time something involving Iran seriously came up before the election. Milley and I kept a careful watch on it, though, concerned about breaching our Four Nos, and were equally pleased to see that Tehran was acting with relative restraint. We needed this uneasy situation to hold.

But now it was October, and on Friday the second, the president revealed that he and the First Lady had tested positive for COVID-19. I learned of this news while in Morocco, on day four of a previously planned trip to North Africa that we had postponed several months due to the pandemic. My travels had me leaving the capital, Rabat, the next day for Kuwait, with a quick stop in Qatar first. The purpose behind my unplanned visit to Kuwait City was to pay my respects on the president's behalf, and to express the condolences of the United States on the recent passing of Sheikh Sabah Al-Ahmad Al-Sabah, the emir of Kuwait. The Kuwaitis had always been good friends of the United States, hosted thousands of American service members in their small oil-rich country, and were a moderating voice in the region. It was important to visit with them during such a difficult time.

I had remained in touch over the weekend with the vice president, and on Sunday, October 4, we had a planned call with the president. He wanted to get an update from his national security team, so Pence, Pompeo, O'Brien, Milley, and I (from the plane on my way back to Washington) joined on a secure call with Trump and Meadows, both of whom were at Walter Reed.

It took a few minutes to get the president on the line, so the rest of us chatted while we waited. I was unsure of what we would hear when he finally did sign on. Based on what the news shows were saying, I was expecting a weak, faint voice to greet us. Maybe struggling ever so slightly to catch a breath. Asking questions but not really engaged, though enough to make this a "check the box" moment that the White House press team could trumpet to the world.

But then Trump jumped on the line, opening with a strong "Hello, everyone" and sharing that he was "feeling great" and that "Melania and I are doing well, never felt better." He sounded surprisingly good and very engaged, much like any other day, a far different profile than what many in the press were conveying. Indeed, one of the reporters traveling with me had tweeted a day or so before that Trump was "incapacitated." In my view, this was a reckless statement, and we had no idea how she was able to make such an assessment thousands of miles away in Morocco.

Trump seemed hardly out of action. He was clearly anxious to work and discuss issues. We started going down the line, each taking turns giving the president a one- to two-minute update. I spoke about our "military readiness around the world," reassuring everyone of our posture, and then took quick dives into the current state of play with China, Russia, North Korea, and Iran.

The president was in good spirits, bouncing around from topic to topic as he normally did. He then focused in on three discrete matters. It was clear they were on his mind. Maybe his stay at Walter Reed gave him time to reflect. They were questions he asked numerous times: "Should we get out of Iraq now?"; When are we "getting out of Africa?"; and "What about our withdrawal from Afghanistan?" We each took turns speaking.

On Iraq, I told the president we "had already reduced our footprint in the country by a couple thousand," to around three thousand, and "were in a much better position from a force protection standpoint than we were a year ago." It was important to stay in Iraq to help them (and us) "ensure ISIS's defeat, but also to counter Iran's malign influence in the country and the region," which was the more strategic and longer-term concern. I said that "if we leave Iraq now, it will look like the militia groups are chasing us out, and it will send the wrong message to friends and foes alike" in the region. The president didn't push back and frankly surprised me by saying, "I agree. Let's not rush."

On Africa, we all knew where he stood on this issue. He wanted all U.S. military personnel off the continent, all diplomats removed, and all embassies closed. He didn't see the value in any Defense or State Department presence. Pompeo and I had argued against doing all this since my earliest days as secretary of defense. And like I had done in the past, I pivoted to the fact that I was "conducting reviews with all my combatant commanders to see where we could free up time, money, and manpower to put back into our highest priorities." Africa Command was the first in the chute, so I was able to update the president on the many adjustments and reductions we had already made, including in Somalia, without jeopardizing our ability to deal with threats to the homeland. Milley joined in with an update on our enhanced efforts to find and rescue an American, Jeff Woodke, whom terrorists were holding hostage in West Africa. The president didn't comment too much on any of this, which would be curious in retrospect given what was ongoing below him and would happen later.

Finally, on Afghanistan, Milley and I briefed that "we are on track to be down to forty-five hundred U.S. military personnel in country by the end of November," as we'd agreed in the summer. Pompeo had covered the diplomatic efforts, and I reinforced his message that "while progress was slow, we were still moving forward." After all, peace talks had begun in Qatar, something that seemed unimaginable a year ago, and no Americans had been killed in nearly nine months. It was nice *not* going to Dover Air Force Base to welcome our deceased service members back home and trying to console their grieving family members. Regarding the timeline for Afghanistan, I added as I usually did that "forty-five hundred remains a good place to pause and assess the situation before making further adjustments." Our commanders were good with this number from a security and mission standpoint, but "we need to determine in November if the conditions warrant any other reductions."

The call ended well, with the president largely (superficially?) in agreement with what we reported, but not really. I still knew he wanted out of all these places; I was just surprised he didn't press us further to get immediately out. Trump thanked us for our efforts and expressed his desire to get back on the campaign trail. We all returned the thanks and wished him well. For some reason, though, O'Brien—the national security adviser—jumped back in as the call was wrapping up to say, "Mr. President, we all love you very much. Get well. We love you. We love you." I couldn't believe it.

As I put down the phone, I reflected upon what we just discussed. We still had a few weeks to go before the election, and while ideas about attacking Iran or Venezuela had faded some, we weren't out of the woods yet. The president's focus on Iraq, Afghanistan, and Africa wasn't unusual, but given the timing, context, and interest,

I took note. Would he try to do something extraordinary in one of these places to fire up the base, deliver on a campaign commitment, or get the country focused on things other than his tax records or COVID? Who knew?

We just needed to be alert and attuned to the period we were now entering, a lesson learned from early June. Incumbent administrations from both parties have done unusual things in the past when it comes to the final weeks of a contested presidential election. After all, that's how we ended up with the phrase "October surprise."

In mid-September, O'Brien had informed me that Trump wanted out of Somalia. There was no explanation why, only that he wanted out. I told O'Brien that we had "already made significant reductions to our forces in East Africa" after having narrowed our forces down to what we needed to train the Somalis, monitor al Shabab's activities, and have "the strike capability to ensure these Islamic insurgents didn't threaten the U.S. homeland." I had explained this to both O'Brien and Trump in the past a few times, but it never seemed to resonate. The president viewed these nations, as he once infamously said, as "shithole countries," and he didn't see much value in having any Americans—whether they be military personnel or diplomats—based anywhere on the continent.[2] The bottom line was that Trump wanted out of Africa . . . completely . . . and Somalia now seemed to be the start point, according to O'Brien.

The U.S. military presence in Africa wasn't big to begin with, with fewer than seven thousand troops on the continent when I became secretary of defense. About half of that number were in Djibouti, a country of only nine thousand square miles on the Horn of Africa that borders Somalia and is composed of fewer than one million people. It was a geostrategic point with an ample port at the southern end of the Red Sea. The Arabian peninsula—Yemen, specifically—sat directly opposite its coastline. U.S. military personnel stationed in Djibouti provided a range of logistical, operational, and command and control support for both AFRICOM and CENTCOM.

The balance of U.S. forces in Africa were spread across the continent, with fewer than 200 personnel in North Africa; 1,400 or so mostly in Somalia and Kenya to deal with al Shabab; and the remainder in West Africa searching for American hostages held captive in the region and supporting French operations to defeat Islamic extremists in Chad, Niger, Mauritania, and Burkina Faso.

The biggest terrorist threat in Africa is al Shabab, an Islamic jihadist group based in the east. The group formed in 2006 in Somalia and forged ties with al Qaeda a few years later, with the aim of controlling this troubled, desperate land, and then spreading its hard-core beliefs on the continent. The United States and other countries had already designated al Shabab a terrorist organization. And with several thousand fighters in its ranks, it controlled large swaths of rural Somalia, occasionally conducting high-profile attacks in urban areas, principally in the capital of Mogadishu.

If I was going to free up time, money, and manpower to implement the National Defense Strategy and shift our focus to China and Russia, then Africa was a good place to start. It was an "economy of force" theater in the Pentagon's strategy to begin with, meaning it was a command where we were willing to accept risk by providing them the minimum essential resources (e.g., people, forces, budget) to accomplish their mission. This last point—their mission—was important, particularly when you need to get into the nitty-gritty work of reforming a large bureaucracy such as the DoD. Like every other command, AFRICOM was operating on hundreds of directives that were many years old that had accumulated over time, like barnacles on a ship's hull. Sometimes these were out of date or in conflict with other instructions. All needed review.

These orders were driving AFRICOM's requirements for troops, equipment, and other resources, however. Therefore, as we began the process of reviewing them and culling the list, one of the biggest decisions I made was to draw the line about when and how to engage terrorist groups around the world, not solely in Africa. In short, if a group had the means and intent to strike the U.S. homeland, then we kept the pressure on. If it had the intent but not the means, then we monitored it and occasionally took out key leaders and critical targets. If it didn't have the intent, let alone the means, then it was time to end the mission.

All agreed that West Africa required monitoring only by the IC. We could make significant reductions in our force presence there. While I was also willing to continue providing air transport, aerial refueling, and overhead surveillance support to the French military for a little while longer, I wanted them to pay full freight for this support, which came to about $50 to $70 million annually. We had a great relationship with the French military on the ground, but it was important to begin weaning them off this "temporary" assistance. We had been providing it for many years without complaint, while their political leaders in France were sticking it to the United States in other areas.

Moreover, my strategic assessment of the situation in West Africa was that the French weren't winning. After so many years, despite their creditable efforts, they had achieved a stalemate at best; mission fatigue in Paris was settling in. In my view, they were setting the stage to leave and were messaging as much. Why wait? I thought. Indeed, in the summer of 2021, Paris would announce that it was curtailing its mission in West Africa and withdrawing most of its troops.[3]

Views about the threat of al Shabab in East Africa were a little mixed, however. My assessment was that al Shabab had some interest in attacking the United States, but they didn't have the means. They should be monitored, with the ability to strike key leaders and critical targets when needed, in the event they evolved over time. But maintaining forces in the region on a steady-state basis at current levels didn't make sense. I heard this often as I spoke with operational leaders who spent time there. Most folks agreed with me.

AFRICOM disagreed, of course. Such an assessment would affect their resources. This was one of the challenges with managing the combatant commands in the broader context of the Defense Department: most complained about being underresourced, some couldn't accept their priority in the bigger scheme of things, and a few would stretch the risk assessment to justify their demands.

Nonetheless, I made the decision—based on an option developed by the commander, General Steve Townsend—to consolidate our forces in southern Somalia and focus on al Shabab's *external* operating capabilities, those most likely to be plotting against the U.S. homeland. This would bring the force in Somalia down below one thousand, yet allow them to keep training the country's armed forces so they could pick up this mission full-time one day. This seemed like a prudent and responsible step for now. After Somalia's elections in early 2021, I wanted to look at going down to two to three hundred personnel in-country, but do so in coordination with our partners on the ground.

I spoke with Mike Pompeo about Somalia during our weekly call on September 21. He wasn't tracking the president's supposed direction either, which surprised me. The DoD didn't operate in a vacuum. State had the lead for U.S. foreign policy, of course, so our presence and activities needed to align with and support them. It was the NSC's responsibility to coordinate these types of decisions, but the interagency process at the principals' level had begun breaking down over the past several months. The NSC held fewer and fewer meetings at the principals' level as the campaign heated up, and O'Brien and others spent more time on the road. With the president in full campaign mode, the opposite should have happened: keep your NSC team back in Washington to coordinate and keep a watchful eye on things.

Given this vacuum, I proposed to Pompeo that he, Mark Milley, Gina Haspel, Robert O'Brien, and I meet to discuss the matter, develop some options, and agree on one. We could then go meet with the president and present our recommendations. After all, State had people and equities on the ground in Somalia as well. Mike agreed. The group planned to meet the afternoon of October 8. O'Brien couldn't make it. He was on a political trip out west, so we invited his deputy, Matt Pottinger. And as fate would have it, the NSC informed Chief of Staff Mark Meadows, who decided to join as well.

When Meadows appeared in one of the squares on the video screen, a collective groan murmured across the Pentagon conference room where Milley, Pompeo—who joined me after a separate meeting we had earlier—and I sat with our line muted. This promised to be tedious at best.

Now the dynamic changed. Instead of having a working discussion about options, the meeting quickly turned into Meadows pushing us for a complete withdrawal before the election—coupled with snarky suggestions that the DoD was "slow-rolling the president," which was ironic since I was the one who pulled the meeting together in the first place. It was a worn-out tune by someone I saw as a political hack, a person who had a reputation for thinking the DoD received too much money and attention in the first place, and who didn't seem to understand the logistics of moving more than one thousand people, as well as hundreds of tons of vehicles, equipment, weapons, and other sensitive items, out of a third-world country on short notice.

The chief of staff went so far as to seemingly accuse us of ignoring this new supposed presidential directive to withdraw from Somalia, but I never received one. Indeed, the first I had heard that such specific direction had been given was from O'Brien just a few weeks earlier. Meadows claimed he had called me about this issue when I was in Hawaii in August earlier to commemorate the seventy-fifth anniversary of the end of World War II—filling in for the president, no less. But my staff never reported a call, and Meadows never tried again or followed up, so it must not have been too important. Even more curious is the fact that Trump did not say anything about Somalia (nor did Meadows) when I briefed him on Africa on October 4, a few days earlier, while he was at Walter Reed and I was flying back to the United States from the Middle East. What was going on at the White House?

On the October 8 call, Meadows was blunt, asking, pressing why a full withdrawal "can't be done in two weeks." Sure, if we walked away from everything, boarded the airplanes, and flew away. The president would never accept leaving behind equipment. We had heard that tune many times before in the past from Trump. So we ended up going round and round on this issue, without even touching on the core questions, though, such as: Why have we been there, why are we there today, why are getting out now, and what happens when/after we depart?

Since this was no longer a working session by principals who understood the issue, I asked Gina Haspel to "please give an overview of al Shabab, their affiliation with al Qaeda, and the overall security environment in the country." She did a good job as always, and I hoped this would set some type of baseline for the broader discussion. I asked Mike Pompeo to go next.

Mike provided us a summary of the foreign partners who were with us on the ground. He said the British and French had caught wind of Trump's alleged directive to exit Somalia and were not happy. He also said, "State is assessing the impact on AMISOM"—the African Union Mission in Somalia, a regional peacekeeping force operating under U.N. Security Council approval. AMISOM was performing a number of tasks, from supporting Somalia's transition to more effective governance and implementing a national security plan to training Somali security forces and facilitating the safe delivery of humanitarian aid. The United States was working closely with AMISOM on the ground, and the U.S. armed forces were integrally involved in much of their work.

I finally asked Milley to give everyone an overview of the U.S. military presence in Somalia. He summarized the logistical scope of "closing five bases, and then moving 4,000 to 5,000 short tons of equipment, 150-plus vehicles, and over 1,000 total U.S. personnel out of country." It was a daunting task. He thought "the quickest we could move out, and not leave anything important behind, was around seventy-five days." But we also had to factor in State's needs, which was one of the purposes of this meeting before it was turned into something else by the White House chief of staff.

Meadows started poking at different parts of what we said, looking for soft spots where he could say we weren't being aggressive enough in our timelines. State said they "needed a minimum of thirty days" to draw down. O'Brien, who had called in some time after the meeting began, piped up and proposed that, rather than withdrawing from Somalia, "why not just move everyone and everything south to Kenya." Pompeo said, "That won't meet the president's intent; he wants out." Mike was right. O'Brien was proposing to play an East Africa shell game with the troops. This wasn't the way to look at the issue; we had to get back to the core questions, especially: What is our purpose, and what do we want to accomplish?

I was anxious to return forces to the United States more than anyone else. After all, they were mostly my people, assets, and budget, and I wanted to focus on China. That said, a complete pullout at this time, at this pace, in this manner, was unwarranted, and I said so. A precipitous withdrawal was worse. Even with the reductions in East Africa I had already decided upon, we could go down to a lower number and still be able to monitor al Shabab and conduct counterterrorism strikes as need be. O'Brien's idea seemed to be the worst of both: the forces would not be best positioned to perform their missions out of Kenya yet also weren't available to bring home. All it did was give the White House the talking point of saying "Trump pulled the United States out of Somalia." It was all politics.

We settled on three options by the end of what had become a contentious meeting: complete withdrawal; maintain a monitoring footprint only; or go heavier with a monitoring and counterterrorism capability. We agreed to get back together in a couple of weeks. NSC planned to organize this follow-up.

The follow-up NSC call never came and the meeting never happened. This was fine with me. And after this most recent episode, I wasn't about to take the lead again and organize another principals meeting for the NSC. I'm sure the White House thought the DoD was slow-rolling the president again; it seemed they never had a mirror to look into. Setting that aside, I hoped that once the election was behind us, we could have a more rational discussion about our mission in Somalia, and Africa writ large, and proceed from there. And if Joe Biden became the president-elect, then our military footprint on the continent was a matter best left for his administration to consider.

I was not surprised, though, to read the news on December 4,

2020, weeks after I left, that Trump was withdrawing all U.S. forces from Somalia. With me out of the way, and his loyalists in place, the president was free to do exactly what he wanted despite the consequences. But this pullout was all a smoke screen, much as Pompeo and I discussed in the October meeting. Withdrawing seven hundred troops from Somalia and repositioning them in Kenya, as was later announced, was a shell game that never really met the president's intent. Instead, it left our operations in East Africa less capable, and the DoD's ability to refocus them on China unfulfilled.[4]

Worse yet, the precipitous nature of the pullout likely damaged our relations with allies on the ground and key partners in the region. All this would have consequences for the security situation in the country, which would impact Somalia's parliamentary elections in January and presidential contest in February. This decision-making approach was the opposite of how policy should be developed, coordinated, and implemented, but it was too often the hallmark of the Trump White House. The president would make a capricious decision, those closest to him would rush about pronouncing and celebrating the decision, and the departments would be left figuring out how to make lemonade out of the rotten lemons that were handed us.

But a quick withdrawal from Somalia, we learned, was only the beginning. On October 7, the day before our Somalia meeting, the president tweeted out that U.S. troops should be home from Afghanistan by Christmas. First Somalia, now this.

As months passed after the February 2020 signing of the peace agreement, and the intra-Afghan talks failed to launch, the United States continued its reductions down to 8,600 troops. Some critics said that we should suspend our drawdown until talks began. That would be a fair point. We took a different view, however. We didn't trust the Taliban. As such, we determined they would cling to any issue, no matter how small, as a reason to avoid moving forward with negotiations, and we didn't want to give them an excuse not to do so. We wanted to take that card out of their hands up front. And besides, I wanted to shrink our footprint in Afghanistan regardless. Therefore, I was anxious to reduce our footprint while the Taliban remained committed to not attacking us.

General Scott Miller (our commander in Afghanistan), James Anderson, Generals McKenzie and Milley, and I had routine update calls on the peace deal's implementation over the succeeding months. General Miller's redeployment plans were well under way and making steady progress. State had the hard job of sorting through prisoner-swap issues and figuring out how to get everyone to begin the intra-Afghan talks.

In June, we had an interagency meeting to discuss reducing the U.S. troop presence further, down to 4,500 service members by the end of November, stopping at that point to assess the situation before making any further decisions, as I argued. The military chain of command felt we could do this, provided the Afghan forces and coalition partners were on board. But going below this would likely jeopardize our key missions, they said, if not force us to abandon the training, advise, and assist role that was important to the Afghans and us.

We discussed this issue again among ourselves after that, and everyone agreed we should pause at 4,500 and not reduce further. I pocketed the win. Adding suspenders to the belt we had in place, I sent a formal letter back to O'Brien in mid-June acknowledging the decision and repeating that we should not go below 4,500 until conditions warranted.

The big breakthrough in the peace process occurred on September 12, 2020, when talks finally began in Doha between the Taliban and the Afghan government. This was significant. General Miller updated my team and me a couple of days later.

Despite the nearly seven-month delay in the negotiations, the Taliban still expected all foreign forces to be out of the country by May 2021. They also wanted more Taliban prisoners released and all sanctions lifted. Meanwhile, Scott Miller reported, the violence perpetrated against the Afghans was as high as ever, and the Taliban had not met all their obligations regarding al Qaeda. We discussed several ideas to help get them in compliance, but there was nothing we could do to move the needle, other than threaten to suspend the peace deal or restart offensive operations.

On October 7, the president surprised everyone with a tweet that declared all American forces should be home by Christmas. His statement contradicted a similar one made hours earlier by Robert O'Brien. So much for the president's statement in August 2017 that "conditions on the ground, not arbitrary timetables, will guide our strategy from now on" or the subsequent agreements we had on this matter during consideration and implementation of the peace deal.[5]

This was a shame, because as slow, erratic, and painful as the intra-Afghan discussions were, at least they were talking. Moreover, no American service members had been killed since the agreement was signed in February 2020. Now we seemed to be giving up the best, if not the only, leverage we had to keep the Taliban at the table. It was a strategic mistake that undermined our efforts to forge a peace agreement between the Afghan government and the Taliban, and it had an odious psychological effect on our Afghan partners and our relationship with them.

Were these rash decisions the nature of the October surprises being planned by the White House, or were they just bucket list items that the president wanted to get done before January 20, 2021? No one knew for sure, but while these decisions were far less onerous than ones that might take us to war, they still were dangerous, uncoordinated, inconsistent with our established policies, damaging to our foreign standing, and signaled strategic retreat. Moreover, given the time of the year, they looked transparently political as desperate acts to further burnish Trump's record with his base and increase his support more broadly.

O'Brien kicked off this latest episode by announcing at the University of Nevada, Las Vegas—why was he even there in the first place?—that "when President Trump took office, there were over 10,000 American troops in Afghanistan. As of today there are under 5,000 and that will go to 2,500 by early next year."[6] Really? Who made that decision? The president had not. The national security adviser was freelancing, and I believed he was putting the peace talks and our troops in jeopardy by doing so.

I quickly spoke with Pompeo about it and he was equally surprised. He told me he "called O'Brien later to ask him about it," as he had done on a few prior occasions. Mike said, in his estimation, "O'Brien basically made it up, deciding to make the statement after speaking with Ric Grenell." Go figure. Staff on the campaign trail were now making strategic decisions with no involvement by the secretary of state or the secretary of defense.

Of course Trump saw O'Brien's comments once they hit the news and decided to double down by tweeting, "We should have the small remaining number of our BRAVE Men and Women serving in Afghanistan home by Christmas!" It was if we were in a bidding war on Twitter.

It was logistically impossible for us to withdraw all our forces and their equipment by December 25; it was also operationally dangerous, and strategically mistaken too. Doing so meant getting out not only 4,500 U.S. troops but other U.S. government personnel as well as American contractors that numbered in the thousands. We also had a commitment to assist our NATO allies with their extraction from the country. "We go in together; we adjust together; we go out together," was a common refrain within NATO. And Christmas was only about two and a half months away.

Finally, we made commitments to our Afghan partners who risked their lives over the years to help us on the ground in Afghanistan. We promised many of them visas and the opportunity to resettle in the United States. There were probably tens of thousands of them and their families that we would also need to withdraw. This would become a massive administrative and logistical operation, one that we couldn't accomplish in seventy-five days. The president's tweets were pure politics. But since the commander in chief said it, it shook the DoD, our forces in Afghanistan (and their families), our allies, and the Afghans. It was reckless in many bad ways.

I organized a call with my commanders for October 9, two days later, to discuss the situation. On the line, once again, were Generals Milley, McKenzie, and Miller, and James Anderson. Miller and McKenzie updated me on the situation, which was as I expected— everyone was surprised ("shocked" may be a better word), anxious about next steps, and unsure about the U.S. position. I asked them their best military advice, and it was that we pause at 4,500 and that we make no further reductions until the Taliban start living up to their end of the peace deal. This was supposed to be a conditions-based plan, and the conditions hadn't been met to go further. Milley completely agreed, as did Anderson. I did too. I asked Miller and McKenzie to put their assessments and recommendations down in writing, for Milley and Anderson to do the same, and to get it all to me by the nineteenth.

My plan was to consider their memos, use them to inform my

decision, and then make a written recommendation to the president so that he could have my views regarding the peace talks, the military state of play, and the further reduction of U.S. forces in Afghanistan. In Washington, D.C., the way to get people's attention is to put it down in writing, and copy others, which was what I planned to do. In the meantime, I asked Policy to schedule a call over the weekend between me and Jens Stoltenberg, the NATO secretary general, to discuss the situation, which we did.

A few days later, General Milley engaged in a public spat with O'Brien about Afghanistan. Milley responded to a question about O'Brien's statement that U.S. forces would be down to 2,500 in January by remarking "Robert O'Brien, or anyone else, can speculate as they see fit, I am not going to engage in speculation, I'm going to engage in the rigorous analysis of the situation based on the conditions and the plans that I'm aware of in my conversations with the president."[7]

Milley was right, of course—we didn't have orders at that time to go below 4,500. Indeed, there was a long-standing agreement that going below that number would be conditions based. I had addressed this formally in writing back to the NSC on at least one occasion, and Pompeo and I both talked about it publicly as well as privately. O'Brien was asserting a change in policy that we had not agreed to, even though he tried to claim that we had. It was true that another stopping point in the plan was to go down to 2,500 troops sometime early in the new year, before May, but that assumed the Taliban were living up to their end of the deal. But no decision had yet been formally made on this.

At a public event on Friday, October 16, O'Brien responded to Milley, stating, "When I speak about troop levels and that sort of thing, I'm a staffer, I staff the president of the United States, so it's not my practice to speculate." He added, "Other people [Milley] can interpret what I say as speculation or not but I wasn't speculating then and I wasn't speculating today."[8]

This public response fired Chairman Milley up. Time and time again Milley and I had to hear the national security adviser in meetings with the president spout off about one thing or another involving the military, and it really grated on the chairman. Too often the NSA's remarks seemed irresponsible and uninformed, if not reckless.

O'Brien was freelancing and playing politics with a very serious issue, plus he was calling into question the chairman's integrity, and it rightfully made Milley angry. He wanted to respond, and loudly, as was his nature. I said to him, "Chairman, let it go." I observed that O'Brien was probably embarrassed by the president when Trump undercut his number, and I added, "All the media wants to do is stir the pot, with you two as the prime ingredients. The last thing we need is for the president to intervene and give us a direct order to withdraw." I added, "Then, we have no maneuver space. Let it go, and we'll follow our last order, which was pause at 4,500 until conditions are met."

These were all the reasons I was trying to stay out of the news. I needed the chairman to do so as well. "Stick with the plan," I kept telling myself, and him. Milley didn't like it, but ended up putting the mission before self, as I knew he would, and stood down. We had made it this far with the Four Nos metric, and the election was right around the corner. There was no need to disrupt it now simply to score some points in the press against someone who dug himself into a hole.

Once I had everyone's input, and made my decision, Policy drafted the classified letter I would send to the president in early November. It was a few pages in length, laying out my views on the state of play in Afghanistan and the perspectives of the commanders on the ground. It made clear that the Taliban was *not* living up to their end of the deal. They had not broken ties with al Qaeda, had not reduced the violence, and were not negotiating in good faith with the Afghan government. My recommendation was that we halt any further reductions until the Taliban met those conditions. After all, the only leverage available to the United States and our Afghan partners was the threat of U.S. forces not leaving Afghanistan and, even more compelling, the resumption of U.S. military operations against the Taliban.

As much as I wanted to get out of Afghanistan, a precipitous withdrawal, I argued, could put our forces at risk, would damage our relations with our allies and partners on the ground, would jeopardize our international standing, and would completely undercut the intra-Afghan negotiations taking place in Qatar. The purpose for invading Afghanistan in the first place was to decimate al Qaeda and ensure that country never again became a safe haven for terrorists who wanted to attack the United States. A peace deal between the Afghan government and the Taliban, one that was conditions based and concluded in good faith, was the only way to achieve that end state in an enduring manner, unless of course we were willing keep U.S. forces there for another twenty years. Nobody wanted that. But we needed strategic patience, and the willingness to step back, employ force, or do whatever else was necessary to ensure compliance with the agreement and help forge an intra-Afghan peace deal, and that meant keeping troops in-country until we felt this path had run its course.

Despite all these issues swirling around, I continued my "inside offense" strategy of moving the National Defense Strategy forward, which made for a busy October. I needed to keep the Pentagon focused on our nation's security, and not the distractions created by the White House and the upcoming election. As such, I held internal reviews of Cyber Command, Transportation Command, Indo-Pacific Command, and, of course, Central Command. International engagements at the Pentagon with several of my foreign counterparts also filled my calendar. I also gave major public speeches on our new strategy for allies and partners, and on our new future naval force structure. We were making solid progress.

As the public flap about Afghanistan troop numbers died down, though, another issue soon emerged. Beginning in late July 2020, we began looking at new ways to find Jeff Woodke, the American missionary performing humanitarian work in Niger whom Islamic terrorists had abducted in 2016.

The White House wasn't happy with State's and CIA's efforts, so they asked the DoD to take the lead. This didn't make sense. The three of us had to work closely together regardless of who was the lead, and the military's role was typically on the back end of a long process—the rescue—if it even ever came to that. We needed to make the system work if we were to be successful.

On the other hand, this was an American citizen and I didn't want to play bureaucratic politics when we might have the chance to bring someone home. Therefore, we accepted the lead. Anderson, Milley, and I did a conference call with General Townsend, the AFRICOM commander, and eventually received a detailed list of his preparatory needs, which we began filling. By early fall, the assets were largely in place and the team was working 24/7 to find Woodke. Meanwhile, Special Operations Command (SOCOM) was planning and rehearsing for a possible rescue operation in West Africa.

On Sunday, October 25, I departed Washington, D.C., on the

long-planned trip to India with Mike Pompeo for the next 2 plus 2 dialogue that I discussed earlier. On the way home, I planned to visit Bahrain, Jordan, and Israel. I had deferred trips to these countries earlier in the year due to COVID, and many critical issues had arisen since then, so I felt it was important to stop in each capital.

On the flight back to the United States on Thursday, October 29, General Milley called me with some breaking news. On Tuesday of that week, an American named Philipe Nathan Walton had been taken from his farm in Massalata in southern Niger, not far from the border with Nigeria. The kidnappers were armed and considered dangerous; they demanded a ransom from the man's father in exchange for his release. The family and Walton's captors were negotiating.

It was unclear how this would end up, but most outcomes seemed bad. If the talks fell through, they could kill Walton, or possibly hand him over to Islamic terrorists in the area for a small sum. If this happened, the dynamics would change for the worse, and Walton could find himself in a situation similar to Woodke. Nobody wanted that to happen.

Milley's breaking news was that we learned where the kidnappers were holding Walton, and the NSC asked that we be prepared to rescue him in the event the negotiations fell through. This made sense to me. The chairman also recommended that we give SO-COM a warning order—which basically provides the command the rough details of the situation and the mission so they can begin planning and preparing—and the okay to deploy forward in theater, which I also approved. The more time we could give our special operators to prepare, the better. We had done this all before.

Jen Stewart, my chief of staff, was on the line too, so I asked her to "make sure that Policy was in the loop both inside the building with the Joint Staff, and with the other players in the interagency," specifically State and FBI. The NSC process had completely broken down at the principals' level at this point, it seemed, and yet we needed to be thoroughly aligned and coordinated in the event this became an approved operation. Plus, I wanted to fully explore all other options before we used the military tool, which the White House had a quick proclivity to employ, despite the potential downsides this sometimes presented.

I had been on the plane for several hours now and needed to get some sleep. We were landing late at night in D.C. and had a long day planned for Friday. I told Jen and Milley to "call me in case anything else came up." The chairman didn't think anything else would. In his view this mission was "a few days to a week away from happening," if at all. This timing would prove off. With that, we ended the call and I tried to get some sleep.

My first meeting the next day, Friday, October 30, was a briefing by SOCOM at 7:30 A.M. on their concept of operations to rescue Walton. They had been working overtime with AFRICOM, and with the benefit of having done most of this planning for Woodke over the previous weeks, their operation was straightforward and well thought through.

Before the call began, however, Milley was informed that Trump had already approved and directed the rescue operation. What? As coincidence would have it, Trump had been at Fort Bragg, North Carolina, on Thursday, the day before, to present an award to the unit that conducted the raid that killed Abu Bakr al-Baghdadi, the brutal leader of ISIS, in October 2019.

The SOCOM commander, General Rich Clarke, was there for the ceremony, and when asked about the Walton situation, Clarke said they were ready to go if ordered. The earliest suitable time to do so would be during the cover of darkness in Niger that Friday night. One thing led to another and sure enough, after a discussion with the SOCOM commander, Trump approved the operation for the evening of October 30, a decision confirmed later by Mark Meadows. It was a terrible way for a last course of action to become the first, and for the concept to become an approved plan. Moreover, as I learned over the following hours, almost no one else in the government seemed to be tracking this.

That said, I wasn't simply going to sign off on the SOCOM plan. The president was never one for details—that was my job—and small things mattered when troops were being asked to risk their lives. I understood his intent. As the secretary of defense, though, I had a responsibility to ensure the plan could accomplish the mission, met the president's aims, was consistent with U.S. policy, and did so in a way that minimized risk.

I also wanted to make sure State, Justice, and the CIA were in the loop and properly coordinated. They had roles to play here, and no one at the DoD knew if they were aware of the president's decision. I wanted to ensure we synchronized the plan with them, and that they supported it. After all, there were some issues they needed to be aware of. For example, one of our biggest concerns was that the kidnappers might kill Walton on the spot if they learned the U.S. military was coming. Everyone needed to understand that before we abandoned the nonmilitary options that State was working, and the "go/no-go" decision point was now only a few hours away, at 1:00 P.M. in D.C., given the time it would take for the special operators to reach their target area.

We could always delay the operation until another date, but that came with risk; the kidnappers might learn of our plans, we could lose track of Walton, they could sell him to terrorists, or his captors could add to their numbers, just to name a few concerns.

We were working hard to conduct the operation in a way that minimized risk, maximized the odds of success, and brought everyone home safely. And if I or any of my cabinet colleagues had serious reservations or concerns, it was my duty to call the president and inform him as we worked through the issues.

It didn't take long to go through the SOCOM plan. I had seen these before, and the basic tactical principles were being applied in ways that I understood well from my own military service. My particular focus, again, was securing Walton quickly so that the kidnappers couldn't harm him or turn him over to a terrorist group. I approved the plan with some minor tweaks and an unresolved question or two—for example, did we have permission from other nations to fly through their airspace en route to the objective?

Often when we would get into big discussions at the White House about the value of our allies and partners, the president measured them solely in terms of their contributions as it related to military spending. This was an important metric, for sure, but one of the many other benefits our allies and partners also offered was their willingness to provide what we called ABO, which was shorthand for access, basing, and overflight rights. We needed these to move people, weapons, or equipment as quickly as possible around the world from point A to point B without any diversions, delays, or obstructions. Sometimes we would stop en route for fuel, repairs, or simply to rest. These permissions made a big difference when planning, conducting, and sustaining combat operations globally.

By contrast, in April 1986, the French had refused to grant U.S. military aircraft overflight rights after President Reagan ordered strikes against Libya in retaliation for a terrorist attack against American citizens in Europe. The denial by Paris required our aircraft to fly an extra 2,400 miles around the western coast of Europe, putting unnecessary stress on the pilots and the aircraft, which raised the risk level of the mission. The African operation before us now, twenty-four years later, was similar in some of those same ways, so we needed these permissions before launching.

One of the issues from the phone call that also needed addressed was the status of the negotiations between the Walton family and the kidnappers. The best outcome was if we could resolve the matter peacefully, without bloodshed. As soon as I ended the call with SOCOM, I dialed up Chris Wray, the FBI director, and explained what was going on.

"Chris," I said over the secure phone, "I'm about to send in our special operators to rescue this guy. Before I do so, and put their lives and his at risk, I want to hear how the negotiations are going on the ground."

Wray wasn't tracking our plans—surprise!—which was important to know, so I updated him. His people were in communication with the Walton family and helping with the talks. He said, "Both sides are still talking, but are very far apart." I asked for his thoughts on our operation. I didn't want to deploy military forces and risk getting either Walton or our service members killed in a firefight if the talks were going well. Chris was reluctant to opine, but said, "Based on everything I'm hearing from my people on the ground, if this was a domestic situation, I would send in an assault team." That was good enough for me. I thanked him, and then commended him for some of the principled positions he had taken in the recent past that caught the president's ire. He thanked me and said something like, "It will probably get me fired at some point," to which I responded, "Welcome to the club." We both chuckled, and with that we hung up.

I called Bill Barr next to tell him what was going on and get his views. He was also unaware of what was unfolding. I informed him of my conversation with the FBI director. Bill asked, "What does

Chris [Wray] think?" I reviewed our conversation, and Wray's view on moving forward, after which the AG said, "I agree. I support it." Two down.

Separately, my folks were trying to reach O'Brien. NSC staff told them he was in Nevada on another campaign trip and wasn't available. Next, they tried Matt Pottinger, his deputy, and were told he was at home without access to a secure phone.

I tried Pompeo next. He was on a return flight from abroad, so his deputy, Steve Biegun, was working the issue for State in his absence. I had known Steve for twenty years. He and I worked together on the Senate Foreign Relations Committee in the early 2000s, so I trusted him and knew he would have the issue well under hand at Foggy Bottom. I called and told him about the mission and our airspace permission needs, and he promised to get right on it.

Finally, I spoke with Gina Haspel. She knew the most of what we were planning. It wasn't surprising, given the close ties between SOCOM and the CIA. However, she was not aware the president decided to launch the rescue operation. She appreciated the call and the readout regarding all the other moving pieces and our timing, and offered the Agency's assistance if we needed any.

I finished all my calls around 11:00 A.M. and then picked up the secure phone to update the president. He was stepping onto the helicopter to go somewhere, so Meadows took the call. It was difficult to hear him with all the background noise on his end, but I told him where things stood, that "I connected with Wray, Barr, Haspel, and Biegun, and all supported moving forward." I said, "We are good to go at this point, except for the overflight permissions, but State is working the matter," and we could always turn around at the last minute. At this point in the decision-making process, I didn't want to cancel the mission and risk Walton's life over an airspace clearance issue we had a few hours to work.

"I recommend we proceed with the mission, given everything I heard from my commanders and my colleagues." I added, "But there are risks. For example, and most notably, Walton and our troops could be hurt or killed in the operation." I asked Meadows to convey this to the president, and said, "I will call back later to confirm." Meadows acknowledged all of this before hustling to join the president on Marine One and update him.

Not long after that, I received word from my Policy shop that "the airspace issues are resolved; we have the clearances." Kash Patel at the NSC reportedly told Tony Tata, the retired Army general who was the acting principal deputy undersecretary for policy, that Pompeo "got the airspace cleared." We were good to go. With that, I called General Milley to pass along my approval for SOCOM and AFRICOM to proceed with the operation. "Tell them it's a go," I said.

A few hours later, though, around 4:45 P.M., I learned some disturbing news. Apparently, we did *not* have permission to enter the airspace of one of the key countries, and the aircraft were only fifteen miles away from the international border. Milley and I spoke and agreed to have the aircraft circle in approved airspace until we received final clearance to proceed. I then called State to find out what happened and get it fixed. Apparently, what Patel reported to Tata was wrong. Pompeo had not secured the clearances. Rather, State was still working the phones to get the proper approval. By the time Mike and I spoke an hour later, he still didn't have the okay from the remaining country. He also didn't know where Patel received his information. Pompeo never spoke with him.

My staff told me that, upon hearing this news, Tata called Patel back and engaged in a heated conversation with him over the NSC staffer's bad report. This was frustratingly rich. Tata had been a good team player in the building since his nomination to become undersecretary of defense for policy was pulled due to bipartisan pushback over outlandish comments he made months and years before on several topics. Trump really liked Tata, so he placed him in this acting role at the Pentagon. But to have him and Patel, two persons considered real Trump loyalists, in verbal fisticuffs yelling at each other was ironic. Regardless, Tata was on the right side of this issue for sure.

There would be time for the forensics of the faux permission later, though. Right now, we were in a bad place. The aircraft had been flying in circles for an hour awaiting permission to cross the border, and if we didn't decide soon, they would have to return to their start point. We would have to reschedule the operation for another evening, which meant that the odds of mission exposure, and Walton being moved (or maybe even killed), would grow with each passing hour and day. Milley had already received an intelligence spot report that suggested those holding Walton were thinking of killing him or giving him to another terrorist group.

Over the preceding hour, I had also been on the phone with my general counsel, Paul Ney, to better understand the legal options available to us if we didn't get the overflight rights. The bottom line, he said, was that "the president can always use his Article II authorities to approve the mission, going into and through foreign airspace without their permission." We went back and forth over this a few times. I didn't doubt Trump would approve this, but I wanted to understand the issue inside and out to my own satisfaction, and especially if the president and I engaged in a deeper discussion on the matter.

Of course, there were also the international politics of the president using his Article II authorities to enter unapproved foreign airspace. I was prepared to discuss all of that too but thought Pompeo should lead that conversation.

The time was creeping closer to 6:00 P.M.—the decision point for the aircraft to go forward or return—so I decided to call the president. I asked Pompeo to join me. General Milley was on the phone too. When the Situation Room connected us with the president, Meadows picked up the call and said, "Hello, Secretary, what's the latest?" I updated him on what happened with the overflight rights and said that "we need to make a decision now regarding the mission." He asked, "How did we receive the bad information in the first place?" clearly annoyed at the situation as much as we were. My team suspected Patel made the approval story up, but they didn't have all the facts. I told Meadows that "Mike [Pompeo] and I want to learn that too, but that is a longer discussion we don't have time for right now."

I gave Meadows a brief rundown on the Article II option and the various considerations. Mike did the same regarding the policy and international politics of proceeding, which would technically be an invasion of a foreign country if they didn't grant us permission. Milley updated him on what was happening on the ground. "With an American's life possibly at stake," I said, "We recommended the mission go forward. But the president needs to make that call. None of us can. And I need to hear that from him," I added, as the time ticked further down. There was a brief pause.

Meadows started asking some questions. Just as he did, the Situation Room intervened with "Break. Break. I have Deputy Secretary of State Steve Biegun on the line. He says he needs to join this call," and asked if Steve could join. "Yes, of course," I said. Steve had breaking news. He had been working this issue all afternoon and knew we were discussing whether to go in or not. He wanted to let us know: "The overflight rights we requested were approved." All was clear to proceed.

Thank goodness! With that news we wrapped up the call. I told Milley to give SOCOM and AFRICOM the green light immediately.

"Yes, sir," he said, jumping off the line to pass the orders. I let everyone know we would keep them apprised.

The tactical mission went off without a hitch. I was concerned that being packed in an aircraft burning holes in the sky for an extra hour or so would wear on the special operators, that it might affect their readiness somehow. I had my share of moments like that during peacetime training missions, and every little thing can take a toll on a person over time. Putting them through that uncertainty and additional wait was unfair, and it was a failure on our part in D.C. to get it right the first time. We couldn't afford to repeat that. Pompeo and I started working to get to the bottom of the airspace clearance issue days later, once the dust settled.

But if SOCOM's success on the objective was the metric that night, and it was, then the additional time in the air didn't affect them. The operation was flawless. Walton was successfully rescued without harm, all the kidnappers but one were killed, and the special operators suffered no casualties. We reunited Walton with his family a day or so later. It was a great day for them, I'm sure, and a good day for the U.S. military, and all thanks to the brave service members who helped make this mission a success.

General Clarke would tell me later that, from the time of Walton's capture until the time of his release, and given everything that happened in between then, especially the movement of forces from the United States to Africa, "It took the U.S. military less than one hundred hours to achieve mission success. It was one of the shortest timelines of any hostage rescue in the history of U.S. special operations," he said. Despite missteps on our end in D.C., they pulled off the near impossible once again and returned Philipe Nathan Walton safely back to his family.

October was a long month, but thankfully it presented no real surprises. We ended on a high note with this successful rescue mission, but we still had to get through November 3 and whatever fallout the election would bring. We had to keep taking it all one day at a time. We made it this far, and through some difficult moments and issues. I just needed to navigate another week or two through this endless minefield.

CHAPTER 23

ENDGAME

"Fox News's decision desk is calling Arizona for Joe Biden," Bret Baier reported. This "changes the math," he added. I couldn't believe it. I had some familiarity with Arizona politics, which traditionally sported two colors in presidential elections: red and redder, but usually not blue. It also seemed to be an early call by the network. This was big news, which immediately begged the question if it was a one-off race or a harbinger of the president's performance in other states. "Trump has to be furious," I thought.

Election Day finally arrived. It was hard to believe I made it this far. After my morning ritual of huddling with my front-office team and reading the morning intelligence updates, I got an update on the security situation around the country. Everything looked good. My biggest, most likely concern, however, wasn't Election Day, but the day after—after partisans and activists reacted to the outcome of November 3. Would the streets fill with protesters from the losing side and claim a stolen election? Would the winning side come out in opposition and rub the victory in their faces? Would violence ensue, with fights in the streets, vandalism in the cities, and mayhem in the states, that Trump would feel the need to "get under control" because it made him "look weak"? If the president won reelection, we certainly expected large crowds in Washington, D.C., and other major cities like Portland, Seattle, Chicago, Philadelphia, and New York, where protesters had gathered and marched in the past.

I went home early that night, planning to sit in front of the TV all evening with Leah, watching the returns and analysis across multiple outlets, and staying close to the phone. The White House was planning a large election watch party for the night, and I had received an invitation, but I had no plans to attend. I didn't like those things to begin with, and if I was going to spend an evening out, I wanted to do so with a small group of close friends. Professionally, I wanted to keep a distance as secretary of defense, to signal the apolitical stance I wanted the DoD to maintain, especially if things got bad over the coming days and the president sought to leverage the armed forces somehow.

After an early dinner, I settled into the comfy leather chair in my living room and began cycling through TV stations to watch the returns from people I thought knew what they were talking about. As the polls closed and reports started coming in around 7:30 P.M., the race was shaping up like many expected. West Virginia, South Carolina, and Alabama quickly fell in Trump's column. Delaware, Connecticut, and New Jersey moved into Biden's. The South and Midwest trended toward the president, while the former vice president racked up states in the Northeast.

Leah moved in and out of our living room throughout the evening, watching with me at times. I also swapped occasional texts, emails, and phone calls with friends and colleagues, digesting an incoming report, and trying to figure out which way this race was headed. No major battleground states were called by 11:00 P.M., though some reports indicated that Florida was trending for Trump. Minutes later, Fox News put the Sunshine State in the president's column. The White House had every reason to be in good spirits.

The Fox News report around 11:30 P.M. regarding Arizona, however, was the game changer. It must have felt like a gut punch—a hard one—that took all of the wind out of Trump and his campaign team. The fact that Fox made the call was interesting in and of itself, adding insult to injury. As many reported later, the president was livid. The White House pulled all the fire alarms and people were scrambling to figure out what was going on.

I was already up past my usual bedtime, and well aware that November 4 could be a very demanding and chaotic day. I wanted to be as ready as possible for what fate—and Donald Trump—threw our way. After all, what was going to be was going to be at this point. I couldn't change it. I just needed to be prepared and rested for the aftermath. I turned the TV off and went to bed a little before midnight, praying once again as I did for a clean and clear outcome.

The next day was unusually calm, or maybe my expectation was that it would be chaotic. Joe Biden had leads in both the electoral vote and the popular vote, but because key states such as Georgia and Pennsylvania were still too close to call, neither candidate was declared the winner. I didn't expect an outcome where the race would be contested in a few critical states, but this occurring in the context of a Biden lead had a salutary tactical effect.

My personal assessment going into Election Day was that if the president won reelection, it was more likely that anti-Trump protesters would fill the streets across America. After four years, the left had had enough, and were going to let the country know. There was no way, I thought, that violence wouldn't break out. And with Trump newly reelected and empowered, I felt sure that he would finally *direct* the deployment of the military. Things would spiral out of control from there. This is all conjecture, but that was what my gut was telling me.

But with Biden in the lead on November 4, and the door(s) not fully closed on the president yet, there wasn't as much reason, it seemed, for people to rush into the streets. There was also no need to seize ballot boxes and do other things that some hard-core Trump loyalists were suggesting. Rather, they went into the state processes, and into the courts, just as they should. In a strange way, the outcome allowed the boiling steam to settle some, enough, while partisans on both sides tried to figure out the best way forward. Over time, this would have a socializing effect on the nation, I thought, before Trump would turn the burners back up with his continued and baseless claims that the election was "stolen" from him.

In the days following the election on November 3, I expected "the call" nearly every time the phone rang. After all, the election was over—except in Donald Trump's mind, perhaps—and I was now expendable. The White House and I had butted heads on issue after issue over the previous months. At a minimum they would at least want to fire me out of spite, or simply to remove an irritant. My dismissal would also clear the way for them to check off a few more bucket list items. I suspected all these motives were at play.

We had accomplished a good deal in the past six months when it came to advancing the Pentagon's National Defense Strategy and other big initiatives that would resonate for years, even though the noise coming out of the White House obscured much of it. For me,

I had made it through the election and kept the military out of politics, implemented my inside offense/outside defense strategy, and hadn't violated any of the Four Nos. If the president was going to fire me, then so be it. I was at peace with myself, knowing that I had tried hard to do the right thing every step of the way.

In the meantime, I wanted to project an aura of calm confidence and business as usual while also monitoring what was happening with the emerging challenges to the election results, keeping a careful watch on our external security, and pushing my internal agenda forward. And if the president dismissed me, I planned to leave professionally, with dignity, and with my sincerest thanks to the department.

Internationally, we still had concerns about Iran, implementation of the Afghan peace plan, and China's activities in the South China Sea and Taiwan Strait. I still had a lot going on within the building too: a meeting with the service secretaries, calls with members of Congress, my weekly Operation Warp Speed update, a review of proposed deployment orders, and an update on our diversity and inclusion initiatives, to name a few.

There were also several things not on my schedule that had been simmering in the previous weeks and months. Media stories would attribute my firing on November 9 to some of these items.

In late October, for example, General Paul Nakasone—the head of both Cyber Command and the National Security Agency (NSA)[*]—wrote asking for my support on an issue boiling over between him and Director of National Intelligence (DNI) John Ratcliffe regarding the release of sensitive information on Russia. Apparently, Trump

---

[*] The NSA is a "national-level intelligence agency of the U.S. Department of Defense, under the authority of the director of National Intelligence, that provides foreign signals intelligence (SIGINT) to our nation's policymakers and military forces."

wanted the intelligence declassified and made public, believing that doing so would rebut long-standing claims that Putin supported him during the 2016 election. It seemed like a silly thing to be worried about four years later.

Nakasone's concern, and mine as well, was that Ratcliffe's release risked exposing very sensitive sources and methods. This information was invaluable not only at the national strategic level but at the operational level as well for U.S. military forces. Its release would hurt national security and impose specific harm to the military. In short, it was too sensitive to declassify, and certainly not for some political issue. After receiving Nakasone's note, I instructed my staff to immediately draft a letter for me to send to the DNI fully supporting the NSA and opposing any release. The team moved out and I had a letter en route to Ratcliffe within forty-eight hours. I later learned that Gina Haspel, backed by Bill Barr, also fought against disclosing the information.

General Nakasone's pushback didn't go over well. This wasn't the first time he was in the White House's gunsights, however. In the run-up to the House impeachment hearings the year before, Representative Devin Nunes (R-CA), who was ranking member on the House Intelligence Committee, reportedly called the White House about Nakasone. It was never clear if he talked to the president or someone else close to Trump, but he apparently complained that the soft-spoken general was playing politics by allegedly giving sensitive information to Representative Adam Schiff, the committee chair, that could be used against Trump.

Schiff was probably Trump's biggest antagonist on Capitol Hill at the time. He was constantly on TV lambasting the president, and many would say he politicized the intelligence committee. As chairman, he made it his mission to investigate Trump's connections to

Russia in the 2016 election, and later became one of the lead investigators in the House impeachment inquiry.

That said, I found this allegation about General Nakasone hard to believe. And based on my experience with some in the White House, I suspected there was no hard evidence to support it. But the drums were starting to beat in the Oval Office for Trump to fire Nakasone, destroying a stellar career based on mere conjecture. This would be both unsurprising and grossly unfair.

The NSA and Cyber Command couldn't afford to lose Nakasone, nor could the country for that matter. He and the rest of the interagency leaders had taken us through the 2018 midterm elections with no hint of external interference. Losing him would also be bad for the military as an institution, and for our plans to grow our cyber offenses and defenses.

I needed to get the facts soonest, so I called him into my office on Wednesday, January 15, 2020, to get the details. Milley joined me in his camouflage fatigues and Nakasone in his Class B dress uniform. Nakasone was sober and straightforward and explained that, beginning in mid-October 2019, in Schiff's role as chair of the House Intelligence Committee, the California Democrat had asked for reams of "NSA information regarding the Russians and the 2016 elections, especially as it involved conversations with U.S. persons."

Some people could call the breadth of information requested a fishing expedition for evidence, while others would say it was lazy staff work by the committee. "Over a period of weeks," Nakasone explained, "my team worked to narrow the scope of the request, not only to get a better understanding of their focus but also to strip away unnecessary work" for the NSA team that had to assemble it. I asked him if Schiff's request "was unusual and out of the norm, especially in light of everything else going on." While it

certainly could look suspect in the context of the pending impeachment, the general said Schiff's request was "not inconsistent with
what previous committee chairmen had asked for in the past."

Nakasone had another concern, one that had been growing over
the past few weeks—Schiff's Intelligence Committee staff, he said
as he sat up in his chair, "are growing impatient with the time it was
taking" to gather the information. Also believing that Nakasone and
the NSA were playing politics, the general felt, Schiff threatened that
he would "use any means necessary to obtain the reports," to include
the issuance of subpoenas, fencing the NSA's funding, and denying
NSA budget reprogramming requests. Any of this would be bad. "I
get it," I said, "such actions would make it look like you and the
NSA are playing politics." I added, "We can't afford to politicize the
intelligence community and their products." General Milley agreed.

The three of us discussed the issue for a while longer until I had
a good understanding of the matter. Nakasone had done nothing
wrong or out of the ordinary, though I did tell him at the end he
needed to "bring these issues to me sooner so that we have more
time to deal with them before they are in crisis stage. That way we'll
all have more maneuver room." Nakasone understood and agreed.

Although both the NSA and Cyber Command that Nakasone led
were in my chain of command, when it came to intelligence matters,
the general took his direction from the DNI. My understanding was
that Nakasone was raising this issue with the acting DNI but wasn't
getting much support—and probably wouldn't, I suspected. My
hunch would prove to be correct.

Despite Schiff's request not being unique, it didn't mean the congressman wasn't trying to use his position as committee chair to get
information he could use against the president in the upcoming impeachment hearing. We simply couldn't prove that. Nakasone was
trapped in the middle between his congressional overseer—Adam

Schiff—and his executive branch boss—Joe Maguire—whose confirmation to become the next director of National Intelligence was pending. As we parted, I thanked him for bringing this to me and said to him, "Just follow your processes and do the right thing. I have your back." With that, we shook hands, and he and Milley left.

A short time later, I called Robert O'Brien and asked that we hold a meeting in his office with all the key civilian players to discuss the situation with Nakasone and the National Security Agency, which he went about organizing. In addition to the two of us, Joe Maguire and John Eisenberg also attended. Pat Cipollone might have been there as well, though I'm sure I had a separate conversation with him about this in his office.

We went back and forth on the issue for thirty minutes in O'Brien's office at the White House. Maguire didn't want to decide one way or the other. He was likely concerned it would become an issue that would affect his Senate confirmation, and he was probably right. If he told Nakasone to ignore Schiff's requests, then this would become an issue for Senate Democrats, and maybe some Republicans. If he told Nakasone to provide Schiff the information, then Trump could easily withdraw his nomination. As a result, Maguire wasn't giving Nakasone direction one way or the other. He was just telling him that the White House didn't want to send up the information, which put the monkey on Nakasone's back.

The NSC legal position was that "any information that Schiff received could be used against the president during the impeachment." They were right, of course, though I told them that "according to Nakasone, he and his team saw nothing in the information that raised any flags." The NSC lawyers acknowledged this, but they were being extra cautious, replying that regardless, they "want to lock down the facts far in advance of the hearing, and are concerned about even a 1 percent chance that Schiff might find something."

"Look," I told them, "I understand what you all are saying, but it's unfair to put Nakasone in this position. We shouldn't ask a uniformed officer to unilaterally make the call on an issue with such heavy political overtones. It puts Nakasone and the NSA in a terrible position, and risks politicizing the intelligence community. We can't afford that. Plus, NSA has a duty to their congressional overseers to provide this information." I added, "We may not like the fact that Schiff is in charge, but we can't do anything about it." I turned to Maguire, a retired admiral and former Navy SEAL, and said, "Joe, I know you get this. You need to make the call. NSA reports to you, not to me, and not to the White House."

There was dead silence. Maguire was clearly uncomfortable, shifting around in his seat and looking around the room for cues. I fully understood why. He was a good guy in a bad spot. I didn't envy him. The meeting was running long, so I said, "This needs to be decided in the next day or two." I continued, "If it's not, then I'm going to send a letter to Nakasone as his 'secondary commander'"—a term I made up on the spot—"directing him to provide the information." As I stood up, I added, "This issue needs [to be] resolved, and he needs top cover." With that, I shook hands with everybody and left O'Brien's corner office.

I went back to the Pentagon and spoke with Milley. I told him about my conversation at the White House, and that I didn't want Nakasone to send anything to the House Intelligence Committee unilaterally. That would surely get him fired. Give it until the end of the week; the ball was now in Maguire's court to act. Milley called Nakasone and conveyed the message, adding that Acting DNI Maguire would provide further guidance in the next twenty-four to forty-eight hours, which was the way I left it at the White House.

I didn't hear any further rumblings about firing Nakasone until after Grenell replaced Maguire as acting DNI in February 2020.

The president raised the matter of the four-star Army general with me later, directly, in an Oval Office meeting one afternoon in the early spring. Trump brought up the matter the way he did with others with whom he was unhappy, first asking "What do you know about this general at the NSA, General Nak-a-so-ne?" He said the name slowly, recalling how to pronounce it, I thought. "Is he doing a good job? What do you think?" he pressed. "Great officer," I said, "The country is lucky to have him." General Milley added a few positive words as well. Trump then looked down—he was writing or signing something as he spoke—and mumbled something like "I don't know. I'm hearing he's helping Schiff and the Democrats. . . ." I suspected Grenell had pointed a finger at Nakasone as he looked to remove "anti-Trump" people at the NSA now that he was acting DNI.

"Mr. President, that's not true," I said, "You're getting some bad information. General Nakasone wouldn't play politics." General Milley responded from a complementary angle, arguing that military officers have a responsibility to remain apolitical, and in this case as head of the NSA, be responsive to their congressional overseers. Trump let it go. Impeachment was behind him by that point, so I assumed the issue wasn't as burning for him. Milley and I left the Oval Office confident that we had beaten this issue back, but Trump had complaints about other four-star officers that we would also have to tackle at times.

The nation was fortunate we didn't lose General Nakasone. He had a distinguished career commanding at multiple levels in the United States and abroad, and few in the military knew or understood cyber warfare like he did. Nakasone also had the leadership credentials to go with it, and the reputation for getting things done. Many months later, on August 24, 2020, I met with him to assess how best to beef up the nation's cyber capabilities. In a series of meetings that would continue into the fall, Nakasone proposed several initiatives to reprioritize his force, grow the number of cyber teams, improve its professional education and training, and ensure greater control of financial resources in the upcoming budget, among other things. They were all smart proposals that would take our defensive and offensive cyber capabilities to the next level, but they also generated some resistance within the Pentagon.

In due course, we would work our way through these matters and I would sign off on his ideas. At the same time, we pressed ahead on Cyber Command's so-called Defend Forward Strategy, ensuring persistent engagement with cyber actors to defeat them online and support a whole-of-government effort to ensure a secure election. It was always a good day when we could focus on the nation's security and make a real difference, and not have to deal with the distractions some at the White House could create. Thank goodness we were able to protect General Nakasone from the personal politics of Trump and his loyalists.

I don't know how much my late October 2020 letter to Ratcliffe in support of Nakasone weighed on Trump's decision about my fate. The same for my back-door communication to the Chinese military leadership in the days prior to the election. My pushback on the precipitous withdrawals from Afghanistan and Somalia was more likely the cause. It was pure vindictiveness—whether from Trump or some of the folks around him, it was hard to know—coupled with a desire by the White House to accomplish some last-minute things they knew I would oppose.

On November 5, one news network published a story that I had prepared a letter of resignation to offer the president.[1] Like many senior officials, I had such a letter prepared for many months, a framework draft, so to speak. In my case, I had one ready in the event that one of the Four Nos was breached and my only option became resignation. It was never my intention to simply step down as the story implied, though I realized certain situations might warrant it. In my mind, and as I later said to a reporter, if my soldiers, sailors, airmen, and Marines couldn't quit when the going got tough, then I wasn't quitting either.

If forced to resign, though, I wanted it to be over something big. Jim Mattis took some flak after stepping aside over what some considered a minor issue—the ordered withdrawal of several hundred troops from northern Syria—which, in fact, we later reversed. I was determined to keep following my game plan until the president fired me. This was the sound advice I was receiving from some of my predecessors—Republicans and Democrats alike—and others outside the Pentagon whom I trusted and respected, and spoke with often.

I wasn't eager to leave, however. We still had work to do, and with a presidential transition expected in about seventy-five days, I wanted to effect the best handoff possible to the Biden team to ensure their success. It was the right thing to do, and what the Pentagon always did. Therefore, I let the White House know that, contrary to what the media was saying, I had no plans to resign.

The story, however, also reported that I was "helping members of Congress draft legislation that will strip names of Confederate leaders from military bases." This was another misstatement that risked inflaming Trump, who opposed renaming any bases.[2]

The president was on the wrong side of this issue. He had asked Milley and me our views on a few occasions, and we told him we supported renaming the bases. Moreover, despite what he was told or believed, or what commitments were made by members of Congress, there was no doubt in my mind that base-renaming language was going to be included in the annual National Defense Authorization Act (NDAA). Both Armed Services Committees included provisions in their annual bills, and support for these measures was bipartisan and widespread. Having worked on the House Armed Services Committee in the past, I had a good sense of how this was going to play out, an instinct confirmed by congressional staff and members with whom I spoke. The president was getting bad advice.

I knew Congress would return right after the election to close out the year, and staffs of the Armed Services Committees had already begun discussing the contours of the final NDAA language in October. Confederate base renaming would be an issue left to the chairmen and ranking members of both committees, and they were expected to wrap this up by mid-November—just a week or so away. That way they could finalize the bill and get it passed in both chambers before Christmas break. I also expected all or some of them would call and ask for my views on the issue.

My biggest concern was that Congress, ever the political body that it was, might include language in the base-renaming provision that risked politicizing the military by, say, keeping open the door to name bases after political persons from the right or left. We needed to keep politics out of the military space. But to have a shot at doing so, we needed to share the views of the Department, and especially of the uniformed leaders, with Congress in advance. This was how things worked.

A few weeks earlier, on October 16, I met privately with Army Secretary Ryan McCarthy and Army Chief of Staff Jim McConville about this matter. The Army had ten bases named after Confederate military leaders: Fort Hood, Fort Bragg, Fort Benning, Fort Gordon, Fort Lee, Fort A. P. Hill, Fort Polk, Fort Rucker, the Virginia National Guard post Fort Pickett, and the Louisiana National Guard's Camp Beauregard. Both leaders were anxious to rename the bases, and they were concerned about how Congress might tell them to change the names. Milley couldn't make it to the meeting, but he shared all these same views as well.

I told McCarthy and McConville that we had to figure out two things. First, what are the criteria by which we would strip names from bases? We had seen over the summer how activists were pulling down statues of Grant and Lincoln, and some were going after Washington and other Founding Fathers. The senior leadership at the Pentagon and I felt that had gone way too far, and we didn't want our military installations to get caught up in that silliness. The second issue was, what should be the criteria that would guide renaming them? I asked McCarthy and McConville to think about this and come back to me in a week with a recommendation.

I knew I was taking a risk—it seemed that someone on the Army staff was intent on leaking sensitive information to the media. I couldn't afford to have that happen; it might appear that the DoD was choosing political sides. I also didn't want to undermine the president on the eve of an election. On the other hand, this issue was too important to not have something ready to share with Congress right after November 3—especially if Trump lost. I needed to give the president options too. And for the recommendations to be credible, they needed the support of the armed services, especially the Army. I asked both men to be very discreet in their deliberations.

As defense secretary, I stated over and over the importance of the DoD remaining apolitical. But taking an apolitical approach doesn't mean I didn't understand politics, wasn't familiar with the political terrain, or didn't operate in this milieu—I had more than two decades of experience in Washington, D.C., after all, including many years on Capitol Hill and service on a presidential campaign.

It also doesn't mean that I didn't engage Congress to advance the administration's and the DoD's agendas. This is all part of what a civilian secretary does. I just saw a huge difference between the politics required of the job to be successful in advancing an effective, nonpartisan national security agenda, as compared to the parochialism, personal attacks, and party stridency that constituted the ugly side of politics and undermined the former. The latter was the type of toxic political gamesmanship now sharply dividing our great country.

On the other hand, I was also a political appointee and expected to advance the president's agenda. That I did also. However, I worked to do so within the limits of my oath—which was my highest duty—and my obligation to the institution, its mission, and its traditions.

November 3 came and went without a story on the Confederate base-renaming matter, but with the results showing a Biden win, and the chance that Democrats could take the Senate in addition to keeping the House, I became even more concerned about this issue being politicized. A divided Congress tended to produce better, more enduring results, rather than a legislative branch controlled by only one party. And if the Democrats ended up controlling the House, Senate, *and* White House, there was no telling where this issue could end up if the far left of the Democratic Party pushed hard.

By Election Day, however, we had general agreement internally on the Department's recommendation, which proposed that the services remove the names of any base or installation named after anyone who committed treason against the United States, rose up in armed opposition to the federal government, was a member of a group that advocated insurrection against the United States, or was convicted of a felony in a U.S. court.

The criteria the military departments would apply in the future, if they decided to name a base after an individual, required that this person meet the following conditions: deceased; awarded the

Silver Star or higher for combat valor, or made an extraordinary contribution to the military while in uniform; had a record of impeccable conduct both in and out of uniform; and reflected the values, attributes, and traditions of his or her military service.

Chairman Milley informed me that the Joint Chiefs supported these criteria. We all agreed that the process for generating nominees needed to be a very inclusive one, and one that involved the surrounding communities where these bases were located. This would take time, but better in these types of situations to build understanding, transparency, and inclusivity into an objective process. I shared all of this with the chairmen and ranking members of the Armed Services Committees the week after I left the Pentagon.

By the end of the first full week in November, I was surprised I was still on the job. I had received several very positive comments, from Republicans and Democrats alike, lauding my steady leadership and urging Trump to keep me on board. I shared with Jen Stewart, my chief of staff, my amazement that we weren't gone yet. After months and months of "last days," we were still standing. Go figure, I thought.

I had accomplished most of what I wanted to do by the third with the help of her steady hand, able assistance, and deft management of the building. If there was a chance I was staying, then what should be our focus in addition to our ongoing plans? Clearly, it would be remaining alert and on guard during a likely turbulent change in administration, which is always a tenuous and uncertain time anyway. At the same time, we would need to get the Biden transition team up to speed so that they could hit the ground running on January 20, 2021.

On Saturday, November 7, *Politico* ran a story headlined, "Trump

Expected to Keep Esper at the Pentagon Despite Clashes."[3] I chuckled to myself. I learned from experience that if this was what *Politico* was reporting, then there was a good chance it was wrong. I had read too many stories about the DoD from *Politico* that I viewed as inaccurate, incomplete, or, in some cases, just plain false.

An omen marked that same day for me, as well. I'm not a superstitious person, but this was the one moment in my life that I really read something into a coincidence. As I went through my bureau at home that morning looking for something to wear for the day, I accidentally knocked my West Point ring off the dresser. It landed hard on the wood floor with a sharp sound and broke apart.

After thirty-five years of wear, tear, and previous drops, I thought it unusual that it would break now. Many times over the previous eighteen months, in some of the darkest of moments and toughest of times, I would look down at the gold ring on my left hand and read the academy motto emblazoned on its side: "Duty, Honor, Country." It would always remind me of General Douglas MacArthur's famous saying, the one we had to memorize as plebes and recite with perfection when grilled by upperclassmen:

> Duty, Honor, Country: Those three hallowed words reverently dictate what you ought to be, what you can be, what you will be. They are your rallying points: to build courage when courage seems to fail; to regain faith when there seems to be little cause for faith; to create hope when hope becomes forlorn.

Those words seemed to sum up many of my experiences as President Trump's secretary of defense, and how I labored to soldier on and lead the department despite all that we faced. As I reached down to pick up the pieces, an inner voice told me it was game over.

I went into work on Monday morning early as usual. The

standard leadership team meeting was on for 8:00 A.M. The news over the weekend was all about Trump and others challenging the election results in a few states, and that the General Services Administration (GSA) had declined to move forward on its duty to make an "ascertainment" decision regarding the outcome. Absent GSA action, the DoD and all other federal agencies and departments were in a holding pattern. That said, we saw the writing on the wall and wanted to lean into the transition.

Without getting out too far over our ski tips, we invited the director of Washington Headquarters Services—the DoD organization responsible for enabling the transition, among many other things—to brief everyone on what they were planning, GSA's role in the process, and what we could expect in the coming days and weeks. The director was a career member of the Senior Executive Service who did a very thorough job explaining the process in a matter-of-fact way.

Of course, the White House was very sensitive to any talk or actions in the departments regarding transition that might signal that Joe Biden was the president-elect. Some news reports said people were being threatened with immediate dismissal if they did so. As such, we limited the questions the director would be asked. With a group this large in the room, every now and then something would leak to the press.

After the director spoke, though, I did follow up with a few short comments, emphasizing that "we would follow the law and our oath to the Constitution. Once GSA makes the ascertainment, and assuming Joe Biden is officially determined to be the winner, I want us to lean hard into the transition process." I added with emphasis, "I want to be transparent and open about everything, and I want this transition to be remembered as the best, most professional ever conducted." This statement seems so naive in retrospect, given what happened from mid-November and into January, and the exact opposite of what would transpire at the Pentagon after my departure. It was a shame.

I returned to my office after the staff meeting in time for my weekly call with Pompeo at 9:30 A.M. We discussed Somalia, security at our embassy in Baghdad, the DoD's plans to deter Iranian aggression during the transition, arms sales to the United Arab Emirates, next steps on Afghanistan, and what to do about the bad info we'd received from the NSC during the Walton rescue mission. He and I had already spoken with O'Brien about this last issue but weren't confident the problem would be addressed.

This sentiment was buttressed by an alarming event that had occurred a couple of weeks earlier involving the National Security Council. Mike and I learned that Trump loyalists, allegedly led by an NSC staffer, went to the British embassy in D.C. for a special meeting, unbeknown to anyone at State. While there, they placed a call to the U.K. Foreign Office to convey the president's supposed plans to take a series of significant actions after the election. First, they reportedly said, Trump would redeploy all U.S. forces from Afghanistan by Christmas. Second, all U.S. forces would be withdrawn from Iraq and Syria. Third, all American troops would be pulled out of Somalia. And finally, Trump would reopen negotiations with Iran. Not surprisingly, the British government was spinning around in circles trying to figure out who these guys were, and how credible their message was.

Pompeo and I couldn't believe it either. We were quite livid. How could these people take such irresponsible and unprofessional actions, ones that completely undermined our own policies and administration? A few days after we found out about this transgression, Pompeo and I gave Robert O'Brien a call one evening to get to the bottom of it. We laid out the facts as they were conveyed to us by the Brits and our folks. The message delivered to them was rippling through the U.K. Foreign and Defense Ministries and was ricocheting back into our own buildings in Washington now as well. None of these ideas were new to the Trump White House, so they weren't hard to believe or easy to dismiss. O'Brien claimed he knew nothing about it.

In terms of damage control, we all agreed to inform our counterparts in the United Kingdom that while these actions had been discussed in the past, the president had made no decisions. Pompeo would take the lead since the Foreign Office took the wayward call. Meanwhile, O'Brien would call in his staff to sort out what happened and hold folks accountable. Neither Pompeo, Milley, nor I had much faith in this, so Mike and I agreed to follow up later with Meadows, or maybe even the president.

From where we stood now on November 9, though, Pompeo and I agreed that the top priority in the coming weeks was Iran and Iraq. We were concerned that Shia militia groups in Baghdad aligned with Tehran would act up during the transition period, and certainly around the anniversary of Soleimani's killing in early January. We had kept a watchful eye over these groups for well over a year now. And while they were armed, equipped, and funded by Iran, and would take direction as well, they didn't always listen to Tehran.

These groups were chomping at the bit to kill Americans, and this created a good deal of instability and unpredictability. We discussed ways to beef up our security of the embassy in Baghdad, and I told Mike we were planning a variety of military activities to demonstrate our resolve and capabilities, to include flying B-52 sorties into the region over the next couple months, as would later be reported by the press.[4] We planned to have a follow-up discussion in a couple of weeks.

As for Afghanistan, Mike and I both agreed that conditions

hadn't been met to go lower than 4,500 troops in the country, but Mike thought the president wouldn't accept that. I mentioned the letter I had sent to Trump on this issue recommending no further reductions, and that I had copied him so that he knew where the DoD and I were on the issue.

Over lunch in my office on November 9, I finished reading the day's intelligence reports. Around 12:50 P.M. or so, my phone began ringing. It was a call from Mark Meadows. Moments before, Jen Stewart had opened an email from the Office of Presidential Personnel. She jumped from her chair and rushed into my office around the second ring in time to say "Meadows is calling you. I just got this email. The president plans on firing you!" Okay, I said, staring back at her. I paused for a second to think. Half smiled. And then, standing, picked up the phone.

Meadows was very businesslike. I had expected this call for a long time. In a steady pitch marked by his North Carolina accent, he said, "The president is firing you this afternoon." He added that Chris Miller (who?) "will be replacing you as acting secretary."

The chief of staff continued, "The president's not happy with you. He feels you haven't supported him enough." He added, "You aren't sufficiently loyal."

I paused, thought, and replied in an even tone, "That's the president's prerogative," but quickly added, "My oath is to the Constitution, not to him." With that, we both hung up.

There, it was done. The time was 12:54 P.M. The president's tweet came out right after that to seal the deal. So much for the good old days when you would have a sit-down with the commander in chief, talk through the matter, agree upon your departure date, and then do everything possible to make sure the new person is on-boarded properly before you left. But that was not Trump. He and his confidants didn't understand personal leadership, didn't realize the impact these things had on organizations and people, and certainly didn't appreciate what it could mean for our nation's security at the end of a hotly contested election in the beginnings of a major transition. Not only didn't Trump understand, but he also didn't care. It was all about him.

The news rattled some folks in my front office and shocked others into silence, with several upset for me and what just happened. We had all formed such close bonds over the many long days and longer months. I was at peace with the situation. The long struggle was over for me, but I was now concerned about those left behind. It had been a hard year and a half; the last six months were extraordinarily difficult. 2020 was probably the most tumultuous year of maybe the most tumultuous presidency in history.

We had somehow endured at the Defense Department, as individuals and as a team. I was proud of everyone; they sacrificed a good deal too. I felt that we remained true to our oath, to our values, to the country. And while I didn't always get it right, I always worked hard to do the right thing. I'll regret the missteps for a long time, for sure. On the other hand, I reflected on the fact that my strategy succeeded, that we didn't violate the Four Nos, and that the military didn't get involved in the election. That would all be behind me now. No more coming in each and every day, as if it were my last, and asking myself: What can I do today to implement the NDS, to make the armed forces better, to take care of our people, to make the nation safer?

I would have time to reflect more deeply later. Right now, however, I had a clock on me. I needed to think through what needed to be done to enable the transition—meet with Norquist; talk with Milley; inform public affairs; gather with my inner team; say goodbye to folks. I needed to let Leah know too. I also wanted to make sure that I left with dignity—that my departure was professional and reflected my respect for the institution and tradition.

I had a Final Message to the Department prepared and asked that it be sent out immediately.* It was my last chance to thank all 2.8 million service members and DoD civilian employees for their service to country and support to me. So much of their great work over the past eighteen months had been obscured by the constant noise coming out of the White House. I wanted them to know that we had accomplished a great deal together despite an uncertain strategic environment, the worst civil unrest in generations, a major economic downturn, and a global pandemic the world hadn't seen the likes of in one hundred years.

In this short note, I told them, "It has been the honor and privilege of a lifetime to serve alongside you as the 27th U.S. secretary of defense these last eighteen months in defense of our great Nation and adherence to our sworn oath to the Constitution." I reminded everyone of the solid progress we made "implementing the National Defense Strategy" and "taking care of our military personnel, spouses, and their families," while also launching "important initiatives" to improve diversity and inclusion in the armed services.

I included in my note the reminder that "we have always put People and Country first"—an important message I thought the White House should hear as well. And I thanked them for remaining apolitical and living up to "those values and behaviors that represent the best of the military profession and mark the character and integrity of the Armed Forces the American people respect and admire"—the same message that I emphasized from day one.

---

* For the Final Message to the Department, see Appendix E.

I also finalized a letter to the president and asked that it be hand-carried to the White House that afternoon.* I wanted the note to be professional, dignified, and focused on the DoD, its people, and what we accomplished. Not Trump. There would be time for that at some future point, I calculated, to share everything else. Now was not that time.

I told the president, "I have served these last few years as both secretary of defense and secretary of the Army in full faith to my sworn oath to support and defend the Constitution, and to safeguard the country and its interests, while keeping the Department out of politics and abiding by the values Americans hold dear."

I outlined the solid progress the DoD made implementing the National Defense Strategy by "modernizing the force, improving its readiness and lethality, strengthening ties with allies and partners, and reforming the Department to make it more efficient." I went on to cite the numerous things we accomplished over the last eighteen months, including the fact that we "stood up the Space Force and Space Command, recapitalized the nuclear triad, expanded the authorities and resources of Cyber Command, launched a readiness and capabilities renaissance in the Army, and proposed a bold vision for a 500+ ship Navy."

And given the tumult of the moment, and the difficult two-plus month transition ahead of the country, I wanted to send a message to the world by adding, "I am confident the Defense Department's progress on all of these initiatives has improved the security of the United States and advanced our interests abroad, and that we would prevail in any conflict if called upon to do so." It was important to make sure our friends and foes alike knew that the U.S. military was on its toes and ready in these uncertain times.

---

* For the November 9, 2020, Letter to the President, see Appendix F.

The memo also acknowledged the president's decision to fire me by stating, "I serve the country in deference to the Constitution, so I accept your decision to replace me."

I closed the letter with what I felt in my heart: "I have never been prouder to serve my country than as a Soldier or Civilian in the Department of Defense."

General Milley stopped by quickly. He walked in my office and shut the door behind him. "I can't believe he fucking fired you," he said. We had talked and joked about this often in the past— gallows humor—but now it was real. He was very angry and upset, saying, "This is complete bullshit" and "I can't believe he did this." He paced back and forth a couple of times, threatening to resign as well. I thanked him—we had been through a lot together over the years, and his emotions reflected the depth of our partnership—but I stood there and said, "You can't do that. You're the only one left now to hold the line. You *have* to stay." It was true, and we both knew it. He had to be around to push back, "especially now that we are entering a particularly dangerous period," I said.

"You have to stay for the military, the institution, and the country." He was steaming, though. Not just with the fact that Trump fired me, but also with the way he did it. I kept telling him "It's fine," that "I never expected the president to be magnanimous." We had seen this movie too many times before with other people Trump dismissed. "I'm sorry about this," he said, as reality settled in. I suspect the chairman was now feeling very exposed and isolated as well, with me heading out the door and a supposed Trump guy on the way in. He was going to be in a tough place for the next seventy days or so. I felt for him.

General Milley wanted to organize a quick "clap out," which is a tradition wherein people throughout the building come down to the Secretary's office and form a cordon running from the second floor down to the front steps outside the building, clapping for the exiting secretary as he departs the Pentagon one last time. I had participated in the clap out for Pat Shanahan, saying goodbye to him right before he climbed in the car. It is a nice, informal, and emotional ceremony folks had done for years.

As nice as it would have been for everyone to do, we couldn't let it happen. By this time, the White House Office of Presidential Personnel had installed their loyalists in the building, and I was getting reports about their seemingly thuggish behavior with other political appointees and career civilians, and even some military personnel in a couple of cases. My folks were concerned that if people showed up for the clap out, hard-core loyalists at the Pentagon would be taking names. I didn't want to put good people in a bad position, possibly jeopardizing their livelihoods by participating in the clap out tradition. So I turned it down, said my final goodbyes to my inner-office team—Jen Stewart, Anne Powers, and Emily Chumaceiro—with a hug, and farewells to Lieutenant General Bryan Fenton, my senior military assistant, and my aide Lieutenant Colonel Caleb Hyatt, with a handshake, grabbed my briefcase, and headed for the back door down to the waiting car. It was around 2:30 P.M.

As we pulled out of the underground garage for the last time, I reminisced about my many years in the Army, and particularly my days at the Pentagon. My first of five assignments in the building began in 1995, twenty-five years earlier, when I'd made the long walk in uniform from the north parking lot to my cubicle in the Army War Plans office every morning. Now here I was a quarter century later, taking the short walk in a business suit from that historic secretary of defense office—where a large portrait of General Marshall watched over my desk from behind for nearly eighteen months—to the black Suburban waiting to take me home. What a journey. What a privilege.

As we drove away from the Pentagon one last time, I thought of Marshall's famous statement about leadership, and hoped that I lived up to it:

The most important factor of all is character, which involves integrity, unselfish and devoted purpose, a sturdiness of bearing when everything goes wrong and all are critical, and a willingness to sacrifice self in the interest of the common good.

And so, the purge began. It was November 10, the day after my dismissal, and the long knives were finally out. Brandished in the open. The White House fired James Anderson as acting undersecretary for policy, the third most important civilian official at the Pentagon, outside of the service secretaries. Next up was Joe Kernan, the retired admiral and SEAL commander who was undersecretary of defense for intelligence. He had been in the gunsights of the White House for a while, and each time they went after him I was able to blunt it. I expected Ellen Lord, the undersecretary of defense for acquisition and sustainment, to also be dismissed. Ellen, who was previously the CEO of an aerospace and defense company, had done a great job at the Pentagon. She was also a team player who worked well with others, but for some reason her name came up at times as well for dismissal. I never could figure out why. Each time I pushed back I was successful, but I had to keep my guard up.

My chief of staff, Jen Stewart, left the Pentagon within days of my firing, and other members of my inner office were reassigned.

Getting rid of good, honest, competent people seemed to be the modus operandi for the Trump administration, especially in 2020. In the final year, a disagreement with some staffer at the White House, or with someone who had connections to the hard-core loyalists working there, and you were quickly branded as a disloyal "never Trumper"—the ultimate scarlet letter.

We all understood that political appointees worked for the president. It was his prerogative to hire, fire, and move people as he saw fit. The American people elected him, after all. But the White House seemingly made personnel decisions in a vacuum, and those decisions were made by personalities who really didn't have the background, understanding or judgment to make good choices. It was both ironic and a shame, but their blind loyalty to Trump resulted in the removal of individuals who were actually making Trump successful by ensuring the government functioned well and implemented the positive parts of his agenda.

The White House planned to fire other senior Pentagon personnel, including David Norquist, but apparently the private intervention by Mitch McConnell, the Senate majority leader, stopped the purge. A lot of damage had already been done, however. It was good for the Department and the country that David Norquist was kept in place as deputy secretary of defense to help transition the incoming Biden team. He would do the right thing.

More harm would occur as the Defense Policy and Defense Business Boards—bipartisan advisory groups of renowned men and women—were dismantled, something I had fended off through the fall. The White House was decapitating the Department and traumatizing the survivors—everyone else—in the process. All were anxious, trying to understand the meaning behind the dismissals, and the schemes of the loyalists the White House was installing to replace them. Meanwhile, all of this was happening in the backdrop of an election, the results of which Trump and his loyalists were hotly contesting with a growing number of bizarre assertions and theories.

As the days and weeks passed, and November turned into December, some of the ideas coming out of the White House were getting more and more desperate. There were credible reports of plans to attack Iran (again) and completely withdraw from Afghanistan (again), for example.

Personnel changes reportedly involved a scheme to replace Gina Haspel's deputy at the CIA with a Trump loyalist, and maybe even doing the same to FBI director Chris Wray. Then there was an attempt to split the National Security Agency and U.S. Cyber Command. General Nakasone, whom the White House didn't like, led both organizations. Taking away the NSA from him would allow Trump to appoint someone to be the acting director of NSA.[1] Why? For what purpose? These were the unanswered questions about all these moves.

As with so many other matters, all this scheming was completely unnecessary, because all the president ever had to do was issue a direct order to effect what he wanted. I never disobeyed a direct order from the president, but then again, I received so few to begin with. Rather, I worked to implement his signed policies and documents, like the National Defense Strategy, which went through a deliberate, coordinated process and had his explicit approval. Trump was, after all, the elected head of government. For some reason, though, the president was always reluctant to issue orders or ask people directly to do something. It seemed he didn't want to own the decision, even though a president is inevitably responsible for everything.

The Trump administration had a lot of shortcomings, but second only to the president's personal style and crass behavior was how the White House treated people who were doing their best to serve the country under difficult circumstances. An organization is only as good as the people who constitute it, and that is true whether you serve in the military, work in a large corporation, are employed at a nonprofit, or are on the government payroll.

Trump had a lot of good people working for him in the departments and agencies across the federal government. But when their values clashed with his, and their priorities turned out to be misaligned, the friction started, and it often started early. It certainly did for me. Nonetheless, even three years into his tenure, long after people were familiar with Trump's shortcomings, good people still wanted to work in the administration. Not necessarily because they supported him, but because many wanted to serve their country.

But by the fourth year, once Trump beat impeachment, and more true believers were brought into the White House, blind loyalty to the president and absolute alignment with his views became the litmus test for everyone. Competence, experience, knowledge of government, integrity, and other attributes that most Americans would (and should) expect of government officials in senior positions were often thrown out the Oval Office window. The White House applied this new filter not only to people coming into the administration but to ones who were already serving—ones who had been vetted by the Trump team before 2020.

The infusion of new loyalists and the replacement of those considered insufficiently obsequious changed the dynamics within the administration. Either you became one of these persons, or you were no longer a member of the team. The president seemed to surround himself with more and more sycophants who would blindly do his bidding, agree with his ideas, and implement his plans regardless of the consequences. This seemed to empower the president and make him even more aggressive during his last several months in office.

The country became like a runaway car, barreling down a hill, with Trump behind the wheel and his loyalists pushing down hard on the accelerator, while others in the White House ripped out the brakes and cut the seat belts. Still, others sat in the backseat, urging the president, "Go faster!"

In the embargoed interview I did right after the election, I explained my strategy for navigating the final half year or so of the Trump presidency—advancing the nation's security, stopping bad things from happening, doing my duty, and honoring my oath, all without disobeying the elected president or giving the White House cause to fire me before we made it through the election. My overarching concern in that regard was "Who's going to come in behind me" and how much time would they have to do permanent damage? I told the reporter, "It's going to be a real 'yes man.' And then God help us."[2]

The White House installed many of the real yes men to aid the others already at the Pentagon and in the administration after November 9, but at least there were only a couple of months remaining at that point. God did help us, or at least me.

The most shocking and troubling event of the Trump presidency was the organization and incitement of a pro-Trump mob that stormed the Capitol on January 6, 2021, and stopped the constitutional process Congress was following to affirm the election and transfer of power to a new president. I never thought I would see what happened on Capitol Hill that day.

It was the worst attack on the Capitol since the War of 1812, and maybe the worst assault on our democracy since the Civil War. And as someone who worked for many years in Congress, and had an office physically in the Capitol, I was shocked, angry, sad, and hurt by what I saw on TV that day. It was doubly hard to believe our fellow Americans conducted these criminal and seditious acts. I would put out my first real tweets as a private citizen that evening, condemning the assault on Congress and those involved in it.*

Just days before, on January 3, 2021, I joined the nine other living former defense secretaries in an opinion piece—the first ever—calling upon the Defense Department to stay out of electoral disputes and to facilitate the peaceful handover of power—reiterating what I had said many times as secretary of defense.† We had no idea, of course, what would happen at the Capitol on January 6, three days later. We were concerned, however, about what was occurring at the time, with Trump loyalists at the Pentagon impeding the transition and Republican lawmakers on Capitol Hill challenging the election results.

The piece cited our oaths to the Constitution—not to a party or an individual—and reminded readers that "there's no role for the U.S. military in determining the outcome of a U.S. election." Unsure of what else Trump might do in his final weeks of office to stay in power, we made sure our former colleagues at the Pentagon understood their solemn duty and that any actions by the DoD to resolve election disputes "would take us into dangerous, unlawful, and unconstitutional duty."[3]

While some at the time thought concerns such as these were hyperbole, we would learn later that Trump entertained a multi-hour discussion in the White House on Friday, December 18, on such issues. This meeting reportedly featured lawyer Sidney Powell, joined by former national security adviser Michael Flynn, who proposed declaring a national security emergency. Powell alleged the voting machines were rigged to work against Trump.

In a televised interview the previous day, Flynn had strongly suggested that Trump declare martial law, and then "he could

---

* For my January 6, 2021, tweets, see Appendix G.
† For this *Washington Post* opinion piece, see Appendix H.

immediately, on his order, seize every single one of these machines."
The former national security adviser then stated that Trump
"could order . . . within the swing states, if he wanted to, he could
take military capabilities and he could place them in those states
and basically rerun an election in each of those states," adding, "I
mean, it's not unprecedented. These people are out there talking
about martial law like it's something that we've never done. Martial law has been instituted . . . sixty-four times."[4] Scary, and real.

At the end of our joint statement, my fellow secretaries and I
called upon senior leaders at the Pentagon "to do as so many generations of Americans have done before them" and "in keeping
with the highest traditions and professionalism of the U.S. armed
forces," to not undermine the results of the election or hinder the
success of the new administration. Such was the request—indeed,
the plea—from ten defense secretaries, Republican and Democrat
alike, spanning over three decades of service to country and multiple, peaceful transitions of power in the world's oldest democracy.

On January 20, 2021, Joe Biden was sworn in as the forty-sixth
president of the United States. Donald Trump did not even bother
to attend the Inauguration—the first sitting and able president to
skip his successor's inauguration since 1869. It was a final act of
petulance that defied tradition, tarnished our democracy, and further damaged Biden's legitimacy with millions of Americans.

The military played its traditional part in the peaceful transfer
of power, however—providing honor cordons and military bands
to welcome the new president and vice president—while also securing the city from those misguided Trump true believers who might
want to interrupt the sanctity of a peaceful, orderly, democratic
transfer of power.

I sat at home, watching carefully, eagerly, and finally, both pleased and relieved that we had made it—the nation made it. We had a new commander in chief. I was proud of what we accomplished at the Department of Defense. Most importantly, I was proud that we did our duty, that we endeavored to do the right thing, and that we stayed out of politics and the election. We honored our sacred oath.

ACKNOWLEDGMENTS

I want to thank my wonderful wife and best friend of more than thirty-two years, Leah, for her unconditional love and support throughout this project. She helped review drafts, offered important inputs, recalled moments I had forgotten, and provided a unique perspective from someone who was "in the arena" with me. This story is as much "ours" as it is "mine," since she experienced the ups and downs, twists and turns, and joys and frustrations of serving right alongside me. But Leah did far more than help me author a book. Much like she did nearly twenty-five years earlier when I was an Army commander in Europe, she played the role of helping me look after spousal, family, and quality-of-life issues for our service members. Without her support, we would not have accomplished as much as we did during my three years in office. The profession of arms is a family business, after all, and the spouses and children carry a different and heavier load than their soldier, sailor, airman, Marine, or guardian. So it was vitally important to have her with me as an active and positive force for families, and she did so with great enthusiasm and commitment for all of the right reasons.

I also want to thank my children, Luke, Jack, and Kate. They are the joy of Leah's and my lives. Leah deserves most of the credit for ensuring they became the wonderful and caring people they are. And while they are unique in many ways, the three of them share at least two common traits: first, the unconditional support and love they have given me throughout their lives; and second, their uncanny ability to keep me humble by finding new ways to make fun of me. Despite this flaw they inherited from their mother, I love them nonetheless and remain their biggest fan and supporter.

A good deal of thanks goes, of course, to my mother, Polly; my sisters, Patty, Donna, and Beth Ann, and their families; my numerous aunts, uncles, and cousins; my parents-in-law, Tom, and his late wife, Von, and my sister-in-law, Lisa; as well as my many friends from Uniontown who encouraged, supported, and stood by me these many years.

My dozens of classmates from the West Point class of 1986 who offered their support and encouragement throughout my career deserve thanks and recognition as well, including an extra special share to David Urban, my good friend and fellow Yinzer of more than forty years; another old friend and former roommate Steve Balentine; and my other longtime friends—former Ranger buddy Justin Whitney and fellow Blue Falcon Brett Barraclough. CNQ! And I would be remiss if I didn't thank two other old friends for their advice and insights along the way: Kori Schake and Matthew Freedman.

I have never written a book before, and doing so has been a journey of learning as much as writing. As such, I want to begin by thanking my terrific agents at Javelin, Matt Latimer and Keith Urbahn, for their insights, explanations, ideas, and assistance. They were the ones who helped jump-start this endeavor, and I appreciate it. The Javelin team also connected me with Emily Kropp Michel, who I came to know and appreciate as a quick and effective fact-checker and researcher who improved my story. Along the same lines, I want to thank my new colleagues at William Morrow, especially Mauro DiPreta, senior vice president and executive editor, who helped encourage and guide my writing, taught me how to "show, not tell," was instrumental to improving the book's organization and clarity, and was a kind, patient, and expert editor. He was aided by many others, I am sure, most of whom I never met.

Of significance, I want to thank the more than two dozen current and former four-star officers and senior civilian officials from across the government who reviewed all or parts of my manuscript They made critical edits, offered vital insights, recounted important moments, and provided helpful additions to improve the book's accuracy, fairness, tone, and completeness. The time and effort they committed to assisting me was invaluable and deeply appreciated. And while I would prefer to publicly recognize and thank each and every one of them, several have requested anonymity. As such, I decided not to list any of them. Regardless, they are all great patriots who put country and mission first, strived to do the right thing during a difficult period in our nation's history, and honored their oaths.

Separately, I want to recognize and thank my core team during my time as defense secretary, beginning with my chiefs of staff, Eric Chewning and Jen Stewart; my senior military assistants, Lieutenant General Bryan Fenton, and earlier Lieutenant General George Smith; my aides, Army Lieutenant Colonel Tim Leone and Marine Lieutenant Colonel Caleb Hyatt; my deputy chiefs of staff, Justin Johnson and Alexis Ross; my executive secretaries, Captain Ollie Lewis and Captain Dave Soldow; and my directors and special assistants, Coleman Lapointe, Liz Cilia, Erin Thomas, Anne Powers, and Emily Chumaceiro. This extraordinary group of people—and many, many others too numerous to list—kept me organized, prepared, and ready for anything and everything. They also ran the department and were a joy to have around. Even during the toughest of days, they were hard at work, optimistic, uplifting, and an inspiration to all, especially me.

I want to publicly thank the senior civilians and officers whom I had the honor and privilege to serve alongside during my tenure, beginning with General Joe Dunford and General Mark Milley. Both men are exceptional officers and extraordinary individuals who always offered great advice, insight, encouragement, and support during their respective tenures as chairman of the Joint Chiefs of Staff. I also want to thank the vice chairmen of the Joint Chiefs of Staff who also served during my tenure, General Paul Selva and especially General John Hyten.

Special thanks go to David Norquist, for the superb work he did as deputy secretary of defense and the incredible assistance he provided me during our eighteen months together. He was a real partner and true public servant who did a great deal with little fanfare. James Anderson, Yisroel Brumer, Dana Deasy, Matt Donovan, Tom Harker, Jonathan Hoffman, Rob Hood, Ann Thomas Johnston, Ellen Lord, Elaine McCusker, Paul Ney, John Rood, James Stewart, and John Whitley served in senior positions at the Pentagon at various times during my tenure. All of them—and others I may have accidentally missed—did a remarkable job helping to implement the National Defense Strategy, develop and execute important policies and plans, and modernize the armed forces during a very complex and challenging period. Many helped me make this book what it is, and I especially value Jonathan Hoffman's continued expert assistance as I navigate the postgovernment media landscape. I deeply appreciate everyone's mission focus, commitment to asserting civilian control, support to me, and service to country during our time together at the Pentagon. We were all assisted by numerous assistant secretaries, deputy assistant secretaries, and many, many others—political appointees and career civilians alike—who were instrumental in making the Department work, supporting our servicemembers, and ensuring mission success.

Finally, I want to thank the service secretaries, Barbara Barrett, Ken Braithwaite, Ryan McCarthy, Richard Spencer, and Heather Wilson; their service chiefs, General David Berger, General C. Q. Brown, Admiral Mike Gilday, General Dave Goldfein, General Jim McConville, General Robert Neller, and General Jay Raymond; and the many combatant commanders who served from 2019 through 2020, several of whom are mentioned in my book. They are all true professionals and dedicated public servants who put country first, took care of the troops, and did their very best to protect the country and advance our nation's security.

I will be forever grateful to all those mentioned above who served with and supported me during my time as the nation's twenty-seventh secretary of defense. Our nation's institutions—and by extension our democracy—are only as strong and capable and principled as those who serve in them. As such, the American people should be eternally thankful for these heroes' service, sacrifice, and commitment to their sacred oaths.

APPENDIX A

THE ARMY VISION

THE ARMY VISION

The United States Army is the most lethal and capable ground combat force in history. It has proven this in multiple conflicts, across a broad spectrum of operations, in various locations around the world, defending the Nation and serving the American people well for over 240 years. The key to this success has been the skill and grit of the American Soldier, the quality of its Leaders, the superiority of its equipment, and the ability of the Army – Regular, National Guard, and Reserve -- to adapt to and dominate a complex and continuously changing environment as a member of the Joint Force.

As we look ahead, near-peer competitors such as China and Russia will increasingly challenge the United States and our allies in Europe, the Middle East, and the Indo-Pacific region. At the same time, we should expect these countries' arms, equipment, and tactics to be used against us by others, including threats such as North Korea and Iran, failed states, and terrorist groups. Our adversaries' ambitions and the accelerating pace of technological change will create challenges and opportunities for the Army's battlefield superiority.

Meanwhile, the many demands on the Nation's resources will put downward pressure on the defense budget in the future, forcing the Army to continue making difficult choices about how it spends scarce dollars to meet national objectives and compelling us to become ever more efficient. A continued commitment to strengthening our alliances and building partnerships will help offset these challenges.

The **Army Mission**—our purpose—remains constant: *To deploy, fight, and win our Nation's wars by providing ready, prompt, and sustained land dominance by Army forces across the full spectrum of conflict as part of the Joint Force.* The Army mission is vital to the Nation because we are a Service capable of defeating enemy ground forces and indefinitely seizing and controlling those things an adversary prizes most – its land, its resources, and its population.

Given the threats and challenges ahead, it is imperative the Army have a clear and coherent vision of where we want to be in the coming years so that we retain our overmatch against all potential adversaries and remain capable of accomplishing our Mission in the future. As such, the **Army Vision**—our future end state—is as follows:

The Army of 2028 will be ready to deploy, fight, and win decisively against any adversary, anytime and anywhere, in a joint, multi-domain, high-intensity conflict, while simultaneously deterring others and maintaining its ability to conduct irregular warfare. The Army will do this through the employment of modern manned and unmanned ground combat vehicles, aircraft, sustainment systems, and weapons, coupled with robust combined arms formations and tactics based on a modern warfighting doctrine and centered on exceptional Leaders and Soldiers of unmatched lethality.

To achieve our Vision, the Army must meet the following objectives in the coming years:

- <u>Man.</u> Grow the Regular Army above 500,000 Soldiers, with associated growth in the National Guard and Army Reserve, by recruiting and retaining high quality, physically fit, mentally tough Soldiers who can deploy, fight, and win decisively on any future battlefield.

- <u>Organize.</u> Ensure warfighting formations have sufficient infantry, armor, engineer, artillery, and air defense assets. Units from brigade through corps must also have the ability to conduct sustained ground and air Intelligence, Surveillance, and Reconnaissance; Electronic Warfare; and cyber operations to shape the battlefield across all domains. Aviation, additional combat support, and robust logistical support must be readily available to units.

- <u>Train.</u> Focus training on high-intensity conflict, with emphasis on operating in dense urban terrain, electronically degraded environments, and under constant surveillance. Training must be tough, realistic, iterative, and dynamic. Continuous movement, battlefield innovation, and leverage of combined arms maneuver with the Joint Force, allies, and partners must be its hallmarks. This training will require rapid expansion of our synthetic training environments and deeper distribution of simulations capabilities down to the company level to significantly enhance Soldier and team lethality.

- <u>Equip.</u> Modernize the force by first reforming the current acquisition system and unifying the modernization enterprise under a single command to focus the Army's efforts on delivering the weapons, combat vehicles, sustainment systems, and equipment that Soldiers need when they need it. This modernization includes experimenting with and developing autonomous systems, artificial intelligence, and robotics to make our Soldiers more effective and our units less logistically dependent.

- <u>Lead.</u> Develop smart, thoughtful, and innovative leaders of character who are comfortable with complexity and capable of operating from the tactical to the strategic level. We will build a new talent management-based personnel system that leverages the knowledge, skills, behaviors, and preferences of its officers and noncommissioned officers. This system, when coupled with more flexible career models, will enable the Army to better attract, identify, develop, and place these leaders to optimize outcomes for all.

To achieve and sustain these objectives given the uncertainty of future budgets, the Army must continually assess everything we do, identifying lower value activities to discontinue and ways to improve what we must do, in order to free up time, money, and manpower for our top priorities. Trusting and empowering subordinate leaders will facilitate both reform and greater performance.

In all these efforts, we will ensure that our Soldiers, civilian workforce, and their Families enjoy the professional opportunities and quality of life they deserve. From the top down we must also remain committed to the Army Values. The Army is at its best when we work and fight as one team, and our Army Values, coupled with our Warrior Ethos, will guide and serve us well as we face the challenges ahead.

Since 1775, the United States Army has proven itself absolutely vital to protecting the American people, safeguarding the Nation, and advancing our interests abroad. This fact remains true today. Our ability to do so will be even more critical in the future as threats continue to emerge and evolve, becoming ever more dangerous and more complex. To remain ready to accomplish our Mission of fighting and winning the Nation's wars, the Army must fulfill the future Army Vision outlined herein. We are confident that with the right leadership, the proper focus, sufficient resources, and sustained effort the U.S. Army will achieve our Vision, remain the world's premier fighting force, and serve the Nation well for decades to come.

Mark A. Milley
General, United States Army
Chief of Staff

Mark T. Esper
Secretary of the Army

APPENDIX B

JUNE 24, 2019, INITIAL MESSAGE TO THE DEPARTMENT[1]

 SECRETARY OF DEFENSE
1000 DEFENSE PENTAGON
WASHINGTON, DC 20301-1000

6/24/19

MEMORANDUM FOR ALL DEPARTMENT OF DEFENSE EMPLOYEES

SUBJECT: Initial Message to the Department

It is the honor and privilege of a lifetime to serve alongside you as the Acting Secretary of Defense.

Since rejoining the Department nearly two years ago as the Secretary of the Army, my confidence in the incredible skill, professionalism, and commitment of our military and civilian workforce has grown even stronger.

As we continue to advance the Nation's security, let me reaffirm our path forward. The National Defense Strategy remains our guiding document and everything we do should support its stated objectives. The Department's priorities remain unchanged. We will continue to expand the competitive space through three mutually reinforcing lines of effort:

- *Build a More Lethal Force* – The surest way to deter adversary aggression is to fully prepare for war. We must continue to build readiness to fight tonight should the Nation call, while modernizing key capabilities for future conflict.

- *Strengthen Alliances and Attract New Partners* – Our Allies and Partners play an essential role in helping us deter conflict and defend freedom around the world. Through continued engagement we will grow these relationships and deepen our interoperability.

- *Reform the Department for Greater Performance and Affordability* – Reform is the means by which we free up time, money, and manpower to reinvest into our top priorities. Look for smarter, more effective ways to do business, and empower your teams to innovate and take prudent risk where necessary.

Having previously served in the Regular Army, National Guard, and Reserve, I understand well the sacrifices our Service Members, Civilians, and their Families make to protect this great country. This is why I am committed to taking care of Families and ensuring they have the resources they need to thrive.

Lastly, I place great importance on a commitment by all – especially Leaders – to those values and behaviors that represent the best of the military profession and mark the character and integrity of the Armed Forces that the American people admire.

I am proud of the great work our Soldiers, Sailors, Airmen, Marines, and Civilians do each and every day around the world. Stay focused on your mission, remain steadfast in your pursuit of excellence, and always do the right thing. Together, we will remain the most ready and capable military force in the world, which is what our Nation expects and deserves.

Mark T. Esper
Acting

APPENDIX C

JUNE 2, 2020, MESSAGE TO THE DEPARTMENT—SUPPORT TO CIVIL AUTHORITIES[1]

SECRETARY OF DEFENSE
1000 DEFENSE PENTAGON
WASHINGTON, DC 20301-1000

JUN – 2 2020

MEMORANDUM FOR ALL DOD PERSONNEL

SUBJECT: Message to the Department – Support to Civil Authorities

The United States military has been the greatest force for good in our Nation's history. While we often see the impact of our efforts overseas, every President has at times deployed military forces for domestic missions as well. In the last few months, for example, America's men and women in uniform – Active Duty, Reserve, and National Guard – have worked day and night across our communities to confront the COVID-19 crisis. This historic mission was just the most recent example of our longstanding support to civilian authorities – from pandemics to hurricanes, and from wildfires to providing security after 9/11.

Throughout these response efforts, I have been incredibly proud of our Service members and their hard work to assist our fellow Americans. This past week, our support to civil authority mission – that had been focused on COVID-19 – changed. Our National Guard are now also being called upon across the country to help protect our communities, businesses, monuments, and places of worship.

Department of Defense personnel have taken an oath to defend the Constitution of the United States. I myself have taken it many times in my military and civilian careers, and believe strongly in it. As part of that oath, we commit to protecting the American people's right to freedom of speech and to peaceful assembly. I, like you, am steadfast in my belief that Americans who are frustrated, angry, and seeking to be heard must be ensured that opportunity. And like you, I am committed to upholding the rule of law and protecting life and liberty, so that the violent actions of a few do not undermine the rights and freedoms of law-abiding citizens.

I appreciate your professionalism and dedication to defending the Constitution for all Americans. Moreover, I am amazed by the countless remarkable accomplishments of the Department of Defense in today's trying times – from repatriating and sheltering Americans who were evacuated from a foreign land, to delivering food and medical supplies to communities in need, and to protecting our cities and communities. In every challenge, and across every mission, the U.S. military has remained ready, capable, and willing to serve.

As I reminded you in February, I ask that you remember at all times our commitment as a Department and as public servants to stay apolitical in these turbulent days. For well over two centuries, the U.S. military has earned the respect of the American people by being there to protect and serve all Americans. Through your steadfast dedication to the mission and our core values, and your enduring support to your fellow Americans, we will safeguard the hard-earned trust and confidence of the public, as our Nation's most respected institution.

Mark T. Esper

APPENDIX D

JUNE 3, 2020, PRESS CONFERENCE IN THE PENTAGON BRIEFING ROOM

SECRETARY OF DEFENSE MARK T. ESPER: Well, good morning, everyone.

Over the past couple days there's been a fair share of reporting, some good, some bad, about what is transpiring—transpiring in our great nation and the role of the Department of Defense and its leaders. I want to take a few minutes to address these issues in person to make clear the facts and offer my views.

First, let me say up front, the killing of George Floyd by a Minneapolis policeman is a horrible crime. The officers on the scene that day should be held accountable for his murder. It is a tragedy that we have seen repeat itself too many times.

With great sympathy, I want to extend the deepest of condolences to the family and friends of George Floyd from me and the Department.

Racism is real in America, and we must all do our very best to recognize it, to confront it, and to eradicate it. I've always been proud to be a member of an institution—the United States military—that embraces diversity and inclusion and prohibits hate and discrimination in all forms.

More often than not, we have led on these issues. And while we still have much to do on this front, leaders across DoD and the services take this responsibility seriously, and we are determined to make a difference.

Every member of this department has sworn an oath to uphold and defend the Constitution of the United States of America. I've taken this oath many times, beginning at the age of eighteen, when I entered West Point. The rights that are embedded in this great document begin with the First Amendment, which guarantees the five freedoms of speech, religion, press, assembly, and the right to petition the government.

The United States military is sworn to defend these and all other rights, and we encourage Americans at all times to exercise them peacefully. It is these rights and freedoms that make our country so special, and it is these rights and freedoms that American service members are willing to fight and die for.

At times, however, the United States military is asked, in support of governors and law enforcement, to help maintain law and order so that other Americans can exercise their rights, free from violence against themselves or their property. That is what thousands of Guardsmen are doing today in cities across America. It is not something we seek to do, but it is our duty and we do it with the utmost skill and professionalism.

I was reminded of that Monday as I visited our National Guardsmen who were on duty, Monday night, protecting our most hallowed grounds and monuments. I am very proud of the men and women of the National Guard who are out on the streets today performing this important task, and, in many ways, at the risk of their own welfare.

I've always believed and continue to believe that the National Guard is best suited for performing domestic support to civil authorities in these situations, in support of local law enforcement. I say this not only as secretary of defense but also as a former soldier and a former member of the National Guard.

The option to use active-duty forces in a law enforcement role should only be used as a matter of last resort, and only in the most urgent and dire of situations. We are not in one of those situations now. I do not support invoking the Insurrection Act.

Last night, a story came out based on a background interview I did earlier in the day. It focused on the events last Monday evening in Lafayette Park, and I found it to be inaccurate in parts. So I want to state very clearly, for all to hear, my account of what happened that Monday afternoon.

I did know that, following the president's remarks on Monday evening, that many of us were going to join President Trump and review the damage in Lafayette Park, and at St. John's Episcopal Church. What I was not aware of was exactly where we were going, when we arrived at the church, and what the plans were once we got there.

It was also my aim—and General Milley's—to meet with and thank the members of the National Guard who were on duty that evening in the park. It is something the president likes to do as well. The path we took to and from the church didn't afford us that opportunity, but I was able to spend a considerable amount of time with our Guardsmen later that evening, as I moved around the city to many of the locations at which they were posted.

I also want to address a few other matters that have been raised about that evening.

First, National Guard forces did not fire rubber bullets or tear gas into the crowd, as reported.

Second, Guardsmen were instructed to wear helmets and personal protective equipment for their own protection, not to serve as some form of intimidation.

Third, military leaders, including the chairman of the Joint Chiefs of Staff, were wearing field uniforms because that is the appropriate uniform when working in a command center and meeting with troops in the streets.

Fourth, it wasn't until yesterday afternoon that we determined it was a National Guard helicopter that hovered low over a city block in

D.C. Within an hour or so of learning of this, I directed the secretary of the Army to conduct an inquiry to determine what happened and why, and to report back to me.

Now, you all have been very generous with your time, so let me wrap up by stating again how very proud I am of our men and women in uniform. The National Guard, over the short span of several months, has gone from tackling natural disasters such as floods, to combating the coronavirus across the country, to now dealing with civil unrest in support of law enforcement on the streets of America, all while many of their fellow Guardsmen are deployed abroad, defending against America's real adversaries.

Most importantly, I want to assure all of you and all Americans that the Department of Defense, the armed services, our uniformed leaders, our civilian leaders, and I take seriously our oath to support and defend the Constitution of the United States and to safeguard those very rights contained in that—that document we cherish so dearly.

This is a tough time for our great country these days, but we will get through it. My hope is that instead of the violence in the streets, we will see peaceful demonstrations that honor George Floyd, that press for accountability for his murder, that move us to reflect about racism in America and that serve as a call to action for us to come together and to address this problem once and for all.

This is the America your military represents. This is the America we aspire to be, and this is the America that we are committed to defending with our lives. Thank you.

STAFF: We'll go to the phones, Bob Burns?

Q: Yeah, thank you, Mr. Secretary. Taking you back to your comments about Monday evening, when you left the White House with the president and others, I think if I heard you correctly, you said you did know that you were going to be going to the St. John's Church, but you didn't know what would happen when you got there. And you've since been criticized by many for essentially participating at a presidential photo op. So my question is, do you regret having participated?

SEC. ESPER: Well, I—I did know that we were going to the church. I was not aware a photo op was happening. Of course, the president drags a large press pool along with him. And look, I did everything I can to try to stay apolitical and to try—trying to stay out of situations that may appear political, and sometimes I'm successful with doing that, and—and sometimes I'm not as successful. But my aim is to keep the Department out of politics, to stay apolitical, and that's what I continue to try and do, as well as my leaders here in the Department.

STAFF: All right. We'll go to Phil Stewart.

Q: Yeah, hi. Mr. Secretary, could you address, there's been a lot of criticism of your use of the word "battlespace" when you describe areas inside the United States where people are protesting. Could you—would you like to take that phrase back? And when you talk about keeping the military apolitical, how do you see, you know, the Department navigating this when the response to protests has become a partisan issue? Thanks.

SEC. ESPER: Well, I'll take your second question first, Phil.

That is the challenge, right? It's—it's a—there—there's a political tone to this. We are in a political season. An election approaches, and this is always a challenge for every Department of Defense in every election year. And so this is something we're going to continue to deal with as we creep closer and closer to election season.

I've been speaking about the importance of staying out of politics by remaining apolitical to my leadership since—since I took office. I reinforced it when I came in, when we started the—the new year, and I've talked about it several times since then. But this will be the ongoing challenge.

With regard to your first question, as—as you rightly said, earlier this week I was quoted as saying the—the best way—way to get street violence under control was by dominating the battlespace, and probably all of you who cover the Pentagon hear us use this phrase often. It's something we use day in and day out. There are other phrases that we use day in, day out that you'll understand, that most people don't understand. It is part of our military lexicon that I grew up with, and it's what we—we routinely use to describe a bounded area of operations. It's not a phrase focused on people, and certainly not on our fellow Americans, as some have suggested.

It is a phrase I used over the weekend when speaking with Minnesota Governor Walz. He and I spoke a couple times on Friday and Saturday as I spoke to him about DoD's support to what was happening there. Keep in mind, it was only a—a—a few short days ago, where Minneapolis was the epicenter and all eyes were focused on—on Minnesota.

But Governor Walz is also a former member of the National Guard, and I was complimenting him on the call with the governors about what he had done. It was his successful use of the Guard in sufficient numbers that really wrested control of the streets from the looters and others breaking the law, and that's—so I was giving him credit for that. And he was doing so so the peaceful demonstrations could be held, so that peaceful demonstrators could share their frustration and their anger.

That's what I was encouraging other governors to consider. In retrospect, I would use different wording so as not to distract from the more important matters at hand or allow some to suggest that we are militarizing the issue.

STAFF: All right, Luis Martinez.

Q: Hi, sir. Thank you much for a very—for doing this briefing. Some of the people that criticized you for the term of "battle space" were some of America's most respected former generals, and they said that that was just inappropriate language. And if I could move on to what you knew about the situation at Lafayette Square, were you aware that the Park Police were going to use such strong measures in pushing back the—the protesters there? And did you express any concern that that may not be exactly what needed to happen to make that photo op possible?

SEC. ESPER: Thanks for the question, Luis. I—I was not aware of law enforcement's plans for the park. I was not briefed on them, nor should I expect to be. But they—they had taken what actions I—I assume they felt was necessary, given what they faced. But I was not briefed on the plans and was—was not aware of what they were doing.

STAFF: All right, Dan Lamothe.

Q: Hi, yes, Mr. Secretary, thanks for your time. I realize you're trying to keep the Department out of politics, but it took you a week to—to say anything along the lines of what you did at the top of this call and—and your strong—strong comments this morning about George Floyd. In—in light of the more than two hundred thousand Black service members in uniform and the pain across the country, why did it take so long? Thanks.

SEC. ESPER: Thanks—thanks, Dan.

It's a fair question. I think you may have written about this, and as you rightly said, I've worked very hard to keep the Department out of politics, which is very hard these days as we move closer and closer to an election.

You know, remaining apolitical means that there are times to speak up and times not to. And as I said in my earlier remarks, what happened to George Floyd happens way too often in this country. And most times, we don't speak about these matters as a department.

But as events have unfolded over the past few days, it became very clear that this is becoming a very combustible national issue. And what I wanted to do—I had made the determination, as events escalated in the last seventy-two hours, that the moment had reached a point where it warranted a clear message to the Department about our approach.

And so, given the dynamics, I wanted to lead by crafting my own statement for the Department first—which I did yesterday, and you all should have seen it and got it, it went out, this piece of paper—my message to the force, which set, I thought was the proper tone for service members and DoD civilians and all, and giving my leaders the space to also craft similar messages, expressing our outrage at what happened, expressing our commitment to the Constitution, expressing our commitment as an institution to—to end racism and hatred in all its forms, and just a general expression with regard to what the Department is about.

So that—that's the timeline, Dan, if you will, and that's why it did, and I do that with great counsel from the—my advisers.

STAFF: We'll go—one more from the phones.

Q: The chiefs, several of the chiefs were interested in speaking up sooner. Sometimes when you say nothing, that says something unto itself. In retrospect, would you have done so more quickly?

SEC. ESPER: Well, we did—we—you know, General Milley, we talked to the chiefs. There was—most of the chiefs wanted to take the lead from me, and—and so what I told them is I was—through the chairman, I was going to take—I was going to send the initial message out, again to set the tone, to express my views and then I'd give them the space to share their views as well, to do so.

And, again, this is—we are a week into this, or so. And when you look at what's escalated, it's been a matter of seventy-two hours, maybe ninety-six or so. So—and we've been consumed with a lot of things between now and then. But I do think it's important to speak up and to speak out and to share what we view, again, as an institution, the racism that exists in America and how we view it as an institution.

Again, I think we've led on these issues over the history of the United States military, and we'll continue to do so, certainly while I'm at the helm.

STAFF: All right, one more from the phone. Tom Bowman? If not Tom, then Nick Schifrin?

Q: Mr. Secretary, thanks very much for doing this. If I could take you back to the other night. I know you're saying that you didn't know exactly what the plans were. But with all due respect, those plans were designed by the commander in chief and also by Bill Barr—of course the fellow cabinet secretary, and someone who is in the command center with you. So how could you not know about those plans and what does it say about those plans, to both clear the park and go to the church and do what the president did? And number two, I know you're conducting an inquiry on the use of the helicopter. You may not want to say this, but do you believe it was inappropriate to use a medevac helicopter to intimidate protesters? Thank you.

SEC. ESPER: On the first thing, Nick, again, I think there's some speculation with regard to what you—what you stated. I'd encourage you to speak to the Department of Justice as, again, it was a law enforcement action.

I had not yet arrived at the command post, I was en route to the command post when I was asked to return to the White House to update the president. I got back to the White House, and within a short period of time, we were—the president went out to give his remarks.

So there was no space in between there, there was no opportunity to get a briefing and again, nor would I expect to get a briefing on what the law enforcement community was planning to do with regard to the clearing of a park. Again, that was not a military decision, it was not a military action. The National Guard was there in support of the—in support of law enforcement.

With regard to your second question, I would just say this much. I'm not going to comment because I've asked that an inquiry be made. I want to make sure I understand why—what happened, who was involved, what orders were they given or not given, was there a safety issue involved, right? With an aircraft hovering that low. So there's a lot of questions that need to be answered. I spoke to Secretary McCarthy last night about it, he is digging into it and we will get the facts, and we'll go back from there.

STAFF: All right. In the room, Tara?

Q: Thank you, Mr. Secretary. So you served in the D.C. National Guard—

SEC. ESPER: I did, that's right.

Q: —to follow on Nick's question, were you surprised that a medical helicopter from the D.C. National Guard was used to intimidate people who were peacefully assembling? And then secondly, as this goes on, you've asked the secretary of the Army to look into this, who tasked the helicopter—

SEC. ESPER: Right.

Q: Was the helicopter under the authority of the Department of Justice? Is that why there's this kind of murkiness about how the helicopter was tasked, how a medical helicopter was used in an aggressive form?

SEC. ESPER: Yeah, so those are some of the details we have to tease out in terms of, you know, who directed it, what was requested, was it at the request of law enforcement. You made a statement that it was to intimidate protesters. I got a report back that they were asked by law enforcement to look at a checkpoint, a National Guard checkpoint to see if there were protesters around.

So there's conflicting reports. I don't want to add to that. I think we need to let the Army conduct its inquiry, and then get back and see what the facts actually are.

Q: But when you looked at the video, if you didn't see it live—

SEC. ESPER: I—look, I think when you're landing that low in a city, it's—it looks unsafe to me, right? But I need to find out—I need to learn more about what's going on. It would not be unsafe if they were a medevac bird picking up somebody who was seriously injured or something like that, right? It would be a different circumstance. So we have to find out all the facts, take it all in, and let the Army do its work and then come back with—with what they discovered.

Let's—

Q: But to your understanding, it was not a medevac mission?

SEC. ESPER: I—that's—right, my understanding, it wasn't. I need to—I'm sorry, but I need to actually head to the White House. So I just want to wrap up by saying something to the—directly to the men and women of the Department of Defense. And let me say this.

As I said in my message to the department yesterday, I appreciate your professionalism and dedication to defending the Constitution for all Americans. Moreover, I am amazed by the countless remarkable accomplishments of the Department of Defense in today's trying times.

From repatriating and sheltering Americans who were evacuated from a foreign land, to delivering food and medical supplies to communities in need, and to protecting our cities and communities, in every challenge and across every mission, the U.S. military has remained ready, capable, and willing to serve.

As I reminded you in February, I ask that you remember at all times our commitment as a department and as public servants, to stay apolitical in these turbulent days. For well over two centuries, the United States military has earned the respect of the American people by being there to protect and serve all Americans.

Through your steadfast dedication to the mission and our core values, and your enduring support to your fellow Americans, we will safeguard the hard-earned trust and confidence of the public as our nation's most respected institution.

Thank you.

APPENDIX E

NOVEMBER 9, 2020, FINAL MESSAGE
TO THE DEPARTMENT

SECRETARY OF DEFENSE
1000 DEFENSE PENTAGON
WASHINGTON, DC 20301-1000

NOV 0 9 2020

MEMORANDUM FOR ALL DEPARTMENT OF DEFENSE EMPLOYEES

SUBJECT: Final Message to the Department

It is has been the honor and privilege of a lifetime to serve alongside you as the 27th U.S. Secretary of Defense these last eighteen months in defense of our great Nation and adherence to our sworn oath to the Constitution.

Together, we have made solid progress implementing the National Defense Strategy by modernizing the force, improving its readiness, strengthening ties with allies and partners, and reforming the Department to make it more efficient. We have also made major strides in taking care of our military personnel, spouses, and their families, and launched important initiatives to improve diversity, inclusion, and equity in the armed services. At the same time, we stood up the Space Force and Space Command, recapitalized the nuclear triad, expanded the authorities and resources of Cyber Command, and proposed a bold vision for a future Navy. As such, I am confident the Defense Department's progress on all of these initiatives has improved the security of the United States and advanced our interests abroad.

I am particularly proud of these accomplishments in light of the challenges we faced along the way: a global pandemic; confrontations with Iran and its proxies throughout the Middle East; continued deployment of troops into conflict zones; domestic civil unrest; malign behavior globally by Russia and China; and a charged political atmosphere here at home. Through thick and thin, however, we have always put People and Country first.

In my first message to the Department in June 2019, I emphasized the great importance I place on a commitment by all, and especially Leaders, to those values and behaviors that represent the best of the military profession and mark the character and integrity of the Armed Forces the American people respect and admire. I want to thank you all for living up to that standard, for remaining apolitical, and for honoring your oath to the Constitution.

While I step aside knowing that there is much more we could accomplish together to advance America's national security, there is much achieved in the time we had to improve the readiness, capabilities, and professionalism of the joint force, while fundamentally transforming and preparing it for the future.

I will always admire and remain forever proud of the great work our Soldiers, Sailors, Airmen, Marines, Space Professionals, and Civilians do each and every day around the world and here at home to keep America safe. Stay focused on your mission, remain steadfast in your pursuit of excellence, and always do the right thing. Following these imperatives will ensure you remain the most ready, respected, and capable military force in the world, which is what our Nation expects and deserves.

Mark T. Esper

APPENDIX F

NOVEMBER 9, 2020,
LETTER TO THE PRESIDENT

SECRETARY OF DEFENSE
1000 DEFENSE PENTAGON
WASHINGTON, DC 20301-1000

NOV 0 9 2020

Mr. President,

It has been a distinct honor to once again serve our great nation and fellow citizens, this time as the 27th Secretary of Defense for the world's premier military force.

I have served these last few years as both Secretary of Defense and Secretary of the Army in full faith to my sworn oath to support and defend the Constitution, and to safeguard the country and its interests, while keeping the Department out of politics and abiding by the values Americans hold dear.

I first took this oath thirty-eight years ago as a Cadet at the United States Military Academy, and many times more since then. I have lived my professional life in accordance with the West Point motto of "Duty, Honor, Country" and have put service to Nation above self as a 21-year Active Duty, Reserve, and National Guard Army officer — in both war and peace, at home and abroad — and as a public servant in the Executive and Legislative branches of government on multiple occasions.

I have been privileged to serve with an outstanding team of military and civilian leaders across the Department of Defense, and alongside the best men and women in uniform the nation has to offer these last few years. Together, we have made solid progress implementing the National Defense Strategy by modernizing the force, improving its readiness and lethality, strengthening ties with allies and partners, and reforming the Department to make it more efficient. We have also made major strides in taking care of our military personnel, spouses, and their families, and launched important initiatives to improve diversity, inclusion, and equity in the Armed Services.

At the same time, we stood up the Space Force and Space Command, recapitalized the nuclear triad, expanded the authorities and resources of Cyber Command, launched a readiness and capabilities renaissance in the Army, and proposed a bold vision for a 500+ ship Navy. As such, I am confident the Defense Department's progress on all of these initiatives has improved the security of the United States and advanced our interests abroad, and that we would prevail in any conflict if called upon to do so.

In addition to these major changes that are underway, I am proud of how the Defense Department handled the following issues in particular:

- Provided full and timely support to the American people in response to COVID-19, while protecting the force and maintaining our military readiness;

- Strengthened allies and partners, defended international rules and norms, and demonstrated U.S. commitment to confront China's bad behavior in the Indo-Pacific;

- Worked closely with NATO to improve allied readiness, deter Russian adventurism, ensure the enduring defeat of ISIS, and chart a new path forward in Afghanistan;

- Acted decisively to restore deterrence with Iran, curtail Tehran's malign behavior, and help defend and reassure regional partners;

- Brought multiple terrorist leaders to justice and focused counter-terrorism operations abroad against threats to the homeland; and,

- Conducted a Defense Wide Review process and Service reforms that freed up time, money, and manpower to put back into the Department's top priorities.

I serve the country in deference to the Constitution, so I accept your decision to replace me. I step aside knowing there is much we achieved at the Defense Department over the last eighteen months to protect the nation and improve the readiness, capabilities, and professionalism of the joint force, while fundamentally transforming and preparing the military for the future.

I have never been prouder to serve my country than as a Soldier or Civilian in the Department of Defense, especially knowing that the military has the faith, confidence, and support of the American people. Moreover, I will always admire and remain forever proud of the great work our Soldiers, Sailors, Airmen, Marines, Space Professionals, and Civilians do each and every day around the world and here at home to keep America safe.

They are all great patriots who are committed to those values and behaviors that represent the best of the military profession and mark the character and integrity of the Armed Forces the American people respect and admire. I want to thank them for living up to that standard, for honoring their oath to the Constitution, and for their support to me and my leadership team.

Sincerely,

Mark T. Esper

APPENDIX G

_____

JANUARY 6, 2021, TWEETS REGARDING THE ASSAULT ON CAPITOL HILL

_____

This afternoon's assault on the US Capitol was appalling and un-American. This is not how citizens of the world's greatest and oldest democracy behave. The perpetrators who committed this illegal act were inspired by partisan misinformation and patently false claims about the election.

This must end now for the good of the republic. I commend Congressional leaders for meeting tonight to complete their Constitutional task of counting the electoral college votes that will affirm Joe Biden as the next president of the United States.

As this transition plays out over the next two weeks, I am confident the U.S. military will stay out of politics, and remain true to its sworn oath to support and defend the Constitution, and the American people, as the most trusted and respected institution in the country.

JANUARY 3, 2021, *WASHINGTON POST* OPINION
PIECE AUTHORED BY THE TEN LIVING FORMER
SECRETARIES OF DEFENSE

ALL 10 LIVING FORMER DEFENSE SECRETARIES: INVOLVING THE MILITARY IN ELECTION DISPUTES WOULD CROSS INTO DANGEROUS TERRITORY

Ashton Carter, Dick Cheney, William Cohen, Mark Esper, Robert Gates, Chuck Hagel, James Mattis, Leon Panetta, William Perry, and Donald Rumsfeld are the 10 living former U.S. secretaries of defense.

As former secretaries of defense, we hold a common view of the solemn obligations of the U.S. armed forces and the Defense Department. Each of us swore an oath to support and defend the Constitution against all enemies, foreign and domestic. We did not swear it to an individual or a party.

American elections and the peaceful transfers of power that result are hallmarks of our democracy. With one singular and tragic exception that cost the lives of more Americans than all of our other wars combined, the United States has had an unbroken record of such transitions since 1789, including in times of partisan strife, war, epidemics, and economic depression. This year should be no exception.

Our elections have occurred. Recounts and audits have been conducted. Appropriate challenges have been addressed by the courts. Governors have certified the results. And the electoral college has voted. The time for questioning the results has passed; the time for the formal counting of the electoral college votes, as prescribed in the Constitution and statute, has arrived.

As senior Defense Department leaders have noted, "there's no role for the U.S. military in determining the outcome of a U.S. election." Efforts to involve the U.S. armed forces in resolving election disputes would take us into dangerous, unlawful, and unconstitutional territory. Civilian and military officials who direct or carry out such measures would be accountable, including potentially facing criminal penalties, for the grave consequences of their actions on our republic.

Transitions, which all of us have experienced, are a crucial part of the successful transfer of power. They often occur at times of international uncertainty about U.S. national security policy and posture. They can be a moment when the nation is vulnerable to actions by adversaries seeking to take advantage of the situation.

Given these factors, particularly at a time when U.S. forces are engaged in active operations around the world, it is all the more imperative that the transition at the Defense Department be carried out fully, cooperatively, and transparently. Acting Defense Secretary Christopher C. Miller and his subordinates—political appointees, officers, and civil servants—are each bound by oath, law, and precedent to facilitate the entry into office of the incoming administration, and to do so wholeheartedly. They must also refrain from any political actions that undermine the results of the election or hinder the success of the new team.

We call upon them, in the strongest terms, to do as so many generations of Americans have done before them. This final action is in keeping with the highest traditions and professionalism of the U.S. armed forces, and the history of democratic transition in our great country.

NOTES

CHAPTER 1: FIRST DAYS, EARLY WARNINGS

1. Ali Vitali, "Trump's 'Nuclear Button' Tweet Sparks Backlash," NBC News, January 3, 2018, https://www.nbcnews.com/politics/white-house/trump-s-nuclear-button-tweet-sparks-backlash-n834321.
2. Courtney Kube and Carol E. Lee, "Trump Weighs Barring U.S. Military in South Korea from Bringing Families," NBC News, February 2, 2018, https://www.nbcnews.com/news/world/trump-weighs-barring-u-s-military-south-korea-bringing-families-n844041.

CHAPTER 2: AN ARMY RENAISSANCE

1. Lolita C. Baldor, "Army Misses Recruiting Goal for First Time Since 2005," Military.com, September 21, 2018, https://www.military.com/daily-news/2018/09/21/army-misses-recruiting-goal-first-time-2005.html; https:// recruiting.army.mil/pao/facts_figures.
2. Nolan Feeney, "Pentagon: 7 in 10 Youths Would Fail to Qualify for Military Service," *Time,* June 29, 2014, https://time.com/2938158/youth-fail-to-qualify-military-service.
3. https://recruiting.army.mil/pao/facts_figures.
4. Meghann Myers, "Only a Third of the Army's BCTs Are Ready to Deploy. Here's How the Service Plans to Fix That," *Army Times,* May 21, 2018, https://www.armytimes.com/news/your-army/2018/05/21/only-a-third-of-the-armys-bcts-are-ready-to-deploy-heres-how-the-service-plans-to-fix-that.
5. Corey Dickstein, "Success of Army's Increase to Basic Infantry Training Fuels More Training for Armor, Cavalry Recruits," Stars and Stripes, January 25, 2019, https://www.stripes.com/success-of-army-s-increase-to-basic-infantry-training-fuels-more-training-for-armor-cavalry-recruits-1.565863.
6. https://www.army.mil/acft.
7. Kyle Rempfer, "Senators Ask for Pause on Army's New Fitness Test, Call it 'Premature,'" *Army Times,* October 21, 2020, https://www.armytimes.com/news/your-army/2020/10/21/senators-ask-for-pause-on-armys-new-fitness-test-call-it-premature.
8. Ibid.
9. Matthew Beinart, "Army's $13.5 Billion 'Night Court' Savings in Budget Request Includes Adjustments to JLTV, AMPV," Defense Daily, February 11, 2020, https://www.defensedaily.com/armys-13-5-billion-night-court-savings-budget-request-includes-adjustments-jltv-ampv/army.
10. https://talent.army.mil/bcap.

CHAPTER 3: WAR WITH IRAN BEGINS IN IRAQ

1. Kevin Liptak and Nicole Gaouette, "Trump Withdraws from Iran Nuclear Deal, Isolating Him Further from World," CNN, May 9, 2018, https://edition.cnn.com/2018/05/08/politics/donald-trump-iran-deal-announcement-decision/index.html.

2. Spencer Kimball, "Trump Warns Iran Not to Fight the US: 'That Will Be the Official End of Iran,'" CNBC, May 19, 2019, https://www.cnbc.com/2019/05/19/trump-warns-iran-not-to-threaten-the-us-that-will-be-the-official-end-of-iran.html.

3. Luis Martinez and Elizabeth McLaughlin, "US to Send 1,000 Additional Troops to the Middle East as Tensions Escalate with Iran," ABC News, June 17, 2019, https://abcnews.go.com/Politics/us-send-1000-additional-troops-middle-east-tensions/story?id=63772858.

4. Peter Baker, Eric Schmitt, and Michael Crowley, "An Abrupt Move That Stunned Aides: Inside Trump's Aborted Attack on Iran," *New York Times*, September 21, 2019, www.nytimes.com/2019/09/21/us/politics/trump-iran-decision.html; Alex Ward, "Trump Confirms He Called Off a Military Strike on Iran," Vox, June 21, 2019, https://www.vox.com/2019/6/21/18700570/trump-iran-attack-drone-twitter.

5. Dr. Mark T. Esper, "Senate Armed Services Committee Advance Policy Questions for Dr. Mark T. Esper Nominee for Appointment to be Secretary of Defense," July 2019, https://www.armed-services.senate.gov/imo/media/doc/Esper_APQs_07-16-19.pdf.

CHAPTER 4: CIVILIAN CONTROL AND REFORM OF THE PENTAGON

1. https://www.youtube.com/watch?v=uLz33hukwvE.

2. https://www.defense.gov/Our-Story/Combatant-Commands.

3. Eric Edelman and Gary Roughead, "Providing for the Common Defense," United States Institute of Peace, November 13, 2018, 47, https://www.usip.org/publications/2018/11/providing-common-defense.

4. Ibid., 48.

5. Ibid.

6. Office of the Secretary of Defense, "Summary of the 2018 National Defense Strategy of the United States of America," January 2018, 1, https://dod.defense.gov/Portals/1/Documents/pubs/2018-National-Defense-Strategy-Summary.pdf.

7. Ibid., 5.

8. https://www.defense.gov/Newsroom/Transcripts/Transcript/Article/2266872/secretary-of-defense-mark-t-esper-message-to-the-force-on-accomplishments-in-im.

9. Loren Dejonge Schulman, Alice Hunt Friend, and Mara E. Karlin, "Two Cheers for Esper's Plan to Reassert Civilian Control of the Pentagon," *Defense One*, September 9, 2019, https://www.defenseone.com/ideas/2019/09/two-cheers-espers-plan-reassert-civilian-control-pentagon/159716.

10. David A. Wemer, "Defense Secretary Unveils a New Strategy for Bolstering Allies and Partnerships in a New Era of Great-Power Competition," Atlantic Council, October 20, 2020, www.atlanticcouncil.org/blogs/new-atlanticist/defense-secretary-unveils-a-new-strategy-for-bolstering-allies-and-partnerships-in-an-era-of-great-power-competition.

CHAPTER 5: TEHRAN ESCALATES

1. https://missilethreat.csis.org/country/iran/.

2. Shawn Snow, "US Withdrawal in Syria is Only a Small Number of Special Operators, Says Trump Administration," *Military Times*, October 7, 2019, https://www.militarytimes.com/flashpoints/2019/10/07/how-the-us-troop-withdrawal-from-northern-syria-could-create-an-isis-resurgence.

3. https://www.cnbc.com/video/2019/10/11/def-sec-esper-greatly-disappointed-in-turkeys-incursion-into-syria.html; https://www.cbsnews.com/news/transcript-secretary-of-defense-mark-esper-on-face-the-nation-october-13-2019.

4. Times of Israel Staff, "Iran Edging Closer to Nuclear Bomb, Israeli Defense Officials Assess—Report," *Times of Israel*, June 14, 2020, https://www.timesofisrael.com/iran-edging-closer-to-nuclear-bomb-israeli-defense-officials-assess-report.

5. Sawsan Morrar and Sam Stanton, "U.S. Contractor Killed in Iraq, Which Led to Strike on Iranian General, Buried in Sacramento," *Sacramento Bee*, January 9, 2020, https://www.sacbee.com/news/local/article239053173.html.

6. Frank Miles, "Trump Orders Attack That Kills Iranian Gen. Qassem Soleimani, Other Military Officials in Baghdad, Pentagon Says," Fox News, January 2, 2020, www.foxnews.com/world/rockets-baghdad-airport-injuries-reported.

7. John Bacon, "Photos Reveal Extensive Damage to US Embassy in Baghdad as American Soldiers Rush to Region," *USA Today*, January 2, 2020, https://www.usatoday.com/story/news/world/2020/01/02/us-embassy-baghdad-attack-damage-fort-bragg-deployment/2793781001.

8. Yaron Steinbuch, "Iraqi Protesters Storm US Embassy in Baghdad, Shouting 'Death to America,'" *New York Post*, December 31, 2019, https://nypost.com/2019/12/31/hundreds-of-iraqis-attempt-to-storm-us-embassy-in-baghdad.

9. Arwa Damon, Jeremy Diamond, Pamela Brown, and Ryan Browne, "Trump Threatens Iran After Protesters Attack US Embassy in Baghdad," CNN, December 31, 2020, https:// www.cnn.com/2019/12/31/middleeast/iraq-protests-us-embassy-intl/index.html.

10. Ibid.

11. "Press Gaggle by Secretary Esper and Chairman Milley, January 2, 2020," Department of Defense, https://www.defense.gov/Newsroom/Transcripts/Transcript/Article/2049496/press-gaggle-by-secretary-esper-and-chairman-milley/.

CHAPTER 6: AMERICA STRIKES

1. Helene Cooper, Eric Schmitt, Maggie Haberman, and Rukmini Callimachi, "As Tensions with Iran Escalated, Trump Opted for Most Extreme Measure," *New York Times*, January 4, 2020, https://www.nytimes.com/2020/01/04/us/politics/trump-suleimani.html.

2. Manu Raju and Ted Barrett, "Top Democratic Leaders Kept in Dark About Soleimani Attack," CNN, January 3, 2020, https://www.cnn.com/2020/01/03/politics/congress-soleimani-attack/index.html.

3. "Press Gaggle with Secretary of Defense Dr. Mark T. Esper and Chairman of the Joint Chiefs of Staff General Mark A. Milley, January 6, 2020," Department of Defense, https://www.defense.gov/Newsroom/Transcripts/Transcript/Article/2051321/press-gaggle-with-secretary-of-defense-dr-mark-t-esper-and-chairman-of-the-join.

4. Katie Rogers, "Trump Says 4 Embassies Had Been Targeted by Iranians," *New York Times*, January 10, 2020, https://www.nytimes.com/2020/01/10/world/middleeast/trump-iran-embassy-attacks.html.

5. David Martin, "Who Would Live and Who Would Die: The Inside Story of the Iranian Attack on Al Asad Airbase," CBS News, February 28, 2021, https://www.cbsnews.com/news/iranian-attack-al-asad-air-base-60-minutes-2021-02-28.

6. Nathan Strout, "Exclusive: How the Space Force Foiled an Iranian Missile Attack with a Critical Early Warning," C4ISR Net, January 7, 2021, https://www.c4isrnet.com/battlefield-tech/space/2021/01/07/exclusive-how-the-space-force-foiled-an-iranian-missile-attack-with-a-critical-early-warning.

7. Martin, "Who Would Live and Who Would Die."

8. Ayesha Rascoe, "After Missile Attack by Iran, President Trump Tweets: All Is Well," NPR, January 8, 2020, https://www.npr.org/2020/01/08/794461182/after-missile-attack-by-iran-trump-tweets-all-is-well.

9. *New York Times,* "Khamenei: Iran Gave U.S. 'Slap on Face,' Calls Missile Strikes 'Day of God,'" January 17, 2020, https://www.nytimes.com/2020/01/17/world/middleeast/iran-ayatollah-khamenei-Friday.html; https://www.reuters.com/article/us-iran-khamenei-usa-slap/khamenei-iran-gave-u-s-slap-on-face-calls-missile-strikes-day-of-god-idUSKBN1ZG0VV.

10. Luis Martinez and Karen Travers, "President Trump Minimizes Concussion-like Injuries in Iraq Attack as Merely 'Headaches,'" ABC News, January 22, 2020, https://abcnews.go.com/Politics/president-trump-minimizes-concussion-injuries-iraq-attack-headaches/story?id=68448853.

11. Martin, "Who Would Live and Who Would Die."

12. https://mfo.org.

13. www.globalsecurity.org/military/agency/dod/unified-com.htm.

14. "U.S. Central Command Statement on the Realignment of the State of Israel," U.S. Central Command, September 1, 2021, www.centcom.mil/media/statements/Statements-View/Article/2762272/us-central-command-statement-on-the-realignment-of-the-state-of-israel.

CHAPTER 7: THE POLITICS OF BUILDING A BETTER NAVY

1. "Navy Maintenance: Persistent and Substantial Ship and Submarine Maintenance Delays Hinder Efforts to Rebuild Readiness," General Accountability Office, December 4, 2019, https://www.gao.gov/products/gao-20-257t#summary.

2. Craig Hooper, "Former Navy Leader Tom Modly Opens Fire on 'Battle Force 2045,'" *Forbes,* October 21, 2020, https://www.forbes.com/sites/craighooper/2020/10/21/former-navy-leader-tom-modly-opens-fire-on-battle-force-2045/?sh=4899a0e6d5dc.

3. David B. Larter, "All US Navy Destroyers Will Get Hypersonic Missiles, Says Trump's National Security Adviser," Defense News, October 21, 2020, https://www.defensenews.com/naval/2020/10/21/all-us-navy-destroyers-will-get-hypersonic-missiles-trumps-national-security-advisor-says.

4. Paul McLeary, "NSA O'Brien's Latest Audible on Navy Plans: Calls for Most Frigates, Faster," Breaking Defense, October 27, 2020, https://breakingdefense.com/2020/10/nsa-obriens-latest-audible-on-navy-plans-calls-for-more-frigates-faster.

5. Paul Sonne, "O'Brien's Travels to Swing States Days Before Election Raise Ethics Concerns," *Washington Post,* October 27, 2020, https://www.washingtonpost.com/national-security/hatch-act-trump-administration-robert-obrien/2020/10/27/5355c9ee-1894-11eb-bb35-2dcfdab0a345_story.html.

6. Russ Vought and Robert O'Brien, "The Navy Stops Taking on Water," *Wall Street Journal,* December 9, 2020, https://www.wsj.com/articles/the-navy-stops-taking-on-water-11607556845.

7. Megan Eckstein, "FY22 Shipbuilding Budget Could Do More to Pave the Way for US Navy Fleet Transformation, Experts Say," Defense News, June 14, 2021, https://www.defensenews.com/congress/budget/2021/06/14/fy22-shipbuilding-budget-could-do-more-to-pave-the-way-for-us-navy-fleet-transformation-experts-say/?utm_source=Sailthru&utm_medium=email&utm_campaign=DNTV%206.14.21&utm_term=Editorial%20-%20Defense%20News%20TV.

CHAPTER 8: THE AFGHANISTAN DILEMMA

1. Jacob Pramuk, "What Trump Said About Afghanistan Before He Became President," CNBC, August 21, 2017, https:// www.cnbc.com/2017/08/21/what -trump-said-about-afghanistan-before-he-became-president.html.
2. "A Timeline of U.S. Troop Levels in Afghanistan Since 2001," Associated Press, September 8, 2019, https://apnews.com/article /fd2ec2085b0b4fd3ae0a3b03c6de9478.
3. "Agreement for Bringing Peace to Afghanistan Between the Islamic Emirate of Afghanistan Which Is Not Recognized by the United States as a State and Is Known as the Taliban and the United States of America," U.S. State Department, February 29, 2020, https://www.state.gov/wp-content/uploads/2020/02/Agreement-For -Bringing-Peace-to-Afghanistan-02.29.20.pdf.
4. Leah Simpson, "Donald Trump Invited the Taliban to Camp David Just Days Before 9/11 Anniversary—but Cancelled the Meeting After They Admitted to Recent Kabul Attack That Killed a US Soldier and 11 Others," *Daily Mail,* September 7, 2019, https://www.dailymail.co.uk/news/article-7439525/President-Trump-cancels -secret-meeting-Taliban-Camp-David-Kabul-attack.html.
5. Chandelis Duster, "Taliban Says It Has Resumed Peace Talks with the US," CNN, December 7, 2019, https://www.cnn.com/2019/12/07/politics/us-taliban-peace -talks-resume-doha-qatar/index.html.
6. "Agreement for Bringing Peace to Afghanistan."
7. Mujib Mashal, "Afghanistan Peace Talks Open in Qatar, Seeking End to Decades of War," *New York Times,* September 12, 2020, https://www.nytimes .com/2020/09/12/world/asia/afghanistan-taliban.html.
8. Susannah George and John Hudson, "Pompeo, Taliban Announce Plan to Sign Peace Deal at the End of the Month," February 21, 2020, *Washington Post,* https:// www.washingtonpost.com/world/violence-reduction-in-afghanistan-set-to-begin -after-midnight-saturday/2020/02/21/c3df0fb2-547d-11ea-80ce-37a8d4266c09 _story.html.
9. Shawn Snow, "Esper Gives Go-ahead to Begin Drawdown of American Forces in Afghanistan," *Military Times,* March 2, 2020, https://www.militarytimes.com /flashpoints/2020/03/02/esper-gives-go-ahead-to-begin-drawdown-of-american -forces-in-afghanistan.

CHAPTER 9: COVID—A TRAGIC, EPIC FIGHT

1. https://www.defense.gov/Newsroom/Transcripts/Transcript/Article/2063275 /in-flight-media-availability-by-secretary-esper; https://www.nytimes.com /2020/01/21/health/cdc-coronavirus.html.
2. Bob Woodward, *Rage* (New York: Simon & Schuster, 2020), 230. This was not a direct quote from an individual in the Woodward book. Rather, they are Woodward's words paraphrasing what was conveyed to Trump. The full passage reads: "At the White House that day. . . chief briefer Beth Sanner told President Trump at that point the intelligence community had a pretty benign take on the coronavirus. 'Just like the flu,' Sanner said in terms of severity. 'We don't think it's as deadly as SARS.' We do not believe this is going to be a global pandemic, she said."
3. Ibid., 230.
4. "Force Health Protection Guidance for the Novel Coronavirus Outbreak" (memorandum), Defense Department, January 30, 2020, https://media.defense .gov/2020/Jan/31/2002242035/-1/-1/1/Force-Protection-Guidance-for-the-Novel -Coronavirus-Outbreak-Jan-30-2020.pdf.

5. "Coronavirus: Timeline," Department of Defense, https://www.defense.gov /Explore/Spotlight/Coronavirus/DOD-Response-Timeline.

6. Hope Hodge Seck, "4 More Military Bases Tapped to House Coronavirus Evacuees," Military.com, February 1, 2020, https://www.military.com/daily -news/2020/02/01/4-more-military-bases-tapped-house-coronavirus-evacuees .html; "Coronavirus: Timeline," Department of Defense.

7. Ronn Blitzer, "Pelosi Says 'No' Regrets After Initial Downplaying of Coronavirus Earlier This Year," Fox News, July 13, 2020, https://www.foxnews.com/politics /pelosi-no-regrets-initial-coronavirus.

8. Woodward, *Rage,* 246. The words "sick people" are Woodward's paraphrasing, and not a direct quote by Fauci.

9. Ibid., 254.

10. Helene Cooper and Eric Schmitt, "Defense Secretary Warns Commanders Not to Surprise Trump on Coronavirus," *New York Times,* March 2, 2020, https://www .nytimes.com/2020/03/02/us/politics/esper-trump-military-coronavirus.html.

11. "Hearing to Receive Testimony on the Department of Defense Budget Posture in Review of the Defense Authorization Request for Fiscal Year 2021 and the Future Years Defense Program" (stenographic transcript), Senate Committee on Armed Services, March 4, 2020, https://www.armed-services.senate.gov/imo/media/doc /20-13_03-04-2020.pdf; Ellen Mitchell, "Pentagon Calls NYT Article on Esper and Coronavirus Response 'Dangerous and Inaccurate,'" The Hill, March 3, 2020, https://thehill.com/policy/defense/485735-pentagon-calls-nyt-article-on-esper-and -coronavirus-response-dangerous-and; Mark T. Esper to James M. Inhofe, May 7, 2020, https://media.defense.gov/2020/Jul/14/2002456734/-1/-1/1/secretary-esper-letter -to-senate-armed-services-committee-chairman-james-inhofe-regarding-covid-19.pdf.

12. Christopher Klein, "How America Struggled to Bury the Dead During the 1918 Flu Pandemic," History, February 12, 2020, www.history.com/news/spanish -flu-pandemic-dead; Andrews Noymer and Michel Garenne, "The 1918 Influenza Epidemic's Effects on Sex Differentials in Mortality in the United States," *Population and Development Review* 26, no. 3 (2000): 565–81, www.ncbi.nlm .nih.gov/pmc/articles/PMC2740912.

13. It was reported later that two additional Americans likely died from COVID in February 2020. Dennis Romero, "1st U.S. Coronavirus Death Was Weeks Earlier Than Initially Believed," April 22, 2020, NBC News, https://www.nbcnews.com /news/us-news/first-u-s-coronavirus-death-happened-weeks-earlier-originally -believed-n1189286.

14. Defense Secretary Esper News Conference, C-Span, March 17, 2020, https:// www.c-span.org/video/?470442-1/defense-secretary-mark-esper-holds-news -conference; "Defense Department Senior Leaders Brief Reporters on DOD Efforts Regarding COVID-19," Defense Department, April 14, 2020, https://www.defense .gov/News/Transcripts/Transcript/Article/2152052/defense-department-senior -leaders-brief-reporters-on-dod-efforts-regarding-covi.

15. https://www.npr.org/sections/coronavirus-live-updates/2020/03/18/817881133 /u-s-navy-hospital-ships-to-deploy-to-new-york-west-coast; https://www.cnn .com/2020/03/18/us/nyc-coronavirus-updates/index.html.

16. Marty Johnson, "Trump Sees USNS *Comfort* Off as It Departs for New York," The Hill, March 28, 2020, thehill.com/homenews/administration/489998-trump -sees-usns-comfort-off-as-it-departs-for-new-york.

17. Lauren Egan, "'70,000-Ton Message of Hope': Trump Sees Off Navy Hospital Ship as It Heads for NYC," NBC News, March 28, 2020, www.nbcnews.com/politics /white-house/70-000-ton-message-hope-trump-sees-navy-hospital-ship-n1171256.

18. "President Trump at USNS *Comfort* Send Off Ceremony," C-SPAN, March 28, 2020, www.c-span.org/video/?470788-1/president-trump-considers-quarantine-york-jersey-connecticut.

19. Meghann Myers, "Exclusive: Esper, on His Way Out, Says He Was No Yes Man," *Military Times,* November 9, 2020, https://www.militarytimes.com/news/your-military/2020/11/09/exclusive-esper-on-his-way-out-says-he-was-no-yes-man.

20. Woodward, *Rage,* 352.

21. "Javits Center Is Now the Country's Largest Hospital," Yahoo News, April 6, 2020, www.news.yahoo.com/javits-center-now-countrys-largest-094246573.html; C. Todd Lopez, "Corps of Engineers Converts NYC's Javits Center into Hospital," Department of Defense, April 1, 2020, www.defense.gov/Explore/News/Article/Article/2133514/corps-of-engineers-converts-nycs-javits-center-into-hospital.

22. "USACE COVID-19 Response Efforts," U.S. Army Corps of Engineers, May 29, 2020, www.usace.army.mil/Coronavirus; Terri Moon Cronk, "Corps of Engineers Takes On 28 COVID-19 Bed Facilities," Department of Defense, April 17, 2020, www.defense.gov/Explore/News/Article/Article/2154305/corps-of-engineers-takes-on-28-covid-19-bed-facilities.

23. Reuters, "Trump Issues Guidelines on '15 Days to Slow the Spread,'" Yahoo News, March 16, 2020, https://news.yahoo.com/trump-issues-guidelines-15-days-205932496.html.

24. Leo Shane III and Howard Altman, "SecDef Issues Guidelines for How Troops Will Start Wearing Face Coverings in Public to Prevent COVID-19 Spread," *Military Times,* April 5, 2020, https://www.militarytimes.com/news/pentagon-congress/2020/04/05/troops-to-start-wearing-face-masks-in-public-to-prevent-coronavirus-spread.

25. Final Report, Command Investigation Concerning Chain of Command Actions with Regard to COVID-19 Onboard USS Theodore Roosevelt (CVN 71), www.secnav.navy.mil/foia/readingroom/SitePages/Home.aspx?RootFolder=%2Ffoia%2Freadingroom%2FHotTopics%2FTR%20INVESTIGATION&Folder CTID=0x012000C9F89F68DF40E744A067873ECF6220C0&View=%7B854 CB8F6-5C90-46E6-A4A1-11FD0F9B23C6%7D.

26. C. Todd Lopez, "Navy: Former USS *Theodore Roosevelt* Commander Will Not Be Reinstated," Department of Defense, June 19, 2020, www.defense.gov/Explore/News/Article/Article/2226839/navy-former-uss-theodore-roosevelt-commander-will-not-be-reinstated.

27. Jamie McIntyre, "As Pentagon Prepares for 'New Normal,' It Shows Dramatic Effect of Early Use of Strict Safety Protocols," *Washington Examiner,* May 29, 2020, https://www.washingtonexaminer.com/policy/defense-national-security/as-pentagon-prepares-for-new-normal-it-shows-dramatic-effect-of-early-use-of-strict-safety-protocols.

28. Ibid.

29. Chris Cillizza, "The Top 10 Women Joe Biden Might Choose as His VP," CNN, April 9, 2020, https://www.cnn.com/2020/04/09/politics/joe-biden-vp-vice-president-pick/index.html; Jon Levine, "The Odds on Who Joe Biden Will Pick as His Female Vice President Candidate," *New York Post,* April 11, 2020, https://nypost.com/2020/04/11/here-are-top-contenders-for-joe-bidens-vice-presidential-candidate; Corey Dickstein, "Senate Democrats Rip Pentagon's Coronavirus Response in Letter to Esper," Stars and Stripes, April 28, 2020, https://www.stripes.com/news/us/senate-democrats-rip-pentagon-s-coronavirus-response-in-letter-to-esper-1.627734.

30. Associated Press, "Esper, in First Trip Since March, Defends Antivirus Efforts," CBS News, May 7, 2020, https://www.cbsnews.com/news/defense-secretary-mark -esper-in-first-trip-since-march-defends-antivirus-efforts.

31. Rebecca Kheel, "Esper Escalates War of Words with Warren, Democratic Senators," The Hill, May 8, 2020, https://thehill.com/policy/defense/496821-esper-escalates -war-of-words-with-warren-democratic-senators; Esper to Inhofe, May 7, 2020.

32. Thomas Burke, Chesley Dycus, Michael E. O'Hanlon, Eric Reid, and Jessica Worst, "COVID-19 and Military Readiness: Preparing for the Long Game," Brookings, April 22, 2020, https://www.brookings.edu/blog/order-from-chaos/2020/04/22 /covid-19-and-military-readiness-preparing-for-the-long-game.

33. https://www.cnn.com/2020/04/30/politics/fauci-states-federal-government -coronavirus-cnntv/index.html.

34. Patricia Kime, "COVID-19 Cases Reaching Record Highs in Military, Among Veterans," Military.com, November 4, 2020, https://www.military.com/daily -news/2020/11/04/covid-19-cases-reaching-record-highs-military-among-veterans .html; Ryan Morgan, "8th US Service Member Dies of COVID-19," American Military News, October 1, 2020, https://americanmilitarynews.com/2020/10/8th -us-service-member-dies-of-covid-19; McIntyre, "As Pentagon Prepares for 'New Normal'"; Associated Press, "Esper, in First Trip Since March."

35. Robert Burns, "Esper: Pentagon Ready for Any New Wave of Coronavirus," Yahoo News, May 7, 2020, https://news.yahoo.com/esper-first-trip-since-march -041205334.html.

36. "Evaluation of the TRICARE Program: FY20 Report to Congress," Military Health System, June 29, 2020, www.health.mil/Military-Health-Topics/Access-Cost -Quality-and-Safety/Health-Care-Program-Evaluation/Annual-Evaluation-of-the -TRICARE-Program.

37. "About DODEA Schools Worldwide," Department of Defense Education Activity, https://www.dodea.edu/aboutDoDEA/today.cfm#:~:text=Did%20you%20 know?%20%20%20%20%20,%20%2021,458%20%201%20more%20rows.

38. Amy Bushatz, "Military Child Care," Military.com, www.military.com/spouse /military-life/military-resources/military-child-care.html#:~:text=DoD%20 Child%20Care%20Centers%20The%20Defense%20Department%20 oversees,Child%20Development%20Centers%20(CDCs)%20on%20military %20installation%20worldwide.

39. Tom Bowman, "U.S. Military Is Sending Medical Staff to COVID-19 Hotspots," NPR, July 13, 2020, https://www.npr.org/sections/coronavirus-live-updates/2020 /07/13/890553905/u-s-military-is-sending-medical-staff-to-covid-19-hotspots.

CHAPTER 10: OPERATION WARP SPEED

1. "Fact Sheet: Explaining Operation Warp Speed," Department of Health and Human Services, December 14, 2020, https://web.archive.org/web/20201219231756 /https://www.hhs.gov/coronavirus/explaining-operation-warp-speed/index .html.

2. Dan Diamond, "The Crash Landing of 'Operation Warp Speed,'" Politico, January 17, 2021, www.politico.com/news/2021/01/17/crash-landing-of-operation -warp-speed-459892.

3. Haley Britzky, "Leaked Pentagon Memo Warns of 'Real Possibility' of COVID-19 Resurgence, Vaccine Not Coming Until Summer 2021," Task & Purpose, May 19, 2020, www.taskandpurpose.com/news/coronavirus-vaccine-pentagon-memo.

4. Kathy Katella, "Comparing the COVID-19 Vaccines: How Are They Different?"

Yale Medicine, December 17, 2021, https://www.yalemedicine.org/news/covid-19 -vaccine-comparison.

5. Bill Whitaker, "How the United States Plans to Increase the Pace of COVID-19 Vaccinations," CBS News, February 28, 2021, https://www.cbsnews.com/news /covid-vaccine-shots-in-arms-60-minutes-2021-02-28.

6. Anne Flaherty and Sasha Pezenik, "'The Mess We Inherited': Biden Leans Heavily on Trump's 'Warp Speed' but Won't Give Credit," ABC News, March 11, 2021, https://abcnews.go.com/Politics/mess-inherited-biden-leans-heavily-trumps-warp -speed/story?id=76186823.

7. Peter Aitken, "Operation Warp Speed Doc: 90% of Biden Vaccine Rollout Plan Was Same as Trump's," Fox News, March 21, 2021, www.foxnews.com/politics /operation-warp-speed-doc-90-of-biden-vaccine-rollout-plan-was-same-as-trumps.

8. Flaherty and Pezenik, "'The Mess We Inherited.'"

9. Samuel Chamberlain, "Fauci Says Operation Warp Speed 'Will Go Down Historically' as 'Highly Successful,'" Fox News, December 22, 2020, https://www .foxnews.com/health/anthony-fauci-covid-vaccine-operation-warp-speed-success.

CHAPTER 11: DESPERATE MEASURES

1. "Trump Alarms Venezuela with Talk of a 'Military Option,'" *New York Times,* August 12, 2017, https://www.nytimes.com/2017/08/12/world/americas/trump -venezuela-military.html.

2. Marie-Danielle Smith, "Canada Introduces New Sanctions on Venezuelan Regime in Wake of Devastating Report on Crimes Against Humanity," *National Post,* May 30, 2018, https://nationalpost.com/news/politics/canada-introduces-new -sanctions-on-venezuelan-regime-in-wake-of-devastating-report-on-crimes-against -humanity.

3. "Trump Alarms Venezuela With Talk of a 'Military Option.'"

4. John Bolton, *The Room Where It Happened* (New York: Simon & Schuster, 2020), 248–49.

5. Joshua Berlinger, "As Guaido Admits He Needs More Military Support, Trump Warns of Worse to Come in Venezuela," CNN, May 2, 2019, https://www.cnn .com/2019/05/02/americas/venezuela-maduro-guaido-intl/index.html.

6. Ibid.

7. Bolton, *The Room Where It Happened,* 254–55, 261.

8. "Trump Threatens 'Full' Embargo on Cuba over Venezuela Security Support," Reuters, April 30, 2019, www.reuters.com/article/us-venezuela-politics-trump -tweet-idUSKCN1S62PD.

9. Bolton, *The Room Where It Happened,* 274.

10. Andrew O'Reilly, "Trump Meets with Venezuelan Opposition Leader Guaidó at White House," Fox News, February 5, 2020, https:// www.foxnews.com/politics /trump-venezuelan-opposition-guaido-white-house. See also Katie Pavlich, "After SOTU Surprise, President Trump Welcomes Juan Guaido to the White House," Town Hall, February 5, 2020, https://townhall.com/tipsheet/katiepavlich/2020 /02/05/after-sotu-president-trump-welcomes-juan-guiado-to-the-white-house -n2560791.

11. Joshua Goodman and Scott Smith, "Ex-Green Beret Claims He Led Foiled Raid into Venezuela," *U.S. News,* May 4, 2020, https://www.usnews.com/news/world /articles/2020-05-03/venezuela-says-it-foiled-attack-by-boat-on-main-port-city.

12. John R. Bolton, "U.S. Efforts to Stop the Spread of Weapons of Mass Destruction," State Department Archive, June 4, 2003, https://2001-2009.state.gov/t/us/rm/21247.html.

13. Al Goodman, "Official: Spain Perplexed by Scud Decision," CNN, December 11, 2002, https://edition.cnn.com/2002/WORLD/europe/12/11/spain.ship.reax.

14. "Democratic Transition Framework for Venezuela," State Department, March 31, 2020, https://2017-2021.state.gov/democratic-transition-framework-for-venezuela/index.html.

15. Jim Garamone, "Trump Visits Southern Command for Briefing on Campaign Against Drugs," Defense Department, July 10, 2020, www.defense.gov/Explore/News/Article/Article/2270397/trump-visits-southern-command-for-briefing-on-campaign-against-drugs.

16. Michel Martin, "How Do Illegal Drugs Cross the U.S.-Mexico Border?" NPR, April 6, 2019, https://www.npr.org/2019/04/06/710712195/how-do-illegal-drugs-cross-the-u-s-mexico-border.

17. Jonathan Landay and Frank Jack Daniel, "Trump Plan to Label Mexican Cartels as Terrorists May Backfire, Mexico, Experts Warn," Reuters, November 27, 2019, https://www.reuters.com/article/us-usa-mexico-cartels-idUSKBN1Y11U2.

18. Sheyla Urdaneta, Anatoly Kurmanaev, and Isayen Herrera, "Venezuela, Once an Oil Giant, Reaches the End of an Era," New York Times, October 7, 2020, https://www.nytimes.com/2020/10/07/world/americas/venezuela-oil-economy-maduro.html.

19. Patricia Laya and Ben Bartenstein, "Iran Is Hauling Gold Bars Out of Venezuela's Almost-Empty Vaults," Bloomberg, April 30, 2020, https://www.bloomberg.com/news/articles/2020-04-30/iran-is-hauling-gold-bars-out-of-venezuela-s-almost-empty-vaults. See also Varun Hukeri, "Iran Sends Oil to Venezuela Despite American Sanctions," Daily Caller, May 18, 2020, https://dailycaller.com/2020/05/18/iran-oil-venezuela-american-sanctions.

20. Parisa Hafezi, "Iran, Venezuela in 'Axis of Unity' Against U.S.," Reuters, July 2, 2007, https://www.reuters.com/article/us-iran-venezuela-idUSDAH23660020070702.

21. Scott Neuman, "U.S. Seizes Iranian Fuel from 4 Tankers Bound for Venezuela," NPR, August 14, 2020, https://www.npr.org/2020/08/14/902532689/u-s-seizes-iranian-fuel-from-4-tankers-bound-for-venezuela.

22. Pamela Falk, "U.N. Security Council Votes Not to Extend Arms Embargo Against Iran," CBS News, August 14, 2020, https://www.cbsnews.com/news/iran-arms-embargo-u-n-security-council-votes-not-to-extend-embargo-indefinitely.

23. Eric Schmitt and Julie Turkewitz, "Navy Warship's Secret Mission off West Africa Aims to Help Punish Venezuela," New York Times, December 22, 2020, https://www.nytimes.com/2020/12/22/us/politics/navy-cape-verde-venezuela.html.

24. Ibid.

25. Vasco Cotovio and Holly Yan, "Alex Saab, Alleged Financier for Venezuela's President, Is Extradited to the US and Due in Court Monday," CNN, October 17, 2021, https://www.cnn.com/2021/10/17/americas/alex-saab-venezuela-cape-verde-extradition/index.html.

CHAPTER 12: THE REPUBLIC WOBBLES

1. "Donald Trump Phone Call Transcript with Governors after Protests: 'You Have to Dominate' and 'Most of You Are Weak,'" Rev, June 1, 2020, https://www.rev.com/blog/transcripts/donald-trump-phone-call-transcript-with-governors-george-floyd-protests.

2. Ibid.

3. Ibid.

4. Ibid.

5. Ibid.
6. Ibid.

CHAPTER 13: A WALK IN THE PARK
1. "FY2021 Defense Budget Request: An Overview," Congressional Research Service, February 20, 2020, https://sgp.fas.org/crs/natsec/IN11224.pdf.

CHAPTER 14: HARD DAYS AND LONG NIGHTS
1. Office of Inspector General, Department of the Interior, "Review of U.S. Park Police Actions at Lafayette Park," June 8, 2021, www.oversight.gov/sites/default/files/oig -reports/DOI/SpecialReviewUSPPActionsAtLafayetteParkPublic.pdf.
2. Grace Segers, "Protestors in D.C. Topple Statue of Confederate General," CBS News, June 20, 2020, https://www.cbsnews.com/news/protesters-washington-dc -topple-statue-confederate-brigadier-general-albert-pike.
3. Ibid.
4. John E. Morrison and Larry L. Meliza, "Foundations of the After Action Review Process" Army Research Institute for the Behavioral and Social Sciences, July 1999, https://apps.dtic.mil/docs/citations/ADA368651.pdf.
5. Tom Vanden Brook, "Defense Secretary Esper Says Beirut Blast Probably an Accident, Breaking with Trump," USA Today, August 5, 2020, www.usatoday.com /story/news/politics/2020/08/05/mark-esper-breaks-trump-says-beirut-blast-likely -accident/3302236001.

CHAPTER 15: MAKING LEMONADE
1. Robin Emmott, "Germany Commits to NATO Spending Goal by 2031 for First Time," Reuters, November 7, 2019, www.reuters.com/article/us-germany-nato /germany-commits-to-nato-spending-goal-by-2031-for-first-time -idUSKBN1XH1IK; Adam Taylor, "Germany Finally Pledges to Increase Military Spending to NATO Levels, but Trump Still Won't Be Happy," Washington Post, November 8, 2019, https://www.washingtonpost.com/world/2019/11/08 /germany-finally-pledges-increase-military-spending-nato-levels-trump-still-wont -be-happy.
2. Allan Smith, "Trump Calls Trudeau 'Two-Faced' After Hot Mic Catches NATO Leaders Speaking Candidly," NBC News, December 4, 2019, www.nbcnews.com /politics/donald-trump/trump-calls-trudeau-two-faced-after-hot-mic-catches -nato-n1095351.
3. Zachary Cohen, Kaitlan Collins, Kevin Liptak, Vivian Salama, and Jim Acosta, "Pentagon Chief on Shaky Ground with White House After Breaking with Trump over Protest Response," CNN, June 3, 2020, www.cnn.com/2020/06/03/politics /esper-insurrection-act-protests/index.html.
4. "Media Availability with Secretary Esper, July 24, 2019," Defense Department, https://www.defense.gov/Newsroom/Transcripts/Transcript/Article/1915743 /media-availability-with-secretary-esper.
5. Luis Martinez, "New Pentagon Guidelines Reaffirm to Top Brass That It's OK to Talk to Press," ABC News, July 26, 2019, https://abcnews.go.com/Politics /pentagon-guidelines-reaffirm-top-brass-talk-press/story?id=64597251.
6. Jennifer Jacobs, "Trump Weighs Replacing Esper at Pentagon After November Election," Bloomberg, August 8, 2020, https://www.bloomberg.com/news/articles /2020-08-12/trump-weighs-replacing-esper-at-pentagon-after-november-election.

CHAPTER 17: PRIDE, PROMOTIONS, AND POLITICS

1. "Remarks by Secretary Esper in a Press Gaggle, Nov. 25, 2019," Defense Department, https://www.defense.gov/Newsroom/Transcripts/Transcript/Article/2026000/remarks-by-secretary-esper-in-a-press-gaggle.
2. Carol E. Lee and Courtney Kube, "White House Officials Sent Document to Pentagon Criticizing Vindman After Impeachment Testimony," NBC News, July 15, 2020, https://www.nbcnews.com/news/military/white-house-officials-sent-document-pentagon-criticizing-vindman-after-impeachment-n1233613.
3. Celine Castronuovo, "Ben Carson Notes Reveal He's 'Not Happy' with White House Official: Report," The Hill, September 25, 2020, https://www.thehill.com/homenews/administration/518303-ben-carson-notes-reveal-hes-not-happy-with-white-house-official.
4. Allum Bokhari, "Democrats to Use Pentagon-Funded AI System to Target Pro-Trump Narratives Online," Breitbart, May 2, 2020, https://www.breitbart.com/tech/2020/05/04/gen-stanley-mcchrystal-advising-democrat-pacs-online-fight-against-trump.
5. Isaac Stanley-Becker, "Technology Once Used to Combat ISIS Propaganda Is Enlisted by Democratic Group to Counter Trump's Coronavirus Messaging," *Washington Post,* May 1, 2020, https://www.washingtonpost.com/politics/technology-once-used-to-combat-isis-propaganda-is-enlisted-by-democratic-group-to-counter-trumps-coronavirus-messaging/2020/05/01/6bed5f70-8a5b-11ea-ac8a-fe9b8088e101_story.html.

CHAPTER 18: LOST CAUSES AND IMPORTANT ONES

1. "See the Stance Candidate Trump Took on Confederate Flag Back in 2015," CNN, www.cnn.com/videos/politics/2020/07/07/trump-confederate-flag-museum-2015-comment-newday-vpx.cnn.
2. Jeanine Santucci, "Trump Says He Won't Consider Renaming Military Bases Named for Confederate Generals," *USA Today,* June 10, 2020, https://www.usatoday.com/story/news/politics/2020/06/10/trump-opposed-renaming-military-bases-named-confederate-leaders/5336093002.
3. "Actions for Improving Diversity and Inclusion in the Department of Defense" (memorandum), Defense Department, June 19, 2020, media.defense.gov/2020/Jun/22/2002319394/-1/-1/1/Actions-for-Improving-Diversity-and-Inclusion-in-the-DOD.pdf.
4. Secretary of Defense Memorandum, "Career Enhancement of Pregnant U.S. Service Members," November 3, 2020, https://dacowits.defense.gov/Portals/48/ODEI%20RFI%2013%20--%20Attachment%201%20CAREER%20ENHANCEMENT%20OF%20PREGNANT%20U_S_%20SERVICE%20MEMBERS.pdf.
5. "Immediate Actions to Address Diversity, Inclusion, and Equal Opportunity in the Military Services" (memorandum), Defense Department, July 14, 20202, media.defense.gov/2020/Jul/15/2002457268/-1/-1/1/Immediate-Actions-to-Address-Diversity-Inclusion-Equal-Opportunity-in-Military-Services.pdf.
6. "Public Display or Depiction of Flags in the Department of Defense" (memorandum), Defense Department, July 16, 2020, media.defense.gov/2020/Jul/17/2002458783/-1/-1/1/200717-Flag-Memo-DTD-200716-final.pdf.
7. Kaitlan Collins and Betsy Klein, "Trump Erupted over Esper's De Facto Ban on Confederate Flag, Sources Say," CNN, July 24, 2020, www.cnn.com/2020/07/24/politics/trump-erupted-esper-defacto-ban-on-confederate-flag/index.html.
8. "SecDef Year in Review," Defense Visual Information Distribution Service, July 1, 2020, www.dvidshub.net/video/758925/secdef-year-review.

9. Barbara Starr, "Esper in Crisis Management Mode amid Turmoil of Trump's Reelection Campaign," CNN, July 23, 2020, www.cnn.com/2020/07/22/politics /esper-crisis-management-trump/index.html.

CHAPTER 19: CHINA, CHINA, CHINA

1. Eric Schmitt, "Amendment Killed, Way Is Cleared for China Trade Bill," *New York Times*, September 14, 2000, https://www.nytimes.com/2000/09/14/world /amendment-killed-way-is-cleared-for-china-trade-bill.html.
2. Donald Trump, "National Security Strategy," December 18, 2017, https:// nssarchive.us/national-security-strategy-2017.
3. Reuters, "Trump Calls U.S.-China Relationship 'Best It's Ever Been,'" Yahoo News, January 15, 2020, www.yahoo.com/lifestyle/trump-calls-u-china-relationship -203719362.html?guccounter=1&guce_referrer=aHR0cHM6Ly93d3cu Z29vZ2xlLmNvbS88&guce_referrer_sig =AQAAAJUpCJBKf3BM01 ZSp8DB5T4WUMMu.
4. "National Security Strategy of the United States of America," December 2017, https://trumpwhitehouse.archives.gov/wp-content/uploads/2017/12/NSS -Final-12-18-2017-0905.pdf.
5. Sherisse Pham, "How Much Has the US Lost from China's IP Theft?" CNN Business, March 23, 2018, https://www.money.cnn.com/2018/03/23/technology /china-us-trump-tariffs-ip-theft/index.html.
6. Rajeswari Pillai Rajagopalan, "The Danger of China's Maritime Aggression amid COVID-19," The Diplomat, April 10, 2020, https://thediplomat.com/2020/04/the -danger-of-chinas-maritime-aggression-amid-covid-19.
7. Jeremy Page, Carol E. Lee, and Gordon Lubold, "President Pledges No Militarization in Disputed Islands," *Wall Street Journal*, September 25, 2015, https://www.wsj.com/articles/china-completes-runway-on-artificial-island-in -south-china-sea-1443184818.
8. Office of the Secretary of Defense, "Military and Security Developments Involving the People's Republic of China, 2020: Annual Report to Congress," https://media .defense.gov/2020/Sep/01/2002488689/-1/-1/1/2020-DOD-China-Military-Power -Report-final.pdf.
9. Trump, "National Security Strategy."
10. "Summary of the 2018 National Defense Strategy of the United States of America," January 2018, https://www.nssarchive.us/wp-content/uploads/2020/04/2018_NDS.pdf.
11. Matthew Lee, "US Tells Russia It Won't Rejoin Open Skies Arms Control Pact," Associated Press, May 27, 2021, www.apnews.com/article/donald-trump-europe -russia-government-and-politics-69038e96de8488f2c759b126c27d1366.
12. Brad Lendon, "China Has Built the World's Largest Navy. Now What's Beijing Going to Do with It?" CNN, March 5, 2021, https://www.cnn.com/2021/03/05 /china/china-world-biggest-navy-intl-hnk-ml-dst/index.html.
13. "China Naval Modernization: Implications for U.S. Navy Capabilities— Background and Issues for Congress," Congressional Research Service, January 27, 2021, https://fas.org/sgp/crs/row/RL33153.pdf.
14. Office of the Secretary of Defense, "Military and Security Developments Involving the People's Republic of China, 2020."
15. Frederico Bartels, "China's Defense Spending Is Larger than It Looks," Defense One, March 25, 2020, www.defenseone.com/ideas/2020/03/chinas-defense -spending-larger-it-looks/164060.
16. United Nations Conference on Trade and Development, "Review of Maritime Transport 2018," https://unctad.org/system/files/official-document/rmt2018_en.pdf.

17. Center for Strategic and International Studies, "Report of the China Power Project," December 1, 2021, https://chinapower.csis.org/tag/shipbuilding.
18. "Secretary of Defense Speech: As Prepared Remarks by Secretary of Defense Mark T. Esper at the Munich Security Conference, Feb. 15, 2020," www.defense.gov /News/Speeches/Speech/Article/2085577/as-prepared-remarks-by-secretary-of -defense-mark-t-esper-at-the-munich-security.
19. Gerry Shih, "China Launches Combat Drills in Taiwan Strait, Warns U.S. Not to 'Play with Fire,'" *Washington Post,* September 18, 2020, https://www .washingtonpost.com/world/asia_pacific/china-launches-combat-drills-in-taiwan -strait-warns-us-not-to-play-with-fire/2020/09/18/6ff46a7e-f977-11ea-85f7 -5941188a98cd_story.html.
20. Ben Westcott, "Chinese President Xi Jinping Tells Troops to Focus on 'Preparing for War,'" CNN, October 14, 2020, https://edition.cnn.com/2020/10/14/asia/xi -jinping-taiwan-us-esper-intl-hnk/index.html.

CHAPTER 20: AMERICA'S STRATEGIC ADVANTAGE

1. "Guidance from the Commander, U.S. Forces Japan," https://www.usfj.mil/About-USFJ.
2. "Burden Sharing: Benefits and Costs Associated with the U.S. Military Presence in Japan and South Korea," Government Accountability Office, March 2021, https:// www.gao.gov/assets/gao-21-270.pdf; John A. Tirpak, "US Pays Most of Shared Defense Costs with Japan, South Korea," Air Force Magazine, March 17, 2021, https://www .airforcemag.com/u-s-pays-most-of-shared-defense-costs-with-japan-south-korea.
3. James R. Holmes, "Defend the First Island Chain," *Proceedings of the U.S. Naval Institute* 140, no. 4, April 2014, https://www.usni.org/magazines/proceedings/2014 /april/defend-first-island-chain.
4. Christine Kim and Ben Blanchard, "China, South Korea Agree to Mend Ties After THAAD Standoff," Reuters, October 30, 2017, https://www.reuters.com/article/us -northkorea-missiles-idUSKBN1D003G.
5. Troy Stangarone, "The US and South Korea Need a Stopgap SMA," The Diplomat, April 1, 2020, https://thediplomat.com/2020/04/the-us-and-south -korea-need-a-stopgap-sma; Robert Burns and Matthew Lee, "U.S. and South Korea Agree on Cost-Sharing Deal for Troops," Associated Press, March 7, 2021, https://apnews.com/article/seoul-south-korea-military-affairs-asia-east-asia -b2216eea05c7a9d3683cb48c9ae83ada.
6. Japan News, "Who Is Moon Jae In? Moon's Reunification Dream Raises Alarm," *Yomiuri Shimbun,* April 18, 2017, https://web.archive.org/web/20170418164630 /http://the-japan-news.com/news/article/0003627269.

CHAPTER 21: UNREST IN THE NORTHWEST

1. Don Bishop, "White House Boosts 5G with DoD Spectrum-Sharing Agreement," AGL Media Group, August 11, 2020, https://www.aglmediagroup.com/white -house-boosts-5g-with-dod-spectrum-sharing-agreement.
2. Mark Guarino, Katie Shepherd, and Griff Witte, "Unrest in Chicago and Portland Shows America's Summer of Protest Is Far from Over," *Washington Post,* August 10, 2020, https://www.washingtonpost.com/national/unrest-in-chicago-and-portland -shows-americas-summer-of-protest-is-far-from-over/2020/08/10/087f48ba-db4e -11ea-8051-d5f887d73381_story.html.
3. General James H. Dickinson, "US Space Command's mission: 'Preparing for the War Not Yet Fought,'" The Hill, April 19, 2021, https://thehill.com/opinion /national-security/549008-us-space-commands-mission-preparing-for-the-war -not-yet-fought.

CHAPTER 22: OCTOBER SURPRISES

1. Russ Buettner, Susanne Craig, and Mike McIntire, "Long-Concealed Records Show Trump's Chronic Losses and Years of Tax Avoidance," *New York Times,* September 27, 2020, https://www.nytimes.com/interactive/2020/09/27/us/donald -trump-taxes.html.
2. Ali Vitali, Kasie Hunt, and Frank Thorp V, "Trump Referred to Haiti and African Nations as 'Shithole' Countries," NBC News, January 11, 2018, www.nbcnews .com/politics/white-house/trump-referred-haiti-african-countries-shithole -nations-n836946.
3. Michele Barbero, "France Bids Adieu to Its Military Mission in West Africa," *Foreign Policy,* July 7, 2021, www.foreignpolicy.com/2021/07/07/france-military -leaving-west-africa-colonialism-macron.
4. Helene Cooper, "Trump Orders All American Troops Out of Somalia," *New York Times*, December 4, 2020, https://www.nytimes.com/2020/12/04/world/africa /trump-somalia-troop-withdrawal.html.
5. "A Timeline of U.S. Troop Levels in Afghanistan Since 2001," Associated Press, September 8, 2019, https://apnews.com/article /fd2ec2085b0b4fd3ae0a3b03c6de9478.
6. "US to reduce troops in Afghanistan to '2,500 by early next year,'" Al Jazeera, October 7, 2020, www.aljazeera.com/news/2020/10/7/us-set-to-reduce-troops -in-afghanistan-to-2500-by-next-year.
7. Ryan Browne, "White House National Security Adviser Takes Shot at Top General in Open Rift on Afghanistan," CNN, October 16, 2020, https://edition.cnn .com/2020/10/16/politics/afghanistan-robert-obrien-mark-milley/index.html.
8. Carol E. Lee and Courtney Kube, "O'Brien Confirms Trump Ordered Pentagon to Cut U.S. troops in Afghanistan to 2,500 by Early 2021," NBC News, October 16, 2020, www.nbcnews.com/news/military/o-brien-confirms-trump-ordered -pentagon-cut-u-s-troops-n1243740.

CHAPTER 23: ENDGAME

1. Courtney Kube and Carol E. Lee, "Long at Odds with Trump, Defense Secretary Esper Has Prepared a Resignation Letter, Defense Officials Say," NBC News, November 5, 2020, https://www.nbcnews.com/politics/donald-trump/long-odds -trump-defense-secretary-esper-has-prepared-resignation-letter-n1245846.
2. Ibid.
3. Lara Seligman and Daniel Lippman, "Trump Expected to Keep Esper at the Pentagon Despite Clashes," *Politico,* November 7, 2020, https://www.politico.com /news/2020/11/07/trump-esper-stay-pentagon-434941.
4. Jacob Knutson, "U.S. Flies B-52 Bombers over Persian Gulf as Show of Force Against Iran," Axios, December 30, 2020, www.axios.com/iran-us-bomber -mission-persian-gulf-fab2b01d-df44-4afe-a147-8d7ca38ba134.html.

EPILOGUE

1. Katie Bo Williams, "Trump Officials Deliver Plan to Split Up Cyber Command, NSA," Defense One, December 19, 2020, https://www.defenseone.com/policy /2020/12/trump-officials-deliver-plan-split-cyber-command-nsa/170913.
2. Meghann Myers, "Exclusive: Esper, on His Way Out, Says He Was No Yes Man," *Military Times,* November 9, 2020, https://www.militarytimes.com/news/your -military/2020/11/09/exclusive-esper-on-his-way-out-says-he-was-no-yes-man.
3. Ashton Carter et. al., "All 10 Living Former Defense Secretaries: Involving the Military in Election Disputes Would Cross into Dangerous Territory," *Washington*

Post, January 3, 2021, www.washingtonpost.com/opinions/10-former-defense
-secretaries-military-peaceful-transfer-of-power/2021/01/03/2a23d52e
-4c4d-11eb-a9f4-0e668b9772ba_story.tl?fbclid=IwAR0qVwPvXlAO9ldruGwdDP
gDb2OgBvCIEAgRYw2nnoi40BZPqtt_Rh4rZwg.

4. Sonam Sheth, "Trump's Former National Security Advisor Says the President
Should Impose Martial Law to Force New Elections in Battleground States,"
Business Insider, December 18, 2020, www.businessinsider.com/michael-flynn
-trump-military-martial-law-overturn-election-2020-12.

APPENDIX B: JUNE 24, 2019, INITIAL MESSAGE TO THE DEPARTMENT

1. "Acting SecDef Esper's First Message to Pentagon," USNI News, June 24,
2019, https://news.usni.org/2019/06/24/acting-secdef-espers-first-message-to
-pentagon#:~:text=The%20following%20is%20Acting%20Secretary%20of
%20Defense%20Mark,alongside%20you%20as%20the%20Acting%20
Secretary%20of%20Defense.

**APPENDIX C: JUNE 2, 2020, MESSAGE TO THE DEPARTMENT—SUPPORT TO
CIVIL AUTHORITIES**

1. "Message to the Department—Support to Civil Authorities" (memorandum),
Defense Department, June 2, 2020, media.defense.gov/2020/Jun/03/2002309686
/-1/-1/1/Message-to-the-Department-on-Support-to-Civil-Authorities.pdf.

INDEX

army readiness. *See also* Army
  advanced training overhaul, 35–36
  basic training overhaul, 34–36
  collective training, 33–34
  for combat, 36–38
  holistic health and fitness plan, 37
  mandatory training, 31–32
  as Milley's top priority, 22
  new systems acquisitions failures, 23
  physical fitness training, 36–38
  recruiting standards, 23
  reliance on foundational combat systems,
    22–23
  Travel Risk Planning System, 32–33
army recruitment
  broadening recruiting base, 29–30
  criteria, 26–27
  declining parent/influencers support, 28
  demographics, 29–30
  failed recruiting goals, 25–26
  marketing campaign overhaul, 28–29
  military spouses and. *See* military
    spouses
  people of color, 29
  recruiting team composition, 29
  trends, 30–31
  "22 City" initiative, 30
  women, 29
Army Senior Leader Conference, 60
Army Talent Alignment Process Program, 51
Army War College, 459
Arreaza, Jorge, 328
ASEAN Defense Ministers' Meeting-Plus, 545
Asia-Pacific Center for Security Studies,
  563–64
Aspen Security Forum, 401
Aspin, Les, 565
Association of Southeast Asian Nations
  defense ministers' conference, 518
AstraZeneca/Oxford, 285
Australia, 502, 520, 555–56
Azar, Alex, 214, 238, 243–45, 276–78. *See
  also* Operation Warp Speed

Baghdad, Iraq. *See* Iraq
Baghdadi, Abu Bakr al-, 138, 162, 316, 622
Bahrain, 182
Baier, Bret, 633
Baker, Stuart, 262–63
ballistic missiles, 169–70
Baltics, 420–21
Barr, Bill
  background of, 343
  drug enforcement and, 309
  Esper and, 581–82
  Lafayette Park protests, Oval Office
    meeting, 334, 336

military police readiness briefing, 583
Milley and, 393
Portland protests Oval Office discussion,
  575
St. John's Episcopal Church photo op, 353
on Trump's eagerness to use military
  force, 571
Venezuela and, 303, 307–9
Venezuela-Iran principals meeting, 320
Walton (Philipe Nathan) rescue operation
  and, 625–26
Barrett, Barbara, 490–91, 497
Basic Exchange and Cooperation
  Agreement for Geo-Spatial Information
  and Services Cooperation (BECA), 562
battalion commander selection, 51–52
Battle Damage Assessment, 119
Battle Force 2045, 200–206, 524, 524n
Battle of Mogadishu, 565
Battle of the Bulge, 297
battle space, Esper's use of the term,
  344–46, 683–84
Biden, Hunter, 454
Biden, Joe, 316, 454, 478, 592–93, 667
Biden administration, 206, 475, 502,
  520, 548
Biegun, Steve, 626, 629
Big 5 weapons systems, 39–40
Bin Laden, Osama, 162
Birx, Deborah, 243–44, 253, 270
Black Lives matter protests. *See* civil unrest
Blake, Jacob, 581
Block II CH-47 helicopters, 48–49
Boehler, Adam, 282
Bolton, John
  Afghan peace agreement meeting, 219,
    223–24
  background of, 70–71
  Esper and, 64, 215
  Maduro regime and, 295–97
  as national security team member, 70
  NSC drone attack response meeting, 72,
    75
  O'Brien replacing, 297
  Pompeo and, 212
  on possible Trump-Taliban meeting, 225
  Room Where It Happened, The, 295–96
  Ukraine security assistance and, 454
  Venezuela's oil reserves and, 296
Bomber Task Forces, 568–69
Bowman, Tom, 687
Bowser, Muriel, 360–61
Braithwaite, Ken, 194–95, 202, 262
Brookings Institute, 267–68
Brown, Kate, 586
Buckley Air Force Base, 169
Bulgaria, 419, 425, 434

Al Asad air base missile strike and,
172–74
as Bolton replacement, 297
China briefing, 365
COVID travel ban meeting, 244
defending U.S. force reductions in
Germany, 418
on defense spending, 367
Embassy Baghdad update call, 146
Esper and, 652–53
Germany force reduction plan briefing,
418, 425
Iran and, 156–57
Iranian uranium enrichment efforts
meeting, 596–97
Iraqi military base rocket attack briefing,
132, 136
on military withdrawal from
Afghanistan, 615
Milley and, 598, 617–18
Nakasone situation and, 641–42
at NATO London Summit, 412
politicizing Battle Force 2045, 202, 204–5
Pompeo and, 123, 652–53
press leaks by, 205
regarding a strike on Iranian officer,
598–600
on Saab's detention, 329–30
as self-stylized "navalist," 197–98
Soleimani strike legal opinion, 149
Somalia withdrawal discussion
principal's meeting, 608–11
St. John's Episcopal Church photo op,
351–54
on targeting western Syria, 599
as Trump loyalist, 471–72
at Trump-Guaidó meeting, 299
Venezuela and, 307
Venezuela-Iran principals meeting,
320–22
Vindman and, 458, 460
Walton (Philipe Nathan) rescue operation
and, 626
Office of the Secretary of Defense (OSD).
See also Defense Department; Esper,
Mark, as defense secretary; Pentagon
press briefings
civilian leadership reasserting control,
101–2
core elements of, 94n
Personnel and Readiness office, 474–78
private outreach to China, 529–30
rigorous COVID protocols, 242
White House Liaison Office (WHLO),
474–75
offset strikes, 133, 135–36
Old Guard soldiers, 207, 337

One China policy, 532–33
Operation Desert Shield, 237, 332
Operation Desert Storm, 33, 48–49, 170–71
Operation Sentinel, 78–80
Operation Warp Speed. *See also*
coronavirus (COVID-19)
Azar's approach to, 275–78
Azar's White House difficulties, 283
clinical trials, 285
communications shortcomings, 289
cyber security, 285
DoD and HHS partnership, 236, 275–76,
279
establishing organization of, 281–84
Fauci's praise for, 290–91
funding for, 279
goals, 275
Kushner providing top cover for, 283
Perna and, 16
president's announcement of, 284
production acceleration, 280
regulatory hurdles, 280
strategies, 275–76
success of, 288
timeline for, 279–80
vaccination prioritization
recommendations, 286
vaccine administration/reporting, 288–90
vaccine development, 282, 285
vaccine distribution, 280–81, 285–88,
290–91
vaccine efficacy, 285, 288
vaccine manufacturing contracts, 285
White House media leaks on, 284

Pahlavi, Mohammad Reza, 65–66
Pakistan, 557
Palau, 564
Park Geun-hye, 542
Patel, Kash, 471–72, 627, 629
Pathfinder school, 34
Patriot missiles, 171, 313n
Pede, Chuck, 467
peer threats, defined, 7n
Pelosi, Nancy, 161–62, 164n, 166–67, 239
Pence, Mike
Abqaiq drone attack and, 119
Afghan peace agreement meeting,
219–20, 223, 226
Al Asad air base missile strike and,
172–74, 176
Azar and, 276
COVID travel ban meeting, 242–43
Embassy Baghdad update, 143, 146
Esper and, 444–45
Iranian uranium enrichment efforts
meeting, 596–97

Author's Note: Some and nearly all parts of this book have been reviewed by more than ten active-duty and retired four-star officers, more than a dozen former Senate-confirmed senior civilian officials—including some of cabinet rank—and a variety of other persons intimately familiar with the events described herein. I deeply appreciate their assistance in helping to ensure this book's accuracy, fairness, and completeness.